The Latin Writings of John Wyclyf: an Annotated Catalog

by
Williell R. Thomson
in part from the notes of the late
S. Harrison Thomson

Since the appearance in 1924 of Johann Loserth's *Revision* of W. W. Shirley's *Catalogue of the Extant Latin Works of John Wyclif*, no sustained effort has been made to analyze and integrate the total *corpus Wyclyfianum* within a single framework. Undertaken initially in 1925 by the late Professor S. Harrison Thomson, the present *Catalog* is the fruit of many years of joint effort with his son. A systematic arrangement of 435 separate writings by one of the chief forerunners of the Reformation into six separate categories (Philosophy, Science and Systematic Theology; *Pastoralia*; *Materia ad Hominem*; *Homo Publicus*; and *Polemica contra Papatum* I, II), followed by a miscellaneous section of *Dubia et Spuria*, embraces the entire range of Wyclyf's concerns. These he voiced with increasing vigor through the 1370s and early 1380s, mixing varying measures of spleen and intellect as occasion demanded. Two massive *summae*, well over two hundred sermons, scores of *opuscula* and a still-unpublished Biblical commentary earned him the sobriquets *doctor evangelicus* and *Johannes Augustini* while he taught at Oxford and battled with mendicants and seculars alike. As "Io. W. curatus de Lutterworth" he upbraided Schism-snared popes, crusading prelates and ignorant fellow-priests with a fury undimmed by paralysis or isolation. Editions, manuscripts, commentary and notes are set forth in a format comparable to the elder Thomson's *Writings of Robert Grosseteste*; five indexes offer maximum accessibility to modern researchers.

SUBSIDIA MEDIAEVALIA 14

THE LATIN WRITINGS OF JOHN WYCLYF

AN ANNOTATED CATALOG

BY

WILLIELL R. THOMSON

in part
from the notes of the late
S. Harrison Thomson

PONTIFICAL INSTITUTE OF MEDIAEVAL STUDIES

ACKNOWLEDGMENT

The publishing program of the Pontifical Institute
is supported through the generosity of the
De Rancé Foundation.

CANADIAN CATALOGUING IN PUBLICATION DATA

Thomson, Williell R., 1941-
　The Latin writings of John Wyclyf

(Subsidia mediaevalia, ISSN 0316-0769 ; 14)
Includes indexes.
ISBN 0-88844-363-3

1. Wycliffe, John, d. 1384 - Bibliography.　　I. Thomson, Samuel Harrison,
1895-1975.　　II. Pontifical Institute of Mediaeval Studies.　　III. Title.
IV. Series.

Z8987.T48　　　　　　　016.282´42574　　　　　　　C83-094110-X

© 1983 by

Pontifical Institute of Mediaeval Studies
59 Queen's Park Crescent East
Toronto, Ontario, Canada M5S 2C4

PRINTED BY UNIVERSA, WETTEREN, BELGIUM

Matri meae, uxori suae:
ambobus lumen in via

Rosamund Dargan Thomson

Table of Contents

Editor's Preface and Acknowledgments XIII
List of Abbreviations XIX

Section A: Philosophy, Science and Systematic Theology 1

 1. A1. *De logica* 4
 2. A2. *Logice continuacio* 5
 3. A3. *De logica tractatus tercius* 6
 4. A4. *De actibus anime* 8
 5. A5. *De proposicionibus insolubilibus* 11
 6. A6. [*Questiones et dubia super viii libros physicorum*] 12
    A7. *Summa de ente* [*Summa intellectualium*] 14
 7. A7.I.a. *De ente in communi* 17
 8. A7.I.b. *De ente primo in communi* 18
 9. A7.I.c. *Purgans errores circa veritates in communi* 18
10. A7.I.d. *Purgans errores circa universalia in communi* 20
11. A7.I.e. *De universalibus* 20
12. A7.I.f. *De tempore* [*De individuacione temporis*] 24
13. A7.I.g. *De ente predicamentali* 26
14. A7.II.a. *De intelleccione dei* 27
15. A7.II.b. *De sciencia dei* 28
16. A7.II.c. *De volucione dei* 29
17. A7.II.d. *De trinitate* [*De personarum distinccione*] 30
18. A7.II.e. *De ydeis* 32
19. A7.II.f. *De potencia productiva dei ad extra* 34
20. A8. *De materia et forma* 35
21. A9. *De composicione hominis* 36
22. A10. *De verbi incarnacione* [*De benedicta incarnacione*] ... 38
23, 24, 25. A11.a, b, c. *De dominio divino* 39
    A12. *Summa theologie* 44
26. A12.a. *De mandatis divinis* [*Decalogus*] 44
27. A12.b. *De statu innocencie* 47

28, 29, 30. A12.c, d, e. *De civili dominio* [*De dominio civili*] [*De dominio humano*] 48
31. A12.f. *De veritate sacre scripture* 55
32. A12.g. *De ecclesia* 58
33. A12.h. *De officio regis* 60
34. A12.i. *De potestate pape* 62
35. A12.j. *De symonia* 63
36. A12.k. *De apostasia* 64
37. A12.l. *De blasfemia* 66
38. A13. *De eucharistia* [*Tractatus maior*] 67
39. A14. *De eucharistia minor confessio* [*De corpore Christi*] ... 69
40. A15. *De fide sacramenti* [*De eucharistia confessio*] 71
41. A16. *De eucharistia conclusiones duodecim* [or: *quindecim*] . 71
42. A17. *Questio ad fratres de sacramento altaris* 73
43. A18. *Errare in materia fidei quod possit ecclesia militans* .. 75
44. A19. *De eucharistia et penitencia* [*Confessio*] 75
45. A20. *De vaticinacione sive de prophecia* 77
46. A21. *De oracione et ecclesie purgacione* 78
47. A22. *Trialogus* [*Summa summe*] 79
48. A23. *De dotacione ecclesie* [*Supplementum trialogi*] 83
49. A24. *De fide catholica* [*De ecclesia (tractatus minor)*] 84
50. A25. *De septem donis spiritus sancti* 86
51. A26. [*Differencia inter peccatum mortale et veniale*] 87
52. A27. *De peccato in spiritum sanctum* 88

Section B: *Pastoralia*: Sermons, Commentaries and Practical Theology 91

53. B1. *De officio pastorali* 94
B2. *Sermones* 96
B2.I. *Sermones super evangelia dominicalia* 97
54-114. B2.I. pref.; B2.I.a.1-B2.I.a.4; B2.I.b.1-B2.I.b.5; B2.I.c.1-B2.I.c.9; B2.I.d.1-B2.I.d.6; B2.I.e.1-B2.I.e.8; B2.I.f.1-B2.I.f.25; B2.I.g.1-B2.I.g.3. 98
B2.II. *Sermones super evangelia de sanctis* 122
115-175. B2.II.1-B2.II.61. 123
B2.III. *Sermones super epistolas* 143
176-234. B2.III.1-B2.III.59. 145

B2.IV. *Sermones miscellanei*	167
235-299. B2.IV.1-B2.IV.65.	169
300. B3. *De demonio meridiano*	191
B4. [*Postilla super totam Bibliam*]	192
301-305. B4.I.a-B4.I.e. [*Politica et legislativa?*]	194
306-319. B4.II.a-B4.II.n. [*Chronicasive historica?*]	194
320-321. B4.III.a, b. *Jb, Ec* [*Dialectica sive disputativa?*]	194
322-324. B4.IV.a-c. *Ps, SS, Lm* [*Hymnidica et quasi poetica et decantativa*]	195
325-327. B4.V.a-c. [*Monastica sive ethica?*]	197
328-344. B4.VI.a-q. *Is, Jr, Baruch, Ezk, Dn, Ho, Jl, Am, Ob, Jnh, Mi, Na, Hk, Zp, Hg, Zc, Ml* [*Prophetica*]	197
345-348. B4.VII.a-d. *Mt, Mk, Lk, Jn* [*Evangelica?*]	204
349-371. B4.VIII.a-w. *Ro, 1 Co, 2 Co, Gl, Ep, Php, Cl, 1 Th, 2 Th, 1 Tm, 2 Tm, Ti, Phm, He, Ac, Ja, 1 P, 2 P, 1 Jn, 2 Jn, 3 Jn, Jde, Rv* [*Epistolaria*]	206
372. B5.a. *Exposicio textus Matthei xxiii* [*De ve octuplici*]	215
373. B5.b. *Exposicio textus Matthei xxiv* [*Longum evangelium*] [*De Antichristo*]	218
374-377. B6.I.a, b; B6.II.a, b. *Opus evangelicum I, II* [*De sermone domini in monte*]; *Opus evangelicum III, IV* [*De Antichristo I, II*]	220
Section C: *Materia ad hominem*: Correspondence and *Responsiones*	225
378, ***379***, **380**. C1.a, [b], c. *Determinaciones contra Kylyngham Carmelitam*	227
381. C2. *Determinacio ad argumenta magistri Outredi*	229
382, 383. C3.a, b. *Ad argumenta Wilelmi Vyrinham determinacio*[*nes*]	231
384. C4. *Responsiones ad xliv conclusiones* [*Responsio ad argucias monachales*]	233
385. C5.a. *Responsio ad decem questiones* [*magistri Strode*]	234
386. C5.b. *Responsiones ad* [*xviii*] *argumenta Radulphi Strode*	235
387. C5.c. *Litera parva ad quendam socium* [*Strode*]	236
388. C5.d. *Responsiones ad argumenta cuiusdam emuli veritatis* [*id est magistri Strode*]	237
389. C6. *Exhortacio cuiusdam doctoris*	239
390. C7. *De octo questionibus pulchris*	240
391. C8. [*Epistola ad quendam socium de sensu mistico Matt. 21º*]	241

392. C9. *De fratribus ad scholares* 241
393. C10. *De amore [Ad quinque questiones]* 242
394. C11. *De gradibus cleri ecclesie* 243
395. C12. *Epistola missa archiepiscopo Cantuariensi* 244
396. C13. *Epistola missa episcopo Lincolniensi* 245

Section D: *Homo publicus*: General Petitions and Protestations ... 247

397. D1. *[De iuramento Arnaldi]* 249
398. D2. *[Responsio] ad quesita regis et concilii [De questione utrum licet thesaurum retinere]* 251
399. D3.a. *Protestacio [or: Declaraciones] Johannes Wyclif* 253
400. D3.b. *[Libellus] ad parliamentum regis* 254
401. D3.c. *De condemnacione xix conclusiones* 255
402. D4. *De paupertate Christi [conclusiones triginta tres]* 257
403. D5. *[Peticio ad regem et parliamentum]* 258
404. D6. *Epistola missa pape Urbano* 259

Section E: *Polemica contra Papatum* I: On Disendowment, the Schism, the Despenser Crusade 261

405. E1. *De servitute civili et dominio seculari* 265
406. E2. *De officio regis conclusio* 266
407. E3. *De clavibus ecclesie [De potestate ligandi et solvendi]* ... 267
408. E4. *Dyalogus [Speculum ecclesie militantis]* 268
409. E5. *Speculum secularium dominorum* 271
410. E6. *De scismate [De dissensione paparum]* 273
411. E7. *De cruciata [Contra bella clericorum]* 275
412. E8. *De Christo et suo adversario Antichristo* 276
413. E9. *De citacionibus frivolis et aliis versuciis Antichristi* 277
414. E10. *De ordine Christiano* 278

Section F: *Polemica contra Papatum* II: On the "Four Sects" and the *Secta Christi* 279

415. F1. *De nova prevaricancia mandatorum* 281
416. F2. *Epistola missa ad simplices sacerdotes* 283
417. F3. *Quattuor imprecaciones [De quattuor imprecacionibus]* . 284
418. F4. *De duobus generibus hereticorum* 285

419. F5. *De mendaciis fratrum* 285
420. F6. *De versuciis Antichristri* 286
421. F7. *De deteccione perfidiarum Antichristi* 287
422. F8. *De novis ordinibus* 289
423. F9. *De contrarietate duorum dominorum* 289
424. F10. *De oracione dominica* 291
425. F11. *De salutacione angelica* 292
426. F12. *De perfeccione statuum* 292
427. F13. *De triplici vinculo amoris* [*sive caritatis*] 294
428. F14. *Purgatorium secte Christi* 295
429. F15. *De quattuor sectis novellis* 296
430. F16. *De dyabolo et membris eius* 297
431. F17. *De fundacione sectarum* 297
432. F18. *De concordacione fratrum* [*cum secta simplici Christi*] [*De sectis monachorum*] [*De ordinacione fratrum*] 298
433. F19. *Descripcio fratris* 300
434. F20. *De religionibus vanis monachorum* [*De fundatore religionis*] 300
435. F21. *De solucione Sathane* 301

Section G: *Dubia et spuria* 303

    GDub.1-18. 305
    GSpur.1-14. 308

Index of Manuscripts 311

Index of Incipits 318

Reverse Index of Explicits 325

Alphabetical Index of Wyclyf's Latin Writings 334

Index of Wyclyf's Writings 336

General Index 339

Preface

Over half a century ago, S. Harrison Thomson submitted his B.Litt. thesis to the theological faculty at Oxford.[1] In the concluding two-page appendix to this thesis, "Additions and Corrections to Loserth's Catalogue of the Extant Latin Works of Wyclif," Thomson singled out a number of errors, both of attribution and of omission, in the canon of Wyclyf's Latin writings as it was then perceived.[2] Such was the genesis of the present *Annotated Catalog*.

---

[1] "The Theological Doctrines of John Wyclif Considered as to their Sources" (1926), 222 pp. (Mostly unpublished MS in the editor's possession.) His preference for the spelling "Wyclyf" dates from a later period: cf. his "Wyclif or Wyclyf?" *EHR* 53 (1938): 675-678; also the concurring article by Joseph H. Dahmus, "Further Evidence for the Spelling 'Wyclyf'," *Speculum* 16 (1941): 224-225; and now Vaclav Mudroch (ed. E. A. Reeves), *The Wyclyf Tradition* (Athens, Ohio, 1979): xi. Useful sources on Thomson's career are Lubomyr R. Wynar, *S. Harrison Thomson: Bio-Bibliography* (Boulder, Colorado, 1963), and the obituary notices in *Speculum* 51 (1976): 578-580, and *AHR* 81 (1976): 707-708. His publications and judgments relevant to the present undertaking are cited below, *passim*.

[2] The first known attempt at a listing of Wyclyf's works appears in three separate MSS now at the ÖNB: 3933, 3935, and 4514, from the first third of the fifteenth century; MS 7980, of the early seventeenth century, is for the most part a copy of MS 4514. Which assiduous Czech scribes executed these helpful lists we do not know; they were no doubt inspired by the example of Peter Payne (see below, 17, n. 4). All four are conveniently transcribed in the first volume produced by the Wyclif Society, Rudolf Buddensieg's *John Wiclif's Polemical Works in Latin* I (1883): LIX-LXXXIV. The indefatigable Bishop of Ossory, John Bale (1495-1563), gave a more extensive listing in the second edition of his *Scriptorum illustrium maioris Brytannię Catalogus* (Basel, 1557-1559): 450-455; it is to our sequential enumeration of these items that reference is made following the commentaries in this *Catalog*. (We should also note R. L. Poole and Mary Bateson's edition of his autograph notebook: *Index Britanniae Scriptorum Quos ex variis bibliothecis non parvo labore collegit Ioannes Balęus, cum aliis* [Oxford, 1902]: 264-275.) Thomas Tanner's posthumous *Bibliotheca Brittanico-Hibernica* ... (London, 1748) took the process a step further, though its organization is at best exasperating.

But the first recognizably *critical* effort to list and place Wyclyf's works was H. H. Baber, *The New Testament, translated from the Latin, In the Year 1380, by John Wiclif, D.D., to which are prefixed, Memoirs of the Life, Opinions, and Writings of Dr. Wiclif; and an historical account of the Saxon and English Versions of the Scriptures, previous to the opening of the fifteenth Century* (London, 1810): xxxviii-liv. Baber's seldom-cited study, and the even more obscure list by Charles Webb Le Bas, *The Life of Wiclif* (London, 1832): 435-450, were far outdistanced, however, by Walter Waddington Shirley's meticulous *A Catalogue of the Original Works of John Wyclif* (Oxford, 1865). This was

Already in the preceding year he had begun to assemble materials for critical texts of the reformer's major philosophical treatises, the *De universalibus*, the *De ydeis*, the *De ente in communi* and the *De ente primo in communi*; of these regrettably only the last two have been published.³ For Thomson always considered Wyclyf not only in his customary guises of theologian and reformer; he also underscored his prominence among the philosophical realists of the fourteenth century. Indeed Thomson urged that in many respects Wyclyf was subtler and more consistent than his English forerunners and preceptors Bradwardine, FitzRalph and Burley.⁴ Although the rapid evolution of Wyclyf's pronouncements on such issues as endowment, the Eucharist, the mendicant orders and the Papacy can be marked with some assurance, it is too often forgotten that these controversial efflorescences were carefully rooted in a dialectical soil, layered according to the categories of the Oxford schools; he tended them with the hand of a master logician.

Although Thomson did participate in the revision of the Wyclyf section in John E. Wells' *A Manual of the Writings in Middle English 1050-1400*,⁵ he cautioned his students and his colleagues against a too-heavy reliance on the English works often laid to Wyclyf's charge.⁶ Careful re-

---

later followed, but not in all respects superseded, by Johann Loserth, *Shirley's Catalogue of the Extant Latin Works of John Wyclif* (WS, n.d., but 1924); also of value is his "Zur Kritik der Wiclifhandschriften," *Zeitschrift des deutschen Vereines für die Geschichte Mährens und Schlesiens* 20 (1916): 247-271. – On the range and diversity of Loserth's scholarship, see W. Erben and A. Kern, "Johann Loserth als Geschichtsforscher. Eine Übersicht seiner wissenschaftlichen Werke," *Zeitschrift des Historischen Vereines für Steiermark* 22 (1926): 3-28. His editions and commentaries will frequently engage us.

³ S. H. Thomson, ed., *Johannis Wyclif Summa de Ente. Libri Primi Tractatus Primus et Secundus* (Oxford, 1930: cf. **7** and **8** below). Thomson's draft editions of the *De universalibus* and *De ydeis*, along with the minor *De insolubilibus* (cf. **5**, **11**, and **18**, below), are in the editor's possession.

⁴ This viewpoint is argued most cogently in S. H. Thomson, "The Philosophical Basis of Wyclif's Theology," *Journal of Religion* (Chicago) 11 (1931): 86-116; *Europe in Renaissance and Reformation* (New York, 1963; German ed., München, 1969): 173-177; "John Wyclyf," in B. A. Gerrish, ed., *Reformers in Profile* (Philadelphia, 1967): 12-39; "Wyclyf, John," in *Encyclopedia of Philosophy* VIII (New York, 1967): 351-352. For bibliography on Bradwardine et al., see below, **4**, nn. 4 and 5; **5**, n. 9; **6**, n. 7; **15**, n. 4; **16**; **23** and n. 12; **51**, n. 2.

⁵ (Orig. ed. 1916; supplements 1-9, 1919-1951.) J. Burke Severs, ed., *A Manual of the Writings in Middle English 1050-1500* II (Hamden, Conn., 1970): especially pp. 354-359, and notes, pp. 517-533: "Wyclyf and his Followers," with Ernest W. Talbert.

⁶ An admonition derived from the standards established long ago by Thomas Arnold, *Select English Works of John Wyclif* I (Oxford, 1869): iii-xiii; III (1871): v-viii; and F. D.

examination of the Lollard Bible, once thought to be chiefly Wyclyf's doing, has shown the hand of his associates Purvey and Hereford to be much greater than their mentor's in both execution and dissemination.[7] From this we may reasonably infer that even the English texts of his sermons, above all those for which we have found no Latin counterparts, should be rigorously tested as to style and thrust before we reach any final verdict.[8] But in any case the restriction of this *Catalog* to the Latin works exclusively is easily defensible on paleographical[9] and methodological grounds alike.

Matthew, *The English Works of Wyclif Hitherto Unprinted* (London, Early English Text Society, 1880): xlix-li. (A comprehensive new edition, under the astute direction of Anne Hudson, is in press at Oxford; see her *Selections from English Wycliffite Writings* [Cambridge, Eng., 1977].) Arnold and Matthew in turn were the foundation for the short but important article by E. D. Jones, "The Authenticity of Some English Works Ascribed to John Wycliffe," *Anglia* (Halle) 30 (1907): 261-268.

[7] Fundamental here is of course Margaret Deanesly, *The Lollard Bible and other Medieval Biblical Versions* (Cambridge, Eng., 1920): 225-315. But see also Sven L. Fristedt, *The Wycliffe Bible*, Part I (all published): *The Principal Problems connected with Forshall and Madden's Edition* (Stockholm Studies in English 4: 1953); Henry Hargreaves, "The Wycliffite Versions," in G. W. H. Lampe, ed., *The Cambridge History of the Bible* II: *The West from the Fathers to the Reformation* (1969): 387-415, and bibliographical notes, pp. 527-528; Peggy Ann Knapp, "John Wyclif as Bible Translator: The Texts for the English Sermons," *Speculum* 46 (1971): 713-720; idem, *The Style of John Wyclif's English Sermons* (The Hague, 1977); Michael J. Wilks, "Misleading Manuscripts: Wyclif and the Non-Wycliffite Bible," in SCH 11: *The Materials, Sources and Methods of Ecclesiastical History*, ed. Derek Baker (Oxford, 1975): 147-161; F. F. Bruce, *History of the Bible in English, From the Earliest Versions* (3rd ed., New York, 1978): 12-23. On Hereford and Purvey, cf. *BRUO* II: 913-915; III: 1526-1527, and now most importantly Anne Hudson, "John Purvey: A Reconsideration of the Evidence for his Life and Writings," *Viator* 12 (1981): 355-380.

A fascinating *quaestio* by Wyclyf's younger Dutch contemporary, Gerard Zerbolt van Zutphen, arguably bears on the larger canonical and societal issue of lay access to Scripture: Carl J. Jellouschek, "Ein mittelalterliches Gutachten über das Lesen der Bibel und sonstiger religiöser Bücher in der Volkssprache," in Albert Lang, J. Lechner and M. Schmaus, edd., *Aus der Geisteswelt des Mittelalters: Studien und Texte Martin Grabmann ... gewidmet* (Münster/Westf., 1935): 1181-1199.

[8] See also below, B2, n. 1.

[9] Cf. S. H. Thomson, *Latin Bookhands of the Later Middle Ages 1100-1500* (Cambridge, Eng., 1969), for his operating criteria in this vital category. It ought to be mentioned here that the editor, while having personally examined over 75 of the MSS mentioned in this volume, as well as many others in photostat or microfilm reproductions, does not claim the degree of paleographical expertise so manifest in *Latin Bookhands*. Throughout, judgments as to date and provenance are almost exclusively those of S. H. Thomson.

The arrangement of, and within, categories in the following pages is still recognizably that of Shirley and Loserth; but almost six decades of serious Wyclyf research have of course dictated considerable restructuring. Here, for the first time, commentaries on individual texts provide also a new kind of focus on the entire *corpus Wyclyfianum*. This is not to say that other authors of the age have been heretofore unfavored: such endeavors have sturdy medieval roots in the many well-worn *accessus ad auctores*,[10] some of which still survive.

It has not been judged necessary, with a few exceptions, to offer detailed descriptions of the manuscripts mentioned in this *Catalog*. Such descriptions may readily be found in the various printed catalogs of the collections themselves (many of which we cite), and as a rule also in the editions of Wyclyf's works to which reference is made under the rubric "III." for each piece. Those wishing a quick overview of the Wyclyf items in particular MSS will find a summary of the *contenta* in the "Index of Manuscripts" at the back of the book.

I wish to express my warmest thanks to Ruth J. Dean, distinguished medievalist and Thomson's close fellow-worker for more than four decades, for her gracious support and repeated help throughout the preparation of this edition. I am also grateful to Heather Phillips at Toronto for timely bibliographic and personal suggestions; to the Penrose Fund of the American Philosophical Society, for support in securing microfilms; to the Center for Medieval and Early Renaissance Studies at the State University of New York at Binghamton, where I was all too briefly a research associate; to Joseph H. Dahmus of The Pennsylvania State University, for his time and encouragement; and most profoundly to my mother, Rosamund Dargan Thomson, to whom this conjoint volume is proudly dedicated.

At the end, a memorandum more than personal, yet more private than public. S. Harrison Thomson was my father. After many seasons of promethean endeavor, he was compelled to struggle for eleven years against a wasting illness which stole away the time and energy he had allotted for the completion of this lifelong labor. I can only hope that the

---

[10] Cf. Edwin A. Quain, "The Medieval Accessus ad Auctores," *Traditio* 3 (1945): 215-264.

form which his scattered notes and partial manuscript (Section A only) have here assumed does justice to his vision. Inevitably, editorial decisions in the interests of uniformity and coherence of style and comprehensiveness of annotation are reflected on every page; for these I take sole responsibility. Over the years we tended Wyclyf's vines together, as occasion offered, and it is certain that of all the multitude of projects at various stages of conception and fruition which occupied him to the end of his fourscore years, he would most emphatically have wished for this companion volume to his celebrated and elegant *Grosseteste*[11] to see at last the light of day.

UNIVERSITY OF NOTRE DAME   W.R.T.

---

[11] *The Writings of Robert Grosseteste, Bishop of Lincoln 1235-1253* (Cambridge, Eng., 1940; reprinted New York, 1971). We have several autographs of Grosseteste; none can surely be attributed to Wyclyf.

Abbreviations

A. PUBLICATIONS AND TEXT COMMENTARY

A	Thomas Arnold, *Select English Works of John Wyclif* (Oxford, 1869), 3 vols.
AHR	*The American Historical Review*
B	Gustav Adolf Benrath, "Die Datierung von elf der sogenannten Quadraginta Sermones Wyclifs," in his *Wyclifs Bibelkommentar* (Berlin, 1966): 378-386
Bale	John Bale, *Scriptorum illustrium maioris Brytannię ... Catalogus. Centuria Sexta* (Basel, 1557-1559): 450-455 (Thomson enumeration of pieces)
BRUO I-III	A. B. Emden, *A Biographical Register of the University of Oxford to A.D. 1500* (Oxford, 1957-1959)
cap., capp.	*capitulum* or *capitula*
CHR	*The Catholic Historical Review*
DNB	*Dictionary of National Biography*
DSB	*Dictionary of Scientific Biography*
EHR	*English Historical Review*
JEH	*The Journal of Ecclesiastical History*
JTS	*Journal of Theological Studies*
L	Johann Loserth, *Johannes Wyclif Sermones* (London, 1887), 4 vols.
Lo	*Shirley's Catalogue of the Extant Latin Works of John Wyclif*, revised by Prof. Johann Loserth (London: WS, n.d., but 1924)
Lohr, "Commentaries..."	Charles H. Lohr, "Medieval Latin Aristotle Commentaries: Authors A-F," *Traditio* 23 (1967): 313-413; "... Authors G-I," *Traditio* 24 (1968): 149-245; "... Authors: Jacobus-Johannes Juff," *Traditio* 26 (1970): 135-216; "... Authors: Johannes de Kanthi-Myngodus," *Traditio* 27 (1971): 251-351; "... Authors: Narcissus-Richardus," *Traditio* 28 (1972): 281-396; "... Authors: Robertus:

	Wilgelmus," *Traditio* 29 (1973): 93-197; "... Supplementary Authors," *Traditio* 30 (1974): 119-144
M	William Mallard, "Dating the *Sermones Quadraginta* of John Wyclif," *MetH* 17 (1966): 86-105
MedSt	*Mediaeval Studies*
MetH	*Medievalia et Humanistica*
n.s.	new series
OHS	Oxford Historical Society
Podlaha	[A. Patera and] A. Podlaha, *Soupis Rukopisů knihovny Metropolitní kapitoly Pražské*, 2 vols. (Praha, 1910 and 1922). Customarily cited without page or volume reference
RS	Rolls Series
SCH	*Studies in Church History*
Sh	Walter Waddington Shirley, *A Catalogue of the Original Works of John Wyclif* (Oxford, 1865)
Truhlář	J. Truhlář, *Catalogus codicum manuscriptorum latinorum qui in C.R. Bibliotheca Publica atque Universitatis Pragensis asservantur*, 2 vols. (Praha, 1905, 1906). Customarily cited without page or volume reference
VC	The "Vienna catalogs": portions of four Wien, ÖNB MSS (3933, 3935, 4514, 7980) listing known *Wyclyfiana* as of about 1415-1430; transcribed in R. Buddensieg, *John Wiclif's Polemical Works in Latin* I (WS, 1883): LIX-LXXXIV
Workman, *JW* I-II	Herbert B. Workman, *John Wyclif. A Study of the English Medieval Church*, 2 vols. (Oxford, 1926; reprinted 1966)
WS	The Wyclif Society (fl. 1882-1924)

NOTE: Abbreviations of books of the Bible follows those of the RSV published by the A. J. Holman Co. of Philadelphia, 1962.

A † after an edition of a piece cited from J. Loserth, *Johannis Wyclif Opera Minora* (WS, 1913) indicates that it was also discussed in his "Wiclifs Sendschreiben, Flugschriften und kleinere Werke kirchenpolitischen Inhalts," *Sitzungsberichte der Kaiserlichen Akademie der Wissenschaften in Wien. Philosophisch-Historische Klasse* 166/6 (1910): 1-96.

Latin orthography is inevitably not wholly consistent throughout. Arabic numerals for Scriptural chapter and verse citations are standard, however (e.g., "8°", "21°"); and "Christus," "Antichristus," "Christianus," etc., are uniform.

ABBREVIATIONS XXI

B. LIBRARIES, ARCHIVES AND MANUSCRIPTS

BCommunale	Biblioteca Communale (Assisi)
BJag	Biblioteka Jagiellońska (Kraków)
BL	British Library (London)
BLaur	Biblioteca Medicea Laurenziana (Firenze)
BLB	Badische Landesbibliothek (Karlsruhe)
BMarc	Biblioteca Nazionale Marciana (Venezia)
BN	Bibliothèque Nationale (Paris)
	Biblioteca Nazionale (Napoli)
BNC	Biblioteca Nazionale Centrale (Firenze)
BPublique	Bibliothèque de la ville (Bruges)
BSB	Bayerische Staatsbibliothek (München)
BU	Biblioteca Universitaria (Pavia)
	Biblioteca Universitaria (Salamanca)
	Biblioteka Uniwersytecka (Wrocław)
C	Cambridge, Trinity College, MS B.16.2
D	Dublin, Trinity College, MS C.1.23
HzglB	Herzog August Bibliothek (Wolfenbüttel)
KapK	Kapitolní knihovna, Olomouc (presently housed in the Statní Archiv, Opava)
KunglB	Kunglig Biblioteket (Stockholm)
MK	Knihovna Metropolitní Kapituli (Praha)
OBod	Oxford, Bodleian Library, MS 716 (S.C. 2630)
OMC	Oxford, Magdalen College, MS 55
ÖNB	Österreichische Nationalbibliothek (Wien)
OSJ	Oxford, St. John's College, MS 171
PMK	Praha, Metropolitní Knihovna MSS
PNM	Praha, Narodny Museum MSS
PUK	Praha, Universitní Knihovna MSS
SBAmpl	Wissenschaftliche Bibliothek der Stadt (Erfurt)
UK	Universitní Knihovna (Brno)
	Universitní Knihovna (Praha)
W	Wien, Österreichische Nationalbibliothek MSS
Wo	Wolfenbüttel, HzglB, Cod.Guelf.

Italicized MSS are normally those not listed in Sh or Lo. MSS under a single rubric are denoted by boldface lower case roman numerals, omitting those MSS of a summary or index type, though providing separate listings for different copies of the same piece within a single codex. The individual pieces themselves are identified by boldface arabic numerals (italicized if no longer extant), though a parallel letter-number system is employed in tandem with these to illustrate relationships within a topical category.

Finally, the term "asc." as it applies to specific MSS signifies that the text in question is actually ascribed to Wyclyf somewhere in the codex itself; JW MS means that a substantial number of items (or a substantial portion of the MS) are by Wyclyf, but the text in question is not there ascribed to him.

Section A

Philosophy, Science and Systematic Theology

Throughout the turbulent twenty-odd years of John Wyclyf's rise to pre-eminence – some would have said then, and others might still say, notoriety – on the Oxford scene, it was always for him a stern imperative to commit his musings on the stubborn intangibles of being, deity, *dominium*, the *lex Christi* and the Eucharist to the disciplined format of chapter and treatise. Even outside the gray walls, in the twilight of his Lutterworth exile, he found time amid the long-range skirmishes of his private wars to structure his *Sermones* and encompass his fundamental articles of faith in the powerful *Trialogus*.

From his first steps in logic through the increasingly adroit *Summa de ente* and on to the massive drama of the *Summa theologie*, Wyclyf applied himself unremittingly to the understanding and voluminous explication of the intellectual issues which vexed his time. That these issues often appear arcane, abstruse and even unintelligible to us does not in the least invalidate his involvement with them – or the almost universal consensus, even among those who strove against his conclusions, that those very questions were *the* proper foci for all their precious training. For us to decry the intrinsic value of those pursuits is to expose our own secular fascinations to the same autocentric dismissal six centuries from now.

We do not have to romanticize the later medieval schoolmen to confirm the magnitude of their achievement. Wyclyf surely embodied the fearfulness, the dogmatism and even to a peculiar degree the feral vengefulness of his time and place. But he saw also the need to transcend those crippling attributes in order to grasp the high prize of blessedness. Wyclyf furthermore never believed that he had said all there was to say, or even everything he might want to say himself, on any subject. Indeed we sense that thought was with him an organic, ramifying process; and this is as good a reason as any to present at least this section in a roughly chronological sequence. That his words are of necessity fixed and frozen in place on the printed or manuscript page, and scattered through dozens of discrete volumes, should not confuse our awareness of their provisional character. He took more sheer delight in ringing changes than any theological bellman since Aquinas. His thought was forged in the fire of debate, cooled by the waters of reflection, and reforged anew in the flames of reassessment. In time he came to doubt the worth of academic exercise, and legalism, and the visible trappings of the *ecclesia militans*, and sought instead the deeper reaches of Spirit itself. That crowning triumph largely eluded him, for he could not long withstand the blighting allure of controversy; but we glimpse the spiritual travail of this essentially private man often enough to credit his sincerity.

1. A1. *De logica*. Ca. 1360.

   I. Inc. proem.: Motus sum per quosdam legis dei amicos ...
      Expl. proem.: × ... perfeccionem tocius operis specialiter me convertam.
      Inc. cap. i: Terminus large loquendo est diccio artificialiter inventa ...
      Expl.: × ... totum maius vel minus: ergo Paulus non erit perfeccior quam Petrus.

   II. MSS:

i	*Erfurt*, SB Ampl.	Q^o 253	ff. 1r-24v	ca. 1410	Asc. So. Ger.[1]
ii	Wien, ÖNB	4523	ff. 1r-16r	1412	Asc. Boh.

   III. Ed. M. H. Dziewicki, *Johannis Wyclif Tractatus de Logica* I (WS, 1893): 1-74. From **ii** only.

   IV. There can be no doubting the authenticity of this short exercise, surely the earliest of Wyclyf's surviving works, despite its absence from the early catalogs. The ÖNB codex contains exclusively ascribed Wyclyfiana and the early Erfurt copy is explicitly ascribed.

   The tractate, in 22 short capp., is rather elementary and not impressive. Yet it is possible to identify at several points the tentative statement of many problems in metaphysics which would engage him more substantially in later years.[2] The year 1360 is here suggested – it was the year he became *magister artium*[3] – though with no pretense to exactitude. None of Wyclyf's other writings is mentioned in it, though it is alluded to in turn in other demonstrably early treatises.

vc: deest   Bale: deest[4]   Sh: 1   Lo: 1

---

[1] Entitled *Summule magistri Joannis Wicleph* in the colophon. MS first noticed by H. Kühn-Steinhausen (= I. H. Stein), "Wyclif-Handschriften in Deutschland," *Zentralblatt für Bibliothekswesen* 47 (1930): 628; she here corrects Loserth's assignment of this MS to **2**; cf. S. H. Thomson, "Unnoticed MSS and Works of Wyclif," *JTS* 38 (1937): 25.

[2] This work, along with the *Trialogus* (**47**), is cited repeatedly in J. Kvačala, "Wiclef a Hus ako filosofi," *Věstník České královské Akademie* 1 (1924): 1-91.

[3] See the documents cited in J. A. Robson, *Wyclif and the Oxford Schools. The Relation of the 'Summa de Ente' to Scholastic Debates at Oxford in the Later Fourteenth Century* (Cambridge, Eng., 1961, reprinted 1966): 13.

[4] Unless we construe his "Logica de aggregatis" (= **30**), listed without incipit, as this treatise.

2. A2. *Logice continuacio.* Between 1360 and 1363.

  i. Inc. proem.: Iuvenum rogatibus quibus afficior superatus, tres tractatus [13wds.] logice propono contexere ...

  Expl. proem.: × ... diffusius priorum logicorum sentenciis, ut plurimum intendo.

  Inc. cap. i: Suppositis autem descripcionibus et distinccionibus [3 wds.] superest primo de probacionibus proposicionum de inesse per ordinem pertractandum ...

  Expl.: × ... in superiore opere meo totum hoc planius pertractatum, huic meo tractatui finem pono.

  ii. MSS:

i	*Assisi, BCommunale*	662	ff. 1ra-27rb	ca. 1385	Asc. Eng.[1]
ii	El Escorial	e.II.6	ff. 1ra-18vb	xiv/2	JW ms Eng.[2]
	[not in the Erfurt ms, *pace* Lo]				
iii	*Praha, MK*	N.19 (1543)	ff. 129ra-166ra	ca. 1410	Asc. Boh.
iv	UK	V.E.14 (908)	ff. 1r-32r	ca. 1400	Asc. Boh.[3]
v		V.H.33 (1010)	ff. 1r-28r	1430	Unasc. Boh.
vi	Wien, ÖNB	4523	ff. 16r-58r	1412	Asc. Boh.

  iii. Ed. M. H. Dziewicki, *Joannis Wyclif Tractatus de Logica* I (WS, 1893): 75-234. From **iv** and **vi** only.

  iv. Dziewicki evidently believed the proemium was tied to the *De logica* (*Summule*: see colophon in Erfurt ms: cf. **1**, n. 1); but a closer reading and comparison with the organization of the text shows that the term "summulas" in the proemium (immediately following our incipit) refers rather to the first part of the present work, capp. i-vii. The second part (confusingly, "tractatus secundus") commences with cap. viii, which deals with exclusive propositions, and extends through cap. xviii, where our explicit appears.[4] There is really no *obiter dictum* in this treatise which would help in dating it (and therefore in providing a *terminus a quo* for **1**). Yet it too is clearly quite early, as Wyclyf here only touches on subjects to be elaborated later in his career. Here his ideas, in contrast to their subsequent maturity of formulation, may properly be called undeveloped and sometimes painfully formal. It is apparent nonetheless that he already had in hand or at least in mind some more extensive treatment of questions he raises and disposes of summarily at this juncture. The expressions "ut alibi probabitur" and "ut post docebitur" occur several times (e.g., pp. 189, 203); these may, of course, be later insertions – though we should in that case expect the references to be more specific.

  The two MSS from which Dziewicki prepared his text are far from satisfactory. A new edition, deploying the four other copies listed above, would eliminate several of the egregious misreadings of which he properly complained.

vc: deest   Bale: 21   Sh: 2   Lo: 2

¹ Thomson, "Unnoticed MSS and Works of Wyclif," 27-28.
² Ibid., p. 27. Annotated by an Italian, ca. 1400: cf. f. 9r.
³ Ends near the conclusion of cap. xii. See ed., p. 176.
⁴ That this is the proper partition of the work as a whole is further substantiated by the visible demarcation into "tractatus primus" and "tractatus secundus," in the oldest extant MS. i.

3. A3. *De logica tractatus tercius*. 1363?

I. Inc.: Sequitur de speciebus ypoteticarum ut prius promiseram, in isto tractatu tercio pertractandum ...

Expl.: × ... huiusmodi parumper desistere, finem tocius operis quiecius inponendo, etc.¹

II. MSS:

i	Assisi,	BCommunale			
		662	ff. 28va-109va	ca. 1385	Asc. Eng.²
ii	El Escorial	e.II.6	ff. 19ra-76vb	xiv/2	JW MS Eng.³
iii	Praha, UK	V.E.14 (908)	ff. 33r-176v	ca. 1400	Asc. Boh.
iv		IX.E.3 (1759)	ff. 1r-176r	ca. 1410	Asc. Boh.⁴

[not in Wien, ÖNB 4523, *pace* Lo⁵]

III. Ed. M. H.Dziewicki, *Joannis Wyclif Tractatus de Logica* II and III (WS, 1896, 1899). From **iii** only.

IV. This work is a simple continuation of the preceding item, deserving of its traditional separate listing chiefly because of its divergent MS history. Internal references to **2** are abundant, e.g., II: 79, 109, 188, 209, 215; III: 52, etc. Evidently Wyclyf's reading had broadened considerably in the meantime, particularly among the medieval commentators on Aristotle. He already voices an opinion on the Real Presence (III: 137), which carries a momentous germ: in calling the remanent bread a "corpus mathematicum" and denying annihilation he hints at the path his more mature thought will follow. Another citation from the same page points in the same direction: "Quia vero ista materia isti loco est inpertinens, ideo non tracto eam ulterius, sed exspecto determinacionem tractare de speciali quidditate illius sacramenti sensibilis remanentis."

Besides the two Hussite scribes of **iii** and **iv**, another Czech student made diligent use of this work. The scribe of Praha, UK IV.H.9 (773), who transcribed several other Wyclyf pieces, also abstracted for his own needs salient arguments from the *Tractatus tercius*. Beginning on f. 259r, we read: "Suppono quedam tradita in tercio tractatu loyce magistri Johannis Wycliff, quorum primum est...." On f. 261r, again: "Si quis autem dilectet videre illam materiam diffusius respiciat tractatum tercium J. J. Wyclyff capitulo de condicionalibus." At the end of three pages of abstracts the scribe has appended (f. 262v): "Explicit quidam modus solvendi insolubilia secundum M. J. Wyclyff doctorem veritatis ewangelice, cuius anime propiciet deus amen," and a postscript: "inveni explicit in exemplari antiquo." (The allusion to insolubilia is almost surely not to **5**, but to II: 194-227 of Dziewicki's edition.)[6]

The statement (III: 183) "et inter terminos illius partis et ipsum nunc sunt mille trecenti et 83 anni" is deeply suspect. I suggest: (a) a copyist, writing in 1383, "corrected" the date from whatever it had been; or (b) the 8 is a mistake for an original 6. The date 1363 would fit nicely with the general course of Wyclyf's known intellectual evolution. But our oldest MS, **i**, has clearly written out (f. 101rb) "mille trecenti octoginta tres anni." A third suggestion therefore seems in order: Wyclyf himself, in the course of recopying his earlier work (not proven!) toward the end of his life, may have added the later date. Yet it is most unlikely that the old schoolman, embattled on several fronts as he was by 1383, would have left his earlier arguments in their original form – or would even have thought at such a remove to revive an interest which we know he regarded as only marginally relevant to his homiletic and polemical preoccupations at that time.

The single MS available to Dziewicki is, as he well knew, of inferior quality; a new edition would be welcome.

VC: deest   Bale: 22, 26[7]   Sh: deest[8]   Lo: 3

---

[1] Colophon follows in **iii**: "Et sic est finis Tercii tractatus Magistri Johannis Wicleff, Doctoris Evangelici, cuius anima habeat eterne visionis iocunditatem. Fideliter correctus, etc." To this Dziewicki wryly adds: "The editor may perhaps be excused here for saying that he thinks the two last words ought, for truth's sake, to have been omitted."

[2] For extraneous interpolations in this MS see Thomson, "Unnoticed MSS and Works of Wyclif," 26.

[3] Ibid., 27.

[4] An original ascription on f. 176r has been erased.

[5] Perhaps an inference from Dziewicki's title-pages; there, however, in all three volumes, it is mistakenly given as 4352.

On 17 March 1411 a commission of twelve Oxford masters and doctors drew up a list of 267 propositions from various of Wyclyf's writings which they deemed heretical or erroneous: David Wilkins, *Concilia Magnae Britanniae et Hiberniae* ... III (London, 1737): 339-349. Of these extracts, nos. 156-175 are charged to the present work (p. 346); but there are distortions in some of them. This commission, which we will call the "committee of twelve," must be distinguished from the twelve who censured some of Wyclyf's teachings at the behest of Chancellor Barton in 1380: see below, **39**, and see also below, for further citations from the 1411 committee, **28-30**; **35**; **47**, n. 10; **374-377**, n. 13; **384**, n. 2; **386**, n. 4; **408**, n. 17; **410**, n. 8; **414**, n. 5; **426**, n. 2; **430**, n. 2. – For the text of the declaration prohibiting the teaching or defense of any of the 267 articles, see H. Anstey, ed., *Munimenta Academica, or Documents Illustrative of Academical Life and Studies at Oxford* I: *Libri Cancellarii et Procuratorum* (London, RS, 1868): 268-270. H. E. Salter, *Medieval Oxford* (Oxford, OHS Publications 100, 1936): 110-112, casts grave doubt on the persistent notion that Wyclyf's influence in the Oxford colleges after his departure late in 1381 was of measurable significance. But if this be true, then why the need for the committee at all, and why did Thomas Netter and so many others labor so assiduously to pick apart his legacy? J. I. Catto's section on "Wyclifism at Oxford, 1360-1430" in the forthcoming work by T. H. Aston, *History of the University of Oxford*, should help to resolve this issue.

[6] Much the same sort of digest appears also in Praha, MK N.19 (1543), ff. 110vb-121ra. See also below, **5**, n. 2, and G*Dub*. 7 for ed. of **iii**.

[7] No. 26, "De distinctivis," corresponds to cap. ii: cf. II: 55-72.
[8] He lists it among "Lost Works" of Wyclyf on p. 51, no. 37, from Bale.

4. A4. *De actibus anime.* Ca. 1365.

I. Inc.: Gracia dicendarum restat tractare de actibus, potenciis, intencionibus et habitibus anime ...

Expl.: × ... cognoscibilis privacione per adnichilacionem substancia sensibilis stantibus accidentibus.

II. MSS:

i   Cambridge, Corpus
    Christi Coll.   103   pp. 47a-87b   xv/1   Asc. Eng.[1]

III. Ed. M. H. Dziewicki, *Johannis Wyclif Miscellanea Philosophica* I (WS, 1902): 1-127. From unique MS.

IV. To this day we still know of only one MS of this important work, wherein it is ascribed to "J. Wicleff" in the rubric of about the turn of the century. But the internal evidence for Wyclyf's authorship is indisputable: there is, for example, an exact reference in the future tense to the *De insolubilibus* (**5**: p. 28) "De hoc dicetur in 1º libro de insolubilibus," which would suggest that the later piece was at least in its first draft.

But a more interesting fact about this essay is that it was apparently intended as a sort of commentary on the *Perspectiva* of the Polish optician "Witelo" (Erazm Ciołek? or Witek?: d. ca. 1270).[2] Wyclyf alludes to "2º libro" and "3º libro," without naming the author, in such a way as to hint that his students were thoroughly conversant with this standard text of the geometry curriculum.[3] See, e.g., at the beginning of cap. iii (p. 38): "Pro responsione ad istud dubium suppono divisionem accionis 3º libro declaratam." The scribe, at some remove from Wyclyf's classroom, has added revealing detail in another context (p. 46): "sicut allegatum est 3º libro (*scilicet liº 3º questione 16ª vitulonis*), visio non fit sine dolore et passione oculi a substancia abiciente." (Emphasis added.) Yet again, in dealing with *motus* as it relates to the "acts of the soul," he says: "quamvis Barlay [= Burley] et precipuis logicis videatur quod auctor sit intelligendus de accionibus corporis quod omnes tales sunt in motu." (P. 49.) Walter Burley certainly also knew "Witelo," but he barely discusses this point in his schematic *De potenciis anime*;[4] perhaps the reference is to his fuller commentary on Aristotle's *De anima*.[5] The beginning of Wyclyf's "pars secunda" (p. 59) confirms this consistent, if curiously tacit, *renvoi* to "Witelo": "Sequitur secunda pars, cuius primam partem quoad veritatem de preterito tractabo isto capitulo. Ponit enim quod summe contingens est me fuisse, et sic de omni veritate de preterito que aliquando potuit non fuisse." The subject of the "ponit," against whose position Wyclyf contends throughout the book, can be none other than "Witelo."

There is a somewhat puzzling reference on p. 80: "Est autem dare multas species obligacionum et multas species posicionum, ut patebit 6to libro." The term "liber" in Wyclyf usually means a larger collection made up of discrete tractates. But if we may presume that it is a general statement in this case, concerning an entire, substantial section in his "sextus liber," it would easily fit capp. ix-xii of the *De universalibus* (**11**), the *fifth* tractate of the first book of the *Summa de ente*. It is hardly an inconceivable error, given the slender reed of our single MS — yet it may indeed not be an error at all, if we accept the suggested rearrangement of the treatises in the first part of the *Summa de ente*.[6]

Wyclyf makes another strange mention of his own labors. In a discussion of time and the delineation of instants, he writes (p. 87): "Sed de hoc in tractatu proximo." One would naturally look for this elaboration in the *De tempore* (**12**), but that is not "proximus" by any collocation thus far suggested. (With Wyclyf, idiosyncratically, "proximus" almost always signifies "just preceding": cf. **3**, II: 209, *et frequenter alibi*.) In fact Wyclyf dwells on the nature of time and the various aspects of the instant in a number of his works, but I suggest that this particular allusion is actually to cap. xiv of the *Logice continuacio* (**2**: 191-202), which, if the tripartite *De logica* (**2, 3**) be regarded as one work, would acceptably explain the "proximo" of our text, and further bolster our assumption that the *De actibus anime* was written shortly after the *De logica*. It is still an indisputably early work, however: on p. 106 we are treated to a rare autobiographical aside: "iam falsum est quod ego vixi 40 annos."

VC: deest   Bale: 37[7]   Sh: 11   Lo: 12.

---

[1] A most intriguing miscellaneous MS. A number of its 20 separate pieces relate to the mendicants. For a summary, see M. R. James, *A Descriptive Catalogue of the Manuscripts in the Library of Corpus Christi College, Cambridge* I (Cambridge, Eng., 1912): 198-201. Immediately preceding our text is a brief, acidulous comment on Wyclyf by Philip Melanchthon; the last items are our **378** and **380**, below. Item 18, identified by James as "Quaedam capitula de summa [theologiae] fratris Alvari de ordine minorum" (pp. 331a-415b), is in fact a sizable portion of the massive *De planctu ecclesiae libri duo*, by the austere Franciscan penitentiary to John XXII, Álvaro Pelayo (Pais), ca. 1275-1352. M. C. Díaz y Díaz, *Index Scriptorum Latinorum Medii Aevi Hispanorum* II (Salamanca, 1959): 406, does not list this MS: it would therefore seem to be the only known MS of English provenance. For bibliography on Álvaro, see W. Holtzmann and R. Morghen, edd., *Repertorium Fontium Historiae Medii Aevi* ... II: *Fontes A-B* (Roma, 1967): 205-206; cf. V. Meneghin, ed., *Scritti inediti di Fra Álvaro Pais* (Lisboa, 1969). Wyclyf may have known, or known of, this harsh critique, but nowhere cites it.

[2] The *Perspectiva* proved to be a durable and highly influential treatise for several centuries. It was printed at Nürnberg in 1535 and again in 1551; then once again at Basel (ed. F. Risner) in 1572. Wyclyf would probably not have used the MS now designated Oxford, Bodleian Ashmolean 424 (*olim* Cambridge, Peterhouse Coll. 250); but the marginalia in Oxford, Merton Coll. 308 (unfoliated) might just conceivably be Wyclyf's own: the codex is English, ca. 1330. (On these and other MSS and editions, see M. R. James, *The Western Manuscripts in the Library of Emmanuel College* [Cambridge, Eng., 1904], item 20; Lynn Thorndike and Pearl Kibre, *A Catalogue of Incipits of Mediaeval Scientific Writings in Latin*, 2nd ed. [Cambridge, Mass., 1963]: cols. 1085, 1547, 1689.) Cf. also Wyclyf's own

explicit citation of "Witelo" in the *De civili dominio* I (**28**): 238-239, 377, *et frequenter alibi*. – On "Witelo" generally, cf. C. Bäumker, *Witelo, ein Philosoph und Naturforscher des XIII. Jahrhunderts* (Münster, 1908); A. Bednarski, "Die astronomischen Augenbilder in den Handschriften des Roger Bacon, Johann Peckham und Witelo," [*Sudhoffs*] *Archiv für Geschichte der Medizin* 24 (1931): 60-78; George Sarton, *Introduction to the History of Science* II/2 (Baltimore, 1931): 1027-1028; A. C. Crombie, *Robert Grosseteste and the Origins of Experimental Science 1100-1700* (Oxford, 1953; reprinted 1962, 1971): 213-232; *Encyclopedia of World Art* IV (New York etc., 1961): 125-126; X (1965): 763; XI (1965): 89-90; D. C. Lindberg, "Lines of Influence in Thirteenth-Century Optics: Bacon, Witelo and Pecham," *Speculum* 46 (1971): 66-83; idem, "Witelo," DSB XIV (New York, 1976): 457-462; Wilfred Theisen, "Witelo's Recension of Euclid's 'De Visu'," *Traditio* 33 (1977): 394-402; idem, "*Liber de Visu*: The Greco-Latin Translation of Euclid's *Optics*," *MedSt* 41 (1979): 44-105. (It was proposed a few years ago that "Witelo" may be a misreading for "Witek": Pierre M. Duhem, *Le système du monde: histoire des doctrines cosmologiques de Platon à Copernic*, 2nd ed., III [Paris, 1954]: 509; cf. II: 120-121; III: 508-511, 514-516; V: 369-373. Ciołek is the reading throughout the *Encyclopedia of World Art*.)

The study of optics and of light was a major scientific concern in the English universities, owing largely to Grosseteste's fascination with the subject. See the several relevant titles examined in Thomson, *The Writings of Robert Grosseteste*, 89-120; C. C. Riedl, trans., *Robert Grosseteste on Light (De Luce)* (Milwaukee, 1942); Crombie, *Robert Grosseteste and the Origins of Experimental Science*, 128-134; idem, *Medieval and Early Modern Science in the Middle Ages: V-XIII Centuries*, 2nd ed. (Cambridge, Mass., 1967): 98-113. Also of value is E. J. Dijksterhuis, *The Mechanization of the World Picture* (Oxford, 1961): 154-162. And behind Grosseteste loomed Augustine: see particularly F.-J. Thonnard, "La notion de lumière en philosophie augustinienne," *Recherches augustiniennes* 2 (1962): 125-175.

But of course any systematic survey of this subject must go back to the seminal Alhazen (= Abû 'Alî al-Ḥasan [or Ḥusayn] ibn al-Haytham al-Baṣri al-Miṣri, ca. 965-1039), whose *Kitāb fi 'l-manāẓir* (= *Thesaurus Opticae libri vii*: trans. 13th cent., Latin ed., F. Risner, Basel, 1572; new Arabic ed. M. N. Bey, Cairo, 1942-1943) surely influenced "Witelo." On extant MSS of his various writings, see Thorndike and Kibre, *A Catalogue of Incipits*, cols. 528, 774, 803, 894, 1021-1022, 1147. Especially valuable are the articles by J. Vernet in *The Encyclopaedia of Islam*, 2nd ed., III (Leiden, 1971): 788-799, and I. Sabra in DSB VI (1972): 189-210. Cf. also H. J. J. Winster, "The Optical Researches of Ibn al-Haitham," *Centaurus* 3 (1954): 190-210; Seyyed Hossein Nasr, *Islamic Science: An Illustrated Study* (Westerham, 1976): *passim*. Jacob Bronowski called Alhazen "the one really original scientific mind that Arab culture produced." (*The Ascent of Man* [Boston and Toronto, 1973]: 179.) Two additional studies require mention here: Joseph A. Mazzeo, "Light Metaphysics, Dante's 'Convivio' and the Letter to Can Grande della Scala," *Traditio* 14 (1958): 191-229; and David C. Lindberg, *A Catalogue of Medieval and Renaissance Optical Manuscripts* (Toronto, PIMS: Subsidia Mediaevalia 4, 1975).

Wyclyf also displayed familiarity with the work of another Arab scholar, the anti-Ptolemaic astronomer Alpetragius (= Nûr ad-Dîn abu-Isḥâq al-Biṭrûji, d. ca. 1204): cf. **3**, III: 23. His *Kitāb fi 'l-Hay'a* was translated by Michael Scot as *De motibus coelorum* in 1217. (Lynn Thorndike, *Michael Scot* [London and Edinburgh, 1965]: 22-24; S. H. Thomson, "Scot, Michael," *Encyclopedia of Philosophy* VII [1967]: 343; L. Minio-Paluello, "Michael Scot," DSB IX [1974]: 361-364.) See, on MSS, Lynn Thorndike, *A History of Magic and Experimental Science* III (New York, 1934): 90; and the ed. by J. J. Carmody, *Al-Bitruji, De Motibus Coelorum* (Berkeley, 1952), and articles by J. Vernet, *The Encyclopedia of Islam*, 2nd ed., I (1960): 1250; Julio Samsó, "Al-Biṭrûji Al-Ishbîli, Abû Isḥâq," DSB XV (1978): 33-36. – But Wyclyf's acquaintance with the translated works of Muslim and Jewish thinkers went beyond this: see the several references in Workman, *JW* I: 336. Touching the much larger question of the crosscultural impact of Islâm, see now Dorothee Metlitzki, *The Matter of Araby in Medieval England* (New Haven and London, 1977).

[3] Pp. 2, 12, 14, 38, 46, 53, 116, 121.

[4] Partial MS listing in James A. Weisheipl, "*Repertorium Mertonense*," *MedSt* 31 (1969): 201-202. L. Bieler at Dublin had an unpublished edition of this work some years ago: C. Martin, "Walter Burley," in *Oxford Studies presented to Daniel Callus* (Oxford, 1964): 203; it was recently edited, however, by M. J. Kitchel, "The 'De potentiis animae' of Walter Burley," *MedSt* 33 (1971): 85-113; cf. ¶¶ 8, 9, 122 (pp. 88, 108). On Burley, see *BRUO* I: 310-314; Herman Shapiro, "Walter Burley and Text 71," *Traditio* 16 (1960): 395-404; and below, **33**, n. 6, and **51**, n. 2.

[5] Cf. Lohr, "Commentaries ... G-I," 182-183; Weisheipl, "*Repertorium Mertonense*," gives one additional MS.

[6] See **13** and n. 2, below.

[7] "Tractatum de anima, Lib. 1. Restat ulterius pertractare de." The incipit is close, and nothing else would quite fit this title.

5. A5. *De proposicionibus insolubilibus*. Ca. 1365.

I. Inc.: Quia omnes homines natura scire desiderant secundum philosophum ... Expl.: × ... pro clarificacione intellectus requirit.

II. MSS:

i	Oxford, Magdalen Coll.	*38*	ff. 23ra-28vb	xiv/2	Unasc. Eng.[1]
ii	Praha, UK	*VIII.E.11 (1536)*	ff. 55v-72v	ca. 1425	Misasc. Boh.[2]
iii	Salamanca, BU	*2358*	ff. 33v-50r	ca. 1400	Asc. Eng.
iv	Wien, ÖNB	*5204*	ff. 76r-96v	ca. 1410	Asc. Boh.
v		*5239*	ff. 146r-147v	ca. 1400	Asc. Boh.[3]

III. Unpublished.[4]

IV. According to Bale,[5] this treatise is supposed to have been in the library of Balliol College, Oxford, but we have had to look elsewhere for our MSS. Until recently it was generally accepted that, if Wyclyf did indeed occupy himself with the subject of insoluble propositions, it was in that portion of his *Tractatus tercius* (**3**: III: 194-227, cap. viii) that we should search.[6] But the discovery of this early and thrice-ascribed text puts any doubts to rest.[7] We also know that the fourth book of John Tarteys' *Logica* "contains a commentary on the *Summa insolubilium* [sic] of J. Wyclif."[8] Indeed it appears that Wyclyf was profoundly concerned with this question and sensitive to the appeals of his students to clarify a very knotty logical technique.[9] He avers, in the opening paragraph: "Ideo ex dei gracia plenam veramque [exposicionem?] insolubilium pro iuvenum erudicione in dei honorem aperte rescribo, promittens primo de proposicionum denominacionibus principia generalia, secundo insolubilium quiditatem pertractans de eorum convertibilitate ac contradiccione principia specialia subiungam. Et tercio ipsa principia insolubili categoriso, deinde insolubili ypotetico finaliter sunt applicanda."

The text of the treatise is not a little peculiar. There is not a single reference to any of Wyclyf's other works, and only one to any other writing – a paraphrase, in our incipit, from the beginning – itself a commonplace – of Aristotle's *Metaphysics*. The work is rigorously limited to the gymnastics of the insolubles.

vc: deest   Bale: 183   Sh: deest[10]   Lo: deest

[1] Incipit begins "Quoniam ..."; an incomplete text.
[2] Part of a Tarteys codex, and asc. to him in the colophon: see below, n. 8. Curiously, the scribe was also careless with the colophon to William Milverley's *Universalia*, f. 140r: "Explicit universalia Wilhelmi Miravelle de Tartis ..." On Milverley, see *BRUO* II: 1287.
[3] A fragment.
[4] S. H. Thomson's transcript of text of iv is in the editor's possession.
[5] Poole and Bateson, edd., *Index Britanniae Scriptorum* ..., 269. Here Bale also indicates lost MSS at Balliol of three books of *Questiones* (= ?), 11, 12, 16 (he mentions too an "Alterum de ydeis"); 20 and 21. Cf. R. A. B. Mynors, *Catalogue of the Manuscripts of Balliol College Oxford* (Oxford, 1963): 384-385.
[6] Cf. the quotation from the scribe of Praha, UK IV.H.9: above, **3**. Paul V. Spade, *The Mediaeval Liar: A Catalogue of the* Insolubilia-*Literature* (Toronto, PIMS: Subsidia Mediaevalia 5, 1975): 76-77, regards it as "doubtful" that *this* piece might be by Wyclyf himself. But it is an extract. The reference to our *De proposicionibus insolubilibus* is also unmistakable in **4** (p. 28: see above).
[7] Thomson, "Unnoticed MSS and Works of Wyclif," 139-144.
[8] A. B. Emden, "Additions and Corrections to *A Biographical Register of the University of Oxford to A.D. 1500*. Supplemental List no. 2," *The Bodleian Library Record* 7 (1964): 160. Not much is known of Tarteys: see *BRUO* III: 1849. The piece attributed to him by Spade, *The Mediaeval Liar*, 70, is actually Wyclyf's: see above, n. 2. Tarteys' work may be found in Praha, MK M.136 (1506), ff. 59v-86v.
[9] It was not an uncommon exercise in the schools. Probably most influential in Wyclyf's background was Burley: cf. *BRUO* I: 314; Weisheipl, "*Repertorium Mertonense*," 196; Spade, *The Mediaeval Liar*, 111-113. Weisheipl and Spade adequately cover the MSS between them; we shall add here only Bruges, BPublique 497, ff. 46ra-59va (William Heytesbury: cf. *BRUO* II: 927-928; Spade, *The Mediaeval Liar*, 105-110); and Oxford, Bodleian Lat. th. C.32, f. 26vb; Canon. misc. 219, ff. 102va-103rb (Peter of Mantua: cf. Spade, *The Mediaeval Liar*, 86). On the growth of this issue in the schools generally, see C. Prantl, *Geschichte der Logik im Abendlande* IV (Leipzig, 1867; reprinted Graz, 1955); s.v. "insolubilia" in index; C. S. Peirce, "Insolubilia," in *Dictionary of Philosophy and Psychology*, ed. J. M. Baldwin, I (New York and London, 1901): 554; I. M. Bocheński, *A History of Formal Logic* (ed. and trans. I. Thomas, Notre Dame, 1961): 237-251; Spade, *The Mediaeval Liar, passim*.

The predilection of the Oxford masters for this sort of logical exercise was evidently well-known in Continental centers by the mid-fourteenth century: cf. Spade, ibid., 69. We may more precisely refer to Vaticano, Vat. lat. 3065, ff. 21ra-31vb ("secundum usum heusonie"); Venezia, BMarc. Z.L.301, ff. 37rb-41rb (a list of "regula solvendi insolubilia secundum usum esoniensem"); Worcester, Cath. Chap. F.118: "Sophistria secundum usum Oxonie."
[10] But listed in his enumeration of "Lost Works, of which the first words are not preserved" (from Bale, i.e.), p. 50, no. 183.

6. A6. [*Questiones et dubia super viii libros physicorum*].[1] Mid- to late 1360s?

I. Inc.: Phylosophia realis dividitur in tres partes ...
   Expl.: × ... et iste est separatus preter supremum intentum que est pars primi animalis celestis et sic est finis.

II. MSS:

i   *Venezia, BMarc.*   *lat. VI.173*   ff. 1ra-58vb   xv/1   Asc. Ger.?[2]

III. Unpublished.[3]

IV. We are not accustomed to thinking of Wyclyf as a close student of the sciences of his day.[4] Always he has worn the somber garb of the theologian, and only more recently the metaphysician's finery. Yet any mind nurtured in the soil of fourteenth-century scholasticism had to absorb formidable quantities of Aristotle and, in somewhat altered form, the phalanx of Arabic commentators on him.[5] Wyclyf's familiarity with optics and astronomy has already engaged us;[6] that he should at some early time in his academic career have paused to wrestle the Philosopher, point by point, through all eight books of the *Physics* is fully consonant with the prevailing pattern of the collegiate curriculum. In view of Wyclyf's thoroughgoing realism, as opposed to the marked nominalist leanings of Aristotle's least discriminating adherents in Wyclyf's day, it is only surprising that a more concerted effort has not hitherto been made to assimilate this collection of 16 *dubia* into our composite image of Wyclyf's intellectual evolution.[7]

Within the work we come upon at least two references to other treatises by Wyclyf himself. On f. 30vb he hints at the *De logica* (= probably **3**): "sicut dixi super loicam." But earlier we read: "hic tamen recitabo communia argumenta concernencia logicam quam adduxi libro predicamentorum." This surely intimates the *De ente predicamentali* (**13**: cf. p. 52) – which itself poses, as we shall see, a thorny dating problem. Whether the composition of these *dubia* – in any case an *ad hoc* effort – ought therefore to be placed prior to the *Summa de ente*, about midway through that enterprise, or even later, cannot be decided on present evidence.

VC: deest   Bale: 196, 197[8]   Sh: deest[9]   Lo: deest

---

[1] Mistakenly given as *Questiones ... super tres primos libros ...* in Thorndike and Kibre, *Catalogue of Incipits*, col. 1043. Our title, as indicated by the brackets, is inferential. Lohr, "Commentaries ... Johannes de Kanthi-Myngodus," 304-305, lists this piece as "of doubtful ascription," without elaboration. It is likely that further substantiation of Wyclyf's authorship may emerge from at least two MSS of a younger Oxford colleague's own *Questiones super libros physicorum*: the German "doctor famosus," John Scharpe, who is known to have opposed Wyclyf on universals. (See the marginalia "opinio Wyclyf" and "contra Wyclyf," ff. 65ra and 67ra of Oxford, Balliol Coll. 93; also cf. Oxford, Bodleian Digby 49, f. 80r ["Wyclyf concordat cum opinione..."].) For bibliography on, and other MSS of, Scharpe, see Lohr, ibid., 279-280; *BRUO* III: 1680.

     J. A. Robson, *Wyclif and the Oxford Schools*, 139, has called our attention to an unmistakable reference to this commentary in M. Bateson, ed., *Catalogue of the Library of Syon Monastery, Isleworth* (Cambridge, Eng., 1898): no. 244: "Wyclyf super tres libros methereorum et super 8 libros phisicorum Aristotelis." But this would seem to be an erroneous indication: it appears only in the index and not in the catalog itself. Both were compiled just before the Dissolution, and very few MSS are known to have survived from this collection. See below, **42**, n. 4.

[2] A mixed hand: see Thomson, "Unnoticed MSS and Works of Wyclif," 145-146.

[3] Extracts in ibid., 146-148.

⁴ George Sarton, of course, conceived of science in the broadest possible sense in his magnificent *Introduction to the History of Science* (3 vols. in 5: Baltimore, 1927-1948). In vol. III/2: 1346, he has in fact next to nothing to say of Wyclyf's science *strictu sensu*. His remark as to the "Joachimite sources of Wycliffe" is arresting – but it must be remembered that Wyclyf was generally critical of the Calabrian abbot; and how well he knew the texts of Joachim is also moot: see Workman, *JW* II: 99n. The references to him are abundant enough: cf. **10**: 47; **13**: 18; **23**: 94; **28**: 325; **30**: III: 258; **31**: I: 140-141; III: 250; **38**: 278; **60**: 35; **373**: 375; **375**: 216. Ranulf Higden's well-thumbed *Polychronicon*, nevertheless, is patently his source in several of these citations.

⁵ The enormous series, *Aristoteles Latinus* (Bruges, 1939 – : to comprise 34 vols.), will be definitive; yet we should still mention the many invaluable contributions of Martin Grabmann. From another angle, the several pertinent papers in Richard Walzer, *Greek into Arabic: Essays on Islamic Philosophy* (Cambridge, Mass., 1962), are also significant here.

⁶ 4, n. 2, above.

⁷ The question of Wyclyf's proximate stimulus for this commentary may not be susceptible of sure solution. Certainly one of two alternative hypotheses seems most likely (and the two are by no means mutually exclusive): any one (or more than one?) of Walter Burley's five separate interpretations of the *Physics* (cf. Lohr, "Commentaries ... G-I," 179-181; S. H. Thomson, "Unnoticed *questiones* of Walter Burley on the *Physics*," *Mitteilungen des Instituts für Österreichische Geschichtsforschung* 62 [1954]: 390-405); or Grosseteste's *Commentarius in viii libros Physicorum Aristotelis*, ed. Richard C. Dales (Boulder, Colorado, 1963): cf. Thomson, *The Writings of Robert Grosseteste*, 82. Grosseteste also wrote a *Summa in viii libros Physicorum Aristotelis*: cf. Thomson, "The *Summa in VIII Libros Physicorum* of Grosseteste," *Isis* 22 (1934): 12-18; *The Writings of Robert Grosseteste*, 83. (To the list of MSS there offered may be added, Assisi, BCommunale 690 and Madrid, BN 2076.)

⁸ There given as *De physica naturali* and *De intentione Physica*.

⁹ Cited as lost from Bale: p. 52, nos. 196, 197.

A7. *Summa de ente* [*Summa intellectualium*]. Ca. 1365 to 1372.

That Wyclyf surely intended to assemble two *summae*, one philosophical and the other a composite treatment of political and theological questions that challenged his interest, is nowhere disputed. So far as we know, however, he himself never actually used the term *summa* for either grouping.¹ But the ordered contents of the Cambridge MS (Trinity Coll. B.16.2), arranged in conspicuous clarity, add evidential weight. (This MS has often been discussed, and is adequately described elsewhere.)² Finally, Wyclyf often refers to treatises within this philosophical *summa* by *liber*, *tractatus* and *capitulum*, e.g.: "ut declaratum est superius libro primo tractatu primo capitulo finali," a *renvoi* to cap. v of the *De ente in communi*.

A great gain in Wyclyf scholarship was registered by J. A. Robson in his very careful study, *Wyclif and the Oxford Schools: The Relation of the "Summa de Ente" to Scholastic Debates at Oxford in the Later Fourteenth Century*.³ Although the sequence of the separate treatises in this *summa* is fairly well established, there remains one interesting aspect of the whole corpus which seems thus far to have been overlooked.

The first *liber* of the *Summa de ente*, containing seven treatises, is devoted to being as it relates to man. Wyclyf's involuted exposition tends to obscure so simple a characterization; yet it does offer us a certain thematic unity. The second *liber* (with six treatises), on the other hand, deals directly with God and His attributes. We may perceive this differentiation most plainly in comparing the two parallel treatises *De universalibus* (**10**) and *De ydeis* (**18**): universals are entities intellected by man; ideas are the same entities, or productive exemplars, as constituted in the mind of God. In the concluding chapter of the *De universalibus* Wyclyf asserts: "ydea est forma eterna in mente divina ad cuius exemplar deus est productivus creature." And the *De ydeis* begins: "Primo oportet querere si sint [i.e., ydee], presupponendo quid nominis tale quod ydea sign[ific]at racionem exemplarem eternam aput deum secundum quod deus est productivus rei ad extra."

In his chapter (pp. 115-140) on the structure of the *Summa de ente* Robson comes to grips with the problems arising from the disjointed organization of *liber* II. He makes the very penetrating suggestion (p. 134) that in the treatises *De trinitate* and *De ydeis* we may have the unfinished first book of a commentary on the *Sentences* of Peter Lombard. Hitherto it has been accepted, though not always without reservation, that the *De verbi incarnacione* (**22**) was Wyclyf's sole sententiary work.[4] Robson's thesis, while it raises some new questions, undeniably has intrinsic merit. We must face the fact that, in the form in which we now have the *Summa de ente*, ordered by *liber* and *tractatus*, its many cross-references are quite specific and apparently definitive. Yet this by no means precludes the possibility that at some earlier stage in his composition, Wyclyf may have structured his various projects otherwise than in the form which has come down to us. In 1929 S. H. Thomson attempted to rationalize the pervasive presence of these cross-references by assuming that the tractates were not published "before the lectures had been delivered and corrected perhaps several times."[5] As previously remarked, we possess no first recension of any of his works, though of course such may yet be unearthed. Perhaps Wyclyf, not satisfied with his text, withheld publication pending revision, and then destroyed his preliminary drafts. In view of the fact that the cross-references do not appear as insertions in any of our MSS – meaning that Wyclyf himself integrated them very carefully – this does not seem too farfetched a supposition. But on this assumption any assignment of specific dates to the component treatises ceases to make much sense. Yet we can, in spite of all this, still argue for an *intended* order of writing, which is reflected in Wyclyf's use of the past or future tenses in the cross-references, e.g., "ut dictum est," "ut dicitur post," "ut patebit post," etc.

Bibliographical details of the thirteen tractates will be offered *seriatim* below.[6]

[1] The term is already in evidence ca. 1415, our date for the completion of the earliest of the vc: cf. Wien, ÖNB 3933 ("Eciam est summa sua in theologia que in Boemia habetur, summa in logica [i.e., **1-3**]. ... Summa ejusdem in theologia continet duodecim libros in se."); 4514 ("Summa theologie hec est et continet in se duodecim libros ..."); cf. Sh: 62, 68. It does not in fact appear in connection with Wyclyf's *philosophical* corpus until Bale's time (Bale: 70), though the parallelism is obvious. (For an

earlier use of the term as applied to Wyclyf's logical tractates – or some combination of them – see Robson, *Wyclif and the Oxford Schools,* 128-129, 225-226.)

[2] First by Shirley (1865), xiii-xvi; then by M. R. James, *Catalogue of the Manuscripts of Trinity College, Cambridge* I (Cambridge, Eng., 1908): 513, no. 378.

[3] Cf. reviews by S. H. Thomson, *Speculum* 38 (1963): 497-499; Gordon Leff, *EHR* 77 (1962): 721-723; D. E. R. Watt, *Philosophical Quarterly* 13 (1963): 175-176; C. H. Lawrence, *History* 47 (1962): 300-301.

[4] But see remarks on this point in **47**, below.

[5] "The Order of Writing of Wyclif's Philosophical Works," in *Českou Minulostí práce, věnované profesoru Karlovy university Václavu Novotnému,* edd. O. Odložilík, J. Prokeš and R. Urbánek (Praha, 1929): 146.

[6] Specific treatments of Wyclyf the philosopher are less plentiful than his stature deserves. Cf. M. H. Dziewicki, "An Essay on Wyclif's Philosophical System" (the preface to his ed., *Johannis Wyclif Miscellanea Philosophica* I [WS, 1902]: v-xxvii); Kvačala, "Wiklef a Hus ako filosofi;" Gotthard Lechler, *Johann von Wiclif und die Vorgeschichte der Reformation* I (Leipzig, 1873: this substantial two-volume biography commanded the field before Workman): 458-466; Victor Vattier, *John Wyclyff D.D. Sa vie – ses œuvres – sa doctrine* (Paris, 1886): 199-222; Workman, *JW* I: 103-150; Thomson "The Philosophical Basis of Wyclif's Theology;" L. H. Rashdall, *The Universities of Europe in the Middle Ages* III (new ed. by F. M. Powicke and A. B. Emden, Oxford, 1936; orig. ed., 1895): 265-272; Etienne Gilson, *History of Christian Philosophy in the Middle Ages* (New York, 1955): 771-772; Michael J. Wilks, "The Early Oxford Wyclif: Papalist or Nominalist?" in *SCH* 5: *The Church and Academic Learning,* ed. G. J. Cuming (Leiden, 1969): 69-98; additional items by S. H. Thomson in n. 4 to the editor's preface, above. – The short article by the Marxist Robert Kalivoda, "Joannes Wyclifs Metaphysik des Extremen Realismus und ihre Bedeutung im Endstadium der mittelalterlichen Philosophie," in *Miscellanea Medievalia* II: *Die Metaphysik im Mittelalter,* ed. R. Wilpert (Berlin, 1963): 716-723, is unfortunately lacking in critical apparatus. Four standard multi-volume surveys – Maurice de Wulf, *Histoire de la philosophie médiévale* (6th ed., 3 vols., Paris, 1934-1947); Bernhard Geyer, ed., *Friedrich Ueberwegs Grundriss der Geschichte der Philosophie* (12th ed., 5 vols., Basel, 1951); Frederick J. Copleston, *A History of Philosophy* (8 vols., New York, 1946-1966); and Wilhelm Totok, *Handbuch der Geschichte der Philosophie* II: *Mittelalter* (Frankfurt, 1973): 600-601, scarcely mention Wyclyf at all.

The question of Wyclyf's ambivalent response to the works of Ockham requires more fine distinctions than those drawn by L. Baudry, "À propos de Guillaume d'Ockham et de Wiclef," *Archives d'histoire doctrinale et littéraire du moyen-âge* 14 (1939): 231-251 – but he did there advance beyond Loserth, "Studien zur Kirchenpolitik Englands im 14. Jahrhundert, I: Bis zum Ausbruch des Grossen Schismas (1378)," *Sitzungsberichte der kaiserlichen Akademie der Wissenschaften in Wien. Philosophisch-historische Classe* 136 (1897): 111-112. On Ockham generally, see Gilson, *History of Christian Philosophy in the Middle Ages,* 487-499 and 783-793; *BRUO* II: 1384-1387; E. M. Buytaert, ed., *Philotheus Boehner ... Collected Articles on Ockham* (St. Bonaventure, N.Y., 1958); Anton C. Pegis, "Concerning William of Ockham," *Traditio* 2 (1944): 465-480; Brian Tierney, "Ockham, the Conciliar Theory and the Canonists," *Journal of the History of Ideas* 15 (1954): 40-70; E. F. Jacob, *Essays in the Conciliar Epoch,* 3rd ed. (Notre Dame and London, 1963): 85-105; 246-248. See now especially Arthur S. McGrade, *The Political Thought of William of Ockham* (Cambridge, Eng., 1974), and, most exhaustively, Gordon Leff, *William of Ockham. The Metamorphosis of Scholastic Discourse* (Manchester, 1975): especially 104-123, on universals.

On philosophical realism, one of the most enduring of all the Western intellectual traditions, see particularly the bibliographies in the articles by A. D. Woozley, "Universals," *The Encyclopedia of Philosophy* VIII: 194-206; and J. Owens and L. H. Starkey, "Realism," *Encyclopaedia Britannica,* 15th ed., *Macropaedia* 15 (Chicago, 1974, or any subsequent year): 539-543. Cf. also J. H. Loewe, "Der Kampf zwischen dem Realismus und Nominalismus im Mittelalter. Sein Ursprung und sein Verlauf,"

Abhandlungen der königlichen böhmischen Gesellschaft der Wissenschaften, 6th ser., 8 (1876): 1-86; R. R. Betts, "The Great Debate about Universals in the Universities of the Fourteenth Century," in R. W. Seton-Watson, ed., *Prague Essays* (Oxford, 1949): 69-80; idem, "The Influence of Realist Philosophy on Jan Hus and his Predecessors in Bohemia," *Slavonic and East European Review* 48 (1970): 402-419 – both articles reprinted in his *Essays in Czech History* (London, 1969): 29-62, and reviewed by S. H. Thomson, *Slavonic and East European Review* 48 (1970): 429-431. Also valuable is M. Markowski, "Problematyka uniwersaliów w polskich piętnastowieczwych pismach nominalistycznych," *Studia Mediewistyczne* 12 (1970): 73-166, and many articles in *Mediaevalia Philosophica Polonorum* (1957 –). Most recently A. A. Maurer, "Some Aspects of Fourteenth-Century Philosophy," *MetH*, 2nd ser., 7 (1976): 175-188, has offered a useful typology, and makes important distinctions between the philosophical agenda of the thirteenth and fourteenth centuries. Gordon Leff, *The Dissolution of the Medieval Outlook: An Essay on the Intellectual and Spiritual Change in the Fourteenth Century* (New York etc., 1976), distils the author's many substantial contributions, although his airy dismissal of Wyclyf (who "sought to put the philosophical clock back to an extreme realism which had long lost any credibility": p. 146) does not seem to be rooted in a direct awareness of Wyclyf's philosophical corpus. Heiko A. Oberman, "Fourteenth-Century Religious Thought: A Premature Profile," *Speculum* 53 (1978): 80-93, despite its modest title, represents an ambitious effort at reassessment which should enjoy considerable success. – An interesting anthology of twentieth-century speculation on universals is Charles Landeman, ed., *The Problem of Universals* (New York and London, 1971).

7. A7.I.a. *De ente in communi*. Ca. 1365.

I. Inc.: In primis supponatur ens esse. Hoc enim nec potest probari nec ignorari ab aliquo cognitivo ...

Expl.: × ... cum non sunt per se in genere, ut patet post.

II. MSS:

i	Cambridge, Trinity Coll.	B.16.2	ff. 4ra-9va	xiv/ex[1]	JW MS Eng.	
ii	Wien, ÖNB	4307	ff. 158r-167v	1433	Asc. Boh.	

III. Ed. S. H. Thomson, *Johannis Wyclif Summa de Ente Libri Primi Tractatus Primus et Secundus* (Oxford, 1930): 1-61. From both MSS.

IV. This first tractate of the *Summa de ente* seems not to have aroused much interest among either English or Czech students. But since both extant MSS carry ascriptions, its authenticity is undoubted. Furthermore, there are references in this work to his own *De intelleccione dei* (**14**) and *De actibus anime* (**4**), both in the future, but in such a way as to apprise the reader that Wyclyf has a fair, if not final, text of the other works at hand. The *De ente in communi*, in turn, is alluded to in Wyclyf's *De sciencia dei* (as "libro primo tractatu primo": **15**: **i**, f. 54rb); in the *De universalibus* (**11**: **xv**, ff. 26r, 31r); and in the *De trinitate* (**17**: p. 125). This is therefore one of the earliest of his more mature efforts, but gives evidence already of wide reading and an awareness of a larger plan into which the more massive and controversial works would fit.

VC: 7980   Bale: 45, 50[2]   Sh: 8.I.1   Lo: 9.I.1

[1] In 1930, in his edition of this treatise, Thomson accepted Loserth's date "end of the xiv[th] or beginning of the xv[th] century" (p. xi). After a number of subsequent examinations of the codex, he inclined without much hesitation to the earlier date. It is one of the very finest of all Wyclyf codices.
[2] Conjectural; the first is entitled *De esse in suo prolixu*, the second *De esse intelligibili creaturae*.

8. A7.I.b. *De ente primo in communi.* Ca. 1365.

I. Inc.: Extenso ente secundum eius maximam ampliacionem possibilem, superest venari in tanto ambitu unum ens ...

Expl.: × ... Immo ex trinitate et misericordia dei sumitur indirecte occasio peccandi.

II. MSS:

i	Cambridge, Trinity Coll.	B.16.2	ff. 9va-13rb	xiv/ex	JW MS Eng.
ii	Wien, ÖNB	4307	ff. 167v-177r	1433	Asc. Boh.

III. Ed. S. H. Thomson, *Johannis Wyclif Summa de Ente Libri Primi Tractatus Primus et Secundus* (Oxford, 1930): 62-112. From both MSS.

IV. This short essay flows immediately from the preceding one. There can be no doubt of its authenticity or of its place in the *schema* of the *Summa* as a whole. There are several references throughout to other treatises within the *Summa*: to the *De intelleccione dei* (**14**: p. 79), the *De ydeis* (**18**: p. 87), and to the *De trinitate* (**17**: p. 93), all correctly in the future tense, save perhaps that to the *De intelleccione dei*, which reads "Vide secundo libro de responsionibus perturbantibus istam materiam." It is difficult to resist the notion that these two opening treatises may actually been written after the main tractates of the *Summa de ente* had either been drafted in considerable detail or even delivered as university lectures one or more times. Wyclyf was thus able to make specific references to capp. of works which had not yet been published, with their texts in front of him in virtually definitive form.

VC: deest   Bale: deest   Sh: 8.I.2   Lo: 9.I.2

9. A7.I.c. *Purgans errores circa veritates in communi.* Between 1366 and 1368?

I. Inc.: Consequens est purgare errores circa instancias quibus decepti putant infringere veritates ...

Expl.: × ... que non convenit siquis logicis; ergo propter talia signa oportet.

II. MSS:

i	Cambridge, Trinity Coll.	B.16.2	ff. 13va-16rb	xiv/ex	JW MS Eng.
ii	Wien, ÖNB	4307	ff. 177v-184r	1433	Asc. Boh.

III. Ed. M. H. Dziewicki, *Johannis Wyclif De Ente: Librorum Duorum Excerpta* ... (WS, 1909): 1-28. From **i** only.

IV. As with the previous two treatises in this first *liber* of the *Summa de ente*, the ascriptions and the internal cross-references in our two MSS vouchsafe the authenticity of the present work. As in the earlier cases also these cross-references are fairly precise, e.g. "vide hoc libro 2° tractatu primo cap. quarto," meaning the *De intelleccione dei* (**14**: p. 7); "et tangetur De universalibus" (**11**: p. 10); and two references by cap. to the *De volucione dei* (**16**: pp. 14, 23). It may be that some subsequent editor's hand was at work, but that must necessarily remain pure speculation in the absence of the archetype. There are also backward glances to the *Purgans errores* in the *De trinitate* (**17**: p. 100) and the *De ydeis* (**18**: **ix**, f. 87r).

Not without interest is his substantial use of Grosseteste's *De veritate* (pp. 6, 8, 19) and *De libero arbitrio* (p. 7).[1] Considering the great debt owed to "Lincolniensis" by so many of the significant English schoolmen of the fourteenth century, and repeatedly admitted in other of Wyclyf's works, perhaps we should not be surprised at this assertion: "utrum autem dicti doctores [meaning, apparently, Bishop Étienne Tempier's condemnation of 219 Averroistic theses at Paris in 1277, an act endorsed by Archbishop Kilwardby at Oxford in March of that year][2] sic senserint, vel non, non contendo. Sed iste sensus patet per Lyncolniensem in tractatu suo de libero arbitrio fuisse de mente Augustini, et sine dubio idem sensit Anselmus, et (ut credo) sanctus Thomas cum aliis." [3]

Given the absence of this piece from the VC, we can only speculate where Peter of Časlav, the scribe of **ii**, might have acquired his sound basis for the numeration of the various treatises throughout this *Summa*.

VC: deest   Bale: deest   Sh: 8.I.3   Lo: 9.I.3.

---

[1] Cf. Thomson, *Writings of Robert Grosseteste*, 90-91, 119-120. Still of considerable worth is Loserth, "Johann von Wiclif und Robert Grosseteste, Bischof von Lincoln," *Sitzungsberichte der Kaiserlichen Akademie der Wissenschaften in Wien. Philosophisch-Historische Klasse* 186/2 (1918). It is time for a fresh look.

[2] Cf. the discussions of this watershed event in Duhem, *Le système du monde*, 2nd ed., VI (Paris, 1954), whole volume; Gilson, *History of Christian Philosophy in the Middle Ages*, 387-407, 717-729; Lohr, "Commentaries ... Robertus-Wilgelmus," 149-150; Gordon Leff, *Paris and Oxford Universities in the Thirteenth and Fourteenth Centuries: An Institutional and Intellectual History* (New York etc., 1967): 229-240; idem, *The Dissolution of the Medieval Outlook*, 24-31. Texts, of course, in H. Denifle and E. Chatelain, *Chartularium Universitatis Parisiensis* ... I: (*1200-1286*) (Paris, 1889): 543-555.

[3] P. 7. In part because of Aquinas' Aristotelian propensities (but on what other grounds is far from obvious), Wyclyf's attitudes toward the great Dominican were not all of a piece. It is a subject worth some further study. A fine MS guide to the early stages of the problem is Franz Ehrle, "Der Kampf um die Lehre des hl. Thomas von Aquin in den ersten fünfzig Jahren nach seinem Tod," brought current by Franz Pelster, ed., *Franz Kard. Ehrle: Gesammelte Aufsätze zur englischen Scholastik* (Roma, 1970): 183-250; cf. Frederick J. Roensch, *Early Thomistic School* (Dubuque, Iowa, 1964): 28-83, 200-265. There are also several fine articles in *St. Thomas Aquinas 1274-1974*, 2 vols. (Toronto, PIMS, 1974).

10. A7.I.d. *Purgans errores circa universalia in communi*. Between 1366 and 1368?

I. Inc.: Obiciencium contra dicta de universalibus quidam nimis pueriliter et quidam subtiliter obiciunt ...
Expl.: × ... et principaliter isti mundo, sed mundo in communi. Unde iste est textus Lyncolniensis.

II. MSS:
i   Cambridge,
    Trinity Coll.   B.16.2   ff. 16va-19va   xiv/ex   JW MS Eng.
ii Wien, ÖNB   4307   ff. 185r-190v   1433   Asc. Boh.

III. Ed. M. H. Dziewicki, *Johannis Wyclif De Ente: Librorum Duorum Excerpta* ... (WS, 1909): 29-48. From i only.[1]

IV. Wyclyf wrote this treatise to rebut such objections as had already arisen to his well-known views on the universals. It is therefore thematically associated with the work which follows it in our preferred ordering of the first *liber* of the *Summa de ente*. More than once, identical arguments appear in both works: e.g., much of p. 31 will be found in cap. iii of the *De universalibus* (**11**: **xv**, f. 16r; p. 32 also corresponds closely to f. 16v); the applicability of the concept of number to species and genera, developed on pp. 44-48 of the present work, also parallels the *De universalibus* (MS cit., ff. 44r-49r). In fact, in the latter treatise (MS cit., f. 44r), cap. v of the *Purgans errores circa universalia* is called "quidam tractatus de speciebus." This expression strengthens our belief that the two pieces may have developed almost *pari passu*. Perhaps the shorter work was a conflation of several *responsiones ad hoc*, as was surely true of many of his polemical works and – as we have intimated – was also likely the case with his *Dubia* on the *Physics* of Aristotle (**6**).

We find unmistakable references to this piece also in the *De ente predicamentali* (**13**: p. 3) and the *De trinitate* (**17**: pp. 129, 140, 150, 156).

vc: deest   Bale: deest[2]   Sh: 8.I.4   Lo: 9.I.4

---

[1] For a considerable portion of the text missing in this MS and consequently in Dziewicki's edition, see S. H. Thomson, "A 'Lost' Chapter of Wyclif's *Summa de Ente*," *Speculum* 4 (1929): 339-346 (from **ii**).

[2] He almost certainly was not pointing to this piece when he mentioned (no. 35) a fanciful *De universo reali*.

11. A7.I.e. *De universalibus*. 1368 or 1369?

I. Inc. proem.: Libellus de universalibus continet quindecim capitula ...
Expl. proem.: × ... ydea est forma eterna in mente divina ad cuius exemplar

deus est productivus creature et declarando descripcionem cum aliis dubiis imponet finem isti tractatui.

Inc. cap. i: In purgando errores circa universalia sunt tria introductoria prenotanda ...

Expl.: × ... pono finem huic superficiali tractatui de universalibus ad alios tractatus prime intencionis, ad quoniam noticiam sentencia ista aperit agressuros.

II. MSS:

i	Cambridge, Gonville & Caius Coll.	337	ff. 1r-47r	xiv/2	Unasc. Eng.[1]
ii	Trinity Coll.	B.16.2	ff. 23ra-44rb	xiv/ex	JW MS Eng.
iii	El Escorial	e.II.6	ff. 104ra-124rb	xiv/2	JW MS Eng.[2]
iv	Kraków, BJag	848	ff. 3ra-36ra	1411	JW MS Boh.[3]
v		1855	ff. 86r-125v	1449	Misasc. Pol.[4]
vi	Lincoln, Cath. Chap.	C.1.15 (159)	ff. 293ra-321va	xiv/2	Unasc. Eng.[5]
vii	Pavia, BU	311	ff. 1ra-35va	xiv/2	Asc. Eng.[6]
viii	Praha, MK	L.36 (1279)	ff. 139ra-169vb	1415	Asc. Boh.
ix		M.54 (1410)	ff. 1r-106r	xv/m	JW MS Boh.
x	UK	III.G.10 (535)	ff. 70r-104r	1397	JW MS Boh.[7]
xi		IV.H.9 (773)	ff. 1ra-56vb	ca. 1400	JW MS Boh.
xii		V.H.16 (993)	ff. 1r-78r	1406	Asc. Boh.
xiii		VIII.F.1 (1555)	ff. 1ra-39rb	1410	Asc. Boh.
xiv		VIII.G.6 (1588)	ff. 1r-57r	ca. 1420	Asc. Boh.
xv		VIII.G.23 (1605)	ff. 1r-84r	1403	Asc. Boh.[8]
xvi		XXIII.F.58 (Lobkovice 153)	ff. 3r-71r	ca. 1410	Asc. Boh.[9]
xvii	Stockholm, KunglB	Lat. A.164	ff. 87r-134r	1398	Asc. Boh.[10]
xviii	Vaticano	Vat.lat.4313	ff. 1ra-31rb	xv/1	Unasc. Boh.[11]
xix	Venezia, BMarc.	Lat. VI.172	ff. 27va-78va	ca. 1400	Asc. Ger.[12]
xx	Wien, ÖNB	4307	ff. 62v-114v	1433	Asc. Boh.
xxi		4523	ff. 58r-132v	1412	Asc. Boh.
xxii		5204	ff. 1r-65v	ca. 1410	Asc. Boh.
xxiii	Wrocław, BU	IV.F.7	ff. 304ra-351rb	xv/2	Misasc. Pol.[13]

III. Unpublished.[14]

IV. The Wyclif Society determined in the early years of this century to forego publication of this treatise, having already produced in *Miscellanea Philosophica* II (1905) a long tractate under this title – which, as it happens, was not by Wyclyf at all, but was a later composition by the Czech Wyclyfite Stanislav of Znojmo.[15] Yet from almost any point of view the *De universalibus* must be reckoned Wyclyf's most important philosophical statement. It is mature, vigorous, elaborate, and rich in its deployment of earlier and near-contemporary philosophers. Nevertheless it is in some ways, like many of his writings, so enmeshed in the ongoing scholastic wrangles at Oxford as to becloud the point of his argumentation time and time again. Given this circumstance, it follows that we cannot accurately assay either the depths of his originality or the antecedents of his approach until we arrive at a definitive sorting-out of those interminable dialectical tests of strength. The pioneering labors of Konstanty Michalski[16] in the philosophical vineyards of fourteenth-century Oxford did not, unfortunately, extend to Wyclyf's time; they can therefore contribute little to any satisfactory resolution of our contextual difficulties. A major monograph is wanting, and only an enterprise of that scope could possibly meet this need.

Wyclyf did not hesitate throughout the *De universalibus* to fall back on several of his own contributions.[17] Naturally, as we have come to expect, this plethora of cross-references does result in some chronological quandaries;[18] but once again we may hope to clarify these by assuming that several of his essays were in process of redaction simultaneously. Assuredly the *De universalibus*, in its received form, was edited by its author with exceptional care.

Our earliest dated copies (1397 and 1398 respectively: **x** and **xvii**) are by Czech scribes, the latter by Hus himself; but some of the English MSS (**i, ii, iii, vi** and **vii**) may be earlier. The *De universalibus* was notably popular with the Czech schoolmen, for it offered a great bulwark for their realism against the nominalism generally upheld by the German "nation" at the University of Prague.[19]

VC: 3933 3935 4514 7980   Bale: 42[20]   Sh: 8.I.5   Lo: 9.I.5

---

[1] First noted in M. R. James, *A Descriptive Catalogue of the Manuscripts in the Library of Gonville & Caius College* I (Cambridge, Eng., 1907): 380-381, and further discussed in S. H. Thomson, "A Gonville and Caius Wyclif Manuscript," *Speculum* 8 (1933): 197-204. The admirable text is followed on ff. 47r-48v by a brief résumé of the *De universalibus*, of unknown authorship.

[2] See Thomson, "Unnoticed MSS and Works of Wyclif," 27.

[3] "Wycleph" is mentioned on f. 2ra, but the identity of both this and the following MS escaped their early cataloger, Władysław Wisłocki, *Katalog Rękopisów Biblijoteki Uniwersytetu Jagiellońskiego* I: *Wstęp. Rękopisy 1-1875* (Kraków, 1877-1881): 249-250, 441-442.

[4] "Tractatus ... Wilhelmi Anglici." As is made more explicit in the colophon, the scribe clearly thought he was dealing here with the *De universalibus* of William Milverley ("mirwelli quoque Wilhelmi"); cf. *BRUO* II: 1284 and Władysław Seńko, "Un traité inconnu 'de esse et essentia'," *Archives d'histoire doctrinale et littéraire du moyen âge* 35 (1960): 238.

[5] The treatise which follows (**12**) is ascribed to "Wyclyff" in the colophon. This codex has undergone excision of whole folia before and following the *De universalibus*: see the description in Reginald M. Woolley, *Catalogue of the Manuscripts of Lincoln Cathedral Chapter Library* (Oxford, 1927): 123-124.

[6] First noticed in I. H. Stein, "Two Notes on Wyclif," *Speculum* 6 (1931): 466-467. S. H. Thomson disagreed with her dating and provenance, placing the script ca. 1380.

[7] Ends in cap. iv.

[8] See, for Praha, UK X.H.9 (1987), n. 19, below; this "Commentarius" covers only capp. i-ix, however.

[9] First discussed in Thomson, "Unnoticed MSS and Works of Wyclif," 29-30.

[10] Explicitly "per manus Johannis Hus de Hussinetz." This codex was first described by G. Stephens, *Förteckning öfver de förnämsta brittiska och fransyska hanskrifterna* (Stockholm, 1847): 35-39; and more helpfully by B. Dudik; *Forschungen in Schweden für Mährens Geschichte* (Brno, 1852):

198-205. Additional analysis, with some corrections, in A. H. Lundström's introduction to M. H. Dziewicki, ed., *Johannis Wyclif Miscellanea Philosophica* I (WS, 1902): XLVII-LXI. See also Thomson, *Latin Bookhands, ad* pl. 48.

[11] First brought to light in Stein, "Two Notes," 465-466.

[12] Analyzed in Thomson, "Unnoticed MSS and Works of Wyclif," 28-29. The scribe was a Michael "Theutonicus," working in Ferrara (?), whose appended lamentation Thomson transcribed *verbatim*.

[13] Ascribed to Egidio de' Colonna (Giles of Rome) in the *contenta*. This MS was first identified by Seńko, "Un traité inconnu," 238.

[14] A critical edition by S. H. Thomson, in MS, is in the editor's possession. Dr. Ivan Mueller of Freiburg has also completed his edition; a collaborative effort under the auspices of the New Wyclif Society is projected.

[15] Cf. M. H. Dziewicki's introduction to the *De ente* (WS, 1909): V-VI. First to establish Stanislav's authorship was Jan Sedlák, *Studie a Texty k Životopisu Husovu* II (Brno, 1914): 119; followed by S. H. Thomson, "Some Latin Works Erroneously Ascribed to Wyclif," *Speculum* 3 (1928): 383-384. On Stanislav – who, like Stephen Páleč, changed from a strong supporter of Hus and Wyclyf to an equally forceful opponent of both – see especially Matthew Spinka, *John Hus' Concept of the Church* (Princeton, 1966): 172-208. There is a brief note too in Lohr, "Commentaries ... Supplementary Authors," 144.

[16] "Les courants philosophiques à Oxford et à Paris pendant le XIVe siècle," *Bulletin international de l'Académie polonaise des sciences et des lettres. Classe de philologie, d'histoire et de philosophie*, années 1919-1920 (Kraków, 1922-1924): 59-88; "Le criticisme et le scepticisme dans la philosophie du XIVe siècle," ibid., année 1925 (Kraków, 1927): 41-122; "Les courants critiques et sceptiques dans la philosophie du XIVe siècle," ibid., 192-242; "La physique nouvelle et les différents courants philosophiques au XIVe siècle," ibid., année 1927 (Kraków, 1928): 93-164; "Le problème de la volonté à Oxford et à Paris au XIVe siècle," *Studia Philosophica* 2 (1937): 233-366 (also published separately at Lwów the same year). There is much of value also in F. M. Powicke, "Master Simon of Faversham," in *Mélanges d'histoire du moyen âge offerts à M. Ferdinand Lot* (Paris, 1925): 649-658 (reprinted, with revisions, in his *Ways of Medieval Life and Thought. Essays and Addresses* [London, 1949]: 230-238), and of course in the many indispensable contributions of Anneliese Maier, among which we shall cite here only "'Ergebnisse' der spätscholastischen Naturphilosophie," *Scholastik* 35 (1960): 161-187 (reprinted in her *Ausgehendes Mittelalter. Gesammelte Aufsätze zur Geistesgeschichte des 14. Jahrhunderts* I [Roma, 1964]: 425-457, 496-500). Several of the recent studies by Gordon Leff offer useful insights; but individual Oxford philosophers are best approached through *BRUO* I-III. Whole sections of this vast field, however, still await their plowman.

That Wyclyf's *De universalibus* indeed became the object of close study at Oxford is evident from remarks in the text of Oxford, Magdalen Coll. 97, ff. 102v-106r, and in a marginal note of MS 47, f. 53v. We know specifically that Richard Lavenham, O.Carm., a colleague of Wyclyf's, was acquainted with his position on the universals: Wien, ÖNB 4878, f. 4v, as cited in Bartolomeu Maria Xiberta, *De Scriptoribus Scholasticis saeculi XIV ex ordine Carmelitarum* (Louvain, 1931): 188; cf. p. 334. On Richard, cf. also *BRUO* II: 1109-1110; Lohr, "Commentaries ... Narcissus-Richardus," 393-394.

[17] To select a few from many, we shall cite here (all from **xv**) **1**: f. 26r; **7**: f. 31r; **8**: f. 46r; **10**: f. 44r; **12**: f. 43v; **17**: f. 19r; **22**: f. 50r.

[18] E.g., as to priority of publication of the *De universalibus* over the *De verbi incarnacione*. Cf. Thomson, "The Order of Writing of Wyclif's Philosophical Works," 158-160.

[19] Cf. the articles by Betts in *Essays in Czech History* (cited above, A7, n. 6). Of general relevance in a preliminary way here are S. H. Thomson, "Cultural Relations of Bohemia with Western Europe before the White Mountain," *Quarterly Bulletin of the Polish Institute of Arts and Sciences in America* (1944): 298-314; idem, "Learning at the Court of Charles IV," *Speculum* 25 (1970): 1-20; Ruben E. Weltsch, *Archbishop John of Jenstein 1348-1400. Papalism, Humanism and Reform in Pre-Hussite*

Prague ('s Gravenhage and Paris, 1968). Immediately pertinent here is an anonymous *Commentarius in J. W. Tractatum de universalibus* in Praha, UK X.H.9 (1887), ff. 1r-68r. A MS at Munich has shed important new light on the early circulation of Wyclyf's writings at Prague: Damasus Trapp, "Clm 27034. Unchristened Nominalism and Wycliffite Realism at Prague in 1381," *Recherches de théologie ancienne et médiévale* 24 (1957): 320-360. Master Zdislav of Zvířetice publicly defended Wyclyf's views on the universals on 6 August 1410 (František Palacký, ed., *Documenta Mag. Joannis Hus ...* [Praha, 1869; reprinted Osnabrück, 1966]: 400; also in J. Loserth, *Hus und Wiclif. Zur Genesis der Husitischen Lehre*, 1st ed. [Praha and Leipzig, 1884]: 285-289.) But Zdislav's loyalty to Wyclyf must have been rather discreet: in 1417 we find him Rector of the University. – On Hus and Wyclyf generally, another issue altogether, see below, **32**, n. 13.

For permutations of this struggle in Poland, see M. Heitzman, "Jana Wyclefa traktat de universalibus i jego wpływ na uniwersytecie praskim i krakowskim," *Archiwum Komisji do Badania Historii Filozofji w Polsce* II/2 (Kraków, 1926): 111-150; Markowski, "Problematyka uniwersaliów"; and incidentally Margaret Schlauch, "A Polish Vernacular Eulogy of Wyclif," *JEH* 8 (1957): 53-75.

[20] Correct incipit, title given as *Logica de singulis*. Another *De universalibus*, without incipit, appears as no. 185.

12. A7.I.f. *De tempore* [*De individuacione temporis*]. Ca. 1368.

I. Inc. proem.: In isto supponendo tempus esse ...
Expl. proem.: × ... de quidditate temporis declarat.
Inc. cap. i: In tractando de tempore sunt aliqua ex dictis superius recapi [or: capienda] ...
Expl. cap. xii: × ... in spiritum sanctum subtrahendo ab eo oracionis suffragia.
Expl. cap. xiii: × ... si unquam erit et per consequens modo instat.

II. MSS:

	Cambridge, Gonville & Caius Coll.	337	f. 48v	xiv/2	Unasc. Eng.[1]
i	Trinity Coll.	B.16.2	ff. 46ra-57ra	xiv/ex	JW MS Eng.
ii	Dublin, Trinity Coll.	C.1.23	pp. 350a-386b	xiv/ex	JW MS Eng.[2]
iii	Kraków, BJag	848	ff. 72va-96vb	1411	JW MS Boh.[3]
iv	Lincoln, Cath.Chap.	C.1.15	ff. 325ra-339va	xiv/2	Asc. Eng.[4]
v	Pavia, BU	311	ff. 48ra-49vb, 51, 50, 52-57, 59, 58, 60ra-61vb, 38ra-42ra	xiv/2	Asc. Eng.
vi	Praha, MK	M.54 (1410)	ff. 170r-210v	xv/m	Unasc. Boh.[5]
vii		N.19 (1543)	ff. 88ra-110va	ca. 1410	Asc. Boh.
viii	UK	III.G.10 (535)	ff. 31r-69v	1397	JW MS Boh.
ix		IV.H.9 (773)	ff. 94ra-113vb	ca. 1400	Asc. Boh.
x		VIII.F.1 (1555)	ff. 87rb-113ra	1410	Asc. Boh.
		X.E.11 (1912)	ff. 174ra-175rb	1433	Boh.[6]
xi		XXIII.F.58 (Lobkovice 153)	ff. 75r-109r	ca. 1410	Asc. Boh.[7]
xii	Stockholm, KunglB	Lat. A.164	ff. 1r-33v	1398	Asc. Boh.

xiii	Venezia, BMarc.	Lat. VI.172	ff. 1ra-27va	ca. 1400	Asc. Ger.
xiv	Wien, ÖNB	4316	ff. 85r-125r	ca. 1430	JW MS Boh.

III. Unpublished.[8]

IV. This work was quite popular among the Hussites; there are also, however, more than the usual number of English copies extant. Its relatively non-controversial nature – at least from the dogmatic point of view – may explain the survival of these MSS. There has arisen a divergent tradition as to the last cap. (xiii): the Continental copies uniformly have only the first twelve capp., whereas the English recensions all have thirteen. Further close examination of the text tradition might determine that this was purely fortuitous.

Wyclyf quotes the following pieces among his own writings in the *De tempore* (all references are to **xiv**): **1**: f. 90r; **4**: f. 107r; **7** (as *De transcendentibus*): f. 104r; and **13** (as *De substancia*): f. 104v. The *De tempore* is itself cited in **13, 15, 18, 19** and **20**.

In view of his later radical position on the impossibility of annihilation of the elements in the Eucharist his assertion (f. 98r) "cum nichil est anichilabile" is of great significance. We know that Wyclyf's lectures "de tempore" which preceded the publication of this treatise were the subject of a lively exchange of views between Wyclyf and the Carmelite John Kenningham.[9] A later Carmelite Prior Provincial, John Keninghale, says that this "strenuus lollii persecutor ... diutinam cum Wycclyff per annos luctam peregit et manuale certamen.... Incepit dulci stilo eum sentire in logicis, sicut de esse suo prolixo, demum si Christus esset eius humanitas; et tunc de dominacione civili et dotacione ecclesie pollicitus est conferre sermonem. Primo sic cepit processum a tempore."[10] Keninghale was, however, confused as to the order in which the debates unfolded. We can identify, in the works he cites, **1-3, 7, 8, 22, 28-30, 32** and the present work, which we are compelled to date several years before the titles drawn from Wyclyf's *Summa theologie* (A12). But Keninghale is trustworthy in his claim that the dispute began over the issue of time and such other metaphysical beguilements as were averred by Wyclyf's critics to be leading him into heresy. The earliest of Kenningham's *determinaciones* which appears in the *FZ* (pp. 4-13) is not really the first in this exchange: in his first sentence he alludes to "quedam superius dicta et recitata in ultima determinacione mea." Lacking this earlier *determinacio* we may provisionally assume that it was in this broadside that Kenningham "cepit processum a tempore," attacking Wyclyf's views as they were shortly to appear in the *De tempore*.[11]

VC: 3933 3935 4515 7980[12]   Bale: 202, 203[13]   Sh: 8.I.6   Lo: 9.I.6

[1] Analysis only; no text.

[2] With *tabula*, p. 387b.

[3] At the end, in another hand, "M Stephani Palecz." On Páleč, who had been a Wyclyfite during the first decade of the fifteenth century, but became Hus' most formidable Czech opponent a few years

before the Council of Constance, see Spinka, *John Hus' Concept of the Church*, 209-251. There are also several references to Páleč in Loserth, *Huss und Wiclif*, 2nd ed. (München and Berlin, 1925: the second ed. actually is missing some of the documentation to be found in the first, and reflected little appreciation of Czech scholarship in the intervening 41 years). Without pretense to exhaustiveness, we may here cite Třeboň, Státní Archiv 17, ff. 160r-167v: "Sermo Magistri Stephani de Palecz, ... contra aliquos articulos Wikleff, reprobando eos," as indicated in J. Weber (= Kadlec), "Soupis Rukopisů Státního Archivu v Třeboni," in *Soupis Rukopisů v Třeboni a v Českém Krumlove* ... (Praha, 1958).

[4] *Proemium* follows text, ff. 339va-340ra.

[5] This and all remaining MSS contain capp. i-xii only.

[6] A *registrum*, but not by Peter Payne: on him, see below, **17**, n. 4.

[7] See Thomson, "Unnoticed MSS and Works of Wyclif," 30.

[8] A critical edition by Allen duPont Breck is promised. (See also his analysis of the MSS in Wolfgang Yourgrau and Allen Breck, edd., *Cosmology, History, and Theology* [New York and London, 1977]: "John Wyclyf on Time," 211-218. His personal helpfulness to the editor is warmly remembered.)

[9] Also the object of Wyclyf's polemical barbs in **378-380**, below. Not to be confused with a Richard Kilingham (Climeton, Kilvington, etc.: d. 1362), whose Aristotelian and sententiary commentaries appear in MSS at Cambridge, Erfurt, Paris, Bruges, Prague, Seville, Vienna and the Vatican: see *BRUO* II: 1050-1051; Lohr, "Commentaries ... Narcissus-Richardus," 392-393. (Our Kenningham is also styled Cuningham, Kynyngham, and Kylyngham in the MSS: *BRUO* II: 1077.)

[10] *FZ*, 3. Shirley's ascription of this compendium to Thomas Netter of Walden, John Keninghale's predecessor as Prior Provincial (a tradition going back to Bale at least), has been recently undermined by the careful study of James Crompton, "Fasciculi Zizaniorum I, II," *JEH* 12 (1961): 35-45; 155-166 – though it did pass through Netter's hands in a less organized form.

[11] It is possible that some at least of Wyclyf's notions in this treatise can be traced to the homonymous work of Robert Kilwardby OP (d. 1279: see *BRUO* II: 1051-1052). Cf. also M. D. Chenu, "Le traité 'De tempore' de R. Kilwardby," in Lang, Lechner and Schmaus, *Aus der Geisteswelt des Mittelalters*, 855-861. Of course Augustine contributed heavily also: see the titles cited below, **17**, n. 10; **55**, n. 2.

[12] Incipit shown in all four VC, however, is that for cap. i.

[13] Gives titles *De temporis quidditate* and *De temporis ampliatione*, without incipits.

13. A7.I.g. *De ente predicamentali*. Ca. 1369?

I. Inc.: Supposito ex superius declaratis et dicendis in posterum, quod ens communissimum possibile equum cum intelligibili ...

Expl.: × ... patet ergo, quod si partes temporis sunt aput deum, tunc vere sunt.

II. MSS:

i   Wien, ÖNB   4307   ff. 190v-242v   1433   Asc. Boh.

III. Ed. Rudolf Beer, *Johannis Wyclif De Ente Praedicamentali* ... (WS, 1901): 1-219. From unique MS.

IV. It has been established for some time now that this treatise does indeed constitute part of the *Summa de ente*.[1] Beer's argument, from evidence in the running titles in our unique MS, that it should properly be denominated the *fifth* tractate of the *liber primus*, is however subject to challenge. Yet we cannot rely on internal chronology to help us unravel this knot: Wyclyf quotes from three treatises of the *liber secundus* (**14**, **16**, **18**), besides **11** and **12** of the first *liber*. We are forced, as in several other instances, to hypothesize later interpolation either by Wyclyf or by an editor. We ought probably not in any case attach much weight to Beer's claim that "at the very spot [in Cambridge, Trinity Coll. B.16.2, normally received as the complete text of the *Summa de ente*] where the *De Ente Predicamentali* should have been several pages have been left blank" (p. ix): in reality, only the verso of f. 36 is blank.[2] Instead of the somewhat involuted conclusions offered by S. H. Thomson in 1929, we should accept now a literal reading of the crucial citation from Wien, ÖNB 4316, f. 108v (**12**): "probatum est tractatu septimo (de quantitate)."[3] The reference must be to capp. vi-vii and xix-xxii of the present work. In the usual deductive manner of many scholastics, Wyclyf is therefore here elaborating specific aspects of time and being which have been schematically mapped out in earlier discussions.

The relative lateness of the single MS does not affect the genuineness of its ascription or contents. It only augments our debt to the Hussite scribe, Peter of Časlav, who transcribed several other works of Wyclyf as well. But in this case, perhaps more acutely than in that of any other text, we feel the need of another and better copy. There is much to be desired in Peter's recension: although his script is quite legible, he seems to have omitted passages he could not read.

vc: deest   Bale: deest[4]   Sh: 4   Lo: 10

[1] Thomson, "Order of Writing," 161; Robson, *Wyclif and the Oxford Schools*, 119.

[2] The cancellation of four leaves from the end of the quire at this point (and also in our Wien MS, as pointed out in Robson, ibid., 125-126), is not conclusive either, though admittedly it does further cloud the issue. It is not at all obvious why this work should have fallen into such obscurity; certainly the contents would not have excited much commotion!

[3] Cf. previous allusion (in the same MS, f. 104v): "tactum est tractatu de substancia et postea tangetur magis plene." Cap. v of the *De ente predicamentali* engages "substancia" at length. (Thomson, "Order of Writing," 161. For other references in this piece, see ibid., 152-153.) An indication of a "capitulum de quantitate" may also be found in Oxford, Corpus Christi Coll. 116, f. 132r – in fact, ff. 132r-140r constitute a series of abstracts from several of Wyclyf's logical and metaphysical works, not always readily identifiable. Cf. Robson, *Wyclif and the Oxford Schools*, 127, 225-226, on these ff., as well as on ff. 48r-56v.

[4] Unless we may so construe, say, his no. 204, *De temporis ampliatione* – but see **12**, n. 13, above.

14. A7.II.a. *De intelleccione dei*. Ca. 1370?

I. Inc.: Illorum que insunt deo communiter quedam insunt sibi soli ...
   Expl.: × ... tales intricaciones rixosas sumus multipliciter involuti.

II. MSS:

i	Cambridge, Trinity Coll.	B.16.2	ff. 59ra-66ra	xiv/ex	JW MS Eng.
ii	*Praha, UK*	*IX.E.6 (1762)*	ff. 1r-15v	ca. 1405	JW MS Boh.[1]

III. Ed. M. H. Dziewicki, *Johannis Wyclif De Ente: Librorum Duorum Excerpta* ... (WS, 1909): 49-112. From **i** only.

IV. In this treatise, five capp. long, the *De ydeis* (**18**) is spoken of as a future undertaking: "De ista materia dicetur tractatu de ydeis" (p. 92), as are **15** (p. 97) and **22** (pp. 75-76). It is itself specifically mentioned in **13** (p. 83): "Ad primum dicetur libro secundo tractatu primo capitulo quarto, quod nichil potest intelligere, nisi quod potest esse." (Cf. p. 70, Dziewicki ed.)

The work may have been too abstruse to achieve much currency either in England or among the Czechs. Our **ii** (not known to Dziewicki)[2] is greatly superior to **i**; it is almost surely the product of the scribe who also penned the excellent copies of **11** and **18** in Praha, UK IV.H.9. This and the two succeeding treatises are written, in his version, without cap. headings, and virtually without indication of beginning or end of the separate treatises themselves.

VC: deest   Bale: deest   Sh: 8.II.1   Lo: 9.II.1

[1] Correctly identified in Truhlař.
[2] Originally discussed in I. H. Stein, "Another 'Lost' Chapter of Wyclif's *Summa de Ente*," *Speculum* 8 (1933): 254-255. See also **15** and **16**, just below.

15. A7.II.b. *De sciencia dei*. Ca. 1370?

I. Inc.: Ex dictis superius satis liquet quod sciencia ...
   Expl.: × ... indigenciam, coaccionem, inevitabilitatem vel huiusmodi connotatum.

II. MSS:

i	Cambridge, Trinity Coll.	B.16.2	ff. 66ra-82vb	xiv/ex	JW MS Eng.
ii	Praha, UK	IX.E.6 (*1762*)	ff. 16r-51r	ca. 1505	JW MS Boh.[1]

III. Unpublished.

IV. In this strongly realist work Wyclyf quotes no fewer than eight of his own works as already completed,[2] and mentions three others in the future tense.[3] We may also remark a larger number of citations of Bradwardine ("doctor profundus") and his *Summa (De causa dei adversus Pelagium)*[4] in this tractate than elsewhere in Wyclyf's *Summa de ente*, excepting only the *De volucione dei* which follows it immediately.

There is some hint that by this time Wyclyf was beginning to focus his analytical faculties on social and political conditions of the day. He writes: "Unde videtur michi multa usurpative dicta de graciis hominum factis suis inferioribus ut delinquentes in dominos exacciones dicuntur ponere se in suis graciis quando subiciunt se extorquative potestati eorum et certum est quod non faciunt illis graciam si minus iniuste extorquent quam poterunt ad eorum indigenciam; nec papa facit graciam suam curato cui dispensat bonum de patrimonio Christi, quia si ista bene fiant recipiens prius naturaliter meretur ubique quia dispensacione indiget sic facere ad augmentum sui meriti." (**i**, f. 63ra.) This is an unaccustomed sort of illustration in Wyclyf's metaphysical canon, and signals for us the broadening of his interests. He is also deeply concerned here with "gracia predestinacionis" – which was, of course, Bradwardine's own distinctive preoccupation.

vc: deest   Bale: deest   Sh: 8.II.2   Lo: 9.II.2

[1] See **14**, n. 2, above. Inc.: "Ex istis...."

[2] **1, 4, 7, 9, 10, 11, 12** and **14**. See Thomson, "Order of Writing," 152-154.

[3] All as cited in **i**: **15**: f. 65vb; **17**: ff. 64rb, 65va; **18**: f. 64vb. There are doubtless others which a careful edition would uncover.

[4] Cf. Gordon Leff, *Bradwardine and the Pelagians. A Study of his 'De Causa Dei' and its Opponents* (Cambridge, Eng., 1957); Heiko A. Oberman, *Archbishop Thomas Bradwardine, A Fourteenth Century Augustinian. A Study of his Theology in its Historical Context* (Utrecht, 1957): especially pp. 198-204, where he suggests that Wyclyf's dependence on Bradwardine became rapidly less marked after 1372, principally owing to his growing absorption with ecclesiological matters where Bradwardine was quite orthodox. – A signpost to Bradwardine's developed views in the *De causa dei* appears in Bartolomeu M. Xiberta, "Fragments d'una qüestió inèdita de Tomàs Bradwardine," in Lang, Lechner and Schmaus, edd., *Aus der Geisteswelt des Mittelalters*, 1169-1180. Still of some use are Justus F. Laun, "Thomas von Bradwardin, der Schüler Augustins und Lehrer Wiclifs," *Zeitschrift für Kirchengeschichte* 47 (1928): 333-356; idem, "Die Prädestination bei Wyclif und Bradwardin," in *Imago Dei. Beiträge zur theologischen Anthropologie. Gustav Krüger zum 70. Geburtstage ...* (Giessen, 1932): 63-84. See also *BRUO* I: 244-246; Lohr, "Commentaries ... Robertus-Wilgelmus," 172-173. The pioneering study of this period was Karl Werner, *Die Scholastik des späteren Mittelalters* III: *Der Augustinismus in der Scholastik des späteren Mittelalters* (Wien, 1883; reprinted New York, 1960): pp. 235-306 deal with Bradwardine, but of that substantial essay only three lines spanning pp. 301-302 allude to his influence on Wyclyf. The "Abschnitt" in his vol. IV/1 (*Der Endausgang der mittelalterlichen Scholastik* [Wien, 1887; reprinted 1960]): 17-58 ("Die theologische Schulbildung auf englischem Boden zur Zeit der Wiclif'schen Unruhen") was a decent effort for its time, but is now far outdistanced by Robson et al.

16. A7.II.c. *De volucione dei*. Ca. 1370?

I. Inc.: Tractando de volucione dei, quem oportet ex dictis supponere, notandum est quod aliquando accipiatur [9 wds.] volucio qua vult res ad extra esse ...

Expl.: × ... vel derisorie vel yronice propter errorem [or: horrorem] blasfeme dixit: benedic deo et morere.

II. MSS:

i	Cambridge, Trinity Coll.	B.16.2	ff. 83ra-104ra	xiv/ex	Asc. Eng.
ii	Praha, UK	IX.E.6 (*1762*)	ff. 56r-96r	ca. 1405	JW MS Boh.[1]

III. Ed. M. H. Dziewicki, *Johannis Wyclif De Ente: Librorum Duorum Excerpta* ... (WS, 1909): 113-286. From **i** only.

IV. This treatise, in 18 capp., was clearly meant to follow the preceding item, to which it alludes at least three times.[2] Three others of Wyclyf's works are also mentioned.[3]

In view of the nature of the subject, one is surprised how little attention is here paid to Duns Scotus, whose voluntarism would have provided Wyclyf many opportunities for drawing fine distinctions.[4] In any case, for a predestinarian like Wyclyf, the question of God's will was supremely important; hence the length and detail of this piece. The work of Bradwardine is copiously deployed throughout; indeed it would not be an exaggeration to call the *De volucione dei* a running commentary on the *De causa dei*.[5] The formidable FitzRalph also crops up occasionally.[6]

vc: deest   Bale: deest   Sh: 8.II.3   Lo: 9.II.3

[1] See above, **14**, n. 2.
[2] Pp. 114, 128, 133.
[3] **4**: pp. 133, 193; **10**: p. 279; and **11**: p. 160.
[4] The "Doctor subtilis" has generated of late an extraordinary degree of interest among modern scholars of fourteenth-century thought. Still of considerable value, however, is the long section on him in D. E. Sharp, *Franciscan Philosophy at Oxford in the Thirteenth Century* (Oxford, 1930): 279-368; and E. Gilson, *Jean Duns Scot. Introduction à ses positions fondamentales* (Paris, 1952), remains indispensable. Further bibliographic and interpretive materials include Gilson, *History of Christian Philosophy in the Middle Ages*, 454-466, 763-764; *BRUO* I: 607-610; J. K. Ryan and B. M. Bonansea, edd., *John Duns Scotus 1265-1965* (Washington, 1965); *Studia Scholastica-Scotistica* I-V (Roma, 1968-1972); Lohr, "Commentaries ... Jacobus-Johannes Juff," 190-195; D. Burr, "Scotus and Transubstantiation," *MedSt* 34 (1972): 336-360; Allan B. Wolter, "Duns Scotus, John," in *The Encyclopedia of Philosophy* II (1967): 427-436; Leff, *The Dissolution of the Medieval Outlook, passim*. (*Franciscan Studies* and *Antonianum* usually feature at least one significant article on Scotus in each issue.)
[5] See the preceding item, n. 4.
[6] See below, **23-25**, and n. 12.

17. A7.II.d. *De trinitate* [*De personarum distinccione*]. Ca. 1370.

I. Inc.: Superest investigare de distinccione et conveniencia personarum quas
credimus plena fide ...

Expl.: × ... intelligendo simpliciter per communem essenciam communi-
cacione essencie.

II. MSS:[1]

i	Cambridge, Trinity Coll.	B.16.2	ff. 108ra-127ra	xiv/ex	Asc. Eng.[2]
ii	Praha, MK	*N.19 (1543)*	ff. 13ra-57ra	ca. 1410	Asc. Boh.[3]
iii	UK	VIII.G.32 (1615)	ff. 83r-143v	1403	Asc. Boh.

iv	Wien, ÖNB	1337	ff. 182ra-243vb	ca. 1410	Asc. Boh.
	[not in 1339, *pace* Lo]				
v		*1387*	ff. 47ra-74vb	ca. 1410	Asc. Boh.[4]
vi		*3935*	ff. 237ra-271rb	ca. 1420	Asc. Boh.
vii		4316	ff. 1r-79v	ca. 1430	Asc. Boh.[5]

III. Ed. Allen duPont Breck, *Johannis Wyclyf Tractatus De Trinitate* (Boulder, Colorado, 1962).[6] From all MSS.

IV. As with other treatises in the *Summa de ente*, Wyclyf's systematic use of cross-references in the *De trinitate* assures us once again of his cohesive purpose. Nine of his earlier works are cited directly or indirectly.[7] His *De eucharistia* (**38**), in finished form at least a decade away from our assigned date for this piece, was nevertheless already more than a gleam in his eye: "sicut nec posse separare accidens inherens a suo subiecto, ut patebit in materia de eucharistia." (P. 111; cf. 121, 123.)[8] Plainly Wyclyf had by now come to acknowledge the necessary conclusions concerning annihilation and the elements to which his realism had inexorably led him. We may confirm this assessment by recalling a remark by one of his ablest adversaries, the Franciscan William Woodford: "dum esset .. magister Johannes sententiarius Oxoniae, ac etiam baccalarius responsalis, publice tenuit et in scholis quod licet accidentia sacramentalia, essent in subjecto, tamen quod panis in consecratione desinit esse." [9] This would push his radical teachings on the Eucharist back sometime into the early 1360s, very near the beginning of his literary odyssey. (But this we have already noted in our commentary on **3**.)

Wyclyf's strong Augustinianism[10] emerges even more forcefully in this treatise than earlier in the *Summa*. The depth and breadth of his reading are by now quite impressive, and surely ballasted the ongoing disputations at Oxford.

vc: 3933[11] 3935[12] 4514[13]   Bale: 49   Sh: 8.II.4   Lo: 9.II.4

[1] For an extended commentary on these MSS, see A. duP. Breck, "The Manuscripts of John Wyclyf's *De Trinitate*," *MetH* 7 (1952): 56-70, and his edition of this work, xvii-xxiv.

[2] Divided into 17 capp.; all Continental MSS have six. Before the Dissolution there was evidently a MS of our work ("Tractatus prolixus & subtilis de trinitate" [unasc.; N 28, ff. 188-238 ?]) at Syon Monastery: Bateson, *Catalogue of the Library of Syon Monastery*, 124.

[3] Inc.: "Nuper est investigare...."

[4] Annotated by Peter Payne. See, on this vital link between England and Bohemia, František M. Bartoš, *Literární Činnost M. Jana Rokycany, M. Jana Příbrama M. Petra Payna* (Praha, 1928): 90-111; idem, *M. Petr Payne, diplomat revoluce husitské* (Praha, 1956); J. Novotný, "Peter Payne, ein englischer Flüchtling in Böhmen im xv. Jahrhundert. Ein Beitrag zu dem Problem der theologischen Abhängigkeit Jan Hus' vom Wycliff," *Zeitschrift für slawische Philologie* 20 (1950): 365-368 (lacking apparatus); R. R. Betts, "Peter Payne in England," *Universitas Carolina, Historia* 3 (1957): 5-14 (reprinted in his *Essays in Czech History*, 236-246); *BRUO* III: 1441-1443; S. H. Thomson "A Note on Peter Payne and Wyclyf," *MetH* 16 (1964): 60-63. On the more general issue of the Wyclyf-Hus nexus, see below, **32**, n. 13.

[5] The colophon reads "Anno domini M°CCCC°," but is evidently incomplete; the hand is clearly later than 1400.

Hus himself wrote a short piece in 1409 or 1410, specifically in defense of the *De trinitate*: "Actus pro defensione libri Ioannis Wiclef de Trinitate sancta ....," ed. in *Joannis Hus et Hieronymi Pragensis, confessorum Christi, historia et monumenta* ... II (Nürnberg: 1st ed. 1558, 2nd ed. 1583): cvr-cviir. For MSS of this "actus," see F. M. Bartoš, *Literární Činnost M. J. Husi* (Praha, 1948): 52.

[6] See the review by Beryl Smalley in *EHR* 79 (1964): 402-403.

[7] See the exact citations in Breck's ed., pp. xxv-xxvii.

[8] The offhand suggestion by James Crompton, "Wyclif, John," in *Lexikon für Theologie und Kirche*, 2nd ed., X (1965): 1280: "Der Tractatus de Trinitate entstand in W.s nich-kontroverser Periode vor 1372, wurde aber später revidiert," is not altogether without merit, but seems less plausible than the hypothesis here advanced.

[9] Quoted by Shirley in his introduction to *FZ*, xv, from Woodford's *72 questiones de sacramento altaris*, in Oxford, Bodleian 703, f. 129r (orthography is that of the edition). On Woodford, see *BRUO* III: 2081-2082; Lohr, "Commentaries ... G-I," 211; Eric Doyle, "A Bibliographical List by William Woodford, O.F.M.," *Franciscan Studies* 35 (1975): 92-105; and below, **23-25** and nn. 16, 21, 22; **28-30**, n. 19; **47**, n. 10; **382** and **383**.

[10] It was not for nothing that Wyclyf was familiarly called "Joannes Augustini" by his students and followers. See Workman, *JW* I: 119, and especially B. Blanciotti, ed., [Thomas Netter of Walden], *Doctrinale Fidei Ecclesiae Catholicae contra Wiclevistas et Hussitas* I (Venezia, 1757: first ed. Venezia, 1571, unpaginated; 1757 ed. reprinted Farnborough, 1967): col. 186. Netter was compelled because of his polemical stance to deny that Wyclyf was really faithful to Augustine; but the 3-volume *Doctrinale* does nevertheless evince a close familiarity with the bulk of the Wyclyf corpus. On Netter, see *BRUO* II: 1343-1344; Lohr, "Commentaries ... Robertus-Wilgelmus," 183-184; and Robson's careful delineation in *Wyclif and the Oxford Schools*, 231-240.

A close survey of Wyclyf's citations will reveal, almost without exception, his manifold reliance on the greatest of the Western Fathers. To be brief, we shall give here only two cases in point: in the *De ecclesia* (**32**), he cites Augustine at least 178 times, in the *De verbi incarnacione* (**22**), 106 – in both instances an overwhelming preponderance. (These figures, and others in the same vein, appear in an unpublished paper by S. H. Thomson, "The Influence of Augustine on Grosseteste and Wyclyf," given before the American Society of Church History on 30 December 1946.) This reliance was previously remarked by F. Loofs, *Leitfaden zum Studien der Dogmengeschichte*, 4th ed. (Halle, 1906): 638-654 (there is a fifth edition of this basic survey, ed. K. Aland, 1953). See now also M. Schmidt, "John Wyclifs Kirchenbegriff. Der *Christus humilis* Augustins bei Wyclif," in F. Hübner, W. Maurer, and E. Kinder, edd., *Gedenkschrift für Werner Elert* (Berlin, 1955): 72-109; Gordon Leff, "Wyclif and the Augustinian Tradition, with Special Reference to his *De Trinitate*," *MetH*, 2nd ser., 1 (1970): 29-39. A very useful summary of Augustine's teaching in one area where Wyclyf's dependence was very strongly marked is Gotthard Nygren, *Das Prädestinationsproblem in der Theologie Augustins* (Lund, 1956).

[11] Misread explicit in Buddensieg's transcription.

[12] Another odd explicit in Buddensieg; no title.

[13] Same explicit as for 3933, again, no title; perhaps these several irregularities in citation explain why the *De trinitate* is not listed in the later vc, 7980.

18. A7.II.e. *De ydeis*. Ca. 1368 ?

I. Inc.: Tractando de ydeis primo oportet querere si sint ...

Expl.: × ... et solum creatura habeat ydeam propriam in deo.

II. MSS:[1]

i   Cambridge,
        Trinity Coll.   B.16.2   ff. 131ra-137va xiv/ex   Asc. Eng.

ii	El Escorial	e.II.6	ff. 97rb-103va	xiv/2	JW MS Eng.[2]
iii	Kraków, BJag	848	ff. 38ra-50rb	1411	JW MS Boh.
iv	Pavia, BU	311	ff. 42rb-47vb; 72ra-76rb	xiv/2	Asc. Eng.
v	Praha, MK	M.54 (1410)	ff. 109r-144v	xv/m	JW MS Boh.
vi		N.19 (1543)	ff. 59ra-71ra	ca. 1410	Asc. Boh.
vii	UK	III.G.10 (535)	ff. 119r-139v	1397	JW MS Boh.
viii		IV.H.9 (773)	ff. 114r-130v	ca. 1400	JW MS Boh.
ix		V.H.16 (993)	ff. 79r-100r	1406	Asc. Boh.
x		VIII.F.1 (1555)	ff. 73va-87rb	1410	Asc. Boh.
		X.E.11 (1912)	ff. 175va-177ra	1433	Boh.[3]
xi		XXIII.F.58 (Lobkovice 153)	ff. 162r-187r	ca. 1410	Asc. Boh.[4]
xii	Stockholm, KunglB Venezia, BMarc.	Lat. A.164 Lat. VI.172[5]	ff. 34r-52v	1398	Asc. Boh.
xiii	Wien, ÖNB	1337	ff. 244ra-258va	ca. 1410	JW MS Boh.
xiv		4002	ff. 42r-52r	1410	Asc. Boh.[6]
xv		4523[7]	ff. 133r-186r	1412	Asc. Boh.

III. Unpublished.[8]

IV. Half a century ago, S. H. Thomson demonstrated that this short piece was composed immediately *before* the much more substantial *De universalibus* (**11**), which frequently refers to it.[9] The treatments are carefully parallel: ideas are the creative categories in God's mind, whereas the universals are their resultant projections in the created cosmos. This differentiation again underlines the basic distinction between the first and second *libri* of the *Summa de ente*: the first embraces the ambience of mortal existence; the second deals with God and His attributes and acts. His own definition of "idea" makes Wyclyf's intent clear: "ydea signat racionem extra rem eternam aput deum secundum quam deus est productivus rei ad extra."[10]

Typically, there are scattered references throughout the work to several other tractates in the *Summa*,[11] further elaborating our already intricate skein of integration.

vc: 3933 3935 4514 7980[12]   Bale: deest   Sh: 8.II.5   Lo: 9.II.5

---

[1] Which of our MSS, if any, once belonged to Matthias Flacius Illyricus, is not now possible to ascertain. Cf. his *Catalogus testium veritatis, qui ante nostram aetatem Pontifici Romano, eiùsque erroribus reclamarunt ...* (Strassburg, 1562): 494: "habeo & De ideis." See below, **36**, n. 8; **53**, n. 7.

[2] Lacking explicit. Cf. Thomson, "Unnoticed MSS and Works of Wyclif," 27.

[3] A *registrum*, but not by Peter Payne.

[4] See Thomson, "Unnoticed MSS and Works of Wyclif," 30.

[5] Listed in Marchanova's *contenta* for ff. 1-13; now lost. See Thomson, ibid., 28.

[6] Asc. scratched out, f. 52r. On ff. 18r-23r a defense of the *De ydeis* by Master Prokop of Plzeň, also dated 1410 (16 July); actually the date is not exactly correct, since we know this *defensio* was part of a week-long Wyclyf round-table or conference (to apply a modern designation: it was quite lively and well-attended) organized by Hus; it was presented there on Thursday, July 31. Ed. in Loserth, *Hus und*

Wiclif, 1st ed., 277-285; cf. 2nd ed., 92-93. Other MSS are Wien, ÖNB 1925, ff. 135v-139r; 4518, ff. 165v-169v.

[7] Not 4533, *pace* Lo.

[8] According to the *Bulletin de Philosophie médiévale* 10-12 (1968-1970): 95, V. Hérold was then preparing an edition of this work. A critical edition by S. H. Thomson, in MS, is in the editor's hands, with future publication anticipated under the auspices of the New Wyclif Society.

[9] "Order of Writing," 158-159.

[10] Continuation of the opening sentence. The phrasing also points toward our next item. We should perhaps note here that Augustine had himself written a *quaestio* on the ideas in his *De diversis quaestionibus lxxxiii*; see Aimé Solignac, "Analyse et sources de la question 'de Ideis'," in *Augustinus Magister. Congrès international augustinien Paris, 21-24 Septembre 1954* I: 307-315. Indeed, one of the reputedly lost works of the Aristotelian canon was also a *De ideis* (περὶ ἰδεῶν) – though it is doubtful that it carried any measurable weight in the medieval controversy.

[11] 7 ("ex primo tractatu primo libri," as in **ix**, f. 79v); **10** (f. 87r, in reference to the introductory section); and **12** (f. 90v: allusion corresponds to **12**: **xiv**, f. 98v).

[12] Here without incipit.

19. A7.II.f. *De potencia productiva dei ad extra*. Late 1371 or early 1372.

I. Inc.: Consequens ad dicta est tractare de potencia productiva dei ad extra ne fiat labor ...

Expl. cap. xi: × ... ad substanciam, qualitatem, quantitatem vel aliud genus creandi.

Inc. cap. xii [beginning of the "de annichilacione"]: Habito quod deus est creativus, restat videre si sit adnichilativus ...

Expl. cap. xvi: × ... adquirit ius vel reservat sibi ius ad taliter dispensandum.

II. MSS:

i	Cambridge, Trinity Coll.	B.16.2	ff. 139vb-157ra	xiv/ex	Asc. Eng.
ii	*Praha, UK*	*IX.E.6 (1762)*	ff. 51r-55v	ca. 1405	JW MS Boh.[1]

III. Ed. (capp. xii-xiv only) M. H. Dziewicki, *Johannis Wyclif de Ente: Librorum Duorum Excerpta* ... (WS, 1909): 287-315. From **i** only.

IV. This treatise, which mentions four of Wyclyf's other works,[2] is both logically and chronologically the last of the *Summa de ente* to be written. It is distinguished from the other twelve constituent tractates in style, spirit, and content. Even compared with the *De ydeis*, immediately preceding, it shows a marked break in orientation. Whereas the earlier elements of the *Summa* incorporate dense masses of the doctrine of Augustine, Grosseteste, Bradwardine, and FitzRalph, the present piece relies chiefly on Scripture itself, and is almost evangelical in tone. We are forced to assume the passing of many months and the development of quite a different outlook on the basic propositions of metaphysics. The *De verbi incarnacione* (**22**), readily assignable to 1372, was probably completed only a few months later. One wishes Wyclyf had been more communicative about his own development! The difference in tone between the

De potencia productiva and the *De ydeis* or the *De trinitate* is indeed so striking as to suggest some experience such as we usually associate with the term "conversion."[3]

Capp. xii-xiv, published as a "Fragmentum de annihilatione" by Dziewicki, has a superficial title to separate discussion. In **i**, although it is an integral part of the whole treatise, the running captions at the top of each righthand page, ff. 135r-140r, do read "de annichilacione." It should be remarked, however, that the titles also are applied to cap. xv, which Dziewicki did not edit – since it does not at all relate to the subject of annihilation. Wyclyf himself, as it happens, terms two of these capp. "de adnichilacione" retrospectively, in the *De verbi incarnacione* (**22**, pp. 76, 78). But in the last analysis there is no persuasive evidence that would lead us to argue that the capp. in question ever constituted a separate "tractatulus." Wyclyf was merely applying a kind of shorthand tag to a distinctive and recognizable portion of a long and somewhat unwieldy treatise.[4] But these capp. do provide us with a valuable *point de départ* for grasping the metaphysics behind the *De eucharistia* (**38**) and other works in that vein.[5]

VC: deest   Bale: deest   Sh: 8.II.6   Lo: 9.II.6

[1] A fragment; expl.: "... nemo dubitaret nec tamen (?) alterum altero."

[2] **12**; cited in **i**, ff. 142rb, 143rb, 144ra, etc. (also twice in Dziewicki ed., p. 293); **15**: f. 140ra; **17**: ff. 141ra, 149ra; **18**: ff. 141va, 142ra.

[3] Conversion has never been a process or event easily amenable to objective measurement. Perhaps our growing awareness that phenomena at the very foundation of the physical universe can by their nature likewise resist exclusive either/or definitions (e.g., Heisenberg's uncertainty principle, etc.) may someday facilitate a more wholesome intellectual deference in the face of undeniably real spiritual occurrences.

[4] An analogous type of citation is Wyclyf's reference to the "De substancia" and "De quantitate" which we have already discussed (**13**, and n. 3) and shown to apply to separate capp. in the *De ente predicamentali*.

[5] Cf. also **3** and **12**, above.

20. A8. *De materia et forma*. Between late 1370 and early 1372.

   I. Inc.: Cum materia et forma sint universalia mundi principia ...
      Expl.: × ... nullum ens dicit prius vel ex equo aliquam essenciam preter deum qui sit benedictus in secula seculorum.

   II. MSS:

i	El Escorial	e.II.6	ff. 78ra-87rb	xiv/2	JW MS Eng.[1]
ii	Praha, MK	M.54 (*1410*)	ff. 145r-169v	xv/m	JW MS Boh.
iii		N.19 (*1543*)	ff. 71rb-88ra	ca. 1410	Asc. Boh.
iv	UK	III.G.10 (535)	ff. 5r-30v	1397	JW MS Boh.
v		IV.H.9 (773)	ff. 56vb-73va	ca. 1400	JW MS Boh.
vi		V.H.16 (993)	ff. 100r-121v	1406	Asc. Boh.
vii		VIII.F.1 (1555)	ff. 39rb-53vb	1410	Asc. Boh.
viii		VIII.G.6 (1588)	ff. 57r-79v	ca. 1420	Asc. Boh.

ix		VIII.G.23 (1605)	ff. 211v-234v	1403	Asc. Boh.
		X.E.11 (1912)	ff. 167vb-173vb,		
			177rb-181va	1433	Boh.²
x		XXIII.F.58			
		(*Lobkovice 153*)	ff. 141r-161v	ca. 1410	Asc. Boh.³
xi	Stockholm, KunglB	Lat. A.164	ff. 53r-76r	1398	Asc. Boh.⁴
	Venezia, BMarc	Lat. VI.172⁵			

III. Ed. M. H. Dziewicki, *Johannis Wyclif Miscellanea Philosophica* I (WS, 1902): 163-242. From **iv, v, vii, viii, xi** only.

IV. Probably our oldest MS is **i**; it is certainly superior textually to **xi** (a Hus autograph), upon which Dziewicki's edition is chiefly based.⁶ The young Master of Arts was evidently working in haste.

There are numerous references in the text to other works of Wyclyf.⁷ In attempting to date it, we cannot expect that the mention or omission of specific treatises will be of much help; yet perhaps the most telling statement appears in cap. iv: "De conversione autem panis in corpus Christi, quam ecclesia vocat transubstancionem, est longus sermo, et mihi adhuc inscrutabilis." (P. 189.) As noted in our evaluation of the preceding item, by 1372 his thought was taking on a more solidly theological and Scriptural cast. Therefore, while it seems safe to assume that the bulk of the *Summa de ente* lay behind him, we ought provisionally to place the completion of the *De materia et forma* (in itself a perfectly orthodox philosophical topic) sometime between late 1370 and early 1372. We are reminded of John Keninghale's observation some time after the event that Wyclyf underwent a progressive change in the temper of his public utterances: "Hoc modo gestum est in primitiis Wyccliff, ut mala semina paulatim crescere sinebantur Oxonie a constudentibus et doctoribus orthodoxis...." ⁸

VC: 3933⁹ 3935 4514 7980   Bale: 36   Sh: 6   Lo: 7

¹ See Thomson, "Unnoticed MSS and Works of Wyclif," 27.
² The first entry is a copy of Peter Payne's *registrum*; the second is another, anonymous, register.
³ See Thomson, "Unnoticed MSS and Works of Wyclif," 30.
⁴ Given in Lo only as "Cod. Holm." It is odd that he overlooked this MS in his listings under other titles.
⁵ Listed in the *contenta* to this MS as occupying ff. 13-37, but long since lost.
⁶ See **11**, n. 9, above.
⁷ **11** (pp. 167, 217); **12** (p. 204); **17** (p. 195); **18** (p. 171); and **22** (p. 205).
⁸ *FZ*, 2. – We have a most curious *defensio* of this treatise (incomplete) by the stalwart Hussite John of Jičin in July of 1410: Loserth, *Hus und Wiclif*, 1st ed., 289-290.
⁹ Incomplete explicit in all four VC.

21. A9. *De composicione hominis.* Ca. 1372.

I. Inc.: Tria movent me tractare [or: ad tractandum] materiam de composicione hominis ...

Expl.: × ... et idem patet 4° et ultimo eiusdem 8^i et alibi satis sepe.

II. MSS:

i	Cambridge, Gonville & Caius Coll.	337	ff. 52r-66r	xiv/2	JW MS Eng.[1]
ii	El Escorial	e.II.6	ff. 87va-97rb	xiv/2	JW MS Eng.[2]
iii	Kraków, BJag	848	ff. 51ra-72ra	1411	JW MS Boh.
iv	Pavia, BU	311	ff. 76rb-88vb, 90, 89, 92, 91ra-b	xiv/2	Asc. Eng.[3]
v	Praha, UK	IV.H.9 (773)	ff. 73va-93rb	ca. 1400	JW MS Boh.
vi		VIII.F.1 (1555)	ff. 53va-73rb	1410	Asc. Boh.
vii		VIII.G.6 (1588)	ff. 81r-109v	ca. 1420	Asc. Boh.
viii		XXIII.F.58 (Lobkovice 153)	ff. 109v-140v	ca. 1410	Asc. Boh.[4]
ix	Wien, ÖNB	4302	ff. 75ra-96ra	xv/m	Asc. Boh.
x		4307	ff. 38v-62r	1433	Asc. Boh.
xi		4504	ff. 121r-153r	xv/1	Asc. Boh.

III. Ed. Rudolf Beer, *Johannis Wyclif De Compositione Hominis* (WS, 1904). From **vi, vii, ix, x, xi** only.

IV. There are a few references in this piece to other of Wyclyf's writings;[5] we have no reason to challenge its authenticity. The modern editor, however, expressed the opinion almost a century ago that the work in its present form "is not a literary work proceeding directly from Wiclif's pen, but that mere notes for lectures formed the source of the work as it has come down to us." (Pp. xv-xvi.) Dr. Beer arrived at this judgment before the bulk of Wyclyf's corpus had appeared in print; he was therefore quite understandably not fully familiar with his nervous and occasionally congested style, and may be allowed the error. We could now, with the five additional MSS that have come to light since Beer's (and Loserth's) time, reconstruct a measurably superior text. Beer's low estimation of Wyclyf's handling of his subject does not take account of the fact, furthermore, that he was expressly introducing here the doctrine of dominion for the first time, aiming at a fuller elaboration in due course.

VC: 3933 3935 4514 7980[6]   Bale: 63   Sh: 5   Lo: 11

---

[1] Inc.: "Tria me movent...." See Thomson, "A Gonville and Caius Manuscript," 198-199; "Unnoticed MSS and Works of Wyclif," 27. We ought perhaps to repeat here his conclusion that the extant text of all MSS (despite occasional colophons) is probably incomplete; the explicit as we now have it may someday yield to another.

[2] See Thomson, "Unnoticed MSS and Works of Wyclif," 27.

[3] See Stein, "Two Notes on Wyclif," 465-468.

[4] See Thomson, "Unnoticed MSS and Works of Wyclif," 30.

[5] **11** (pp. 5, 10-11, 14, 28, 48, 103, 114); **17** (pp. 1, 114); **22** (pp. 1, 114); **28-30** (p. 2: "quia antecedit ad tractatum humani dominii...").

[6] Without incipit in 7980.

22. A10. *De verbi incarnacione* [*De benedicta incarnacione*].[1] 1372.

I. Inc. proem.: Prelibato tractatu de anima qui introductorius est [4 wds.] restat tractatum de benedicta incarnacione operosius aggredi ...
Expl. proem.: × ... propter incarnacionis misterium cognoscendum.
Inc. cap. i: Quia autem spiritualiter viantibus in discendo necesse est primo removere prohibens disciplinam ...
Expl.: × ... sint formidine impugnacionis sophistice procedere in dicenda ad laudem, gloriam et honorem eiusdem domini nostri Jesu Christi.

II. MSS:[2]

i	Cambridge, Gonville & Caius Coll.	*337*	ff. 128r-178r	xiv/2	JW MS Eng.[3]
ii	London, BL	Royal 7 B.III	ff. 66r-75r	ca. 1400	Asc. Eng.[4]
iii	Oxford, Oriel Coll.	15	ff. 225ra-243ra	xiv/2	Asc. Eng.[5]
iv	Pavia, BU	*311*	ff. 91va-b, 93ra-97vb, 62ra-71vb, 108ra-130rb	xiv/2	Unasc. Eng.
v	Praha, MK	*D.35 (600)*	ff. 1r-77v	ca. 1410	Unasc. Boh.
vi	Wien, ÖNB	1387	ff. 75ra-104vb	ca. 1410	Asc. Boh.[6]
vii		4307	ff. 115r-157v	1433	Asc. Boh.
viii		4504	ff. 37r-110v	xv/1	Asc. Boh.

III. Ed. E. Harris, *Johannis Wyclif Tractatus de Benedicta Incarnacione* (WS, 1886). From **ii, iii, vi, vii, viii** only.

IV. This treatise was, in all likelihood, Wyclyf's first exclusively theological essay. It is generally accepted that it represented his prescribed commentary on the fourth book of the *Sentences*; we suggest that it was completed probably by the fall of 1372, before he commenced his year as Regent-doctor.[7] The whole of the *Summa de ente* lay behind him now, as well as his early efforts in logic; his philosophical realism is clear and confirmed in his mind. Its extension into the realm of theology has begun to engage him. He has not yet taken an irreversible stand on the remanence of the elements; but, from the retrospective position of the later 1370s, we can now trace his growing doubts and the direction his thought would soon take (cf., e.g., pp. 44, 189-191). There was emphatically no question in anyone else's mind by that time, however, as to the implications of his doctrine of annihilation, which he had published just before the *De verbi incarnacione* in the *De potencia productiva dei ad extra* (**19**). The parallels between the axiomatic duality of Christ's nature and the suppressed ambiguities in the doctrine of the Eucharist were all too obvious to Wyclyf's probing eye.

He quotes at least four of his earlier works,[8] and has by now reached an age at which he is beginning to deprecate, in the manner of Augustine, his youthful vagaries.

VC: 3933 3935[9] 4514[10] 7980   Bale: 75   Sh: 12   Lo: 13

[1] The weight of evidence presently available inclines us to prefer the first of these two interchangeable titles. (All four vc give *De incarnacione verbi.*) Against Harris, we may also cite R. L. Poole, ed., *Johannis Wyclif De Dominio Divino* (WS, 1890): 55, and Aubrey Gwynn, *The English Austin Friars in the Time of Wyclif* (London, 1940): 211. Finally, all three English MSS (i, ii, iii) have our preferred title.

[2] Bateson, *Catalogue of the Library of Syon Monastery*, no. N 28, ff. 142-187, claims a lost "Tractatus prolixus et subtilis de incarnacione verbi" at that institute before the Dissolution. This may well have been our piece.

[3] See Thomson, "A Gonville and Caius Wyclif Manuscript," 200-201.

[4] Abridged; see Harris ed., xiii-xiv.

[5] See the note on the erasure of the terminal ascription in L. Minio-Paluello, "Two Erasures in MS. Oriel College 15," *The Bodleian Library Record* 4 (1953): 207. Good general description in Harris ed., xiv-xvi.

[6] Annotated by Peter Payne.

[7] Our line of reasoning here follows Workman's close argument, *JW* I: 203; he inclines, however, to "about 1370" (pp. 97, 332). He seems in turn to have been accepted here as in other particulars by R. H. Hodgkin, *Six Centuries of an Oxford College. A History of the Queen's College 1340-1940* (Oxford, 1949): 29-30. Robson, without supporting citations, avers that "all scholars date [the *De verbi incarnacione*] to *c.* 1374." (*Wyclif and the Oxford Schools*, 194.)

[8] 4, 11, 12 and 19. On p. 53 he alludes to a *De continuacione*, which we would normally construe as the third of Wyclyf's logical treatises (3), though the context does not quite fit.

[9] Inc.: "Oportet autem ..."; expl.: "... eisdem domini nostri...."

[10] Expl.: "... eius Domini mei ..."; the same for 7980, with the addition of "18. conclusiones" at the end, an obvious elision with the following item from 4514.

23, 24, 25. A11.a, b, c. *De dominio divino.* 1373-1374.

I. Inc. proem.: Cum quilibet Christianus et specialiter theologus mori debeat virtuosus ...

Expl. proem.: × ... sanctorum doctorum aput ecclesiam approbate.

Liber I inc.: In tractando de dominio oportet inprimis supponere ipsum esse ...

Liber I expl.: × ... horum trium est eternum simpliciter sed contingens ...[1]

Liber II inc.: Iam secundo restat lacius disserere de dominio divino ...

Liber II expl.: × ... dicta philosophorum de magis noto homine et nature ...[2]

Liber III inc.: Redeundo iam tercio ad materiam que direccius concernit dominium ...

Liber III expl.: × ... sine debito secundum legem humanam donare dicitur.[3]

II. MSS:

i	Cambridge, Gonville & Caius Coll.	*337*	ff. 68r-127v	xiv/2	JW MS Eng.
	Praha, MK	*C.118 (550)*	ff. 110r-130v	ca. 1410	Boh.[4]
	UK	*X.E.11 (1912)*	ff. 183ra-205vb	1433	Boh.[5]
ii	Wien, ÖNB	1294	ff. 212ra-251vb	xiv/2	JW MS Eng.[6]
iii		1339	ff. 1ra-89vb	ca. 1410	Asc. Boh.
		1725	ff. 1r-31v	xv/1	Boh.[7]

iv	3929	ff. 114rb-170rb	1409	Asc. Boh.[8]
v	3935	ff. 13ra-48ra	1423	Asc. Boh.[9]

III. Ed. Reginald Lane Poole, *Johannis Wyclif De Dominio Divino* (WS, 1890): 1-256. From all MSS except **i**.

IV. This major effort was intended as a point of departure for Wyclyf's second great *summa*, the *Summa theologie* (A12). He had already published the *De verbi incarnacione* (**22**),[10] and alludes, toward the end of the *De dominio divino*, to a future treatise *De dominio humano* (**28-30**),[11] signalling that his plans for a more focused treatment of dominion in its secular aspects were already well advanced.

There is a particularly thorny chronological thicket to penetrate in attempting to fix with any precision the date of composition of this work. Although, as with virtually all of Wyclyf's writings, real exactitude is a chimerical expectation, we may strive to clarify here at least the sequence of publication of several closely related works on dominion, both by Wyclyf and by his opponents in debate. It is to be hoped that more of the latter will soon be discovered or published.

Richard FitzRalph, Archbishop of Armagh (1348-1360), eloquent Oxford scholar and resourceful adversary of the mendicants both there and at the Curia, provided much grist for Wyclyf's mill with his important *De pauperie salvatoris*, appropriately printed (though only in part) as an appendix to Poole's text of the *De dominio divino*.[12] FitzRalph, for his part, leaned on the striking essay of the papalist Giles of Rome, *De potestate ecclesiastica*, who had himself marshalled first Augustine, then Aristotle, the Bible, and the canonists.[13] Professor Leff has rightly stressed the startling metamorphosis in the three-quarters of a century between Giles and Wyclyf: radically different conclusions could spring from similar (if not identical) premises; Professor Wilks also reminds us that Wyclyf "could never resist the temptation to play a game of cat and mouse with his readers ... he always delighted in proving the opposite of what he apparently set out to demonstrate."[14] We should therefore not be too quick to deny Wyclyf a considerable measure of originality, if not in thematic interest, then certainly in the application of new lines of ratiocination to old dialectical exercises. Indeed it would appear to have been inherent in that sort of discipline to delight in the spontaneous efflorescence of variations on a common theme.

The *De dominio divino* may have begun to germinate in Wyclyf's mind within a few months after the completion of the *De verbi incarnacione*, which points to early in 1373; its first *liber* (19 capp.; the last, however, of only thirteen lines) was probably in finished form, or close to it, before he was commissioned by the king to go to Bruges on 26 July 1374.[15] The second and third *libri* (with only five and six capp. respectively) are almost surely unfinished, though they may perhaps have been completed either during his three months' stay in Bruges or upon his return to Oxford. A complete MS may yet surface, though its putative massiveness is not likely to have escaped any cataloger!

His views in any case were well known at Oxford, and the Franciscan scholar William Woodford, with whom Wyclyf remained on amicable terms until sometime in 1377, composed a rather pointed *Defensorium contra Armachanum pro mendicitate Christi*,[16] in which he assailed a number of FitzRalph's conclusions, some of which had just appeared anew in the *De dominio divino*. This *Defensorium* probably saw the light of day early in 1375. Wyclyf, in turn, had already declared his intention to prepare a study on civil dominion, and the first two *libri* of this very weighty treatise were actually published late in 1375 or early in 1376.[17] In the meantime the stout peripatetic Benedictine of Durham, Uthred of Boldon, had attacked Wyclyf's restrictive view of clerical authority in a *tractatulus* which has evidently not survived; the same oblivion has also befallen the simultaneous diatribe of another Benedictine, William Binham, the prior of a house at Wallingford and an Oxford scholar as well.[18] Against each of these Wyclyf launched separate counterthrusts in a series of *Determinaciones* (**381-383**) which have themselves experienced a fragmentary MS tradition. (The piece by Binham, probably titled *Contra posiciones Wiclivi*, provoked much the sharper response.) These *Determinaciones* offer a more radical approach to the problem of dominion than appears in either of his two major tractates on the question, and must therefore be the last works in our series. This inference, which incidentally runs counter to Workman[19] and modifies the conclusions in Loserth's edition of the *Determinaciones*,[20] is solidified by the reference at the outset of the first *Determinacio* against Binham to the animadversions of Woodford, which Wyclyf states he had dealt with the previous year.[21] Now by this we are to assume some systematic interchange, as the language of his allusion clearly implies familiarity with a published piece of some kind. It was, in fact, not Woodford's *Defensorium* which is implied here – to it Wyclyf may have been content to reply in some oral forum – but rather Woodford's more substantial *De dominio civili clericorum*, a frontal assault on the first two *libri* of Wyclyf's own *De civili dominio*.[22] And Wyclyf's reply to Woodford was in turn the third *liber* of that omnibus treatise, wherein we find no fewer than 30 specific *responsiones* to Woodford's assertions. The latter's polemic has been persuasively dated between April and June of 1376; the third *liber* of the *De civili dominio* must consequently have been written in the last half of that year, and the *Determinaciones* sometime early in 1377.

Wyclyf plainly regarded the completion of the *Summa theologie* as the balance of his life's work. The statement is there, in the first paragraph of the *De dominio divino*, which serves, as we have noted, as a kind of prolegomenon to the *Summa*: "Tempus est mihi per totum residuum vite mee tam speculative quam practice ..." The speculative part had been his logical and philosophical exercises; the practical would be for him the fulfilment of all that went before. It is not beside the point to observe that this sequence might give pause to those who have tended to view medieval thinkers, and particularly those who labored in the twilight of Scholasticism, as men with scant regard for practical matters.

vc: 3933[23] 3935 4514   Bale: 71[24]   Sh: 14   Lo: 15

[1] See text, p. 40, and nn. 3 and 23, below.
[2] Ibid.
[3] The vc, discussed below, n. 23, offer a different explicit; this confirms our suspicion that the work as we have it is truncated somewhat. Even the Cambridge ms, which is arguably archetypal for the rest, has the same format. It is quite probable that the concluding cap. of each of the three *libri* is wanting. A very tentative reconstruction of their contents might conceivably be attempted from such scattered references to it as surface in Wyclyf's other works and those of his opponents in debate.
[4] A copy of Peter Payne's *registrum*.
[5] Ibid.
[6] The only English ms of Wyclyf material in either Prague or Vienna. It was brought to Prague from England by the Czech copyists Mikuláš Faulfiš and Jiří of Knĕhnic in 1408. During the preceding year they had been engaged in transcribing a number of Wyclyf's works at Braybrook in Northamptonshire. For them, see *BRUO* II: 670, 1059; Thomson, "A Note on Peter Payne and Wyclyf," 60-61.
[7] A copy of Peter Payne's *registrum*.
[8] Textually very close to ii; however not identical. The marginalia (many in Czech), the *contenta*, and the missing capitular divisions in iv all distinguish this ms from its presumed prototype.
[9] Annotated by Peter Payne; index, ff. 1ra-11va.
[10] "... et de istis patet tractatu de incarnacione verbi." (P. 55.) He also mentions his *De perplexitate* (= perhaps **1-3**, but possibly **5** [p. 126]); **12** (p. 112); and **18** (p. 197).
[11] Pp. 204, 224, 255; see **22**, above.
[12] Pp. 257-476. (From Cambridge, Corpus Christi Coll. 180.) For the remainder of this great polemic, see R. O. Brock, Jr., "An Edition of Richard FitzRalph's *De Pauperie Salvatoris*, Books V, VI and VII" (unpublished Ph.D. dissertation, University of Colorado, Boulder, 1953). There exists, we now know, an eighth book, added at Avignon in 1358 or 1359: Katherine Walsh, "The *De vita evangelica* of Geoffrey Hardeby oesa (c. 1320-1385). A Study in the Mendicant Controversies of the Fourteenth Century," *Analecta Augustiniana* 33 (1970): 227; ms is Paris, BN f.l. 3222, ff. 1-78. – On FitzRalph, see the several articles by Aubrey Gwynn in *Studies: An Irish Quarterly Review* 22 (1933): 389-405, 591-607; 23 (1934): 395-411; 24 (1935): 25-42, 558-572; 25 (1936): 81-96; 26 (1937): 50-67; idem, "The Sermon-Diary of Richard FitzRalph," *Proceedings of the Royal Irish Academy* 44 (1937): 1-57; "Two Sermons of Primate Ric. FitzRalph," *Archivia Hibernica* 14 (1949): 50-65; L. L. Hammerich, *The Beginning of the Strife between Richard fitzRalph and the Mendicants* (Det kongelige Danske Videnskabernes Selskab, Historisk-filologiske Meddelser 26/3: København, 1938); R. R. Betts, "Richard FitzRalph, Archbishop of Armagh, and the Doctrine of Dominion," in H. A. Cronne, T. W. Moody, and D. B. Quinn, edd., *Essays in British and Irish History in Honour of James Eadie Todd* (London, 1949: 46-60; reprinted in his *Essays in Czech History*, 160-175); *BRUO* II: 692-694. We are now further favored by the superb study of Katherine Walsh, "Archbishop FitzRalph and the Friars at the Papal Court in Avignon, 1357-1360," *Traditio* 31 (1975): 223-245.
It has been pointed out by Workman, *JW* I: 119, and Sarton, *Introduction to the History of Science* III/1 (1947): 562, that a lesser source of Wyclyf's notion of the "subordination of clerical to royal power" was John Baconthorpe. On him, see especially Xiberta, *De Scriptoribus ... ex ordine Carmelitarum*, 167-240; *BRUO* I: 88-89; James Etzwiler, "Baconthorpe and Latin Averroism," *Carmelus* 18 (1971): 235-292; idem, "John Baconthorpe, 'Prince of the Averroists'," *Franciscan Studies* 36 (1976): 145-176; and Walter Ullmann, "John Baconthorpe as a Canonist," in C. N. L. Brooke et al., edd., *Church and Government in the Middle Ages. Essays Presented to C. R. Cheney on his 70th Birthday* (Cambridge, Eng., etc., 1976): 223-246.
[13] See Richard Scholz, *Aegidius Romanus De Ecclesiastica Potestate* (Weimar, 1929; reprinted Aalen 1961); Holtzmann and Morgen, *Repertorium ...* II: *Fontes A-B*: 136-137. The line of descent is briefly traced in William A. Pantin, *The English Church in the Fourteenth Century* (Cambridge, Eng., 1955); and more fully in Gordon Leff, "John Wyclif: the Path to Dissent," *Proceedings of the British*

Academy 52 (1966): 174-175. We must add, nevertheless, that we possess no firm proof that Wyclyf himself knew Giles' work at first hand. – The same caveat must also extend, *pari passu*, to the Dominican John (Quidort) of Paris (d. 1306), whose *De potestate regia et papali* deals in substantial detail (from the opposing side) with the issue of clerical dominion. (Ed. Jean Leclercq, *Jean de Paris et l'ecclésiologie du XIIIe siècle* [Paris, 1942]: 168-260; and Fritz Bleienstein, *Johannes Quidort von Paris Über königliche und päpstliche Gewalt (De Regia potestate et papali)* [Stuttgart, 1969].) See also Brian Tierney, *Foundations of the Conciliar Theory: The Contribution of the Medieval Canonists from Gratian to the Great Schism* (Cambridge, Eng., 1965; reprinted 1968): 157-178. Finally, see also below, **406**, n. 5.

[14] Michael J. Wilks, "Predestination, Property and Power: Wyclif's Theory of Dominion and Grace," in G. J. Cuming, ed., SCH 2 (1965): 225, 228 – a very careful article. This cautionary note would seem to have been heeded by John Gilchrist in his all-too-brief "The Social Doctrine of John Wyclif," *The Canadian Historical Association: Historical Papers* (1969): 157-165.

[15] The context and unfolding of this singular event in Wyclyf's life are discussed, with many asides, by Workman, *JW* I: 209-256. The standard treatment of the episode from the angle of international relations remains E. Perroy, ed., *The Anglo-French Negotiations at Bruges 1374-1377* (Camden Historical Society 80 = Camden Miscellany 19: London, 1952).

[16] We know of a least two MSS of this work, one at Oxford, Magdalen Coll. 75, the other at Cambridge, Univ. Ff.1.21; both MSS have appended a short additional polemic by Woodford, *De erroribus eiusdem Armachani*. (See on Woodford **17**, n. 9, above, and n. 22, below.) The title strongly intimates, however, that he was also taking issue with FitzRalph's *Defensorium curatorum contra eos qui privilegiatos se dicunt* (i.e., the mendicants) of 1357: this piece ed. by Edward Brown, *Fasciculus Rerum Expetendarum et Fugiendarum* II (London, 1690): 466-486. For MSS of the latter, see Gwynn, "The Sermon-Diary..."; Walsh, "Archbishop FitzRalph...," 223n.

[17] See below, **28-30**.

[18] On Uthred, see A. F. Pollard, "Uhtred, Utred or Owtred," DNB VIII (1899): 17-18 (erroneous at several points); Loserth, "Die ältesten Streitschriften Wiclifs. Studien über die Anfänge der kirchenpolitischen Tätigkeit Wiclifs und die Überlieferung seiner Schriften," *Sitzungsberichte der kaiserlichen Akademie der Wissenschaften in Wien. Philosophisch-historische Klasse* 160/2 (1908): 7-23; Workman, *JW* I: 222-224; C. H. Thompson, "Uthred of Boldon (A Study in Fourteenth Century Political Theory)" (unpublished Ph.D. dissertation, Victoria Univ., Manchester, 1936); Mildred E. Marcett, *Uhtred of Boldon Friar William Jordan and Piers Plowman* (New York, 1938); W. A. Pantin, "Two Treatises of Uthred of Boldon on the Monastic Life," in R. W. Hunt, W. A. Pantin, and R. W. Southern, edd., *Studies in Medieval History presented to Frederick Maurice Powicke* (Oxford, 1948; reprinted 1961): 363-385; Michael David Knowles, "The Censured Opinions of Utred of Boldon," *Proceedings of the British Academy* 37 (1951): 305-342; idem, *The Religious Orders in England* II: *The End of the Middle Ages* (Cambridge, Eng., 1961): 48-54, 66-67, 272 (partially reprinted in his *Saints and Scholars: Twenty-Five Medieval Portraits* [Cambridge, Eng., 1962]: 132-141); Pantin, *The English Church in the Fourteenth Century*, 166-175; *BRUO* I: 212-213. On William Binham, see R. L. Poole, "Binham or Bynham, William," DNB V (1886): 56; Loserth, "Die ältesten Streitschriften," 23-37; Workman, *JW* I: 231-232; *BRUO* I: 189.

[19] "But this was only the skeleton of a larger work, his vast treatises on *Divine and Civil Dominion*." (*JW* I: 257.)

[20] *Johannis Wyclif Opera Minora* (WS, 1913): L-LVI.

[21] "Quantum ad istud, declaravi proximo anno respondendo ad argumenta doctoris mei reverendi fratris Wilelmi Weldeforde, quomodo patenter deficit." (Ibid., 415-416.)

[22] The Berlin MS is scrutinized in Eric Doyle, "A Manuscript of William Woodford's De dominio civili clericorum," *Archivum Franciscanum Historicum* 62 (1969): 377-381; it is collated with the London, BL Lansdowne 409 text in the same author's "William Woodford's 'De dominio civili clericorum' against John Wyclif," *Archivum Franciscanum Historicum* 66 (1973): 49-109; text ed., 76-109. Other controversial exchanges between the two men are discussed below, **28-30**, n. 19.

[23] All three vc show the explicit "habentur hic"; likewise all three show 7 capp. for the second *liber*; and all indicate as well that the three *libri* served as prefatory material for the *Summa theologie*. 4514 shows 29 capp. for book I; probably a scribal misreading for 19.

[24] Inc. given as "Quoniam plerique pseudoglossatores."

A12. *Summa theologie*. 1375-1381.

Whether Wyclyf ever consciously planned his academic or scholarly life at its beginning, we may never surely know. Yet it does appear that early in life he began to organize his thought on a grand scale. He began with logic in its manifold aspects, sharpening the dialectical tool without which no schoolman could communicate with his fellows or hope to command their attention. Sustained in this discipline, he went to work with a furious intensity, aiming to recast English scholastic thought on the metaphysical ponderables which loomed largest in his day. The outcome was a series of lectures, over a span of a decade (more or less), on being, the universals, the Trinity, and the attributes and creative ideas of God, all considered philosophically. This was a necessary preface to the application of these same concepts to earthly concerns and institutions. Frequently we find him closing a demonstrative argument in a theological treatise with language to this effect: "This will be clear to anyone *nutritus in materia de universalibus* [or *de ydeis*]."[1] The *Summa theologie*,[2] as we shall see in analyzing its constituent treatises, is not therefore a strictly theological work at all, but an extended dissection of the leading religious and political problems of his day, seen through the lens of an Augustinian realist. It is a vital schematization of the ecclesiological concerns foremost at Oxford and, by extension, throughout the realm. As such it stands in need of a more thoroughgoing appreciation than it has heretofore received.[3]

The twelve (or ten, if we count the enormous *De civili dominio* as a single work) treatises of which the *Summa* is composed were prepared over a period of about seven years, beginning in 1375. Wyclyf, as will become apparent in our subsequent examination of his sermons and polemical pieces, was engaged on several other fronts at the same time. It was a momentous era in English and European history: we need only mention the continuing imbroglio with the French, the Schism, and the Peasants' Revolt. Wyclyf's *Summa theologie* rather broods above it all on a lonely crag; and arduous though our ascent may be, we must allow it a central place in the keen controversies of later scholasticism and the Reformation alike.

[1] Harris, ed., *Johannis Wyclif Tractatus de Benedicta Incarnacione*, 81.

[2] For the early use of this term see A7, n. 1, above.

[3] Still useful, so far as they go, are the three essays by Loserth in the *Sitzungsberichte der kaiserlichen Akademie der Wissenschaften in Wien, Philosophisch-historische Klasse*: "Studien zur Kirchenpolitik Englands im 14. Jahrhunderts, I: bis zum Ausbruch des Grossen Schismas (1378)," 136

(1897); "Studien ... II: Die Genesis von Wiclifs Summa Theologiae und seine Lehre vom wahren und falschen Papsttum," 156/6 (1907); "Johann von Wiclif und Guilelmus Peraldus. Studien zur Geschichte der Entstehung von Wiclifs Summa Theologiae," 180/3 (1916). It should be remarked that this last article was of major significance in identifying the extent of Wyclyf's indebtedness to the compendious *Summa viciorum et virtutum* of Peraldus. (Cf. Workman, *JW* I: 342.) See, for MSS of this popular work, Morton W. Bloomfield, "A Preliminary List of Incipits of Latin Works on the Virtues and Vices, mainly of the Thirteenth, Fourteenth and Fifteenth Centuries," *Traditio* 11 (1955): 292-293, 298 (for his *Speculum religiosorum*, otherwise *De eruditione religiosorum*), 329, 332, 362-363.

For such scattered bibliography as does exist on this general subject, see A. Molnár, "Recent Literature on Wyclif's Theology," *Communio Viatorum* 7 (1964): 186-192. There is a substantial new study of this whole subject: William Farr, *John Wyclif as Legal Reformer* (Leiden, 1974); see also Gunnar Westin, *John Wyclif och hans Reformidéer* (2 parts in 1 vol.; Uppsala, 1936) and John Stacey, *Wyclif and Reform* (London, 1964), 94-127.

26. A12.a. *De mandatis divinis* [*Decalogus*]. 1375-early 1376.

I. Inc. proem.: Sentenciam humani dominii sicut duorum priorum decrevi in tres tractatus ...[1]

Expl. proem.: × ... allegans scripturas multiplices exponit illud Deuteronomii 21° quomodo iure ecclesia debet ...

Inc. cap. I: Premissa sentencia de dominio in communi ac speculativa de spiritu qui est homo et per consequens subiectum humani dominii restat [5 wds.] discutere ...

Expl.: × ... ideo infidelitas facit quod lege ista contemptu discitur aliena.

II. MSS:

i	Cambridge, Univ.	*Ii.iii.29*	ff. 2ra-45vb	ca. 1400	Unasc. Eng.[2]
ii		Ll.v.13	ff. 2ra-108va	xiv/2	Misasc. Eng.[3]
iii	Gonville & Caius Coll.	337	ff. 181r-277v	xiv/2	JW MS Eng.
iv	Trinity Coll.	B.15.28	ff. 1r-128r	xiv/ex	Unasc. Eng.[4]
v	Oxford, Bodleian	333 (S.C. 2245)	ff. 109ra-186va	xiv/ex	Asc. Eng.[5]
vi	Magdalen Coll.	98	ff. 117ra-206va	xv/1	Asc. Eng.
vii	Paris, BN	*f.l. 15869*	ff. 109r-120v	xiv/ex	Unasc. Fr.[6]
viii	Praha, MK	A.70 (116)	ff. 192r-275v	xv/1	Asc. Boh.[7]
ix		C.38 (462)	ff. 18ra-107va	ca. 1410	JW MS Boh.[8]
x	UK	IV.D.21 (675)	ff. 2ra-105vb	ca. 1420	Asc. Boh.
xi		IV.D.22 (676)	ff. 1ra-129va	1405	Asc. Boh.
		IV.G.27 (759)	ff. 125ra-146va	1446	Boh.[9]
xii		V.A.3 (794)	ff. 1r-121v	1404	Asc. Boh.
xiii		V.E.17 (911)	ff. 2r-180r	ca. 1410	Asc. Boh.
		X.E.11 (1912)	ff. 206ra-230vb	1433	Boh.[10]
xiv		X.G.1 (1955)	ff. 20r-158v	xv/1	Asc. Boh.[11]
xv		XIV.C.26 (2493)	ff. 141r-236v	xv/1	Unasc. Boh.
xvi	Wien, ÖNB	1339	ff. 91ra-234rb	ca. 1410	Asc. Boh.[12]
xvii		1598	ff. 1r-78v	xv/1	Asc. Boh.[13]
		1725	ff. 33r-67v	xv/1	Boh.[14]

III. Ed. J. Loserth and F. D. Matthew, *Johannis Wyclif Tractatus de Mandatis Divinis accedit Tractatus de Statu Innocencie* (WS, 1922): 1-474. From all MSS except **i**, **iii** and **vii**.

IV. The tradition that Wyclyf intended the *De mandatis divinis*[15] to be the first book of his theological *summa* was firmly fixed by the time it began to be copied by Czech scribes. The rubric at the beginning of the work in **xvi**, f. 91r, reads: "Incipit liber mandatorum qui est primus in ordine summe sue, et presupponit istos tres tractatus de divino dominio precedentes." The tone of the treatise is careful and conservative; there is virtually nothing in it which could plausibly have been castigated as heretical at the time – probably this is why so many copies have survived. His dependence on Grosseteste's homonymous work is obvious throughout.[16] Wyclyf does allude a few times to the superiority of the king over the pope *in temporalibus*; but this position was scarcely extraordinary in the decades after Provisors and *Praemunire*.[17]

Although we do not claim with absolute certitude that Wyclyf foresaw the direction his sharpening ecclesiological perceptions would take him, we do encounter once again his habit of referring ahead to future works – specifically here to the *De civili dominio* (**28-30**): "Vide de hoc tractatu tercio capitulo x." (P. 40.) Loserth placed the date of composition "about 1375/6,"[18] linking it with the circumstances in which the Good Parliament of 1376 convened. The internal reference to the papal collector (almost surely the same Arnold Garnier who had vexed the English in 1371 and again in 1374) accords well with this approximate date;[19] to allow time for the implicit partial completion of the *De civili dominio* we would be well advised to fix the spring and summer of 1376 as the safest *terminus ad quem*.

The chief aim of the *De mandatis divinis* was to examine the hoary subject of *ius*, of which God is both source and essence. This *ius* is best understood, as it pertains to man, in its reflection in the ten commandments, which Wyclyf then proceeds to elucidate in their manifold aspects. His systematic approach appears to good advantage in this exposition.

VC: 3933 3935 4514   Bale: 132   Sh: 15.I   Lo: 16.I

[1] The *proemium* appears only in **i** (even there incomplete), and is therefore not in Loserth's edition. (Ed. Thomson, "A Gonville & Caius Wyclif Manuscript," 201-202.) It is actually a composite prologue to **26**, **27** and **28-30**, written probably in 1378.

[2] Exclusive of the *proemium* (for which see the preceding note); begins with cap. xv, "Detectis utrumque parumque arris...."

[3] Asc. to Grosseteste (inside front cover and colophon). Index follows, ff. 112r-129v.

[4] Begins with cap. xv: see n. 2, above.

[5] S.C. says xv/early. On f. 109r there is a compendium, with erased asc. It was evidently from this MS that Richard James took notes in Bodleian, James 3 (S.C. 3840), pp. 89-106 (ca. 1620-1636): and see below, **31**, n. 7.

[6] A fragment: first remarked in Thomson, "Unnoticed MSS and Works of Wyclif," 30.

[7] A fragment. Followed by a short *registrum*, ff. 277r-279v.
[8] Complete *registrum* of the *De mandatis divinis* on ff. 1ra-16va; and "sentencia decalogi," ff. 173ra-174va. Our text actually begins on f. 17ra, and runs to p. 3, line 10 in Loserth's ed.; then begins again on f. 18ra.
[9] A copy of Peter Payne's *registrum*. On ff. 1ra-35vb, an admirable register of Wyclyf's Scriptural references, by books of the Bible, drawn from **23-26, 28-34, 36, 37, 47** and **395**. Cf. also Wien, ÖNB 4522, ff. 24r-108v.
[10] Ibid.
[11] *Registrum* precedes text, ff. 1ra-19rb.
[12] *Registrum* follows, ff. 234rb-236rb.
[13] The last leaf has been cut out. Ends on p. 251, line 20 of Loserth's ed.
[14] A copy of Peter Payne's *registrum*. – Lo: 100 notes that the so-called "lost" *De virtute orandi* is really cap. xix of the *De mandatis divinis*. We have no indication that an autocephalous work by this title ever experienced a separate MS tradition.
Jakoubek of Stříbro defended the *De mandatis divinis* at Prague on 28 July 1410: partially reproduced text, from Praha, UK X.E.24, in Loserth, *Hus und Wiclif*, 1st ed., 271.
[15] The B.Litt.Oxon. (St Catherine's) dissertation by J. F. McCristal, "A Study of John Wyclif's Treatise *De Mandatis Divinis*" (1958), especially chapter 3, "Wyclif's Use of Grosseteste's Treatise *De Decem Mandatis*," 258-371, emphasized Wyclyf's free rearrangement of "Lincolniensis." See next note.
[16] Cf. Thomson, *The Writings of Robert Grosseteste*, 131-132. Neil Ker has noted a copy of the *De mandatis* "cum aliis contentis" (also Wyclyf?) in the library of the Queen's College at Oxford which was pledged as a loan in 1401: "Wyclif Manuscripts in Oxford in the Fifteenth Century," *Bodleian Library Record* 4 (1953): 293. Beryl Smalley has also discussed Grosseteste's unpublished commentary in "The Biblical Scholar," in D. A. Callus, ed., *Robert Grosseteste Scholar and Bishop: Essays in Commemoration of the Seventh Centenary of his Death* (Oxford, 1955): 82-83.
[17] He treads lightly here too, e.g., p. 381: "Excommunicaciones autem quas fulminat [i.e., the pope] ad terrendum laicos, sicut tota ista materia, sunt alibi denudanda."
[18] P. xxxii.
[19] P. 381; see Workman, *JW* I: 220, 270, and especially below, **397**.

27. A12.b. *De statu innocencie*. Mid-1376.

I. Inc.: Ut supradicta magis appareant, oportet parumper disgredi ...

Expl.: × ... de dominio hominis lapsi videtur diffusius pertractandum de dominio clericorum.

II. MSS:

i	Cambridge, Gonville &Caius Coll.	337	ff. 278r-287v	xiv/2	JW MS Eng.
ii	Dublin, Trinity Coll.	C.1.23	pp. 332b-350a	xiv/ex	Asc. Eng.
iii	Praha, UK	III.G.11 (536)	ff. 72r-85v	xv/1	JW MS Boh.[1]
iv	Wien, ÖNB	1339	ff. 237ra-248vb	ca. 1410	JW MS Boh.[2]
v		1622	ff. 73r-75r	1410	JW MS Boh.[3]
vi		3929	ff. 267rb-274va	1409	JW MS Boh.[4]
vii		3935	ff. 225ra-231ra	1423	JW MS Boh.[5]

III. Ed. J. Loserth and F. D. Matthew, *Johannis Wyclif Tractatus de Mandatis Divinis accedit Tractatus de Statu Innocencie* (WS, 1922): 475-524. From all MSS except **i**.

IV. This, the shortest of the books in the *Summa theologie*, appears to have arisen as an afterthought to the *De mandatis divinis*. As he explains in his first paragraph, Wyclyf became aware of the fact that the *De mandatis* had failed to present in their proper order the steps in the drama of God's dealings with his creatures when demanding of them strict obedience to His commandments. Wyclyf then describes, under this self-imposed imperative, the conditions of life before the Fall. As we read at the outset: "Ut supradicta [i.e., God's demands of man] magis appareant, oportet parumper disgredi, videndo quomodo homo debuit in statu innocencie conversari. Sicut enim ex medicorum principiis oportet statuere hominem equalis complexionis simpliciter quoad iusticiam, cuius complexionis temperamentum sit metrum et regula aliorum; sic oportet videre que conversacio fuit homini debita ex institucione primaria; et secundum accessum ad illam vel ab illa distanciam debent aliorum iusticie vel iniusticie mensurari." (There follows in due course a labored examination of the categorically impossible origin of the liberal arts in the state of innocence.)

Wyclyf mentions a previous discussion of annihilation early in the treatise (p. 476): "et hoc diffuse prosecutus sum in materia de adnichilacione"; in all likelihood the reference is to capp. xii-xiv of the *De potencia productiva dei ad extra* (**19**), although he had also brushed the topic in the *De logica tractatus tercius* (**3**), and would again in the *De eucharistia* (**38**), the *Trialogus* (**47**), and many other works – and there much more in depth.

We may assign a date of summer or early fall of 1376 to this composition.

VC: 3933 3935 4514   Bale: 54   Sh: 15.II   Lo: 16.II

[1] Expl.: "... et sic de consimilibus." Included under 16.II in Lo; but not mentioned at all in his edition. Also overlooked in Truhlař; see below, **202**, n. 1.
[2] "Incipit tractatus de statu innocencie quid est secundus in ordine summe sue." (F. 237ra.) Breaks off in cap. vi; in the *contenta* (inside front cover): "... liber de statu innocencie eciam incompletus."
[3] A fragment; ends in cap. ii.
[4] Ends in cap. vi.
[5] Ibid.

28-30. A12.c, d, e. *De civili dominio* [*De dominio civili*] [*De dominio humano*]. Late 1375-late 1376.

I. Liber I inc.: Tractando de civili dominio hominis superaddito naturali, oportet in primo videre si civile dominium presupponat dominium naturale ...

Liber I expl.: × ... Quid elucidant me vitam eternam habebunt, quam nobis conferat liber vite.[1]

Liber II inc.: Licet capitulo 37º rogarem obnixius omne genus auditorii fovere evangelicam veritatem ...

Liber II expl.: × ... in bono vincere adversarios crucis Christi.[2]

Liber III inc.: Ut supradicta de lege Christi in genere plus lucescant, oportet
ordiri secundum aliam formam ...
Liber III expl.: × ... in quo non sit necesse procuratorie sic orare.[3]

II. MSS:[4]

i	Durham, Dean & Chap. Muniments	—	ff. 110r-125v	xv/1	Unasc. Eng.[5]
ii	Firenze, BLaur	*Plut. XIX.33*	ff. 174r-182v	1408	JW MS Eng.[6]
iii	Paris, BN	*f.l. 15869*	ff. 70r-103r, 120v-125r	xiv/ex	Unasc. Fr.[7]
iv	Praha, MK	*O.29 (1613)*	ff. 234v-236r	ca. 1430	JW MS Boh.[8]
	UK	*IV.G.27 (759)*	ff. 36ra-124vb	1446	Boh.[9]
v		*V.H.27 (1004)*	ff. 59r-65r	xv/1	Unasc. Boh.[10]
vi		*X.E.6 (1907)*	f. 61v	1452	Asc. Boh.[11]
		X.E.11 (1912)	ff. 230vb-359ra	1433	Boh.[12]
vii	Wien, ÖNB	*1340*	ff. 1ra-260vb	ca.1410	Unasc. Boh.[13]
viii		*1341*	ff. 1ra-251vb	ca. 1410	Unasc. Boh.[14]
		1725	ff. 81r-236r	xv/1	Boh.[15]
ix		*4488*	ff. 11r, 36r	ca. 1435	Boh.[16]

III. *Liber* I ed. R. L. Poole, *Iohannis Wycliffe Tractatus de Civili Dominio Liber Primus* (WS, 1885);[17] *libri* II and III ed. J. Loserth, *Iohannis Wyclif De Civili Dominio Liber Secundus; Liber Tercius* (3 vols.: WS, 1900, 1902, 1904).[18] From vii and viii only.

IV. The present work, in its totality[19] surely the most massive of Wyclyf's treatises, has been customarily regarded by later scholars as a kind of watershed event in his intellectual development. We shall cite here only Loserth: "Wyclif's book *De civili dominio* in its origin is most closely connected with the great agitation of men's minds which was brought about by the proceedings of the Good Parliament (1376), and which gave a new direction to Wyclif's life and work."[20] While we would not discount for a moment the impact of the dramatic incidents of April-July 1376[21] upon Wyclyf's consciousness, perhaps too much emphasis has been placed on the distinctive character of the circumstances surrounding the composition of this work. Thematically the *De civili dominio* flows naturally from the *De dominio divino* (**23-25**) – indeed, as we have already demonstrated,[22] the publication of the last part of the *De dominio divino* and the first *liber* of the *De civili dominio* probably occurred within a year of each other. A detailed examination of the unfolding of his argument in the latter work affords us no direct indication at all, in fact, that any part of it sprang from the contemporary debates over ecclesiastical property that occupied the Good Parliament and the subsequent session of the Great Council.[23]

The first *liber*, as we may accept from Poole's notes, contained either *verbatim* or by extension all nineteen of Wyclyf's "theses," so violently stigmatized by Gregory XI in his five bulls from Rome on 22 May 1377.[24] Unquestionably the pope had had time (before or after his return to Rome on 17 January?) to examine a copy of the *De civili dominio, liber* I: the excerpts he cites do appear in the sequence he gives them in the treatise itself.[25] That Wyclyf honed his arguments further in the second and third *libri* we may confidently attribute to the growing heat of debate at Oxford: an anonymous Benedictine (John de Aclyff? William Binham?[26]) and William Woodford OFM, both figure explicitly in his lengthy extrapolations in those two *libri*. Later, of course – after the confrontation at St Pauls in February of 1377, and after the parliamentary *contretemps* in the following months, and after the publication of the five bulls in England only in December – Wyclyf would defend those nineteen propositions in at least three separate tracts which shall engage us below (see **399-401**).

Three aspects of the *De civili dominio*, quite apart from its contingent circumstances, demand our attention; all three bear on his concept of the law in its manifold relationships to the twin principles of dominion and Grace. Preeminent among these three, naturally, is the *lex Christi*, which is at once source and standard for all earthly laws, secular and canonical alike. The term in one or another guise appears dozens of times throughout the *De civili dominio*. It is a dynamic, compelling concept, which itself seems to have provided much of the impetus for the radicalization of Wyclyf's subsequent pronouncements on the sacraments and the friars.[27]

The second aspect of this treatise which concerns us is his new emphasis on canon law and, to a lesser extent, on the common law and Roman civil law.[28] As to the former, his citations from Gratian, the *Decretales* and later canonists such as Hostiensis are sufficient both in number and in precision (beginning in cap. xl of *liber* I and running throughout the rest of the treatise) to reflect a sustained exposure to the standard texts. It is significant, however, that the great preponderance of these references incorporates patristic quotations: clearly he availed himself of canonical texts for the most part to buttress the chief edifice of his argument, which remained sturdily Scriptural. (At one point, indeed, he paused to lament his youthful ignorance of the rich meanings of Scripture: now, he affirms, he realized the powerful "loyca Christi."[29]) His deployment of the common law of the Realm and (very rarely) of the *Codex*[30] tended, on the other hand, to underscore his insistence on the legitimate delimitation of ecclesiastical jurisdiction in the secular sphere.

Finally, we ought to note briefly that one rendering of Wyclyf's thematic *dominium* (depending, of course, on context) is "sovereignty." Several modern students of medieval political theory have occupied themselves quite fruitfully in pursuing the twists and turns of this elusive but perdurable notion into the Renaissance and even the twentieth century. I will only suggest here that Wyclyf's observations on this topic (which Gregory XI believed echoed all too clearly the pernicious opinions of Marsiglio of Padua and John of Jandun)[31] deserve their place in our retrospective estimation of scholastic contributions to the theory of sovereignty.[32]

There are several allusions in the *De civili dominio* to preceding *libri* of the *Summa theologie* (as "primus," "secundus huius") and sometimes promises to go into a subject later (e.g., in vol. III, p. 380, a reference to **34**; and in vol. IV, p. 598, to **32**). Wyclyf's story of the prebend in Lincolnshire which was given to "alienigene ydiote" is found in vol. III, p. 334.[33]

vc: 3933 3935 4514   Bale: 68   Sh: 15.III-V   Lo: 16: III-V

[1] At the end of all three *libri* in **vii** and **viii** will be found what appear to have been Wyclyf's own *registra*, consisting of cap.-by-cap. summaries. The incipit for the first *liber* is "Capitulum primum probat tripliciter ...," and the explicit is "... et narrat eius commendacionem multiplicem."

[2] Inc. reg.: "Capitulum primum introducendo causam ..."; expl.: × "... hortans ad ipsum obiciens et dissolvens."

[3] Inc. reg.: "Capitulum primum premittit supposicionem ..."; expl.: × "... nisi de quanto mens orantis magis attenditur."

[4] The *Differencia inter peccatum mortale et veniale* (= Sh: 28; Lo: 29) is actually a fragment of *liber* III; for those MSS and separate ed., see **51**, below.

[5] The MS is entitled, according to a communication from Dean Jeremy I. Catto of Oriel College, Oxford, *Registrum papireum*; the fragment contains capp. xxiv, xxvi and xxvii of *liber* III. First noticed in H. E. Salter, W. A. Pantin, and H. G. Richardson, *Formularies which bear on the History of Oxford c. 1204-1420* I (OHS, new ser., 4: Oxford, 1939): 218-226.

[6] Last cap. of *liber* III only. See I. H. Stein, "The Wyclif Manuscript in Florence," *Speculum* 5 (1930): 96. This and the Durham fragment are the only MSS of any part of the *De civili dominio* now known in an English hand. On 14 February 1454 Andrew Mankswell, a fellow of Oriel College (cf. *BRUO* II: 1215), sold to his colleague Thomas Wyche (cf. *BRUO* III: 2102) a MS containing the present work and **37** too; Ker, "Wyclif Manuscripts in Oxford," 293. He also purchased from John More, the Oxford stationer, another book "cum multis continentis Wycliff" on 10 March. What this may have been is impossible to tell; and the MSS in question may even have been Continental in provenance.

[7] *Liber* I only; but extracts from *liber* III on ff. 120v-125r. See Thomson, "Unnoticed MSS and Works of Wyclif," 30; W. P. Reeves, "A Second MS. of Wyclif's *De Dominio Civili*," *Modern Language Notes* 50 (1935): 96-97. Ff. 103r-108r contain a fascinating *quaestio disputata* on Wyclyf's doctrine of dominion, debated at Paris on 16 January 1381 (sic!); the script, unfortunately, is atrocious. (There is no mention of this episode in Denifle and Chatelain, *Chartularium Universitatis Parisiensis .. III: Ab anno MCCL usque ad annum MCCCLXXXXIII* [Paris, 1891; reprinted Brussels, 1964].)

[8] An extract.

[9] A copy of Peter Payne's *registrum*.

[10] Cap. xv of *liber* II only.

[11] A fragment of *liber* III, cap. xxvii.

[12] A copy of Peter Payne's *registrum*.

[13] *Liber* III only. On ff. 261ra-266ra the *registrum* (cf. above, n. 1).

[14] *Libri* I and II. *Registra* are at ff. 144rb-152vb and 252ra-254vb (above, n. 1). The lack of a specific ascription is of no moment. The rubric reads: "Primus liber de civili dominio de summa sua in theologia." The MS bears marginalia in the hand of Peter Payne (Thomson, "A Note on Peter Payne and Wyclyf," 62), and is part of a projected Wyclyf corpus, done by two or by at most three scribes using the same codex specifications and style.

[15] A copy of Peter Payne's *registrum*.

[16] This MS is a Hussite compilation: on the ff. indicated, and probably on several others as well, specific citations from different capp. are made.

A sizeable number of citations from the *De civili dominio* were singled out by the "committee of twelve" at Oxford in 1411 as erroneous or heretical: Wilkins, *Concilia...* III: 346-348 (nos. 176-219).

Undoubtedly close examination of these would disclose the usual mix of exact quotation and paraphrase – always out of context, of course.

[17] Ed. from **viii** only.

[18] Ed. from **vii** and **viii** only. – Brief extracts trans. in A. R. Myers, ed., *English Historical Documents* IV: *1327-1485* (New York, 1969): 885-887. (**39** is also partially trans. in this collection [p. 839], as is part of **398** [pp. 656-657].)

[19] Eric Doyle, in his recent "William Woodford, o.f.m. and John Wyclif's *De religione*," *Speculum* 52 (1977): 329-336, has argued on contextual grounds that the first three capp. of *liber* III of the *De civili dominio*, followed by the first two capp. of the *De apostasia* (**36**), "were originally one whole" work known to Woodford as the *De religione*. This is a serious suggestion. It is certainly true that some case can be made on the basis of the mss themselves – but it is not ultimately convincing: after all, the ms tradition of many of Wyclyf's writings is as variegated and supposititious as it is here. But we may marshal a number of facts overlooked by Doyle which together militate against his proposed introduction of a new piece into the Wyclyf canon. First among these is Wyclyf's failure ever to allude to any *De religione* as such – though of course this is by itself not conclusive! Much more weight must be assigned to the fact that Wyclyf (premise: not the copyists – though actually this would not damage our case) no less than three times within the third *liber* of the *De civili dominio* itself refers explicitly to two of the three capp. in question: vol. III: 199 = cap. iii, vol. IV: 477 = cap. i; vol. IV: 477 = cap. iii. Elsewhere in the third *liber* he alludes to later capp. by their accepted numbers: pp. 233, 303, 411, 440, 454, 473. (He is wrong only once, on p. 151, where he gives viii instead of ix.) In cap. xiv of **37** (p. 203), we come upon clear *renvois* to the *De civili dominio* III, cap. iii, and to the *De apostasia*, cap. ii. Peter Payne, Bale and the recent catalogers ascribe no such work to Wyclyf. I would not for a moment deny that perhaps quite soon after the *Summa theologie* began to circulate, some perceptive and enterprising schoolman may have lifted the five capp. in question out of context and retitled them *De religione*, detecting for his own purposes a certain continuity in subject matter. Woodford would then himself (or was he the artificer?) have come upon this version (*which is in any case no longer extant*) and cited it under the novel rubric in his *Quattuor determinaciones* (1389/1390; ed. cit. in Doyle, pp. 329-330). But Wyclyf himself almost surely never penned an autocephalous *De religione*.

[20] From his very thorough introduction in vol. IV: V. Other studies of this subject include R. L. Poole, "Wyclif's Doctrine of Dominion," in his *Illustrations of the History of Medieval Thought*, 246-268; Westin, *John Wyclif och hans Reformidéer* I: 124-145; Lowrie J. Daly, *The Political Theory of John Wyclif* (Chicago, 1962: but see the review by S. H. Thomson in *Speculum* 40 [1965]: 344-345); Howard Kaminsky, "Wyclifism as Ideology of Revolution," *Church History* 32 (1963): 57-74; Wilks, "Predestination, Property and Power," 220-236.

[21] Most conveniently reviewed in May McKisack, *The Fourteenth Century 1307-1399* (Oxford History of England 5: Oxford, 1959): 384-403; cf. bibliographical note, p. 387. Also of value is T. J. Hanrahan, "John Wyclif's Political Activity," *MedSt* 20 (1958): 154-166.

[22] Above, **23-25**.

[23] It met in the fall of 1376, and succeeded under John of Gaunt's prodding in undoing many of the actions of the Commons during the Good Parliament.

[24] Usefully translated *seriatim* in Joseph H. Dahmus, *The Prosecution of John Wyclyf* (New Haven, 1952: see review by S. H. Thomson, *Speculum* 28 [1953]: 563-566), 39-50; text of the nineteen theses, pp. 49-50 – see his note about the persistent confusion over their number. Dahmus also probes the circumstances of the years 1376-1377 in his other major study, *William Courtenay Archbishop of Canterbury 1381-1396* (University Park, Pa., and London, 1966), 31-63.

[25] It ought to be remarked here that a sketchy commentary on *liber* I appears in L. J. Daly, "Walter Burley and John Wyclif on Some Aspects of Kingship," in *Mélanges Eugène Tisserant* IV (Studi e Testi 234: Città del Vaticano, 1964): 170-173; also see below, **33**, n. 6.

[26] See **23-25**, n. 18, above. The reference is to "illum dominum et socium de ordine sancti Benedicti inter omnes valentes Oxonienses." (vol. II: 1.) The attached note refers us to an appendix; and

Loserth explains in his introduction to vol. IV: xxi, that Poole had promised such an appendix to pin down the identity of this "socius," but never wrote it – "and so the passage remains as dark as before." It is virtually impossible that Wyclyf could have meant William Woodford, whom he generally limned as "doctor meus reverendus magister" or some such – and Woodford was a Franciscan in any case. The shadowy John de Aclyff was an associate of Uthred of Boldon's at Durham who perhaps incepted in theology at Oxford in 1377 or 1378: see W. A. Pantin, "A Benedictine Opponent of John Wyclif," *EHR* 43 (1928): 73-77; *BRUO* I: 10-11. Then again, as maintained by Michael Hurley, "'Scriptura Sola': Wyclif and his Critics," *Traditio* 16 (1960): 290n., it may have been Henry Crump, O.Cist.: see for him *BRUO* I: 524-525; H. E. Salter, ed., *Medieval Archives of the University of Oxford* I (OHS 70: Oxford, 1917): 223-225; also **384**, n. 1, below.

[27] There are three quite inadequate monographs on these topics, which of course figure prominently in many other treatments of Wyclyf: Edward A. Block, *John Wyclif Radical Dissenter* (San Diego, 1962); Eduardo D. McShane, *A Critical Appraisal of the Antimendicantism of John Wyclif* (an extract from his Gregorian University dissertation: Roma, 1950); and, most remotely, A Dakin, *Die Beziehungen Johann Wyclifs und der Lollarden zu den Bettel-mönchen* (London, 1911). There are some useful observations in Knowles, *Saints and Scholars*, 142-152, and Gilchrist, "The Social Doctrines of John Wyclif," 163-164.

[28] Most germane here are Frederick W. Maitland, "Wyclif on English and Roman Law," in his *Collected Papers* III (ed. H. A. L. Fisher, Cambridge, Eng., 1911): 50-53 (originally published in 1896, before the second and third *libri* were printed by the WS); Edith C. Tatnall, "John Wyclif and *Ecclesia Anglicana*," *JEH* 20 (1969): 19-43. Harry Pressfield, "Wyclif and the Common Law," *Bibliotheca Sacra* 90 (1933): 175-184, is grossly elementary and of less than no value.

Wyclyf's own copy of the *Decretum* (London, BL Royal 10.E.II), pledged as a *cautio* on 23 October 1381 (about the time of his final departure to Lutterworth), attests his close interest in the subject. And we may also point to a revealing indication of Wyclyf's feelings toward the law of the church in the next treatise of the *Summa theologie*: "Et sic concedo, quod expedit, multa adiscere iura canonica, sed primo omnium secundum illam partem, in qua expressius docetur lex ewangelica, et sic forent omnes decretiste pure, sed grossi theologi. Et de quarto fuerint plures eorum secundum gradus sapiencie, quos deus eis instillaverit, de tanto iocundium procederet sancta mater ecclesie." (R. Buddensieg, ed., *John Wyclif's De Veritate Sacrae Scripturae* II [WS, 1906]: 271.) Yet his judgment would soon be much harsher: see, e.g., Loserth, ed., *Iohannis Wyclif Tractatus de Ecclesia* (WS, 1886): 237 (quoted below, **32**).

[29] Vol. IV: 443.

[30] See **397**, n. 6, below.

[31] No explicit connection has even been proven; but the matter of estimating intellectual inheritance or influence, in the absence of direct quotation or acknowledgment, is delicate in the extreme. Kaminsky cites Emerton and Bartoš as two recent scholars who have singled out some affinities between Wyclyf and Marsiglio ("Wyclifism as Ideology of Revolution," 5, 17; and cf. Sarton, *Introduction to the History of Science* III/1: 988, "John Wycliffe was much influenced by it"); Daly has also assumed some link (*The Political Theory of John Wyclif*, 20-23). Workman, however (*JW* I: 132-134), doubts that Wyclyf was at all acquainted with Marsiglio's work. Of course it is still possible that a very close parallel reading of the *Defensor pacis* and *liber* I of the *De civili dominio* might uncover some tacit borrowing. In general it must be said, though, that Marsiglio's focus of influence remained on the Continent until the Reformation awakened the interest of Henry VIII's abettors in its strident antipapalism. (See C. W. Previté-Orton, "Marsilius of Padua," *Proceedings of the British Academy* 21 [1935]: 3-49. Of major significance is Nicolai Rubinstein, "Marsilius of Padua and Italian Political Thought of His Time," in John R. Hale, J. R. L. Highfield, and Beryl Smalley, edd., *Europe in the Late Middle Ages* [Evanston, Ill., 1965]: 44-75; and Carlo Pincin, *Marsiglio* [Pubblicazioni dell'Istituto di Scienze Politiche dell'Università di Torino 17: 1967] is quite thorough. But the short article by E. S. Molnar, "Marsiglio of Padua, Wyclyf and Hus," *Anglican Theological Review* 44 [1962]: 33-43, offers little of substance.)

John of Jandun is another case altogether. Here we must revert to the text of Gregory's letter. After marking Wyclyf as the author of several "propositiones et conclusiones erroneas et falsas, in fide male sonantes, que statum totius ecclesie subvertere et enervare conantur," he continues: "quarum alique, licet aliquibus mutatis terminis, sentire videntur perversas opiniones et doctrinam indoctam damnate memorie Marsilii de Padua, et Joannis de Ganduno, quorum liber per ... Joannem PP. XXII ... reprobatus extitit et damnatus..." (J. D. Mansi, ed., *Sacrorum conciliorum nova et amplissima collectio...* XXVI [Venezia, 1784]: 562). Yet it has been firmly established that John of Jandun, despite his close association with Marsiglio at Paris at the time of publication of the *Defensor pacis* (1320-1324), had virtually nothing to do with its actual authorship: A. Gewirth, "John of Jandun and the *Defensor Pacis*," *Speculum* 23 (1948): 267-272. On John, see Gilson, *History of Christian Philosophy*, 522-524, 797; S. MacClintock, "John of Jandun," *The Encyclopedia of Philosophy* IV: 280-282; Lohr, "Commentaries ... Jacobus-Johannes Juff," 208-215. (Note too: the "Januensis" actually cited by Wyclyf in the *De civili dominio*, vol. IV, cap. xxi, p. 425, is *not* John of Jandun but John of Genoa OP. The same caveat should probably be extended to his *Determinacio [prima] contra Kylyngham Carmelitam* [**378**]: *FZ*, 462.)

Medieval men were not nearly so strict in demanding proof of attribution or association as we are, however; it therefore come as no particular surprise to find the first *liber* of the *De civili dominio* actually bound with the *Defensor pacis* in **iii** (see above, n. 7); or the latter text in turn bound with the "Articuli erronei Johs Wycleff heresiarche damnati Londiniis in Anglia a. do. mccc octagesimo" in BN f.l. 14619. We even find Wyclyf's *[Questiones et dubia...]* (**6**) bound with John of Jandun's *Tractatus et questiones in Averrois* (Venezia, BMarc Lat. VI.173). (Reeves, "A Second MS of Wyclif's De Dominio Civili," 96-98.)

[32] Important studies of this vital topic are Ernest H. Kantorowicz, *The King's Two Bodies. A Study in Medieval Political Theology* (Princeton, 1957); M. J. Wilks, *The Problem of Sovereignty in the Later Middle Ages* (Cambridge, Eng., 1963); Gaines Post, *Studies in Medieval Legal Thought. Public Law and the State, 1100-1322* (Princeton, 1964); idem, "Vincentius Hispanus, 'Pro Ratione Voluntas', and Medieval and Early Modern Theories of Sovereignty," *Traditio* 28 (1972): 159-184; Walter Ullmann, *A History of Political Thought: The Middle Ages* (Baltimore, 1965): 200-228; Beryl Smalley, "Church and State 1300-1377: Theory and Fact," in Hale, Highfield and Smalley, edd., *Europe in the Late Middle Ages*, 15-43; Joseph R. Strayer, *On the Medieval Origins of the Modern State* (Princeton, 1970).

[33] By "ydiota" is usually meant "layman," though not in this instance: the individual in question was Philip de Thornbury, a priest in the diocese of Modena. (See Workman, *JW* I: 206.) For Wyclyf's customary usage of the term, cf. **384**: pp. 201, 203.

A number of things have been said in extenuation of Wyclyf's holding of several offices in the church simultaneously: it was a very common practice in the decades following the Black Death. Yet once again the serious dearth of autobiographical asides in Wyclyf's writings reduces us to inference: could he in fact somehow have met the obligation of the *cura animarum* in his various livings at Fillingham, Aust, Ludgershall, and (before 1379) Lutterworth? Might he not have canonically delegated some of these duties? See, for various shades of opinion, S. A. Twemlow, "Wycliffe's Preferments and University Degrees," *EHR* 15 (1900): 529-530; H. S. Cronin, "John Wycliffe, the Reformer, and Canterbury Hall," *Transactions of the Royal Historical Society*, 3rd ser., 8 (1914): 55-76; H. E. Salter, "John Wyclif, Canon of Lincoln," *EHR* 35 (1920): 98; and, in the same issue, Cronin again (disagreeing with Salter), "Wycliffe's Canonry at Lincoln," 563-569; J. J. Wilkins, *Was John Wycliffe a Negligent Pluralist? Also John de Trevisa, His Life and Work* (London, 1915): 1-67; M. E. H. Lloyd, "John Wyclif and the Prebend of Lincoln," *EHR* 61 (1946): 388-394; A. Hamilton Thompson, *The English Clergy and their Organization in the Later Middle Ages* (Oxford, 1947): 101n., 103n.; K. B. McFarlane, *John Wycliffe and the Beginnings of English Nonconformity* (New York, 1953: the most hostile of recent monographs): 25-27, 30, 63, 66-69; J. R. Dahmus, "Wyclyf was a Negligent Pluralist," *Speculum* 28 (1953): 378-381. With slight corrections, nevertheless, Workman, *JW* I: 79-80, 151-206, still offers the most comprehensive survey of this vexed question. For a supplementary comment, see also below, **397**, n. 10.

That absenteeism was a major deficiency in the years after 1349 is universally conceded; that it was at times grossly inexcusable may be gathered from, *inter alia*, the *De corrupto ecclesie statu* (ca. 1398), by Nicolas de Clamanges, or a contemporary: ed. E. Brown in *Fasciculus Rerum Expetendarum et Fugiendarum* II: especially pp. 562-563.

31. A12.f. *De veritate sacre scripture.* Late 1377-end of 1378.

I. Inc.: Restat parumper discutere errores et concordias ...
   Expl.: × ... quam, si deus voluerit, propono diffusius pertractare.

II. MSS:

i	Bautzen, Stadt- und Kreisbibliothek?	*Q° 24*	ff. 228v-229v	xv/ex	Unasc. So. Ger.[1]
ii	Cambridge, Peterhouse Coll.	*223*	ff. 179r-281v	ca. 1400	Unasc. Eng.[2]
iii	Queen's Coll.	15 (Horne 27)	ff. 1r-190r	xv/1	Unasc. Eng.[3]
iv	Dublin, Trinity Coll.	C.1.24	pp. 1-3, 8a-248b	xiv/2	Asc. Eng.[4]
v	London, BL	Royal 7 E.x	ff. 166ra-213vb	xiv/2	Unasc. Eng.[5]
vi	*Olomouc, KapK*	*C.O.115*	ff. 2v-296v	xv/1	Unasc. Pol.[6]
vii	Oxford, Bodleian	924 (S.C. 3021)	pp. 1-621	xiv/ex	Asc. Eng.[7]
viii	*Praha, MK*	*A.84 (158)*	ff. 122ra-149rb	ca. 1420	Unasc. Boh.[8]
ix		*B.53 (359)*	ff. 1r-274r	ca. 1415	Unasc. Boh.[9]
x		*C.38 (462)*	ff. 107va-158va	ca. 1410	JW ms Boh.[10]
xi		*O.29 (1613)*	ff. 161r-162r	ca. 1430	Unasc. Boh.[11]
xii	UK	III.B.5 (414)	ff. 7ra-155vb	xv/1	Unasc. Boh.[12]
xiii		VIII.C.3 (1472)	ff. 2ra-222rb	ca. 1410	Asc. Boh.
		X.E.11 (1912)	ff. 1ra-30va	1432	Boh.[13]
xiv	Wien, ÖNB	1294	ff. 1ra-119vb	1407	JW ms Eng.[14]

III. Ed. Rudolf Buddensieg, *John Wyclif's De Veritate Sacrae Scripturae* (3 vols.: WS, 1905, 1906, 1907; German ed., 1904, 1905).[15] From **iii, iv, vii** and **xiv** only.

IV. The masterly edition of this treatise by Rudolf Buddensieg, begun in 1882 and completed more than twenty years later, appears to have left little to add to the MS tradition, despite the subsequent discovery of several additional codices. Almost alone among the major works of Wyclyf, nearly half of the MS copies of the *De veritate sacre scripture* were executed by English scribes. Buddensieg ventured very modestly on the provenance of **xiv**, which quite properly he selected as his "A" text, that it "was written in England." It is indisputably the work of an English copyist – in fact it is the only Wyclyf MS of English origin in either Prague or Vienna – and deserves therefore a certain priority in details of textual precision.[16]

Buddensieg examined also the question of the authenticity of the tractate. Beyond the fact of the attribution in the Oxford MS and all four of the vc, the internal evidence really obviates the necessity of further inquiry: he refers several times to other of his writings; and his intense devotion to Scripture (which, incidentally, he had already personalized in such expressions as "ut dicit Veritas" in earlier pieces)[17] caused him to be known in the schools and to many later scribes and commentators as "Doctor evangelicus." A recent study has observed that Wyclyf "proclaims the perfection and sufficiency of Scripture as God's law. But what in effect he proclaims is the perfection and sufficiency of God's moral law, of the evangelical law of charity." [18] Seldom is this emphasis more evident than in the *De veritate sacre scripture*.

The date of composition is, however, despite Buddensieg's confidence in the matter,[19] open to some discussion. A number of fixed internal dates can be usefully deployed: the five bulls of Gregory XI condemning Wyclyf's teaching on dominion[20] reached England in late December of 1377; a reference to 24 March 1378 as "hodie" in the middle of cap. xi;[21] the election of Urban VI at Rome on 8 April 1378; and the inception of the Schism with the election of Clement VII at Fondi on 13 September 1378. Capp. i-xix, though occasionally quite direct in the assertion of controversial opinions, remain reasonably within the permissible latitudes of debate; but beginning in cap. xx he launches a number of separate sorties against papal claims and the *clerici possessionati*, stressing the power of the laity over the property of the church. It would thus appear from these and other indications that capp. i-x fit best into the fall and winter of 1377, rather earlier than Buddensieg fixes them; capp. xi-xv may be placed safely in March and April of 1378; and the balance probably took up the rest of the year. This last period witnessed Wyclyf's change of heart toward Urban VI from cautious approval to a markedly stronger disapprobation. The colophon in **xiii**, not known to Buddensieg, reads: "Anno millenesimo trecentesimo septuagintaque [*sic*] octo." It would thus appear either that Wyclyf took no time to revise the composition at a later date, or that he was content to let it stand as a clear reminder of his own evolving attitude toward the Papacy in the first year of the Schism.

VC: 3933 3935 4514 7980   Bale: 51   Sh: 15.VI   Lo: 16.VI

---

[1] A fragment of cap. xiv. The slightly anachronistic use of such epithets as "pseudofratres" and "episcopi simoniaci" betrays Hussite interpolation: see S. H. Thomson, "Unnoticed Manuscripts of Wyclyf's *De Veritate Sacre Scripture*," *Medium Aevum* 13 (1944): 69-70. (Editor unable to confirm current particulars of this MS. Bautzen, DDR, was once Budyšin, chief city of the Lusatian Sorbs.)

[2] Leaves off in cap. xxiv (= vol. II: 246, line 5). See Thomson, "Unnoticed MSS and Works of Wyclif," 32. In this MS Robson has spotted an important marginal note identifying William Barton, who would become Chancellor at Oxford in 1379 (and shortly thereafter one of Wyclyf's more formidable adversaries; the two men had been fellows at Merton College together), as the unnamed "quodam doctore" who crops up in cap. xiv: *Wyclif and the Oxford Schools*, 223, and bibliography there cited. See also **39**, below.

[3] Asc. *recentiori manu* (1722) "I take it to be Wicleff and never published." (Cf. vol. I: LX.)

[4] Pp. 1-3 are a fragment of capp. viii and vii: see Thomson, "Unnoticed MSS and Works of Wyclif," 30-31. On pp. 4-7 Wyclyf's own compendium of this work.

[5] Thomson, "Unnoticed MSS and Works of Wyclif," 31. This MS is incomplete, and some capp. are out of sequence.

[6] This octave MS has not been previously known to Wyclyf scholars. It is a remarkably clean text, written by three scribes, which occupies the entire codex. There are few marginalia; occasional commentary at the top of the ff. begins only on f. 97v, then more frequently from f. 134r by the second copyist and later by the third as well. The editor possesses microfilm of this text courtesy of the Státní Archiv, Opava, where this collection is housed today.

[7] Starts in cap. iv (= vol. I: 77, line 9). Asc. in colophon erased. From this MS Richard James took substantial notes, ca. 1620-1636: Oxford, Bodleian, James 3 (S.C. 3840), pp. 107-227.

[8] Ends in cap. xii. See Thomson, "Unnoticed Manuscripts of Wyclyf's *De Veritate Sacre Scripture*," 68.

[9] A compendium follows, ff. 274r-278r.

[10] Ends in cap. xiv (= vol. I: 368, line 18); followed by $1^1/_2$ blank cols.

[11] Short extract from cap. xii.

[12] Compendium, ff. 1ra-3ra.

[13] A copy of Peter Payne's *registrum*.

[14] Index, ff. 120ra-125rb; analysis, ff. 125va-127rb.

[15] A portion of cap. xiv (= vol. I: 343-375) was printed in Lechler, *Johann von Wiclif und die Vorgeschichte der Reformation* II: 605-621, from **xiv** only. – An unpretentious but well-conceived commentary on this treatise is William Mallard, "John Wyclif and the Tradition of Biblical Authority," *Church History* 30 (1961): 50-60. For a comparison between Buddensieg's two versions of this edition, see Hurley, "'Scriptura Sola': Wyclif and his Critics," 294n.

[16] See **23-25**, n. 6, above.

[17] E.g., **23-25** (p. 18); **26** (p. 19); **27** (p. 480); and frequently throughout, **28-30**. He also repeatedly avails himself here of the concept of the "lex Christi," as before.

Absolutely fundamental here is Hurley, "'Scriptura Sola': Wyclif and his Critics," 275-352. This long article is in part a critique of Paul de Vooght, *Les sources de la doctrine chrétienne d'après les théologiens du XIVe siècle et du début du XVe avec le texte intégral des XII premières questions de la Summa inédite de Gérard de Bologne (†1317)* (Paris, 1954): 168-199 (and cf. also the critical review by M. D. Knowles in *JTS*, new ser., 6 [1955]: 314-316); and an endorsement of F. Kropatschek, *Das Schriftprinzip der lutherischen Kirche* I: *Die Vorgeschichte. Das Erbe des Mittelalters* (Leipzig, 1904): 326-359, who regarded Wyclyf's use of this principle as legalistic in the extreme. Yet in view of his subsequent hostility to just such legalism and his continued thematic deployment of the "lex Christi," we must question the validity of this interpretation to some degree. (Heiko Oberman, *The Harvest of Medieval Theology. Gabriel Biel and Late Medieval Nominalism* [Cambridge, Mass., 1963]: 371-375, submits the provocative distinction between "Tradition I" and "Tradition II," which is illuminating on this point.)

A more general survey of the place of Scripture in the thought of later medieval churchmen is Hermann Schüssler, *Der Primat der Heiligen Schrift als theologisches und kanonistisches Problem im Spätmittelalter* (Wiesbaden, 1977); and of course, for different reasons, we cannot omit to mention here also Friedrich Stegmüller's epic *Repertorium Biblicum Medii Aevi* (7 vols.: Madrid, 1950-1961) and Beryl Smalley, *The Study of the Bible in the Middle Ages*, 2nd ed. (Oxford, 1952; reprinted Notre Dame, 1964). We have already alluded to G. W. H. Lampe, ed., *The Cambridge History of the Bible* II: *The West from the Fathers to the Reformation*.

[18] Hurley, "'Scriptura Sola': Wyclif and his Critics," 350.

[19] As expressed in his Introduction, pp. XLVIII-LIV.

[20] Of 22 May 1377; see above, **28-30**, n. 24.

[21] Vol. I: 258.

32. A12.g. *De ecclesia.* Early 1378-early 1379.

I. Inc.: Quia nonnulli, eciam illi qui videntur esse aliquid, discordant in materia de quiditate ecclesie ...

Expl.: × ... demerentur, licet prosint per accidens. De isto alibi.

II. MSS:

i	Dublin, Trinity Coll.	C.1.23	pp. 398b-403b	xiv/2	JW MS Eng.[1]
ii	Firenze, BLaur	Plut.XIX.33	ff. 29v-30r	1408	JW MS Eng.[2]
iii	Praha, UK	X.D.11 (1890)	ff. 1ra-130rb	ca. 1410	JW MS Boh.[3]
		X.E.11 (1912)	ff. 30vb-45rb	1432	Boh.[4]
iv	Wien, ÖNB	1294	ff. 128ra-207vb	1407	JW MS Eng.[5]
v		3929	ff. 1ra-114ra	1409	JW MS Boh.
vi		3934	ff. 148r-151r	xv/1	Asc. Boh.[6]
vii	Wolfenbüttel, HzglB	Cod. Guelf. 1126 (1233)	ff. 46r-84v	xv/1	Unasc. Ger.[7]

III. Ed. J. Loserth, *Iohannis Wyclif Tractatus de Ecclesia* (WS, 1886).[8] From i, iii, iv and v only.

IV. One of the most vigorous of Wyclyf's mature works, the *De ecclesia* is also among the less well organized. It doubtless was vaguely projected from the inception of his *Summa theologie*, but the events of the return of the Papacy to Rome and the subsequent Schism strongly shaped his treatment of the nature and mission of the church.[9] Certain parts of the work may be separately dated, at least with reference to a *terminus ante quem*. Cap. xxiii (the concluding one, on indulgences: see below, n. 13) refers to Pope Gregory XI as still living (pp. 564, 571, etc.); cap. ii speaks of Urban VI and his zeal in *rectificando instantem ecclesiam* (p. 37); yet in cap. xiii we find (interpolated?) reference to the Schism as having broken out *per duos pseudomonachos* (p. 290; cf. p. 309). The composition of the *De ecclesia* thus extended in all probability from the spring of 1378 until sometime early in 1379; evidently the capp. were not composed in the order in which we now have them.

The treatise strikes us as disorganized largely because of his major digression, beginning in cap. vii and running through cap. xvi, to deal with the explosive case of the two knights, John Haulay and Richard Shakyl, who had escaped from the Tower and taken sanctuary in Westminster Abbey, where the king's men caught up with them and cut Haulay down by the altar.[10] Sometime late in October or early in November of 1378 Wyclyf, along with several other clerics, appeared before Parliament at Gloucester to depose concerning the limitations of sanctuary. Cap. vii seems to be the main text of Wyclyf's brief on that occasion, while the next nine capp. represent his later development of the implications of his position.[11] Both the *De ecclesia* and the preceding *De veritate sacre scripture* (to say nothing of the *De civili dominio*), therefore, offer insights into the active interplay between current events and their philosophical ramifications in

Wyclyf's applied thought. (It ought to be mentioned too that much of the rest of the treatise is devoted to an energetic point-by-point rebuttal of an unnamed scholastic doctor's contentions as to the true nature of the church. This conforms neatly to Wyclyf's well-established pattern of academic disputation.)

John Hus' use of this work in his own *De ecclesia* (1413) and in other writings has already engaged us elsewhere;[12] we do not believe that a further belaboring of Loserth's cavalier dismissal of Hus as a simple plagiarist[13] would serve any useful end. The Czech reformer had a fertile native tradition to draw upon; and, while he unquestionably derived inspiration and even extensive (often unacknowledged) passages from his English exemplar, he consistently maintained his own orthodoxy on, for example, the Eucharist to the end. Curiously enough, the principal doctrine which he did extract from the Wyclyfite arsenal – that the true church was the whole body of those predestined[14] – found condemnation at Constance in 1415 not as Wyclyf's doctrine (and of course not as Augustine's!), but as Hus' own.[15]

vc: 3933 3935 4514 7980   Bale: deest   Sh: 15.VII   Lo: 16.VII

[1] Listed as n. 66 in Sh, with the Dublin MS identification; and as n. 167 in Lo, without; it is in fact cap. vii, appearing under the rubric "De Captivo Hispanensi"; see n. 11, below.

[2] Cap. vii only (i.e., the "De Captivo Hispanensi": see the preceding note). See Stein, "The Wyclif Manuscript in Florence," 95, for Mabillon's note on this text.

[3] Compendium, ff. 212ra-214vb.

[4] A copy of Peter Payne's *registrum*.

[5] On ff. 208ra-210va a summary of capp. i-xii. The Czech *correctores*, Faulfiš and Knĕhnic, evidently divided this MS into capp. (See above, **28-30**, n. 4.)

[6] An extract.

[7] Asc. mutilated; text breaks off toward the end of cap. iii: see Kühn-Steinhausen, "Wyclif Handschriften in Deutschland," 625.

[8] Part of cap. xii (pp. 370-371) was printed by Lechler, *Johann von Wiclif und die Vorgeschichte der Reformation* II: 574-575.

[9] See now R. Stalder, "Le concept de l'église selon le 'de Ecclesia' de Wiclif," *Bijdragen. Tijdschrift voor Filosofie en Theologie* 22 (1962): 38-81, 287-302. Still useful, though not based solely on the *De ecclesia*, are Friedrich Wiegand, *De Ecclesiae Notione quid Wiclif docuerit* (Leipzig, 1892); H. Fürstenau, *Johann von Wiclifs Lehren von der Einteilung der Kirche und von der Stellung der weltlichen Gewalt* (Berlin, 1900); more recently we have P. de Vooght, "Le caractère sacerdotal selon Wiclif," in his *Hussiana* (Bibliothèque de la Revue d'histoire ecclésiastique 35: Louvain, 1960): 241-260; and W. Eckermann, "Augustus Favaroni von Rom und Johannes Wyclif. Der Ansatz ihrer Lehre über die Kirche," in *Scientia Augustiniana. Festschrift Adolar Zumkeller* (Würzburg, 1975): 323-348.

[10] The antecedents of this bizarre episode are summarized in E. Perroy, "Gras profits et rançons pendant la guerre de cent ans: l'affaire du Comte de Denia," in *Mélanges d'histoire du Moyen Âge dédiés à la mémoire de Louis Halphen* (Paris, 1951): 573-580; see also J. Charles Cox, *The Sanctuaries and Sanctuary Seekers of Mediaeval England* (London, 1911): 51-53; Workman, *JW* I: 314-324; Dahmus, *The Prosecution of John Wyclyf*, 74-78.

[11] This seventh cap., under the title of "De captivo Hispanensi," has experienced an independent MS tradition; see nn. 1 and 2, above.

[12] S. H. Thomson, *Magistri Johannis Hus Tractatus de Ecclesia* (Boulder, Colo., 1956): viii-ix. See the next note.

[13] Chiefly in his *Hus und Wiclif* (1st ed., 159-287; again, more than forty years later, in the second ed., 131-192 – without appreciable modification in his stance, despite the major corrective labors of such Czech scholars as Sedlák and Novotný). See also reviews by S. H. Thomson of F. M. Bartoš' *Literární Činnost M. J. Husi* in *Speculum* 24 (1949): 419; Paul de Vooght's *L'Hérésie de Jean Huss* in *Speculum* 38 (1963): 118; and Matthew Spinka's *John Hus. A Biography* in *Archiv für Reformationsgeschichte* 61 (1969): 291. (The last author's *John Hus' Concept of the Church* [Princeton, 1966] is of enduring worth.) See in this connection also Otakar Odložilik, "Wycliffe's Influence upon Central and Eastern Europe," *The Slavonic (and East European) Review* 7 (1929): 634-648, especially p. 635, where he observes that Vojtěch Raňků of Ježov, an acquaintance of FitzRalph's, had established at some point two stipends for Czech students either at Paris or Oxford (but how these funds were administered we do not know); idem, "Wyclif and Bohemia," *Věstník královské česke společnosti nauk: Třida filosoficko-historicka* I, 1935 (pub. 1936): 1-14; P. de Vooght, "La notion wiclifienne de l'épiscopat dans l'interprétation de Jean Huss," *Irénikon* 28 (1955): 290-300 (reprinted in his *Hussiana*, 231-240). W. R. Cannon, "John Wyclif and John Hus," *Emory University Quarterly* 15 (1959): 80-87, is without apparatus and of little interest; of greater substance are Gustav A. Benrath, "Wyclif und Hus," *Zeitschrift für Theologie und Kirche* 72 (1965): 196-216; Gordon Leff, "Wyclif and Hus: A Doctrinal Comparison," *Bulletin of the John Rylands Library* 50 (1967-1968): 387-410; F. Šmahel, "'Doctor evangelicus super omnes evangelistas': Wyclif's Fortune in Hussite Bohemia," *Bulletin of the Institute of Historical Research* 43 (1970): 16-34; M. J. Wilks, "*Reformatio regni*: Wyclif and Hus as leaders of religious protest movements," in Derek Baker, ed., SCH 9: *Schism Heresy and Religious Protest* (Cambridge, Engl., 1972): 109-130; W. R. Cook, "John Wyclif and Hussite Theology 1415-1436," *Church History* 42 (1973): 335-349. (František M. Bartoš, *Viklef a Čechy. Průvodce Výstavou Veřejné a Universitní Knihovny v Praze. 15.-31. Leden 1935* [Praha, 1935] is only a summary exhibit catalog.) I have not seen M. Kaňak, *John Viklef. Život a dílo anglického Husova předchůdce* (Praha, 1973), reviewed by P. de Vooght in *Revue d'histoire ecclésiastique* 70 (1975): 359. Kaminsky, *A History of the Hussite Revolution*, 35-37, has analyzed this tangled skein of doctrinal dependence with some care; yet we cannot unreservedly subscribe to his conclusions. Finally, see also below, **42**, n. 3; and, for a summary of recent Czech literature, de Vooght, "Hus et Wiclif: état de la question," in his *Hussiana*, 1-6. Somewhat later and broader overviews are B. A. Vermaseren, "Nieuwe Studies over Wyclif en Hus," *Tijdschrift voor Geschiedenis* 76 (1963): 190-212; Carl Berkhout and J. B. Russell, edd., *Medieval Heresies: A Bibliography 1960-1979*, Subsidia Mediaevalia 11 (Toronto: PIMS, 1981): 87-95 and 100-110.

[14] Cf. the present piece, p. 2: "... congregacione omnium predestinatorum"; *et frequenter alibi*.

[15] Edith C. Tatnall, "The Condemnation of John Wyclif at the Council of Constance," in G. J. Cuming and Derek Baker, edd., SCH 7: *Councils and Assemblies* (1971): 209-217.

33. A12.h. *De officio regis*. Mid-1379.

I. Inc.: Consequenter ad ordinem clericalem restat de militari ordine pertractandum ...

Expl.: × ... contra pseudo Christianos defendere partem suam.

II. MSS:

i	Praha, UK	X.D.11 (1890)	ff. 130rb-210va	ca. 1410	JW MS Boh.[1]
		X.E.11 (1912)	ff. 45va-55ra	1432/1433	Boh.[2]
ii	Wien, ÖNB	3933	ff. 1ra-57rb	ca. 1415	JW MS Boh.[3]
iii		4514	ff. 105r-182r	1432	Asc. Boh.[4]

III. Edd. Alfred W. Pollard and Charles Sayle, *Iohannis Wyclif Tractatus de Officio Regis* (WS, 1887).[5] From **ii** and **iii** only.

IV. This treatise is an application of Wyclyf's philosophical and theological premises to a special case: the basic conditions of the governance of society according to Scriptural dictates. Of course most medieval political theorists – whether availing themselves primarily of classical or of Scriptural sources – settled on monarchy in one or another guise as their paradigm; here Wyclyf was no exception.[6] The circumstances of the summer of 1379, when in all likelihood this treatise was completed, were volatile at best: the grinding French war, impending social revolt, a regency, and the Schism all lent urgency and point to Wyclyf's extended argumentation. It is rather surprising that the work survives in only three copies, none of them in an English hand. It is perhaps owing to the diligence of Peter Payne that any trace of the *De officio regis* remains at all.

Its authenticity is certain: in it he refers, for instance, to his own *De ecclesia* (**32**: p. 1) and the *De civili dominio* (**28-30**: pp. 55-56); and it has been urged that several lines of speculation first apparent in his *De paupertate Christi* (**402**) took on greater substance in the *De officio regis*.[7]

Much of his dialectic displays close familiarity with Gratian and the *Decretales*. He rounds suddenly on both civil and canon lawyers, however, in cap. x: "Unde videtur quod si rex Anglie non permitteret canonistas vel civilistas ad hoc sustentari de suis elemosinis vel patrimonio crucifixi ut studeant tales leges (hoc enim non sustinet de lege propria cui racionabiliter plus faveret), non dubium quin clerus foret utilior sibi et ad ecclesiasticam promocionem humilior ex noticia civilitatis proprie quam ex noticia civilitatis duplicis aliene." (P. 237.)[8] This marks the beginning of a deepening disaffection.

VC: 3933 3935 4514 7980   Bale: deest   Sh: 15.VIII   Lo: 16.VIII

---

[1] Compendium, ff. 210va-212ra. See n. 5, below.

[2] A copy of Peter Payne's *registrum*.

[3] Index, ff. 58ra-62va.

[4] Compendium, ff. 182r-184r.

[5] This edition is plainly one of the less fortunate productions of the WS. Pollard and Sayle themselves, as they admit, never saw any of the MSS of the *De officio regis* at all, but depended on two European scholars, Drs. Stange and Herzberg-Fränkel, for their transcripts of **ii** and **iii**. The late Dr. Edith Tatnall went to some lengths to demonstrate the clear textual superiority of **i** (editor in possession of several recensions of a substantial article detailing this thesis); cf. Loserth's comments to the same effect in his introduction to Wyclyf's *De ecclesia* (**32**): xxxI. See also in general Tatnall's unpublished Ph.D. dissertation, "Church and State according to John Wyclif" (University of Colorado, 1964).

[6] The brief study by L. J. Daly, "Walter Burley and John Wyclif on Some Aspects of Kingship," 163-184, fails adequately to incorporate the *De officio regis*: all but two of his citations of Wyclyf come from the *De civili dominio*, which obviously represented earlier stages in the evolution of his outlook on this topic. While Daly's excerpts from and commentary on the *De officio regis* are more extensive in his *The Political Theory of John Wyclif*, 97-181, much more of value might have been said concerning Wyclyf's use of sources. For remarks of considerable suggestive force in this connection, see Jean

Dunbabin, "Aristotle in the Schools," in Beryl Smalley, ed., *Trends in Medieval Political Thought* (Oxford, 1965): 65-85.
[7] Loserth ed., *Johannes Wyclif Opera Minora* (WS, 1913): VIII.
[8] See **28-30**, n. 28, above.

34. A12.i. *De potestate pape*. Fall 1379.

I. Inc.: Iam ultimo restat videre quomodo Christus dominus noster caput universalis ecclesie ordinavit sponsam suam secundum gradus ecclesiastice hierarchie ...

Expl.: × ... viam, que ducit membrum dyaboli ad infernum.

II. MSS:

i	Dublin, Trinity Coll.	A.5.3 (115)	pp. 176-179	ca. 1380	Asc. Eng.[1]
ii	Praha, MK	C.73 (504)	ff. 161rb-259va	xv/1	Asc. Boh.[2]
		C.118 (550)	f. 96v	ca. 1410	Boh.[3]
iii		O.29 (1613)	ff. 166r-177v	ca. 1430	Unasc. Boh.[4]
iv	UK	III.F.11 (514)	ff. 134vb-223ra	ca. 1410	Asc. Boh.[5]
v		III.G.16 (541)	f. 15v	1414	Asc. Boh.[6]
		X.E.11 (1912)	ff. 55rb-72va	1433	Boh.[7]
vi		XI.E.3 (2050)	f. 58v	1416	JW MS Boh.[8]

III. Ed. J. Loserth, *Johannis Wyclif Tractatus de Potestate Pape* (WS, 1907). From **ii** and **iv** only.

IV. Loserth regarded this work as basic to any understanding of Wyclyf's rapidly developing doctrine of the church. He promised "to deal with Wyclif's doctrine in a special treatise," which would have been most welcome; Loserth seems, however, never to have published such a monograph. But his introduction is quite detailed, and we have also a few remarks by Workman touching the contextual significance of the *De potestate pape*.[9]

That it fits in the sequence customarily ascribed to it since the preparation of the VC is plain enough: **31** and **33** are alluded to as already published on p. 1; the reader's familiarity with **32** is assumed throughout. The *De symonia* (**35**), on the other hand, we know to have seen the light of day late in 1379 or early in 1380: it alludes twice to the *De potestate pape* (pp. 42, 59) as a finished work. Throughout the piece he manifests an increasing alienation not only from individual popes – this we have already encountered – but even from the very institution of the Papacy itself. He begins also to express a new antagonism toward the mendicants. His fateful rupture with them over the Eucharist was only a few months away.[10]

VC: 3933 3935 4514 7980   Bale: deest   Sh: 15.IX   Lo: 16.IX

[1] An extract from cap. vi. See Stein, "Two Notes on Wyclif," 467; Thomson, "Unnoticed MSS and Works of Wyclif," 32.
[2] Compendium, ff. 263ra-264va.

³ A copy of Peter Payne's *registrum*.
⁴ An extract: see n. 1, above.
⁵ Compendium, ff. 226va-228rb.
⁶ An extract.
⁷ A copy of Peter Payne's *registrum*.
⁸ An extract.
⁹ *JW* II: 74-79. M. J. Wilks, "The *Apostolicus* and the Bishop of Rome," *JTS*, new ser., 14 (1963): 349, notes that Wyclyf, while still granting at this time the legitimacy of the Petrine succession, was unique in his insistence that a truly apostolic power must be limited by a corresponding apostolic poverty and humility. But of course the whole "poverty question" was very much in the air: FitzRalph and the mendicants had quarreled about it (see **23-25**, n. 12, above); we need mention here only M. D. Lambert, *Franciscan Poverty, The Doctrine of the Absolute Poverty of Christ and the Apostles in the Franciscan Order 1210-1323* (London, 1961); Michel Mollat, ed., *Études sur l'histoire de la Pauvreté: Moyen Âge-XVIᵉ siècle* (2 vols.: Paris, 1974); and Lester K. Little, *Religious Poverty and the Profit Economy in Medieval Europe* (London, 1978). Also see below, **382-383**, n. 13.

¹⁰ Henry of Ghent, who had fought the friars at Paris almost a century before, had been driven by the exigencies of that episode into an interesting perception of the limitations of papal authority: see J. Marrone, "The Absolute and the Ordained Powers of the Pope: An Unedited Text of Henry of Ghent," *MedSt* 36 (1974): 7-27. For broader treatments of the *dramatis personae* in this continuing debate, see Brian Tierney, *Origins of Papal Infallibility, 1150-1350: A Study on the Concepts of Infallibility, Sovereignty and Tradition in the Middle Ages* (Leiden, 1972). A long and critical review of Tierney's assumptions by A. Stickler appeared in *CHR* 60 (1974): 427-441; the controversy continues, and is summarized in part in Heiko Oberman, "'Et tibi dabo claves regni caelorum.' Kirche und Konzil von Augustin bis Luther. Tendenzen und Ergebnisse, II," *Nederlands Theologisch Tijdschrift* 29 (1975): 92-118. Of great utility also is W. E. McCready, "Papalists and Antipapalists: Aspects of the Church/State Controversy in the Later Middle Ages," *Viator* 6 (1975): 241-273.

35. A12.j. *De symonia*. Early 1380.

I. Inc.: Post generalem sermonem de heresi restat de eius partibus pertractandum ...

Expl.: × ... moveat, qui super totam ecclesiam semper regnat.

II. MSS:

i	Dublin, Trinity Coll.	C.1.24	pp. 249a-293a	xiv/2	JW MS Eng.¹
ii	Praha, MK	*O.29 (1613)*	ff. 149v-152v	ca. 1430	Unasc. Boh.²
iii	UK	X.E.9 (1910)	ff. 70v-126r	xv/1	Unasc. Boh.³
		X.E.11 (1912)	ff. 72va-76ra	1433	Boh.⁴
iv	Wien, ÖNB	1343	ff. 1ra-35rb	ca. 1410	JW MS Boh.⁵
v		1622	ff. 83r-127v	1410	JW MS Boh.
vi		3927	ff. 53ra-74rb	ca. 1410	JW MS Boh.⁶
vii		3937	ff. 115ra-137va	1401	Asc. Boh.
viii		4504	ff. 2r-36r	xv/1	JW MS Boh.⁷
ix		4515	ff. 27r-67v	ca. 1420	JW MS Boh.
x		4536	ff. 132r-187va	xv/1	JW MS Boh.⁸

III. Edd. [S.] Herzberg-Fränkel and M. H. Dziewicki, *Iohannis Wyclif Tractatus de Simonia* (WS, 1898). From all MSS except **ii**. Translation by Terrence McVeigh forthcoming.

IV. This work is the first of a topically self-contained trilogy, embracing *libri* X, XI and XII of the *Summa theologie*. Wyclyf heralded his three-pronged attack in this manner (continuing from the incipit): "Tres autem sunt maneries heresis plus famose: scilicet symonia, apostasia et blasfemia, nec distinguuntur isti ex opposito, eum tam virtutum quam viciorum species sint connexe." It has been stressed that Wyclyf's concept of simony extended far beyond the usual bounds: it served him as a vehicle for assaulting almost every perceived excess in the church of his day.[9] His attitude toward the mendicants, however, is still relatively moderate: he writes that "maior pars fratrum vel omnes et speculativi cuiuscumque status" are nonetheless simoniacs if they even suppress knowledge of simony or do not reprove those who are guilty of it. (P. 98.) Early 1380 best fits the temper and evident circumstances of this piece.

VC: 3933 3935 4514   Bale: 104[10]   Sh: 15.X   Lo: 16.X

[1] *Tabula*, ff. 310v-311v.
[2] An extract.
[3] *Registrum* on ff. 126r-131r; capp. headings ff. 69r-70r. Asc. in *contenta*.
[4] A copy of Peter Payne's *registrum*.
[5] F. 1ra, in Peter Payne's hand: "Incipit de symonia et est liber x in ordine summe sue." (*Sentencia tractatus* added, ff. 35va-36vb.)
[6] Index follows, f. 74va-b.
[7] *Registrum* on ff. 1r-2r. Asc. on flyleaf is *per recentiorem manum*.
[8] *Registrum* on ff. 187va-191va. – The "committee of twelve" picked out 24 of Wyclyf's propositions in the *De symonia* as offensive or worse: Wilkins, *Concilia* ... III: 343-344, nos. 75-98. (See above, **3**, n. 5.) These extracts are sometimes *verbatim*, but more often paraphrased or condensed. I give herewith first the number attached to the quotation, followed by the page number in our edition: 75: 5-6, 82; 76: 6; 77: 6; 78: 7; 79: 7; 80: 8; 81: 19; 82: 19; 83: no close parallel; 84: 24; 85: 24; 86: no close parallel; 87: 28-29; 88: 38; 89: 40-41; 90: 50; 91: 50-51; 92: 75-76; 93: 76; 94: 76; 95: 94; 96: 99 (perhaps); 97: 112; 98: 113. The selection seems odd, as there are several other passages throughout the *De symonia* which the twelve theologians could easily have isolated as more *male sonantes* to the church establishment than those actually chosen.
[9] A recent and very thorough study of Wyclyf's doctrine and antecedents here is Friedrich de Boor, *Wyclifs Simoniebegriff: Die theologische und Kirchenpolitische Grundlage der Kirchenkritik John Wyclifs* (Halle, 1970); see the review by M. J. Wilks in *JEH* 29 (1973): 70-71. See also P. de Vooght, "La 'simoniaca haeresis' de saint Thomas d'Aquin à Jean Huss," in his *Hussiana*, 379-399. We might mention here the likelihood that this piece and Wyclyf's much shorter and almost certainly fragmentary *De duobus generibus hereticorum* (**418**, below) were composed at about the same time.
[10] Title given as "De simonia sacerdotum"; wrong incipit.

36. A12.k. *De apostasia*. Late 1380.

I. Inc.: Restat ulterius ponere aliud principium pro ambitu heresis symoniace pertractando ...
    Expl.: × ... multiplicanda est errorum varietas in hoc venerabili sacramento.

II. MSS:

i	Dublin, Trinity Coll.	C.1.24	pp. 293a-310b	xiv/2	JW MS Eng.[1]
ii	Praha, MK	C.73 (504)	ff. 86va-161ra	xv/1	Asc. Boh.[2]
		C.118 (550)	ff. 96v-110r	ca. 1410	Boh.[3]
iii		O.29 (1613)	ff. 142r-149r	ca. 1430	Unasc. Boh.[4]
iv	UK	III.F.11 (514)	ff. 69vb-134rb	ca. 1410	Asc. Boh.
v		III.G.11 (536)	ff. 208v-220v	xv/1	JW MS Boh.[5]
		X.E.11 (1912)	ff. 76rb-92rb	1433	Boh.[6]
vi	Wien, ÖNB	1343	ff. 37ra-124vb	ca. 1410	Asc. Boh.
vii		3935	ff. 49ra-128vb	1423	Asc. Boh.[7]
viii	Wolfenbüttel, HzglB	Cod. Guelf. 306 (340)	ff. 268rb-369vb	xv/1	Asc. Pol.[8]

III. Ed. M. H. Dziewicki, *Iohannis Wyclif Tractatus De Apostasia* (WS, 1889). From all MSS except **iii** and **viii**.

IV. This is the second of Wyclyf's three treatments of the touchstones of heresy, springing from his long, more abstract excursus in the concluding cap. of the *De veritate sacre scripture* (**31**). He here conceives of apostasy in a markedly idiosyncratic fashion: in capp. i-ii he assails the failure of the orders to live up to their vows, while capp. iii-xvi dwell at length on a multitude of errors on the Eucharist then current.[9]

In his edition of this treatise Dziewicki dated its composition in 1383 (p. VI); four years later, however, in his edition of the *De blasfemia*, he revised this estimate to 1380 (p. VIII). The latter date better suits the relatively mild tone; it is arguable that the *De apostasia* assumed its final form early in 1381, but surely no later.

VC: 3933 3935 4514   Bale: 187   Sh: 15.XI   Lo: 16.XI

---

[1] Runs only through the end of cap. ii, p. 45.

[2] The scribe of Praha, MK B.86 (401), cites the *De apostasia* and several other of Wyclyf's works on f. 45v.

[3] A copy of Peter Payne's *registrum*.

[4] An extract.

[5] A fragment; ends in the middle of cap. ii, p. 30.

[6] A copy of Peter Payne's *registrum*.

[7] Bears marginalia by Peter Payne.

[8] Belonged to Matthew Flacius Illyricus. What use he may have made of it in his various Lutheran compositions is moot; his attitude toward Wyclyf was quite critical on the whole. (For an exception, however, see his *Catalogus Testium Veritatis, qui ante nostram aetatem reclamarunt Papae* [Basel, 1556; reed. J. C. Dietericus, 1672]: 493-494.) For bibliography on Flacius, see H. Scheible, *Die Anfänge der reformatorischen Geschichtsschreibung. Melanchthon, Flacius und die Magdeburger Zenturien* (Gütersloh, 1966): 9-10; cf. also above, **18**, n. 1, and below, **53**, n. 7.

[9] But there is not the sharp break in subject matter or tone between capp. **ii** and **iii** which this description would imply; see above, **28-30**, n. 19.

37. A12.1. *De blasfemia.* Mid-1381.

I. Inc.: Restat succincte de blasfemia pertractandum ...
Expl.: × ... quam sibi placuerit ad hoc ministerium limitare.

II. MSS:

i	Dublin, Trinity Coll.	C.1.24	pp. 312a-422b	xiv/2	JW MS Eng.[1]
ii	Praha, MK	C.73 (504)	ff. 11ra-86rb	xv/1	Asc. Boh.
iii		O.29 *(1613)*	ff. 118r-129v	ca. 1430	Unasc. Boh.[2]
iv	UK	III.F.11 (514)	ff. 1ra-69va	ca. 1410	Asc. Boh.
		X.E.11 (1912)	ff. 92va-113vb	1433	Boh.[3]
v	Wien, ÖNB	1343	ff. 125ra-230va	ca. 1410	Asc. Boh.
vi		3933	ff. 117ra-183va	ca. 1415	Asc. Boh.[4]
vii		3935	ff. 129ra-223ra	1423	JW MS Boh.[5]
viii		4514	ff. 29r-86r	1432	Asc. Boh.[6]

III. Ed. M. H. Dziewicki, *Iohannis Wyclif Tractatus de Blasphemia* (WS, 1893). From **i, v, vi, vii** and **viii** only.[7]

IV. This treatise, the last of Wyclyf's subordinate trilogy on simony, apostasy and blasphemy, also concludes the *Summa theologie* itself. It continues and broadens his attack on the orders and the hierarchy, with particular emphases on their blatant abuses of sacramental authority, disregard of Scriptural imperatives, and erroneous doctrine concerning the Eucharist. As in the *De apostasia*, he is repetitious to a fault: we must assume either hasty composition or a stridently polemical mood.

It appears that the trilogy had been conceived early in 1380; its completion in all likelihood should be assigned to the late summer or fall of 1381. Dziewicki, in his preface, corrects his earlier estimate of 1383 for the *De apostasia*, stressing the long excursus (pp. 190-200) into the aftermath of the Peasants' Revolt and the murder of Archbishop Sudbury (June 1381) in the present piece. (Pp. vii-viii.) As for the puzzling reference to the "cruciatum [sic] langwidum infinitum" on p. 177 of the *De apostasia*, he postulates a later, garbled interpolation.[8] If a second English MS of early date were to come to light a clear resolution of the question might be possible.[9]

vc: 3933 3935 4514   Bale: 186   Sh: 15.XII   Lo: 16.XII

---

[1] For a lost English MS once at Oriel College, Oxford, see above, **28-30**, n. 6.

[2] An extract.

[3] A copy of Peter Payne's *registrum*.

[4] Followed by a *registrum*, ff. 185ra-195rb.

[5] Annotated by Peter Payne.

[6] *Tabula*, ff. 86r-102v.

[7] Dziewicki knew of **ii** and **iv**, and used **vi** and **vii** only through cap. ii. The reasons for their exclusion were chiefly financial: see his introduction, p. v.

[8] It may also be, on the other hand, that Wyclyf was here referring to one of the many "crusades" launched in Italy by Clement vii against Urban vi or vice versa. From an Englishman's point of view it

all must have seemed as remote as Czechoslovakia seemed to Neville Chamberlain in 1938. We may argue too that word of the first bulls sent to Bishop Henry Despenser (25 March 1381), urging a crusade, replete with indulgences, in Flanders, had percolated at Oxford and provoked Wyclyf's irritation. See William E. Lunt, *Studies in Anglo-Papal Relations during the Middle Ages* II: *Financial Relations of the Papacy with England 1327-1534* (Mediaeval Academy of America Publications 74: Cambridge, Mass., 1962): 535-536; also below, **48**, n. 4.

[9] Wyclyf's redoubtable German antagonist, John Scharpe, the "doctor famosus" of Queen's College, took issue specifically with cap. viii of the *De blasfemia*: see his unpublished *De suffragiis viatorum ecclesie militantis* in Oxford, Merton Coll. K.33 (175), ff. 261vb-262ra. On Scharpe, see above, **6**, n. 1.

38. A13. *De eucharistia* [*Tractatus maior*]. Mid- to late 1380.

I. Inc. prol.: Sentencia tractatus de eucharistia in compendio sic habetur ...
Expl. prol.: × ... et recitat tres sophisticaciones cleri in quibus populus est illusus.
Inc. cap. i: Tractando de eucharistia oportet premittere quedam communia ...
Expl.: × ... adiuvando deum conficere et in Christo Jesu finaliter observare.

II. MSS:

	Praha, MK	C.118 (550)	ff. 1r-?	ca. 1430	Boh.[1]
i		O.29 (1613)	ff. 153r-160v	ca. 1430	Unasc. Boh.[2]
ii	UK	IV.D.22 (676)	ff. 130bisra-207rb	1405	JW MS Boh.
iii		VIII.G.32 (1615)	ff. 1r-82v	1403	Asc. Boh.
		X.E.11 (1912)	ff. 146rb-167va	1433	Boh.[3]
iv		XI.E.3 (2050)	ff. 15r-54r	1416	Asc. Boh.
v	Vaticano	Vat.lat. 4313	ff. 31rb-70va	xv/1	Unasc. Boh.[4]
vi	Wien, ÖNB	1387	ff. 1ra-43rb	ca. 1410	JW MS Boh.[5]
vii		3927	ff. 77ra-122ra	ca. 1410	JW MS Boh.[6]
viii		3932	ff. 157ra-207va	1418	Asc. Boh.

III. Ed. J. Loserth, *Iohannis Wyclif De Eucharistia Tractatus Maior. Accedit Tractatus De Eucharistia et Poenitentia sive De Confessione* (WS, 1892): 1-326. From all MSS except **i**, **iii** and **v**. Translation of some sections in M. Spinka, ed., *Advocates of Reform* (Library of Christian Classics 14: Philadelphia, 1953): 61-88.

IV. The sacrament of the Eucharist, in both its philosophical and theological ramifications, exercised Wyclyf's subtle mind for many years. Although the concluding capp. of his *De potencia productiva dei ad extra* (**19**), a section he entitled "De annihilacione," already pointed toward a perceived strain in his efforts to resolve orthodox teaching and his own thoroughgoing philosophical realism as early as 1372, it was only after seven more years[7] that the dialectical pressures at Oxford drove him first to declare his views in the schools, and after several more months finally to publish the momentous treatise here considered. All modern authorities more or less concur that the *De eucharistia* was the primary catalyst both of his expulsion from Oxford and consequent retirement to his rectory at Lutterworth,[8] and of a virtually unanimous closing of ranks among the mendicants against him.[9] Hereafter the imperative of further, generally more succinct, treatment of the Eucharist and of the "apostasy" of the friars preoccupies him almost to the exclusion of all else, save the supervision of Hereford and Purvey in their work of translation and some connection, evasive of definition, with the Poor Priests.[10]

The *De eucharistia* is only the most weighty of the six we have from his pen which carry the subject in their titles.[11] And in a great many sermons, in other shorter tracts on church government or against the "four sects"[12] he devoted ample time to an ongoing assault on what he deeply felt to be the root of much malicious latter-day damage to the *lex evangelica*. Since the composition of this piece fell outside the structure of the *Summa theologie* (though clearly before its completion), we must fall back on internal evidence to fit it into the overall scheme of his writings. He does refer to his own *De ecclesia, De officio regis, De potestate pape,* and *De symonia* (**32-35**), while his choice of texts in several cases closely parallels his selection in the *De apostasia* (**36**). As we might expect, he continues to display a thorough familiarity with canon law, but his citations from that *corpus* are by preference, as we have previously noted, heavily Scriptural and patristic in content.[13]

VC: 3933 3935 4514   Bale: deest   Sh: 18   Lo: 19

[1] A *registrum*. Editor unable to ascertain exact foliation.
[2] An extract.
[3] A copy of Peter Payne's *registrum*.
[4] See Stein, "Two Notes on Wyclif," 465-466.
[5] Heavily annotated by Peter Payne.
[6] Index follows, ff. 122ra-123vb.
[7] Loserth marshals the evidence in his introduction, pp. III-IX; he relies here heavily on the note by his sometime collaborator, F. D. Matthew, "The Date of Wyclif's Attack on Transubstantiation," *EHR* 5 (1890): 328-330. Workman, *JW* II: 408-409, argues for 1379, but this seems less defensible. Cf. also above, **3**, and below, n. 12.

[8] The pulpit, vestment, table and chair still at the parish church of St Marys in Lutterworth in the last century were long attributed to him: see John Nichols, *The History and Antiquities of the County of Leicester* IV/1: *containing Guthlaxton Hundred* (London, 1810; reprinted East Ardsley [Yorks], 1971): 264, and figs. 38-40, Pl. xxxviii; cf. Workman, *JW* II: 298-302. The chances of this attribution being correct, nevertheless, are very remote.

[9] He probably left Oxford shortly after pledging a copy of the *Decretum* on 23 October 1381 (above, **28-30**, n. 28). It is perhaps significant that this act occurred almost two weeks into the Michaelmas term: had Wyclyf actually commenced his fall lectures? For the fixed dates of the Oxford academic year, see C. Wordsworth, ed., *The Ancient Kalendar of the University of Oxford from Documents of the Fourteenth to the Seventeenth Century* (OHS Publications 45: 1904): 24.

Robert Southey, the Poet-laureate, exclaimed in his *The Book of the Church*, 3rd ed., I (London, 1825): "At first [Wyclyf] exercised himself in disputing against the Friars upon scholastic subtleties and questions which, ending in nothing, as they begin, exercise the intellect without enriching it." Southey's abiding anti-Romanism aside, it goes almost without saying that to Wyclyf and his colleagues, and to many generations of scholars before and after their day, it was precisely these "subtleties and questions" which enriched the intellect *through exercising it*.

[10] Still the only close examination of this amorphous and largely acephalic body is H. L. Cannon, "The Poor Priests: A Study in the Rise of English Lollardy," *Annual Report of the American Historical Association for 1899* I (Washington, 1900): 451-482. For additional cautious observations on Wyclyf's ill-documented links with this group (perhaps, though not necessarily, identical with his "simplices sacerdotes," and probably *not* to be equated with his "secta Christi"), cf. introductions to Secs. B and F, below.

[11] See **39-42**, **44**, below.

[12] See below, **50**, n. 6. For other writings bearing on the Eucharist, see **39-44**, **47**, as well as many sermons and polemical pieces. Dr Heather Phillips has recently examined the whole issue in her 1980 Toronto dissertation, "John Wyclif's *De eucharistia* in its Medieval Setting" (Centre for Medieval Studies).

[13] See above, **28-30**; **33**.

39. A14. *De eucharistia minor confessio (De corpore Christi)*. 10 May 1381.

I. Inc.: Sepe confessus sum et adhuc confiteor quod idem corpus Christi [46 wds.] est vere et realiter panis sacramentalis ...

Expl.: × ... sed credo quod finaliter veritas vincet eos.

II. MSS:

i	Cambridge, Jesus Coll.	59 (*Q.G.11*)	ff. 140v-144v	xiv/ex	Asc. Eng.[1]
ii	Eton Coll.	47	ff. 119r-121v	xv/m	Asc. Eng.[2]
iii	London, BL	Royal 7 B.III	ff. 75r-76v	ca. 1400	Asc. Eng.[3]
iv	Oxford, Bodleian	703 (S.C. 2766)	ff. 57ra-58vb	xiv/ex	Asc. Eng.[4]
v	e Musaeo	86 (S.C. 3629)	ff. 36vb-39va	1439	Asc. Eng.[5]
vi		*James 3 (S.C. 3840)* pp. 261-262		1636	Asc. Eng.[6]
vii	Praha, UK	XI.E.3 (2050)	ff. 54v-58r	1416	Asc. Boh.
viii			ff. 69r-76r		Asc. Boh.[7]
ix	Wien, ÖNB	1387	ff. 43rb-46rb	ca. 1410	JW MS Boh.
x		4343	ff. 225r-234r	1433	Asc. Boh.[8]

III. Ed. John Lewis, *The History of the Life and Sufferings of the Reverend and Learned John Wicliffe, D.D.* ... (London, 1720): 272-281; idem, 2nd ed. (Oxford, 1820): 323-332; Robert Vaughan, *The Life and Opinions of John de Wycliffe, D.D.* ... II (London, 1828): 445-453; idem, *John de Wycliffe, D.D. A Monograph* ... (London, 1853): 564-570. All from **iii** and/or **iv** only. Also ed. in *FZ*, 115-132, from **v** only.

IV. Where the *De eucharistia* (**38**) was a long, discursive collection of Wyclyf's accumulated thoughts on the sacrament of the altar that crystallized for his Oxford public – and beyond – his academic position, the present, much shorter, piece, appearing in its most comprehensive context in the *Fasciculi zizaniorum*, was clearly *pro occasione*, prepared in response to the condemnation of his two principal teachings on the Eucharist by a committee of twelve theologians appointed by Chancellor William Barton at Oxford, probably late in 1380.[9] Wyclyf, says our hostile source, was taken aback by the condemnation, read to him in the school of the Austin friars, but quickly recovered. Hard upon the heels of this setback, his redoubtable patron, John of Gaunt, entwined as he surely was in the chronic intrigues of his nephew's minority, came personally to Oxford to urge the irascible doctor's compliance with the prohibitions of the chancellor's edict. The *Confessio* was Wyclyf's unbending reply to both censure and suasion: it was published on 10 May 1381, and is therefore by far the most precisely datable of any of his works, except for a handful of the *Sermones*. Sections of it were excerpted from the *De apostasia* (**36**).

In its turn this *Confessio* provoked the Franciscan John Tissington, who had served as a member of the chancellor's committee, to pen a *Confessio* of his own; perhaps more tellingly, the Carmelite Thomas Winterton, who had stood at Wyclyf's side before that day, now set down a sorrowful *Absolucio*.[10] Within a few months Wyclyf would retire to Lutterworth, forbidden to teach or preach within the confines of the University. The last phase of his turbulent career would then begin.

VC: 3933 3935[11]   Bale: 18   Sh: 19   Lo: 20

[1] Inc.: "Corpus Christi est idem in numero quod fuit assumptum...." In fact it is our piece, contrary to the observations in Thomson, "Unnoticed MSS and Works of Wyclif," 32-34, where the text is reproduced.

[2] See the thorough description of this text and of Nicholas Radcliff's and William Woodford's subsequent commentaries (ff. 121v-131v) in Neil Ker, *Medieval Manuscripts in British Libraries* II: *Abbotsford-Keele* (Oxford, 1977): 686-687.

[3] Followed by a commentary, f. 77r, relating to the doctrines in the *Confessio* which were themselves condemned at Blackfriars (the "Earthquake Synod") in mid-1382. See also BL, Harley 31, 206.

[4] The scribe, though frequently careless in transcription (cf. Shirley's remarks, *FZ*, lxxx), nonetheless did take pains to identify Wyclyf's sources in the margin. (These are not, however, beyond challenge.) Tissington's *Confessio* follows, ff. 59ra-65vb.

[5] This is the handsome codex utilized as the basis for Shirley's edition. See **12**, n. 10, above.

[6] Copied from **iv**; perhaps it is James' "later" hand which erased the terminal "I" from that MS. (Cf. Loserth's introduction, p. VIII.)

[7] This is the second transcription of our text in this codex, in a different hand. Both are asc., and also incomplete.

[8] The twelve masters and doctors at Oxford who drew up a bill of particulars against Wyclyf in 1411 found five objectionable propositions in this tract: Wilkins, *Concilia...* III: 349. They correspond to Shirley's edition as follows (number in Wilkins followed by page in *FZ*): 259: 117 (distorted); 260: 118; 216: 123 (distorted); 262: 125-126 (a loose paraphrase); 263: 129.

[9] The condemnation precedes the *Confessio* in *FZ*: 110-113; it is interesting that Wyclyf is not mentioned by name. But its promulgation leaves no doubt that he was its principal target. The circumstances are discussed in Gwynn, *The English Austin Friars in the Time of Wyclif*, 258-261; Dahmus, *The Prosecution of John Wyclif*, 129-135 (his translation omits the names of the twelve masters, six of whom were mendicants: Workman, *JW* II: 140-148, gives useful data on them, and on the sequence of events generally; but cf. now also the appropriate entries in *BRUO*).

[10] Published in *FZ*: 133-180. Part of Tissington's *Confessio* also in Oxford, Bodleian James 12 (S.C. 3849), pp. 103-107; cf. *FZ*, 181-238. See *BRUO* III: 1879-1880 on Tissington and 2062 on Winterton.
[11] The expl. given in both MSS. "quantum in episcopis est," does not correspond to anything in the accepted text.

40. A15. *De fide sacramenti* [*De eucharistia confessio*]. Late 1381?

I. Inc.: Illa hostia alba et rotunda a sacerdote consecrata dicitur post consecracionem corpus Christi ...
Expl.: × ... in primo articulo fidei et in multis aliis.

II. MSS:

| i | Cambridge, Trinity Coll. | B.14.50 | ff. 56r-58r | xv/1 | Unasc. Eng. |

III. Ed. S. H. Thomson, "John Wyclif's 'Lost' *De Fide Sacramentorum*," *JTS* 33 (1932): 359-365. From unique MS.

IV. The ascription of this work to Wyclyf rests perhaps on less secure ground than we might wish. Bale gives it no incipit, and it is extant, so far as we know, in only one MS. In it, along with the present short piece, there are a number of works in English from the same hand.[1] The terminology – especially the reliance on patristic sources in the *Decretum*, on Scripture, and on the sort of illustrations also to be found in the *De apostasia* and the *De eucharistia* (**36, 38**), embracing even his polemical use of such terms as "solucionem sathane" – clearly points to Wyclyf as its author. We have also a much shorter English text, printed now by Anne Hudson in a critical recension, which does somewhat parallel the *De fide sacramenti*;[2] but it mentions a "consayle of freres at London," i.e., Blackfriars in 1382; our Latin version belongs to a slightly earlier period.

VC: deest   Bale: 233   Sh: 20   Lo: 21

[1] M. R. James, *The Western Manuscripts in the Library of Trinity College, Cambridge: A Descriptive Catalogue* I (Cambridge, Eng., 1900): 457-459, listed this codex simply as "Lollard Tracts." It has recently received closer examination by Anne Hudson, ed., *Selections from English Wycliffite Writings*, 141, 145 (book reviewed by Janet Coleman in *Medium Ævum* 49 [1980]: 142-145). Cf. also below, **433**, n. 3.
[2] Hudson, *Selections from English Wycliffite Writings*, 17-19.

41. A16. *De eucharistia conclusiones duodecim* [or: *quindecim*]. Mid- or late 1381?

I. Inc.: Hostia consecrata quam videmus in altari nec est Christus, nec aliqua sui pars ...
Expl.: × ... quorum uterque in natura est perfeccior accidente.
Expl. alt.: × ... quilibet articulus fidei Christiane.

II. MSS:

i	Oxford, Bodleian e Musaeo	86 (S.C. 3629)	ff. 34va-35ra	1439	Asc. Eng.
ii	Praha, MK	C.73 (504)	f. 161ra	xv/1	Asc. Boh.[1]
iii	UK	III.F.11 (514)	f. 134va	ca. 1410	JW MS Boh.[2]
iv	Wolfenbüttel, HzglB	Cod. Guelf. 306 (340)	ff. 369vb-370ra	xv/1	Asc. Pol.[3]

III. Ed. John Lewis, *The History of the Life and Sufferings of the Reverend and Learned John Wiclif, D.D.* ... (2nd ed., Oxford, 1820): 318-319; R. Vaughan, *The Life and Opinions of John de Wycliffe, D.D.* ... (London, 1828): 436-437;[4] idem, *John de Wycliffe, D.D. A Monograph* ... (London, 1853): 560-561;[5] *FZ*, 105-106. All from **i** only.

IV. This work is hardly a tract in any customary sense of the word; it is rather a list of *determinationes* for academic disputation, and is so designated by Bale. John Keninghale, in the running commentary which precedes his text in the *Fasciculi zizaniorum*, avers that Wyclyf "incepit ... sub anno domini MCCLXXXI, in estate, determinare materiam de sacramento altaris, in qua materia subscriptas posuit conclusiones." There is obviously some confusion as to dates here: it is arguable that Wyclyf may have proposed these heads of discussion even before he began to write the major *De eucharistia* in 1380. Alternatively, it may just as well be urged that the twelve *conclusiones* in fact constituted the subject-matter of his disputation at the school of the Austin friars in Oxford at the very time he was officially notified that Chancellor Barton had condemned his latest teaching on the Eucharist (in the spring of 1381).[6] We suggest a slightly later date with considerable diffidence, based only on the very slender evidence adduced by Keninghale (with the proviso that we allow the date of 1380 for Wyclyf's *first* public debates on the subject, but the summer of 1381 for these particular *determinaciones*).

The issue is further clouded by the fact that only the Oxford text then proceeds to give an additional three *conclusiones* – preceded, however, by another of Keninghale's interpolations: "Et in uno die, in publica sua determinacione, has tres subsequentes posuit conclusiones, ex quibus sequuntur ille tres prime condemnate per Willelmum archiepiscopum...." But the language of these three propositions does not at all correspond to the first three heresies singled out at the Blackfriars Synod on 21 May 1382.[7] They actually repeat, almost verbatim, *conclusiones* 7-9 among the original twelve. Hence our suggested modification in what must be in any case a tentative title. It is also likely that the "Willelmum" mentioned in the Oxford commentary was not the archbishop (i.e., Courtenay), but rather the chancellor, Barton, whose committee would thus have had a very convenient catalog of Wyclyf's teachings on the Eucharist in this summary form. Finally, *conclusio* 8 (= 14), by its uncharacteristic imprecision and uncritical use of the term "transubstanciatur," further evokes the suspicion that someone else was putting words in Wyclyf's mouth.

All Continental MSS, incidentally, lack *conclusiones* 7-12.

vc: deest   Bale: 19   Sh: 19   Lo: 22

[1] Presents only the first six *conclusiones*.
[2] Ibid.
[3] First noticed in Kühn-Steinhausen, "Wyclif-Handschriften in Deutschland," 626; likewise contains only six *conclusiones*. Signature of "W. Hamoczan" at the end; ff. 370rb-373v blank. F. 374r not a Wyclyf piece.
[4] Prints only the twelve *conclusiones*.
[5] Ibid.
[6] See **39**, above.
[7] Text in *FZ*, 275-282; other sources and the circumstances of this "Earthquake Synod" are discussed in Dahmus, *William Courtenay Archbishop of Canterbury 1381-1396*, 78-83, 299, n. 15; idem, *The Prosecution of John Wyclyf*, 88-99. Two very caustic poems about this assemblage are published in Thomas Wright, ed., *Political Poems and Songs relating to English History, composed during the Period from the Accession of Edw. III to that of Ric. III* I (RS, 1859): 250-263. Again, for extended examination of the 51 men who participated at Courtenay's behest in the London synod, see Workman, *JW* II: 253-273 (the complete list of those in attendance appears in *FZ*, 286-288 – and see also, of course, the entries scattered throughout the three vols. of *BRUO*). The second through fifth (last) sessions of the synod eventually engaged more than 22 additional luminaries before the final condemnations were promulgated in July. It should be noted once again that Wyclyf's name never appears in any of the quasi-official documents that have come down to us from Blackfriars; nor was he ever required to attend personally. The response of Richard II on 13 July was to second the archbishop's directive to the chancellor to expel any defenders of Wyclyf, Hereford, Purvey or Aston: H. E. Salter, ed., *Mediaeval Archives of the University of Oxford*, 216-217. For Wyclyf's acidulous retort from Lutterworth to news of the synod's action, see *FZ*, 283-285, and below, **216, 218, 219, 225, 392**.

42. A17. *Questio ad fratres de sacramento altaris.* 1381 ?

I. Inc.: Quid in natura sua est hoc album et rotundum ...
   Expl.: × ... est increata trinitas que est melior corpore salvatoris etc.

II. MSS:

i	Praha, UK	III.G.11 (536)	f. 86r	xv/1	JW MS Boh.
ii	Wien, ÖNB	4343	ff. 234v-235r	1433	Asc. Boh.
iii		4522	f. 139v	1423	Asc. Boh.[1]

III. Ed. J. Loserth, *Iohannis Wyclif de Eucharistia Tractatus Maior. Accedit Tractatus de Eucharistia et Poenitentia sive de Confessione* (WS, 1892): 347-348. From **i** only.

IV. This is a puzzling piece. It was not written by Wyclyf himself; the two third-person allusions to him preclude that. ("Sepe quesivit idem Johannes et adhuc queritur a fratribus ... quia idem Johannes est certus ex fide quod ille panis est realiter corpus Domini Jesu Christi....") Shirley (who gives an inappropriate explicit) seems to have thought that it was the work of Richard Wyche, a priest of Hereford, whose recantation of Wyclyfite views occupies pp. 501-505 of the *FZ*. But this judgment would seem to rest on the terminal ascription: a like ascription ("Rychardo Vicz") in the *contenta* of **i**, however, was clearly written over an erasure of "Joh. Wycleph." [2] Loserth avers in his revision of Shirley's *Catalogue*, and also in his introduction to his edition of this piece (p. LXV), that "it is from the pen of a Bohemian Wyclifite." Nevertheless, although in his introduction to the *De eucharistia* (**38**) Loserth attempted to indict the Czechs in Hus' circle of a Wyclyfite position on the remanence of the bread (pp. XLV-LX), it is extremely improbable that more than a handful among them even speculated philosophically in this vein.[3] Besides, the unmistakable present-tense allusions to Wyclyf and the unnamed Oxford friars (Kenningham? Woodford? Tissington? Winterton?) with whom he was then seeking to join the issue of the real presence militates strongly against any later Czech authorship. Wyclyf was little known in Bohemia during his lifetime, and began to be widely read there only after 1407. In **ii**, unknown both to Shirley and to Loserth, it is firmly ascribed to Wyclyf, and is sandwiched between the *De eucharistia minor confessio* (**39**) and the *De paupertate Christi* (**402**), all by the same scribe in the same year. Much the same observations could be made anent **iii**. Though late, both Wien MSS considerably strengthen its attribution to Wyclyf – not as a work of his own pen, but of an amanuensis carefully recording yet another of his master's peremptory challenges to his mendicant opponents, probably still in 1381 – though a case for late 1380 would not be out of court.

VC: deest   Bale: deest   Sh: 22   Lo: 23

---

[1] There was evidently at one time a "de sacramento altaris" by Wyclyf (which may or may not have been this piece) in Syon Monastery MS 86, f. 11: see Bateson, *Catalogue of the Library of Syon Monastery*, 244 (index: not in catalogue itself). And see above, **6**, n. 1.

[2] For Wyche, see *BRUO* III: 2101.

[3] On the development of a strong indigenous Czech tradition which acted to qualify the Hussite acceptance of Wyclyf, especially regarding the Eucharist, see V. Kybal, "Étude sur les origines du mouvement Hussite en Bohême. Matthias de Ianov," *Revue historique* 103 (1910): 1-31 (taken here as emblematic of early Czech scholarship, but more accessible than most); S. H. Thomson, "Pre-Hussite Heresy in Bohemia," *EHR* 48 (1933): 23-42; E. Peschke, "Die Bedeutung Wiclefs für die Theologie der Böhmen," *Zeitschrift für Kirchengeschichte* 54 (1935): 462-483; and especially R. R. Betts, "English and Čech Influences on the Hussite Movement," *Transactions of the Royal Historical Society*, 4th ser., 21 (1939): 71-102 (reprinted in his *Essays in Czech History*, 132-159); and now William R. Cook, "John Wyclif and Hussite Theology"; idem, "The Eucharist in Hussite Theology," *Archiv für Reformationsgeschichte* 66 (1975): 23-35. For direct links, many of them admittedly conjectural, between Oxford and Prague, see Robert F. Young, "Bohemian Scholars and Students at the English Universities from 1347 to 1750," *EHR* 38 (1923): 72-84. Loserth further explicated his own position in "Die Wiclif'sche Abendmahlslehre und ihre Augname in Böhmen," *Mitteilungen des Vereins für Geschichte der Deutschen in Böhmen* 30 (1892): 1-33 (and see above, **32**, n. 13). Yet although on the

matter of the Eucharist Loserth's claims fell an early casualty to Czech rectification, much of his unfortunate bias against Hus still lingers. The two volumes by P. de Vooght, *L'Hérésie de Jean Huss* and *Hussiana*, are a useful corrective. It is much to be regretted therefore that de Vooght's position is misrepresented in the otherwise excellent survey by Howard Kaminsky, *A History of the Hussite Revolution*, 35-37.

43. A18. *Errare in materia fidei quod possit ecclesia militans.* Late 1381.

   I. Inc.: Arguitur sic: ecclesia militans potuit olym determinare quod panis remaneat ...

      Expl.: × ... aut fidem suam de certo determinacioni commiserunt successorum.

II. MSS:

i	Praha, UK	XI.E.3 (2050)	f. 61v	1416	JW MS Boh.

III. Ed. S. H. Thomson, "Three Unprinted Opuscula of John Wyclif," *Speculum* 3 (1928): 250. From unique MS.

IV. It is unlikely that Wyclyf himself wrote this opusculum; rather it seems a student took notes on some *disputatio in scholis* between the Evangelical Doctor and an unidentified "adversarius," shortly before Wyclyf left Oxford in the fall of 1381. The central argument, repeated several times, is simply that if the church once taught as the Apostles did concerning the remanence of the bread, but now teaches accidents without substance, it can err. It was just this sort of thinking which had impelled Wyclyf to his lonely eminence in the first place.

vc: deest   Bale: deest   Sh: 32   Lo: 33

44. A19. *De eucharistia et penitencia* [*Confessio*]. Early 1382?

   I. Inc.: Duo sunt sacramenta precipua in quibus ecclesia est illusa ...

      Expl.: × ... dimittere et contrarium constancius confiteri.

II. MSS:

i	Bautzen, Stadt- und KreisB	M.St.80.7	ff. 13r-19v	xv/1	Asc. Boh.[1]
ii	Karlsruhe, BLB	*343*	f. 8v	xv/1	Unasc. Boh.[2]
iii	Praha, MK	D.123 (693)	ff. 72v-82v	xv/1	JW MS Boh.
iv	UK	III.G.11 (536)	ff. 234r-238r	xv/1	Asc. Boh.
v		IV.H.7 (771)	ff. 93r-98r	ca. 1410	JW MS Boh.
vi		*V.F.9 (931)*	ff. 126r-130r	1408	Asc. Boh.
vii	Wien, ÖNB	1337	ff. 47rb-50vb	ca. 1410	JW MS Boh.
viii		3927	ff. 5vb-8rb	ca. 1410	JW MS Boh.
ix		3930	ff. 217va-221ra	1412	Asc. Boh.
x		4527	ff. 107r-110v	1410	Asc. Boh.

III. Ed. J. Loserth, *Iohannis Wyclif de Eucharistia Tractatus Maior. Accedit Tractatus de Eucharistia et Poenitentia sive de Confessione* (WS, 1892): 329-343. From all MSS except **ii, iii, v** and **vi**.

IV. Among Wyclyf's several treatises devoted to the subject of the Eucharist, it seems plain that the present essay was the last written, probably after he had retired to Lutterworth.[3] Here he deals with the subject in less than two pages. His allusion to "talia ... ridicula infinita que fideles evacuant" (p. 329) seems to imply a period of time during which he had satisfied himself as to the soundness of Eucharistic doctrine among the laity.

But ninety percent of the tract focuses on penance, and here he breaks new ground. Analytically we may regard these pages as an extended commentary on *Omnis utriusque sexus*, the pronouncement of IV Lateran (1215) on auricular annual confession which soon found its way into the *Decretales* of Gregory IX (X.5.38.12).[4] He observes that oral confession before a priest may be salutary in certain cases, but often is not; that the institution has become commercialized and is the occasion of all manner of sexual improprieties; and it is finally the cause of unwarranted neglect of preaching by the priesthood generally. In connection with a renewed indictment of the mendicants ('quattuor religionibus privatis sepedictis," p. 334; cf. p. 343), he argues that the institutionalization of the confessional has gravely infringed upon man's free will.[5] His logic is remorseless: if this new ordinance was justified in the time of Innocent III, then all the saints who were so ill-favored as to have lived before its issuance surely sinned.

VC: deest   Bale: deest   Sh: 23   Lo: 24

[1] Editor unable to visit this library or otherwise confirm MS particulars; see above, **31**, n. 1, and description in Loserth's introduction, p. LXVI.

[2] This MS first described by Wilhelm Brambach, ed., *Die Handschriften der Grossherzoglich Badischen Hof- und Landesbibliothek in Karlsruhe* IV: *Die Karlsruher Handschriften* (Karlsruhe, 1896): 37-38; see also Kühn-Steinhausen, "Wyclif-Handschriften in Deutschland," 628 – cited there as "De confessione." The MS itself clearly labels this fragment (which breaks off on p. 331, line 9 of our edition: "... quam de lege gracie. Et sic videtur") cap. vi of the *De ordine Christiano* (**424**), but there would appear to exist no contextual or other basis in fact for this unique arrangement. We must bear in mind that such hypothetical constructions are not at all extraordinary in the Wyclyf MS tradition generally, and that he himself on several occasions saw fit to shift individual works around to suit his purposes. The *Sermones* (**54-299**) perhaps best illustrate this practice.

[3] Although a substantial portion of his *Responsiones ad argumenta cuiusdam emuli veritatis* (**388**), against Strode, dating from mid-1384, touch the issue retrospectively; see especially Loserth, ed., *Johannis Wyclif Opera Minora*, 307-312. The same might be said of the cognate piece, *Responsiones ad xliv conclusiones* (**384**).

[4] A. Friedberg, ed., *Corpus Iuris Canonici* II (Leipzig, 1881): 87. Additional literature cited in Carl Mirbt, *Quellen zur Geschichte des Papsttums und des römischen Katholizismus*, 4th ed. (Tübingen, 1924): 181; B. Poschmann, *Penance and the Anointing of the Sick*, trans. and revised by F. Courteney (New York, 1964).

[5] Wyclyf's Augustinian predilections come to the fore here. (Cf. **17**, n. 10, above.) "Deus enim dedit homini liberum arbitrium et multis specialem instinctum, quando et qualiter debent taliter

operari." (P. 336; cf. p. 335.) He had touched on the subject as early as the *De mandatis divinis* (**26**: p. 36), and again in the *De veritate sacre scripture* (**31**: vol. II: 223; vol. III: 218). In a practical way, his belief in this cardinal tenet compelled Wyclyf, as it would Luther, consistently to minimize the valid functions of the hierarchy; to spread the Gospel among the laity; and to insist upon the fidelity of the mendicants to the high standards established for them by their founders.

45. A20. *De vaticinacione sive de prophecia.* Late 1382?

I. Inc.: Cum secundum sanctos spectat ad officium doctoris evangelici prophetare ...

Expl.: × ... ad statum apostolorum, per quorum oracionis suffragium perturbacio ecclesia sit sedata.

II. MSS:

i	Praha, MK	C.73 (504)	ff. 259va-262vb xv/1	JW	MS Boh.
ii	UK	III.F.11 (514)	ff. 223va-226va ca. 1410	JW	MS Boh.
iii		III.G.11 (536)	ff. 223r-227r xv/1	JW	MS Boh.
iv	Wien, ÖNB	1337	ff. 20vb-23va ca. 1410	JW	MS Boh.
v		1387	ff. 113rb-114vb ca. 1410	JW	MS Boh.
vi		3933	ff. 99ra-101va ca. 1415	JW	MS Boh.

III. Ed. J. Loserth, *Johannis Wyclif Opera Minora* (WS, 1913): 165-174.† From all MSS.

IV. Since his colleagues choose to prophesy concerning the state of the church, Wyclyf avers, he will too – but with a difference: where they rely on the hoary sayings of Merlin, Hildegard of Bingen,[1] and the like, he will trust Scripture itself to be his guide. It is obvious, he continues, that not only the friars, but all the clergy, having drifted so far from the moorings of apostolic poverty, are in imminent jeopardy. The people are shamefully served, and so he declares with Augustine that "erit consumata destruccio per complices Antichristi." (P. 167.) Really this treatise is less of an exposition of prophecy than simply another occasion for Wyclyf to lament the desuetude of the *ecclesia militans* in his own time.

Loserth infers from Wyclyf's support of disendowment that this work should be dated "about 1378" (p. xxx). But Wyclyf consistently urged this drastic step throughout at least the last six years of his life. One reference in the text, immediately following the remark quoted above, hints strongly at an appreciably later date: "... ut alias exposui secundum propheciam Danialis [sic] 2° quam Christus precipit, ut *is qui legit intelligat.*" (P. 167; cf. also Mt 24:15.) The allusion would appear to be to his *De antichristo* I (**376**), capp. xxxv-xxxvi; or perhaps to his *Exposicio textus Matthei xxiv* (**373**), cap. iii. The former is incomplete, broken off at his death in 1384; the latter was composed in 1383. Finally, the tone of his invective against the mendicants is far too harsh to fit the circumstances of any year before the synod at Blackfriars in the spring and summer of 1382.

VC: 3933 3935 4514 7980   Bale: deest[2]   Sh: 24   Lo: 25

[1] Pp. 165, 169. Other references to the abbess of St. Rupert's (1098-1179) in Wyclyf's writings are given in Workman, *JW* II: 93n; see now also H. D. Rauh, *Das Bild des Antichrist im Mittelalter: von Tyconius zum deutschen Symbolismus* (Beiträge zur Geschichte der Philosophie und Theologie des Mittelalters, n.F. 9: Münster, 1973): 474-527. Wyclyf's specific reference here is to the widely-known *Revelatio Hildegardis de fratribus mendicantium*, an early thirteenth-century forgery. (Cf. literature cited in McShane, *A Critical Appraisal of the Antimendicantism of John Wyclif*, 35n. M. Schrader and A. Führkötter, *Die Echtheit des Schrifttums des heiligen Hildegard von Bingen* [Köln and Graz, 1956], do not even mention the *Revelatio*.) In any case Wyclyf regarded this source as of little worth.

[2] Bale's no. 79, entitled "In prophetiam Hildegardis," has the incipit "Beata virgo Hildegardis cuius haec." In his section of spurious works he observes that our present tract could not be by Wyclyf because it has a different incipit from the "In prophetiam" – which is lost in any case! Whether Wyclyf ever wrote a separate piece on Hildegard is moot; but in light of his generally sceptical attitude toward her (presumed) *Revelatio*, we may doubt it. (See the preceding note.)

The possibility is worth exploring that Wyclyf might have had some passing acquaintance with one or more of the popular *vaticinia de summis pontificibus*: cf. Bernard McGinn, "Angel Pope and Papal Antichrist," *Church History* 47 (1978): 171.

46. A21. *De oracione et ecclesie purgacione.* Late 1383.

I. Inc.: Dicturus de oracione suppono inprimis eius quidditatem ...
Expl.: × ... ac tercio, quomodo sunt ab ecclesia expellende.

II. MSS:

i   Wien, ÖNB   1337   ff. 68ra-71rb   ca. 1410   JW MS Boh.

III. Ed. R. Buddensieg, *John Wiclif's Polemical Works in Latin* I (WS, 1883): 343-354.[1] From unique MS.

IV. Although we still know of only one MS of this opusculum, its authenticity is secure. It is not, however, one of Wyclyf's more convincing efforts. The first three capp. deal with the three forms of prayer grounded in Scripture ("mentalis, vocalis, et vitalis"), and advance his argument that the last is preferable, but not at the expense of the others; the fourth cap. is a sustained invective against the "four sects"[2] which so vexed him in the last three years of his life; and the fifth and last cap. urges their radical excision from the body of the faithful. Any attempt to assign a firm date to this piece must take account of two things: its strident temper and its four separate references (all on p. 350) to the present pope as "iste refuga." This latter term crops up also in several other demonstrably late works; here the language is so unbending, his bridges so patently burnt behind him, that we must opt with Buddensieg for the last few months of 1383, and construe "iste refuga" as applying to Urban VI, then in Naples.[3]

VC: 3933 3935 4514 7980[4]   Bale: deest   Sh: 25   Lo: 26

[1] This, the first volume produced under the auspices of the Wyclif Society, appeared also the same year in a German edition, published at Leipzig: *Johann Wiclifs lateinische Streitschriften*, which

comprised in a single volume the material contained in vols. I and II of the English version. Since pagination is identical, we shall henceforth refer only to the WS vols.

[2] I.e., the "possessionati" or "clerus cesareus" (secular clergy); monks; canons; and friars. Confusion occasionally arises in the literature, since Wyclyf's attacks on the mendicants also embraced the four orders of the Franciscans (preeminently!), Dominicans, Carmelites, and Austin Friars.

[3] He had earlier discussed prayer (in quite different wise) in the *De ecclesia* (**32**: pp. 523-541). On the phrase "iste refuga," cf. **405**, n. 3, below.

[4] All four vc indicate seven, not five, capp.; and give besides our explicit an additional one, "dictum est de gradibus ecclesie." (Reminiscent of **394**, below.) With only one MS now known, we may perhaps be justified in suspecting that it is incomplete. But why then would the vc also give our explicit?

47. A22. *Trialogus* [*Summa summe*]. Late 1382 or early 1383.

I. Inc. prol.: Cum locucio ad personam multis plus complacet quam locucio generalis ...

Expl. prol.: × ... theologus et maturus tanquam Phronesis decideret veritatem.

Inc. liber I: Alithia. Licet dixit insipiens in corde suo, non est Deus ...

Expl.: × ... de quo evangelium, satians quemlibet sensum beatorum.

II. MSS:[1]

i	*Firenze, BLaur*	*Plut. XIX.33*	ff. 57v-165v	1408	JW MS Eng.[2]
ii	Oxford, Bodleian e Musaeo	86 (S.C. 3629)	ff. 71vb-72rb	1439	Asc. Eng.[3]
iii	*Praha, MK*	*O.29 (1613)*	ff. 162r-166r	ca. 1430	Unasc. Boh.[4]
	UK	*XI.E.3 (1912)*	ff. 113rb-146ra	1433	Boh.[5]
iv	Wien, ÖNB	1387	ff. 163ra-215ra	ca. 1410	JW MS Boh.[6]
v		3930	ff. 23ra-124vb	1412	Asc. Boh.[7]
vi		3932	ff. 1ra-72rb	1418	Asc. Boh.[8]
vii		4505	ff. 34r-187v	1439	Asc. Boh.[9]
viii		4516	ff. 88r-203v	1440	Asc. Boh.[10]

III. Ed. Johann Froben (?) or Otto Brunfels (?), *Io. Wiclefi viri undiquaque piis. dialogoru̅ libri q̅ttuor* ... (Basel [?], 1525);[11] L. P. Wirth, *Ioannis Wiclefi viri undiquaque piissimi, Dialogorum Libri Quatuor* ... (Frankfurt and Leipzig, 1753);[12] Gotthard Lechler, *Joannis Wiclif Trialogus cum Supplemento Trialogi* (Oxford, 1869).

IV. Cast out from Oxford, censured by the leading churchmen of the realm, cut off by his own choice from the friars who had stood at his side in previous clashes, and to all appearances maintaining only the most tenuous of connections with John of Gaunt, Wyclyf yet chose to spend his last feverish years flying still in the teeth of this gale of adversity. Certainly one of the most substantial products of this final stage of his career – and by all odds the most readable! – was the *Trialogus*. In it, as its alternate title suggests, Wyclyf (speaking as the dominant character, Phronesis) touches on almost every issue – philosophical, theological, or political – which had exercised him during more than two decades of running disputation. He had earlier employed the device of dialogue in the *Dyalogus* (**408**), there between a transparent "Veritas" and "Mendacium": here, however, there is some subtlety. His prefatory wooden characterizations of "Alithia" ("solidus philosophus" – though of course the Greek term signifies "truth"), "Pseustis" ("infidelis captiosus"; Gk. "lie") and "Phronesis" ("subtilis theologus et maturus"; but Gk. simply "intelligence")[13] tend to mask Alithia's real function as both foil and prod to her "brother" Phronesis; Pseustis' sharp insight into the heart of a problem; and Phronesis' own human predilection for dilating upon whatever strikes his fancy, regardless of the ostensible topic of the moment. While Wyclyf, in thus deploying three mouthpieces, calls to mind the Thomistic technique and its Greek antecedents, not to mention Anselm and perhaps his beloved Grosseteste[14] too, still we might be well advised to seek more immediate inspiration in such works as the *De pauperie salvatoris* of Richard FitzRalph[15] and, of course, the ongoing dialectic of the schools themselves.

The organization of the *Trialogus* roughly parallels that of the *Libri quattuor sententiarum* of Peter Lombard: *liber* I, "De Deo"; II, "De mundo"; III, "De virtutibus peccatisque et de salvatore"; and IV, "De signis." He cites the Lombard directly only twice, however; Scripture and Augustine as usual are his mainstays.[16] Here his austere teaching on the sacraments clearly springs immediately from his philosophical realism; while his predestinarianism, his harsh opposition to every claim of the mendicants – even against the motives of the founders, Francis and Dominic[17] – and his sturdy rejection of the institutional church as it had developed since the "solucio Sathane" in the eleventh century[18] all mark the *Trialogus* as a massive effort at personal doctrinal synthesis. A term much exercised throughout the *Trialogus* is "viator." Although the concept of the wayfaring Christian was a commonplace of the later Middle Ages – its origin appears in Augustine, if not earlier[19] – Wyclyf's frequent and flexible use of the word elevates it to a thematic level in the present work.[20]

As to the date of composition, it plainly falls after the "Earthquake Synod" at Blackfriars (May 1382): that episode is mentioned with his customary disdain at least three times.[21] His incidental allusions to his other writings are often so imprecise as to be of very little help yet in some instances they seem to suggest a very late *terminus ante quem*, perhaps as late as 1384.[22] The calamitous crusade of Bishop Despenser, on the other hand, receives no notice at all;[23] and, given both his habitual reference to it in later pieces and the appropriate subject matter at certain junctures in the *Trialogus*, we may urge adequate grounds for assigning its completion to the end of 1382 or the first few months of 1383.

vc: 3963 3935 4514 7980   Bale: 1   Sh: 16   Lo: 17

---

[1] A MS of the *Trialogus* was once to be seen at Trinity College, Cambridge; it is now lost, and Sh and Lo both mention it as lost in their day as well. Perhaps this MS was the one alluded to in [G. H.

Wanley]. *A Catalogue of the Harleian Collection of Manuscripts* I (London, 1759): *ad* MS 1731: "I hear there is a copy of the Trialogus now remaining; being found some years since, in an old Monastery. Moreover, my Lord Weymouth hath lately bought the Trialogus (or at least a great part of it) of a very old Print: Perhaps sett forth by the Hussites in Bohemia." (This last doubtless points to our 1525 *editio princeps*.)

[2] See, for mention of Mabillon's first notice of this MS, Stein, "The Wyclif Manuscript in Florence," 95.

[3] A fragment of *liber* IV, capp. 36, 37, 27; this is the *FZ* MS. Cf. Shirley ed., 283-285.

[4] An extract.

[5] A copy of Peter Payne's *registrum*.

[6] Heavily annotated by Peter Payne. It should be remarked here that Hus may have translated the *Trialogus*, or some of it, into Czech as early as 1403: Workman, *JW* I: 18; and see also his comments in II: 291, 309-310, 344.

[7] *Registrum* at ff. 1ra-2rb.

[8] Index, ff. 91ra-92ra.

[9] Detailed index, ff. 209ra-227va.

[10] On 28 February 1397, the new archbishop of Canterbury, Thomas Arundel, declared heretical eighteen articles drawn from the *Trialogus* by Wyclyf's old adversary, William Woodford OFM. The formal pronouncement took place at the conclusion of a provincial synod in St Pauls, convened for that express purpose: cf., *inter alia*, Paris, BN f.l. 14619, ff. 167v-168v; Melk, E.20, ff. 173v-175v. Printed in Wilkins, *Concilia...* III: 226-230; Lewis, *A History of the Life and Sufferings of John Wiclif, D.D.* (1820 ed.): 372-381 (with parallel passages); Lechler, *Johann Wiclif und die Vorgeschichte der Reformation* II: 46-49 (cf. English version, *John Wycliffe and his English Precursors* [London, 1884]: 450-451). Commentary also in Hurley, "'Scriptura Sola': Wyclif and his Critics," 320-329; Margaret Aston, *Thomas Arundel. A Study of Church Life in the Reign of Richard II* (Oxford, 1967): 331-334. Woodford, foil now to a man long dead, could not let the matter rest, and produced after several more years a substantial *Tractatus contra errores Wyclefi in Trialogo*, printed in E. Brown's ed. of Ortuinus Gratius, *Fasciculus Rerum Expetendarum et Fugiendarum* I: 190-265 (on p. 190 the 18 articles; the *Tractatus* is an extended commentary on them).

In 1411, Arundel was still determined to aid Rome in the extirpation of Wyclyf's memory: the Oxford theologians sent him a compendium of some 267 heresies and errors drawn, often quite loosely (see above, **3**, n. 5) from a number of his works, including the *Trialogus* (= articles 121-140: Wilkins, *Concilia...* III: 344-345). This aspect of Arundel's life has been less thoroughly examined than it deserves to be. For some useful remarks, however, see W. A. Pantin, *Oxford Life in Oxford Archives* (Oxford, 1972): 70-72.

[11] Only the date is certain. Lechler (and, after him, Workman, *JW* I: 13n.) ventured both Basel and Froben. However there were a number of other printers active in Basel in the first quarter of the sixteenth century (fifteen were censured in the *Index* of 1559: Heinrich Reusch, *Die Indices Librorum Prohibitorum des Sechszehnten Jahrhunderts* [Tübingen, 1886]: 206-208). The editor has examined the copy in the Firestone Library at Princeton University. No really distinctive emblem or any traceable clue leaps to the eye. By way of negative evidence, we may observe that P. Heitz and C. C. Bernouilli, *Basler Büchermarken bis zum Anfang des 17. Jahrhunderts* (Strassburg, 1895) portray no analogous logotype. A fine undated catalog of H. P. Kraus, *The Cradle of Printing. From Mainz and Bamberg to Westminster and St. Albans. One Hundred Incunabula and Manuscripts Important for the Development of Early Printing*; and Lawrence C. Wroth, ed., *A History of the Printed Book* (The Dolphin 3: New York, 1938) are likewise of little help here. [A. F. Johnson and Victor Scholderer], *Short-Title Catalogue of Books Printed in the German-Speaking Countries and German Books printed in Other Countries from 1455 to 1600 now in the British Museum* (London, 1962): 913, write [P. Schoeffer: Worms] in their description of the BL copy. On Peter Schöffer (not to be confused with Gutenberg's associate and successor at Mainz), see Josef Benzing, *Buchdruckerlexikon des 16. Jahrhunderts*

(Deutsches Sprachgebiet) (Frankfurt/M., 1953): 187; he gives five printers besides Froben actually active in Basel in 1525, pp. 21-24. In any event, there are quite a number of glaring slips in this *editio princeps* which are difficult to reconcile with Froben's reputation for care and accuracy.

Sarton, *Introduction to the History of Science* III/2: 1347-1348, says it was edited by Otto Brunfels, "one of the fathers of the botanic renaissance," and a Reformation enthusiast; he cites the copy in the Boston Public Library. This ascription is also given in the catalog excerpt attached to the Princeton copy. On Brunfels, see Jerry Stannard, "Brunfels, Otto" in DSB II (1970): 535-538. The three-page preface, when carefully compared with Brunfels' known writings, may conceivably yield some stylistic parallels. It is quite possible that Brunfels may have edited it for Froben or some other Protestant printer. Surely it was this edition which was listed among a number of Luther's and other Reformers' tracts in London in 1529 (?): Reusch, *Die Indices Librorum Prohibitorum*, 6 (summarily described).

[12] The text bears this date. There was bound with it a biography of Wyclyf by Wirth, dated 1754; J. J. Vierling printed both.

[13] *Prologus*, p. 38 (Lechler ed.). Wyclyf's acquaintance with Greek was superficial at best: cf. **17**, p. 102; **23**, p. 19; **26**, p. 117; **36**, p. 1; **37**, p. 1; **61**, p. 43; **79**, p. 170; **420**, p. 101; etc. Wyclyf did come, nevertheless, to hold a high opinion of the sacramental and non-papal aspects of the Orthodox Church as he understood it: cf. **36**, p. 89; **48**, p. 446; **208**, p. 275; **408**, p. 91. It would be sheer speculation to state that he either reflected or influenced wider sentiments in Oxford in this matter; the last two decades of the fourteenth century saw little ecumenical progress in the Latin West. For a broad assessment of the impact of Byzantine culture on the Occident generally, see now Deno John Geanakoplos, *Interaction of the "Sibling" Byzantine and Western Cultures in the Middle Ages and Italian Renaissance (330-1600)* (New Haven and London, 1976): 55-94 and notes.

[14] Cf. his *Dialogus de contemptu mundi* (unpubl.; ref. S. H. Thomson, *The Writings of Robert Grosseteste*, 129-130). R. W. Hunt believed this may have been a version of a dialogue by Hugh of St. Victor, which appears in J. P. Migne, ed., *PL* 176: 703. "Lincolniensis" is cited several times in the *Trialogus* – but only by "Phronesis." The references might usefully be traced.

[15] There the disputants are "Iohannes" and "Ricardus": see **28-30**, n. 12, above.

[16] References in Lechler's indices, 457-465. There is a definitive edition of the *Sentences* underway: *Magistri Petri Lombardi Parisiensis Episcopi Sententiae in IV. Libris Distinctae* I/1: *Prolegomena*; I/2: *Liber I et II* (Spicilegium Bonaventuriana 4; Rome, 1971); the concluding *libri* are under the direction of Fr. Ignatius Brady.

[17] Slighting remarks on pp. 343 and 361.

[18] Cf. pp. 153, 361; also the whole tract *De solucione Sathane* (**435**), below.

[19] See the excellent overview by Gerhart B. Ladner, "*Homo Viator*: Medieval Ideas on Alienation and Order," *Speculum* 42 (1967): 233-259, especially p. 236, n. 14. *Piers Plowman* and the *Pilgrim's Progress* are other manifestations of this persistent image. For two virtually contemporary instances (almost surely known to Wyclyf), see Arnold Williams, "*Protectorium Pauperis*, a Defense of the Begging Friars by Richard of Maidstone, O.Carm. (d. 1396)," *Carmelus* 5 (1958): 151; and Uthred of Boldon's *Contra querelas fratrum* (ed. Marcett, *Uhtred de Boldon*, 29).

[20] Cf. pp. 128, 134-136, 138-139, 145, 159, 163-164, 171, 173, 175, 178, 181, 186, 188, 191, 194-195, 198, 204, 211-212, 236, 240, 246, 271, 282, 285, 296, 305, 325, 352-353, 357-359, 383, 397, 401; and, from the *De dotacione ecclesie* (**48**), 408, 456; *et frequenter alibi*.

[21] Pp. 339, 374, 376.

[22] P. 225: "ut suppono ex declaratis in tractatu de incarnacione" signifies **22**, pp. 13-28; p. 263: "Ideo misi alias satrapis in ista materia istas tres conclusiones..." appears roughly to fit the letters to the archbishop of Canterbury and the bishop of Lincoln (**395**, **396**: but the former must date from the spring of 1383 at the earliest); p. 289: "Ideo dixi quando fui iunior quod quantitas..." could refer to **26** or to any of several other treatises or sermons; p. 327: "Mihi autem videtur, ut explanavi diffusius..." clearly points to **44**; p. 330: "De contricione autem dixi in tercia parte sermonum LXIV..." puzzles until

we come upon an almost exact parallel passage in the *fourth* sermon of the third part (**179**), which on internal evidence seems quite late; p. 341: "Dixi alias in lingua multiplici, quomodo mendicacio est satis equivoca, sicut oracio.... Unde alias descripsi mendicacionem..." – the English allusion I cannot pin down, but the Latin was evidently **427**; p. 349: "Placet de illis dicere in latino, quod quondam expressi in anglico..." touches the so-called "letters of fraternity": these are discussed at greatest length in the English work *De blasphemia, contra fratres* (in Arnold, *Select English Works* III [1871]: 420-429); and there are other, incidental, mentions of this topic in three other, also late, works in Matthew, *The English Works of Wyclif Hitherto Unprinted*, 5, 7, 12, 27, 160, 262. But in favor of a somewhat earlier date of composition – which does not rule out later insertions – we read on p. 374: "videtur quod fratres generaliter pro anno Domini millesimo trecentesimo octogesimo secundo recenter et particulariter in suo concilio terremotus Londiniis intoxicaverunt regnum nostrum." Lechler believed the *Trialogus* was published in 1381 (clearly not possible!) or 1382 (p. 476), and Loserth concurred: *Johannes Wyclif Sermones* I (WS, 1887): xxxiv.

[23] Discussed below, **48** (especially n. 4); **49**.

48. A23. *De dotacione ecclesie* (*Supplementum Trialogi*). Late 1382.

I. Inc.: Utrum clerus debuit dotacionem, quam modo occupat, a dominis temporalibus recepisse ...

Expl.: × ... in isto maximo periculo pro dei adiutorio postulando.

II. MSS:

i	Wien, ÖNB	1338	ff. 82ra-99rb	ca. 1410	JW MS Boh.[1]
ii		1387	ff. 115ra-123rb	ca. 1410	JW MS Boh.[2]
iii		3929	ff. 170va-181vb	1409	JW MS Boh.
iv		4505	ff. 188r-207r	1439	Asc. Boh.[3]

III. Ed. Gotthard Lechler, *Joannis Wyclif Trialogus cum Supplemento Trialogi* (Oxford, 1869): 407-456. From all MSS.

IV. Although all of our MSS use the title *Supplementum Trialogi* at some point, and the usage is well established, only in one text (**iv**) does this piece actually follow the *Trialogus*. It is difficult to demonstrate that it was ever intended by Wyclyf as any kind of sequel or supplement to the latter work: it is cast in the form of a scholastic *quaestio*, not a dialogue; it relates only peripherally to the subject-matter of *liber* IV, cap. xvii (concluding) of the *Trialogus* (to all appearances, quite self-contained); and makes no reference at all to the larger work. The title *De dotacione ecclesie* does appear in at least one of the MSS in a contemporary hand (**i**, f. 82ra), and is much more revealing as to content; it is therefore preferred here.

Like the bulk of his compositions in the Lutterworth years, the present treatise is a broadside against the mendicants. In this instance, however, we come upon one of his clearest statements of motive (p. 447): "Si igitur iste due extremitates ecclesie malignancium, papa et fratres, fuerint emendate, tunc foret facilius medios errores corrigere, et statum ecclesie ad ordinacionem Christi pure secundum legem suam reducere, quod attendere desidero." His sturdy avowal of the separation of powers is prominent too, as we might expect (p. 427): "Unde principes seculi debent regna sua a spoliacione huius diaboli [i.e., the pope] potenter defendere, et clericos titulo huius Antichristi promotos prudenter expellere, et nullo modo expensis laboribus vel favore fovere talem diabolum vel iuvare."

It is possible to fix the date of the *De dotacione ecclesie* with some precision, from an indication on p. 449 that Pope Urban had issued his call to arms against Clement, and that the friars were active in this endeavor: the very end of 1382.[4] A few months after this time, Bishop Henry Despenser of Norwich stormed into Flanders at the head of one of the most poorly-coordinated and impulsive of England's Continental misadventures, and Wyclyf would make this sorry débâcle the centerpiece of several of his last writings.

The issue of endowment remained touchy for decades: in 1401, the redoubtable Oxonian Richard Ullerston fired off a *Defensorium dotacionis ecclesie* against the Lollards.[5] Henry VIII, of course, rendered further deliberation nugatory in 1536.

VC: 3933[6] 3935[7] 4514[8]   Bale: 61, 95[9]   Sh: 17   Lo: 18

[1] Marginalia by Peter Payne.
[2] Ibid.
[3] Wilkins, *Concilia...* III: 348, gives articles 225-238 as suspect propositions in 1411, from the "De dotacione Cesarea."
[4] Walsingham, Knighton, the *Chronicon Anglie*, and other narratives tell the story; modern accounts are scarce, but see George M. Wrong, *The Crusade of MCCCLXXXIII., known as that of the Bishop of Norwich* (London, 1892); Gerhard Skalweit, *Der Kreuzzug des Bischofs Heinrich von Norwich im Jahre 1383* (Königsberg, 1898; thorough review of sources, 74-83); É. Perroy, *L'Angleterre et le grand Schisme d'Occident. Étude sur la politique religieuse de l'Angleterre sous Richard II (1378-1399)* (Paris, 1933): 166-209; R. A. Edwards, "Henry Despenser: The Fighting Bishop," *The Church Quarterly Review* 159 (1958): 26-38 (very elementary); Lunt, *Financial Relations*, 535-543.
[5] Unpublished: MSS are London, BL Lansdowne 409, ff. 39r-69v; Berlin-Dahlem, Stiftung Preussischer Kulturbesitz, Theol. Fol. 580, ff. 375r-401v (cf. Eric Doyle, "William Woodford's 'De dominio civili clericorum' against John Wyclif," 53, 62). On Ullerston, see *BRUO* III: 1928-1929.
[6] Identified as "Supplementum trialogi id est de dotacione ecclesie et debet stare inmediate post trialogum."
[7] Proper incipit attributed to preceding title; reference garbled.
[8] "De dotacione ecclesie seu supplementum trialogi." Gives correct incipit and explicit – followed, however, by incipit and explicit for **27**.
[9] A separate listing for each of our two titles; no. 61 has the proper incipit.

49. A24. *De fide catholica* [*De ecclesia (Tractatus minor)*]. Mid-1383.

1. Inc.: Suppositis dictis de fide tam in symbolo apostolorum quam in symbolo ecclesie [10 wds.] notandus videtur secundus articulus ...
   Expl.: × ... nec possunt confederacionem Christi et diaboli stabilire.

II. MSS:

i	Brno, UK	Mk II.44 (62)	ff. 241v-252v	xv/m	Unasc. Boh.[1]
ii	London, Lambeth Pal.	1058	pp. 1-23	xvii/2	Asc. Eng.[2]
iii	Praha, UK	III.G.11 (536)	ff. 238v-250r	xv/1	JW MS Boh.
iv		IV.H.7 (771)	ff. 49r-55v	ca. 1410	JW MS Boh.[3]
v		V.F.9 (931)	ff. 112r-122v	1408	JW MS Boh.
vi	Wien, ÖNB	1337	ff. 150va-161ra	ca. 1410	JW MS Boh.
vii		3927	ff. 43ra-49vb	ca. 1410	JW MS Boh.
viii		3930	ff. 221ra-230ra	1412	Asc. Boh.[4]
ix		4527	ff. 110v-120v	1410	JW MS Boh.[5]

III. Ed. J. Loserth, *Johannis Wyclif Opera Minora* (WS, 1913): 98-128.† From all MSS except **i** and **ii**.

IV. This telescoped compendium of Wyclyf's ecclesiology appears in several copies under the alternative title of *De ecclesia*. Loserth emphasized in his introduction (pp. xviii-xx) the close relation of this shorter work to the *De ecclesia* (**32**) which is part of the *Summa theologie*. His demonstration does not convince: Wyclyf never cites the earlier treatment at any point, and such random parallelism of argumentation or even of wording as does occur can easily be explained by recalling that the nature of the church and its hierarchical manifestations here below formed part of his intellectual stock in trade over many years. In fact, besides predestination and disendowment – the old themes – we encounter considerable discussion of newer topics as well: the Eucharist and the crusade in Flanders, both of which evoke the usual diatribes against the friars. It is interesting, however, that he bases his opposition to the Urbanist warmongering on a relatively well-structured Scriptural commentary: 1 Co 13:4-8, Paul's powerful descant on the nature of *caritas*.[6]

His citation of the *Trialogus* (**47**: p. 116) is his only reference to his own writings, and urges Loserth's date of summer 1383, or perhaps even a few months later.

VC: 3933 3935 4514[7]   Bale: 3[8]   Sh: 13   Lo: 14

---

[1] First noticed by Jan Sedlák, *Studie a Texty k náboženským dějinám českým* I: *Studie a texty k životopisu husovu* (Olomouc, 1914): p. XVII (interleaved). His variant readings from this MS appear on pp. XVII-XIX; none seriously affect the meaning. (Item overlooked in V. Dokoupil, *Soupis Rukopisů Mikulovní Dietrichsteinské Knihovny* [Praha, 1958]; his personal helpfulness to the editor is gratefully acknowledged.)

[2] Loserth elected not to use this MS in his edition because of its late date (1692?); he furthermore misidentifies it as MS 1038. It is entitled *De Ecclesia Confessio Johannis Wickleff*. At several points the copyist left lacunae, and the text breaks off at "similiter nullus fidelis vel ethnicus..." = p. 108, line 26 in Loserth ed. Was there an English exemplar?

[3] Capp. i-iv and part of v are lacking. It begins abruptly "Papa Iohannes XXIIus dicitur dampnasse ..." (p. 113).

[4] Entitled *De Ecclesia*.

[5] Ibid.

[6] The theme recurs many times in Wyclyf's writings; other commentaries on this specific Epistolary passage will be found in **47**: pp. 134, 137, 413, 428; **141**: p. 198; **148**: pp. 244-247; **180**: p. 32; **187**: p. 92; **193**: p. 142; **238**: p. 36; **246**: p. 98; **255**: p. 180; **265**: p. 266; **376**: p. 196; **408**: p. 28; and **431**: p. 460.
[7] Correct incipit and explicit followed by those for **17**, though not so specified.
[8] Title given as *De ecclesia et membris*.

50. A25. *De septem donis spiritus sancti.* Late 1383.

I. Inc.: Cum spiritus sit tercia persona trinitatis ...
   Expl.: × ... illarum errorem multipliciter prophetavit.

II. MSS:

i	Praha, UK	III.G.11 (536)	ff. 154r-160v	xv/1	JW MS Boh.
		V.F.9 *(931)*	f. 130v	1408	Boh.[1]
ii		X.E.9 (1910)	ff. 132r-136v	ca. 1420	JW MS Boh.[2]
iii	Wien, ÖNB	1337	ff. 104vb-110ra	ca. 1410	JW MS Boh.
iv		3929	ff. 208vb-212ra	1409	JW MS Boh.
v		3930	ff. 300ra-303vb	1412	JW MS Boh.
vi		3933	ff. 76vb-80vb	ca. 1415	Asc. Boh.
vii		4515	ff. 204v-207v, 210r-212ra	ca. 1420	JW MS Boh.[3]
viii		4527	ff. 157v-162r	1410	JW MS Boh.[4]

III. Ed. R. Buddensieg, *John Wiclif's Polemical Works in Latin* I (WS, 1883): 208-230. From all MSS.

IV. This is one of the best-organized of Wyclyf's shorter tracts. Taking for his text Is 11:2,[5] he examines each of the seven "gifts" (sapientia, intellectus, spiritus consilii, animi fortitudo, scientia, pietas, timor domini) in turn, urging them upon the "viator" or "fidelis" of the "sect or order of Christ." As might be anticipated, he insists that the "novelli ordines" (monks) and the "four sects" generally (priests, monks, canons and friars)[6] are not only utterly bereft of these gifts, but even by their actions uphold their opposites, diabolical instruments that they are. He advocates their peremptory dissolution, which would indeed be "to their profit and that of the whole church militant; nonetheless I do not agree that any individual should be killed, unless I should happen to have a divine revelation" (p. 225) – a rare touch of humor?[7] More than a hint of violence on the other side surfaces two pages later, when he mentions an assassination attempt against the Duke of Lancaster, his erstwhile patron. Buddensieg could not place this, and almost a century after him the reference still eludes verification[8] – but a chronological fix on the incident, obviously, would materially aid in dating the *De septem donis* more exactly. For now, we must like Buddensieg pick Wyclyf's allusion to the *De fundacione sectarum* (**431**) in the concluding sentence as our benchmark, and assign this piece to late 1383.

VC: 3933[9] 3935[10] 4514[11] 7980   Bale: 232   Sh: 27   Lo: 28

¹ Title given, followed by a simple listing of the seven "gifts."
² The treatise begins on f. 132r, then begins again on the verso.
³ See Buddensieg's n. 32, p. 230, on the ending of the text in this MS.
⁴ Marginalia by Peter Payne.
⁵ There is a listing of *nine* gifts in 1 Co 12:7-10; see below, **219**.
⁶ See above, **46**, n. 2; cf. also **429**, *et frequenter alibi*. Of some value here is V. F. Janssen, "Die Four Sects und die Sect of Crist bei Wiclif," *Zeitschrift für Kirchengeschichte* 3rd ser., 56 (1937): 354-360 (based chiefly on Arnold, *Select English Works*, II).
⁷ But see a similar remark in **71**: p. 118.
⁸ In the spring of 1384, during the Salisbury Parliament, an Irish Carmelite friar, John Latemar, disclosed the details of a conspiracy against Richard II which he averred to have been orchestrated by the Duke himself – but he soon died in the royal torture chamber, refusing to implicate others. The Duke's own registers (at least those that survive) are empty between October of 1383 and April of 1387, and are not in any case the sort of document likely to illuminate the problem: E. C. Lodge and R. Somerville, edd., *John of Gaunt's Register 1379-1383* (Camden Society, 3rd ser., 56-57: London, 1937).
⁹ Expl.: "... multipliciter prophetat."
¹⁰ Ibid.
¹¹ Ibid.

51. A26. [*Differencia inter peccatum mortale et veniale*]. Late 1376.

I. Inc.: Restat nunc [promissa] discutere differenciam inter peccatum veniale et mortale ...

Expl.: × ... quando sine discrimine nesciuntur.

II. MSS:

i	Praha, MK	A.70 (116)	ff. 275v-276v	ca. 1410	Unasc. Boh.
ii		C.38 (462)	ff. 182va-183rb	ca. 1410	Asc. Boh.
iii	UK	V.E.17 (911)	ff. 180r-183v	ca. 1410	Unasc. Boh.

III. Ed. J. Loserth and F. D. Matthew, *Johannis Wyclif Tractatus de Mandatis Divinis accedit Tractatus de Statu Innocencie* (WS, 1922): 527-532. From all MSS.

IV. Wyclyf, it appears, seldom resisted the temptation to dilate upon a subject once broached, leaving no stone unturned in his continuing quest for refinement and amplification. The subject of the present *tractatulus* is no exception; our major task is to establish some clear lines of filiation in the development of his argument. In *liber* III, capp. v-vi, of the *Trialogus* (**47**: pp. 144-150) and again in one of the *Sermones* (**198**: pp. 179-184),¹ the topic of the present work is treated at length, but in quite a different fashion. Loserth pointed out in his introduction (pp. xxix-xxx) that Wyclyf mentioned the *Differencia* three times in the sermon (pp. 180, 181); the priority of the *Differencia* vis-à-vis the sermon is therefore self-evident.

But to return to the *Trialogus*: on p. 148 Wyclyf (as "Phronesis") dismisses a cavil of "Pseustis" by retorting: "Ad terciam instanciam tollebam eam diffuse, quando fui logicus ....," which leads us back into his Oxford years. In cap. xviii of the *De veritate sacre scripture* (**31**: vol. II: 96) we read: "Unde correspondenter dicendum est de distinccione mendaciorum mortalium et venialium, sicut dictum est libro quinto capitulo de distinccione gravedinis peccatorum...." And finally, by this circuitous route, we arrive at the *De civili dominio* III (**30**: vol. IV: 512-518), where the entire text of the present work will be found almost verbatim ! Cap. xxiv begins "Ulterius restat iuxta promissa discutere differenciam inter peccatum ..." and our explicit comes only about one-eighth of the way into the cap. Along the way a few of Wyclyf's references to Augustine, obscure in the *De civili dominio*, are given more precisely in the *Differencia*. It is strange that Loserth, who edited both, should have missed the connection: the incipit itself, as well as the complete absence of any mention of the friars, ought to have alerted him. We list it here as a separate, acephalous piece only because of its distinct MS tradition and its inclusion in all three of the early vc.[2] (See **28-30**, n. 5, on the Durham MS.)

VC: 3933 3935 4514   Bale: deest   Sh: 28   Lo: 29

[1] The English version of this sermon, "On Passioun Sondai Pistle" (Arnold, *Select English Works* II: 280-281), does not contain this material.

[2] The reference to Empedocles (p. 528, line 10), missing from the *De civili dominio* text, seems superficial at first glance. But in the *De intelleccione dei* (**14**: p. 87, line 33), Wyclyf does demonstrate a familiarity with an Empedoclean fragment in the *Physics* of Aristotle (= B8, 198b29) – see G. S. Kirk and J. E. Raven, *The Presocratic Philosophers* (Cambridge, Eng., 1969): 337; and, for extended commentary on the central problems in dealing with the fragments, the two essays by A. A. Long and C. H. Kahn in Alexander P. D. Mourelatos, ed., *The Pre-Socratics: A Collection of Critical Essays* (Garden City, N.Y., 1974): 397-456. The most exhaustive compendium remains, however, Hermann Diels, *Die Fragmente der Vorsokratiker* I (6th ed. by Walther Kranz: Berlin, 1951): 276-374.

Wyclyf may have known the *Physics* in the translation of Michael Scot, though the earlier version of James of Venice remains a possibility: cf. Lohr, "Commentaries ... Johannis de Kanthi-Myngodus," 347-350 (on Michael Scot cf. also **4**, n. 2, above); but idem, "Commentaries ... Jacobus-Johannes Juff," 149, does not mention the *Physics* by James of Venice: for this see L. Minio-Paluello, "Iacobus Veneticus Grecus, Canonist and Translator of Aristotle," *Traditio* 8 (1952): 265-295. (For Wyclyf's own *Dubia* on the *Physics*, see **6**, n. 7, above.)

Empedocles also merited mention in Burley's *De vita et moribus philosophorum*, a compendium much copied on the Continent, but little known in England before the turn of the fifteenth century. See John O. Stigall, "The Manuscript Tradition of the *De Vita et Moribus Philosophorum* of Walter Burley," *MetH* 11 (1957): 44-57; Cora E. Lutz, "Walter Burley's *De Vita et Moribus Philosophorum*," in her *Essays on Manuscripts and Rare Books* (Hamden, Conn., 1975): 50-56. (There is now an edition and translation by Paul Theiner, *Walter Burley. On the Lives and Characters of the Philosophers* [New York, 1982].) It also happens that Burley's section on Empedocles was adopted verbatim in Lucas Brandeis' popular *Rudimentum Novitiorum* (1475): Curt F. Bühler, "Greek Philosophers in the Literature of the Later Middle Ages," *Speculum* 12 (1937): 441. Burley himself wrote no fewer than five commentaries on the *Physics*: see above, **6**, n. 7; and on Burley generally, **4**, n. 5. – Of course the possibility cannot be excluded that Wyclyf might have encountered Empedocles in another commentary.

52. A27. *De peccato in spiritum sanctum*. Early 1377 ?

1. Inc.: Nemo peccat in spiritum sanctum ad sensum evangelii ...
   Expl.: × ... ut prescitos ecclesiam cuiusmodi sunt prelati.

II. MSS:

i	Praha, MK	D.123 (693)	f. 150r	xv/1	JW MS Boh.
ii		*O.29 (1613)*	f. 228r	ca. 1430	Unasc. Boh.
iii	UK	V.F.17 (939)	f. 213r-v	1412	JW MS Boh.[1]
iv	Wien, ÖNB	1337	f. 53va-b	ca. 1410	JW MS Boh.
v		1387	f. 107ra	ca. 1410	JW MS Boh.
vi		3929	f. 208rb-va	1409	JW MS Boh.
vii		4527	f. 146r-v	1410	JW MS Boh.

III. Ed. J. Loserth, *Johannis Wyclif Opera Minora* (WS, 1913): 11-12.† From all MSS except **i** and **ii**.

IV. The theme of this short work is simple and direct: many of the "Caesarean clergy" in England are devils, foreknown to damnation, divorced from the true church. As to a final determination of the proper place of the *De peccato* in the Wyclyf canon, that is far less easily resolved. Although grouped by both Shirley and Loserth among the *Epistolae*, and indeed so appearing in several MSS, it shows no trace of epistolary form or intent – Loserth even admits as much in his introduction, p. VI. It seems rather to represent Wyclyf's position in a kind of truncated scholastic *dubium*. His one Scriptural citation, to Jn 6:71, appears also in several of his other works.[2] His paraphrase from Augustine's sixteenth homily on John, however, leads us in an interesting direction. It will be recalled that we have just established the identity of **51** with the first part of cap. xxiv of *liber* III of the *De civili dominio*. There likewise (p. 516) he mentions Augustine's *twelfth* homily on John; and on p. 514 we read "Sed hii ... dicunt quod omne peccatum *preter peccatum in spiritum sanctum* est veniale ..." (my emphasis). Now not only the remainder of cap. xxiv, but all of the two following capp., extending to p. 626, deal with the topic of sin – yet nowhere is this gravest of all sins addressed. Is it not conceivable that Wyclyf meant to remedy this omission shortly after the completion of the *De civili dominio* (i.e., 1376), while still *in scholis*, and before his break with the mendicants? The tone of his censure against the "prelati cesarii" is not at all incompatible with such a supposition: cf. *De civili dominio*, vol. III: pp. 497, 532, etc. *De peccato* thus recommends itself most persuasively as a slightly later insertion into the larger work, though it has not come down to us that way in MS.

VC: 3933 3935 4514 7980[3]   Bale: deest   Sh: 61.6   Lo: 62.7

---

[1] This MS gives the title *Sequitur dubium contra cavillantes quod presciti sunt ecclesia* (see Loserth's n. to line 6); this would appear to strengthen our suspicion that the piece was in its original form a *dubium*.

[2] E.g., **431**: p. 16; **377**: pp. 315, 322; **34**: p. 216.

[3] All four VC give *De eo qui in spiritum sanctum peccat* (*peccavit*); but there is little support for this more prolix title in the MSS themselves.

Section B

Pastoralia
Sermons, Commentaries and Practical Theology

With his foundations in philosophy securely laid, and with a theological superstructure rapidly taking form by 1375, Wyclyf felt confident in a new, aggressive application of both philosophy and theology to the daily life of the church militant. Through all his mature works there runs a visible awareness that the Gospel – the *lex* or *doctrina Christi* – only lightly, and often better not at all, adorned by the embellishments of post-patristic commentary – must be communicated to the people, to his *fideles* and *viatores*, in all its essential vigor and vitality.[1] The ministry of the pulpit therefore extended far beyond the narrow calling of the scholar's podium.

There are few churchmen of the later Middle Ages who could match the sheer mass of Wyclyf's own preaching: in Latin for the literate clergy and the scholar, in the terse vernacular of the day for the townsmen and the whole fair field of country folk.[2] Nor is it without significance that whereas the mendicants, and above all the Franciscans, had given such a great impetus to the whole *genre* of sermon-literature in the thirteenth century,[3] by the waning decades of the fourteenth Wyclyf's own reforming urge drove him to upbraid the friars who shared those years with him for their vicious abuses of the pastoral imperative. The Poor Priests (*simplices sacerdotes*, to use perhaps his most frequent designation) whom he may have encouraged as early as 1374 were those he believed most suited outside the schools to carry an unvarnished *evangelium* to those presumably most ripe for it: the poor, the wretched, and the discontent. Just exactly those who had experienced most abrasively the arrogance and the manipulation of the hierarchy were, in his view, the ones who stood most immediately to benefit from the comforting message he found for them in Christ's counsels.[4] It is all very well to insist that John Wyclyf the man was not above hypocrisy, bitterness, obscurantism or invidious raillery; yet to omit from any summary judgment his earnest compassion and fine sense of justice, which suffuse so many of his writings if we will but look for them, is to miss a fundamental reason for the enduring magic of his name among both the Lollards and the Hussites.

Although the pieces in this section cannot yet – and may never – be fixed along a sure chronological continuum, some modification of the sequence in which they are listed in Shirley and Loserth has been necessary. Particularly is this true of our first title below, the *De officio pastorali*, which Wyclyf himself intended should serve as a kind of vademecum, and in which most of his themes pertaining to the *cura spiritualis* are articulated.

---

[1] See, e.g., the *Speculum secularium dominorum* (**409**: p. 76): "Constat quidem ex fide, quod nihil vivacius nutrit ecclesiam quam predicacio verbi dei."

² Sometimes Wyclyf himself did not observe this trite distinction: see Loserth's introduction to the *Sermones super evangelia dominicalia* (B2.I: p. IX); and pp. 9, 72, and 73 of the *Opera Minora* edition.
 A valuable observation from a somewhat different perspective appears in Peter Auksi, "Wyclif's Sermons and the Plain Style," *Archiv für Reformationsgeschichte* 66 (1975): 6: "His hold on our attention stems from the ability of his Latin sermons to illustrate how the Christian reinterpretation of classical rhetorical theory offered by St. Augustine among others, was kept alive and indeed extended by a program of startlingly comprehensive religious reform, before it resurfaced, fully formed, in the seminal work of William Perkins and Richard Baxter." On the English sermons, see below, B2, n. 1.
 ³ Especially evident in the various *libri exemplorum* that have come down to us: Andrew G. Little, *Liber Exemplorum ad usum Praedicantium saeculo XIII compositus a quodam Fratre Minore anglico de Provincia Hiberniae* (British Society of Franciscan Studies 1: Aberdeen, 1908); J. T. Welter, "Un recueil d'exempla du XIIIe siècle," *Études franciscaines* 30 (1913): 646-665; 31 (1914): 194-213, 312-320; idem, "Un nouveau recueil ....," ibid., 42 (1930): 432-476, 595-625; Livario Oliger, "Liber Exemplorum Fratrum Minorum saeculi XIII (excerpta e cod. Ottob. Lat. 522)," *Antonianum* 2 (1927): 203-274; S. L. Forte, "A Cambridge Dominican Collectio of Exempla in the Thirteenth Century," *Archivum Fratrum Praedicatorum* 28 (1958): 115-148. One of the most encyclopedic of the treatises dealing with the methodology of preaching (*artes praedicandi*) was drawn up by the Dominican Master-General, Humbert de Romans (d. 1263); the *De eruditione predicatorum*, ed. M. de La Bigne, *Maxima Bibliotheca Veterum Patrum et Antiquorum Scriptorum Ecclesiasticorum* XXV (Lyon, 1677): 424-567. On the *artes praedicandi* generally, see Harry Caplan, *Mediaeval* Artes Praedicandi. *A Hand-List* (Cornell Studies in Classical Philology 24; Ithaca, 1934); idem, *Mediaeval* Artes Praedicandi. *A Supplementary Hand-List* (Cornell Studies ... 25: Ithaca, 1936); T.-M. Charland, *Artes Praedicandi. Contribution à l'histoire de la rhétorique au Moyen Âge* (Publications de l'Institut d'Études médiévales d'Ottawa 7: 1936). See also Lucy T. Smith, "English Popular Preaching in the Fourteenth Century," *EHR* 7 (1892): 25-36; Hans G. Pfander, *The Popular Sermon of the Medieval Friar in England* (privately printed Ph.D. dissertation, New York University, 1937); Peter C. Erb, "Vernacular Material for Preaching in MS Cambridge University Library Ii.III.8," *MedSt* 33 (1971): 63-84; Beryl Smalley, "Oxford University Sermons 1290-1293," in J. J. G. Alexander and M. T. Gibson, edd., *Medieval Learning and Literature. Essays presented to Richard William Hunt* (Oxford, 1976): 307-327; D. L. D'Avray, "Sermons to the Upper Bourgeoisie by a Thirteenth-Century Franciscan" (i.e., Guibert de Tournai), in Derek Baker, ed., *The Church in Town and Countryside* (SCH 16: Oxford, 1979): 187-199; Janet Coleman, *Medieval Readers and Writers* (London and New York, 1981): 204-231.
 By far the most exhaustive survey of the entire field now, and of enormous value in its identification of sermon MSS, is Johann B. Schneyer, *Repertorium der lateinischen Sermones des Mittelalters für die Zeit 1150-1350* (8 vols.: Münster-in-Westfalen, 1969-1978) – preceded by his *Die Unterweisung der Gemeinde über die Predigt bei scholastischen Predigern. Eine Homiletik aus scholastischen Prothemen* (München, 1968). But still of great value for our period are the two classic studies by G. R. Owst, *Preaching in Medieval England* (Cambridge, Eng., 1926), and *Literature and Pulpit in Medieval England* (Cambridge, Eng., 1933; reprinted 1961).
 ⁴ The actual identity of the poor Priests remains elusive; see above, **38**, n. 10, and below, introduction to Section F.

53. B1. *De officio pastorali.* Early 1379.

    1. Inc. pars I: Cum duplex debet esse officium Christiani ...
        Expl. pars I: × ...et sic sunt mundo dediti tanquam speciales filii Antichristi.
        Inc. pars II: Tacto superficialiter de prima parte sacerdotalis officii [8 wds.],
            restat videre de secunda parte pertinencie pastoris ...
        Expl. pars II: × ... et Christi nostri domini regis regum.

II. MSS:

i	Brno, UK	Mk II.44 (62)	ff. 253r-276v	xv/m[1]	Asc. Boh.
ii	Cambridge, Corpus Christi Coll.	436	ff. 97r-135r	ca. 1400	Unasc. Eng.
iii	Olomouc, Státní vědecká Knihovna	I.V.34	ff. 26r-48v	1411	Unasc. Boh.[2]
iv	Praha, MK	F.20 (866)	ff. 136r-155v	xv/1	Asc. Boh.
v	UK	III.G.11 (536)	ff. 1r-27v	xv/1	Asc. Boh.
vi		V.F.9 (931)	ff. 131r-147r	1408	JW MS Boh.[3]
vii		X.C.23 (1876)	ff. 183ra-194ra	1410	JW MS Boh.
viii		X.E.9 (1910)	ff. 37r-67r	ca. 1420	Asc. Boh.[4]
ix		X.H.17 (1995)	ff. 37r-57r	ca. 1410	Unasc. Boh.
x		XII.F.21 (2359)	ff. 35r-61v	ca. 1410	Unasc. Boh.
xi	Wien, ÖNB	1337	ff. 1ra-20vb	ca. 1410	JW MS Boh.[5]
xii		3933	ff. 101va-117ra	ca. 1415	JW MS Boh.
xiii		4302	ff. 53v-74r	xv/m	Asc. Boh.
xiv		4302	ff. 133r-156v	1410	Asc. Boh.
xv		4522	ff. 109r-131v	1423	JW MS Boh.
xvi		4527	ff. 209v-226ra	1410	JW MS Boh.[6]
xvii		4536	ff. 67v-96v	xv/1	Asc. Boh.[7]
xviii	Wolfenbüttel, HzglB	Cod.Guelf. 1126 (1223)	ff. 1r-46r	xv/1	Unasc. Ger.[8]

III. Ed. Gotthard Lechler, *Johannis de Wiclif Tractatus de Officio Pastorali* (Leipzig, 1863). From **x** only. Trans. of some sections in M. Spinka, ed., *Advocates of Reform* (Library of Christian Classics 14: Philadelphia, 1953): 32-60.

IV. This treatise, divided into two parts of 19 and 12 capp. respectively, sets forth Wyclyf's views on the proper character and doctrine of the curate. The former constitutes the theme of the first part, and is summarized at the outset (p. 7): "Debet enim esse sanctus, in omni genere virtutum adeo confirmatus, ut pocius omnia genera confederacionis humane, omnia mundi temporalia, eciam vitam mortalem deseret, antequam a veritate Christi culpabiliter declinaret." The latter is the point of departure for the second part, and is epitomized on p. 31: "pastor habet triplex officium: primo verbo dei pascere spiritualiter oves suas, ac si per pascua semper virencia ad beatitudinem patrie initiarentur. Secundum officium pastorale est purgare prudenter oves suas a scabie, ne sese et alias magis inficiant. Et tercium est, pastorem defendere oves suas a lupis rapacibus tam sensibilibus quam insensibilibus. Et utrobique precipuum officium pastoris videtur seminare suis ovibus verbum dei." The "four sects" are interjected several times, and in capp. iv and v of the second part the friars come in for their share of sharp criticism – but there is nowhere any hint of the Eucharistic controversy.

In his preface, Lechler suggested a date between 1367 and 1378 (pp. 3-5); of course at the time of his edition no other work of Wyclyf's, save only two minor pieces on the Eucharist (**39, 41**) and the *Trialogus* (**47**) were in print, and the yeoman labors of the Wyclif Society were still almost a generation in the future;

so any more precise estimate would then have been premature. We are today in a much better position to assign a reasonably firm date of composition. On an aspect of secular dominion, he remarks (p. 9): "... ut patet in tractatu de servis...." This is evidently the *De servitute civili et dominio seculari* (**405**), which we place in 1378; that year is therefore a reliable *terminus a quo*. For an equally firm *terminus ante quem*, we may cite the *De officio regis* (**33**), p. 163: "Patet ista lex ex lege priori et ex dictis libro [sic] vi° De pastorali officio." That part of the *Summa theologie*, as we have seen, dates from the summer of 1379; the reference corresponds to pp. 13-14 of Lechler's edition. Because of his budding antipathy here toward the mendicant "pseudofratres," the spring of 1379 seems the most likely date for this piece.[9]

vc: 3933 3935 4514 7980   Bale: 99   Sh: 41   Lo: 47

[1] Codex dated 1494, f. 33v; almost surely an error for 1444: see f. 210r.
[2] First remarked in Buddensieg's edition of the *Polemical Works* I: lvii. He stigmatized it as an inferior text (not, however, from the paleographical standpoint; it is easily legible); but it is nonetheless surprising that Loserth, who added several mss to Shirley's listing, should have overlooked this one. Inc.: Cum triplex debet esse ...
[3] Capitular index follows, ff. 147v-148r.
[4] *Registrum*, ff. 67r-68v.
[5] The sole ms used in Lechler's edition. Obviously a close examination of the other codd. would clear up most of his lacunae and uncertain readings.
[6] *Registrum*, f. 226ra-vb.
[7] *Registrum*, ff. 96v-98r.
[8] Annotated by Matthias Flacius Illyricus (see above, **36**, n. 8). First correctly asc. to Wyclyf by Kühn-Steinhausen, "Wyclif-Handschriften in Deutschland," 625.
[9] If not a later interpolation, this may in fact be the earliest use of this term in Wyclyf's polemical lexicon. He also employs the term "viator" a number of times (pp. 8, 10, 20, 21, 33, 34, 43-45) – a stylistic hallmark of his later years (cf. **47**, nn. 19, 20). An interesting suggestion of what we might construe as a growing discontent with the Oxford scene appears on p. 45: "Utrum autem dampnati sint obligati deo per suam dampnacionem perpetuam et viatores propter quamcunque penam quam infert ex sua iusticia, est apud scolasticos difficultas. Sed tales difficultates non multum apprecior, sed contempno." Does this alienation perhaps reflect his still-recent "conversion"? (See **19**, above.)

54-299. B2. *Sermones*. 1375-1383.

The quadripartite arrangement of the *Sermones* in Loserth's fine four-volume edition – reproducing the structure which Wyclyf himself finally imposed on this disparate mass of homiletic material – has been preserved in this *Catalog* as well. Commentary on dating, content and format appears where appropriate in the individual sermon listings below. The Vulgate citations are abbreviated (though it is they which are usually rubricated in several of the mss; our incipits are often difficult to distinguish). Certain shorthand designations employed here to minimize redundancy are as follows:

C = Cambridge, Trinity Coll. B.16.2, xiv/ex, the only complete text, wanting only **54** and **299**, of all four collections of *Sermones*; it is the basis of Loserth's edition.
D = Dublin, Trinity Coll. C.1.23, xiv/2, containing portions of B2.III and B2.IV. (Neither of these English MSS is ascribed, though the sermons appear in exclusively Wyclyfite *contenta*.)
W = Wien, ÖNB (several MSS).
PUK and PMK = respectively, Praha, Universitní Knihovna and Metropolitní Knihovna; several MSS.
Wo = Wolfenbüttel, HzglB, Cod.Guelf. (catalog designations omitted).

Particulars of the MSS in question are given *in extenso* only at the outset of B2.I, II, III or IV; thereafter only the foliation (and sometimes textual peculiarities) are remarked. Finally, L, followed by page numbers, and with another number beneath (= his numbering sequence) points to Loserth's edition; and A = Arnold, *Select English Works*, followed by volume number (I-III) and pages of his edition of an English sermon corresponding to the Latin text (but never exactly, and often with major omissions).[1]

Wyclyf did not always, it seems, observe the lectionary requirements of the Sarum Missal. The basic references here are F. H. Dickinson, ed., *Missale ad Usum insignis et praeclarae ecclesiae Sarum* (Burntisland, 1861-1883); J. Wickham Legg, *The Sarum Missal, edited from Three Early Manuscripts* (Oxford, 1916); and Walter Howard Frere, *The Use of Sarum* (2 vols.: Cambridge, Eng., 1898, 1901).[2] But this is indeed a thorny thicket.

We have assigned specific dates to individual sermons only when clearly warranted by internal evidence; this is most often the case with the so-called *sermones quadraginta* (**257-296**).

---

[1] We do not wish here either to defend or to oppose the thesis that Wyclyf himself bore any responsibility for the present form and appearance of the English sermons. Useful literature includes E. W. Talbert, "The Date of the Composition of the English Wyclyfite Collection of Sermons," *Speculum* 12 (1937): 464-474; Margaret W. Ransom, "The Chronology of Wyclif's English Sermons," *Research Studies of the State College of Washington* 16 (1948): 67-114 – both essentially superseded by Anne Hudson, "A Lollard Sermon-Cycle and its Implications," *Medium Ævum* 40 (1971): 142-156. See the Preface, above, for further remarks on the whole question of Wyclyf's English *corpus*.

[2] A staunch critic of Wyclyf's, who yet on occasion saw the same evils in the *ecclesia militans* as he did, was Bishop Thomas Brinton of Rochester (1373-1389): see Mary A. Devlin, "Bishop Thomas Brunton and his Sermons," *Speculum* 14 (1939): 324-344, and her edition of the sermons, as cited in William J. Brandt, "Remarks on Bishop Thomas Brinton's authorship of the Sermons in MS Harley 3760," *MedSt* 21 (1959): 291n.; article continues to p. 296.

54-114. B2.I. *Sermones super evangelia dominicalia*. 1381-1382.

1. Inc.: Cum deus undiquaque plenus abhorret vacuum ...
   Expl.: × ... ut in febre ethica est sua inanicio impercepta.

II. MSS:

i	C		ff. 142ra-184rb	xiv/ex	JW MS Eng.[1]
ii	W	3928	ff. 131va-139ra	ca. 1410	JW MS Boh.
iii		3931	ff. 145vb-153vb	ca. 1410	JW MS Boh.
iv		3934	ff. 1ra-132vb	xv/1	Asc. Boh.
v		4529	ff. 1r-165r	ca. 1420	Asc. Boh.
vi	Wo	565 (*613*)	ff. 1ra-109vb	xv/1	JW MS Boh.[2]

III. Ed. J. Loserth, *Iohannis Wyclif Sermones* I: *Super Evangelia Dominicalia* (WS, 1887). From all MSS except **vi**.

IV. (See commentary on individual sermons below.)

VC: 3933 3935 4514 7980   Bale: 10? 13?   Sh: 33   Lo: 34

[1] The ink foliation observed by Loserth; there are also an occasional pencil foliation (which includes excised folios throughout) and a running pencil pagination.

[2] First noticed in Kühn-Steinhausen, "Wyclif-Handschriften in Deutschland," 626-627; she corrects Heinemann's catalog of the collection.

54. B2.I.pref. *Prefacio*.

Cum deus undiquaque plenus abhorret vacuum ... × ... salutabo dubia que ex evangelia possent capi.

L:	2 pp. before first sermon, unpaginated	C:	deest[1]
		W 3934:	f. 1ra-b
		W 4529:	f. 1r
		Wo 565:	f. 1ra-b

In this succinct preface Wyclyf sets forth the considerations which had impelled him to assemble these "sermones rudes ad populum ... per singulas dominicas per anni circulum ..."; chief among them was his sense of duty in doing what he had a talent for: "quilibet fidelis secundum talentum sibi creditum daret operam ...." The arrangement of this first collection into six parts corresponds, of course, to the liturgical calendar; we observe the subdivision in our sequence hereinafter (but not in B2.II-IV, where the divisions in the MSS are not marked as they are in B2.I); but **112-114** seem to have been included as an afterthought.

As was not unusual in sermons of the time, Wyclyf declares his intention in commenting a particular Scriptural passage to (a) presuppose (and therefore not elucidate) a literal meaning; (b) explain its mystical sense; and (c) resolve questions arising from the text, "secundo more Augustini."

[1] F. 141v is blank, save for the reminder "Cum appropinquasset" at the bottom.

55. B2.I.a.1. *First Sunday in Advent*.

Text: Mt. 21:1 – Cum appropinquasset ...
Constat ex evangelio quod tribus vicibus Christus advenit humanitus ... × ... et subtilem tractatum huius materie relinquo aliis declarandum.[1]

L:	1-8	C:	f. 142ra-va
	1	W 3934:	ff. 1rb-3ra
		W 4529:	ff. 1r-3v
A I:	65-68	*Wo 565*:	ff 1rb-3rb

The two disciples Christ sent to Jerusalem, Wyclyf proposes, are to be understood as figures for secular lords and priests, cooperating in His name. His poverty, as prefigured in Zc 9:19 (and realized in Mk 11:7, Lk 19:30), testifies against the practice of clerical endowment. From these observations he progresses to an exposition of Gn 1, relying heavily on Augustine's *De Genesi ad literam* against the later doctors.[2] The link between the two parts of this sermon – as we shall often note below – is tenuous at best; the exigency of the occasion (his first remarks of the Advent season) seems to have inspired this prosaic reflection on the advent of the universe itself. His tendency to fall back upon logical terminology – as in the definition of time (p. 8; cf. his *De tempore*, **12**) – is quite pronounced. Finally, here as in the substantial majority of his Latin sermons, we encounter the expression "circa hoc evangelium [or epistolam, etc.] dubitatur ..." (p. 3). It may be possible someday to pinpoint just which compendious commentaries were at his elbow in Lutterworth (or in some cases at Oxford; but we must remember that his editorial compilation of the *Sermones* happened between 1382 and 1384); we know he was partial to Nicholas of Lyra, Jerome, Augustine and Chrysostom.

[1] "Declarandum" is obviously correct, and is given in C; but the other three mss agree on "alias declarandas."

[2] Most easily accessible in P. Agaësse and A. Solignac, edd., *Œuvres de Saint Augustin* 48, 49: *De Genesi ad litteram libri duodecim* (Paris, 1972: French and Latin on facing pp.); the section dealing with the seven days of creation appears on pp. 84-334. And see also E. Gilson, *Introduction à l'étude de Saint Augustin* (3rd ed.: Études de philosophie médiévale 11: Paris, 1949): 246-255; Albert Mitterer, *Die Entwicklungslehre Augustins im Vergleich mit dem Weltbild des Hl. Thomas und dem der Gegenwart* (Wien and Freiburg, 1956). Lacking Wyclyf's own postil on Genesis, we can only speculate as to his early sources in this area. It is not likely that he would have been familiar with Bonaventure's important *Collationes in Hexaemeron* (ed. F. Delorme, Quaracchi, 1934); but Grosseteste's *Hexameron* we know Wyclyf to have consulted on several occasions: cf. Thomson, *The Writings of Robert Grosseteste*, 100-101 (add to references also his *De universalibus* [**11**], cap. v); Joseph T. Muckle, "The Hexameron of Robert Grosseteste," *MedSt* 6 (1944): 151-174; idem, "Robert Grosseteste's Use of Greek Sources in his *Hexameron*," *MetH* 3 (1945): 33-48.

56. B2.I.a.2. *Second Sunday in Advent*.

Text: Lk 21:25-26 – Erunt signa...
Hoc evangelium facit mencionem de tercio Christi adventu ... × ... quod deus sit omnium mobilium primus motor.

L:	9-15	C:	ff. 142va-143rb
	2	W 3934:	ff. 3ra-4va
		W 4529:	ff. 3v-6r
A I:	68-70	*Wo 565*:	ff. 3rb-5rb

From creation we pass to judgment, and this *viancium* too, with all else, must come to pass: here, as on numerous other occasions, Wyclyf remarks "Scimus quidem quod omnia futura necessario evenient" (p. 12).[1] And indeed all is in flux: the Trinity itself commenced at creation. This he demonstrates with a coolly Aristotelian abstraction.

[1] From this volume alone we may cite pp. 64, 114, 219, 231 and 282; the similar expression "omne quod fuit vel erit est in suo tempore" appears on pp. 208, 318, etc.; one or the other of these axioms may be found also in vol. II: 335 and vol. IV: 183 of the *Sermones*, as well as in **375**: 352, 451 and **388**: 175, 181; and so on. But see especially **373**, n. 8, below.

57. B2.I.a.3. *Third Sunday in Advent*.

Text: Mt 11:2-3 – Cum audisset ...
Hoc evangelium facit mencionem de primo illorum ... × ... stabilivit sibi edificium quasi perpetuum hic in terris.

L:	15-22	C:	f. 143rb-vb
	3	W 3934:	ff. 4va-6rb
		W 4529:	ff. 6r-8v
A I:	71-73	Wo 565:	ff. 5rb-7ra

John the Baptist was a prophet, and an ascetic: Wyclyf drily notes that the spirit of prophecy[1] may fall on the unrighteous, while the friars wear "mollia vestimenta" and raise extravagant churches – which nevertheless shall not prevail against the true church of Christ, "edificium quasi perpetuum hic in terris."

[1] Cf., his *De vaticinacione sive de prophecia* (**45**).

58. B2.I.a.4. *Fourth Sunday in Advent*.

Text: Jn 1:19 – Miserunt Judei ...
Constat ad literam quomodo in nativitate Johannis miraculum rutilabat ... × ... plus instant ad observandum ipsa quam ceteri Christiani.

L:	22-28	C:	ff. 143vb-144va
	4	W 3934:	ff. 6rb-8ra
		W 4529:	ff. 8v-10v
A I:	74	Wo 565:	ff. 7ra-8vb[1]

Wyclyf continues in this sermon with the figure of John the Baptist, who said that he was unworthy to loose His sandal (Jn 1:27); this aside leads Wyclyf to exclaim at the foolish dispute between the Franciscans and the Dominicans over Christ's footwear or lack thereof (as also in **62**, pp. 53-55, below). He then elaborates the significance of baptism – and from there, by a characteristically abrupt change of subject, he passes to the impermissibility of lying, a grave sin often indulged in by friars and possessioners alike. It is no wonder that he set heads spinning! Yet it is well to recall that the dialectical method that was the very ground of his training encouraged just such oscillations in argument.

[1] Followed by the same comment which appears as a marginalium in iv and v; cf. Loserth ed., p. 28, n. to line 24.

59. B2.I.b.1. *Sunday within Octave of Christmas Day.*

Text: Lk 2:33 – Erant Joseph ...
Illa pauca que narrant evangelia ... × ... oportet aptari populo secundum quod estimatum fuerit eis plus prodesse.

L:	28-35	C:	ff. 144va-145rb
	5	W 3934:	ff. 8ra-9vb
		W 4529:	ff. 10v-13r
A I:	332-334	*Wo 565*:	ff. 8vb-10vb

As is frequently the case with these sermons, Wyclyf uses the verse of his text as an entree to the discussion of issues raised in later but associated verses. In this instance his chief concern is with the elucidation of verse 40: "And the child grew and became strong, filled with wisdom ...." At the end, however, he avers that such an approach may be safely put aside in construing the text passage for popular edification – a clear sign of his purpose in assembling this collection in the first place.

60. B2.I.b.2. *The Circumcision.*

Text: Lk 2:21 – Postquam consumati ...
In hoc brevi evangelio notatur Christi circumcisio ... × ... equivoci sunt varii varie respondentes.

L:	35-43	C:	ff. 145rb-146ra
	6	W 3934:	ff. 9vb-11vb
		W 4529:	ff. 13v-15v
A I:	335-337	*Wo 565*:	ff. 10vb-12vb

From the obligatory consideration of circumcision as a prefiguring of crucifixion, Wyclyf passes to an examination of the negative impact of Christ's preaching on many who heard it. The friars "et quicunque muti presbyteri aut vecordes" (p. 42) of today fail to defend God's law, despairing of His wisdom and mercy.

61. B2.I.b.3. *The Epiphany.*

Text: Mt 2:1 – Cum natus ...
Patet quod in tribus commendatur solempnitas ... × ... certificatur fidelis ex fide quod vita contemplative sit melior quam activa.

L:	43-49	C:	f. 146ra-vb
	7	W 3934:	ff. 11vb-13vb
		W 4529:	ff. 15v-18r
A I:	339-342	*Wo 565:*	ff. 13ra-15ra

Taking the wretched circumstances of Christ's birth as his point of departure, Wyclyf says here some very significant things about the imperative of poverty and the relative merits of the active and contemplative lives. We see an image of his own career in his concluding verdict: all "active" clerics aim at the "bonum patrie" ultimately, but immediately at the "bonum corporis hic in via"; the contemplative (who may also preach, of course!) finds less value in such tangible gratifications.[1]

[1] Wyclyf here betrays no acquaintance with Aquinas, *Summa theologiae*, 2a2ae, 182, which would have lent great strength to his argument.

62. B2.I.b.4. *Sunday within Octave of the Epiphany*.

Text: Jn 1:29 – Vidit Johannes ...
Hoc evangelium facit mencionem de secunda causa ... × ... ex ipsis inficitur et Christiana religio deturpatur.

L:	49-57	C:	ff. 146vb-147va
	8	W 3934:	ff. 13vb-16ra
		W 4529:	ff. 18r-21v
A I:	77-79	*Wo 565:*	ff. 15ra-17va

Wyclyf here expounds the threefold meaning of the term "lamb" as applied to Christ, and then scrutinizes John the Baptist's relationship to Jesus as a contemporary and as to "dignitas." He reproves the friars (as above, **58**) and declares that the act of fasting is less meritorious than abstinence from sin.

63. B2.I.b.5. *Octave of the Epiphany*.

Text: Mt 3:13 – Venit Jesus ...
In hoc evangelio replicatur sentencia dicta proximo sermone ... × ... ut patet noscenti harum religionum observancias singillatim.

L:	57-66	C:	ff. 147va-148va
	9	W 3934:	ff. 16ra-18vb
		W 4529:	ff. 21v-25r
A I:	80-83	*Wo 565:*	ff. 17ra-20ra

From John's baptism in the Jordan of one greater than himself Wyclyf turns to a discussion of baptism in general. As elsewhere he cautions against over-reliance on forms, pointing to Jn 3:3: the "private orders" (meaning mostly the friars in this context) conveniently ignore this passage. Their mendicancy is blatantly illicit, making the "egeni" even more miserable.

64. B2.I.c.1. *First Sunday after the Octave.*

Text: Lk 2:42 – Cum factus ...
Constat quod Lucas ex informacione Pauli ... × ... secundum sapienciam et graciam in processu temporis prodessentem.

L:	66-72	C:	ff. 148va-149rb
	10	W 3934:	ff. 18vb-20vb
		W 4529:	ff. 25r-27v
A I:	83-86	*Wo* 565:	ff. 20ra-22ra

The learned men with whom Jesus was found expounding holy matters come off much better than the modern doctors, "qui nec prudenter audiunt nec interrogant nec respondent" (p. 67) – especially as regards the Eucharist. The rest is a homily on obedience, with one rare (for the *Sermones*, at least) canonical citation (p. 69).

65. B2.I.c.2. *Second Sunday after the Octave.*

Text: Jn 2:1 – Nupcie facte ...
Miraculum huius evangelii creditur esse cause ... × ... quod doctrina evangelica que currit cum silencio est proscripta.

L:	72-78	C:	f. 149rb-vb
	11	W 3934:	ff. 20vb-22rb
		W 4529:	ff. 27v-29v
A I:	86-89	*Wo* 565:	ff. 22ra-23vb

A disquisition on the lawfulness of marriage leads Wyclyf to consider the miracle at Cana, which in turn provides ample opportunity to underline his affinity for the Platonist concept of substance. It is interesting that he chooses not to interject the Eucharist; yet he does indulge his reflexive spleen against the friars. It is just such anomalous juxtapositions that make it difficult for us to date the delivery of the sermons in this collection; some interpolation seems plausible.

66. B2.I.c.3. *Third Sunday after the Octave.*

Text: Mt. 8:1 – Cum descendisset ...
In hoc evangelio narratur instructivum et doctrinale miraculum ... × ... sed secundum gradum disparem noticie vel disparem racionem.

L:	78-86	C:	ff. 149vb-150vb
	12	W 3934:	ff. 22rb-24va
		W 4529:	ff. 29v-32v
A I:	89-92	*Wo* 565:	ff. 23vb-26ra

There is little effort here at structure. Wyclyf reflects variously on Christ's power of salvation; confession; the torments of the damned; the literal meaning of Scripture (cf. **54**, above; he finds this the surest);[1] and the inadequacies of our knowledge of the last things.

[1] We are somewhat reminded (though again with no claim to have found a source for Wyclyf's ruminations) of Aquinas, *Summa theologiae*, 1a.1.10: a consensus statement, incorporating Augustine and Hugh of St. Victor.

67. B2.I.c.4. *Fourth Sunday after the Octave*.

Text: Mt 8:23 – Ascendente Jesu ...
In isto evangelio docetur ecclesia salubriter et compendiose ... × ... quod solius dei est reservatum ad statum in patria.

L:	86-92	C:	ff. 150vb-151va
	13	W 3934:	ff. 24va-26va
		W 4529:	ff. 32v-35v
A I:	92-95	*Wo 565*:	ff. 26ra-28ra

Want of faith leads to every sin; the friars show forth this want "in monstruositate suorum conventuum" (p. 88).[1] At this juncture Wyclyf suddenly remembers that a "certain devout layman" has asked him to expound the Commandments (and here is inserted a plainly retrospective reference to his own *De mandatis divinis* **[26]**). The rest of the sermon therefore deals with idolatry, which offers a convenient opening for another assault on the fraudulent dissemblings of the mendicants on the Eucharist. He promises to take up the remaining verses of the Decalogue in the nine succeeding sermons (**68-76**, below).

[1] For a quotation from St. Bonaventure more than a century previously which validates at least this dimension of Wyclyf's disquietude, see W. R. Thomson, "The Image of the Mendicants in the Chronicles of Matthew Paris," *Archivum Franciscanum Historicum* 70 (1977): 32-33. See generally A. R. Martin, *Franciscan Architecture in England* (British Society of Franciscan Studies 18: Manchester, 1933-1934).

68. B2.I.c.5. *Fifth Sunday after the Octave*.

Text: Mt 13:24 – Simile est ...
Hoc regnum celorum est in predicacione secundum essenciam rex regum ... × ... cum ut sic oportet arma domini deturpare.

L:	93-99	C:	ff. 151va-152ra
	14	W 3934:	ff. 26va-28va
		W 4529:	ff. 35v-38r
A I:	95-98	*Wo 565*:	ff. 28ra-29vb

The parable of the tares naturally draws Wyclyf to consider heresy, wherein he cautions that "pauci vel nulli sciunt utrum plus prodesset ecclesie quod tales peccatores forent superstites quam quod corporaliter occidantur." (P. 97.) The last part of the sermon, as promised the preceding Sunday, deals with the second commandment: in what cases (at law, e.g.) are oaths permissible?

69. B2.I.c.6. *Septuagesima Sunday*.

Text: Mt 20:1 – Simile est ...
Hoc regnum celorum est filius dei (ut supra) ... × ... in vinea atque continuam continenciam exhortari.

L:	99-107	C:	f. 152ra-vb
	15	W 3934:	ff. 28va-30vb
		W 4529:	ff. 38r-41r
A I:	98-102	*Wo* 565:	ff. 29vb-32ra

The kingdom of heaven evokes here the image of the vineyard (the "ecclesia viatorum") and of the judgment to come. The friars and many prelates neglect their duties. The third commandment enjoins the Sabbath observance, but does not always forbid honest labor on that day.

70. B2.I.c.7. *Sexagesima Sunday*.

Text: Lk 8:5 – Exiit qui ...
Hec est prima septem parabolarum ... × ... lex Christi sit vera et lex sibi contraria nimis falsa.

L:	107-114	C:	f. 153ra-va
	16	W 3934:	ff. 31ra-32vb
		W 4529:	ff. 41r-43v
A I:	102-105 (on Lk 8:4)	*Wo* 565:	ff. 32ra-34ra

The literal sower of seed becomes the preacher of the word, "nam cum hoc verbum sit cibus quo homo interior pascitur" (p. 110). Preaching is therefore the most important human act – here he follows Grosseteste.[1] Then he examines the fourth commandment, and explains the three types of parents that may be signified thereby.

[1] On this topic, see especially Knapp, *The Style of John Wyclif's English Sermons*, 23-34; still of value is Bernard L. Manning, *The People's Faith in the Time of Wyclif* (Cambridge, Eng., 1919). Also cf. above, Section B, introduction and n. 1.

71. B2.I.c.8. *Quinquagesima Sunday*.

Text: Lk 18:31 – Assumpsit Jesus ...
Doctrina huius evangelii nedum spectat principaliter ad prelatos ... × ... ipsi enim post nactum dominium sunt multipliciter homicide.

L:	114-121	C:	ff. 153va-154rb
	17	W 3934:	ff. 32vb-34va
		W 4529:	ff. 43v-46v
A I:	106-108	Wo 565:	ff. 34ra-36ra

Wyclyf's concern here is with the figure of the blind man beside the road to Jericho, who symbolizes both the uncomprehending apostles and the Gentiles generally. An exposition of the fifth commandment follows, with special emphasis on Wyclyf's censure of those priests who commit spiritual manslaughter by failing their flocks.

72. B2.I.c.9. *First Sunday in Lent*.

Text: Mt 4:1 – Ductus est ...
Hoc evangelium narrat triplicem penalitatem ... × ... potest evangelisans secundum pertinenciam auditorii dilatare.

L:	121-128	C:	ff. 154rb-155ra
	18	W 3924:	ff. 34va-36vb
		W 4529:	ff. 46v-49v
A I:	109-112	Wo 565:	ff. 36ra-38ra

As Christ withstood the temptations in the desert, so should we resist the temptations of Antichrist today. When Wyclyf speaks particularly of the beguilement of benefices and the imposition of first fruits, however, we sense a personal note: was he thinking of the exactions of the papal collector, Arnold Garnier, against him ? (See **397**, below.) The sixth commandment follows, and here as earlier he looks to Grosseteste's *Decalogus* for inspiration. (Cf. **26**, nn. 15, 16, above.)

73. B2.I.d.1. *Second Sunday in Lent*.

Text: Mt 15:21 – Egressus Jesus ...
Quantum ad sensum literalem huius evangelii est plana litera ... × ... Et ista materia modo inennarrabilis est de generibus latrocinii prelatorum.

L:	128-133	C:	f. 155ra-vb
	19	W 3934:	ff. 36vb-38rb
		W 4529:	ff. 49v-51v
A I:	113-116	Wo 565:	ff. 38ra-39va

Wyclyf chooses this text as a basis for reflecting on the meaning of prayer, a subject he also discusses elsewhere (e.g., **46**). The second half of this sermon examines the seventh commandment, and offers a very broad definition of theft: anyone on earth who "consumando bona huius domini et non ministrando sibi fideliter," is to that degree a thief. The property-poverty nexus comes naturally under scrutiny again.

74. B2.I.d.2. *Third Sunday in Lent.*

Text: Lk 11:14 – Erat Jesus ...
Supponendum est ut fides quod hoc evangelium sicut tota vita Christi sonat ... ×
... nisi quod in proximi occisionem vulneri vulnus addiderit.

L:	133-140	C:	ff. 155vb-156rb
	20	W 3934:	ff. 38rb-40vb
		W 4529:	ff. 51v-54v
A I:	116-120	*Wo 565:*	ff. 39va-41rb

This sermon is one of Wyclyf's most significant shorter Scriptural commentaries. Unhappily we have no sure idea what his sources were, though Jerome and Chrysostom appear elsewhere with some frequency in this collection. From Satan's ascendancy in Christ's day it was for Wyclyf a logical step to the flourishing evils of his own. He concludes with an excursus on the eighth commandment, remarking that "lex nature dedit nobis loquelam, ut caritativius communicemus cum proximis" (p. 140). This driest of humor shows its fleeting face all too rarely.

75. B2.I.d.3. *Fourth Sunday in Lent.*

Text: Jn 6:1 – Abiit Jesus ...
Sensus literalis huius evangelii patet plurimum ... × ... ultimum peccatum interioris hominis per quod dyabolo simulatur.

L:	140-146	C:	ff. 156rb-157ra
	21	W 3934:	ff. 40vb-42va
		W 4529:	ff. 54v-56v
A I:	120-123	*Wo 565:*	ff. 41rb-43ra

After dilating briefly on this text, Wyclyf seems compelled to add to what he had said on the first Sunday in Lent (**72**) concerning the temptations of a kingdom of this earth. Augustine then buttresses his construction of the ninth commandment.

76. B2.I.d.4. *Fifth Sunday in Lent.*

Text: Jn 8:42 – Dicebat Jesus ...
Istum sermonem direxit dominus tam inferioribus ... × ... quod posset faciliter fictam elemosinam abnegando.

L:	146-154	C:	ff. 157ra-158ra
	22	W 3934:	ff. 42va-45va

		W 4529:	ff. 56v-60r
A I:	124-128	*Wo 565*:	ff. 43ra-45rb

The wickedness of the Jews takes up the first part of the sermon; the tenth commandment opens the door for yet another barrage against the mendicancy of the friars. The paradox of Jn 8:58 ("Before Abraham was, I am") caught his eye, and he was moved to exclaim: "considero quod quantumcunque longevus fuero et ab ineunte etate cum quibuscunque doctoribus studuero vix sufficiam superficiem istorum verborum Christi attingere." (P. 152.) It seems that with advancing years Wyclyf was more and more inclined to challenge the assumptions that had underpinned his long years in the schools; an inner revolution was at work here, never quite consummated. We can never know how much more evangelical or simply pastoral he would have become without the savage intervention of his first stroke in 1382.

77. B2.I.d.5. *Palm Sunday*.

Text: Mt 27:62 – Altera autem ...
In fine patet ad literam quomodo Christo ... × ... et Antichristi discipuli sacerdotes legis veteris in malicia antecellunt.

L:	154-160	C:	f. 158ra-vb
	23	W 3934:	ff. 45va-47va
		W 4529:	ff. 60r-62v
A I:	128-131	*Wo 565*:	ff. 45rb-47ra

The tropological construction of Pilate's abdication of responsibility for the judgment of Christ most concerns Wyclyf here. We have in consequence a relatively coherent exposition of his thoughts on the permanence of Christ's ordinances, the imperative model of His actions, and the indefensibility of clerical dominion. He notes in passing that the knights of his day appear stalwart in their reception of evangelical truth despite all the efforts of the clergy to obscure it.

78. B2.I.d.6. *Easter Day*.

Text: Mk 61:1 – Maria Magdalene ...
Claret historia quomodo Christo ... × ... fidelem ministrare et accipere huiusmodi sacramenta.

L:	160-166	C:	ff. 158vb-159va
	24	W 3934:	ff. 47va-49rb
		W 4529:	ff. 62v-64v
A I:	131-134	*Wo 565*:	ff. 47rb-48vb

The observance of the central day of the entire Christian calendar moved Wyclyf to cite three heavy-handed stanzas (Loserth suggests Higden's *Polychronicon* as a likely source) by way of illumination (p. 161); we look in vain for drama. As in the *De eucharistia et penitencia* (**44**), he seizes upon the hoary decretal of Innocent III (*Omnis utriusque sexus*) as a wrongful compulsion: John the Baptist, after all, never took communion! The friars' views on the subject, oddly enough, do not figure here at all.

79. B2.I.e.1. *First Sunday after Easter*.

Text: Jn 20:19 – Cum esset ...
Hoc evangelium et multa alia narrat Christi ... × ... de tanto sit in eius laudibus et fide amplius stabilitus.

L:	166-172	C:	ff. 159va-160rb
	25	W 3934:	ff. 49rb-51rb
		W 4529:	ff. 64v-67v
A I:	134-137	*Wo 565*:	ff. 48vb-50va

This sermon represents one of Wyclyf's most sustained exegetical efforts, and concludes with an important statement of his position on the faith-and-reason dichotomy. We are again reminded that he never ceased to be a philosopher, though his emphases shifted in later years. For someone accustomed to thinking of Wyclyf as prolix and often redundant, this affirmation of the Augustinian view on illumination is refreshingly brief and to the point: "veritas est quod lumen naturale ordinatum a deo ut inducat in fidem non est contrarium lumini fidei, sed in fidem catholicam inductivum." (P. 170; and cf. the Thonnard article cited in **4**, n. 2, above.)

80. B2.I.e.2. *Second Sunday after Easter*.

Text: Jn 10:11 – Ego sum ...
Hoc evangelium sicut est clarissimum speculum ... × ... iudicium de novellis ministris et suis variacionibus introductis.

L:	172-179	C:	ff. 160rb-161rb
	26	W 3934:	ff. 51rb-53rb
		W 4529:	ff. 67v-70r
A I:	138-141	*Wo 565*:	ff. 50vb-52vb

Perhaps nowhere else in Wyclyf's writings, save for the *De officio pastorali* (**53**), does he disclose so plainly his conception of the true shepherd in the church, or denounce so uncompromisingly the inadequacies of "human traditions" as opposed to Gospel truth. He even resorts to the term "sola fide" (p. 179), though of course we should not label him a solifideist on this account!

81. B2.I.e.3. *Third Sunday after Easter.*

Text: Jn 16:16 – Modicum et ...
Constat ex multis capitulis in die cene domini ... × ... de quanto ad eius discenciam promoverent.

L:	179-185	C:	ff. 161rb-162ra
	27	W 3934:	ff. 53rb-55ra
		W 4529:	ff. 70r-72v
A I:	141-144	Wo 565:	ff. 52vb-54va

This sermon chiefly addresses the proper definitions of knowledge and ignorance as they relate to the striving of the *viator* (cf. **47**, nn. 19, 20, above) after perfection.

82. B2.I.e.4. *Fourth Sunday after Easter.*

Text: Jn 16:5 – Vado ad ...
Sensus istius evangelii est eiusdem cum priori ... × ... secundum auditorii capacitatem congruam sunt aptande.

L:	185-192	C:	f. 162ra-vb
	28	W 3934:	ff. 55ra-56vb
		W 4529:	ff. 72v-75r
A I:	144-147	Wo 565:	ff. 54va-56rb

"Vado" propels Wyclyf into discourse on the subtleties of motion, and even an aside on the Eucharist. Reproving then the uncritical worship of relics, which stems from the overhumanizing of Christ, he turns to consider the indivisibility of the Trinity, and declares more than once that eternal truth must be imparted as befits the hearer. So who was his audience on this occasion, when he waxed so formidably scholastic?

83. B2.I.e.5. *Fifth Sunday after Easter.*

Text: Jn 16:23 – Amen, amen ...
Mos est Johannis inter ceteros evangelistas hoc adverbium Amen singulariter et regulariter geminare ... × ... sophisticatur in vendicione oracionis [noviter introducte].[1]

L:	192-199	C:	ff. 162vb-163vb
	29	W 3934:	ff. 57ra-59ra
		W 4529:	ff. 75r-78r
A I:	148-151	Wo 565:	ff. 56va-58vb

The ascension offers Wyclyf further grist for his homiletic mill: predestination, universal love and the Trinity engage him here. But the bulk of this sermon is an exegesis on the Lord's Prayer; it parallels his polemical piece *De oracione dominica* (**424**).

¹ Only **iv** has this explicit.

84. B2.I.e.6. *Sixth Sunday after Easter*.

Text: Jn 15:26 – Cum venerit ...
In hoc evangelio cum sit in uno de quinque capitulis supradictis inculcat Christus ... × ... invasionem hominis vel dyaboli insultantis.

L:	199-207	C:	ff. 163vb-164vb
	30	W 3934:	ff. 59ra-61va
		W 4529:	ff. 78r-81v
A I:	151-154	*Wo 565*:	ff. 58vb-60vb

Persecution, as by the Jews of Christ – and latterly among Christians themselves – and the ignorance of God which spurs it, absorb Wyclyf here. Naturally his reflections on the topic of ignorance lead him to speak of the senses, in particular sight and hearing, and how we may be deceived through them.

85. B2.I.e.7. *Whit Sunday*.

Text: Jn 14:23 – Si quis ...
Cum Christi dileccio includit utrumque tabulam mandatorum ... × ... ad illuminacionem spiritus defectus in hiis sensibus devitare.

L:	207-214	C:	ff. 164vb-165vb
	31	W 3934:	ff. 61va-63vb
		W 4529:	ff. 81v-84v
A I:	155-158	*Wo 565*:	ff. 60vb-63ra

Neither the grammarians nor the logicians can rightly claim to interpret the true meaning of this saying, but only the orthodox theologians: it is they who have prepared men for the coming of a true peace. By an implausible construction Wyclyf then moves to consider the application of the three remaining carnal senses to man's readiness to accept the peace of the Spirit. Loserth's notes identify some parallelisms with the *Trialogus* (**47**).

86. B2.I.e.8. *Trinity Sunday*.

Text: Jn 3:1 – Erat homo ...
Quia fides trinitatis est fundamentum fidelibus ... × ... sic exemplatum a trinitate deficere quin finaliter sit beata.

L:	215-223	C:	ff. 165vb-166vb
	32	W 3934:	ff. 63vb-66ra

| | | W 4529: | ff. 84v-88r |
| A I: | 158-162 | Wo 565: | ff. 63ra-65rb |

Of all Wyclyf's Sunday Gospel sermons this is the most cohesive, examining the meaning of baptism and the second birth. He also enunciates his hermeneutic axiom: where individual words or passages seem to contradict the general sense, that sense must prevail; and herein he claims to oppose the "moderne regule" (p. 218).

87. B2.I.f.1. *First Sunday after Trinity.*

Text: Lk 16:19 – Homo quidam ...
Constat ex parabola hac evangelica quomodo stulti mundo divites reprobantur ... × ... Ideo necesse est populum tenere se in limitibus ordinis Christiani.

L:	223-228	C:	ff. 166vb-167rb
	33	W 3934:	ff. 66rb-67vb
		W 4529:	ff. 88r-90v
A I:	1-3	Wo 565:	ff. 65rb-67ra

The stock contrast of Dives and Lazarus provides Wyclyf with a springboard for yet another plunge into the mendicant imbroglio. This is, however, one of his more succinct tirades.

88. B2.I.f.2. *Second Sunday after Trinity.*

Text: Lk 14:16 – Homo quidam ...
Homo iste singularis est Christus ... × ... cum per timorem servilem ipsam generant sicut seta.

L:	228-234	C:	ff. 167rb-168ra
	34	W 3934:	ff. 68ra-69va
		W 4529:	ff. 90v-93r
A I:	3-6	Wo 565:	ff. 67ra-68vb

The initial exposition in this sermon is both direct and impressive, and exemplifies for us the attractive aspects of metaphorical homiletics. Wyclyf's secondary themes are the issue of predestination and the proper place of secular rulers in the cosmic order.

89. B2.I.f.3. *Third Sunday after Trinity.*

Text: Lk 15:1 – Erant appropinquantes ...
Celestis medicus et incontaminibilis videns quod publicani et peccatores sunt sanabiles ... × ... prius noti querunt hoc angeli se reciproce consolantes.

L:	235-240	C:	f. 168ra-vb
	35	W 3934:	ff. 69va-71rb
		W 4529:	ff. 93r-95v
A I:	7-9	*Wo* 565:	ff. 68vb-70va

Jesus' association with sinners is clarified by reference to his parables of the lost sheep and the ten pieces of silver. Wyclyf also remarks that excommunication by human agency is often wrongful; in any case to converse and reason together with excommunicates should be allowed – a notably humane position.

90. B2.I.f.4. *Fourth Sunday after Trinity*.

Text: Lk 6:36 – Estote ergo ...
Notatis verbis huius evangelii patet quomodo Christus hortatur ... × ... credendo quod sit medium ad amplius [pro]merendum.[1]

L:	240-246	C:	ff. 168rb-169rb
	36	W 3934:	ff. 71rb-73va
		W4529:	ff. 95v-98r
A I:	9-12	*Wo* 565:	ff. 70va-72ra

A summary definition of Christian mercy and of its rewards opens the door to an examination of prelates who fail their flocks, and herein we encounter again Wyclyf's premise: "Debent [i.e., the higher clergy] enim primo attendere quod superest populum in sciencia et virtute, et per consequens quod istas virtuose applicent ad subditos regulandum." (P. 243.) Hence he urges withholding the tithe from unworthy churchmen. It is rather surprising that we find so little indication in the official records of the time that Wyclyf was prone to argue in this neo-Donatist vein.

[1] All three Continental MSS have "merendum."

91. B2.I.f.5. *Fifth Sunday after Trinity*.

Text: Lk 5:1 – Cum turbe ...
Patet primo notata historia quomodo ad sensum allegoricum ... × ... quod fideles capiant in verbo Christi.

L:	246-252	C:	ff. 169rb-170ra
	37	W 3934:	ff. 73va-75vb
		W 4529:	ff. 98r-100v
A I:	12-14	*Wo* 565:	ff. 72ra-73vb

For a man who trumpeted so often and so assertively his conviction that the literal sense of Scripture was the soundest, Wyclyf wandered off into the uncharted wilds of allegory and tropology with unnerving frequency. This sermon betrays that tendency quite strikingly through its first half; and the latter half is devoted to a recitation of the seven works of mercy, which he closes by predictably urging the merciful correction of the "Pharisees" of his own day.

92. B2.I.f.6. *Sixth Sunday after Trinity.*

Text: Mt 5:20 – Nisi habundaverit ...
Constat quod ecclesia integratur ex tribus partibus ... × ... nichil ex facto vel dicto tali est magis hereticum et blasfemum.

L:	252-258	C:	f. 170ra-vb
	38	W 3934:	ff. 75vb-79rb[1]
		W 4529:	ff. 100v-103v
A I:	14-17	Wo 565:	ff. 73vb-75va

The orthodox conception of the tripartite church allows Wyclyf to excoriate the clergy, so fallen away from Christ's poverty. Justice and anger are also thematic; and he remarks in an aside that "nullus foret prelatus ecclesie vel custos anime nisi theologus" (p. 257), the better to expose true heresy.

[1] There is no f. 77 in this codex.

93. B2.I.f.7. *Seventh Sunday after Trinity.*

Text: Mk 8:2 – Misereor super ...
Tria possunt notari super literalem sensum ... × ... militum Christi foret aspere predicandum.

L:	259-265	C:	ff. 170vb-171rb
	39	W 3934:	ff. 79rb-81va
		W 4529:	ff. 103v-106r
A I:	17-19	Wo 565:	ff. 75va-77rb

The seven works of mercy (cf. **91**, above) and the meaning of the "two lords" in Mt 6:24 occupy Wyclyf here. The friars, "specialiter obligantur ad defensionem partis domini expurgando vicia et imprimendo virtutes in populo ut prophete" (p. 264), fall far short of fulfilling their duties.

94. B2.I.f.8. *Eighth Sunday after Trinity.*

Text: Mt 7:15 – Attendite ad ...
Constat ex fide quod Christus est summe sapiens ... × ... quod seculares defuncti renuncient in manu fidelium omnibus bonis suis.

L:	265-271	C:	ff. 171rb-172ra
	40	W 3934:	ff. 81va-84ra

| | | W 4529: | ff. 106r-109r |
| A I: | 19-21 | *Wo 565:* | ff. 77rb-79rb |

Simoniacal bishops and friars who extort legacies from a man's dying breath here incur Wyclyf's spleen: it werefar better for a man to distribute his goods while yet alive.

95. B2.I.f.9. *Ninth Sunday after Trinity.*

Text: Lk 16:1 – Homo quidam ...
Notata litera evangelica patet ad sensum misticum ... × ... quod fecerunt Christus aut eius apostoli foret sollicitudo plus culpanda.

L:	271-278	C:	f. 172ra-vb
	41	W 3934:	ff. 84ra-86va
		W 4529:	ff. 109r-112r
A I:	22-24	*Wo 565:*	ff. 79rb-81rb

Stewardship, alms and endowment make up the substance of this sermon, which in its cohesiveness seems more of a *tractatulus* than do most of the *Sermones*.

96. B2.I.f.10. *Tenth Sunday after Trinity.*

Text: Lk 19:41 – Cum appropinquaret ...
Notata historia patent tria ad edificacionem ecclesie ... × ... non facit religionis vel ordinis novitatem.

L:	278-284	C:	ff. 172vb-173va
	42	W 3934:	ff. 86va-88vb
		W 4529:	ff. 112r-114v
A I:	24-26	*Wo 565:*	ff. 81rb-83ra

A mixed disquisition on sin, foreordination, and collective responsibility.

97. B2.I.f.11. *Eleventh Sunday after Trinity.*

Text: Lk 18:14 – Omnis qui ...
Notata historia patet quomodo fidelis in tribus instruitur ... × ... instanter alia forma hec temporalia mendaciter blasfemamus.

L:	284-291	C:	ff. 173va-174rb
	43	W 3934:	ff. 88vb-91rb
[*pace* L, A I: 27-29, on Lk 18:9, does		W 4529:	ff. 114v-117v
not at all correspond to our text]		*Wo 565:*	ff. 83ra-85ra

A peroration on Judgment and humility drives Wyclyf yet again to impugn the pharisaical mendicants; here, however, he has more than usual to say about their ill-treatment of his "sacerdotes simplices."

98. B2.I.f.12. *Twelfth Sunday after Trinity.*

Text: Mk 7:37 – Bene omnia ...
Notata historia potest allegorice intelligi ... × ... et mutescunt sunt magis culpabiles ut falsi Christiani.

L:	291-297	C:	ff. 174rb-175ra
	44	W 3934:	ff. 91rb-93va
[A I:	29-31 relates to Mk 7:31	W 4529:	ff. 117v-120v
	for this Sunday]	Wo 565:	ff. 85ra-87ra

Chiefly an exposition of the articles of the Credo, interwoven with a brief examination of the nature of faith itself.

99. B2.I.f.13. *Thirteenth Sunday after Trinity.*

Text: Lk 10:23 – Beati oculi ...
Licet hoc evangelium sit gravidatum multiformi sentencia ... × ... cum sit iniquior spoliorum receptabilis est iniquus.

L:	298-304	C:	f. 175ra-vb
	45	W 3934:	ff. 93va-96ra
		W 4529:	ff. 121r-123r
A I:	31-33	Wo 565:	ff. 87ra-88vb

The *lex et liga* of Christ are sufficient guidance to the faithful; the friars acknowledge neither.

100. B2.I.f.14. *Fourteenth Sunday after Trinity.*

Text: Lk 17:11 – Dum iret ...
Sensus huius evangelii potest allegorice sic notari ... × ... non foret tantus zelus mercandie audiendi confessiones sicut hodie palliatur.[1]

L:	304-310	C:	ff. 175vb-176va
	46	W 3934:	ff. 96ra-98rb
		W 4529:	ff. 123r-125v
A I:	34-36	Wo 565:	ff. 88vb-90vb

As repeatedly throughout these sermons, Wyclyf's professed fidelity to the literal signification of his text is again obscured here by a moth-and-candle fascination with allegory. His real focus, however, is on confession, penance and forgiveness;

he is sharply critical of current practice in these spheres, and especially of indulgences.

[1] L reads "polliatur"; but our reading is plain in all four MSS.

101. B2.I.f.15. *Fifteenth Sunday after Trinity.*

Text: Mt 6:24 – Nemo potest ...
Constat quod Christus intelligit de duobus dominis contrariis non secundum naturam ... × ... angusta in conservacione et finaliter tribulacione in amissione.

L:	311-317	C:	ff. 176va-177rb
	47	W 3934:	ff. 98rb-100vb
		W 4529:	ff. 125v-128r
A I:	36-38	Wo 565:	ff. 90vb-92vb

The property-poverty dialectic Wyclyf views here in ineluctable association with avarice and service; the sermon does constitute one of his better short essays on disendowment. (Cf. **93**, above.)

102. B2.I.f.16. *Sixteenth Sunday after Trinity.*

Text: Lk 7:11 – Ibat Jesus ...
Patet ex processu evangelii quod Christus tres mortuos suscitavit ... × ... et plures pro parte sua contra dominum procurantes.

L:	317-324	C:	ff. 177rb-178ra
	48	W 3934:	ff. 100vb-103ra
		W 4529:	ff. 128v-131r
A I:	38-41	Wo 565:	ff. 92vb-94vb

The state of Grace and a scholastic analysis of the six modes of consent to sin engage Wyclyf in this sermon.

103. B2.I.f.17. *Seventeenth Sunday after Trinity.*

Text: Lk 14:1 – Cum intraret ...
Constat ex textu evangelii quomodo ipsum est trimembre ... × ... Et patet quod necessitamur consilium dei instanter expetere.

L:	324-330	C:	f. 178ra-vb
	49	W 3934:	ff. 103ra-105rb
		W 4529:	ff. 131r-133v
A I:	41-43	Wo 565:	ff. 94vb-96va

Another diatribe against avarice, directed this time mainly at the "Caesarean clergy."

104. B2.I.f.18. *Eighteenth Sunday after Trinity.*

Text: Mt 22:34 – Accesserunt ad ...
Constat quod in prima parte huius evangelii Christus reducit ad binarium totum decalogum ... × ... sicut ipsum esse hominem, quod est minus quam deitas.

L:	330-336	C:	ff. 178vb-179va
	50	W 3934:	ff. 105rb-107rb
		W 4529:	ff. 133v-136r
A I:	43-46	Wo 565:	ff. 96va-98ra

Wyclyf focuses here quite singlemindedly on Christ's distillation of the Decalogue into the two commandments of divine and fraternal love.

105. B2.I.f.19. *Nineteenth Sunday after Trinity.*

Text: Mt 9:1 – Ascendens Jesus ...
Navicula ista potest intelligi ad sensum misticum ... × ... est validior quam sensus hominum quibus argucie cuncte seducuntur.[1]

L:	336-342	C:	ff. 179va-180ra
	51	W 3934:	ff. 107va-109vb
		W 4529:	ff. 136r-138v
A I:	46-48	Wo 565:	ff. 98ra-99vb

Wyclyf applies the metaphor of the mustard seed to the Church itself, with qualifications: there is no real growth without the poverty which Christ embodied. And not even the pope can truly absolve men in the utterly direct manner of Christ Himself.

[1] All three Continental MSS so read; i has "cuncte cedunt."

106. B2.I.f.20. *Twentieth Sunday after Trinity.*

Text: Mt 22:1 – Loquebatur Jesus ...
Constat per dicta sanctorum quomodo regnum celorum est ecclesia ... × ... si fuerit animatus primum eligeret.[1]

L:	342-348	C:	f. 180ra-vb
	52	W 3934:	ff. 109vb-112ra
		W 4529:	ff. 138v-141r
A I:	48-51	Wo 565:	ff. 99vb-101va

A typically oblique approach, via the parable of the wedding feast and the Incarnation, to the damnation of the foreknown. It would take us too far afield into medieval rhetoric and psychology to establish the point beyond cavil, yet it is not amiss at least to remark that at times in these sermons one is struck by the fundamental differences in the reasoning process itself between that age and our own.

[1] As in the Continental MSS; i adds (in a different hand) "non secundum."

107. B2.I.f.21. *Twenty-first Sunday after Trinity.*

Text: Jn 4:46 – Erat quidam ...
Regulus iste potest notare mistice ... × ... suo vicario potestatem absolvendi a culpa.

L:	348-354	C:	ff. 180vb-181va
	53	W 3934:	ff. 112ra-114rb
		W 4529:	ff. 141r-143v
A I:	51-53	*Wo* 565:	ff. 101va-103rb

A neo-Aristotelian exercise, observing the traditional distinctions between "intellectus" and "affectus." Why Wyclyf chose this approach is far from self-evident; but cf. Aquinas, *Summa theologiae*, 1a, 84-89. Some of Aquinas' categories of course derived from Arabic commentators such as Ibn Sînâ and al-Fârâbî.

108. B2.I.f.22. *Twenty-second Sunday after Trinity.*

Text: Mt 18:23 – Simile est ...
Patet ex dictis quod regnum celorum hoc est ecclesia catholica figuratur ... × ... cum ducit eos insolubiliter ad contradiccionem palam infinitam.

L:	354-360	C:	ff. 181va-182ra
	54	W 3934:	ff. 114rb-116va
		W 4529:	ff. 143v-146r
A I:	54-56	*Wo* 565:	ff. 103rb-104vb

The parable of the talents here provokes Wyclyf to unwonted introspection: "Quando autem fui iunior, negavi quod quidquam sit debitum nisi debeatur simpliciter quoad deum .... Et consequenter locutus sum cum aliis ... et sic exposui scripturam et negavi de virtute sermonis verba doctorum in ista materia." (P. 357: cf. p. 358, 11, 19-22.) Again he has become the outsider, alienated from the stormy schools.

109. B2.I.f.23. *Twenty-third Sunday after Trinity.*

Text: Mt 22:15 – Abeuntes pharisei ...
Patet ex hoc evangelio quomodo pharisei machinati sunt ... × ... impetere sive persequi et cruciare dominum Jesum Christum.

L:	360-366	C:	f. 182ra-vb
	55	W 3934:	ff. 116va-118vb
		W 4529:	ff. 146r-148v
A I:	56-58	*Wo 565:*	ff. 104vb-106va

Wyclyf cites William of Auvergne ("Parisiensis" – not John [Quidort] of Paris, as in Loserth's n., p. 364) on hypocrisy, then applies these definitions both to the "new sects" and endowment.

110. B2.I.f.24. *Twenty-fourth Sunday after Trinity.*

Text: Mt 9:18 – Ecce princeps ...
Notata historia huius evangelii patet ad sensum misticum quomodo filia ... × ... fideles istam tradicionis repugnanciam detestantes.

L:	366-372	C:	ff. 182vb-183va
	56	W 3934:	ff. 118vb-121ra
		W 4529:	ff. 148v-151r
A I:	59-61	*Wo 565:*	ff. 106va-108ra

Wyclyf is initially absorbed here with the *sensus misticus* of his text; afterwards he launches yet another discourse on the participation of act and intent in sin.

111. B2.I.f.25. *Twenty-fifth Sunday after Trinity.*

Text: Jn 6:5 – Cum sublevasset ...
Notata historia huius evangelii cum aliis patet quod Christus ... × ... perveniatur ad regnum sempiternum.

L:	372-377	C:	ff. 183va-184rb
	57	W 3934:	ff. 121ra-123ra
		W 4529:	ff. 151r-153v
A I:	62-64	*Wo 565:*	ff. 108ra-109vb[1]

We encounter here a surprising analogy: just as the grains of English wheat are harder to crack, yet are better for making bread, so is English theology: "concordando curie propinquior ceremoniis ordeaceis sed racione subtilitatis et explanacionis cum fuerit purgata sit planior ac pastui populi secundum panem vite clarior atque fertilior." (P. 374.) This bears on the whole issue of Scriptural as against patristic, canonistic, etc., *auctoritas*.

[1] Text concluded "Amen"; over half a column (ruled) left vacant.

112. B2.I.g.1. *Dedication of a Church.*

Text: Lk 19:1 – Egressus Jesus ...
Patenti litera potest hoc evangelium ad sensum allegoricum sic exponi ... × ... in testamento suo solvi docuit ut patet ad Rom. 13° et 1ª Petri 2°.

L:	378-385	C:	ff. 234va-235rb
	58 (= *Sermones mixti*, 2)	W 3928:	ff. 131va-133va
		W 3931:	ff. 145vb-148ra
		W 3934:	ff. 123ra-125vb
A II:	208-209	W 4529:	ff. 153v-157r

One of Wyclyf's more sharply focused examinations of the alleged mendicancy of Christ,[1] this sermon ends with a vigorous denunciation of papal bulls: "nam plumbum mutum et litera mortua non equivalent vivis operibus." – The inclusion of this and the following two sermons from the *sermones mixti* (most of which will be found in B2.IV, below) follows L and **iv** and **v**; wanting in **vi** altogether, and in **i** and the two other Wien MSS, **ii** and **iii**, they appear at the end of the *Sermones super evangelia de sanctis* (B2.II, below). I would not venture to insist that our arrangement is necessarily the only one conceivable; Wyclyf's preface in any case (**54**) does not mention them at all.

[1] Cf. general overview in J. Leclercq, "Les controverses sur la pauvreté du Christ," in Mollat, ed., *Études sur l'histoire de la Pauvreté* I: 45-56.

113. B2.I.g.2. *Sunday after Dedication Day*.

Text: Lk 6:47 – Omnis qui ...
Constat ex evangelio Matth. 7° et Luce 6° duplice esse domum ... × ... Ergo quilibet misericorditer elemosinans debet a Christo auctoritatem expetere et exemplum.

L:	385-393	C:	ff. 235rb-236ra
	59 (= *Sermones mixti*, 3)	W 3928:	ff. 133ra-135vb
		W 3931:	ff. 148ra-150va
A II:	210	W 3934:	ff. 126ra-128vb
		W 4529:	ff. 157r-160v

Until his pedestrian concluding aside on the endowment of colleges and convents, Wyclyf almost achieves the sublime in his grand conception of the physical and spiritual universes. The first half of this sermon surely ranks among the most pleasing parts of the entire *corpus Wyclyfianum*.

114. B2.I.g.3. *Octave of the Dedication*.

Text: Jn 10:22 – Facta sunt ...
Omnia ista tria evangelia alludunt dedicacioni ecclesie ... × ... ut in febre ethica est sua inanicio impercepta.

L:	393-404	C:	ff. 236ra-237rb
	60 (= *Sermones mixti*, 4)	W 3928:	ff. 135vb-139ra
		W 3931:	ff. 150va-153vb

A II: 105-107 (very few points   W 3934:   ff. 128vb-132vb
        of correlation)   W 4529:   ff. 160v-165r

The longest sermon in this first collection, it is also among the most censorious: the Eucharist is grossly mistaught, and the entire structure of the Church as it existed in his time – most particularly the mendicant orders – must be pulled out root and branch. The reformer is in full cry.

115-175. B2.II. *Sermones super evangelia de sanctis.* 1378 ?-1384.

  I. Inc.: Continuando sermones sanctorum cum sermonibus dominicis incipien-
       dum videtur a festo Sancti Sanctorum ...
     Expl.: × ... unum vagum accidens sine aliquo subiectante.

  II. MSS: (those which contain the *De sex iugis* [cf. 141, below] are marked with an asterisk):

i	C		ff. 184va-234va	xiv/ex	JW MS Eng.
ii	PMK	C.116 (548)*	ff. 333r-337r	ca. 1400	Asc. Boh.
iii		D.123 (693)* [1]	ff. 29r-42r	xv/1	JW MS Boh.
iv		N.48 (1572)*	ff. 155r-160r	1422	Unasc. Boh.[2]
	[not in PUK III.B.19 (428), *pace* Lo]				
v	W	1337*	ff. 161ra-165vb	ca. 1410	JW MS Boh.
vi		3928	ff. 1ra-123ra, 128rb-131rb	ca. 1410	JW MS Boh.
vii		3928*	ff. 186va-189ra		
viii		3931	ff. 1ra-137rb, 142va-145vb	ca. 1410	JW MS Boh.[3]
ix		3932*	ff. 153ra-155va	1418	JW MS Boh.
x		4343*	ff. 270r-271v	1433	Unasc. Boh.
xi		4522*	ff. 139v-144v	1423	JW MS Boh.

  III. Ed. J. Loserth, *Iohannis Wyclif Sermones* II: *Super Evangelia de Sanctis* (WS, 1888). From **i, vi** and **viii** only.

  IV. See commentary on individual sermons below. – But it is appropriate in this place to remark that Loserth's claim that this collection "contains the most interesting and important of all Wyclif's Latin sermons" (Introduction, p. III) is debatable; such a determination to have any meaning must be strictly limited to one or another aspect of just what is "interesting and important."

  VC: 3933 3935 4514 7980   Bale: 102   Sh: 34   Lo: 35

---

[1] Lo reads 623.
[2] A Hus MS; asc. rubbed out.
[3] A few notes by Peter Payne throughout; there are four excised ff. between the flyleaf and f. 1.

115. B2.II.1. *Christmas Day*.

Text: Lk 2:1 – Exiit edictum ...
Continuando sermones sanctorum cum sermonibus dominicis incipiencum videtur a festo ... × ... calidissimis et falsissimis spoliacionibus Antichristi.

L:	1-7	C:	ff. 184va-185ra
	1	W 3928:	ff. 1ra-2vb
		W 3931:	ff. 1ra-2vb
A I:	316-322		

It is prognostic of the temper of this collection that Wyclyf begins it with an attack on the practice of arbitrary canonization ("pro lucro": p. 1) by the Papacy. There follows a surprisingly literal exposition of the Christmas story; while the power of Jesus' poverty serves as a descant throughout.

116. B2.II.2. *St Stephen* (26 December).

Text: Mt 23:34 – Ecce ego ...
Post nativitatem Sancti sanctorum [12 wds.] sollempnizat ecclesia proximo natalem ... × ... inter alios martyrem gloriosum.

L:	7-14	C:	ff. 185ra-186ra
	2	W 3928:	ff. 2vb-4va
		W 3931:	ff. 2vb-4vb
A I:	322-324		

Persecution is here analyzed, and Wyclyf shows how St. Stephen met the three orthodox criteria for martyrdom.

117. B2.II.3. *St John the Evangelist* (27 December).

Text: Jn 21:15 – Dixit Jesus ...
Cum triplex dicatur martyrium ... × ... dando eis temporale dominium conquisitum.

L:	14-21	C:	f. 186ra-vb
	3	W 3928:	ff. 4va-6va
		W 3931:	ff. 4vb-6vb
A I:	325-327		

There are many paths to Christ, but Wyclyf here charges the priesthood of his day with missing most of them, and wasting their calling in sterile intellectual enticements, business ventures, law and war.

118. B2.II.4. *The Holy Innocents* (28 December).

Text: Mt 2:13 – Angelus Domini ...
Hoc evangelium narrat de triplici martyrio ... × ... ut fecerunt apostoli ad instar Christi.

L:	22-28	C:	ff. 186vb-187va
	4	W 3928:	ff. 6va-8rb
		W 3931:	ff. 6vb-8vb
A I:	327-331		

A straightforward account of the Herodian slaughter; we are to persevere in the faith in the teeth of all adversities.

119. B2.II.5. *St Thomas [à Becket]* (December 29).

Text: Lk 19:12 – Homo quidam ...
Homo iste est indubie dominus Jesus ... × ... et specialiter caritati fervide quam habuit hora mortis.

L:	28-35	C:	ff. 187va-188rb
	5	W 3928:	ff. 8rb-10ra
		W 3931:	ff. 8vb-11ra
A I:	257-261		

How the parable of the talents discloses the nature of God to us; and how St Thomas' martyrdom emphatically did not connote the endowment of the church, but rather the defense of justice.

120. B2.II.6. *St Sylvester* (31 December).

Text: Mt 25:14 – Homo quidam ...
Homo iste est Christus indubie qui peregrinavit ... × ... Et hii sunt qui scandalizant partes ecclesie triumphantis.

L:	35-44	C:	ff. 188rb-189rb
	6	W 3928:	ff. 10ra-12rb
		W 3931:	ff. 11ra-13va
A I:	252-257		

Parallel parable, different conclusion: Pope Sylvester was wrong to accept Constantine's endowment,[1] but the secular rulers, who enjoy dominion prescriptively, have laxly allowed the lords of the Church to wield that same dominion. This sermon offers one of the clearest possible indications that after his bootless appeal to Richard II against the verdict of Blackfriars (1382), Wyclyf came to trust at last only the redress of Scripture itself. His reforming drive then, far from becoming exclusively activistic and immediate (as we might expect from his labors of translation and on behalf of the Poor Priests), actually struck root even more deeply in the stern imperatives of literal Christianity.

[1] Cf. **412**, n. 7, below.

121. B2.II.7. *The Conversion of St Paul* (25 January).

Text: Mt 19:27 – Dixit Simon ...
Constat ex fide quod mundus perditus est ... × ... et promovent rapinam [plurem quam exhibent Antichristo].[1]

L:	44-52	C:	ff. 189rb-190rb
	7	W 3928:	ff. 12rb-14rb
		W 3931:	ff. 13va-15vb
A I:	342-345		

The friars impoverish all England, and most of all the English poor; how much better would it be if they bent their backs to honest labor, as enjoined by Paul in 2 Th 3:8.

[1] The shorter explicit only in **viii**.

122. B2.II.8. *Candlemas Day* (2 February).

Text: Lk 2:22 – Postquam impleti ...
Inter quinque festa beate Marie virginis hoc festum Purificacionis videtur tenere ... × ... et alia ad hoc necessitancia removendo.

L:	52-59	C:	ff. 190rb-191ra
	8	W 3928:	ff. 14rb-16rb
		W 3931:	ff. 15vb-17vb
A I:	345-347		

Mary's vow of virginity leads Wyclyf to examine the unscriptural origins of the mendicant orders, and in particular their seven chief failings as preachers.

123. B2.II.9. *St Peter's Chair* (22 February).

Text: Mt 16:13 – Venit Jesus ...
Hec civitas primo dicta est Lachis ... × ... patet quod sunt ypocrite contrarii Veritati.

L:	59-66	C:	f. 191ra-vb
	9	W 3928:	ff. 16rb-18ra
		W 3931:	ff. 17vb-19vb
A I:	347-350		

A sturdily antipapal dissertation on the power of the keys; Wyclyf's distinction between the efficaciousness of acts done by prelates in the "true church" and those outside it is quite predictable. Ordination, he continues, is nowadays too elaborate; it should be as it was "antequam erant privati libri papales editi" (p. 64).

124. B2.II.10. *St Matthias* (24 or 25 February).

Text: Mt 11:25 – Confiteor tibi ...
Constat ex fide scripture Act. 1º, 26 ... × ... sit dampnabilis et mortalis.

L:	66-73	C:	ff. 191vb-192va
	10	W 3928:	f. 18ra-va[1]
		W 3931:	ff. 19vb-21va
A I:	350-353		

In passing, a defense of Urban vi's legitimacy; this is therefore one of the earliest sermons in this collection, dating from 1378 or 1379.

[1] Despite Loserth's fairly regular references to this MS in his edition, it seems that it must somehow be abbreviated, owing to the foliation; close examination should resolve the discrepancy.

125. B2.II.11. *Annunciation of the Blessed Virgin Mary* (25 March).

Text: Lk 1:26 – Missus est ...
Istud est festum tercium beate virginis ... × ... duplex interpretacio nominis Marie virginis satis iuvat.

L:	73-79	C:	ff. 192va-193rb
	11	W 3928:	ff. 18va-21rb
		W 3931:	ff. 21vb-23va
A I:	353-356		

The Assumption is here examined; but Wyclyf puts off his customary *dubia*, quite uncharacteristically, to the concluding paragraph.

126. B2.II.12. *St Mark* (25 April).

Text: Jn 15:1 – Ego sum ...
Christus consolando suos contra tribulaciones illis imminentes post mortem suam narrat parabolam ... × ... ipsos decipiunt cum quibus communicant.

L:	79-86	C:	ff. 193rb-194ra
	12	W 3928:	ff. 21rb-22vb
		W 3931:	ff. 23va-25va
A I:	165-168		

The mendicants are guilty of many transgressions, including the persecution of their own dissident members and false teaching on the Eucharist.

127. B2.II.13. *St Philip and St James* (1 May).

Text: Jn 14:1 – Non turbetur ...
Sentencia huius evangelii est inclusa ... × ... ut pannus menstruus sine virtute informative mortiferi.

L:	86-95	C:	ff. 194ra-195ra
	13	W 3928:	ff. 22vb-25rb
		W 3931:	ff. 25va-28rb
A I:	357-359		

On those circumstances which undermine a preacher's effectiveness; a good deal also appears in this sermon on the pitfalls in the path of the *viator* (cf. **47**, nn. 19, 20, above).

128. B2.II.14. *Vigil of St John the Baptist* (23 June).

Text: Lk 1:5 – Fuit in ...
Cum genealogia cuiuscunque persone que in scriptura sacra inseritur terminatur ... × ... exhinc est accepcio personarum.

L:	95-104	C:	ff. 195ra-196ra
	14	W 3928:	ff. 25rb-27vb
		W 3931:	ff. 28rb-31ra
A I:	362-364		

One of Wyclyf's more intriguing arguments against the "novelli ordines" emerges here: the plethora of requirements within the orders deprives their members of the exemplary freedom of action which Christ allowed His followers.

129. B2.II.15. *St John the Baptist* (24 June).

Text: Lk 1:57 – Elizabeth impletum ...
In isto evangelio exprimitur promissio dei ... × ... sicut patet de instantibus quoad tempus.

L:	105-113	C:	ff. 196ra-197ra
	15	W 3928:	ff. 27vb-30rb
		W 3931:	ff. 31ra-33vb
A I:	364-365		

Certainly one of Wyclyf's most sustained and immoderate outbursts against the mendicants, and tangentially against the doctors and decretals of the Church.

130. B2.II.16. *St Peter and St Paul* (29 June).

Text: Jn 21:15 – Dixit Jesus ...
Hoc evangelium notificat ecclesie ... × ... ad finem religionis Domini totum residuum dimittentes.

L:	113-123	C:	ff. 197ra-198ra
	16	W 3928:	ff. 30rb-32vb
		W 3931:	ff. 33vb-36vb
A I:	366-367		

On the pastoral office again (cf. **53**, etc.); a condemnation of both monks and friars predictably ensues.

131. B2.II.17. *Translation of St Martin* (4 July).

Text: Lk 12:32 – Nolite timere ...
Christus stabilit suam ecclesiam ... × ... cum ignoramus singuli horam mortis.

L:	123-132	C:	ff. 198ra-199ra
	17	W 3928:	ff. 32vb-35ra
		W 3931:	ff. 36vb-39ra
A I:	370-373		

Christ's rule is superior to all others; the friars, again, are superfluous and hypocritical.

132. B2.II.18. *St Mary Magdalene* (22 July).

Text: Lk 7:36 – Rogabat Jesum ...
Cum Salvator ordinatus est ex eterno dei consilio ... × ... secundum evangelium Matth. 7° Attendite.

L:	132-140	C:	f. 199ra-vb
	18	W 3928:	ff. 35ra-37ra
		W 3931:	ff. 39ra-41ra
A:	deest		

The hazards of penance as currently enjoined and interpreted; cf. **44**, above.

133. B2.II.19. *St James* (25 July).

Text: Mt 20:20 – Accessit ad ...
Constat quomodo Jacobus et Johannes per rogacionem muliebrem pecierant ... × ... pure et virtuose conformiter legi Christi.

L:	140-146	C:	ff. 199vb-200va

	19	W 3928:	ff. 37rb-38vb
		W 3931:	ff. 41rb-42vb
A I:	377-379		

Both endowment and the friars torment the true Church.

134. B2.II.20. *Assumption of the Virgin* (15 August).

Text: Lk 10:38 – Intravit Jesus ...
Hoc evangelium potest intelligi in sensu multiplici ... × ... et ad peccata plurima inductiva.

L:	146-152	C:	ff. 200va-201rb
	20	W 3928:	ff. 38vb-40va
		W 3931:	ff. 42vb-44va
A I:	382-385		

On the three virtues of humility, chastity and reticence – and their contraries.

135. B2.II.21. *St Bartholomew* (24 August).

Text: Lk 22:24 – Facta est ...
Ista contencio sicut filiorum Zebedei procuracio de maioritate erat occasionaliter benedicta ... × ... quos voluerit illustret in ista sentencia.

L:	152-159	C:	ff. 201rb-202ra
	21	W 3928:	ff. 40va-42rb
		W 3931:	ff. 44va-46rb
A I:	385-387		

The hierarchy and the laws of the church defy the true meaning and example of Christ's life and purpose.

136. B2.II.22. *Beheading of St John the Baptist* (29 August).

Text: Mk 6:17 – Misit Herodes ...
Fidelibus recte evangelizantibus est necessarium historiam ... × ... per generacionem adulteram ecclesia est seducta.

L:	159-165	C:	f. 202ra-vb
	22	W 3928:	ff. 42rb-44ra
		W 3931:	ff. 46rb-48ra
A I:	387-389		

An exceptionally close commentary on the text – prefaced however by a rambling excursus on the puzzling nature of women. Undoubtedly that whole question ill suited the scholastic temperament![1]

[1] Cf. his deliberate avoidance of the subject in **423**, below. Yet certain aspects of Wyclyf's teaching strongly appealed to women: see now Claire Cross, "'Great reasoners in scripture': the activities of women lollards 1380-1530," in Derek Baker ed., *Medieval Women* (SCH, Subsidia 1: Oxford, 1978): 359-380.

137. B2.II.23. *Nativity of the Blessed Virgin Mary* (8 September).

Text: Mt 1:1 – Liber generacionis ...
De quinque festis beate virginis hoc secundum festum sue nativitatis genealogizat generacionem Joseph ... × ... ideo totus homo debet dirigi ad virtutes.

L:	165-172	C:	ff. 202vb-203va
	23	W 3928:	ff. 44ra-45vb
		W 3931:	ff. 48ra-49vb
A I:	390-392		

Wyclyf here outdoes most of his contemporaries in a convoluted and contrived effort to reconcile the genealogies of Jesus as given in Mt 1:1-16 and Lk 3:23-38. A frank admission that there remain irreducible differences between the two accounts, such as is almost universal in historical New Testament scholarship today,[1] was beyond imagining for virtually all medieval exegetes. Indeed the prevailing mentality is epitomized in Wyclyf's own airy dismissal of the entire issue (p. 172): "Nec dubium quin ex serie utriusque testamenti Christus fuit filius David, nec oportet genealogiam ulteriorem scrutari quam dicit evangelium."

[1] Though Ernest Renan's *Vie de Jésus* (Paris, 1863), ch. xv, went too far in asserting that the line of David was in fact extinct, yet his bold formulations did provide a basic agenda for subsequent more careful investigators. A good recent source on the genealogies is Michael Grant, *Jesus. An Historian's Review of the Gospels* (New York, 1977): 96-102.

138. B2.II.24. *Exaltation of the Cross* (14 September).

Text: Jn 12:31 – Nunc iudicium ...
Hoc evangelium facit mencionem de crucifixione ... × ... sequentes vivunt conformiter istis sanctis.[1]

L:	172-179	C:	ff. 203va-204rb
	24	W 3928:	ff. 46ra-47va
		W 3931:	ff. 49vb-51vb
A I:	392-394		

A pithy statement of ecclesiastical politics: "nec Romano pontifici nec alicui prelato ecclesie militantis debet amplius vel aliter obediri, nisi de quanto sonat ex fide scripture in obedienciam domino Jesu Christo ..." (p. 177). Both popes are moreover suspect regarding the Eucharist.

[1] L acknowledges that the concluding phrase of his edition of this sermon, "quod est difficile demonstrare," is probably a later addendum in **i**, and it appears there only. We may safely exclude it.

139. B2.II.25. *St Matthew* (21 September).

Text: Mt 9:9 – Cum transiret ...
In hoc evangelio exprimitur Matthei eleccio ... × ... quando superhabundanter spiritualem retribuit recompensam.

L:	179-188	C:	ff. 204rb-205ra
	25	W 3928:	ff. 47vb-50ra
		W 3931:	ff. 51vb-54ra
A I:	397-398		

Prelates ought not to lay out lavish banquets, since their wealth is expropriated from the poor, whom Christ fed. The logic is both stern and ineluctable, and was the sinew of Wyclyf's strength.

140. B2.II.26. *Michaelmas Day* (29 September).

Text: Mt 18:1 – Accesserunt ad ...
Quia conturbati sunt discipuli ... × ... machinacione iniurietur heredibus tanti regni.[1]

L:	188-195	C:	ff. 205ra-206ra
	26	W 3928:	ff. 50ra-52ra
		W 3931:	ff. 54ra-55vb
A I:	398-402		

A homily on humility, with an aside on accidents as they relate to both the Eucharist and the Incarnation.

[1] Both **vi** and **viii** have "regis," but here **i** is contextually correct.

141. B2.II.27. *All Saints' Day* (1 November).

Text: Mt 5:1 – Videns Jesus ...
Hoc evangelium continet legem Christi ... × ... patet superius parte prima.

L:	195-203[1]	C:	f. 206ra-vb
	27	W 3928:	ff. 52ra-54rb
		W 3931:	ff. 55vb-57vb
A I:	406-412		

An exposition of the beatitudes; the first of the six "yokes" (see note below).

[1] P. 202, l. 21 – p. 203, l. 38, inc.: "Ut idiote et simplices ...," is the first part of an autocephalous piece, *De sex iugis*, ed. G. Lechler, *Johann von Wiclif und die Vorgeschichte der Reformation* II: 591-605. The MSS in their entirety are cited above, B2.II (asterisked). The remainder of the piece corresponds to **142**: p. 206, l. 1 – p. 210, l. 25; **145**: p. 232, l. 8 – p. 234, l. 6; **146**: p. 237, l. 21 – p. 240, l. 30; and **147**: p. 244, l. 6 – p. 247, l. 12; expl.: × ... contra huiusmodi novitates.

142. B2.II.28. *St Andrew* (30 November).

Text: Mt 4:18 – Ambulans Jesus ...
Huius evangelii plana est historia ... × ... in filiis suis inducere paulative.

L:	204-210[1]	C:	ff. 206vb-207va[2]
	28	W 3928:	ff. 54rb-56rb
		W 3931:	ff. 57vb-59va
A I:	301-306		

On the calling of the apostles; the second and third of the six "yokes" (see n. 1, below).

[1] Other MSS. alluded to in the note to **141**, just above, contain a portion of this sermon as part of the *De sex iugis*.
[2] At the end of this sermon: "Explicit secunda pars. Incipit tercia" (as L notes, crossed out – but followed by a gold-rubricated "H" at the beginning of what our copyist later [i.e., after **154**, f. 218vb] discovered to be **143** – though it might equally well have stood for "Hora iam ..." at the opening of **176**). It all could conceivably have been a simple scribal error, but perhaps from it we may glean some indication of his examplar? (And we must also allow the possibility that there is here a logical line of demarcation, after all: this sermon is the last in this collection corresponding to a particular saint's day.)

143. B2.II.29. *Common of an Apostle*.

Text: Jn 15:12 – Hoc est ...
Quia autem finis mandatorum est caritas ... × ... preter istam sentenciam sicut libet.

L:	210-219	C:	ff. 207va-208va
	29	W 3928:	ff. 56rb-58vb
		W 3931:	ff. 59va-61vb
A I:	168-171		

On the six proper objects of man's love.

144. B2.II.30. *Common of an apostle*.

Text: Jn 15:17 – Hec mando ...
Premittit Christus specialiter suis apostolis et in eis cunctis Christicolis ut diligant se mutuo ... × ... ad bonum utile ordinandi.

L:	219-226	C:	ff. 208va-209rb
	30	W 3928:	ff. 58vb-60va
		W 3931:	ff. 62ra-64ra
A I:	172-175		

An essay on the paradoxes of sin and persecution.

145. B2.II.31. *Common of an apostle.*

Text: Mt 10:16 – Ecce ego ...
Hoc evangelium docet apostolus ... × ... comminatorie ab ipso conducti.

L:	227-234[1]	C:	ff. 209rb-210ra
	31	W 3928:	ff. 60va-62va
		W 3931:	ff. 64ra-66va
A I:	deest		

The friars are the wolves in the Church; they signify four evils prophesied by Christ. The fourth of the six "yokes" (see note).

[1] For other MSS containing the *De six iugis*, of which a portion of this sermon is a part, see above, **141**, n.

146. B2.II.32. *Common of an evangelist.*

Text: Lk 10.1 – Designavit dominus ...
Hoc evangelium docet quale ministerium ... × ... propter malum retribuere bonum.[1]

L:	234-240[2]	C:	f. 210ra-vb
	32	W 3928:	ff. 62va-64va
		W 3931:	ff. 66va-67vb
A I:	175-178		

How the friars violate Christ's injunction to preach, as given to His disciples. The fifth of the six "yokes" (see n. 2, below).

[1] "Bonum" lacking in **vi** and **viii**; but the sense demands it.
[2] For other MSS containing the *De sex iugis*, of which a portion of this sermon is a part, see above, **141**, n.

147. B2.II.33. *Common of one martyr.*

Text: Jn 12:24-25 – Nisi granum ...
In isto evangelio monet Christus electos suos ... × ... exequeretur ecclesia contra huiusmodi novitates.[1]

L:	240-247[2]	C:	ff. 210vb-211va
	33	W 3928:	ff. 64va-66rb
		W 3931:	ff. 67vb-69vb
A I:	179-182		

The vicarious martyrdom of following the *via Christi*; last of the "six yokes" (see n. 2, below).

[1] Only **i** of all MSS (including those of the *De sex iugis*: see next note) adds, as L observes, in a later hand, "ex consilio Antichristi fallaciter introductos."

[2] For other mss containing the *De sex iugis*, of which a portion of this sermon forms the conclusion, see above, 141, n.

148. B2.II.34. *Common of one martyr.*

Text: Lk 10:16 – Qui vos ...
In hoc evangelio ostenditur auctoritas predicantis ... × ... inflaciones superbie contra regulas caritatis?

L:	247-254	C:	ff. 211va-212rb
	34	W 3928:	ff. 66rb-68va
		W 3931:	ff. 69vb-71vb
A I:	185-189		

Of predestination, pride and indulgences.

149. B2.II.35. *Common of one martyr.*

Text: Mt 16:24 – Si quis ...
Hoc evangelium ut priora hortatur ad paciendum ... × ... quia regula sibi contrarians sit heresis manifesta?

L:	254-261	C:	ff. 212rb-213ra
	35	W 3928:	ff. 68va-70va
		W 3931:	ff. 72ra-74rb
A I:	182-185		

This sermon distils much of Wyclyf's doctrine in a single sentence: "videtur mihi (ut sepius) quod necesse est omnem salvandum crucem suam tollere et penaliter sequi Christum." (P. 257.) On p. 259 there is a reference to Grosseteste's *De cessatione legalium*.[1]

[1] Cf. Thomson, *The Writings of Robert Grosseteste*, 121-122; Smalley, "The Biblical Scholar," 81-82. This work was also of great help to Wyclyf in the composition of his *De veritate sacre scripture* (**31**); it is likely that this sermon dates from the same period.

150. B2.II.36. *Common of one Martyr.*

Text: Lk 14:26 – Si quis ...
Hoc evangelium docet quante et qualiter omnis fidelis debet Christum diligere ... × ... et sanctorum oportet oppositum evenire.

L:	261-269	C:	ff. 213ra-214ra
	36	W 3928:	ff. 70va-73ra
		W 3931:	ff. 74rb-77rb
A I:	189-193		

Always a difficult text; Wyclyf's construction is rigorous here. It furnishes also ample occasion for another attack on clerical endowment: "nec caverent clerici qui ad totum cleri ministerium plene sufficerent suffragio temporali, cum cotidiane elemosine sanctitas sue vite et labores manuales (si oportet) instar Apostoli de omnibus istis vite necessariis cum dei providencia providerent." (P. 269.)

151. B2.II.37. *Common of one Martyr.*

Text: Mt 10:26 – Nichil opertum ...
Hoc evangelium docet per que media Christi servus ad martyrium roboratur ... × ... pauca relinquo aliis pertractanda.

L:	269-277	C:	f. 214ra-vb
	37	W 3928:	ff. 73ra-75vb
		W 3931:	ff. 77rb-80ra
A I:	194-197		

Wyclyf's extended obbligato on divine omniscience, human trepidation and the fate of the damned made this sermon a gloomy ordeal for his parishioners.

152. B2.II.38. *Common of one Martyr and Bishop.*

Text: Mt 9:35 – Circuibat Jesus ...
Hoc evangelium dat formam multiplicem ... × ... et sermone 30° prime partis.[1]

L:	277-285	C:	ff. 214vb-215va
	38	W 3928:	ff. 75vb-77va
		W 3931:	ff. 80ra-82vb
A I:	197-201		

A lamentation on the canonical obstacles to the full exercise of the preacher's gifts: episcopal jurisdiction, arbitrary limitation of the cure, and the reluctance of preachers themselves to travel to remote places. Wyclyf then exhorts his listeners to the ministry of healing, purifying and raising the dead – all construed, in his age of brass, figuratively.

[1] This is the corrected explicit in L; see his note.

153. B2.II.39. *Common of many Martyrs.*

Text: Lk 6:20 – Elevatis Jesus ...
Istud creditur esse evangelium ... × ... congruenciam loci et temporis adaptari.

L:	285	C:	f. 215va-vb
	39	W 3928:	f. 77va-vb
		W 3931:	ff. 82vb-83ra
A I:	201-205		

This shortest of Wyclyf's sermons (though not in its English version) refers back to **141**, treating the texts synoptically.

154. B2.II.40. *Common of many Martyrs.*

Text: Mt 10:23 – Cum persequentur ...
Hoc evangelium docet martyres quomodo debent laborare ... × ... ad statum hominis non attingens.

L:	285-293	C:	ff. 215vb-216va
	40	W 3928:	ff. 77vb-80ra[1]
		W 3931:	ff. 83ra-86ra
A I:	206-209		

A dialectical presentation of martyrdom and suicide; Augustine and the devil are the chief protagonists. This seems to be the only use of this device in any of Wyclyf's sermons.

[1] The two folios neatly excised between 78 and 79 do not interrupt the text.

155. B2.II.41. *Common of many Martyrs.*

Text: Lk 21:14 – Ponite in ...
Dictum est superius sermone 31° ... × ... ad persecuciones suorum membrorum fideliter tollerando.

L:	293-300	C:	ff. 216va-217rb
	41	W 3928:	ff. 80ra-82ra
		W 3931:	ff. 86ra-88vb
A I:	209-214		

Among diverse other matters, Wyclyf remarks that Christians are seriously outweighed by the Saracens: "illi sunt plures, potenciores et mundo graviores quam nos ..." (p. 297) – for an insular man, a commendably objective view. For that reason, he continues, we ought all the more faithfully to follow the example of the first Christians, "nam per consideracionem ad particularia et affeccionem ad bona propria caritas fere extinguitur et fides que debet esse longa, lata et profunda nimium ecclipsatur."

156. B2.II.42. *Common of many Martyrs.*

Text: Lk 6:17 – Descendens Jesus ...
Cotidie legimus evangelium attestans ... × ... in officio curati fructuosius.

L:	300-308	C:	ff. 217rb-218rb
	42	W 3928:	ff. 82ra-84rb
		W 3931:	ff. 88vb-91va
A I:	214-217		

The poverty of Christ contrasted to the opulence of the clergy.

157. B2.II.43. *Common of many Martyrs*.

Text: Lk 21:9 – Cum audieritis ...
Ista sentencia reseratur sepe a Domino ... × ... ex revelacione Domini cognoverunt.

L:	308-314	C:	ff. 218rb-219ra
	43	W 3928:	ff. 84rb-86ra
		W 3931:	ff. 91va-93vb
A I:	218-222		

On wrongful excommunications: Wyclyf alludes once to his own *De symonia* (**35**: p. 312), thereby providing a *terminus a quo*.

158. B2.II.44. *Common of many Martyrs*.

Text: Lk 12:1 – Attendite a ...
Hoc evangelium ut priora hortatur ad prudenter paciendum martyrium ... × ... nostris sectis pharisaicis avidius prosecuta.

L:	314-322	C:	f. 219ra-vb
	44	W 3928:	ff. 86ra-88rb
		W 3931:	ff. 94ra-96vb
A I:	222-226		

Hypocrisy suffuses all other sins; the orders are full of it: "Ex quo patet, cum tota via viantis debet esse elemosinaria et Deo abscondita, quod tota religio privata sit ypocrisi maculata." (P. 320.) This sermon is separately listed in Bale (= no. 102).

159. B2.II.45. *Common of many Martyrs*.

Text: Mt 24:3 – Sedente Jesu ...
Hoc evangelium enucleat martyribus materiam paciendi ... × ... spoliat populum atque fraudat.

L:	322-330	C:	ff. 219vb-220vb
	45	W 3928:	ff. 88rb-90vb
		W 3931:	ff. 96vb-99vb
A I:	225-230		

Strongly anti-papal; concludes with another attack on the great edifices of the orders (cf. **57** and **67**, n., above).

160. B2.II.46. *Common of many Martyrs*.

Text: Mt 10:34 – Nolite arbitrari ...
Hoc evangelium dirigit amorem hominis ... × quod alios cum prudencia moderanda.

L: 330-339   C: ff. 220vb-221va
        46   W 3928:   ff. 90vb-93rb
                             W 3931:   ff. 99vb-102vb
A I: 231-234

A reasonably close exegesis, followed by a solid exposition of Wyclyf's teaching on alms.

161. B2.II.47. *Common of many Martyrs.*

Text: Mt 24:1 – Egressus Jesus ...
Hoc evangelium ut priora docet formam ... × ... solucio istorum patet diffuse alibi.

L: 339-345   C: ff. 221va-222rb
        47   W 3928:   ff. 93rb-95ra
                             W 3931:   ff. 102vb-105ra
A I: 235-239

A continuation of the preceding treatment of alms and mendicancy. The implication in the explicit that he has treated an aspect of the question elsewhere more comprehensively does *not* correspond to his *Exposicio super textus Matthei xxiv* (**373**, below); in fact the reference is to several passages outside Mt 24 altogether: cf., e.g., **87**, *et frequenter alibi*.

162. B2.II.48. *Common of many Martyrs.*

Text: Lk 11:29 – Dixit Jesus ...
Hoc evangelium ut priora docet quomodo usque ad martyrium sunt inimici ecclesie arguendi ... × ... virtutem moralem particularis prudencia comitetur.

L: 345-354   C: ff. 222rb-223ra
        48   W 3928:   ff. 95ra-97rb
                             W 3931:   ff. 103ra-107vb
A I: 239-242

The keys of heaven are the true knowledge of Scripture and a consequent sound theology; a man may indeed be pope by virtue of such *sciencia*, though not purely by sitting at Rome: there is in fact no need for an institutional pope in the true church at all.

163. B2.II.49. *Common of many Martyrs.*

Text: Mk 13:1 – Egrediente Jesu ...
Exposicio huius evangelii dicta est ... × ... et continuacionem observancie legis Christi.

L:	353-360	C:	f. 223ra-vb
	49	W 3928:	ff. 97rb-99rb
		W 3931:	ff. 107vb-110ra
A I:	243-248		

Wyclyf here defines the three aspects of the church (triumphant, sleeping, militant), and observes that all the laws of the Gospel bear on the last of these, *hic in via*. Again, the orders in the church, and the Papacy itself, have fallen on evil times: "Que enim secta tam presens non declinat a sanctitate observancie primitive?" (P. 359.) Seldom will we come upon such a clear assertion of the essentially retrospective heart of any reformer in the Christian context.

164. B2.II.50. *Common of a Confessor and a Bishop*.

Text: Mt 24:42 – Vigilate, quia ...
Expedito superficialiter de sentencia [6 wds.] superest declarare sentenciam ... ×
... Et patet posterius solucio ad alia argumenta [que sequuntur].[1]

L:	360-368	C:	ff. 223vb-224vb
	50	W 3928:	ff. 99rb-101va
		W 3931:	ff. 110ra-112va
A I:	248-252		

The watchful wayfarer is like the faithful servant; the endowment of prelates is a great snare.

[1] **vi** lacks the last two words; they do seem redundant.

165. B2.II.51. *Common of a Confessor and a Bishop*.

Text: Mk 13:33 – Videte, vigilate ...
Exposicio huius evangelii patet in parte ... × ... ad maiorem profectum ecclesia amplius insordescat.

L:	368-376	C:	ff. 224rb-225va
	51:	W 3928:	ff. 101va-103vb
		W 3931:	ff. 112va-115rb
A I:	261-266		

A continuation of the preceding sermon. Wyclyf twice refers to canon law (p. 369); this is rare in the later sermons.

166. B2.II.52. *Common of a Confessor and Doctor*.

Text: Mt 5:13 – Vos estis ...
Hoc evangelium docet in exemplo quadruplici ... × ... quelibet veritas philosophica includitur in scriptura.

L:	376-384	C:	ff. 225va-226rb
	52	W 3928:	ff. 103vb-106ra
		W 3931:	ff. 115rb-118ra
A I:	266-271		

A good prelate, rare though he be, is truly the salt of the earth; a good Christian (*viator*, again) is the light of the world.[1]

[1] For an earlier discourse on light, see above, **4**, and especially n. 2; the following sermon in this collection also dilates on this topic. Wyclyf would later quote portions of his discussion of light in this sermon in **374**: 80-89.

167. B2.II.53. *Common of a Confessor and a Doctor.*

Text: Mt 5:14 – Vos estis ...
Quando fui iunior et in delectacione vaga magis sollicitus ... × ... est indubie vasallus perpetuus principis tenebrarum.

L:	384-392	C:	ff. 226rb-227rb
	53	W 3928:	ff. 106ra-108rb
		W 3931:	ff. 118ra-120va
A I:	deest		

"Witelo" (cf. **4**, n. 2, above) remarked upon the twelve aspects of light; there are twelve analogous aspects of human love.

168. B2.II.54. *Common of a Confessor and a Doctor.*

Text: Mt 5:14 – Non potest ...
Duo sunt quibus Christus comparat suos apostolos ... × ... ipsos esse debere sub pena dampnacionis perpetue.

L:	392-400	C:	ff. 227rb-228ra
	54	W 3928:	ff. 108rb-110rb
		W 3931:	ff. 120va-123ra
A I:	deest		

Christ came to fulfil the law; we are bound to follow His commandments, despite the forces which threaten always to extinguish His light in us. (See the two preceding commentaries.)

169. B2.II.55. *Common of a Confessor and Abbot.*

Text: Lk 11:33 – Nemo accendit ...
Hoc evangelium docet quomodo quicunque confessor vel Christianus debet dirigi quoad Deum ... × ... vel eius procuratorem sufficere improbare.

L:	400-408	C:	f. 228ra-vb
	55	W 3928:	ff. 110rb-112vb
		W 3931:	ff. 123ra-126ra
A I:	271-274		

Further ruminations on the manifold meanings of *lux*; the state should illuminate the actions of the church if, as surely true in Wyclyf's England, the church is herself thick with shadows.

170. B2.II.56. *Common of many Confessors.*

Text: Lk 12: 35 – Sint lumbi ...
Hoc evangelium excitat et informat viatores ... × ... a vidente inconveniencia que sequuntur.

L:	409-416	C:	ff. 228vb-229vb
	56	W 3928:	ff. 112vb-114vb
		W 3931:	ff. 126ra-128rb
A I:	275-279		

More on the duties of secular lords to defend the *populus ac pauperes* against papal rapacity; a counsel of peace with other governments: "... pro temporalibus non pugnare" (p. 416).

171. B2.II.57. *Common of many Confessors.*

Text: Mt 10:5 – Misit Jesus ...
Ordo autem caritatis exigit quod homo ... × ... tam spiritualem quam eciam corporalem.

L:	416-425	C:	ff. 229vb-230va
	57	W 3928:	ff. 114vb-117va
		W 3931:	ff. 128rb-131rb
A I:	280-284		

The first of three commentaries on the kingdom of heaven; the last of three on the rightful sphere of secular power. Of course this theme recurs with great regularity in the Wyclyf canon; besides **28-30** and **33**, we should cite here also the *Peticio ad regem et parliamentum* (**403**).

172. B2.II.58. *Common of one Virgin and Martyr.*

Text: Mt 13:44 – Simile est ...
Constat quod inter septem parabolas Salvatoris quas loquitur Matthei 13° tres in isto evangelio [5 wds.] inculcantur ... × ... ne ab infidelibus illudantur.

L:	426-435	C:	ff. 230vb-231vb
	58	W 3928:	ff. 117va-120va
		W 3931:	ff. 131va-134va
A I:	284-289		

Perhaps the most attractive of Wyclyf's sermons, at least to the middle of p. 433, where he slips into his customary raillery at the popes and especially the friars; on p. 435 we come upon one of his calculations of their financial drain on the English nation. It was exaggerated to a degree, but we shall probably never possess a sufficiently accurate estimate of such recondite entities as the GNP, per capita annual income, or net personal worth in late fourteenth-century England to know just how far off the mark his round numbers were.

173. B2.II.59. *Common of a Virgin not a Martyr*.

Text: Mt 25:1 – Simile est ...
Hoc evangelium docet statum ecclesie ... × ... ex diurnitate defensio.

L:	436-444	C:	ff. 231vb-232va
	59	W 3928:	ff. 120va-123ra
		W 3931:	ff. 134va-137rb
A I:	289-294		

A gloomy panorama of death, judgment and large-scale damnation; cf. **153**, above.

174. B2.II.60. *Ascension Day* (40th day after Easter).

Text: Mk 16:14 – Recumbentibus undecim ...
Ante ascensionem valefaciens suis discipulis ipsos in fide et suo officio informavit ... × ... ut salventur a vicio quadruplici cardinali.

L:	445-452	C:	ff. 232va-233va[1]
	60		
A I:	360-362		

On preaching as the manifestation of the Holy Spirit.

[1] Deest in both **vi** and **vii**; at this point **236** and **245** are inserted.

175. B2.II.61. *Corpus Christi Day* (Thursday after Trinity Sunday).

Text: Jn 6:56 – Caro mea ...
Hoc evangelium alludit fundacioni et sensui ... × ... unum vagum accidens sine aliquo subiectante.

L:	453-463	C:	ff. 233va-234va

61 (= *Sermones mixti*, 1)   W 3928:   ff. 128ra-131rb[1]
                                   W 3931:   ff. 142va-145vb
A II: 169-170

The occasion offered the obvious text for a concluding and quite coherent discourse on the true identity of the Eucharist.[2] Dismissing all contrary views as "deliramenta puerilia," Wyclyf closes with: "Nos enim ponimus quod hoc sacramentum virtute verborum Christi est vere corpus Domini; ... quod hoc sacramentum est in natura sua verus panis; ... quod virtute benediccionis Christi et verborum suorum sacramentalium panis melioratur, quia fit quodammodo corpus Christi...."

[1] Before this sermon, both **vi** and **viii** have "Expliciunt ewangelia de sanctis." After it, i.e., as nos. **62-64** of this collection, **i** gives the sermons identified as **112-114**, above. Our inclusion of it here is, like Loserth's, admittedly arbitrary, but it is defensible.

[2] Cf. **209**, below; **38-44**, **47**, above, etc.

176-234. B2.III. *Sermones super epistolas*. 1378?-1382.

  I. Inc.: Omnes quatuordecim libri Apostoli et septem epistole [9 wds.] sunt paris auctoritatis ...
  Expl.: × ... Hii sunt illi. De isto inferius.

  II. MSS (those which contain the *De prelatis contencionum* [= a part of **202**; also known as *De incarcerandis fidelibus*] are marked by an asterisk; those containing the *De religione privata II* [= a part of **204**] are marked by a dagger):

i	C		ff. 238ra-290va, 347ra-352bisr	xiv/ex	JW MS Eng.
ii	D		pp. 387a-398a	xiv/2	JW MS Eng.
iii	Herrnhut, Archiv der Brüder-Unität	ABII.R.1.16.a	ff. 35r-38r, 41r-43v, 48r-52r, 55r-56v, 145r-147r	1412	Unasc. Boh.[1]
iv	Olomouc, KapK	C.O.118*	ff. 202v-204v	xv/1	Unasc. Boh.[2]
v	Oxford, Bodleian	e Musaeo 86	f. 71vb	1439	Asc. Eng.[3]
vi	PMK	D.123 (693)*	ff. 23r-28v	xv/1	JW MS Boh.
vii	PUK	III.G.11 (536)*	ff. 69v-72r	xv/1	JW MS Boh.
viii		X.E.9 (1910)†	ff. 202r-206r	ca. 1420	JW MS Boh.
ix	W	1337*	ff. 168va-170rb	ca. 1410	JW MS Boh.
x		1387*	ff. 110va-111va	ca. 1410	JW MS Boh.
xi		3930†	ff. 197vb-202ra	1412	JW MS Boh.
xii		4483	ff. 67v-69r	1408	Asc. Boh.
xiii		4527†	ff. 226v-229v	1410	JW MS Boh.
xiv	Wo	306 (340)	ff. 3ra-197vb	xv/1	Asc. Pol.[4]
xv		565 (613)	ff. 110ra-292va	xv/1	JW MS Boh.
xvi		669 (719)†	ff. 175v-179v	1417	Asc. Boh.[5]

III. Ed. J. Loserth, *Iohannis Wyclif Sermones* III. *Super Epistolas* (WS, 1889); and as indicated below for specific sermons of a divergent MS tradition. From all MSS except **iii, iv, xii, xiv, xv** and **xvi**.

IV. See commentary on individual sermons below.

VC: 3933 3935 4514 7980   Bale: 9?   Sh: 35   Lo: 36

[1] Not fully identified in Lo and not used in L (although briefly remarked in his introduction to vol. IV of the *Sermones*, p. XII). I wish here to acknowledge the helpfulness of Pastorin Ingeborg Baldauf at the Moravian Archives in confirming the foliation.

[2] First remarked by Sedlák, *Studie a Texty* I: XVII (interleaved); he offers no corrections of Loserth's readings.

[3] The *FZ* MS; a fragment, noted in L but not in Lo.

[4] A Wyclyf hymn in Polish and a Polish commentary occupy most of f. 1r. Throughout L there are many identifiable lacunae in **i**; after carefully checking both major Wo MSS (**xiv, xv**) against a clear majority of those noted by Loserth, I do not hesitate to assert that the later Continental scribes had a superior text before them. There are sufficient differences from clear readings in **i** to exclude the possibility that the Wo scribes simply copied more carefully than the writer of **i**.

[5] See, as for **xiv** and **xv** also, Kühn-Steinhausen, "Wyclif-Handschriften in Deutschland," 625 (-627).

176. B2.III.1. *First Sunday in Advent*.

Text: Ro 13:11 – Hora est ...
Omnes quatuordecim libri Apostoli et septem epistole [9 wds.] sunt paris auctoritatis ... × ... operum quantum ad graciam promerendum.

L:	1-9	C:	f. 238ra-vb[1]
	1	Wo 306:	ff. 3ra-5vb
		Wo 565:	ff. 110ra-112va
A II:	221-225		

A rather abstract disquisition on sin; lacks any current points of reference.

[1] F. 237v is blank.

177. B2.III.2. *Second Sunday in Advent*.

Text: Ro 15:4 – Quecunque scripta ...
Ista epistola sicut quelibet scripture particula docet tamquam conclusionem ... × ... et in speculo scripture rectitudinem eorum perficere ne declinent.

L:	9-16	C:	ff. 238vb-239va
	2	Wo 306:	ff. 5vb-8rb
		Wo 565:	ff. 112va-114vb
A II:	225-228		

A linear development *ex textu* into a gentle reflection on Christ as the incarnation of faith, hope and charity.

178. B2.III.3. *Third Sunday in Advent.*

Text: 1 Co 4:1 – Sic nos ...
Quamvis autem sentencia istius epistole dirigi possit ... × ... et prelati precipue infideliter ipsam negant.

L:	16-23	C:	ff. 239va-240rb
	3	*Wo 306:*	ff. 8rb-11ra
		Wo 565:	ff. 114vb-117rb
A II:	228-231		

A lamentation upon the snares of temporalities, extending even to a rare indictment of secular lordship: "nostri principes et seculare brachium non laborant ad stabiliendum cleri ecclesiam conformiter legi Christi, sed potentes indubie ex parte diaboli nituntur ipsos trahere ad mundanum officium et hinc ipsos ditare de Christi patrimonio contra ipsum." (P. 16.)

179. B2.III.4. *Fourth Sunday in Advent.*

Text: Php 4:4 – Gaudete in ...
Ista epistola tamquam clavis tocius religionis Christiane docet quomodo passiones animi debeant moderari ... × ... et opera consequencia in eo sanccius fundabuntur.

L:	25-31	C:	ff. 240rb-241rb
	4	*Wo 306:*	ff. 11ra-13vb
		Wo 565:	ff. 117rb-119vb
A II:	232-236		

An excursus on the four ruling passions here affords Wyclyf an opening to charge the sects and confessors alike with deceitful practices. The reference to "Sermone LXXX°" on p. 26 is actually a *renvoi* to *sermo* 60 of the first part (= **114**, pp. 402-403); while a reference in the *Trialogus* (**47**, p. 330) to *sermo* LXIV "in tercia parte" is actually to pp. 26-27 of this sermon.

180. B2.III.5. *Christmas Day.*

Text: Ti 2.11 – Apparuit gracia ...
Ista epistola docet specialius quomodo Christiani viantes debent predictam pacem Domini custodire ... × ... usque ad fundamentum destruit suas feces.

L:	31-40	C:	ff. 241rb-242rb
	5	D:	pp. 387a-390a
		Wo 306:	ff. 13vb-16vb
A II:	deest	*Wo 565:*	ff. 119vb-122va

Then as now, it is safe to assume a more numerous *congregatio fidelium* at Christmas; it should not therefore surprise to find that Wyclyf has seized the occasion to dilate upon a number of issues uppermost in his mind: grace, predestination, disendowment, and the friars' excesses – in this case, those of "quidam pseudofrater idiota nimis ignarus" (p. 37), who had evidently written some sort of commentary on 2 Ch. Further research may unearth the identity of this minor luminary.

181. B2.III.6. *Sunday within Octave of Christmas Day*.

Text: Ti 3:4 – Apparuit benignitas ...
Ista epistola ut prior docet quomodo debemus in virtutibus nos servare ... × ... plus ponderatur humana suspensio quam divina.

L:	40-48	C:	ff. 242rb-243ra
	6	D:	pp. 390a-393b
		Wo 306:	ff. 16vb-19vb
A II:	deest	*Wo 565*:	ff. 122ra-125ra

The depth of Wyclyf's conviction in the matter of prelates "suspended by God" is not now, nor was then, subject to challenge. What is most noteworthy is the artlessness of his resolution of the hoary issue of their worthiness to administer the sacraments: "solebam dicere quod sicut fidelis non debet de talibus nimium mussitare, sic non debet partem affirmativam talium ut fidem accipere, sed citra fidem ex bonis operibus vel malis partem sequentem tamquam probabilem reputare, quia certus sum quod nec auctoritas nec racio subducta revelacione necessitat ad unam partem disiunctive vel aliam." (P. 47.) His measure of faith in man's inerrant faculty for distinguishing good and evil fruits seems to have been uncommonly ample; that very faith, provoked and tested so frequently as it surely was by massive evidence of mischief, informed his remedial resolve and inflamed his wrath.

182. B2.III.7. *The Circumcision* (1 January).

Text: He 1:1, 2 – Multiphariam, multisque ...
In ista epistola docet Paulus Hebreos ... × ... nec proporcionem aliarum graciarum hominum et gracie unionis.

L:	48-55	C:	f. 243ra-vb
	7	D:	pp. 393b-396b
		Wo 306:	ff. 19vb-22rb
A II:	deest	*Wo 565*:	ff. 125ra-127rb

A dense, totally apolitical Christological thicket. Wyclyf also remarks on the unknown authorship of the epistle as a whole, with no evident interest in resolving this vexing question: "Tacet autem in ista epistola singulariter nomen suum, ne propter hoc quod fuit a pluribus sui generis exprobatus sentencia sua plus pateret contemptui." (P. 19.)[1]

[1] A compact and unbiased summary of the current state of the question is John Wick Bowman, *Hebrews James 1 Peter 2 Peter* (The Layman's Bible Commentary 24: Atlanta, 1962): 7-10.

183. B2.III.8. *The Epiphany*.

Text: Gl 4:1 – Quanto tempore ...
In ista epistola declarat Apostolus libertatem ... × ... redire ad puram ordinacionem et simplicem legis Christi.

L:	54-62	C:	ff. 243vb-244vb
	8	*Wo 306*:	ff. 22rb-24rb
		Wo 565:	ff. 127rb-129vb
A II:	238-240		

A highly charged antipapal polemic, heavily laced with canonical citations – several of which, however, are surprisingly inexact. His conclusion epitomizes the bulk of his argumentation: "sepe dixi quod habentes conscienciam rectam tam in religiosis quam in prelatis cesariis necessitabuntur redire ad puram ordinacionem et simplicem legis Christi."

184. B2.III.9. *Sunday within Octave of Epiphany*.

Text: Is 60:1 – Surge, illuminare ...
Epistola ista prophetica narrat quid contingeret de Messia ... × ... quod salus stat in prima confessione et primo medico animarum.

L:	62-69	C:	ff. 244vb-245va
	9	*Wo 306*:	ff. 24rb-27rb
		Wo 565:	ff. 129vb-132rb
A II:	241-244		

The customary *dubium* provides a platform for predictable remarks on confession, as then construed by the Curia and "prelati qui vendicant se" (p. 69).

185. B2.III.10. *Octave of Epiphany*.

Text: Is 25:1, etc. – Domine deus ...
Istud autem verbum fuit prophete eximii Isaie ... × ... de quanto fundate fuerint in scriptura.

L:	69-78	C:	ff. 245va-246va
	10	D:	pp. 396b-398a

		Wo 306:	ff. 27rb-30vb
A II:	deest	Wo 565:	ff. 132rb-135rb

The chief function of the priest is preaching; therefore Wyclyf here defends the homiletic rights of the *simplices sacerdotes*, i.e., the Poor Priests.

186. B2.III.11. *First Sunday after the Octave.*

Text: Ro 12:1 – Obsecro vos ...
Apostolus in ista epistola instruit Romanos ... × ... et illam ordinacionem defendere et fovere.

L:	78-88	C:	ff. 246va-247va
	11	Wo 306:	ff. 30vb-34ra
		Wo 565:	ff. 135rb-137rb[1]
A II:	244-246		

It is more than usually difficult to trace a line of reasoning through this sermon. One is reduced to the frank admission that Wyclyf's mental processes sometimes deviated from strict linearity. He passes here from the sevenfold aspect of service to God, through an artless monothelite musing, to a furious metaphysical exercise on the venerable multiplicity-unity paradoxes.

[1] There are two ff. 136 in the extant numeration.

187. B2.III.12. *Second Sunday after the Octave.*

Text: Ro 12:6 – Habentes donaciones ...
In ista epistola que immediate sequitur epistolam proximam in eodem capitulo docet Apostolus viginti septem condiciones ... × ... ut instruamur in mediis et in finem ultimum beatifice elevemur.

L:	88-97	C:	ff. 247va-248va
	12	Wo 306:	ff. 34ra-37rb
		Wo 565:	ff. 137rb-140va
A II:	246-249		

This sermon is in actuality a rapid scan of Ro 12:6-16, with sulfurous invective for once subordinated to straightforward exposition.

188. B2.III.13. *Third Sunday after the Octave.*

Text: Ro 12:16 – Nolite esse ...
In ista epistola immediate sequente post proximam in capitulo 12° ad Romanos docet Apostolus gentiles ... × ... tamen sunt ad breviores epistolas differenda.

L:	97-105	C:	ff. 248va-249va
	13	Wo 306:	ff. 37rb-40rb
		Wo 565:	ff. 140va-143va
A II:	249-251		

Wyclyf's feelings on the just war,[1] though not precisely datable in this sermon, are of considerable interest in that they do clearly predate his more topical argumentation subsequent to the Flanders crusade of 1383. In pursuing his commentary from the sixteenth through the twenty-first verse of Ro 12, he chose to stress his own pacific bent: "Numquam enim sum ausus ad bellum vel pugnam corporalem consulere sed ad partem securiorem ad quem ortatur Apostolus." (P. 101.)

[1] Cf. in general Frederick H. Russell, *The Just War in the Middle Ages* (Cambridge, Eng., 1976).

189. B2.III.14. *Fourth Sunday after the Octave.*

Text: Ro 13:8 – Nemini quicquam ...
In ista epistola pro finali conclusione trium precedencium Apostolus epilogat caritatem ... × ... et illibertacionem legis veteris est gravata.

L:	105-114	C:	ff. 249va-250va
	14	Wo 306:	ff. 40rb-43rb
		Wo 565:	ff. 143va-146va
A II:	252-254		

This is one of several opportunities Wyclyf seized in his *Sermones* and in his polemical writings to impugn the friars' practice of and rationale for mendicancy. Here rather more than elsewhere he targets specific Scriptural passages often cited by the mendicant apologists (cf. **161**, above), turning their substance to his own ends. His skill in this exercise is formidable.

190. B2.III.15. *Fifth Sunday after the Octave.*

Text: Cl 3:12 – Induite vos ...
Dictum est sermone 12° huius de viginti vestibus ... × ... ac blasfemo mendacio Jesu Christi nostri cicius revocaret.

L:	114-122	C:	ff. 250va-251va
	15	Wo 306:	ff. 43rb-46ra
		Wo 565:	ff. 146va-149rb
A II:	255-257		

Save for the stern concluding paragraph, this sermon is notably free of personal rancor; owing to its subject (the thirteen garments needful for the true Christian) and this singular absence of vitriol, it must rank as one of Wyclyf's most coherent and pleasing exegetical efforts.

191. B2.III.16. *Septuagesima Sunday*.

Text: 1 Co 9:24 – Nescitis quod ...
In ista epistola Apostolus hortatur racione exemplari fideles ... × ... quam sciunt pro parte sua ex evangelio fabricare.

L:	122-129	C:	ff. 251va-252va
	16	*Wo 306*:	ff. 46ra-48vb
		Wo 565:	ff. 149rb-152ra
A II:	257-260		

This sermon may be viewed, from the pronouncement of the *dubium* on p. 126 to its conclusion, as a further extension of Wyclyf's offensive against the friars in **189**, above. His concern here is chiefly with their alleged mendacity. The references to the Beguines and Beghards[1] and Grosseteste (unidentifiable; probably from a letter) on p. 128 disclose once again his wonted eclecticism.

[1] Cf. Ernest W. McDonnell, *The Beguines and Beghards in Medieval Culture, with special emphasis on the Belgian Scene* (New Brunswick, N.J., 1954); Little, *Religious Poverty and the Profit Economy in Medieval Europe*, 128-134; and below, **224**, p. 417.

192. B2.III.17. *Sexagesima Sunday*.

Text: 2 Co 11:19; 12 – Libenter suffertis ...
In ista epistola videtur multis quod Apostolus more suo increpat ironice ipsos Corinthios ... × ... ut virtus pacientis similiter habitet copiosius in viante.

L:	129-136	C:	ff. 252va-253rb
	17	*Wo 306*:	ff. 48vb-51va
		Wo 565:	ff. 152ra-154vb
A II:	260-264		

Fools need not be suffered without recourse: kings and lords, bishops and the people themselves may limit the evils of today's false and foolish teachers (i.e., the mendicants). These observations are followed by a fervent apostrophe to St. Paul.

193. B2.III.18. *Quinquagesima Sunday*.

Text: 1 Co 13:1 – Si linguis ...
Ista epistola magnificat caritatem quomodo excellit omnis virtutes ... × ... tam in via quam in patria superat ambo ista.

L:	137-144	C:	ff. 253rb-254rb
	18	Wo 306:	ff. 51va-53va
		Wo 565:	ff. 154vb-157vb
A II:	265-269		

A commentary on 1 Co 13:1-12, the Pauline descant on love and knowledge.[1] Twice, on pp. 139 and 144, Wyclyf touches on the issue of self-existing accidents – which from 1379 on would have led him inexorably into an excursus on the Eucharist; here it does not. Interesting sidelights are cast on his belief concerning the connections between *caritas* and predestination.

[1] Cf. **49**, n. 1, above.

194. B2.III.19. *Quadragesima Sunday*.

Text: 2 Co 6:1 – Hortamur vos ...
Dictus est in communi verbo de gracia ... × ... licet in persona sua peccare non potuit.

L:	145-152	C:	ff. 254rb-255rb
	19	Wo 306:	ff. 53va-56rb
		Wo 565:	ff. 157vb-160vb
A II:	deest		

I am not sure whence Wyclyf may have derived his pithy definition of grace (p. 145): "michi tamen videtur quod satis pertinenter potest tempus idoneum datum homini ad merendum vocari ista dei gracia ..."; in any case it provides him a precipitous *point de départ* for a dizzy plunge into both the subtleties of grace and of the practical means of strengthening witness to it. Assuredly it is resident neither at Rome nor at Avignon; nor does it abide in the bosom of the orders.

195. B2.III.20. *Second Sunday in Lent*.

Text: 1 Th 4:1 – Rogamus vos ...
In ista epistola hortatur Apostolus Thessalonicos ... × ... quousque secundum leges superioris pape medici finaliter sit sanatus.

L:	152-161	C:	ff. 255rb-256rb
	20	Wo 306:	ff. 56rb-59vb
		Wo 565:	ff. 161ra-163vb
A II:	272-274		

A plague is invoked upon both papal houses; and excommunications by prelates today are grounded in any case on dubious Scriptural antecedents, and are tainted by larcenous motives as well.

196. B2.III.21. *Third Sunday in Lent.*

Text: Ep 5:1 – Estote imitatores ...
In hac epistola Apostolus docet Ephesios ... × ... ostendens pulcritudinem diligibilem omnium in qua lucet.

L:	162-169	C:	ff. 256rb-257ra
	21	*Wo 306*:	ff. 59vb-62va
		Wo 565:	ff. 163vb-166rb
A II:	274-277		

An unsparing, slashing assault on the pretensions of the Franciscans, and on sin generally.

197. B2.III.22. *Fourth Sunday in Lent.*

Text: Gl 4:22 – Scriptum est ...
Constat ex serie huius epistole quomodo Apostolus intendit quod legalia legis veteris cessare debuerant ... × ... pro hac pulcra et facili libertate.

L:	169-176	C:	f. 257ra-vb
	22	*Wo 306*:	ff. 62va-65rb
		Wo 565:	ff. 166va-169ra
A II:	277-280		

A basic elucidation of Wyclyf's own hermeneutic principles. The old law has been supplanted by Christ's new law, though the new sects do not by their actions acknowledge this.

198. B2.III.23. *Passion Sunday.*

Text: He 9:11 – Christus assistens ...
In ista epistola commendat primo Apostolus ex sex excellenciis pontificium ... × ... sicut peccatum finalis inpenitencie est gravissimum.

L:	176-184	C:	ff. 257vb-258vb
	23	*Wo 306*:	ff. 65rb-68ra
		Wo 565:	ff. 169ra-171va
A II:	280-383		

On mortal and venial sins; cf. **51**, above.

199. B2.III.24. *Palm Sunday.*

Text: Php 2:5 – Hoc sentite ...
In ista epistola docet Apostolus singulos Christianos ... × ... addiscere linguam et logicam quam ignorant.

L:	184-191	C:	ff. 258vb-259rb
	24	*Wo 306*:	ff. 68ra-70rb
		Wo 565:	ff. 171va-174ra
A II:	283-285		

Reflections on the Incarnation lead to an extended *obiter dictum* (pp. 188-190) on the woeful ignorance of a certain "canis niger," styled "tolstanus" both in the printed text (p. 189, line 5) and in **xiv** and **xv**, who allegedly delated Wyclyf's *Libellus* (**400**) to the Roman Curia, probably in 1378. J. P. Whitney suggested that "tolosanus" is a more plausible reading, and points to the figure of Robert Waldby as the probable target.[1] This worldly Austin divine, who had indeed studied at Toulouse, would in the years before his death in 1397 hold successively the offices of Bishop of Aire and of Chichester; Archbishop of Dublin and of York; and Chancellor of Aquitaine and of Ireland.[2] One is compelled to wonder at the recklessness with which Wyclyf alienated men of influence who might arguably have been persuaded to his point of view by gentler tactics.

[1] "A Note on the Work of the Wyclif Society," in H. W. C. Davis, ed., *Essays in History Presented to Reginald Lane Poole* (Oxford, 1927; reprinted 1969): 107n.

[2] Aubrey Gwynn, *The English Austin Friars in the Time of Wyclif* (Oxford, 1940): 271-272; but the record here is not quite so complete as in *BRUO* III: 1958.

200. B2.III.25. *Easter Day*.

Text: 1 Co 5:7 – Expurgate vetus ...
Ista epistola docet fideles quomodo se debeant ad esum eukaristie preparare ... ×
... cum suis premissis ex sensu Apostoli.

L:	191-197	C:	ff. 259rb-260ra
	25	*Herrnhut*:	ff. 35r-38r
		W 4483:	ff. 67v-69r[1]
		Wo 306:	ff. 70va-72vb
A II:	286-289	*Wo 565*:	ff. 174ra-176va

A stalwart defense of his position on the Eucharist provides an opening for Wyclyf's most elaborate known attempt at humor (p. 194): "Hec eciam est racio quare fideles burgenses non permittunt fratres penetrantes domos intrare celaria sua vinaria ad vinum, ne forte benedicendo vino in calice convertant totam doliorum congeriem in pura accidencia...." It is pleasant to imagine that on the Easter in 1381 or 1382 when Wyclyf delivered this message, his flock may have enjoyed the Paschal observance more than he intended!

[1] Garbled; entitled "sermo de sacramento corporis et sanguinis."

201. B2.III.26. *First Sunday after Easter.*

Text: 1 Jn 5:4 – Omne quod ...
Beatus iste Johannes tractans specialiter de dileccione dei et proximi dat in epistola ista principium ... × ... et sic ista testificacio excedit omnes probaciones politicas.

L:	197-205	C:	f. 260ra-vb
	26	*Herrnhut*:	ff. 41r-43v[1]
		Wo 306:	ff. 72vb-75vb
A II:	289-291	*Wo 565*:	ff. 176va-179rb

Wyclyf here sets forth in exceptionally clear language the axiom which most impelled him to reform the Church Militant of his day: "Et unum sepe prenosticavi et adhuc prenostico quod ecclesia numquam erit sine perturbacione notabili, antequam Christi ordinacio que tantum hiis diebus despicitur ad institucionem secundum formam primariam sit reducta." (P. 201.) Endowment and the humanity of Christ come under scrutiny again.

[1] Different incipit.

202. B2.III.27. *Second Sunday after Easter.*[1]

Text: 1 P 2:21 – Christus semel ...
Ista epistola sicut multe alie docet quomodo debemus imitari Christum ... × ... et prudenciam legios suos acucius puniendi.

L:	206-212	C:	ff. 260vb-261va
	27	*Herrnhut*:	ff. 48r-52r
		Olomouc:	ff. 202r-204v
		PMK:	ff. 23r-28v
		PUK III.G.11:	ff. 69v-72r[2]
		W 1337:	ff. 168va-170rb
		W 1387:	ff. 110va-111ra
		Wo 306:	ff. 75vb-79ra
A II:	292-294	*Wo 565*:	ff. 179rb-182rb

The deviant MS tradition of this text is explicable largely by its truncated, autocephalous appearance under the alternate titles of *De prelatis contencionum* and *De incarcerandis fidelibus*. (See n. 1, below.) The latter differs from the sermon which contains it (= p. 209, line 11 *usque ad finem*) only in a few words, and in the insertion of an obviously later diatribe against the "disciples of Antichrist."[3] The telltale allusion to the "refuga" (meaning Urban VI: see **405**, n. 3, below) strengthens our assumption that Wyclyf excerpted and modified this section in 1383. His chief concern throughout is to limit the authority of bishops, particularly with regard to incarceration and excommunication.

¹ Over half of this sermon appears separately as a polemical piece, titled as indicated in the commentary, and so published by Loserth, *Johannis Wyclif Opera Minora* (WS, 1913): 92-97†; see his remarks on the date and circumstances of this redaction, pp. xvi-xvii. The title is given more fully in **x** as "De sentencia incarcerando fideles propter excommunicacionem post 40 dies." It appears in all four vc as an "Epistola"; deest in Bale; and is no. 92 in Sh and 93 in Lo.

² End of text on f. 85v reads "Explicit tractatus de incarcerando fideles ..."; this has misled both Sh and Truhlař. Actually this marks the end of the *De statu innocencie* (**27**).

³ After the word "suos" in line 13, p. 121 of L. The passage in the *Opera Minora* runs from p. 95, line 26, to p. 97, line 9.

203. B2.III.28. *Third Sunday after Easter.*

Text: 1 P 2:11 – Obsecro vos ...
Docet beatus Petrus quod Christiani debent [9 wds.] diffundere legem Christi ... ×
... sed spiritualis quo principaliter timeant deum suum.

L:	213-224	C:	ff. 261va-262vb
	28	*Herrnhut*:	ff. 55r-56v¹
		Wo 306:	ff. 79ra-83rb
A II:	294-296	*Wo 565*:	ff. 182va-186va

The theme of humble subjection to a righteous king carries over from the preceding sermon. An assault on the friars' superficial learning and criminal behavior ensues – but not all the friars are vicious: one indeed, an unnamed Carmelite doctor (p. 223), is undeniably a good man. In his last years, after the Blackfriars Synod, Wyclyf rarely bothered with such fine distinctions.

¹ An incomplete text.

204. B2.III.29. *Fourth Sunday after Easter.*[1]

Text: Jn 1:17 – Omne datum ...
Constat ex doctrina Augustini quomodo de tribus modis bonorum bona fortune sunt infima ... × ... in suis descripcionibus et racionibus quare ordines sunt privati.

L:	224-239	C:	ff. 262vb-264va
	29	PUK X.E.9:	ff. 202r-206r
		W 3930:	ff. 197vb-202ra
		W 4527:	ff. 227v-229v
		Wo 306:	ff. 83rb-88vb
		Wo 565:	ff. 186va-192ra
A II:	297-298	*Wo 669*:	ff. 175v-179v

The circumstances here are comparable to those of **202**, above. The bulk of this sermon (from p. 230, line 21, *usque ad finem*) is identical with a piece commonly identified as *De religione privata II* (see note below). The separate listing would appear to be defensible on the grounds of the diverse MS tradition, which does link it more than once to the *De religione privata* [*I*] (G*Dub*.1). On contextual grounds this association surely has warrant as well. But its inclusion (unaltered) as part of this sermon in the form of the usual *dubium* commentary, is plainly integral, given the immediate connection with the text (p. 230): "... utrum privata religio *sit datum optimum, descendens a patre luminum*" (emphasis added). The mention of the "materia de eukaristia," i.e., his treatise by that name (**38**) on p. 225, vouchsafes a relatively late date for the sermon itself, and is consonant with his vendetta against the friars in the *dubium*. It is an exceptionally long sermon – but so are **265** and **287**, and the integrity of the latter has never been contested.

[1] Separately published as an autocephalous piece, *De religione privata II*, in R. Buddensieg, ed., *John Wiclif's Polemical Works in Latin* II: 524-536. Not in vc or Bale; = Sh: 81; Lo: 82.

205. B2.III.30. *Fifth Sunday after Easter.*

Text: Jn 1:22 – Estote factores ...
Constat ex processu epistole huius sancti quomodo commendat actum ... × ... qui ipsam destruerent nimis generaliter obligat viatores.

L:	239-248	C:	ff. 264va-265va
	30	Oxford:	f. —[1]
		Wo 306:	ff. 88vb-92rb
A II:	299-301	*Wo 565*:	ff. 192ra-195ra

This and the following sermon evidently became part of an ongoing row between Wyclyf and John Wells OSB[2] on the pretensions of the orders. But Loserth's identification of the "Carmelita" (also on p. 246) as Peter Stokes[3] is by no means secure; his reference to Lechler does not in fact substantiate any such inference. It is possible Stephen Patrington[4] or even Richard Maidstone[5] may have been intended. He also cites his old vademecum "Witelo"[6] again, and gives a rare nod to Scotus as well.[7]

[1] A fragment; runs from p. 246, line 28 ("Unde ...") to p.247, line 3. Published in *FZ*, p. 239. See the next sermon also. Exact f. not determined by editor.
[2] Cf. Workman, *JW* II: 412; *BRUO* III: 2008. The identification is confirmed by *FZ*, p. 239.
[3] Cf. Workman, *JW* II: 275-277; *BRUO* III: 1783-1784.
[4] Cf. Workman, *JW* II: 247-248; *BRUO* III: 1435-1436.
[5] Cf. Workman, *JW* II: 249; *BRUO* II: 1208; and see now especially Arnold Williams, "*Protectorium Pauperis*: A Defense of the Begging Friars by Richard of Maidstone, O.Carm.," as cited in **47**, n. 19, above. The fact that our only complete MS of this *apologia* appears in the *FZ* probably should not sway our verdict, however.
[6] See **4**, n. 2, above. (Cited on p. 244.)
[7] See **16**, n. 4, above.

206. B2.III.31. *Sunday after Ascension.*

Text: 1 P 4:7 – Estote prudentes ...
Secundum philosophos patet quod prudencia est quinta virtus ... × ... sed impertinens est dicendum vel efficaciter invehendum.

L:	248-257	C:	ff. 265va-266rb
	31	Oxford:	f. —[1]
		Wo 306:	ff. 92rb-95va
A II:	302-305	*Wo 565*:	ff. 195va-198vb

See the previous commentary on the context of this sermon; here he brusquely rebuts seven of Well's objections. But of course the virtue of prudence is the nominal pretext for this fusillade.

[1] A fragment; published previously in *FZ*, pp. 239-241; corresponds to p. 251, ll. 31-33; p. 252, ll. 10-15; p. 253, ll. 1-5, 25-31, 34-36 (more or less); p. 254, ll. 21-26; p. 255, ll. 26-28; p. 256, ll. 3-5, 32-? (the final quotation has no analogue). Wells' citations, like those of the 1411 "committee of twelve," are often specious and of course highly selective. – Exact foliation not ascertained by editor.

207. B2.III.32. *Whitsunday.*

Text: Ac 2:1 – Cum complerentur ...
Ystoria actuum apostolorum licet superflua vel superficialis videatur aliquibus ... × ... sed legis Christi prudenter hoc facere in mensura.

L:	257-267	C:	ff. 266rb-267va
	32	*Wo 306*:	ff. 95vb-99va
		Wo 565:	ff. 198vb-202va
A II:	305-307		

Wyclyf complains here of invidious misrepresentations by his enemies of his views of law and Scripture. He summarizes them in this way: "Credimus autem ex fide quod licet tota veritas et lex Dei sit in prioribus scriptis evangelica implicite, Deus tamen eternaliter ordinavit quod sint secundum illam mensuram adeo implicite." (P. 266.)

208. B2.III.33. *Trinity Sunday.*

Text: Rv 4:1 – Vidi hostium ...
Cum exposicio huius libri requirit revelacionem novam ... × ... in domibus possessionatorum ordinum per fratrum negligenciam incastrata.

L:	267-277	C:	ff. 267va-268va
	33	*Herrnhut*:	ff. 145r-147r[1]
		Wo 306:	ff. 99va-103va
A II:	308-312	*Wo 565*:	ff. 202va-206va

Wyclyf tries his hand at the mystical sense of Rv 4:1-9; and he says too that endowment, commencing with the Donation of Constantine,[2] and the poorly-rationalized proliferation of new sects are today hopelessly compounded by the Schism. His own marginal allegiance to "Urbanus noster" (p. 276) is still evident, however.

[1] Captioned "Explicacio capitis Apocalypsis 4."
[2] See **412**, n. 7, below.

209. B2.III.34. *Corpus Christi Day*. 1382.

Text: 1 Co 11:23 – Ego enim ...
In ista epistola docet Apostolus nedum grecos sed cunctos fideles ... × ... quantum in ipsis est corpus Christi.

L:	277-286	C:	ff. 268va-269va
	34	*Wo 306*:	ff. 103va-107ra
		Wo 565:	ff. 206va-209vb
A II:	deest		

As in another sermon for this day (**175**, above), the doctrine of the Eucharist is the self-evident focus. Here he alludes much more frequently than is common in the *Sermones* to his own writings (pp. 279-280): **11**, **17** and **22** are clearly signified, and there is also an unidentifiable *De fide* (**xiv** and **xv**, unfortunately, do not illuminate this). He also intimates his own presence at a "consili[um] perfid[um]" during which a certain "adversarius scripture cum suis catulis" opposed his views on remanence. One is strongly tempted to venture that this was Peter Stokes, or some other Carmelite (cf. **205**, n. 3, above), but there is no way to declare this with any certainty. In any case he is openly contemptuous of those he regards as abysmally deficient even in the rudiments of logic. If we may extrapolate from his example that such reciprocal *ad hominem* barrages were not uncommon *in scholis*, "academic freedom," had the issue arisen in his time, would surely have meant something radically different from what we take it to mean today.

210. B2.III.35. *First Sunday after Trinity*.

Text 1 Jn 4:8 – Deus caritas ...
Johannes evangelista more suo tractat specialiter de perfectissima virtute ... × ... et ex hoc patet quam vana est eorum religio.

L:	286-297	C:	ff. 269va-270vb
	35	*Wo 306*:	ff. 107ra-111rb
		Wo 565:	ff. 209vb-213va
A II:	312-316		

Caritas was unquestionably at the very quick of Wyclyf's response to the Christian imperative. In the midst of excoriating the friars and the *possessionati*, not only here but in many other places as well, he suddenly stops to reflect on their real defects: lack of love, excess of base fear. "Sed qui sic timet non est perfectus in caritate, sed ut Deum non diligat toto corde." (P. 295.) It is at times a hard task for the modern commentator justly to assess this lively consciousness of *caritas*, neutralized as it so often is by his notorious rancor and vituperation; but it plainly did fortify him in the face of real adversity. − It is possible that the allusion to the "Earthquake Synod" (p. 292) is a slightly later insertion; but cf. also **216**, **218**, **219**, **229**, below, which we have all confidently assigned to 1382. It may be that all of the Sunday *Sermones super epistolas* after Trinity Sunday were delivered in that year.

211. B2.III.36. *Second Sunday after Trinity*.

Text: 1 Jn 3:13 − Nolite mirari ...
Verba huius epistole possunt tam ad bonos dirigi quam ad malos ... × ... regna principum atque ecclesiam que est regnum celorum?

L:	297-305	C:	ff. 270vb-271vb
	36	*Wo 306*:	ff. 111rb-114va
		Wo 565:	ff. 213va-216vb
A II:	317-320		

We are bound to love even the odious and lying friars, though we hate their evil works. (He reiterates this in **214**, p. 326.) On p. 302 there is a rare citation from St. Basil the Great.

212. B2.III.37. *Third Sunday after Trinity*.

Text: 1 P 5:6 − Humiliamini sub ...
Ista epistola docet humilitatem viancium in opere ... × ... et ad ista attencio sunt omisse.

L:	306-314	C:	ff. 271vb-273ra
	37	*Wo 306*:	ff. 114va-118ra
		Wo 565:	ff. 216vb-220ra
A II:	321-323		

The friars violate humility in their rapacity, in their exaggerated claims to sanctity (though he does not here deny that the founders, Francis and Dominic, were holy men), and in their endless schemes of self-aggrandizement.

213. B2.III.38. *Fourth Sunday after Trinity.*

Text: Ro 8:18 – Estimo quod ...
In ista epistola hortatur Apostolus quod voluntarie sine murmure ministrent ... × ... et talibus illusionibus decipiunt activos ecclesie.

L:	315-323	C:	ff. 273ra-274ra
	38	*Wo 306*:	ff. 118ra-121va
		Wo 565:	ff. 220ra-223ra
A II:	323-325		

The vanity of men raises barriers to their acceptance of grace. The friars particularly are arrogant in their begging; this is most reprehensible in the able-bodied, a practice for which there can exist no plausible warrant.

214. B2.III.39. *Fifth Sunday after Trinity.*

Text: 1 P 3:8 – Omnes unanimes ...
Cum nemo salvabitur nisi dona Spiritus Sancti habuerit ... × ... secundum fidem caritate formatam et indefectibiliter adheretis.

L:	323-331	C:	ff. 274ra-275ra
	39	*Wo 306*:	ff. 121va-124va
		Wo 565:	ff. 223ra-226rb
A II:	325-328		

There are six conditions for efficacious prayer; the friars and possessioners manifest none of them.

215. B2.III.40. *Sixth Sunday after Trinity.*

Text: Ro 6:3 – Quicunque baptizati ...
Cum quecunque scripta sunt ad nostram doctrinam ... × ... et sepeliret eius egenciam clamorosa et licite mendicare.

L:	331-340	C:	ff. 275ra-276ra
	40	*Wo 306*:	ff. 124ra-128ra
		Wo 565:	ff. 226rb-229va
A II:	328-329		

We must be dead to sin to arise in new life, after the example of Christ. God of course does not will sin, "sed vult quod informet ad creature profectum quoad esse secundum peccati." (P. 337.) As often elsewhere, he argues that Christ did not truly beg (i.e., as the friars do), because He was already perfect in dominion.

216. B2.III.41. *Seventh Sunday after Trinity.* 1382.

Text: Ro 6:19 – umanum dico ...
Ista epistola docet media et medicinas ... × ... ideo lex paciencie quam Christus docuit est secura.

L:	341-352	C:	ff. 276ra-277rb
	41	*Wo 306*:	ff. 128ra-132rb
		Wo 565:	ff. 229va-233va
A II:	330-331		

Here Wyclyf responds to hostile accusations (by John Wells? or Peter Stokes? or Stephen Patrington?)[1] at the Blackfriars Synod in 1382. He takes special care to define *religio*; and he distinguishes most notably "common" from "private" religion, regarding the former as "religionem quam omnis fidelis debet sub pena amissionis beatitudinis observare, et illa intellecta primo modo est lex mandatorum Domini, sed intellecta secundo modo est vel actualis complecio huius mandatorum vel universalis observancia sine prevaricacione in aliquo individuo legis Dei ..." (pp. 344-345). To this law all additions are superfluous or even deleterious.

[1] Cf. **205**, nn. 2-4, and **206**, above.

217. B2.III.42. *Eighth Sunday after Trinity.*

Text: Ro 8:12 – Debitores sumus ...
In ista epistola docet Apostolus quomodo vita nostra aptabitur ... × ... palliaciones iste diaboli per sectas fallacie introducte.

L:	352-365	C:	ff. 277rb-278va
	42	*Wo 306*:	ff. 132rb-137ra
		Wo 565:	ff. 233va-238vb
A II:	331-333		

The mendicant letters of fraternity[1] here provoke Wyclyf's ire; he likewise is incensed at their assertions on the Eucharist.

[1] See the literature on this subject cited by John Moorman, *A History of the Franciscan Order from its Origins to the Year 1517* (Oxford, 1968): **515**, n. 8; cf. also **47**, n. 22; **224**, p. 425; **238**, p. 503.

218. B2.III.43. *Ninth Sunday after Trinity.* 1382.

Text: 1 Co 10:6 – Non simus ...
Paulus in ista epistola tamquam speculator providus predicit ecclesie ... × ... non attenderet ad tales prepositos Antichristi.

L:	365-374	C:	ff. 278va-279va
	43	*Wo 306*:	ff. 137ra-140va
		Wo 565:	ff. 239ra-241vb
A II:	333-336		

The Blackfriars Synod twice draws Wyclyf's fire (pp. 370, 373); but there runs throughout this sermon a rather uncharacteristic *fin de siècle* fatalism: on p. 367 he even makes a rare mention in passing of the plague.[1] (But cf. also **257**, p. 203.) Yet, as he adds with a fillip of hope, in such morbid times the lures of the devil are less potent!

[1] More refined figures than those we have been accustomed to appear in William J. Courtenay, "The Effect of the Black Death on English Higher Education," *Speculum* 55 (1980): 696-714.

219. B2.III.44. *Tenth Sunday after Trinity*. 1382.

Text: 1 Co 12:2 – Scitis quoniam ...
In epistola ista docemur quomodo debemus ex recepcione prioris beneficiencie grati esse Christo ... × ... graviter ad retardaciones ecclesie militantis.[1]

L:	375-384	C:	ff. 279va-280vb
	44	*Wo 306*:	ff. 140va-143vb
		Wo 565:	ff. 241vb-245ra
A II:	336-339		

This homiletic review of 1 Co 12:2-11 focuses on the efficaciousness of prayers. He deplores the facile acceptance of special prayers by the Blackfriars Synod, and even laments the ease with which kings and lords "ducuntur ut bos ad iugum diaboli" to the allurements of false religion.

[1] Expl: × "... tardacionem ecclesie." – In both **xiv** and **xv**.

220. B2.III.45. *Eleventh Sunday after Trinity*. 1382.

Text: 1 Co 15:45 – Notum facio ...
In ista epistola Apostolus innuens commendacionem sui evangelii racione quadruplici docet fructum ... × ... quod non errent in concilio quam in vita.

L:	384-393	C:	ff. 280vb-281vb
	45	*Wo 306*:	ff. 143vb-147ra
		Wo 565:	ff. 245ra-248ra
A II:	339-341		

The Pauline writ runs on a level with that of the Gospels themselves, and the words of the Apostle should be universally preached. The Eucharist today is heretically misconstrued: "Numquam autem pertinaciter defendebam quod esset substancia panis materialis; sed quod sit panis ex auctoritate Apostoli usque ad mortem volo defendere." (P. 392.)

221. B2.III.46. *Twelfth Sunday after Trinity*.

Text: 2 Co 3:4, 5 – Fiduciam talem ...
Ista epistola multipliciter docet ecclesiam ... × ... ne ista sentencia secularibus dominis predicetur.

L:	393-401	C:	ff. 281vb-282va
	46	Wo 306:	ff. 147ra-150ra
		Wo 565:	ff. 248ra-251ra
A II:	342-345		

Human laws and the law of the Old Testament gave way on Pentecost to the new law of Christ, "levis, brevis et utilis" (p. 401). Priests especially, but the secular lords also, tragically turn away from this new dispensation.

222. B2.III.47. *Thirteenth Sunday after Trinity*.

Text: Gl 3:16 – Abrahe dicte ...
In ista epistola docet Apostolus quod per graciam domini Jesu Christi datur eterna hereditas ... × ... et eorum fictas elemosinas nutriant sua facinora [vel defendunt].[1]

L:	402-410	C:	ff. 282va-283vb
	47	Wo 306:	ff. 150rb-153va
		Wo 565:	ff. 251rb-254rb
A II:	345-347		

A continuation of the preceding sermon on the law, sonship in Christ, and the waywardness of the orders.

[1] The last two words omitted in **xiv** and **xv**; in the corrector's hand in **i**.

223. B2.III.48. *Fourteenth Sunday after Trinity*.

Text: Gl 5:16 – Spiritu ambulante ...
In ista epistola intendit Apostolus docere viantes ... × ... humanitatem vel crucifixionem remota similitudine et mistica sequi illum.

L:	411-420	C:	ff. 283vb-284vb
	48	Wo 306:	ff. 153va-157rb
		Wo 565:	ff. 254rb-257vb
A II:	348-351		

Time and time again in the last five years of his life Wyclyf demanded of the spokesmen of the orders that they stand forth and declare without equivocation their real views on the Eucharist and endowment. It seems that they did, more than once – though not necessarily in response to the don's importuning. What Wyclyf hoped for was evidently a kind of *purgatio errorum* from their side; given his standing as the lone *vox clamans*, it is not surprising that he was disappointed.

224. B2.III.49. *Fifteenth Sunday after Trinity.*

Text: Gl 5:25 – Si spiritu ...
In ista epistola docet Apostolus ipsos Galatas ... × ... sed fidem Christi cum modestia reserare.

L:	420-429	C:	ff. 284vb-285vb
	49	*Wo 306*:	ff. 157rb-161ra
		Wo 565:	ff. 257vb-261ra
A II:	351-354		

A dithyramb on justice and *caritas*.

225. B2.III.50. *Sixteenth Sunday after Trinity.* 1382.

Text: Ep 3:13 – Obsecro vos ...
Dictum est in proxima epistola ex auctoritate Apostoli ... × ... Sed que sanctitas vel sciencia in tali ecclesia Antichristi?

L:	429-438	C:	ff. 285vb-286vb
	50	*Wo 306*:	ff. 161ra-164va
		Wo 565:	ff. 261ra-264ra
A II:	354-356		

After a protracted discussion of Ep 3:13-21, Wyclyf introduces some new metaphysical arguments against the Eucharistic pronouncements of the Blackfriars Synod.

226. B2.III.51. *Seventeenth Sunday after Trinity.*

Text: Ep 4:1 – Obsecro vos ...
Apostolus in ista epistola hortatur nedum Ephesios ... × ... ista sedes posset in materia fidei vel alia derivare.

L:	438-447	C:	ff. 286vb-287vb
	51	*Wo 306*:	ff. 164va-167vb
		Wo 565:	ff. 264ra-266vb
A II:	356-359		

Sixteenth through nineteenth-century Protestants seized upon this passage as one of the most pertinent to the vexed issue of the Christian *vocatio*. Wyclyf's remoteness from his successors is seldom more apparent than in his brief, perfunctory notice of the significance of this term. He turns the occasion instead into a sermon more concentrated than any other around the Eucharist.

227. B2.III.52. *Eighteenth Sunday after Trinity*.

Text: 1 Co 1:4 – Gracias ago ...
Corinthi dicuntur esse Achaici et sunt Greci ... × ... et quomodocumque Spiritus Sanctus consulit sanctam ecclesiam adiuvando.

L:	447-455	C:	ff. 287vb-288va
	52	*Wo 306*:	ff. 167vb-171ra
		Wo 565:	ff. 266vb-269va
A II:	359-360		

This is rather more colorful than his customary denunciation of the "four sects": on p. 453 we find his enumeration of the "twelve daughters of the leech": "popes, cardinals, bishops, archdeacons, officials and deans, rectors, priests, possessioners and beggars [*mendici*, not *mendicantes*], clerks and pardoners." It is odd that in such a detailed listing he should have omitted his personal scourge, the papal collectors (cf. **397**, below).

228. B2.III.53. *Nineteenth Sunday after Trinity*.

Text: Ep 4:23 – Renovamini spiritu ...
Pro exposicione illius epistole oportet primo notare terminos ... × ... ut patet Act. 20° et secunda ad Thessal. ultimo.

L:	455-464	C:	ff. 288va-289va
	53	*Wo 306*:	ff. 171ra-175ra
		Wo 565:	ff. 269va-273ra
A II:	360-362		

A dissertation on the four cardinal virtues, and on the sins of lying and anger.

229. B2.III.54. *Twentieth Sunday after Trinity*.

Text: Ep 5:15 – Videte quomodo ...
In ista epistola docet Apostolus quomodo Christiani debent spiritualiter ambulare ... × ... sed ut pure elemosinas gratis datas.

L:	465-473	C:	ff. 289va-290va
	54	Oxford:	f. 71vb[1]
		Wo 306:	ff. 175ra-178va
A II:	362-365	*Wo 565*:	ff. 273ra-276ra

On temptations, and the Eucharist.

[1] A fragment, separately published in *FZ*, p. 283. Corresponds to p. 468, line 30 - p. 469, line 2 in L.

230. B2.III.55. *Twenty-first Sunday after Trinity.*

Text: Ep 6:10 – Confortamini in ...
Ista epistola docet fideles viantes quomodo debent pugnare ... × ... cum plus participant racionis dyaboli?

L:	473-482	C:	ff. 347ra-348ra[1]
	55	*Wo 306*:	ff. 178va-182va
		Wo 565:	ff. 276ra-279rb
A II:	365-368		

Ep. 6:10-17 leads Wyclyf to ruminate on the fallen estate of the prelacy.

[1] The corrector's marginalium on f. 290va, as reproduced in L, p. 473 n., clearly indicates that he realized his omission; "pars III." appears at the top of ff. 347-352.

231. B2.III.56. *Twenty-second Sunday after Trinity.*

Text: Php 1:6 – Confidimus in ...
In ista epistola ostendit et exemplificat Apostolus caritatem ... × ... ac defensione ordinacionis contrarii acutissime laborare?

L:	483-491	C:	ff. 348ra-349rb
	56	*Wo 306*:	ff. 182ra-186ra
		Wo 565:	ff. 279va-282va
A II:	368-370		

Poverty is the condition which best fosters sincerity and "a macula conservat" (p. 488); endowment and the avarice of the friars lead to the opposite ends.

232. B2.III.57. *Twenty-third Sunday after Trinity.*

Text: Php 3:17 – Imitatores mei ...
In ista epistola hortatur Apostolus fideles quomodo ipsum imitari debent ... × ... et ita ut patet superius sunt manifesti heretici et raptores.

L:	491-501	C:	ff. 349rb-350va
	57	*Wo 306*:	ff. 186ra-189vb
		Wo 565:	ff. 282va-285vb
A II:	370-373		

Further on the arrogance and hypocrisy of the friars.

233. B2.III.58. *Twenty-fourth Sunday after Trinity.*

Text: Cl 1:9 – Non cessamus ...
In ista epistola ostendit Apostolus tam affeccionem quam operacionem ... × ... et cuncta que inferre poterunt humiliter paciendo.

L:	502-510	C:	ff. 350va-351vb
	58	*Wo 306*:	ff. 189vb-193va
		Wo 565:	ff. 285vb-289ra
A II:	373-378		

Improper judgment that a man is a heretic makes the judge himself heretical. The fiction of Roman impeccability, "specialiter in materia fidei" (p. 509), has encouraged a widespread heretical belief about the Eucharist, though in the days of Nicholas II "valde servit Romana ecclesia in illa materia" (p. 507). To all of this he rejoins: "Istam ergo blasphemiam de inpeccabilitate Romane ecclesie placuit Deo dissolvere. Ideo teneamus pristinam libertatem et antiquos articulos fidei in Christo fundatos qui peccare non poterit vel suos fideles decipere." (P. 510.) There are parallels to these passages in the *De blasfemia* (**36**: pp. 72-73).

234. B2.III.59. *Twenty-fifth Sunday after Trinity.*

Text: Jr 23:5 – Ecce dies ...
Quia ista est ultima dominica anni precedentis ... × ... contra quos reges et regna debent insurgere, hii sunt illi. De isto inferius.

L:	511-520	C:	ff. 351vb-352bis-r[1]
	59	*Wo 306*:	ff. 193va-197va
		Wo 565:	ff. 289ra-292va
A II:	375-376		

Since the cornerstone of the papal claim to punitive jurisdiction in cases of heresy is the papal share in imperial power (presumably the Donation of Constantine is meant here)[2] – and the Empire's laws do not hold in England, then the pope may not prosecute heresy there. By extension, the papal inquisitors have no rights in England.

[1] A fragment (given by L as 352ᵉ), inserted before the *Opus evangelicum*.
[2] Cf. **412**, n. 7, below.

235-299. B2.IV. *Sermones miscellanei.*[1] 1375-1383.

I. Inc.: Consuetudo gentilis superstitum tam in clero quam vulgo exuberat ...
Expl.: × ... in terra vivencium cum corpore resumendum.

II. MSS (as very few of these sermons have counterparts in A II, that listing is given only when such is the case: B² and M³ apply specifically to the *Sermones quadraginta*):

i	C		ff. 290va-346rb	xiv/ex	JW MS Eng.
ii	D		pp. 404a-413a	xiv/2	JW MS Eng.
iii	London, Lambeth Pal.	23	ff. 258ra-280vb	ca. 1400	Asc. Eng.
iv	PUK	III.G.11 (536)	ff. 52r-53v, 112r-141r, 260v-271v	xv/1	JW MS Boh.
v		V.H.27 *(1004)*	ff. 65v-77r	xv/1	Unasc. Boh.
vi	W	1337	ff. 95ra-96vb	ca. 1410	JW MS Boh.
vii		*1337*	ff. 170rb-174va		
viii		3928	ff. 123rb-128rb, 139ra-186rb, 193ra-253rb	ca. 1410	Asc. Boh.
ix		*3929*	ff. 205va-206va	1409	JW MS Boh.⁴
x		3931	ff. 137rb-203ra	ca. 1410	Asc. Boh.⁵
xi		3932	ff. 92va-151vb, 207va-209rb	1418	Asc. Boh.
xii	*Wo*	306 *(340)*	ff. 197va-209va	xv/1	Asc. Pol.
xiii		565 *(613)*	ff. 292v-303r	xv/1	Asc. Boh.⁶

III. Ed. J. Loserth, *Iohannis Wyclif Sermones* IV. *Sermones Miscellanei (Quadraginta Sermones de Tempore. Sermones Mixti XXIV)* (WS, 1890). From all MSS except **v, vii, xii** and **xiii**.

IV. See commentary on individual sermons below.

VC: 3933 3935 4514 7980⁷   Balè: deest   Sh: 36, 37   Lo: 37

---

¹ This is a most disparate assemblage, offering sermons from both the earliest (1375) and, probably, latest (1383?) years of his preaching activity. Their appearance together in this final volume of the *Sermones*, artificially joining together as it does the *sermones quadraginta* (early: **257-296**) and 20 of the 24 *sermones mixti* (late: **237-244, 246-256, 299**; for the sequential listing of all 24, see L IV, 509-510); and even five sermons of neither affiliation (**235-236, 245, 297-298**), is awkward but conventionally well established.

² B = the "Exkurs" by Gustav Adolf Benrath, "Die Datierung von elf der sogenannten Quadraginta Sermones Wyclifs," in his *Wyclifs Bibelkommentar* (Berlin, 1966): 378-386.

³ M = William Mallard, "Dating the *Sermones Quadraginta* of John Wyclif," *MetH* 17 (1966): 86-105. We reproduce also his conjectural sequence (seq:). See also his "Charity and Dilemma: The *Forty Sermons* of John Wyclif," in G. H. Shriver, ed., *Contemporary Reflections on the Medieval Christian Tradition. Essays in Honor of Ray C. Petry* (Durham, N.C., 1974): 19-38.

⁴ Used in L, omitted from Lo.

⁵ Annotated by Peter Payne.

⁶ Both Wo MSS offer sequence: **297 - 235 - 236**.

⁷ Almost invariably listed in the VC as "XL sermones compositi dum stetit in scolis ..." and "sermones XX compositi in fine vite sue."

235. B2.IV.1. *Epistle of the Missa pro defunctis*.

Text: 1 Th 4:12 – Nolumus vos ...
Consuetudo gentilis superstitum tam in clero quam vulgo exuberat ... × ... nobilissimus et strenuissimus affectus fuit specialiter trinitati.

L:	1-11	C:	ff. 290va-291vb
	1	D:	pp. 404a-408b
		Wo 306:	ff. 201rb-205rb[1]
		Wo 565:	ff. 296r-299v

Dating this anomalous sermon is far from simple: p. 10, line 29 - p. 11, line 1 may or may not be an oblique reference to the Flanders crusade of 1383; but the style of reference to Richard II on p. 11 is much more appropriate to 1376 or 1377, while the specific *renvoi* on p. 9 to his own writings on simony, apostasy and blasphemy (= **35-37**) must date from 1379 or 1380.

[1] Given in **xii** and **xiii** as no. 61 of B2.III.

236. B2.IV.2. *Gospel of the Missa pro defunctis*.

Text: Jn 11:21 – Dixit Martha ...
Constat ex fide evangelii quod Christus tres mortuos suscitavit ... × ... de Salomone et multis similibus veteris testamenti.

L:	11-24	C:	ff. 291vb-293ra
	2	D:	pp. 408a-413a
		W 3928:	ff. 123rb-126va
		W 3931:	ff. 137rb-140vb
		Wo 306:	ff. 205rb-209va[1]
A II:	212-214	*Wo 565*:	ff. 299v-303r

After asides against mendicancy and the usual Eucharistic errors, Wyclyf expounds topically on the inappropriateness of sumptuous funerals.

[1] Given as no. 62 (i.e., of B2.III) in **xii** and **xiii**; col. 209vb of **xii** is blank; at conclusion of this sermon we read "et sic est finis epistole."

237. B2.IV.3.

Text: Ps 121:6 – Rogate que ...
Verbum istud prophete tripliciter potest sane intelligi ... × ... Locus autem est impertinens, ubi anima custoditur.

L:	24-33	C:	ff. 293ra-294ra
	3 (= *sermones mixti*, 10)	PUK III.G.11:	ff. 112r-116r
		W 3928:	ff. 152va-155ra
		W 3931:	ff. 167vb-170va

No occasion is indicated for this or the following two sermons on Ps 121:6-8. In its subject matter, his preference for general as against special prayer, it echoes **219**, above.

238. B2.IV.4.

Text: Ps 121:7 – Fiat pax ...
Constat ex fundamento fidei quod fundamentum vere pacis est fides ... × ... ad peccandum nisi gratis consenserit.

L:	34-42	C:	ff. 294ra-295ra
	4 (= *sermones mixti*, 11)	PUK III.G.11:	ff. 116r-119v
		W 3928:	ff. 155rb-157va
		W 3931:	ff. 170va-173ra

The evils of war are here recounted (cf. **188-191**); the friars support both popes in the Schism, and abet the baneful crusading fervor. (But evidently this sermon preceded Despenser's crusade in 1383.)

239. B2.IV.5.

Text: Ps 121:8 – Proper fratres ...
Videtur sanctum prophetam celesti lumine inspiratum de sancta matre ecclesia dicere ... × ... usque ad mortem factus erit in pace perpetua locus eius.

L:	42-49	C:	f. 295ra-vb
	5 (= *sermones mixti*, 12)	PUK III.G.11:	ff. 119v-122v
		W 3928:	ff. 157va-159va
		W 3931:	ff. 173ra-175ra

On predestination – a state of which the *viator* can never be certain! – and the evils of war, again; on p. 46 he cites the *Trialogus* (**47**), which assures a late date for the sermon.

240. B2.IV.6. *Gospel for Ash Wednesday.*

Text: Mt 6:18 – Cum ieiunatis ...
Hoc evangelium docet quomodo est a fidelibus ieiunandum ... × ... ad fructuose de suo crimine conterendum.

L:	49-57	C:	ff. 295vb-296ra
	6 (= *sermones mixti*, 13)	W 3928:	ff. 159va-161vb
		W 3931:	ff. 175ra-177va
A II:	38-40		

The hypocritical friars are the Pharisees of this age; among the new rites and sacraments "sine fundacione ex lege Domini" is confession to a priest.

241. B2.IV.7. *Gospel for Good Friday.*

Text: Mt 26:49 – Ave Raby ...
Constat ex fide scripture quod instante nativitate Christi (quia statim post) preconisavit ipse pacem ... × ... sanguinem eius de manu tua requiram; et patet conclusio.

L:	58-66	C:	ff. 296va-297va
	7 (= *sermones mixti*, 14)	PUK III.G.11:	ff. 122v-126v
		PUK V.H.27:	ff. 65v-68v[1]
		W 3928:	ff. 161vb-164ra
		W 3931:	ff. 177va-180ra

One of the most virulently anti-mendicant of the *Sermones*; Wyclyf finds little to choose between the warring popes.

[1] One of four sermons by Wyclyf in this codex; in margin of f. 65v: "de pace." See **273-275**, below.

242. B2.IV.8. *Gospel for Easter Monday.*

Text: Lk 24:13 – Duo ex ...
Plana est historia quomodo ista apparicio quarta in ordine fuit ... × ... nisi gratis et vecorditer nos reddiderimus sine causa.

L:	66-74	C:	ff. 297va-298va
	8 (= *sermones mixti*, 15)	PUK III.G.11:	ff. 126v-130r
		W 3928:	ff. 164ra-166rb
A II:	133-135	W 3931:	ff. 180ra-182rb

An intriguing guide to the good life, decrying undue asceticism, flimsy learning and the delusions of solitude.

243. B2.IV.9. *Gospel for Rogation Monday.*

Text: Lk 11:5 – Quis vestrum ...
Hoc evangelium docet fideles formam orandi et declarat parabolice ... × ... est in omni temptacione hominis periculosa mendacia seminare.

L:	74-81	C:	ff. 298va-299rb
	9 (= *sermones mixti*, 16)	PUK III.G.11:	ff. 130r-133v
		W 3928:	ff. 166rb-168va
A II:	153-155	W 3931:	ff. 182rb-184va

Further considerations on the virtues of right prayer, guided by Scripture. We need not complicate matters by introducing "lex ... fallax pape vel cesaris" (p. 80).

244. B2.IV.10. *Gospel for Whitmonday.*

Text: Jn 3:16 – Sic deus ...
Hoc evangelium dat fulcimenta fidelibus ... × ... vite vel operis est Deo placencior quam vocalis.

L:	81-89	C:	ff. 299rb-300ra
	10 (= *sermones mixti*, 17)	PUK III.G.11:	ff. 133v-137r
		W 3928:	ff. 168va-170rb
A II:	161-162	W 3931:	ff. 184va-186vb

There is very little concern here with current affairs; the substance of the message is rather that faith banishes despair, though the Christian may have just cause to weep at times.

245. B2.IV.11. *Mass for the Dead, Tuesday Gospel.*

Text: Jn 6:37 – Omne quod ...
Multiplex ponitur causa quare fiunt in ecclesia exequia martirorum ... × ... bene vixerit non poterit male mori.

L:	89-95	C:	f. 300ra-vb
	11	W 3928:	ff. 126va-128rb
		W 3931:	ff. 140vb-142va

In tone and topic (funeral rites), this is reminiscent of **236**, above.

246. B2.IV.12. *Epistle for Ash Wednesday.*

Text: Jl 2:12 – Convertimini ad ...
Sicut dictum est de sacramento Eukaristie secundum fidem evangelii ... × ... et totum fundatur in luciferina superbia, non in fide.

L:	95-104	C:	ff. 300vb-301va
	12 (= *sermones mixti*, 18)	PUK III.G.11:	ff. 268v-271v
		W 3928:	ff. 170vb-173ra
		W 3931:	ff. 186vb-189ra

Penance and confession are commonly misunderstood and abused. Not so harsh as **240**, above, hence surely earlier.

247. B2.IV.13. *Epistle for Ash Wednesday.* 18 March 1383.

Text: Is 58:7 – Frange esurienti ...
Post generalem sentenciam de penitencia vel confessione dicendum est specialius ... × ... est frustatorium et demeritorium quicquid agunt.

L:	104-112	C:	ff. 301va-302va
	13 (=*sermones mixti*, 19)	PUK III.G.11:	ff. 137r-141r
		W 3928:	ff. 173ra-175rb
		W 3931:	ff. 189ra-191va

The friars, who claim the right to alms spuriously, undermine the realm also in preaching on behalf of Despenser's crusade; this allusion fixes our date.

248. B2.IV.14. *Epistle for St Andrew's Day.* 30 November 1382.

Text: Ro 10:10 – Corde creditur ...
Iste sanctus apostolus Andreas habuit quandam primitatem ... × ... et intrepide promulgant istam sentenciam tamquam fidem.

L:	113-121	C:	ff. 302va-303va
	14 (=*sermones mixti*, 20)	W 3928:	ff. 175rb-177vb
		W 3931:	ff. 191va-194ra

The connection with St. Andrew's Day allows us also to date two other works in the Wyclyf canon: *De dissensione paparum* and *De cruciata* (**411, 412,** below) as necessarily prior to this sermon, since his reference to "tres conclusiones in ista materia" already published by him (pp. 117-118) fits most nearly (though not *verbatim*) portions of the latter piece (pp. 592-597 in Buddensieg's edition).

249. B2.IV.15. *Epistle for the Purification.* 2 February 1383.

Text: Ml 3:1 – Hec dicit ...
Sive autem a verisimili fratres in ista perturbacione ecclesie de voluntate Dei menciuntur ... × ... sic creditur beatam virginem in labore femineo alternasse.

L:	122-129	C:	ff. 303va-304rb
	15 (=*sermones mixti*, 21)	W 3928:	ff. 177vb-179vb
		W 3931:	ff. 194va-196rb

This sermon is another attack on the friars' preaching of Despenser's crusade, and especially on their liberal indulgences. Priests too should shun lavish banqueting; in a picturesque image, Wyclyf observes that "Non enim video quod plus pertinet sacerdoti Christi taliter populum convivare quam super vaccam sellatam hominem equitare." (P. 128.)

250. B2.IV.16. *Epistle for St John Baptist.* 24 June 1383.

Text: Is 49:1 – Audite insule ...
Sicut iste textus potest sane intelligi de persona ... × ... et populus contra regaliam illius domini sic delinquunt?

L:	129-138	C:	ff. 304rb-305rb
	16 (= *sermones mixti*, 22)	W 3928:	ff. 179vb-182va
		W 3931:	ff. 196rb-199ra

This sermon continues Wyclyf's invective against unwarranted absolutions and indulgences by both popes (of whom at least one must patently be wrong!) in the Flanders crusade.

251. B2.IV.17. *Epistle for Sts Peter and Paul*. 29 June 1383.

Text: Ac 12:1 – Misit Herodes ...
Iste fuit Herodes tercius iuxta hoc metricum ... × ... de lege Christi dictante quod clerus non est taliter prediandus.

L:	138-148	C:	ff. 305rb-306rb
	17 (= *sermones mixti*, 23)	W 3928:	ff. 182va-185ra
		W 3931:	ff. 199ra-201vb

On this occasion, Wyclyf condemned the crusade yet again, suggesting that "in factis paparum recentibus patet quod non querunt salutem ecclesie sed sua temporalia vel seculi dignitates." (P. 146.) The friars, furthermore, are suspect in their teaching that the apostles went barefoot. (St. Francis himself, of course, believed this; the Italian Observantists of the fourteenth century[1] and the Discalced Friars of sixteenth-century Spain did too.)

[1] Most recent comprehensive coverage in Duncan Nimmo, "Poverty and Politics: The Motivation of Fourteenth-Century Franciscan Reform in Italy," in Derek Baker, ed., *Religious Motivation: Biographical and Sociological Problems for the Church Historian* (SCH 15: Oxford, 1978): 161-178.

252. B2.IV.18. *Epistle for the Mass de non Virginibus*.

Text: Pr 31:10 – Mulierem fortem ...
Constat ex evidencia huius scripture et concordi sanctorum testimonio quod ista epistola loquitur de Christo ... × ... quam ipse cum suis apostolis observavit.

L:	147-157	C:	ff. 306va-307va
	18 (= *sermones mixti*, 5)	W 3928:	ff. 139ra-141vb
		W 3931:	ff. 153vb-156va
		W 3932:	ff. 207va-209rb[1]

An unusually protracted commentary, covering Pr 31:10-31; this part may be earlier than the rest of the sermon, which again chides both popes for their unseemly involvement in the Flanders crusade – but since the *missa de non virginibus* is a votive mass, it is not possible to fix its date here. There would not appear to have been any compelling reason for its unique separate appearance in **xi**.

[1] Here in isolation; titled from the text "Mulierem fortem quis inveniet?" Listed as no. 41 in both Sh and Lo. In this MS it wants the last sentence; hence expl.: × "... restitucio ablate cesarie dignitatis."

253. B2.IV.19. *Epistle for the Assumption* (15 August).

Text: Ec 24:11 – In omnibus ...
Videtur ex processu huius auctoris quod ista verba loquitur Sapiencia ... × ... assumi ab ipso dyabolo renuebat.

L:	158-167	C:	ff. 307va-308va
	19 (= *sermones mixti*, 6)	W 3928:	ff. 141vb-144rb
		W 3931:	ff. 156va-159ra

A harsh assignment of guilt to both popes for the Schism.

254. B2.IV.20. *Epistle for the Nativity of the Virgin Mary*. 8 September 1383.

Text: Ec 24:23 – Ego quasi ...
Communiter exponitur ista epistola et satis catholice ... × ... laboret viriliter contra istam blasfemiam.

L:	167-177	C:	ff. 308va-309va
	20 (= *sermones mixti*, 7)	W 3928:	ff. 144rb-147rb
		W 3931:	ff. 159ra-162vb

A paean to wisdom yields, by a transition less abrupt than usual, to a broadside against the crusade, endowment, both popes and the treasury of merit.

255. B2.IV.21. *Epistle for Michaelmas Day* (29 September).

Text: Rv 1:1 – Significavit Deus ...
Constat ex fide scripture cum pauca probabilitate propinqua fidei quomodo Johannes Evangelista edidit librum ... × ... quod propter complecionem istius peccati tanta indulgencia sit concessa.

L:	177-188	C:	ff. 309vb-310vb
	21 (= *sermones mixti*, 8)	PUK III.G.11:	ff. 260v-264v
		W 3928:	ff. 147rb-150ra
		W 3931:	ff. 162va-165rb

The contrast in tone between the commentary on Rv 1:1-5, which takes up about two-thirds of the sermon and is heavily exegetical, and the *dubium*, which occupies the remainder and is violently splenetic against the mendicant and papal doctrine of indulgences, is so startling as to prompt the suspicion that most of the *dubium* as it is presently received was not a part of the sermon when it was first delivered.

256. B2.IV.22. *Epistle for All Saints Day* (1 November).

Text: Rv 7:2 – Ecce ego ...
Aliqua in ista epistola capienda sunt ut fides ... × ... ad execucionem istius vocate indulgencie congregati.

L:	188-197	C:	ff. 310vb-311vb
	22 (= *sermones mixti*, 9)	PUK III.G.11:	ff. 264v-268v
		W 3928:	ff. 150rb-152va
		W 3931:	ff. 165va-167vb

At first glance, the references on pp. 195 and 197 to fighting bishops would lead us to conclude that the Despenser crusade is meant. This is not possible, however: apparently even the Schism lay still in the future, since mention is made only of one pope; and the friars make no appearance whatever. But the strictures against episcopal bellicosity do reveal that Wyclyf was committed to the irenic ideal even in 1377, or perhaps earlier. (Cf. also **258**, below.)

257. B2.IV.23. *Epistle for first Sunday in Advent*. Dates in M.

Text: Ro 13:11 – Hora est ...
Ecclesia facit hodie mencionem de adventu ... × ... sed ibi nacta possessione habebimus plenum ius in re.

L:	197-206	C:	ff. 311vb-312vb
	23 (= *sermones XL*, 1)	London:	f. 258ra-vb
B:	382-383: 30 Nov. 1376	W 3928:	ff. 193ra-195ra
M:	99-101: 30 Nov. 1376, "the greater part"; part also 27 Nov. 1379	W 3932:	ff. 92va-94rb

Two allusions *in textu* (p. 202, line 5; p. 205, line 11) are unequivocally insertions at the time of the integration of this first of the *sermones quadraginta* (cf. above, B2.IV, n. 1) into the final omnibus plan of the *sermones* in 1383. Another reference (p. 199, line 26) is perhaps to the *Postilla super totam Bibliam* (B4, below), which surely preceded the earliest suggested date for this sermon. His later habit in the *sermones* of using the *dubium* (e.g., "circa hoc evangelium/hac epistolam dubitatur ...") as a peg on which to air his prejudices is nowhere evident in the *sermones quadraginta*.

258. B2.IV.24. *Epistle for first Sunday in Advent*. 29 November 1377.

Text: Ro 13:12 – Induamur arma ...
In sermone proximo dicetur quomodo necesse est omnem Christianum negociari ... × ... ad plenitudinem lucis spiritualis et corporalis in patria.

L:	206-212	C:	ff. 312vb-313va
	24 (= *sermones XL*, 2)	London:	ff. 258vb-259va
B:	384: 29 Nov. 1377	W 3928:	ff. 195ra-196va
M:	88-89: ibid.; seq.: 61-24-25	W 3932:	ff. 94rb-95vb

On the narrow limits within which a just man may be legitimately urged to war. It is far better to conduct a spiritual campaign against the evils of the world by inner discipline.

259. B2.IV.25. *Epistle for second Sunday in Advent.* 6 December 1377.

Text: Ro 15:4 – Per pacienciam ...
Ut dicetur infra sermone xxxix° ... × ... quod nobis concedat [omnipotens Pater et Filius et Spiritus Sanctus].[1]

L:	213-222	C:	ff. 313va-314rb
	24 (= *sermones XL*, 3)	London:	ff. 259va-260va
B:	383: 6 Dec. 1377[2]	W 3928:	ff. 196va-198va
M:	89: ibid.; seq.: 61-24-25	W 3932:	ff. 95vb-97va

On patience and hope.

[1] i and iii both stop at "concedat"; but the sense demands the rest of it.
[2] *Pace* L, p. 217n., who implies 1383.

260. B2.IV.26. *Epistle for second Sunday of Advent.* 7 December 1376.

Text: Ro 15:5 – Deus autem ...
Constat quod per pacienciam et tribulacionem et consolacionem premiorum prosperatur vita ... × ... suos pacientes bonum regimen eis imposuisse observasse.

L:	222-231	C:	ff. 314rb-315va
	26 (= *sermones XL*, 4)	London:	ff. 260va-261vb
		W 3928:	ff. 198va-200vb
M:	89-90: 7 Dec. 1376	W 3932:	ff. 97va-99va

Of the savor of Scripture and the bitterness of ill-speaking; for slanderers ("fictatores et zelatores mendacii") he suggests a heavy iron collar around the neck, inscribed with their nonsensical utterances, "sicut audivi quoddam Londinii consuetum fieri" (p. 229).

261. B2.IV.27. *Gospel for second Sunday after Octave of Epiphany.*

Text: Jn 2:3 – Vinum non ...
Constat ex historia quomodo dominus noster Jesus Christus cum sua familia

[6 wds.] dignatus est adesse nupciis ... × ... ad cenam novissimam ad quam nos perducat [Jesus Christus].

L:	232-238	C:	ff. 315-316ra
	27 (=*sermones XL*, 5)	London:	ff. 261vb-262va
M:	102: 21 Jan. 1375 ("doubtful")[1]	W 3928:	ff. 200vb-202rb
		W 3932:	ff. 99va-101ra

On the superior force of the *lex Christi*. In the mid- to late 1370s this was an issue of equal magnitude with *dominium* on the Wyclyf agenda: cf. **31**, above.

[1] On the likelihood that this sermon dates from January in 1378 or even 1379, see W. R. Thomson, "An Unknown Letter by John Wyclyf in Manchester, John Rylands University Library MS. Eng. 86," *MedSt* 43 (1981): 536, n. 29.

262. B2.IV.28. *Gospel for third Sunday after Octave of Epiphany*. 28 January 1375.

Text: Mt 8:13 – Sanatus est ...
Istud evangelium continet historice duo miracula ... × ... scilicet in presente et gloriam in futuro.

L:	238-245	C:	f. 316ra-vb
	28 (=*sermones XL*, 6)	London:	ff. 262va-263rb
		W 3928:	ff. 202rb-203vb
M:	91-92: 28 Jan. 1375	W 3932:	ff. 101ra-102va

On faith and humility. This sermon closes with a reflection that would often be repeated in Wyclyf's last years: God is no accepter of persons.

263. B2.IV.29. *Gospel for Septuagesima Sunday*. 25 January 1377.

Text: Mt 20:6 – Quid hic ...
Constat ex serie evangelii quomodo Veritas docet suos discipulos ... × ... et in servitorem spiritui redigere.

L:	245-255	C:	ff. 316vb-318ra
	29 (=*sermones XL*, 7)	London:	ff. 263rb-264va
M:	90-91: 25 Jan. 1377;	W 3928:	ff. 203vb-206ra
	seq.: 29-30-32-33	W 3932:	ff. 102va-104va

If we are truly to manifest our faith, it must be in the energetic service of God.

264. B2.IV.30. *Gospel for Sexagesima Sunday*. 1 February 1377.

Text: Lk 8:11 – Semen est ...
Dictum est superiori dominica quomodo operarii in ecclesia Domini debent vites

suffodere ... × ... usque ad mortem pro nobis Deus benedictus in secula seculorum.

L:	256-262	C:	f. 318ra-vb
	30 (= *sermones XL*, 8)	London:	ff. 264va-265va
M:	90-91: 1 Feb. 1377;	W 3928:	ff. 206ra-207va
	seq.: 29-30-32-33	W 3932:	ff. 104va-105vb

Pride is a subtle sin, for several reasons – but is nonetheless devastating.

265. B2.IV.31. *Gospel for Sexagesima Sunday*.[1] 16 February 1376.

Text: Lk 8:11 – Semen est ...
Constat ex serie evangelii quod salvator noster dominus Jesus Christus crebro locutus est ... × ... quorum nobis concedat dominus Deus noster.

L:	262-275	C:	ff. 318vb-320ra
	31 (= *sermones XL*, 9)	London:	ff. 265va-267ra
		W 1337:	ff. 170rb-174va[2]
M:	92-94: 16 Feb. 1376;	W 3928:	ff. 207va-210rb
	seq.: 31-34-35-38-39	W 3932:	ff. 105vb-108va

This sermon, on the same text as the preceding one but delivered a year earlier, is more preoccupied with the task of the preacher and the right use of his sources, i.e., Scripture. But there is on p. 270 an interesting denunciation of the monks, based on an unidentified citation from Grosseteste. The form of address incidentally employed on p. 273 ("fraternitati vestre") is unusual in Wyclyf's writings (but cf. also **271**, p. 312); it is in fact the formal corporate designation common in papal rescripts.

[1] Separately printed also in Lechler, *Johann von Wiclif und die Vorgeschichte der Reformation* II: 580-590, from **viii** only.
[2] Called here "sermo pulcher," a designation generally applied to **299**, below. Overlooked by L.

266. B2.IV.32. *Gospel for Quinquagesima Sunday*. 8 February 1377.

Text: Lk 18:42 – Respice fides ...
Superiori dominica docuit Christus ecclesiam ... × ... quod primo erit in die iudicii unanimiter laudat Deum.

L:	275-283	C:	f. 320ra-vb
	32 (= *sermones XL*, 10)	London:	f. 267ra-vb
M:	90-91: 8 Feb. 1377;	W 3928:	ff. 210rb-212ra
	seq.: 29-30-32-33	W 3932:	ff. 108va-110ra

More on the guises of pride, with predictable citations from Boethius, Augustine and Bede.

267. B2.IV.33. *Gospel for first Sunday in Lent*. 15 February 1377.

Text: Mt 4:10 – Dominum Deum ...
Superiori dominica dictum est quomodo cecus restitutus est ... × ... patet quantum malum infert gula.

L:	283-290	C:	ff. 320vb-321va
	33 (=*sermones XL*, 11)	London:	ff. 267vb-268va
M:	90-91: 15 Feb. 1377;	W 3928:	ff. 212ra-213va
	seq.: 29-30-32-33	W 3932:	ff. 110ra-111va

Wyclyf's later polemical absorption with alms and fasting would lead him to treat those topics with much less conventionality than he does here.

268. B2.IV.34. *Epistle for Midlent Sunday*. 16 March 1376.

Text: Gl 4:28 – Nos autem ...
Nota est historia Gen. 17° et 21° quomodo sanctus Abraham [7 wds.] genuerant filium ... × ... et tunc non dubium quin sumus filii Dei, quod si filii et heredes.

L:	290-296	C:	ff. 321va-322rb
	34 (=*sermones XL*, 12)	London:	ff. 268va-269rb
M:	92-94: 16 Mar. 1376;	W 3928:	ff. 213va-214vb
	seq.: 31-34-35-38-39	W 3932:	ff. 111va-112vb

A temperate consideration of the central significance of faith.

269. B2.IV.35. *Epistle for Passion Sunday*. 30 March 1376.

Text: He 9:12 – Christus per ...
Exodi 26° describitur tabernaculum ... × ... sine intermissione pro peccati suo et tocius populi.

L:	296-304	C:	ff. 322rb-323rb
	35 (=*sermones XL*, 13)	London:	ff. 269rb-270rb
M:	92-94: 30 Mar. 1376;	W 3928:	ff. 215ra-216va
	seq.: 31-34-35-38-39	W 3932:	ff. 112vb-114va

A thoroughly orthodox delineation of the necessity for confession. Later, of course, he would stress the imperative of an inner confession, without priestly mediation.

270. B2.IV.36. *Gospel for Passion Sunday*. 15 March 1377.

Text: Jn 8:47 – Qui ex ...
In istis verbis tria sunt declaranda ... × ... beati qui audiunt verbum Dei et custodiunt illud.

L:	304-309	C:	f. 323rb-vb
	36 (= *sermones XL*, 14)	London:	f. 270rb-vb
M:	95-97: 15 Mar. 1377;	W 3928:	ff. 216va-217va
	seq.: 36-37-41-44-45	W 3932:	ff. 114va-115rb

On free will, obedience and the first three commandments; cf. **26** and **67-69**, above.

271. B2.IV.37. *Epistle for Psalm Sunday*. 22 March 1377.

Text: Php 2:5 – Hoc sentite ...
Dictum est dominica proxima quomodo omnis Christianus tenetur audire verbum ... × ... ut vel sic adquiramus beatitudinem [ad quam perducat].[1]

L:	307-314	C:	ff. 323va-324rb
	37 (= *sermones XL*, 15)	London:	ff. 270vb-271rb
M:	95-97: 22 Mar. 1377	W 3928:	ff. 217va-218va
	seq.: 36-37-41-44-45	W 3932:	ff. 115rb-116rb

His yoke is easy, and His burden is light; thou shalt not kill.

[1] The last three words in **viii** and **xi**, as noted by L; they are not essential.

272. B2.IV.38. *Epistle for Palm Sunday*. 6 April 1376.

Text: Php 2:5 – Hoc sentite ...
In epistola hodierna tria genera imperfectorum reperio ... × ... requiescat in te; quod nobis concedat.

L:	314-321	C:	ff. 324rb-325ra
	38 (= *sermones XL*, 16)	London:	ff. 271rb-272ra
M:	92-94: 6 Apr. 1376;	W 3928:	ff. 218va-220ra
	seq.: 31-34-35-38-39	W 3932:	ff. 116rb-117vb

Here an instructive comparison is possible with the foregoing sermon, since both are on the same text, a year apart. This sermon focuses on the sources and entrapments of pride (cf. **264** and **266**, above).

273. B2.IV.39. *Gospel for Good Friday*. 11 April 1376.

Text: Jn 19:18 – Crucifixerunt eum ...
Proxima dominica dixi fraternitati vestre de Christi humilitate ... × ... quo ipse ingressus est necessarie perveniet.

L:	321-328	C:	f. 325ra-vb
	39 (= *sermones XL*, 17)	London:	ff. 272ra-273ra
		PUK V.H.27:	ff. 68v-71v[1]

M: 92-94: 11 Apr. 1376;   W 3928:   ff. 220ra-221va
        seq.: 31-34-35-38-39   W 3932:   ff. 117vb-119ra

A somber portrait of the Man of Sorrows.

¹ See **241**, above.

274. B2.IV.40. *Gospel for Good Friday*. 16 April 1378.

Text: Jn 19:27 – Ecce mater ...
Constat iuxta historiam quod aliis discipulis [5 wds.] Evangelista carissimus affuit sibi ... × ... qui crucis patibulo passus est dira pro redempcione nostra.

L: 328-337   C: ff. 325vb-327ra
        40 (= *sermones XL*, 18)   London: ff. 273ra-274ra
                                        PUK V.H. 27: ff. 71v-75r
M: 94-95: 16 Apr. 1378;   W 3928:   ff. 221va-223va
        seq.: 40-42-46-47   W 3932:   ff. 119ra-121ra

Strict avoidance of the cardinal sins (and for Englishmen, gluttony in particular!) is an ineluctable requirement of all true Christians.

275. B2.IV.41. *Gospel for Good Friday*. 27 March 1377.

Text: Jn 19:30 – Consummatum est ...
Supponitur illud esse ultimum verbum ... × ... de quibus patet superius sermone proximo.

L: 338-343   C: f. 327ra-va
        41(= *sermones XL*, 19)   London: f. 274ra-vb
                                        PUK V.H. 27: ff. 75v-77r¹
M: 95-97: 27 Mar. 1377;   W 3928:   ff. 223ra-224vb
        seq.: 36-37-41-44-45   W 3932:   ff. 121ra-122ra

This, the third of Wyclyf's Good Friday sermons in the *sermones quadraginta*, dwells on the purpose of Christ's suffering for us.

¹ This last of the four unascribed sermons in this codex is followed by a conventional definition of the seven cardinal sins, which is ascribed to Wyclyf.

276. B2.IV.42. *Gospel for Easter Sunday*. 18 April 1378.

Text: Mk 16:2 – Veniunt ad ...
Qui pasceret corporaliter magnum populum ... × ... quo nos perducat via veritas et vita.

L: 343-355   C: ff. 327va-328vb
        42 (= *sermones XL*, 20)   London: ff. 274vb-276ra

M:	94-95: 18 Apr. 1378;	W 3928:	ff. 224vb-227rb
	seq.: 40-42-46-47	W 3932:	ff. 122ra-124va

This Easter meditation offers a perception of the Eucharist anticipating his more detailed treatment in the *De eucharistia* (**38**, above); it is notably lacking in animosity toward the defenders of "wrong" views. He also reflects on the pitfalls of warfare.

277. B2.IV.43. *Gospel for first Sunday after Easter.*

Text: Jn 20:21 – Pax vobis ...
Die Parasceues dictum est de Christi passione ... × ... facit tam Deo quam proximo manifestam iniuriam.[1]

L:	355-360	C:	ff. 328vb-329rb
	43 (= *sermones XL*, 21)	London:	f. 276ra-va
		W 3928:	ff. 227rb-228rb
M:	102: 20 Apr. 1376 ("doubtful")	W 3932:	ff. 124va-125va

Inner peace is most desirable; but it may be thwarted by a contentious clergy. A later date than that offered by M is surely possible, though not later than 1379.

[1] "iniuriam manifestam" in **viii**.

278. B2.IV.44. *Gospel for first Sunday after Easter.* 5 April 1377.

Text: Jn 20:21 – Pax vobis ...
Duobus modis solet Christus dicere verba ... × ... et nota pro ista sentencia dilatanda.[1]

L:	360-365	C:	ff. 329rb-330ra
	44 (= *sermones XL*, 22)	London:	ff. 276va-277rb
M:	95-97: 5 Apr. 1377;	W 3928:	ff. 228rb-229va
	seq.: 36-37-41-44-45	W 3932:	ff. 125va-126vb

On peace, again; quarrels motivated by avarice are senseless.

[1] Last word "declaranda" in **viii** and **xi**.

279. B2.IV.45. *Gospel for second Sunday after Easter.* 12 April 1377.

Text: 1 P 2:21 – Christus passus ...
In istis verbis patet primo racio gratitudinis ... × ... iste probatus est sed quem Deus commendat.

L:	365-370	C:	f. 330ra-va
	45 (= *sermones XL*, 23)	London:	f. 277rb-vb

M: 95-97: 12 Apr. 1377;   W 3928:   ff. 229va-232ra[1]
    seq.: 36-37-41-44-45   W 3932:   ff. 126vb-129rb

More than the usual freight of patristics: Gregory the Great here provides the bulk of the citations. Wyclyf exclaims at the failings of the pastorate, and laments man's stubborn myopias.

[1] Both **viii** and **xi** tack on a number of miscellaneous quotations (expl.: × "... implevit officium ministrans Christo ut in eternam sit cum ipso."); L asserts that these were inserted "a quodam (ut videtur) Hussita." But to judge in this vein on the basis of the material's irrelevance to the ostensible thrust of the sermon, as he seems to do, is not sufficient warrant to exclude Wyclyf himself as the compiler.

280. B2.IV.46. *Gospel for second Sunday after Trinity*. 27 June 1378.

Text: Lk 14:16 – Homo quidam ...
Notata historia evangelii hodierni constat quod homo iste tam singulariter notatus est dominus ... × ... quod nobis concedat conviva dominus Jesus Christus.

L:	370-379	C:	ff. 330va-331va
	46 (=*sermones XL*, 24)	London:	ff. 277vb-278vb
M:	94-95: 27 Jun. 1378;	W 3928:	ff. 232ra-233vb
	seq.: 40-42-46-47	W 3932:	ff. 129rb-131rb

Here we encounter (especially on p. 375) an early form of his later polemical refrain that the unjust man ("omnis criminosus") possesses the "bona Dei" unlawfully. Of course this perception had in its turn grown out of the systematic exposition in his two major treatises on *dominium* (**23-25**, **28-30**, above).

281. B2.IV.47. *Gospel for third Sunday after Trinity*. 4 July 1378.

Text: Lk 15:7 – Gaudium est ...
Constat ex evangelica historia quomodo publicani et peccatores appropinquant ad Jerusalem ... × ... omnes enim tales in finali iudicio collocabit a dextris.

L:	379-387	C:	ff. 331va-332va
	47 (=*sermones XL*, 25)	London:	ff. 278vb-279vb
M:	94-95: 4 Jul. 1378;	W 3928:	ff. 233vb-235rb
	seq.: 40-42-46-47	W 3932:	ff. 131rb-133ra

It is axiomatic that we shall never fully penetrate to the source of all of Wyclyf's homiletic – let alone philosophical, historical, legal or theological – observations. But the transformation of the ninety-and-nine sheep that were not lost into the nine angelic orders may be original with him.

282. B2.IV.48. *Gospel for the Assumption* (15 August).

Text: Lk 10:42 – Maria optimam ...
Constat quod tota servitus qua ecclesia militans servit sponso ecclesie dividitur in tres partes ... × ... nisi qui optimam partem cum ipsa elegerit.

L:	387-392	C:	ff. 332va-333ra
	48 (= *sermones XL*, 26)	London:	ff. 279vb-280rb
		W 3928:	ff. 235rb-236rb
M:	101: 15 Aug. 1378 ("doubtful")	W 3932:	ff. 133ra-134ra

There is an arresting topical allusion to his own St Mary's parish on p. 391; naturally the subject of the sermon throughout is the paramount significance of Mary. But for him it is an exceptional emphasis, seldom matched elsewhere in the *corpus Wyclyfianum*.

283. B2.IV.49. *Gospel for the tenth Sunday after Trinity*.

Text: Lk 19:41 – Videns civitatem ...
Tria possunt dici caritati vestre ... × ... docent nos noster magister et dominus qui sic flevit.

L:	392-396	C:	f. 333ra-va
	49 (= *sermones XL*, 27)	London:	f. 280rb-vb
M:	101-102: 14 Aug. 1379	W 3928:	ff. 236rb-237rb
	("doubtful")	W 3932:	ff. 134ra-135ra

A comparison with **96** on the same text will quickly disclose Wyclyf's political evolution. The present short sermon is pensive and even devotional by contrast. (Indeed the same metamorphosis appears in comparing **284** and **97**.)

284. B2.IV.50. *Gospel for the eleventh Sunday after Trinity*.

Text: Lk 18:14 – Omnis qui ...
Constat ex serie evangelii quomodo duo homines scilicet publicanus et phariseus ascenderunt in domum ... × ... cum eius familia consequente, quod nobis concedat [Christus Jesus].[1]

L:	396-400	C:	ff. 333va-334ra
	50 (= *sermones XL*, 28)	London:	f. 280vb[2]
M:	101-102: 21 Aug. 1379	W 3928:	ff. 237rb-238ra
	("doubtful")	W 3932:	f. 135vb

On the futility of boasting, given the limitations of our knowledge of the last things.

---
[1] The last two words only in **i**, but the sense demands them.
[2] A fragment; breaks off: × "... et adulter lex"; = p. 397, line 3 of our edition.

285. B2.IV.51. *Gospel for twelfth Sunday after Trinity*. 28 August 1379.

Text: Mk 7:37 – Surdos fecit ...
Constat ex serie evangelii quomodo Salvator non solum edificavit Judeam ... × ...
Quando enim Deus non premiat, propria dona coronat.

L:	401-405	C:	f. 334ra-va
	51 (= *sermones XL*, 29)	W 3928:	f. 238ra-vb
B:	385: 28 Aug. 1379	W 3932:	ff. 135vb-136vb
M:	97: idem		

Bede on Lk provides grist for a mystical construction: we are all deaf and dumb, but Christ has touched us with the gifts of preaching and of intelligent obedience.

286. B2.IV.52. *Gospel for thirteenth Sunday after Trinity*.

Text: Lk 10:25 – Magister quid ...
Istam questionem quam quesivit legisperitus a Christo potest quilibet subditus a suo prelato querere ... × ... dominus fideliter constituit super omnia bona sua.

L:	405-409	C:	ff. 334va-335ra
	52 (= *sermones XL*, 30)	W 3928:	ff. 238vb-239vb
M:	101-102: 4 Sept. 1379	W 3932:	ff. 136vb-137va
	("doubtful")		

On the full measure of love, which is the chief requirement for salvation.

287. B2.IV.53. *Gospel for eighteenth Sunday after Trinity*.

Text: Mt 22:38 – Quod est ...
Constat ex serie evangelii quomodo pharisei subdole, derisorie et inutiliter temptarunt Christum ... × ... ubi intrabunt celum cum domino eternaliter regnaturi.[1]

L:	409-422	C:	ff. 335ra-336va
	53 (= *sermones XL*, 31)	W 3928:	ff. 239vb-242va
M:	102-103: not 1376;	W 3932:	ff. 137va-140va
	seq.: 53-54		

More on love; on improper oaths; on the third commandment. We may safely exclude 1379 also from consideration, leaving 1377 or 1378.

[1] Expl. in **viii** and **ix**: × "... hic vexati audient vocem populi amabilem etc." – this occurs just before the expl. in **i** given here.

288. B2.IV.54. *Epistle for nineteenth Sunday after Trinity.*

Text: Ep 4:13 – Renovamini spiritu ...
Constat ex testimonio scripture Ecclus. 17°, 1 quod Deus creavit hominem ... × ... cum ipso Deo eternaliter conregnabimus in gloria.[1]

L:	423-425	C:	ff. 336va-337ra
	54 (= *sermones XL*, 32)	W 3928:	ff. 242va-243rb
M:	102-103: not 1376;	W 3932:	ff. 140va-141rb
	seq.: 53-54		

A comparison with **228**, on the same text, is again illuminating: the present sermon is irenic, the other brooding. This may be the earlier of the two.

[1] **viii** and **xi** add: "... quod nobis concedat primus dominus [Deus - **xi**]."

289. B2.IV.55. *Gospel for twentieth Sunday after Trinity.* 26 October 1376.

Text: Mt 22:2 – Simile est ...
Constat ex sensu literali huius evangelii quomodo quidam rex terrenus fecit nupcias ... × ... corpus in ignobilitate, surget autem in gloria.

L:	426-434	C:	ff. 337ra-338ra
	55 (= *sermones XL*, 33)	W 3928:	ff. 234rb-245ra
B:	380: 26 Oct. 1376	W 3932:	ff. 141rb-143ra
M:	98-99: idem; seq.:		
	59-55-56-57-62-60		

The tone is sharper here than we would expect for this early date; both legacies and expensive funerals come under his withering eye. But as yet the friars do not.

290. B2.IV.56. *Gospel for twenty-first Sunday after Trinity.* 2 November 1376.

Text: Jn 4:49 – Domine, descende ...
Constat ex serie evangelii quomodo quidam regulus [29 wds.] audivit correpcionem ... × ... amplexus summe gaudiosos gloriosius introducta.

L:	434-443	C:	ff. 338ra-339ra
	56 (= *sermones XL*, 34)	W 3928:	ff. 245ra-247ra
B:	380: 2 Nov. 1376	W 3932:	ff. 143ra-145ra
M:	98-99: idem; seq.:		
	59-55-56-57-62-60		

A moderate commentary on the first part of the Lord's Prayer; for a more strident statement, cf. the *De oracione dominica* (**414**, below).

291. B2.IV.57. *Epistle for twenty-second Sunday after Trinity*. 9 November 1376.

Text: Php 1:19 – Hoc oro ...
Proximo die dominico introducta est materia oracionis ... × ... ad quam consequitur vita corporis immortalis.

L:	443-450	C:	f. 339ra-vb
	57 (= *sermones XL*, 35)	W 3928:	ff. 247ra-248rb
B:	381: 9 Nov. 1376	W 3932:	ff. 145ra-146va
M:	98-99: idem; seq.:		
	59-55-56-57-62-60		

A continuation of the preceding; it occasionally forces the text.

292. B2.IV.58. *Gospel for twenty-second Sunday after Trinity*.

Text: Mt 18:33 – Oportuit et ...
Constat ex dicto capitulo quomodo Christus docuit Petrum ... × ... et per Dei graciam fructus glorie et gaudium materiale in patria.

L:	450-460	C:	ff. 339vb-341ra
	58 (= *sermones XL*, 36)	W 3928:	ff. 248rb-250va
M:	103: 25 Oct. 1377; alt.:	W 3932:	ff. 146va-148va
	14 Nov. 1378		

A mild catechism for the admonition and correction of wrongdoers.

293. B2.IV.59. *Gospel for nineteenth Sunday after Trinity*. 19 October 1376.

Text: Mt 9:2 – Confide fili ...
Ex serie evangelii hodierni cum supplecione evangelii Marci $2°$ patet quomodo Christus intravit Capharnaum ... × ... quibus homo ditabitur plene in patria.

L:	460-467	C:	f. 341ra-vb
	59 (= *sermones XL*, 37)	W 3928:	ff. 250va-252ra
B:	380: 19 Oct. 1376	W 3932:	ff. 148va-150ra
M:	98-99: idem; seq.:		
	59-55-56-57-62-60		

Where we fail, God is strong.

294. B2.IV.60. *Gospel for the Sunday before Advent*. 23 November 1376.

Text: Jn 6:11 – Distribuit discumbentibus ...
Constat ex serie evangelii quod Christus conversans in terris fuit tria convivia ... × ... est vigilia ad sanctum sabbatum post diem iudicii.

L:	468-476	C:	ff. 341vb-342vb
	60 (= *sermones XL*, 38)	W 3928:	ff. 252ra-253rb[1]
B:	382: 23 Nov. 1376	W 3932:	ff. 150ra-151vb
M:	98-99: idem; seq.:		
	59-55-56-57-62-60		

Aside from a mild stricture upon indulgences, this is an acceptably orthodox disquisition on the perils of sin and the rewards of virtue.

[1] Expl.: × "... et sic licet videatur in principio." This is p. 475, line 2 in L. F. 253v is blank; f. 254r is numbered. At the bottom of f. 253rb, in another hand, we read "qui desunt duo sermones."

295. B2.IV.61. *Gospel for Common for a Virgin and a Martyr*.

Text: Mt 13:45 - Simile est ...
Licet regnum sumatur multipliciter in scriptura ... × ... quam possessionem nobis concedat sponsus virginum Jesus Christus.

L:	476-482	C:	ff. 342vb-343va
	61 (= *sermones XL*, 39)	W 3932:	ff. 151vb-152vb[1]
B:	384: 22 Nov. 1377?		
M:	88-89: idem; seq.: 61-24-25		

On true riches, and on the option - not the requirement - of almsgiving. In later years he would become fiercely antagonistic to this practice.

[1] The last of the *sermones* in this MS.

296. B2.IV.62. *Gospel for Dedication of a Church*. 16 November 1376.

Text: Lk 19:9 - Hodie salus ...
Constat ex serie evangelii quomodo Christo redituro in Jerico quidam princeps [5 wds.] cupit videre Salvatorem ... × ... venerandum et super omnia diligendum in secula seculorum.

L:	482-492	C:	ff. 343va-344vb
	62 (= *sermones XL*, 40)		
B:	381: 16 Nov. 1376		
M:	98-99: idem; seq.:		
	59-55-56-57-62-60		

In the midst of a peroration on prayer and faith, Wyclyf avers "Ideo est sciencia theologica pernecessaria sine qua non potest salvari respublica, quia per illam crevit ecclesia et post ex eius carencia minoratur. Unde errant notabiliter qui dicunt quod theologi sunt Anglie inutiles, quia sine illis non potest pax Dei ad hominem confirmari." (P. 486.) There lurks a sense of mission in these impassioned words. This is the last of the *sermones quadraginta*.

297. B2.IV.63. *Epistle for Dedication of a Church*.

Text: Rv 21:2 – Vidi civitatem ...
Propheta Johannes in ista epistola narrando statum finalem ecclesie incipit in isto capitulo statum orbis sublunaris declarare ... × ... et in hoc potissime stabit regnum.

L:	492-501	C:	ff. 344vb-346ra
	63	Wo 306:	ff. 197va-201rb[1]
		Wo 565:	ff. 292v-296r

This is not one of the *sermones quadraginta*, but rather a votive sermon, and as such it is intrinsically undatable – but his scalding of the friars, and of the schismatic popes in the matter of the Eucharist, clearly dictates a time after 1380.

[1] Given in **xii** and **xiii** as no. 60 (i.e., of B2.III).

298. B2.IV.64. *Gospel for Tuesday in Whitsun Week*.

Text: Jn 10:1 – Qui non ...
Christus qui mentiri non poterit asserit quod quicunque qui intraverit in ovile ... × ... et prudentem ipsum populum secundum legem domini regulantem.

L:	502-505	C:	f. 346ra-rb
	64		
A II:	163-16		

This last sermon in the Cambridge codex harps on simony and the four sects; it should probably be dated in the spring of 1382. (F. 346v is blank.)

299. B2.IV.65. *An Act Sermon*.[1]

Text: Ru 2:4 – Dominis vobiscum ...
Secundum philosophos finis est actus ... × ... in terra vivencium cum corpore resumendum.

L:	511-515	PUK III.G.11	ff. 52r-53v
	unnumbered	W 1337:	ff. 95ra-96vb
	(= *sermones mixti*, 24)	W 3928:	ff. 185ra-186rb
		W 3929:	ff. 205va-206va
		W 3931:	ff. 201vb-203ra

An early sermon, concerned with the proper mode of accommodation to the indwelling Spirit.

[1] Commonly designated the "sermo pulcher"; but we have seen this same term is also applied in **vi** to **265**, and in **iv** to **239**, above.

300. B3. *De demonio meridiano.* Mid-1376.

I. Inc.: Frons meretricis facta est populo ex scelere antiquato ...
Expl.: × ... contra clemenciam persone tercie impedit caritatem in Anglia germinare.

II. MSS:

i	München, BSB	*clm 15771*	ff. 27r-28r	ca. 1435	Asc. So. Ger.[1]
ii	Praha, MK	*B.6.3 (293)*	ff. 241r-242v	1421	Asc. Boh.[2]
iii		D.123 (693)	ff. 87v-92r	xv/1	JW MS Boh.
iv	UK	X.C.23 (1876)	ff. 195va-196va	1410	JW MS Boh.
v		XI.E.3 (2050)	ff. 11v-12r	1416	JW MS Boh.
vi	Vaticano	Borgh. lat. 29	ff. 71r-72v[3]	xv/1	Asc. Fr.
vii	Wien, ÖNB	1337	ff. 37vb-39va	ca. 1410	JW MS Boh.
viii		*1622*	ff. 181v-183v	1410	JW MS Boh.
ix		3927	ff. 9va-10vb	ca. 1410	JW MS Boh.
x		4527	ff. 169v-171r	1410	JW MS Boh.
xi		*4937*	ff. 80r-82v	ca. 1420	Asc. Boh.
xii	Wolfenbüttel, HzglB	Cod. Guelf. 306 *(340)*	ff. 256vb-259ra	xv/1	Asc. Pol.[4]

III. Ed. R. Buddensieg, *John Wiclif's Polemical Works in Latin* II (WS, 1883): 417-425; From **v, vii, ix** and **x** only.

IV. Buddensieg refrained from fixing a date for this short piece; but the two references to Prince Edward's death (8 June 1376, i.e., Trinity Sunday – on pp. 417, 418), in combination with the thematic use of the Trinity here, argue very strongly for a date soon after that shattering event. His harshness toward the secular clergy – reaching even to their condemnation for wholesale sins against charity, or the Holy Spirit[5] – his utter silence on the Eucharist, and his two incidental (probably interpolated) allusions to the friars (pp. 421, 424) all urge a date several years prior to 1382.[6] A sustained solicitousness toward the poor manifests his early awareness of their plight. An obscure exclamation that a "sacerdos fidelis volens predicare ewangelium Iesu Christi erit statim prohibitus predicare *in ista dyocesi*" (pp. 424-425; emphasis added) might perhaps clarify the issue; and this indication of some *particular* diocese (London or Lincoln?) in turn, when added to the explicits and colophons of several MSS ("verbum communiter dicendum clero et dominis et populo"),[7] finally impels us to classify this piece as a hitherto unrecognized *sermon*. The exegetical content germane to Ps 90:6[8] is uncharacteristically slight, but it is possible that the audience on this occasion was an exceptionally illustrious one, at this apex of Wyclyf's notoriety in such circles; he may therefore have seized the commemoration opportunity to challenge his early tormentors among the seculars.

VC: 3933 3935 4514 7980[9]   Bale: deest[10]   Sh: 73   Lo: 74

[1] Noticed in Kühn-Steinhausen, "Wyclif-Handschriften in Deutschland," 627.
[2] Discussed in Thomson, "Unnoticed MSS and Works of Wyclif," 36 – but misidentified there as MS 243.
[3] Previously ff. 11r-12v: I. H. Stein, "The Vatican Manuscript Borghese 29 and the tractate 'De Versuciis Anti-Christi'," *EHR* 47 (1932): 95.
[4] First noticed in Kühn-Steinhausen, "Wyclif-Handschriften in Deutschland," 626.
[5] Here (pp. 422-424) he is markedly Thomistic: see the essay by T. C. O'Brien in vol. 27 of the Blackfriars edition of the *Summa theologiae* (London, 1974): 110-117. Of course, as we have repeatedly emphasized, this does not prove any direct source dependence.
[6] Workman, *JW* II: 278, also leans toward 1377.
[7] Cf. **iii, iv, x** and **xiii**; and perhaps others as well.
[8] The term "d[a]emonio meridiano" is from the Septuagint Vulgate sources; the Hebrew is rendered "a morsu insanientis meridie." For literature on this recurrent theme in medieval homiletics, see Pierre de Labriolle, "Le démon de midi," *Bulletin du Cange* 9 (1934): 46-54; Roger Caillois, "Les démons de midi," *Revue de l'histoire des religions* 115 (1937): 142-173; 116 (1937): 54-83, 143-186; Rudolf Arbesmann, "The 'Daemonium Meridianum' and Greek and Latin Patristic Exegesis," *Traditio* 14 (1958): 17-31.
[9] A truncated version, inc. "Cum autem Spiritui Sancto appropriatur ...," with the correct expl., is also given, without title, in all four VC, immediately following **401**.
[10] Unless no. 66, "De diabolo millenario," inc.: "Cum consummati fuerint mille anni ...,' be accepted as our piece.

301-371. B4. [*Postilla super totam Bibliam*].[1] 1371-1376.

I. Inc.: [...] Tercia vero pars Scripture disputativa et dialectica continetur librorum binario ...[2]

Expl.: × ... et finaliter pro omnibus fidelibus ecclesie orando graciam finem imponit. Deo gracias.

II. MSS (abbreviated in subsequent citations, as with B2):

i	Oxford, Bodleian	716 (*S.C. 2630*)	ff. 1ra-171vb	1403	Asc. Eng.[3]
ii	Magdalen Coll.	55	ff. 1ra-248va	xv/1	Unasc. Eng.[4]
iii		117	ff. 1ra-319ra	xv/1	Unasc. Eng.[5]
iv	St John's Coll.	171	ff. 1r-374v	xv/1	Unasc. Eng.
v	Praha, Národný Mus.	XXX.F.9 (*3356*)	ff. 1r-180v	xv/1	Asc. Boh.[6]
vi	UK	III.F.20 (*523*)	ff. 1r-202v	ca. 1410	Asc. Boh.[7]
vii		VIII.F.9 (*1563*)	ff. 1r-200r	xv/1	Asc. Boh.[8]
viii	Wien, ÖNB	1342	ff. 1ra-348vb	xv/1	Asc. Boh.[9]

III. Selected passages ed. Beryl Smalley, "John Wyclif's *Postilla super Totam Bibliam*," *The Bodleian Library Record* 4 (1953): 186-205; idem, "Wyclif's *Postilla* on the Old Testament and his *Principium*," in *Oxford Studies Presented to Daniel Callus* (OHS: new ser, 16; 1964): 253-296; other passages as identified below in Gustav Adolf Benrath, *Wyclifs Bibelkommentar* (Berlin, 1966): *passim*. All MSS except **v, vi** and **vii** used.

IV. Miss Beryl Smalley has rightly stressed the uniqueness of Wyclyf's achievement as a Biblical commentator for his time and place: Nicholas of Lyra (who was Wyclyf's chief source in this enterprise) was the last great postillator before him, and his omnibus *Postilla litteralis* had been completed at Paris by 1331. Truly no English scholar in his century strove so diligently as Wyclyf to encompass every dimension of Scripture. As his philosophy broadened and deepened into his theology, so did his unequalled facility with the Vulgate texts inform his sermons and undergird his social and political pronouncements.

We are most fortunate that in the last fifteen years an enterprising German scholar, Gustav Adolf Benrath at Heidelberg, has elected to follow in the track of Lechler, Buddensieg and Loserth with his superb monograph, *Wyclifs Bibilkommentar*.[10] Although it is of necessity selective in its analysis of portions of the scattered MSS, which even together embrace only five of the eight parts composed by Wyclyf from his lectures in the years between 1371 and 1376, it nevertheless provides an absolutely indispensable point of departure for any future edition or further commentary.

Miss Smalley's three articles[11] are, in the customary manner of that astute and exacting scholar, replete with suggestions for the pursuit of sundry tantalizing *obiter dicta in textu*. At this time it is the editor's firm conviction that his most valuable contribution in this vein will be the careful identification of incipits, explicits, and textual variations in them. (He has examined *in situ* or on microfilm all eight of the known codices.)

The first effort in that direction was, it should be mentioned, Friedrich Stegmüller's massive *Repertorium Biblicum Medii Aevi* III (Madrid, 1951): 452-460. His references are identified as St: below, followed by his item number.

vc: 3933 3935 4514[12]   Bale: 129? 207?[13]   Sh: 45[14]   Lo: 45[15]

---

[1] The title is, of course, conjectural, since we do lack the first two parts; but it is so designated in the (early) vc. Wyclyf may have himself called it *Commentarius in Veterem/Novum Testamentum*, or indeed any other plausible title; he never refers to it explicitly in his later writings. – The most authoritative *textus criticus* of the Vulgate, against which Wyclyf's occasional variant readings should be checked, is that produced by the Württembergische Bibelanstalt, Stuttgart, edd.: B. Fischer, J. Gribomont, H. F. D. Sparks, W. Thiele, and R. Weber: *Biblia Sacra iuxta Vulgatam Versionem* (2 vols.; 2nd ed., 1975).

[2] This is the incipit of the Prologue to Jb. Naturally it is subject to supercession by any authenticated text from parts 1 or 2 that may turn up.

[3] Asc. brought out from f. 22rb by ultraviolet, as demonstrated in Smalley, "John Wyclif's *Postilla Super Totam Bibliam*," 188 and p. XIII (a). See also the description of this MS in F. Madan and H. H. E. Craster, edd., *A Summary Catalogue of Western Manuscripts in the Bodleian Library at Oxford* II/1 (Oxford, 1922): 459.

[4] Neither this nor the following MS were identified as Wyclyf pieces in H. O. Coxe, *Catalogus codicum manuscriptorum qui in collegiis aulisque Oxoniensibus hodie adservantur* II (Oxford, 1852): *Collegii B. Mariae Magdalenae*: 33, 61-62. Stegmüller may have been the first (1951) to make this identification, and then tentatively; Smalley's 1953 article is decisive.

[5] See the preceding note.

[6] František M. Bartoš, *Soupis Rukopisů Národního Musea v Praze* II (Praha, 1927): 276-277, was the first to note the asc. to Wyclyf; cf. Thomson, "Unnoticed MSS and Works of Wyclif," 35.

⁷ Truhlář properly noted the asc. in this and the following MS; cf., Thomson, "Unnoticed MSS and Works of Wyclif," 35. Neither Benrath nor Smalley was able to utilize any of the Praha MSS.

⁸ See the preceding note.

⁹ This codex provided the foundation for both Sh's and Lo's erroneous assumption that Wyclyf's Biblical commentaries comprised only the New Testament, "preter Apocalypsin." See n. 14, below.

¹⁰ See the useful reviews by James Crompton in *JEH* 18 (1967): 263-266; and Siegfried Wenzel in *Speculum* 43 (1968): 121-123.

¹¹ Including, besides the two cited in III, just above, her "The Bible and Eternity: John Wyclif's Dilemma," *Journal of the Warburg and Courtauld Institutes* 37 (1964): 73-89.

¹² Cited most revealingly in W 3933 as "postilla super totam bibliam que hodie non habetur," without incipit.

¹³ No. 129 = *Commentarios vulgares*; inc.: Stabat Johannes, et ex discipulis ... (see the remarks by Smalley, "John Wyclif's *Postilla Super Totam Bibliam*," 186); no. 130 = *Scholia scripturarum* (no inc.); no. 207 = *Glossas scripturarum* (no inc.).

¹⁴ Given as *In Omnes Novi Testamenti libros, praeter Apocalypsin, Commentarius*, from **viii** only. Of course Rv is commented in both OBod and OMC 55; but see below, G*Spur*.5.

¹⁵ Offered more briefly than in Sh.

301-305. B4.I.a-e. [*Gn-Ex-Lv-Nu-Dt: Politica et legislativa ?*]

Not known to have survived.

306-319. B4.II.a-n. [*Jsh-Jg-Ru(1,2)-S(1,2)-K(1,2)-Ch (= Paralipomenon)(1,2)-Ezr-Tobias-Judith-Es: Chronica sive historica ?*]

Not known to have survived.

320. B4.III.a. *Jb* (St: deest   Benrath: 13-18)

Inc. prol.: Tercia vero pars scripture disputativa et dialectica continetur librorum binario. Omnis namque disputacio vel est inter opponentem ...

Expl. prol.: × ... vult ergo quod ex divina providencia aliquando malis bona concedentur et bonis mala penalia ut declaratur infra.

    OMC 117:   f. 274ra-va
    OSJ: f. 1r-v

Inc. *Postilla super libro Job*: < Vir erat in terra hus nomine Job >¹ Genesis 22° patet quod melcha peperit nachor frater abrahe hus primogenitum ...

Expl.: × ... usus est ad virtutem et augmentum bonorum gracie quibus perductus est ad futuram gloriam. Que durat per omnia secula seculorum.

    OMC 117:   ff. 274va-319ra
    OSJ: ff. 2r-64v

[1] All of the postills commence with the first verse of the book in question. Henceforth these shall be indicated as follows: " < Vir ... > ," etc.

321. B4.III.b. *Ec* (St: deest   Benrath: 18-22)

Inc. prol.: Iste liber dicitur soliloquium salomonis nunc loquentis in persona sapientis nunc in persona stulti ...
Expl. prol.: × ... et appetitum floride iuventutis: capitulo 11° et 12°. Dividitur autem liber totalis in prohemium et tractatum qui incipit ibi Vanitas vanitatum sanctum Jeronimum.

   OSJ: f. 64v

Inc. *Postilla super Ecclesiastes*: < Verba ... > In titulo enim describitur autor huius libri ex nomine et genere ...
Expl.: × ... et vincet cum iudicabit Ps. 90°. Cui iudicanti et vincenti et viventi in sancta sanctorum. Sint laus et honor in eternum dominum.

   OSJ: ff. 64v-108v[1]

[1] After our expl.: "Explicit Postilla super ecclesiastes et finitur tercia pars scripture."

322. B4.IV.a. *Ps* (St: deest   Benrath: 23-42; 337-338)

Inc. prol.: Quarta vero pars scripture que est ymnidica et quasi poetica et decantativa sub numero librorum ternario ...
Expl. prol.: × ... et tercio in partem tractantem de sacerdocio Christi a principio dixit dominus usque in finem.

   OSJ: ff. 108v-109v

Inc. *Postilla super Psalterium*: < Beatus... > Primo genus hortatur sive David sive Esdras quasi propheciatur ad hanc doctrinam ...
Expl.: × ... Omnis spiritus angelicus seu humanus laudet dominum, quia ibi continue laudant deum. Ps. 83°. Beati qui habitant in domo tua domine in sancta sanctorum. Lau[dabunt] te ad quam gloria nos perducat qui sine fine vivit et regnat.

   OSJ: ff. 109v-311**v

323. B4.IV.b. *SS* (St: deest   Benrath: 42-58; 338-349; Smalley, "Wyclif's *Postilla* ...,": 268-281; 288-296)

Inc. prol. [primus]: Iste est secundus liber inter libros hymnidicos continens x partes ...

Expl. prol. [primus]: × ... De una parte ecclesie ad aliam. De ecclesia ad deum et e contra.

OSJ: f. 312r

Inc. *Postilla [prima] super Cantica Canticorum*: < Osculetur... > In primo ergo Dragmate loquitur sponsa primo volens liberare de egiptica servitute ...
Expl.: × ... Cui creanti, recreanti et finaliter iudicanti sit honor in eternum.

OSJ: ff. 312r-323r

Inc. *Prefacio introductoria ad intellectum Cantici Canticorum seu pocius totius scripture* [= *prologus secundus*]:[1] Tria sunt que magis conferunt mundicordibus ...
Expl.: × ... et habitus librum vite indefectibiliter intuentes.

OSJ: ff. 323v-326v

Inc. *Exposicio tropologica super Cantica Canticorum* [= *postilla secunda*]: < Osculetur ... > Notandum quod triplex est osculum ...
Expl.: × ... Vide allegoriam seu tropologiam supra in exposicione prima.[2]

OSJ: ff. 326v-362r

[1] This was Wyclyf's inaugural lecture, or *principium*, for the D.D. It is thoroughly edited in both Benrath and Smalley, and evinces his growing dexterity in handling Scriptural matter.

[2] This is obviously an editorial comment and not by Wyclyf; it stands at the beginning of the exposition of cap. iv in the SS. The expl. for his treatment of cap. iii reads: × "... ut die mulieres sorde originalis peccati."

324. B4.IV.c. *Lm* (St: deest Benrath: 58-63; 349-351; Smalley, "Wyclif's *Postilla* ...": 283-284)

Inc. prol.: Liber tercius hymnidicus scripture est liber Threnorum ...
Expl. prol.: × ... Et hinc Salomonis Cantica Canticorum metrico contex[er]int.

OSJ: ff. 362v-363r

Inc. *Postilla super libro Drenorum*: < Quomodo > Utitur autem liber iste secundum Gelbertum omnibus coloribus rethoricis ...
Expl.: × ... Deo ergo qui fines mundi intuetur ut dicitur Job. 28° sit honor et gloria per infinita secula seculorum.[1]

OSJ: ff. 363r-374v

[1] There then follows "Explicit quarta pars scripture qua dicitur hymnidica sive decantativa." The next folio is blank, and the codex ends.

325-327. B4.V.a-c. [*Pv-Sapiencia-Sirach* (= *Ecclesiasticus*): *Monastica sive ethica ?*]

Not known to have survived.

328. B4.VI.a. *Is* (St: 5076   Benrath: 64-89, intermittently)

Inc. prol. [primus]: Est autem triplex calumpnia ...
Expl. prol. [primus]: × ... processus huius evangeliste in compendio.

        OMC 55:   ff. 1ra-2va
        OMC 117:   ff. 1ra-2vb[1]

Inc. prol. [secundus]: In prefacione huius libri tanguntur quattuor principi...
Expl. prol. [secundus]: × ... ignis succedentis templum sum aliquo extinguente.

        OMC 55:   ff. 2va-3rb

Inc. *Postilla super Ysaiam*: < Visio ... > In prophetando de exaltacione ecclesie per Christum dicit quod in novissimis diebus ...
Expl.: × ... pocius quam illud gaudat intret in eos [perducat sine fine vivat et regnat].[2]

        OMC 55:   ff. 3rb-30ra
        OMC 117:   ff. 2vb-71ra

[1] Truncated; inc.: "Nemo cum prophetas ..." (also lacks second prologue altogether).
[2] Portion in brackets added in **iii**.

329. B4.VI.b. *Jr* (St: 5077   Benrath: 64-89, intermittently; Smalley, "Wyclif's *Postilla* ...": 287-288)

Inc. prol. primus: Eremias propheta cui hic prologus inscribitur vero sacerdos ex sacerdotibus ...
Expl. prol. primus: × ... dei magnalia quidam peccata sua.

        OMC 55:   f. 30ra-vb[1]
        OMC 117:   ff. 71ra-72rb

Inc. prol. secundus: Liber jeremie prophete dividitur in partes 16. Principaliter in prima parte legacio prophete imponitur ...
Expl. prol. secundus: × ... liber alius trenorum superius parte quarta divisus est.

        OMC 117:   f. 72rb-vb

Inc. *Postilla super propheciam jeremie*: < Verba ... > De 16 partibus in quas dividitur iste liber, prima continet prohemium ...

Expl.: × ... ad continuandum summam cum trenis quorum exposicio patet supra parte quarta. Benedictus sit dominus veritatis.[2]

    OMC 55:   ff. 30vb-50vb
    OMC 117:   ff. 72vb-123**va

[1] Truncated inc. and expl. No second prologue in this MS.
[2] ii expl.: × "... tunc sunt filii abrahe sed diu post."

330. B4.VI.c. *Baruch* (St: 5078   Benrath: 64-89, intermittently)

Inc. [prol.]: Liber Baruch dividitur in septem partes secundum septem conclusiones quas intendit ...

Expl. [prol.]: × ... quam destinavit jeremias captivitatis pro ydolatria declinanda.

    OMC 117:   f. 123**va-vb

Inc. *Postilla super Baruch*: < Et ... > Baruch sequitur librum jeremie[1] secundum ordinem temporis ...

Expl.: × ... talis homo erit honorabilis coram deo et angelis omnibus cui sit honor qui est latera in secula seculorum.[2]

    OMC 55:   ff. 50vb-52va
    OMC 117:   ff. 123**vb-131va

[1] ii has: "... thobie ..."
[2] ii, obviously incomplete, has expl.: × "... usque post mortem yeremie quam et legit eam coram captivis."

331. B4.VI.d. *Ezk* (St: 5079   Benrath: 64-89, intermittently)

Inc. prol.: Prima pars Ezechielis [divisi in septem partes] introducit grande oraculum ...[1]

Expl. prol.: × ... illud mt. ultimo datum est mihi omnis potestas in celo et in terra.[2]

    OMC 55:   f. 52va-vb
    OMC 117:   ff. 131va-132ra

Inc. *Postilla super Ezechielem prophetam*: < Et ... > Dividitur autem liber iste in prohemium et tractatum ... [3]

Expl.: × ... per opera et condiciones personarum que soli deo sunt nota quo ad omnia, qui sit honor et gloria in secula seculorum.

    OMC 55:   ff. 52vb-69ra
    OMC 117:   ff. 132ra-184ra

[1] The words in brackets not in ii.
[2] Prologue truncated in ii.
[3] No division between prologue and the postill itself in ii; it begins "In prohemio tanguntur ...." I suspect the postill is also abbreviated in this MS, though the expl. does correspond to that found in iii.

332. B4.VI.e. *Dn* (St: 5080, 5080, 1   Benrath: 64-89, intermittently)

Inc. prol. [primus]: Danielem prophetam iuxta Septuaginta interpretes et secundum eorum interpretacionem domini salvatoris ecclesie non legunt ...[1]

Expl. prol. [primus]: × ... quia aut convenienter laudant quod amant aut inconvenienter vituperantur quod oderint.

    OMC 117:   ff. 184rb-185vb

Inc. prol. [secundus]: Prima pars libri Danielis divisi in quinque partes ostendit adquisicionem intellectus ...

Expl. prol. [secundus]: × ... Et Ps. 94°: Quoniam dominus magnus dominus et rex magnus super omnes deos.

    OMC 117:   ff. 185vb-186ra

Inc. *Postilla super Danielem*: < Anno ... > In primo capitulo ponitur quasi prohemialiter adquisicionem intellectus Danieli ...[2]

Expl.: × ... Et sic per hoc miraculum rex gentilis et populo sibi subditus inducti sunt ad laudandum deum. Cui deo sic in sanctis suis glorioso: sit laus in evum.[3]

    OMC 55:   ff. 69ra-76vb
    OMC 117:   ff. 186ra-214va[4]

[1] Introduced as "expositio prologi beati jeronimi super Danielem." Of course Jerome's prologues constituted an integral part of the Vulgate text; it is interesting here to see how Wyclyf adapts his prototype's remarks on Chaldaic and Hebrew to French and English; cf. **397**, n. 4, below.
[2] Again ii seems abbreviated: inc.: "Deus ut rex supereminens ...."
[3] ii expl.: × "... Nam primum ydolem dictum est belus." While this does pertain to cap. 14 of Dn, the commentary here runs to less than 10 lines, while in iii the coverage extends to almost six cols. A close parallel examination of both MSS might conceivably disclose that ii is not merely an abridgement of iii, but a separate commentary altogether. This should surely be ascertained before any attempt at an edition is made.
[4] Most of f. 214va and all of 214vb is blank; there then follow ff. 214* and 214** – also blank.

B4.VI.Prol. *Prologus super libro 12 prophetarum.*

Inc.: Liber 12 prophetarum dividitur in tres partes quarum prima est comminatoria secunda consolatoria tercia revocatoria ...

Expl.: × ... omnes filii jacob id est dei subplantatis sub pedibus suis omnes creaturas.

          OMC 117:   f. 215ra-rb

333. B4.VI.f. *Ho* (St: 5081[1]   Benrath: 69-84, intermittently)

Inc. prol.: Liber Osee dividitur in 5 partes. In prima autem parte assumit personam vatis ...

Expl. prol.: × ... Qui sapiens et intelligit ista.

          OMC 117:   f. 215rb-vb

Inc. *Postilla super Osee*: < Verbum ... > Osee fuit filius prophete beeri quamvis hoc tacetur ...

Expl.: × ... et diligencia tenende sunt ille vie recte duces ambulantes in eis ad vitam eternam.

          OMC 117:   f. 216ra-226va

[1] St (and Benrath too, in his description of this MS, p. 388) lumps all the minor prophets together, without folio distinctions. Jerome's prologue was also inclusive.

334. B4.VI.g. *Jl* (St: 5081   Benrath: 69-84, intermittently)

Inc. prol.: Prima pars Johel est comminativa pene et captivitatis, secunda vero promissiva venie et jocunditatis ...

Expl. prol.: × ... Et erit in die illa stillabunt montes dulcedinem.

          OMC 117:   f. 226va-vb

Inc. *Postilla super Johelem*: < Verbum ... > Secundum Jeronimum in epistola ad paulinum de studio scripture sacre, Johel prophetavit ...

Expl.: × ... videbitur a sanctis in fruicione beatifica cui sit honor et gloria in secula seculorum.

          OMC 117:   ff. 226vb-231rb

335. B4.VI.h. *Am* (St: 5081   Benrath: 69-84, intermittently; Smalley, "Wyclif's *Postilla* ...",: 284-286).

Inc. prol.: Liber Amos prophete dividitur in 8 partes. In prima namque parte comminatur generaliter 8 gentibus ...

Expl. prol.: × ... et maxime super reliquias credituras in Christum capitulo nono.

          OMC 117:   f. 231rb-va

Inc. *Postilla super Amos prophetam*: < Verba ... > Hac prophecia dividitur in prohemium et tractatum qui incipit ibi ...

Expl.: × ... de terra sua quam dedi eis dicitur dominus deus. In qua ecclesia sit ei honor et gloria in secula seculorum.

    OMC 117:   ff. 231va-239vb

336. B4.VI.i. *Ob* (St: 5081   Benrath: 69-84, intermittently)

Inc. prol.: Abdias prophetando contra ydumeos ad iudeorum consolacionem ...

Expl. prol.: × ... per Ihesu Christi salvatoris presenciam ibi. Et in monte syon erit salvacio.

    OMC 117:   ff. 239vb-240ra

Inc. *Postilla super Abdiam*: < Visio ... > Secundum doctores hebraicos et latinos iste Abdias dispensator fuit domus Arhab regis ...

Expl.: × ... in finali iudicio iudicancium infidelitates et peccata dampnandorum eodem nomine signatorum. Et erit domino regnum tunc enim perfecte subicietur domino omne regnum ineternum.

    OMC 117:   ff. 240ra-241ra

337. B4.VI.j. *Jnh* (St: 5081   Benrath: 69-84, intermittently)

Inc. prol.: Prima pars libri jone prophete divisi in 7. Introducit ipsum jonam de imperio resistentem ...

Expl. prol.: × ... et sub edre viridis iudicio deviliscentem.

    OMC 117:   f. 241ra

Inc. *Postilla super Jona*: < Et ... > In hoc capitulo primo describitur jone rebellio secundo rebellantis deprehensio ...

Expl.: × ... ab eius misericordiam ineternum cantantibus sit honor et gloria in secula seculorum.

    OMC 117:   ff. 241ra-243va

338. B4.VI.k. *Mi* (St: 5081   Benrath: 69-84, intermittently)

Inc. prol.: Prima pars prophecie Michee est comminativa per capitula tria secunda repromissiva per capitula quattuor ...

Expl. prol.: × ... pasce populum tuum in virga tua in fine capituli septimi.

    OMC 117:   f. 243va-vb

Inc. *Postilla super Michea*: < Verbum ... > Lira dividit hunc librum in prohemium et tractatum ...

Expl.: × ... que tunc fuerant adimplende et nunc implete sunt. In domino Ihesu Christo cui sit honor et gloria in secula seculorum.

OMC 117: ff. 244ra-250rb

339. B4.VI.l. *Na* (St: 5081   Benrath: 69-84, intermittently)

Inc. prol.: Prophecia Naum dividitur in quinque partes primo premittat in omnem gentem peccativem (?) comminacionem generalem ...

Expl. prol.: × ... Et erit omnis qui videret te resiliet a te.

OMC 117: f. 250rb

Inc. *Postilla super Naum*: < Onus ... > Lira dividit hunc librum in duas partes in prohemium et tractatum. In prohemio primo tangitur materia prophecie ...

Expl.: × ... omnes debent gaudere dei iusticie applaudentes cui ineternum sit accio graciarum.

OMC 117: f.250rb-252va

340. B4.VI.m. *Hk* (St: 5081   Benrath: 69-84, intermittently)

Inc. prol.: Liber abacuch dividitur in tres partes. Primo assumit propheta contra dominum querelam ...

Expl. prol.: × ... Tercia pars ostendit prophetam domino propter hoc regnaciantem et devotum canticum componentem capitulo tercio.

OMC 117: f. 252va

Inc. *Postilla super Abacuch*: < Onus ... > Liber iste secundum liram dividitur in prohemium et tractatum. Onus est prophecia de malo pene caldeorum ...

Expl.: × ... Et finaliter concludit cum laude dei ibi. Ego autem in domino gaudebo, cui sit honor et gloria in secula seculorum.

OMC 117: ff. 252va-255vb

341. B4.VI.n. *Zp* (St: 5081   Benrath: 69-84, intermittently)

Inc. prol.: Prima pars sophonie divisa in quinque partes ponit generalem comminacionem super omnes populos ...

Expl. prol.: × ... Et eius excellenciam describit. In die illa dicetur ierusalem.

OMC 117: ff. 255vb-256ra

Inc. *Postilla super Sophonia*: < Verbum ... > Lira dividit hanc propheciam in prohemium et tractatum. In prohemio notantur condicio seu status ...

Expl.: × ... quod omnino oportuit implevi quia hoc dicit dominus qui est ipsa veritas, qui est benedictus in secula.

OMC 117: ff. 256ra-258vb

342. B4.VI.o. *Hg* (St: 5081   Benrath: 69-84, intermittently)

Inc. prol.: Aggei prophecia dividitur in sex partes. Prima est reprehensiva ...

Expl. prol.: × ... Sexta pars est iterum Christi repromissiam zorobabeli cum esset de eius semine [?] incarnandus.

OMC 117: f. 258vb

Inc. *Postilla super Aggeum*: < In ... > Paralipomenon 36° et jeremie 39° patet de periurio ...

Expl.: × ... Illud inquam fuit a domino impositum ab angelo nunciatum a parentibus et pastoribus promulgatum illud cuius nomen sit benedictum in secula.

OMC 117: ff. 258vb-260va

343. B4.VI.p. *Zc* (St: 5081   Benrath: 69-84, intermittently)

Inc. prol.: Prophecia zacharie dividitur in quattuor, primo ponuntur prophecie spectantes ad tempus presentis edificacionis templi ...

Expl. prol.: × ... spectant ad tempora romanorum succedencia post machabeos et dividitur in quattuor ultima capitula.

OMC 117: f. 260va-vb

Inc. *Postilla super Zachariam*: < In ... > In prohemio primo notatur tempus quo facta fuerat prophecia ...

Expl.: × ... scilicet Christi et ecclesie qui sibi romanum imperium subiugavit cui ineternum regnanti sit honor et imperium nunc et in evum.

OMC 117: ff. 260vb-271rb

344. B4.VI.q. *Ml* (St: 5081   Benrath: 69-84, intermittently)

Inc. prol.: Malachia ultimus duodecim prophetarum continet duodecim particulas principales. Nam primo reprehendit ingratitudinem iudeorum ...

Expl. prol.: × ... ad hunc errorem introducit diem judicii in quo nulli bono erit male et nulli malo erit bene.

OMC 117: f. 271rb-va

Inc. *Postilla super Malachia propheta*: < Onus ... > Dividitur in prohemium et tractatum. In prohemio ponitur primo malachie officium prophetandi ...

Expl.: × ... Electi autem adherebunt deo sempiterna fruicione quam nobis concedat qui sine fine vivit et regnat.[1]

        OMC 117:   ff. 271va-273***ra

[1] Followed by: "Explicit postilla super 12 prophetas et sic explicit sexta pars scripture que dicitur prophetica exclamatoria et declarativa." The rest of this folio as well as f. 273**** is blank; then Job commences on f. 274 (above, **320**) and completes the codex. – There is no indication that Wyclyf postillated either (1, 2) Macchabees or (3, 4) Ezr, though he was fond of quoting 3 Ezr 3:12 ("super omnia vincit veritas") in his later works.

345. B4.VII.a. *Mt* (St: 5088, 5091   Benrath: 91-156, 167-285 *passim*; 352-362)

Inc. prol. [primus]: Matheus ex Judea sicut in ordine. Iste prologus est beati jeronimi qui dividitur principaliter in 4 partes ...
Expl. prol. [primus]: × ...et quattuor virtutibus cardinalibus inchoati [...][1]

    PUK III.F.20:   f. 3r[2]
    W: f. 1ra-vb

Inc. prol. [secundus]: Matheus qui interpretatur datus primo inter quattuor evangelistas scripsit ...
Expl. prol. [secundus]: × ... dicit ergo subintelligendo verbum more prophetarum.

    OBod: ff. 1ra-2ra
    OMC 55:   ff. 77ra-78rb
    W: ff. 1vb-2ra[3]

Inc. *Postilla super Matheum*: < Liber ... > Triplex autem ponitur racio [or: causa] quare [i adds: qualiter] David premittitur ...
Expl.: × ... fuit thesauria tocius fidei gerens personam tunc filii sepulti.

    OBod: ff. 2ra-22rb
    OMC 55:   ff. 78rb-100rb
    PUK III.F.20:   ff. 3r-70r
    W: ff. 4ra-54va

[1] Incomplete, as noted by Benrath, p. 388; his foliation is slightly off.
[2] Preceded, ff. 1r-3r, by a related (Hussite?) commentary which cites Wyclyf's *Trialogus* (**47**), cap. xx. It is possible that I may have, given the limited time which I allotted to the examination of this MS, overlooked the second prologue.
[3] Incomplete, as noted by Benrath, p. 388. But ff. 2ra-4ra are not part of the second prologue, but rather a false start on Mt, cap i.

346. B4.VII.b. *Mk* (St: 5092   Benrath: 91-156, 167-285 *passim*)

Inc. prol.: Marcus fuit a domino ordinatus scribere evangelium et institutus a Petro ...
Expl. prol.: × ... et sic dividitur in 19 partes.

OBod:	ff. 22rb-23ra
OMC 55:	ff. 100rb-101ra
PUK III.F.20:	ff. 70r-72r
W:	ff. 54va-56ra

Inc. *Postilla super Marcum*: < nb: Initium ... not in any MS > Evangelium dicitur bonum nuncium quia in illo enunciatur summum bonum ...
Expl.: × ... ut novo homini conformando ut veteri innovando.

OBod:	ff. 23ra-32va
OMC 55:	ff. 101ra-111rb
PUK III.F.20:	ff. 72r-104r[1]
W:	ff. 56ra-78ra

[1] Expl.: × "... a quibus universa Job quinto." But this is from the commentary on cap. xvi, so the text is almost complete.

347. B4.VII.c. *Lk* (St: 5093   Benrath: 91-156, 167-285 *passim*; 362-365)

Inc. prol.: Lucas intendit principaliter quod homo iste qui dicitur Ihesus fuit salvator et medicus animarum ...
Expl. prol.: × ... predicacionem sileret quia lex et prophete usque ad johannem.

OBod:	ff. 32va-34rb
OMC 55:	ff. 111rb-113ra
PUK III.F.20:	ff. 104v-108v
W:	ff. 78ra-82ra

Inc. *Postilla super Lucam*: < Fuit ... >[1] Notatur temporis adventus Christi per hoc quod in diebus herodis ...
Expl.: × ... a die ascensionis usque ad diem pentacostes in oracione.

OBod:	ff. 34rb-51ra
OMC 55:	ff. 113ra-131ra
PUK III.F.20:	ff. 108v-153r
W:	ff. 82ra-120ra

[1] The citation is from the beginning of v. 5.

348. B4.VII.d. *Jn* (St: 5094   Benrath: 156-167, 366-369)

Inc. prol.: Evangelium Johannis ultimo scriptum excellit alia in subtilitate et sublimitate ...

Expl. prol.: × ... Johannes ergo [or: igitur] evangelista declarans filium dei esse sic orditur.

        OBod: f. 51ra-vb
        OMC 55:   f. 131rb-vb
        PUK III.F.20: ff. 153v-155r
        W: ff. 120ra-121rb

Inc. *Postilla in Johannem*: < In ... > Pro quo notandum quod solum racionalis vere est verbum principaliter causare ...

Expl.: × ... esse causam beatificacionis in trinitate vide luce 5°.[1]

        OBod: ff. 51vb-69va[2]
        OMC 55:   ff. 131vb-149ra[3]
        PUK III.F.20: ff. 155r-199r[4]
        W: ff. 121rb-160va

[1] vi expl.: × "... et semper remanet quantumlibet postilandum."
[2] Ff. 69vb-72v are blank; Ro, which follows, and the rest of the codex, are in a second hand, considerably more regular – much like that of **ii**, in fact.
[3] A short epilogue follows, evidently editorial.
[4] Truhlař says this ends on f. 187r, and doubts Wyclyf's authorship.

349. B4.VIII.a. *Ro*[1] (St: 5097   Benrath: 242-285 *passim*)

Inc. prol.: Octava et ultima pars scripture est epistolaris divisa in quattuor libros ...

Expl. prol.: × ... vide sapienciam 13° et 3° Regum 11 et interpretacionem 8°.

        OBod: f. 73ra-vb
        OMC 55:   f. 149ra-vb
        PNM: ff. 1r-2r
        PUK VIII.F.9: ff. 1r-3r
        W: ff. 160va-162rb

Inc. [*Postilla super*] *epistola*[*m*] *ad Romanos*: < nb: text cit. only in **v** and **vii**: Paulus ... > Paulus in prohemio reddit romanos benivolos dociles et attentos ...

Expl.: × ... sed ut obediatur sibi et totum hoc fit per dominum Ihesum Christum.

        OBod: ff. 73vb-83vb
        OMC 55:   ff. 149vb-159vb

PNM:	ff. 2r-27r
PUK VIII.F.9:	ff. 3r-29r
W:	ff. 162rb-183vb

[1] Ac (below, **363**) constitutes in this arrangement the *second* of the four "libri" of this "octava pars scripture." For a general survey of earlier Ro commentaries, cf. Werner Affeldt, "Verzeichnis der Römerbriefkommentare der lateinischen Kirche bis zu Nikolaus von Lyra," *Traditio* 13 (1957): 369-406.

350. B4.VIII.b. *1 Co* (St: 5098   Benrath: 242-285 *passim*; 369-370[1])

Inc. [*Postilla super*] *epistola*[*m*] *prima*[*m*] *ad Corinthios*: < Paulus ...: in **v** and **vii** only > Apostolus noscens omnia genera linguarum sicut scripsit epistolam ...

Expl.: × ... vide secunda[m] ad corinthios 8°, ad Romanos 15°.

OBod:	ff. 83vb-93va
OMC 55:	ff. 160ra-170vb
PNM:	ff. 27r-52v
PUK VIII.F.9:	ff. 29r-55v
W:	ff. 183vb-207ra

[1] An important early statement on the Eucharist. No prologue extant for this postill.

351. B4.VIII.c. *2 Co* (St: 5099   Benrath: 242-285 *passim*)

Inc. [*Postilla super*] *secunda*[*m*] *epistola*[*m*] *ad Corinthios*: < nb: no text cit. in any MS > Informatis corinthiis de quattuor sacramentis in hac secunda epistola instruit eos ...

Expl.: × ... in mittendo filium et communio spiritus in uniendo fideles.

OBod:	ff. 93va-101va
OMC 55:	ff. 170vb-178ra
PNM:	ff. 52v-77r
PUK VIII.F.9:	ff. 55v-71v
W:	ff. 207ra-222va

352. B4.VIII.d. *Gl* (St: 5100   Benrath: 242-285 *passim*; 371-373[1])

Inc. prol.: Apostolus intendit pro finali conclusione in ista epistola quod circumcisio et cetera legalia non sunt observanda ...

Expl. prol.: × ... et ille dividitur in prosecucionem et confirmacionem.

OBod:	f. 101va-vb
OMC 55:	f. 178ra-rb
PNM:	f. 77r-v

            PUK VIII.F.9:   ff. 71v-72r
            W: f. 222va-vb

Inc. [*Postilla super epistolam*] *ad Galathas*: < nb: text cit. only in v > Paulus vero authonomatice dictus est apostolus nec electus est ad hoc ad hominibus ...

Expl.: × ... et inde stigare quasi stimulare et producit stigam sicut et sua composita [et sequitur aliud].

            OBod: ff. 101vb-105rb
            OMC 55:   ff. 178rb-182ra
            PNM: ff. 77v-87r
            PUK VIII.F.9:   ff. 72r-80r
            W: ff. 222vb-230vb

[1] An important statement of Wyclyf's hermeneutic principles.

353. B4.VIII.e. *Ep* (St: 5101   Benrath: 242-285 *passim*)

Inc. prol.: Asia Minor pars est grecie. Hii conversi sunt ...
Expl. prol.: × ... de quiditate scripture et eius sensibilitate.[1]

            OBod: f. 105va
            OMC 55:   f. 182ra-rb
            PNM: f. 87r-v
            PUK VIII.F.9:   f. 80r-v
            W: ff. 230vb-231ra

Inc. [*Postilla super epistolam*] *ad Ephesios*: < nb: texts henceforth appear usually only in **v**, and there at the beginning of the prologue, relatively detached from the body of the postill; they shall be omitted hereafter > Habitacio [or: Salutacio] patet ex predictis illa [or: ista] epistola ...

Expl.: × ... sanctitas per Christum qui est unctus.

            OBod: ff. 105va-108vb
            OMC 55:   ff. 182rb-185vb
            PNM: ff. 87v-95r
            PUK VIII.F.9:   ff. 80v-88r
            W: ff. 231ra-238ra

[1] **i** and **v** are cut off before our expl., much shorter than the full prologue text.

354. B4.VIII.f. *Php* (St: 5102   Benrath: 242-285 *passim*)

Inc. prol.: Paulus hortatur Philippenses principaliter ad tolleranciam passionum ...

Expl. prol.: × ... et affeccio patris per dominum nostrum Ihesum Christum.

>   *OBod*: f. 108vb
>   *OMC 55*: ff. 185vb-186ra
>   *PNM*: f. 95r
>   *PUK VIII.F.9*: f. 88r-v
>   *W*: f. 238ra

Inc. [*Postilla super epistolam*] *ad Philippenses*: Incipit ergo partem executivam a graciarum accione confitendo more suo omnia bona ...

Expl.: × ... dabit graciam et gloriam in spiritu et redundanter in corpus.

>   *OBod*: ff. 108vb-111rb
>   *OMC 55*: ff. 186ra-188rb
>   *PNM*: ff. 95r-100r
>   *PUK VIII.F.9*: ff. 88v-93v
>   *W*: ff. 238ra-243ra

355. B4.VIII.g. *Cl* (St: 5103 Benrath: 242-285 *passim*)

Inc. [*Postilla super epistolam*] *ad Collocenses*:[1] Ista epistola dividitur in quattuor in salutacionem in graciarum accionem ...

Expl.: × ... et salvator Matth. 25 in carcere et visitastis me.

>   *OBod*: ff. 111rb-113rb
>   *OMC 55*: ff. 188rb-190va
>   *PNM*: ff. 100r-104v
>   *PUK VIII.F.9*: ff. 93v-98v
>   *W*: ff. 243rb-247vb

[1] None of the MSS indicates a prologue, though this sort of inc. is typical of one. It ought also to be mentioned that only the English MSS, and then only occasionally, clearly divide prologue from body of postill.

356. B4.VIII.h. *1 Th* (St: 5104 Benrath: 242-285 *passim*)

Inc. [*Postilla super*] *prima*[*m*] *epistola*[*m*] *ad Thessalonicenses*: Paulus more solito premittet salutacionem secundo maiorum in bonis ...

Expl.: × ... et hoc signat communicacio pacis in ecclesiis vide marcum 10°.

>   *OBod*: ff. 113rb-115vb
>   *OMC 55*: ff. 190va-193rb
>   *PNM*: ff. 104v-110r
>   *PUK VIII.F.9*: ff. 98v-104r
>   *W*: ff. 247vb-253rb

357. B4.VIII.i. *2 Th* (St: 5105   Benrath: 242-285 *passim*)

Inc. [*Postilla super*] *secunda*[*m*] *epistola*[*m*] *ad Thessalonicenses*: Paulus apostolus in salutando premittit Silvanum qui est Sylas ...
Expl.: × ... compilasse sed terminatur ab ecclesia quod non in synodo nicena vide Hebreos 1°.[1]

OBod:	ff. 116ra-117rb
OMC 55:	ff. 193rb-194vb
PNM:	ff. 110r-112v
PUK VIII.F.9:	ff. 104r-107r
W:	ff. 253rb-256ra

[1] ii does not have our expl., though it appears to be of about the same length as the other MS versions.

358. B4.VIII.j. *1 Tm* (St: 5106   Benrath: 242-285 *passim*)

Inc. [*Postilla super*] *prima*[*m*] *epistola*[*m*] *ad Thymotheum*: Epistola ad Thymotheum dividitur in quattuor primo enim ponit salutacionem ...
Expl.: × ... et inficiendo quo ad fructus toxicos.

OBod:	ff. 117rb-120vb
OMC 55:	ff. 194vb-198va
PNM:	ff. 113r-120r
PUK VIII.F.9:	ff. 107r-115r
W:	ff. 256ra-264ra

359. B4.VIII.k. *2 Tm* (St: 5106   Benrath: 242-285 *passim*)

Inc. [*Postilla super*] *secunda*[*m*] *epistola*[*m*] *ad Thymotheum*: Secunda epistola scribitur a Roma per apostolum incarceratum ...
Expl.: × ... salutans Timotheum fuit secundus episcopus Romanus post Petrum ut dicit Chrisostomus.

OBod:	ff. 120vb-122vb
OMC 55:	ff. 198va-200vb
PNM:	ff. 120v-124v
PUK VIII.F.9:	ff. 115r-119v
W:	ff. 264ra-268va

360. B4.VIII.l. *Ti* (St: 5108   Benrath: 242-285 *passim*)

Inc. [*Postilla super*] *epistola*[*m*] *ad Titum*: Titus fuit ordinatus archiepiscopus in creta a beato Paulo ...
Expl.: × ... quam prius fidelis dogmatisat pertinaciter operum fidei Christiane.

OBod:	ff. 122vb-124rb
OMC 55:	ff. 200vb-202rb
PNM:	ff. 124v-127r
PUK VIII.F.9:	ff. 120r-123r
W:	ff. 268vb-272rb

361. B4.VIII.m. *Phm* (St: 5109   Benrath: 242-285 *passim*)

Inc. [*Postilla super*] *epistola*[*m*] *ad Philemonem* [*pro Onesimo*][1]: Intencio apostoli in ista epistola est impetrare veniam onesimo servo philemonis ...

Expl.: × ... et per consequens foret donum et non onus veniendo de carcere.

OBod:	f. 124rb-vb
OMC 55:	f. 202rb-vb
PNM:	ff. 127v-128r
PUK VIII.F.9:	ff. 123r-124r
W:	ff. 272rb-273rb

[1] Last words added only in colophon to **ii**; do not correspond to any received Vulgate text.

362. B4.VIII.n. *He* (St: 5110   Benrath: 242-285 *passim*)

Inc. prol.: Apostolus scripsit hanc epistolam hebreis hebraice sicut priores epistolas scripsit latinis ...[1]

Expl. prol.: × ... de observanciis legalium scripsit hanc epistolam secundum Crisostomum.

OBod:	ff. 124vb-125ra
OMC 55:	ff. 202vb-203ra
PNM:	f. 128r-v
PUK VIII.F.9:	f. 124r-v
W:	f. 273rb-vb

Inc. [*Postilla super*] *epistola*[*m*] *ad Hebreos*: Quo supposito potest dividi hec epistola in quattuor ...

Expl.: × ... pro isto nuncio ex rogatu apostoli salutate omnes.

OBod:	ff. 125ra-133rb
OMC 55:	ff. 203ra-212ra
PNM:	ff. 128v-143r
PUK VIII.F.9:	ff. 124v-143r
W:	ff. 273vb-292va

[1] Cf. **182**, n. 1, above, regarding Wyclyf's uncritical attitude on the authorship of He.

363. B4.VIII.o. *Ac* (St: 5096   Benrath: 285-300; 373-377)

Inc. prol.: Nota quod prelati debent vigilare primo in proprie consciencie purgacione ...
Expl. prol.: × ... quam Philargiam postpositis mundialibus deus vendicat sibi soli vide luce 7°.

OBod:	ff. 133va-134rb
OMC 55:	ff. 212ra-213ra
PNM:	ff. 143r-144v
PUK VIII.F.9:	ff. 143r-145r
W:	ff. 292va-294vb

Inc. *Postilla super Actus Apostolorum*: Beatus Lucas intendit principaliter istam conclusionem quod fides Christi introivit miraculose in orbem ...
Expl.: × ... in illo suscipiebat omnes qui ingrediebantur.[1]

OBod:	ff. 134rb-147ra
OMC 55:	ff. 213ra-227rb
PNM:	ff. 144v-168r
PUK VIII.F.9:	ff. 145r-172v
W:	ff. 294vb-323ra

[1] **v** and **viii** expl.: × "... redeundo Romam martirisatum fuisse cum Petro." This is the sentence preceding the expl. in the other MSS.

364. B4.VIII.p. *Ja* (St: 5111   Benrath: 242-285 *passim*)

Inc. prol.: Omnes isti quattuor apostoli in septem epistolis volunt informare ecclesiam ...[1] ...
Expl. prol.: × ... ubique terrarum scripsit hanc epistolam.

OBod:	f. 147ra
OMC 55:	f. 227rb
PNM:	f. 168r
PUK VIII.F.9:	f. 172v
W:	f. 323ra

Inc. *Postilla super epistolam Jacobi*: In tractatu vero informat eos primo ...
Expl.: × ... salvat quidem occasionaliter et instrumentaliter sed non donative.

OBod:	ff. 147ra-150ra
OMC 55:	ff. 227rb-230va
PNM:	ff. 168r-173v
PUK VIII.F.9:	ff. 172v-178v
W:	ff. 323ra-329va

[1] Identified in the colophon to **i** as "prologus ad epistolas canonicas"; in **ii** as "prologus septem epistolarum et Jacobi primo"; etc.

365. B4.VIII.q. *1 P* (St: 5112   Benrath: 242-285 *passim*)

Inc. *Postilla super primam epistolam Petri*: In hac prima canonica tractat Petrus de virtutibus moralibus ...

Expl.: × ... que est causa continentis ut aqua in mixtis.

OBod:	ff. 150ra-153ra
OMC 55:	ff. 230vb-234ra
PNM:	ff. 173v-179r
PUK VIII.F.9:	ff. 178v-184v
W:	ff. 329va-334rb

366. B4.VIII.r. *2 P* (St: 5113   Benrath: 242-285 *passim*)

Inc. *Postilla super secundam epistolam Petri*: In hac secunda epistola petri informatur ecclesia in moralibus ...

Expl.: × ... contingenti que sunt diffinitive sunt nobis noscibiles.

OBod:	ff. 153ra-155ra
OMC 55:	ff. 234ra-236rb
PNM:	ff. 179v-183v
PUK VIII.F.9:	ff. 185r-189v
W:	ff. 334rb-339rb

367. B4.VIII.s. *1 Jn* (St: 5114   Benrath: 242-285 *passim*)

Inc. prol.: Beatus Johannes affectus numero ternario propter misterium trinitatis ...

Expl. prol.: × ... duorum vel trium stat omne verbum testificandi.

OBod:	f. 155ra-rb
OMC 55:	f. 236rb-va
PNM:	ff. 183v-184r
PUK VIII.F.9:	ff. 189v-190r
W:	f. 339rb-vb

Inc. *Postilla super primam epistolam Johannis*: Tractatus dividitur in tria secundum tria tacta in prohemio ...

Expl.: × ... de quocunque predicante moraliter, ideo est doctrinalis conclusio.[1]

OBod:	ff. 155rb-158rb
OMC 55:	ff. 236va-238vb
PNM:	ff. 184r-189r

PUK VIII.F.9:	ff. 190r-196v
W:	ff. 339vb-345vb

[1] Expl. of all Continental MSS: × "... simulacris Marco 14º."

368. B4.VIII.t. *2 Jn* (St: 5115   Benrath: 242-285 *passim*)

Inc. [*Postilla super*] *secunda*[m] *epistola*[m] *Johannis*: Hanc secundam epistolam scripsit beatus Johannes [cuidam] domine [de Babilonia] cum sua familia ...

Expl.: × ... sub se septem metropolitanos quibus scripsit Apocalypsim.[1]

OBod:	f. 158rb-vb
OMC 55:	ff. 238vb-239ra
PNM:	ff. 189r-190r
PUK VIII.F.9:	ff. 196v-197v
W:	ff. 345vb-346vb

[1] Expl. in ii: × "... fuit enim Johannes archiepiscopus tocius Asie Minoris."

369. B4.VIII.u. *3 Jn* (St: 5116   Benrath: 242-285 *passim*)

Inc. [*Postilla super*] *tercia*[m] *epistola*[m] *Johannis*: Hanc terciam epistolam scribit Johannes cuidam fideli Corintho nomine Gayo ...

Expl.: × ... prophetavit per triplex medium ut patet in prologo proximo sequente.

OBod:	ff. 158vb-159ra
OMC 55:	f. 239ra-rb
PNM:	f. 190r-v
PUK VIII.F.9:	ff. 197v-198v
W:	ff. 346vb-347rb

370. B4.VIII.v. *Jde* (St: 5117   Benrath: 242-285 *passim*)

Inc. [*Postilla super*] *epistola*[m] *Jude*: Hec septima epistola Jude movet principaliter permanere in doctrina apostolica ...

Expl.: × ... nullam essenciam dicunt aliquod istorum preter deum.

OBod:	f. 159ra-va
OMC 55:	f. 239rb-vb
PNM:	ff. 190v-191v[1]
PUK VIII.F.9:	ff. 198v-200r[2]
W:	ff. 347va-348vb[3]

[1] A small portion at the bottom of the column is blank; no provision for Rv.
[2] The remaining two-thirds of f. 200r; all of f. 200v and ff. 201 and 202 (not numbered) are blank.

[3] End of the codex; no provision, apparently, for Rv. Since this was the sole MS of any part of B4 known to Sh and Lo, it is not surprising that it strengthened their assumption that Wyclyf had not commented the Apocalypse. But in this curious vacuum it began to be thought that the commentary beginning "Opus arduum valde ..." was the missing piece: cf. below, G*Spur*5.

371. B4.VIII.w. *Rv* (St: 5119   Benrath: 300-309)

Inc. *Postilla super Apocalipsim*: Conclusio quam intendit Johannes in hoc [or: isto] libro est [hec] instruere ecclesiam ...

Expl.: × ... et fideliter pro omnibus fidelibus ecclesie orando gracia[m] finem imponit.

    OBod: ff. 159vb-171vb
    OMC 55:   ff. 239vb-248va

372. B5.a. *Exposicio textus Matthei xxiii* [*De ve octuplici*].[1] Late 1381?

I. Inc.: Cum sapiencia dei patris sit nucleus veritatis ...

Expl.: × ... ex ista memorata ingratitudine erit pena in istis perfidiis sine fine.

II. MSS (those containing the *De magisterio Christi* marked *):

i	Manchester, John Rylands Lib.	Eng. 86	ff. 69r-82v	xv/1	JW MS Eng.
ii	Praha, MK	N.48 (1572)*	ff. 175v-178r	1422	Unasc. Boh.[2]
iii	UK	III.G.11 (536)*	ff. 174v-178v	xv/1	JW MS Boh.
iv			ff. 178v-190v		
v		IV.H.7 (771)	ff. 58r-80r	ca. 1410	JW MS Boh.

[not in UK V.F.9 (931), *pace* Loserth, introduction, p. LVIII, and Lo: 95]

vi	Wien, ÖNB	1337*	ff. 110rb-114ra	ca. 1410	JW MS Boh.
vii		1338	ff. 31ra-44va	ca. 1410	JW MS Boh.
viii		1387	ff. 138ra-144vb	ca. 1410	JW MS Boh.
ix		3929*	ff. 247va-250ra	1409	JW MS Boh.
x		3930	ff. 125ra-141rb	1412	JW MS Boh.
xi		4527	ff. 85r-98v	1410	JW MS Boh.
xii		*	ff. 191r-194v		
xiii	Wolfenbüttel, HzglB	Cod.Guelf. 306 (340)	ff. 213va-229va	xv/1	Asc. Pol.[3]

III. Ed. J. Loserth, *Johannis Wyclif Opera Minora* (WS, 1913): 313-353†; the *De magisterio Christi* ed. separately in idem, 439-449. From all MSS except **ii, ix** and **xiii**.

IV. Loserth observes in his introduction (p. XXXVII) that in Sh this *Exposicio* was "wrongly" bracketed with the exegetical works and sermons – yet he himself in his revision of the *Catalogue* sustained his predecessor's judgment. The present piece might with reason be assigned to the general category of polemical works; yet we ought not on that account to overlook its significant parallelisms with the *Opus evangelicum* III (= *De Antichristo* I: **376**), and the fact that almost all of the short treatise *De magisterio Christi* [*De graduacionibus*][4] is an extract from the *Exposicio*. It is worthwhile to put these connections in tabular form:[5]

De magisterio Christi	*Exposicio ... Mt xxiii*	*De Antichristo* I
p. 439 - p. 448, l. 14	p. 323, l. 17 - p. 333, l. 26 (= part of cap. iv; all of capp. v, vi)	[no parallel]
p. 448, l. 14 - p. 449, l. 21 (end)	[no parallel]	[no parallel]
[no parallels]	p. 314, ll. 14-17; in cap. i	p. 1, ll. 18-21; in cap. i
	p. 316, ll. 19-21; in cap. ii	p. 8, ll. 30-32; in cap. ii
	p. 319, ll. 24-26 ; in cap. iii	p. 12, l. 37 - p. 13, l. 2; in cap. iv
	[see above for capp. iv-vi]	[no parallels]
	p. 333, ll. 30-32; in cap. vii	p. 28, ll. 21-23; in cap. viii
	p. 337, ll. 25-29; in cap. viii	p. 39, ll. 20-24; in cap. xi
	p. 338, l. 36 - p. 339, l. 2; In cap. viii	p. 42, ll. 25-28; in cap. xii
	p. 340, ll. 25-28; in cap. ix	p. 45, ll. 33-36; in cap. xiii
	p. 344, ll. 17-21; in cap. x	p. 49, ll. 17-21; in cap. xiv
	p. 344, ll. 21-22; in cap. x	p. 53, l. 33; in cap. xiv
	p. 346, ll. 24-28; in cap. xi	p. 54, ll. 28-33; in cap. xv
	p. 347, ll. 18-23; in cap. xii	p. 57, ll. 2-7; in cap. xvi
	p. 348, l. 32 - p. 349, l. 4 in cap. xiii	p. 60, ll. 13-17; in cap. xvii
	p. 350, ll. 23-26; in cap. xiv	p. 76, ll. 25-27; in cap. xxi
	p. 353, l. 8; in cap. xiv	p. 94, ll. 26-27; in cap. xxvi

The table demonstrates clearly that not only can fourteen identical citations from the *Exposicio* and the *De Antichristo* be noted, but also that they appear in the same sequence – though even a cursory examination would reveal that the passages in question are exclusively Scriptural in content, and that the contextual adaptation is often quite different. So we may safely conclude that the *Exposicio* furnished a ready arsenal of Biblical embellishment, but little more, for Wyclyf's last great exegetical effort, the *De Antichristo*.

On balance wa have therefore elected to maintain the earlier classification of the *Exposicio* (and obviously also of its sister piece, **373**, just below) as a commentary; in truth it is a verse-by-verse gloss on Mt 23.

We would much oversimplify the issue of Wyclyf's animosity toward the "four sects"[6] if we were to assume that he became progressively more bitter against all of them right up to his dying day. It was more a matter of mutation, of perceptible alterations in quality and degree in response to challenges and change. His first outbursts against the friars, for example, flowed directly from their rupture with him over the Eucharist (though tension had certainly been building over the matter of Christ's poverty); and with the catalytic events of the Blackfriars Synod of mid-1382 and the mendicant flogging of the Flanders crusade in mid-1383 he found fresh causes for revilement. But neither the Eucharist, nor the Blackfriars, nor the crusade appears even once in the *Exposicio*. There is in fact nowhere any allusion to any specific datable occurrence, not even the Schism[7] – though his rancor toward the secular clergy is extreme. What we do discover are two typically oblique *obiter dicta* on pp. 324 and 325: "Quis ergo est ille qui *contra iuramentum* proprium nidum inficeret .... Et quantum ad infeccionem nidi proprii dicit fidelis, confitens humiliter crimina que commisit, quod tenetur ex lege caritatis corrigere in que peccaverat, et premunire alios ne incidunt in istud periculum sicut ipse." (Emphasis added.) Considering the context – the problem of the *magisterium* of teaching generally – two things are plain: the ease with which this section could have been, indeed was, extracted, and then developed a separate MS tradition as the *De magisterio Christi*; and its close chronological link with Wyclyf's departure from Oxford. (There can, incidentally, be no suspicion that the *De magisterio* was arbitrarily inserted into, rather than lifted from, the *Exposicio*: its running commentary on Mt 23: 8-12 fits precisely between capp. iii and vii.) We submit therefore early 1382, or quite late in 1381, as the most plausible time of composition.[8]

vc: 3933 3935 4515 7980   Bale: 88[9]   Sh: 43   Lo: 43

---

[1] An alternate title appearing in several MSS; the reference is specifically to Mt 23:13-36. Cf. Loserth's introduction, p. xxxvii.

[2] Podlaha gives the correct explicit and folio no., but overlooks the piece itself; cf. **416**, n. 5, below.

[3] Cf. Kühn-Steinhausen, "Wyclif-Handschriften in Deutschland," 626.

[4] In **xii**, it appears under the rubric *De gradibus cleri*. We have indicated a preference for *De magisterio Christi* throughout, as the other is too easily confused with **394**, below. Cf. Sh: 94 and Lo: 95.

[5] The portion of Wyclyf's *Postilla super Matheum* (**345**) that deals with Mt 23 has little bearing on any of these later writings.

[6] Cf. above, **46**, n. 2; **50**, n. 6; Section F, below.

[7] Nor are there any easily recognizable *renvois* to his own work, though Mt 23 was discussed both in his earlier *Postilla* ... (above, n. 5) and in the *De veritate sacre scripture* I (**31**: p. 334). Cf. also the Scriptural indices in all four vols. of the *Sermones* (B2.I-IV), and several other eds. by the WS.

[8] The reference of the beginning of the *Exposicio textus Matthei xxiv* (**373**: p. 354) to "quomodo Christus in capitulo proximo precedente interpretatur Ve octuplex scribis et Phariseis" does not presuppose the present piece, but the elapse of more than a year between the two commentaries is not thereby called into question.

[9] Inc. given as the first words of the Vulgate text.

373. B5.b. *Exposicio textus Matthei xxiv* [*Longum evangelium*] [*De Antichristo*].[1] Mid-1383 ?

I. Inc.: Quia evangelium istud est multis absconditum ...
Expl.: × ... ut fides huius evangelii sit melius intellecta.

II. MSS:

i	Manchester, John Rylands Lib.	Eng. 86	ff. 55r-64v	xv/1	JW MS Eng.
ii	Praha, UK	III.G.11 (536)	ff. 190v-201r	xv/1	JW MS Boh.
iii		IV.H.7 (771)	ff. 103r-116r	ca. 1410	JW MS Boh.
iv	Wien, ÖNB	1338	ff. 44va-54ra	ca. 1410	JW MS Boh.
v		1387	ff. 145ra-149rb	ca. 1410	JW MS Boh.
vi		3930	ff. 141rb-150va	1412	JW MS Boh.[2]
vii		4527	ff. 98v-107r	1410	JW MS Boh.
viii			ff. 178r-181r[3]		
ix	Wolfenbüttel, HzglB	Cod. Guelf. 306 (340)	ff. 229va-240vb	xv/1	Asc. Pol.[4]

III. Ed. J. Loserth, *Johannis Wyclif Opera Minora* (WS, 1913): 354-382†. From all MSS except **viii** and **ix**.

IV. This piece is indeed a gloss on Mt 24 but, like the preceding item, it is strongly polemical in tone, and glaringly antipapal throughout. There is one specific problem in connection with this work which requires exploration, and some effort at resolution. In the *Opus evangelicum* III (= *De Antichristo* I: **376**, below: pp. 132-134) the introduction to cap. xxxvi concludes with the phrase "Unde sic legimus in quodam opere magistrali ..."; and the cap. itself ends "Ego autem nescio importare racione vel scriptura supposita veritate gestus papalis istam sentenciam magistralem." (The composition of this part of the *Opus evangelicum* clearly fell around mid-1384.) The passage enclosed by these quotations runs "Licet autem textus ... × ... pro racione voluntas"[5] – and it also appears *verbatim* in the present *Exposicio*, p. 359, l. 33 - p. 362, l. 27. There can be no cavil at its appositeness here: as a commentary on Mt 24:15, it fits logically into the linear flow. And since in the *Exposicio* there is no effort to identify the passage as borrowed from some earlier source, we are naturally led to conclude that the *Exposicio* was itself that "opus magistrale" twice alluded to in the *Opus evangelicum*. The problem is that the *Exposicio* patently dates from mid-1383 at the earliest: it abounds in allusions to the Flanders crusade and to Urban VI as "iste refuga" (p. 368).⁶ In what sense Wyclyf may have intended the term "opus magistrale" to apply to his own gloss, on which the ink was barely dry, it is difficult to imagine. One would ordinarily construe it as a kind of thesis, which in Wyclyf's *cursus honorum* much predated the controversial imbroglios of which the *Exposicio* is as typical as any other of his Lutterworth productions. His only previous commentaries on Mt 24:15 both seem to be excluded: in the *Postilla super Matheum* (**345**) he had no polemical and certainly no antipapal axe to grind; in the *De potestate pape* (**33**: pp. 221, 228, 322), while loosely equivalent phraseology touching the "abhominacio desolacionis" is employed, it is arguably no closer to the thematic development of the *Exposicio* than are the elliptical references in the much later *De fundacione sectarum* (**431**: p. 75); the *De novis ordinibus* (**422**: pp. 332-333); or the *Trialogus* (**47**: pp. 181, 268, 425).⁷ Allowing then for the possibility that his use of the term "opus magistrale" may be a deliberate bit of obfuscation, we are left with the disquieting inference that he may have lifted this substantial extract in the *Exposicio* (with no attribution whatever) from some unknown *magister* whose own antipapal "opus" would assuredly not have enjoyed official favor at Oxford or anywhere else! Somehow this does not satisfy the conditions; "opus magistrale" must have meant something else to Wyclyf here than what we normally take it for.

Those wishing to pursue Wyclyf's metaphysical postulate that "omnia que evenient de necessitate evenient"⁸ will find its most mature exposition on pp. 376-377.

VC: 3933 3935 4514   Bale: 6 ?⁹   Sh: 44   Lo: 44

¹ The latter title, of course, suggests a strong affinity with the second half of the *Opus evangelicum* (**376-377**); indeed in his edition of the latter work Loserth identifies several parallel passages, as we did for the preceding item: see his introduction, pp. XXVI-XXIX.

² After our expl., the text continues "... de quibus dictum est sufficienter."

³ A fragment; ends at the conclusion of cap. iii, p. 362.

⁴ Cf. Kühn-Steinhausen, "Wyclif-Handschriften in Deutschland," 626.

⁵ The latter is part of a quotation from Juvenal that crops up also in the *De officio regis* (**33**: p. 227), and in the *De blasfemia* (**37**: p. 162) as well.

⁶ See below, **405**, n. 3, for a clarification of this sobriquet.

⁷ On the last-enumerated page, we begin to encounter in turn some parallelisms with Wyclyf's *De Christo et suo adversario Antichristo* (**412**), which also coincide with cap. iv of this *Exposicio* – all of which only proves that he never hesitated to rework earlier (here, nearly simultaneous) formulations. But this only deepens our problem with the "Licet ... voluntas" passage, since *it* is clearly not a reworking at all.

⁸ Cf. above, **56**, n. 1. We might add that certainly one of the *earliest* formulations of this position appears in the *De volucione dei* (**16**: p. 117, ll. 20-21: "omnia que erunt vel fuerunt, sunt in tempore sempiterno"). That tractate, as we have already remarked, was essentially a commentary on Bradwardine's *De causa dei*. It is therefore intriguing to find that Bradwardine himself regarded the matter in quite another light: "et quidam heretici moliuntur destruere universaliter liberum arbitrium tam in deo quam in creatura et omnem graciam ac gratuitam et liberam accionem, dicentes quod

omnia que evenient de necessitate evenient." (Ed. H. Savile [London, 1618]: 637; plate of MS Oxford, Merton Coll. 71, f. 200ra, reproduced in Thomson, *Latin Bookhands*, pl. 101.) Probably Wyclyf also touched upon this issue in his *De tempore* (**12**) and *De sciencia dei* (**15**); future editions of those treatises should set the matter to rest.

[9] Tit.: *De Christo & Antichristo*; inc. "Egressus Jesus ...," the opening words of Mt 24:1. But cf. **162**; and two other sermons in that collection also relate to Mt 24 (:3 and :42 respectively): **160**, **165**.

374-377. B6.I.a, b; II.a, b. *Opus evangelicum* I, II [*De sermone domini in monte*]; III, IV [*De Antichristo* I, II]. 1383- end of 1384.

I. Inc. I: Licet totum evangelium annuatim deferat sua spiritualia ...
Expl. I: × ... Sed iste tres sufficiunt pro presenti.
Inc. II: Sequitur in textu evangelii: Attendite ...
Expl. II: × ... faciliter possunt ex gracia dei resurgere.
Inc. III: Completo tractatu primo evangelii de sermone domini in monte [14 wds.] restat cum spe divini adiutorii aggredi secundum tractatum ...
Expl. III: × ... quod habent a domino non appetent se non esse.
Inc. IV: Dictus est superius quod tercius tractatus evangelii stat in sermone ...
Expl. IV: × ... sed differre pocius disputator. Hec Augustinus.[1]

II. MSS (as the *Opus evangelicum* is complete in all four MSS,[2] we shall give the sequence of the four parts individually in each case):

i	Cambridge, Trinity Coll.	B.16.2	ff. 353ra-379rb; 379rb-404rb; 404rb-432ra; 432ra-437vb	xiv/ex	JW MS Eng.[3]
ii	Dublin, Trinity Coll.	C.1.23	pp. 3a-100b; 100b-195b; 195b-313a; 313a-332a	xiv/2	JW MS Eng.[4]
iii	Praha, UK	IV.A.18 (594)	ff. 1ra-63ra; 63ra-123rb; 123rb-191rb; 191rb-202va	ca. 1400	Asc. Boh.[5]
iv	Wien, ÖNB	1647	ff. 1ra-88ra; 88ra-176vb; 177ra-279va; 279va-298va	ca. 1400	Unasc. Boh.[6]

III. Ed. J. Loserth, *Iohannis Wyclif Opus Evangelicum* (WS, 1895): 1-234, 235-471; idem, *Iohannis Wyclif Operis Evangelici liber tertius et quartus sive De Antichristo liber primus et secundus* (WS, 1896): 1-283, 287-336. From **i** and **ii** only.

IV. It is a peculiarity of many of Wyclyf's works, especially during the years following the *Summa theologie* (A12), that they may with equal cogency be assigned to any of several topical classifications. The *Opus evangelicum*, both massive and unfinished, also exemplifies this characteristic. On its face, it is an exhaustive commentary on Mt 5-7 (= *De sermone domini in monte*), Mt 23-25 (= *pars* I of the *De Antichristo*), and Jn 13-17 (so intended: the commentary breaks off at Jn 13:31 – = *pars* II of the *De Antichristo*). It is heavily larded with long excerpts from Chrysostom's *Opus Imperfectum*,[7] Jerome,[8] and Augustine's celebrated *De sermone domini in monte*.[9] Grosseteste[10] is also pressed into service on many occasions. From the sheer mass of these citations, and the structure of the work as a whole, we have determined to place the *Opus evangelicum* once more under its traditional exegetical rubric. But in tone it is stridently and repeatedly antipapal and anti-mendicant – and could therefore defensibly be inserted into the polemical canon. Finally, in its range and diversity of subordinate topic coverage, it is reminiscent of the *Trialogus* (**47**), which would dictate its inclusion among the philosophical and theological tractates. It is well to remind ourselves that the categories here adopted are a matter of retrospective analytical convenience and at best arbitrary; certainly Wyclyf himself would have been puzzled at our contemporary arrangement.

Thematic throughout **374** and **375** is his contention that the precepts of the Sermon on the Mount are adequate law in themselves: "et sic sufficeret eciam sermo domini in monte regulare perfecte sine tradicione humana quotlibet viatores." (II, p. 368.) The *De Antichristo*, on the other hand, shifts emphasis to the theme of hypocrisy, a vice he saw rampant throughout the institutional church of his own day. A frequent phrase here is "versucie Antichristi,"[11] his code-phrase for the multitude of iniquities crowding him.

Perhaps on the very day of his fatal stroke late in December of 1384, he reflected yet again, along with "quidam theologi" otherwise unidentified, on the right upbringing of a true theologian: "necesse est theologum in recta logica, philosophia et metaphisica esse instructum et quod cognoscat istam quintuplicem armaturam, primo quod cognoscat universalia ex parte rei; et per hoc potest cognoscere verba Moysi locuta de genere et specie .... Secundo cognoscat secundum rectam metaphisicam scole Christi veritatem de quiditate temporis et aliorum accidencium ... et confunditur ista heresis quod hostia consecrata sit accidens sine subiectante substancia sive nichil. Tercio quod cognoscat quod apud deum et creatos spiritus omnia que fuerunt vel erunt sunt in magno tempore sibi presencia,[12] et per hoc potest cognosci sensus huius evangelii: Antequam Abraham fieret, ego sum .... Quarto quod cognoscat quod creature habent in deo esse ydeale eternum existenciam in suo genere eternaliter antecedens; et per hoc potest cognosci huius sensus evangelii Johannis: quod factum est in ipso, vita erat .... Et quinto quod cognoscat naturalem essenciam esse perpetuam et ex non quantis esse compositam et formas materiales esse eius disposiciones .... Per hec quinque cum suis appendiciis potest subtilis logicus defendere catholice textus theologicos scripturarum." (IV, pp. 325-326.) The startling expression "secundum rectam metaphisicam scole Christi veritatem" is perhaps more revealing of the distance between his age and our own than any other single phrase in the entire *corpus Wyclyfianum*.[13]

vc: 3933 3935 4514 7980[14]   Bale: 15[15]   Sh: 42   Lo: 42

[1] Both English mss add: "Auctoris vita finitur et hoc opus ita." The circumstances of Wyclyf's death (and of the stroke which presaged it two years previously) are documented in Workman, *JW* II: 316 and n. 3. The *Opus evangelicum* would appear to be the only unfinished work in the entire Wyclyf canon – arguably excepting *libri* II and III of the *De civili dominio* (**29, 30**) – surely a remarkable testimony to his persistence and discipline.

[2] *Pace* Lo, who says the Praha ms is incomplete.

[3] As with the *Sermones* (B2.I-IV), we observe here the older foliation also employed by Loserth in his edition.

[4] There is an index on pp. 414a-422b.

[5] The foliation is odd: facing pages bear the same number. We observe here the usual style.

[6] There exists a ms, previously misidentified, which excerpts and arranges the *Opus evangelicum* in much the same manner as the English Lollard *florilegia* identified by Anne Hudson, "A Lollard Compilation and the Dissemination of Wycliffite Thought," *JTS*, new ser., 23 (1972): 65-81; it is in turn strikingly close in concept to London, BL Harley 401, for which see Thomson, *Latin Bookhands*, pl. 103. The ms (ca. 1400, Eng.) is Oxford, Magdalen Coll. Lat. 99, ff. 176ra-178vb. The scribe quite understandably chose to identify our work as an [anonymous] commentary on Mt 5-7, 23-29 [sic] and Jn 13-17. It is emphatically *not*, as stated in Coxe, *Catalogus codicum manuscriptorum* ... II: 54, a "condemnatio articulorum variorum ex Joh. Wiclevi de simonia, de perfectione statuum et aliis operibus extractorum;" all references in the ms are to the *Opus evangelicum*.

[7] Basic here are Bernard de Montfaucon, ed., Τοῦ ἐν Πατρὸς ἡμῶν, Ἰωαννοῦ τοῦ χρυσοστόμου ... τὰ εὑρισκόμενα πάντα VII (Paris, 1836): cols. 212-347 (also in Migne, *Patrologia ... Graeco-Latina*); John Chrysostom, *Commentary on Saint John the Apostle and Evangelist; Homilies 1-88* (2 vols., New York, 1957, 1959); Jaroslav Pelikan, ed., *The Preaching of Chrysostom* (Philadelphia, 1967).

[8] Jerome was of course central to Wyclyf's much earlier *Postilla super totam Bibliam* (B4); the references here are occasional, and may be picked out in Migne; his various commentaries are being re-edited in the *Corpus Christianorum Series Latina* (Turnholt: cf. vols. 72-78).

[9] Dennis J. Kavanaugh, trans., *Augustine. Commentary on the Lord's Sermon on the Mount, with 17 related Sermons* (The Fathers of the Church 11: New York, 1951). This commentary became an indispensable model for medieval homiletics. (On Augustine and Wyclyf generally, see **17**, n. 10, above.)

[10] Around a dozen explicit citations appear s.v. "Lincolniensis" in Loserth's "Index of Names" to both vols. (On Grosseteste and Wyclyf generally, see **4**, n. 2; **6**, n. 7; **26**, nn. 15, 16; and **55**, n. 2, above.)

[11] Cf. pp. 5, 98, 127, 180, 199, 200, 328; also **420**, below.

[12] See **373**, n. 8, above.

[13] By far the largest number of erroneous and heretical propositions extracted from any of his books is represented by the *Opus evangelicum* in the proceedings of the 1411 committee of twelve: Wilkins, *Concilia* ... III: 339-343 (nos. 1-74). (See above, **3**, n. 5.)

Loserth observes in his introduction to vol. I, p. III, that Hus' *De sufficiencia legis Christi* (for which see Bartoš, *Literární Činnost M. J. Husi*, p. 89), was "merely a feeble extract from the present work." (Workman makes basically the same observation in *JW* II: 313.) Once again Loserth has overstated his case for Hus' dependence on Wyclyf's thought. The synthesis, the application and the thrust remained essentially Hus' own. Citation, acknowledged or not, was hardly equivalent to total identification with the author cited. Medieval theologians customarily incorporated substantial excerpts from texts – Scriptural, patristic, canonical, or whatever – into their own screeds; and they often did so, incidentally, as Eusebius and others had done centuries before, with the sole purpose of discrediting them. It is to this practice that we owe the very survival of many texts that came to be viewed as suspect or heretical outright.

[14] The text in the first three varies; all, however, distinguish the four parts separately.

[15] Tit. *De sermone Domini in monte*; no inc.; the *De Antichristo* could be no. 7 or 8. Bale was often very casual in his citation.

Section C

Materia ad hominem
Correspondence and *Responsiones*

The disparate pieces in this section, which span the last twelve or thirteen years of Wyclyf's life, fall naturally into three subgroups. The first, **378-384**, precede and encompass the specifically *ad hominem* debates *in scholis*, commencing with Kenningham in about 1372 and focusing increasingly on the dominion issue. (In this connection we should also mention at a minimum **23-25** and **28-30** above, as well as **399, 400, 405, 408** and **409** below.)

The second grouping, **385-388**, illuminates the most sustained intellectual discourse of Wyclyf's career, that with the logician and lawyer Ralph Strode, who may well have been Wyclyf's closest friend (at least before his association with Hereford and Purvey, who were in any case junior men). Wyclyf seems never to have broken off relations with Strode despite the cataclysms of his waning years. Evidently Strode was a man of no small forbearance and a generous humor.

Our third and last cluster is **389-396**, a miscellaneous assemblage of *ad hoc* perceptions of current concerns.

The sequence here represents a considerable revamping of Sh and Lo, in keeping with both topical and chronological imperatives. Indeed this will hold true on to the end of this *Catalog*.

378, 379, 380. Cl.a, [b], c. *Determinacio*[*nes*] *contra Kylyngham Carmelitam*. 1372.

    I. Inc. Determinacio [prima]: Tres sunt nidi in quibus ego cum aliis pullis Christi adhuc volare nescientibus nutrior ...

    Expl. Determinacio [prima]: × ... igitur omne tale est sibi presens et per consequens est.

    [Determinacio secunda: not yet found]

    Inc. Determinacio [tercia]: Tercium nidum supremum non querit doctor disrumpere ...

    Expl. Determinacio [tercia]: × ... quod multi non imperatores Romani dotant ecclesiam. Hoc tamen ...[1]

II. MS:

i	Cambridge, Corpus Christi Coll.	103	pp. 419a-428b	xv/1	Asc. Eng.[2]

III. Ed. W. W. Shirley, *FZ* (RS, 1958): 453-476, 477-480. From unique MS.

IV. Our principal effort here must be to arrive at the context of these two extant *determinaciones* against Wyclyf's first known opponent in debate, John Kenningham, O. Carm.[3] Precisely because a reconstructive attempt of this nature has not previously been ventured, we shall at this time offer a tentative schematization of these exchanges:

(1) An initial *determinacio*, or *quodlibet*, or something perhaps less formal, by Wyclyf *in scholis*: no longer extant in any form.

(2) The opening *responsio* by Kenningham, apparently now lost but unambiguously signified in the first sentence of his subsequent *Ingressus* (in *FZ*, p. 4: "... et recitata in ultima determinacione mea contra reverendum Magistrum meum Wycclyff").

(3) A probable, though nowhere explicitly confirmed, rejoinder by Wyclyf to Kenningham's first critique; I suspect this may have come in the form of extemporaneous remarks *in scholis*. In this rejoinder he may well have made use of Lm 5:7 – this verse was already a bone of contention in the *Ingressus* (p. 8), and was again in our piece (p. 469), and would be yet once more in the first *Actum* (p. 29).

(4) Kenningham's *Ingressus* is the first extant document of this protracted exchange: it is published in *FZ*, pp. 4-13, from a single defective MS.[4] Here he seizes the opportunity to elaborate on certain points he had originally wished to develop elsewhere, "sed temporis brevitas non permisit" (p. 4). Evidently the debate was accelerating.

(5) Our present piece, originally three separate but closely connected *determinaciones*. (The second, touching the second "nidus" – i.e., "naturalis", between the "logicus" and "metaphysicus"; given above as *379* – is wanting, while the third is probably less than half complete as it has come down to us.[5]) In his first "nidus" he is chiefly concerned with rebutting thirteen specific *argumenta* (perhaps in the missing portion of the *Ingressus*?) by Kenningham; in the third he deals with another five.

(6) Evidently in his three subsequent *Acta* (*FZ*, pp. 14-42, 43-72, 73-103), Kenningham was content to let his earlier logical *argumenta* stand without reprise; he concentrated instead on the metaphysical dimension stressed by Wyclyf in the third *determinacio*.[6] (Some short span of time, with a concomitant opportunity for Wyclyf to interject addenda, may have intervened between *Acta* I and II, or between II and III – especially since by II Wyclyf is a *doctor*, but in I still only a *magister*.[7]) One is tempted to apply Ockham's razor to the whole tangled web.[8]

From this point onward, the debate became more political in substance, involving other participants such as William Binham and Uthred of Boldon (see the next two items).

The date of composition of Wyclyf's three *determinaciones* fell perforce sometime in 1372: he refers to his own *De ydeis* (**18**) as completed and to the *De materia et forma* (**20**) as in train (p. 464); the systematic treatment of dominion is yet in the future (p. 456). So the *Determinaciones* rightly emerge as our first hint of Wyclyf's conduct in the heated atmosphere of scholastic parry and riposte. Kenningham would appear to have been a most mettlesome opponent, though his deference to the man who was probably his mentor ("magister meus," so frequently apostrophized, seems a token of acknowledged academic subordination) is quite marked in both the *Ingressus* and the *Acta*.

VC: deest   Bale: 212   Sh: 53   Lo: 54

¹ There seems to be no space allowed for the second *determinacio* in our unique MS, though the sense demands it.
² Lo has 303, an obvious error. Pp. 419a-427b the first *determinacio*; p. 428a-b the third.
³ On him see above, 12, n. 9.
⁴ See notes on *lacunae*, pp. 8 and 13.
⁵ There are extensive paraphrases and even direct quotations in Kenningham's *Acta*: e.g., pp. 52, 88, 99-102; from these a partial reconstruction might be essayed.
⁶ His whimsical reference to "Herodis" (p. 14: it is so emended by Shirley, who, however, acknowledges the clear text reading of "herodii") prompted an article by Bernard L. Manning, "Wyclif and the House of Herod," *Cambridge Historical Journal* 2 (1926): 66-67, which showed that the reference is clearly to Ps 103:17. The only conceivable justification for applying the passage to John of Gaunt (whose confessor Kenningham later became) would seem to be the humorous *Wortspiel* immediately preceding: "Verumtamen ut mihi videtur magister meus nidificavit in excelsis ...."
⁷ Workman, *JW* I: 121n., errs in discerning the dividing line between II and III. But Kenningham was also *doctor* by this time.
⁸ The time-smoothed phrase has blurred the fact that Ockham, if he ever in fact employed it himself in any meaningful way, owed it to others: see now Roger Ariew, "Did Ockham Use His Razor?" *Franciscan Studies* 37 (1977): 5-17.

381. C2. *Determinacio ad argumenta magistri Outredi.*¹ 1377 or 1378.

I. Inc.: Doctor meus reverendus et magister specialis dominus Outredus inter alias pulcras veritates [12 wds.] tres conclusiones catholicas tangentes materiam quam ostendi alia inculcavit ...

Expl.: × ... dixerim doctori meo reverendo ad conclusiones et subtilia argumenta.

II. MS:

| i | Paris, BN | f.l. 3184 | ff. 46v-48r | 1396 |

Asc. No. Fr.²

III. Ed. J. Loserth, "Die ältesten Streitschriften Wiclifs. Studien über die Anfänge der kirchenpolitischen Tätigkeit Wiclifs und die Überlieferung seiner Schriften," *Sitzungsberichte der Kaiserlichen Akademie der Wissenschaften in Wien. Philosophisch-Historische Klasse* 160/2 (1908): 37-47; idem, *Johannis Wyclif Opera Minora* (WS, 1913): 405-414. From unique MS.

IV. Uthred of Boldon has already occupied us.³ This formidable Benedictine was probably, according to our incipit, one of Wyclyf's masters at Oxford. His clash with Archbishop Langham over the poverty issue had culminated in his retreat from the Oxford scene in 1368; in 1373, however, he was among the papal delegates sent to Avignon to represent the English position on subsidies and provisions. In May of 1374 he delivered a redoubtable speech at London, in which he pleaded the papal side to a gathering of mixed notables. From Wyclyf's clear allusions (two on the opening page: "quam intendi alias" and "ut alias intendi"; cf. p. 410, l. 34: "specificavi ...," and p. 414, ll. 35-36: "dixi alias diffuse") it is obvious that he had already addressed the question of dominion in some other forum: Loserth has traced only one of these references, to the *De civili dominio* III (**30**: p. 375; reference on p. 405 of the present work), but he has also found a number of other parallel passages in all three *libri* of that monumental treatise; we should add here only *De civili dominio* I: 265-266, which corresponds in emphasis to p. 406, ll. 13-18 of our piece. As to the source of the three *conclusiones* by Uthred, cited at the outset of this *Determinacio*, the first comes from his *De naturali et necessaria connexione ac ordine sacerdotalis officii et regalis*;[4] the second is perhaps a paraphrase from a later passage in the same work;[5] and it has been suggested that the third was drawn from his *De non auferendis ecclesie bonis*.[6] C. H. Thompson believed these tracts were composed around 1367 or 1368, at the height of Uthred's struggle with the mendicants,[7] and so inferred from this that Wyclyf's reply must date from the same period – a startling revision of the accepted range between 1374 and 1377, if it should be sustained. But the internal evidence, cited above, belies this judgment. It is enough to mention Uthred's reemergence into public view at Avignon and London as an adequate stimulus for Wyclyf's recalling the monk's earlier polemical utterances – of course we may safely presume he had known of them at the earlier date. *Dominium* remained a warm issue for many years at Oxford – both Wyclyf and Uthred saw to that. (We shall defer the arguments for a more precise fix on 1377 or 1378 to the next item.)

One wishes for another MS as a control; doubtless some *renvois* would fall into place. Bur ours is early, ascribed and reasonably legible.

VC: 3933 3935 4514 7980[8]   Bale: 217[9]   Sh: 54   Lo: 55

[1] The MS actually says "Outredi de Omesima" (quite clearly, *pace* the *Bibliothèque Nationale. Catalogue général des Manuscrits latins* IV: (*nos. 3017 à 3277*) [Paris, 1958]: 328, which reads "Omefina"; Workman, *JW* I: 223n., says this was a Czech misreading of "Oxoniensis" or some such – but the scribe was French. Perhaps a guess at "Dunelmensis"?).

[2] One of Uthred's own writings, the *Contra fratrum mendicitatem*, appears in BN, f.l. 1383, ff. 160v-168v.

[3] **23-25**, n. 18, above.

[4] C. H. Thompson, *Uthred of Boldon*, p. 55.

[5] Ibid., p. 64n.

[6] Ibid., p. 28. It is not now extant under this title, but is perhaps identical with Uthred's *Contra garrulos dotacionem ecclesie impugnantes*: cf. Pantin, "Two Treatises," p. 365.

[7] It is not unlikely that despite their falling-out Wyclyf would have availed himself of arguments from these early writings (in conjunction with the more massive efforts of FitzRalph: above, **23-25**, n. 12) in his later broadsides against the friars. Again we witness the price he paid for his short temper: Uthred would have been a doughty ally in the trenches. – In this connection we should cite Otto Hüttebräuker, *Der Minoritenorden zur Zeit des grossen Schismas* (Berlin, 1893: a slight effort); and Carolly Erickson, "The Fourteenth-Century Franciscans and their Critics," *Franciscan Studies* 35 (1975): 107-135; 36 (1976): 108-147.

[8] None mention Uthred.
[9] Tit.: *Contra monachum Dunelmensem*; no inc.

382, 383. C3.a, b. *Ad argumenta Wilelmi Vyrinham determinacio*[*nes*]. 1378.

I. Inc. Determinacio [prima]: Secundus doctor meus reverendus Wilelmus Wiham arguit contra eandem conclusionem ...

Expl. Determinacio [prima]: × ... Et ista sentencia patet per Hugonem De sacramentis libro secundo parte secunda capitulo septimo. Vide originale.

Inc. Determinacio [secunda]: Inter alia doctor meus reverendus intromittit se de iure ...

Expl.: × ... quod hec condicio fuerit racionabilis et honesta.

II. MSS:[1]

i	Firenze, BLaur	Plut.XIX.33	ff. 22r-23v	1408	JW MS Eng.[2]
ii	London, Lambeth Pal.	537	pp. 1-24	1609	Asc. Eng.[3]
iii	Oxford, Bodleian	703 (S.C.2766)	ff. 66va-68vb	xiv/ex	Asc. Eng.[4]
iv	Arch. Selden	B.26 (S.C.3340)	ff. 88ra-90ra	xv/1	Asc. Eng.[5]
v	Paris, BN	f.l. 3184	ff. 49r-52v	1396	Asc. No. Fr.[6]

III. Ed. J. Lewis, *The History of the Life and Sufferings of the Reverend and Learned John Wicliffe, D.D. ...*, 1st ed. (London, 1720): 363-371;[7] idem, revised ed. (London, 1820): 349-356[8] (both from **iv** only); J. Loserth, "Die ältesten Streitschriften Wiclifs. Studien über die Anfänge der kirchenpolitischen Tätigkeit Wiclifs und die Überlieferung seiner Schriften," *Sitzungsberichte der Kaiserlichen Akademie der Wissenschaften in Wien. Philosophisch-Historische Klasse* 160/2 (1908): 47-62; idem, *Johannis Wyclif Opera Minora* (WS, 1913): 415-430.[9] From **v** only.

IV. This piece (edited by Loserth in the *Opera Minora* and his "Streitschriften" alike as one item, though its MS tradition is quite otherwise), is a manifest extension of Wyclyf's more courteous and deferential debate with Uthred of Boldon, and therefore immediately follows it here. In it (p. 415) he also says "declaravi proximo anno[10] respondendo ad argumenta doctoris mei reverendi fratris Wilelmi Weldeforde ..." – meaning Woodford of course; Loserth's *renvoi* at this point to the *De civili dominio*[11] is well taken. This would target 1378 for the present piece; so by implication the prior response to Uthred must have fallen within the months or even weeks leading up to the exchange with Binham.[12] But we ought perhaps to allow for some scribal interpolation at the outset of this riposte to Binham, or even for Wyclyf's own realization in a subsequent redaction that the subject matter of the two *determinaciones* was such as to facilitate a rhetorical bridge between them.

Two areas are of particular interest in the contents: Wyclyf's oblique concern with the theoretical property rights (papally vested) of the Franciscans[13] and the imputed speeches of seven lords given "in quodam concilio" (pp. 425-429). The former may well represent Wyclyf's earliest specific observations on the subject, and contain therefore the germ of much future disturbance; while as to the latter we may second Workman[14] in assuming that it was merely an artful dialectical device. And we shall here further dissipate his doubts[15] as to the "ambiguous" clause "quam [i.e., solucionem] audivi in quodam concilio a dominis secularibus *esse datam*" (emphasis added): the whole scenario is suspect and rather uncharacteristic of Wyclyf, though not inconsonant with his transparent attempt at mouthpiecing in the *Dyalogus* (**408**) a year or so later. Granted there may indeed have been a conference of sorts in the standing council under Gaunt's direction, but Wyclyf was surely not privy to it, and his imagination, normally fully engaged in the realms of metaphysics and theology, evidently extended here to the enticements of regency intrigue.[16]

vc: 3933 3935 4514 7980[17]   Bale: 213   Sh: 55, 56   Lo: 56, 57

[1] Bateson, *Catalogue of the Library of Syon Monastery*, no. N 28 (ff. 116-117 ?): "inieccio eiusdem [i.e., Wyclyf] contra quemdam doctorem de non soluendo tributum romano pontifici." Undoubtedly this signifies the second *determinacio*.

[2] Second *determinacio* only. Noticed in Stein, "The Wyclif Manuscript in Florence," 95.

[3] In the hand of Thomas James, the Bodleian librarian; his preface speculates that John Tissington or Woodford was Wyclyf's foil. It takes up the whole ms, but contains only the second *determinacio*, which does not in fact mention Binham by name. (Another transcription, by Richard James, is in Oxford, Bodleian James 3, pp. 262-268.)

[4] Second *determinacio* only.

[5] Ibid., the basis for Lewis' ed. Cf. n. 7, below.

[6] Cf. **381**, above, and n. 9, below.

[7] Edits the second *determinacio* only. It is odd that Loserth himself did not use this ms in either of his editions, preferring instead to harp on Lewis' poor transcription; cf. introduction to the *Opera Minora*, pp. L-LII.

[8] Ibid.

[9] The text of v probably caused him to overlook the break between the two *determinaciones*. Actually only v has the first *determinacio* at all.

[10] By which he almost always meant "preceding": cf. above, **4**.

[11] III (ed. Loserth): 351 etc. Cf., for Woodford, **17**, n. 9, etc., above.

[12] On Binham, see **23-25**, n. 18, above.

[13] Pp. 416-417. – It is difficult to say whether Wyclyf's growing preoccupation with this issue grew out of his general hostility to endowment or from a more specific awareness that in its beginnings the Franciscan order had adhered to very strict standards in regard to the holding of property. (Certainly Wyclyf was aware of this; whether the English piece "The Rule and Testament of St. Francis" [in F. D. Matthew, ed., *The English Works of Wyclif Hitherto Unprinted*, 40-51] was by him is moot. Cf. Severs, *A Manual of the Writings in Middle English*... II: 372, 530.) Pope John XXII had practically laid the matter to rest in the sweeping bull *Cum inter nonnullos* of 12 November 1323, but tensions continued within the order nonetheless, and of them Wyclyf was surely aware. FitzRalph's animadversions were well known to him: cf. above, **23-25**, n. 12. Basic to any effort at understanding the problem is Lambert, *Franciscan Poverty* and useful also are Burkhard von Wolfenschiessen, "Das franziskanische Privilegienrecht," *Collectanea Franciscana* 4 (1934): 337-362; A. van Hove, *De Privilegiis. De Dispensationibus* (Commentarium Lovaniense I/5: Malines, 1939); Burkhard Mathis, *Die Privilegien des Franziskanerordens bis zum Konzil von Vienne (1311), im Zusammenhang mit dem*

Privilegienrecht der früheren Orden dargestellt (Paderborn, 1927). Arnold Williams, "Relations between the Mendicant Friars and the Secular Clergy in England in the Later Fourteenth Century," *Annuale Mediaevale* 1 (1960): 22-95, remains of the greatest importance. See also **34**, n. 9, and **381**, n. 12, above.

[14] *JW* II: 233-237.

[15] Ibid., p. 233, n. 3.

[16] The circumstances of these *determinaciones* are further scrutinized in Loserth, "The Beginnings of Wyclif's Activity in Ecclesiastical Politics," *EHR* 11œ – !i: 319-328; and in his introduction to the *Opera Minora*, LII-LVI.

[17] The first three give separate (and varying) titles and incipits for the two *determinaciones*; 7980, because incomplete, gives the first one only, after 4514.

384. C4. *Responsiones ad xliv conclusiones* [*Responsio ad argucias monachales*]. Late 1383.

I. Inc.: Quidam doctor utinam veritatis nititur impugnare sentenciam ...

Expl.: × ... ut dei gracia subtrahetur et patris mendacii nequicia dominetur.

II. MSS:

i	Wien, ÖNB	1338	ff. 123va-141rb	ca. 1400	JW MS Boh.
ii		1622	ff. 157v-179v	1410	JW MS Boh.
iii		3927	ff. 11va-24rb	ca. 1410	JW MS Boh.
iv		4527	ff. 46v-65v	1410	JW MS Boh.

III. Ed. J. Loserth, *Johannis Wyclif Opera Minora* (WS, 1913): 201-257†. From all MSS.

IV. Considering both the splenetic temper and the wide range of this broadside against the Cistercian doctor and former Oxford Chancellor (1372-1373), William de Rymyngton,[1] it is surprising that the Oxford Commission in 1411 chose to single out for opprobrium only eleven of the statements herein contained.[2]

That no love was lost between Wyclyf and Rymyngton is obvious from numerous slighting asides, and even from an atypical snatch of personal raillery: "Vellem autem quod doctor poneret in suo lato liripipio ius civile, quia certum est mihi quod nec ipsum nec ius canonicum valet homini nisi in iure domini fuerit fundatum."[3] The epithet "merdosus," attached to anything from Rymyngton's sophistical reasoning to the "four sects,"[4] crops up at least four times;[5] and his pet phrase "versucie Antichristi," six.[6] Explanation if not excuse for this floodtide of venom lies in the evident aim of Rymyngton's *conclusiones* themselves: to discredit the Poor Priests (styled throughout Wyclyf's text "sacerdotes simplices" – or, more cryptically, the "secta Christi"). He was defending not merely his own beliefs or interpretations of Catholic doctrine this time, but that considerable number of sympathizers, chiefly *extra scholas*, who for many reasons had come to see in him a champion.

The references to the Flanders crusade *in progress*[7] warrant a relatively precise date: the fall of 1383. There are discernible similarities of sentiment (though the personal hostility here unbalances their expression) with **388**, below. Wyclyf, from afar, is still settling an old score – though it is impossible to date Rymyngton's *conclusiones* themselves with any assurance; and the mechanism of transmission from Oxford to Lutterworth we can only guess at.

vc: 3933 3935 4514   Bale: 211 ?[8]   Sh: 59   Lo: 60

[1] Cf. Workman, *JW* II: 122-123; *BRUO* III: 1617. None of our MSS states outright that Rymyngton was the target of this attack, but both the Oxford censure of 1411 ("... ad argumenta monachi de Sally") and the allusion *in textu* (p. 222, line 34) to Henry Crumpe, O.Cist. (cf. Workman, *JW* II: 124; and **28-30**, n. 26, above) as "suo socio" render the identification virtually certain.

[2] Wilkins, *Concilia*... III: 348-349 (nos. 239-249).

[3] P. 240. This is incidentally Wyclyf's most succinct and acerbic condemnation of human laws: cf. above, **28-30**, n. 28. But because Rymyngton's own text, as here transcribed, relies heavily on canonical citations, Wyclyf himself makes greater use of it here than in any other of his post-Oxford writings.

[4] Cf. above, **46**, n. 2; **50**, n. 6; Section F, below.

[5] Pp. 214, 217, 219, 248.

[6] Pp. 202, 205, 223, 246 (twice), 247. Cf. **374-377**, above, and **420**, below.

[7] The implication is quite clear on p. 206, and stated outright on 230 and 246.

[8] Tit. *Responsiones argumentorum*; no inc.

385. C5.a. *Responsio ad decem questiones* [*magistri Strode*].[1] Mid-1378.

I. Inc.: Magister reverende et amice precarissime. Ad primam decem questionum [13 wds.] dixi, quod triplex est proprietas ...

Expl.: × ... quem rogo ut ipsam construat illuminet et conservet.

II. MSS:

i	Praha, UK	III.G.16 (541)	ff. 86r-87v	1414	JW MS Boh.
ii		V.G.19 (971)[2]	ff. 256v-258v	ca. 1420	Unasc. Boh.
iii	Wien, ÖNB	3929[3]	ff. 274va-275ra	1409	JW MS Boh.

III. Ed. J. Loserth, *Johannis Wyclif Opera Minora* (WS, 1913); 398-404†.[4] From all MSS.

IV. The format of this piece is indisputably epistolary, though this fact has been surprisingly ignored by Shirley and Loserth (both in his revision of Sh and in his preface to the edition, p. XLVII); we offer it here as the first of four exchanges from Wyclyf's side – none from Strode seem to have survived.

Ralph Strode had earned his spurs as a logician at Oxford, and became thereafter a prominent lawyer in the service of the City of London. For a dozen years before his death in 1387, he was also a friend of Chaucer's.[5] He was also a close contemporary of Wyclyf's, and in this and the other works addressed by Wyclyf to him their enduring mutual high regard is often apparent. This earliest *responsio* in the series – which, however, presupposes years of acquaintanceship – bears chiefly on the dominion issue, and by extension on papal prerogative and penance. Twice he abbreviates his reply by remarking simply "in ista materia sum diffusus nunc in scolis" [6] – an unmistakable *renvoi* not only to the *De civili dominio* (**28-30**) but equally also to the exchanges with Kenningham (**378-380**), Woodford (in the *De civili dominio*),[7] Uthred of Boldon (**381**) and William Binham (**382-383**), and of course to the nineteen propositions drawn from the *De civili dominio* I-II by Gregory XI.[8] Although his formulations here remain well within the permissible bounds of orthodox speculation, the date portends a rapid radicalization, and the seeds of his later and far less compromising views are broadcast in his terse exclamation (p. 401): "Legibus autem quibusdam humanis contigit meritorie rebellare. Unde ad detrimentum fidei et ista infidelitas que surrepsit ad defendendum monstruosum cleri dominium...."

VC: deest[9]   Bale: deest   Sh: 60   Lo: 61

[1] ii reads "magistri Ricardi Strade."

[2] Lo has 941 in error; in his ed, p. XLVII, he gives V.G.9, a Hus MS.

[3] Given as 3926 in the article on Strode in the *Encyclopaedia Britannica*, 11th ed., XXV (1910-1911): 1040.

[4] Lo says this is "unprinted"!

[5] Cf. *BRUO* III: 1807-1808 (the best compact summary); C. Prantl, *Geschichte der Logik im Abendlande* IV (Leipzig, 1867; reprinted Graz, 1955): 45-56; Workman, *JW* II: 125-129; 412-414; Sarton, *Introduction to the History of Science* III/2: 1412-1413; E. A. Moody, *Truth and Consequence in Mediaeval Logic* (Amsterdam, 1953): 85, 87-89, 91; Spade, *The Medieval Liar*, 87-91. Strode's friendship with Chaucer is attested by the latter's dedication of *Troilus and Criseyde* to him (and John Gower): Bk. V: 266 ("... and to the philosophical Strode"); it is emblematic of the pitfalls awaiting the unwary scholar in such regions that even the normally careful G. G. Coulton should have called Strode "a distinguished philosopher and *anti*-Wycliffite controversialist" (*Chaucer and His England*, 8th ed. [London and New York, 1963]; emphasis added). Almost certainly Wyclyf and Strode knew each other at Merton in the early 1360s. On the possibility of his being the elusive *Pearl*-Poet, cf. Marie P. Hamilton, "The *Pearl* Poet," in Severs, ed., *Manual of Writings in Middle English* II: 339-348, 505-506, 509-511. Strode's *Consequencie* and *Obligaciones* much intrigued Renaissance logicians in Italy; on two of these, Paul of Venice and Cajetan of Thiene, cf. Gilson, *History of Christian Philosophy*, 527, 798.

[6] Pp. 400, 401.

[7] III (ed. Loserth): 321.

[8] **28-30**, n. 24, above; and see also **399-401**, below.

[9] It is a bit curious that the VC should have overlooked this piece; but neither that fact nor the lack of specific attribution in the MSS weighs in this instance against Wyclyf's authorship. Tone and internal reference to the *De civili dominio* suffice to confirm it.

386. C5.b. *Responsiones ad* [*xviii*] *argumenta Radulphi Strode.* Early 1379?

I. Inc.: Quia secundum philosophum sanctum est prehonorare veritatem ...
   Expl.: × ... sunt prevaricatores ingratissimi et discrasie tocius ecclesie causativi.

II. MSS:

i	Praha, UK	III.G.11 (536)	ff. 160v-170v	xv/1	JW MS Boh.
ii		V.G.10 (962)	ff. 138r-148v	xv/1	Asc. Boh.[1]

iii	Wien, ÖNB	1338	ff. 116ra-123rb	ca. 1410	Asc. Boh.
iv		3929	ff. 218rb-223rb	1409	JW MS Boh.
v		4527	ff. 67r-75r	1410	Asc. Boh.

III. Ed. J. Loserth, *Johannis Wyclif Opera Minora* (WS, 1913): 175-200†. From all MSS except **ii**.

IV. Although after 1373 – or even before then – Ralph Strode[2] was no longer embroiled in Oxford affairs, it is plain that he still considered himself competent to pronounce upon the worth of Wyclyf's ecclesio-political ruminations. Having earlier animadverted upon the *De civili dominio* (**28-30**; in **385**, just above), he ventured now to target the *De ecclesia* (**32**) in a work which twentieth-century scholarship has conveniently titled *XVIII posiciones contra Wiclevum*.[3] Portions of this critique are quoted *verbatim* in the present *Responsiones*, quasi-epistolary in form. What contribution it may have made to the ongoing hubbub *in scholis* is moot; the Oxford commission in 1411 found nine dubious propositions in it.[4] Evidently Strode had singled out three groups of six propositions each, relating respectively to 1) the position of the *predestinati* within the church; 2) endowment and the proper duties of the clergy; and 3) the necessity for *reformatio* according to evangelical standards, involving a great reliance on the vigorous oversight of the king and the lords – redounding finally to the advantage of the *tenentes pauperes* or *tenentes simplices* (p. 200). There is an edge to Wyclyf's tone, though in a remarkable passage – one which he would not have written to an avowed enemy – he does grant that at times in the schools he has sinned against charity; in his elliptical third-person mode, he "confitetur tamen se multipliciter peccasse presumpcione et arrogancia." (P. 197.)

VC: 3933 3935 4514   Bale: 214?[5]   Sh: 57   Lo: 58

[1] Identified only as "Fragmenta" in Truhlař; tit. *in textu: De predestinacione, presciencia, de dotacione...*; f. 146v is blank, probably indicating a gap.
[2] Cf. **385**, n. 5, above.
[3] Tit. suggested by Workman, *JW* II: 128; no independent copies are known.
[4] Wilkins, *Concilia...* III: 349 (nos. 250-258; reasonably faithful).
[5] Tit.: *Ad 14* [sic] *argumenta Strodae*; no inc.

387. C5.c. *Litera parva ad quendam socium* [*Strode*]. Late 1381?

I. Inc.: Amice carissime. Vobis in nomine dei regracior ...
   Expl.: × ... Vester servus et socius in labore [Io. W.][1] curatus de Lutterworth.

II. MSS:

i	Praha, MK	D.123 (693)	f. 151r	xv/1	JW MS Boh.
ii	UK	X.G.11 (1965)	f. 302r	ca. 1420	Asc. Boh.
iii	Wien, ÖNB	1338	f. 30rb	ca. 1410	JW MS Boh.

iv		1387	f. 107ra	ca. 1410	JW MS Boh.
v		*3929*	f. 208vb	1409	Asc. Boh.²
vi		4527	f. 147r	1410	Asc. Boh.

III. Ed. J. Loserth, *Johannis Wyclif Opera Minora* (WS, 1913): 10-11†. From all MSS except **i** and **v**.

IV. All of our MSS indicate either in the title or in the colophon that this letter was sent in fact to Ralph Strode; yet Loserth expresses doubt in his introduction (p. v): "We must remember that Strode was by no means friendly to Wyclif's teaching." But we possess in fact no real evidence that Wyclyf's continuing relationship with his presumed Merton colleague was ever distinguished by less than the utmost courtesy. The present short letter (nine lines in Loserth's edition) simply urges its recipient to persevere "in causa sua, conformiter legi Christi"; it is perhaps in response to some unfortunate bit of personal news. That Wyclyf signed as rector of Lutterworth does argue for the dispatch of this letter sometime after his retirement to that place, i.e., after the fall of 1381 – but probably not much later than that time. He was no doubt still stung by the twists of fortune which forced him there.

VC: 3933 3935 4514 7980   Bale: deest   Sh: 61.7   Lo: 62.6

[1] Clearly so indicated in **ii**; "Jo." in colophon of **vi**.
[2] Identified as "Epistola missa per Jo. W. ad quendam consortem suum"; expl.: × "... concedat dominus Ihesus Christus." – Without giving reasons, Workman, *JW* II: 308, n. 3, states "this friend cannot be ... Ralph Strode."

388. C5.d. *Responsiones ad argumenta cuiusdam emuli veritatis* [*id est magistri Strode*].[1] Mid-1383 - late 1384?

I. Inc.: Quidam socius quem suppono esse emulum veritatis invehit multipliciter contra sentencias ...
   Expl.: × ... Et hec dicta sufficiant pro presenti.

II. MSS:

i	Cambridge, Trinity Coll.	O.4.43	——²	xiv/2	Unasc. Eng.
ii	Praha, UK	V.F.9 (931)	ff. 18v-39r	1408	JW MS Boh.
iii		X.E.9 (1910)	ff. 156v-174r	xv/1	JW MS Boh.
iv	Vaticano	Borgh.lat. 29	ff. 7r-23v	xv/1	Asc. Fr.³
v	Wien, ÖNB	1338	ff. 100ra-116ra	ca. 1410	JW MS Boh.
vi		*3929*	ff. 192rb-203va	1409	JW MS Boh.
vii		4527	ff. 1r-17r	1410	JW MS Boh.⁴
viii		4536	ff. 193r-216r	xv/1	Asc. Boh.

III. Ed. J. Loserth, *Johannis Wyclif Opera Minora* (WS, 1913): 258-312†. From all MSS except **i** and **iv**.

IV. There is plentiful internal evidence in this lengthy series of *responsiones* to compel the acceptance of Loserth's contention (p. XXXVII) supporting a date much later than 1379 (Shirley's preference): the thematic use of the phrase "four sects"[5] as well as frequent recourse to his latter-day image of the ideal pope as humble, poor and obedient[6] – if we must have a pope at all! – go far beyond the cautionary wording of the *De ecclesia* (**32**) or even the *De potestate pape* (**34**). The unmistakable reference to the *early stages* of the Flanders crusade on p. 304 directs us to the spring or early summer of 1383 as the date of composition for the major part of the work; but the *renvoi* to his own *De Antichristo*[7] directs us to mid- or late 1384 as the proper frame for capp. XVI and XVII, pp. 307-312.[8] Nevertheless, the occasional piece by Strode[9] – itself no longer extant beyond the substantial extracts here – to which this is responsive cannot possibly allude to any part of Wyclyf's writings subsequent to the *De eucharistia* (**38**), and may in fact not have touched on any specific works at all, as at three vital junctures Wyclyf identifies the source of Strode's anxiety as "sentencia[m] quam *concipit me dixisse*" – hearsay plain and simple.[10] But at no point does Wyclyf deny having made any of those inflammatory declarations about the Papacy, the church or the Eucharist; indeed in these *responsiones* he carries them to further extremes. Quite understandably he must have wanted his old friend to hear at first hand just where his priorities lay in his last months. How Strode reacted to such a grim perspective we may only surmise.

We do glimpse for just an instant Wyclyf's wistful vision of a harmonious Christian society: "... nunquam habundabit concordia in contrata nostra occidua, antequam discordia inter papas reducto populo ad legem domini funditus sit destructa; et sic foret unio tam inter clericos, quam inter laycos, et altrinsecus in se ipsos, quia clerici sequentes unanimiter Christum in humilitate, et pauperie non spoliarent laycos sicut modo, sed darent sollicitudinem ad humiliter predicandum legem domini in pace atque concordia, gloriam vel lucrum proprium non querentes..." (p. 290).

vc: 3933 3935 4514[11]   Bale: 211 ?[12]   Sh: 58   Lo: 59

[1] The portion in brackets has been rubbed out in **v**, but is not difficult to make out. Loserth seems to have overlooked it.

[2] Front and back pastedowns; recto and verso of front flyleaf. I wish to thank Dr. Frank Mantello of the Catholic University of America for kindly calling his discovery of this item to my attention. For a description of the whole MS, see James, *The Western Manuscripts in the Library of Trinity College, Cambridge* III: *Containing an Account of the Manuscripts standing in Class O* (1902): 291; but also see now Mantello's concise note, "The Endleaves of Trinity College Cambridge MS 0.4.43 and John Wyclif's *Responsiones ad argumenta cuiusdam emuli veritatis*," *Speculum* 54 (1979): 100-103, with commentary on missing portions of the text. A new edition, incorporating the *varia* of this and the Vatican MS, would not be amiss.

[3] Previously at ff. 49r-59v and 67r-72v, as in Stein, "The Vatican Manuscript...," 97. S. H. Thomson believed at one time that the hand was German; but there is no convincing paleographical

ground for rejecting the French hand here indicated. Cf. Anneliese Maier, *Codices Burghesiani Bibliothecae Vaticanae* (Città del Vaticano, 1952).

[4] Annotated by Peter Payne.
[5] Cf. above, **50**, n. 6, and often elsewhere. Here on pp. 280, 281, 282, 288, 293, and 295.
[6] Pp. 266, 270-271, 289, 290, 304; cf. also **384**, pp. 204 and 208.
[7] I.e., 376, 377: specifically p. 165, as noted by Loserth. There is no parallel passage in his contemporaneous *De Christo et suo adversario Antichristo* (**413**, below).
[8] See above, **44**, n. 3.
[9] There is no compelling reason to question the unique ascription: above, n. 1.
[10] Pp. 258, 290 and 307; emphasis added.
[11] All assign this work 18 capp. but expl. precedes ours by one sentence.
[12] Cf. **384**, n. 8, above.

389. C6. *Exhortacio cuiusdam doctoris.*[1] 1378?

I. Inc.: < Labora sicut bonus miles Christi ... >[2] Post fructum benedicionis sequi debet thema laudacionis ...

Expl.: × ... cuius risus participium nobis concedat dominus veritatis.

II. MSS:

i	Praha, UK	III.G.11 (536)	ff. 53v-55v	xv/1	JW MS Boh.
ii	Wien, ÖNB	1337	ff. 71va-72vb	ca. 1410	JW MS Boh.
iii		3929	ff. 206va-207va	1409	JW MS Boh.
iv		3933	f. 87ra-vb	ca. 1415	JW MS Boh.

III. Ed. J. Loserth, *Johannis Wyclif Opera Minora* (WS, 1913): 413-435†. From all MSS.

IV. Loserth called this short piece a sermon; Shirley confined himself to the designation of *exhortacio*, as in the MSS. It is not a sermon, but rather a short disquisition on the meaning of the text in 2 Tm 2:3, clearly addressed to a younger man (perhaps a favorite student?): the second person singular is not to be found in his other letters – not even to Strode – but it crops up several times in the last two pages of our edition. The structure of the first sentence itself implies either a previous correspondence (or conversation), or the loss of the first part of the letter itself, which would have dissected the meaning of the term "benediccio" in similarly literal language. The style of the piece is not unlike that of Wyclyf's *[Postilla super] secunda[m] epistola[m] ad Thymotheum* (**359**), but as to the specific passage from 2 Tm, there is no parallelism of treatment at all. His concern here is rather to encourage his protégé to uphold truth and rejoice in it. In fact the *Exhortacio* had been originally directed to a newly incepting doctor (unnamed: "Unde consului dominum inceptorem et alios...": p. 433), and this letter seems to be a résumé of his advice on that occasion. It is not strident in temper and would seem best to fit the period around 1378 when Wyclyf was deeply involved in writing the *De veritate sacre scripture* (**31**).

VC: 3933 3935 4514 7980   Bale: deest   Sh: 38   Lo: 38[3]

¹ The title given in all four vc and in **iv**; *Exhortacio doctoris cuiusdam* in **ii**; *Novi exhortacio doctoris* in **iii**; untit. in **i**.
² We enclose the Scriptural citation which is the incipit after the fashion of the texts in the *Postilla super totam Bibliam* (B4); it is conceivable that a text beginning "Post fructum..." may surface.
³ In his ed. of the *Sermones* IV, p. xi, he stated that this piece was "not by Wyclif;" but he came around to the opposite view in his introduction to this piece, p. lvii. Though none of the mss happens to be asc., they are all in JW mss, and it is asc. in all four of the vc.

390. C7. *De octo questionibus pulchris*. Early 1382?

I. Inc.: Amice preclare ex scripturis vestris concipio quod queritis pulcre et compendiose multas difficilis questiones ...

Expl.: × ... multum dampnum ecclesie insensibiliter introducunt.

II. MSS:

i	Praha, MK	*D.123 (693)*	——¹	xv/1	JW ms Boh.
ii	Wien, ÖNB	1337	ff. 114ra-115rb	ca. 1410	JW ms Boh.
iii		1387	f. 106rb-vb	ca. 1410	JW ms Boh.
iv		3929	ff. 266rb-267ra	1409	JW ms Boh.
v		*4937*	ff. 26v-28r	ca. 1420	Asc. Boh.²

III. Ed. J. Loserth, *Johannis Wyclif Opera Minora* (WS, 1913): 12-15. From **ii, iii** and **iv** only.

IV. The anonymous recipient of this letter had asked eight questions concerning the propriety and extent of tithes; these queries Wyclyf quoted or paraphrased in his replies.³ His response to the second question, regarding tithes given to soldiers, is such as to hint that the piece must precede the crusade of 1383. His concern with the poor in dealing with the third, seventh and eighth questions points to an active involvement in parish duties at Lutterworth – probably late in 1381 or in 1382 prior to his first stroke. Who the "eminent friend" may have been we can only surmise; conceivably it was Strode (cf. **385-388**, above).

vc: 3933 3935 4514 7980⁴   Bale: deest   Sh: 61.8   Lo: 62.8

¹ Not in Podlaha; identified in ms by Thomson, "Unnoticed mss and Works of Wyclif," 36. Due to the fact that this collection is now combined with classified modern documents at the Chancery, access to it is quite difficult; nor did the editor receive any response to a request for microfilm. But this particular codex contains many JW pieces; the brevity of **390** renders its unremarkable appearance therein quite conceivable.

² Tit. *in textu* as in the first three vc.

³ This would appear to be the only one of Wyclyf's writings devoted exclusively to the topic, though of course it impinges directly on both endowment and alms, which often absorbed his critical faculties. For remarks elsewhere on the subject, cf. *Dyalogus* (**408**: pp. 2, 6, 76, 97); *Sermones* (**229**: pp. 471-473; **247**: p. 105); *Trialogus* (**47**: pp. 298, 417-418); *Responsiones ad xliv conclusiones* (**384**: pp. 244, 245); *Responsiones ad argumenta cuiusdam emuli veritatis* (**388**: pp. 260, 261); *De paupertate Christi* (**400**: pp. 60, 64).

⁴ First three tit.: *De octo questionibus propositis discipulo*; 7980 tit.: *De octo questionibus propositis populo* [sic].

391. C8. [*Epistola ad quendam socium de sensu mistico Matt. 21º*]. 1378 or 1379.

I. Inc.: Unus amicus fidelis in domino quesivit sensum misticum huius evangelii ...

Expl.: × ... vel ut fingatur quod lex domini compleatur.

II. MS:

i	Manchester, John Rylands Lib.	Eng. 86	f. 117r	ca. 1400	JW MS Eng.

III. Ed. W. R. Thomson, "John Rylands Library MS Eng. 86: An Unnoticed Piece by John Wyclyf," *MedSt* 43 (1981): 531-536. From unique MS.

IV. This letter, from a codex known to contain exclusively Wyclyfiana since 1880, has only very recently seen the light of day. Its recipient is unknown; the use of the "four sects" and other peculiarly Wyclyfian turns of phrase, beside the verbatim recurrence of several portions in another indubitably authentic piece, vouchsafes its place in the canon. The editor's article and edition offer further surmises and particulars.

VC: deest   Bale: deest   Sh: deest   Lo: deest

392. C9. *De fratribus ad scholares*. Mid-1382.

I. Inc.: Subito aurugine prima a parte sinistra venit quidam turbo ...

Expl.: × ... et ne honoris me causa scripsisse videar, valeatis.

II. MSS:

i	Praha, MK	B.48.2 (352)	ff. 137v-138v	ca. 1415	Unasc. Boh.[1]
ii	UK	III.G.11 (536)	ff. 60r-61v	xv/1	JW MS Boh.[2]
iii		*V.E.3 (895)*	ff. 166r-167v	ca. 1400	Unasc. Boh.[3]
iv		X.D.10 (1889)	ff. 106v-107r	ca. 1415	Asc. Boh.[4]

III. Ed. J. Loserth, *Johannis Wyclif Opera Minora* (WS, 1913): 15-18. From **ii** and **iv** only.

IV. To which "scholares" this outpouring may have been directed is not clear; we would however be safe in assuming that it was intended for sympathizers still at Oxford after his retirement late in 1381. His *alma mater* still evoked sufficient nostalgia in him to prompt a rare rhapsody: "Locus amenus fertilis et optimus et habitacioni deorum convenientissimus domus dei et porta celi congrue vocitata..." (p. 18). It is perhaps of all his diatribes against the mendicants the most unbridled: Rv 7:2-3, on the four angels "who had been given power to harm the land and the sea"; Dn 7:3-8 on the four beasts arising from the sea, and Bernard's *De consideratione* IV: cap. ii[5] all provide both imagery and fuel for his verbal incendiarism. Oddly enough he reserves his special wrath for the Carmelites, and after them the Dominicans: the Friars Minor, so often elsewhere heaped with abuse, are here passed over with no more than a contemptuous sniff. But a likely explanation for this unwonted inversion of priorities emerges from the fact that the condemnation of Wyclyf's teachings at Blackfriars in London in May and June of 1382 was chiefly engineered by Peter Stokes[6] and Stephen Patrington,[7] both Oxford Carmelites. In fact the present invective may well be Wyclyf's initial response to the news of the proceedings of that stern assembly.

It should be noted that Buddensieg[8] believed this piece not to be by Wyclyf at all; but certain turns of phrase ("Caym," "pseudoprophete," "validi mendicantes"), as well as the heavy reliance on the *De consideratione*, and the clear ascription in **iv**, all undermine his contention. Certainly our premise that Wyclyf, feeling the chill of outer darkness and bitter from the covert assaults on him at Blackfriars, should have sought at least once to let his beleaguered adherents know where he chose to fix the blame for his and their misfortune, is easily defensible. Yet once again we lack vital specifics.

vc: deest   Bale: deest   Sh: 90[9]   Lo: 62.9, 91[10]

[1] Tit.: *Scripta ad scolares Oxonienses*.

[2] Contrary to Sh's reading, this MS does begin and end as in our inc. and expl.

[3] Tit.: *De fratribus Jacobitarum*; see Thomson, "Unnoticed MSS and Works of Wyclif," 36. (The allusion is to the Dominicans.)

[4] Inc. and expl. as in Sh: 90 (n. 9, below).

[5] Wyclyf cited this reformist piece far more often than any other of Bernard's works: cf. **26** (p. 430); **28** (pp. 260 [?], 390, 393); **29** (p. 212); **30** (pp. 25, 193, 397, 402, 445); **32** (pp. 13, 109, 136, 316, 317, 328, 516); **33** (pp. 36-38, 40, 43, 47, 68, 98, 123, 134, 146); **34** (pp. 86, 87, 92, 136, 138-140, 144, 170, 171, 225, 265, 269, 278, 302, 343, 361, 388); **35** (pp. 63, 64); **47** (p. 300); **384** (pp. 229-232, 236); **398** (pp. 259, 261, 264, 266, 267); **402** (pp. 22-24, 26, 27, 29, 35, 51); **412** (p. 609). The definitive edition is J. Leclercq and H. M. Rochais, edd., *S. Bernardi Opera* III: *Tractatus et Opuscula* (Roma, 1963): 369-493; the fifteen MSS of this popular work presently in English libraries are listed on pp. 382-384. Further analysis in Ignatius Geraedts, "Gedachten rond 'De Consideratione'," in *Sint Bernardus van Clairvaux Gedenkboek ... bij het achtste eeuwfeest van Sint Bernardus' Dood* (Rotterdam, 1953): 141-151; Elizabeth T. Kennan, "Antithesis and Argument in the *De Consideratione*," in *Bernard of Clairvaux. Studies presented to Dom Jean Leclercq* (Cistercian Studies Series 23: Washington, 1973): 91-109; and her earlier, well-documented "The *De Consideratione* of St. Bernard of Clairvaux and the Papacy in the mid-Twelfth Century: A Review of Scholarship," *Traditio* 23 (1967): 73-115.

[6] Cf. **205**, n. 3, above.

[7] Cf. ibid., n. 4, above.

[8] *John Wiclif's Polemical Works in Latin* II: 486-487.

[9] Inc.: "Nimis olens nomen Caym ..."; expl.: × "... vix medietatem facinorum." Our inc. immediately precedes his, and our expl. comes just after his.

[10] No. 91 corresponds to Sh: 90 (see the preceding note); he says there "Not yet printed." Such lapses not infrequently vitiated this catalogue.

393. C10. *De amore [Ad quinque questiones]*. 1383 or 1384?

I. Inc.: Quidam fidelis in domino querit caritative ut estimo quintuplicem questionem ...

Expl.: × ... in hoc statu miserie dirrumpamus.[1]

II. MSS:

i	Praha, MK	D.123 (693)	ff. 92r-94v	xv/1	JW MS Boh.
ii	UK	V.F.9 (931)	ff. 100r-101r	1408	Asc. Boh.
iii	Wien, ÖNB	1337	ff. 52vb-53va	ca. 1410	JW MS Boh.
iv		1387	ff. 105vb-106rb	ca. 1410	JW MS Boh.
v		*1622*	ff. 179v-180r	1410	JW MS Boh.
vi		3927	ff. 24va-25ra	ca. 1410	JW MS Boh.
vii		4527	ff. 147v-148r	1410	JW MS Boh.

III. Ed. J. Loserth, *Johannis Wyclif Opera Minora* (WS, 1913): 8-10†. From all MSS except **ii** and **v**.

IV. Loserth remarks in his introduction (p. v) that "This is the translation of the English tractate: 'Five questions on Love';" but it is in fact the other way around.[2] The *De amore* begins by mentioning that an unnamed friend has raised five questions touching the nature of love. His answers to the first four are terse, but to the fifth, "in quo statu patet homo congruencius diligere deum suum," he offers a fuller reply, grounded in the orthodox premise that a man's manner of expressing his love of God springs first of all from his condition in society: while the best state is that of Christ Himself – priestly and virginal – the least desirable is that of the "four sects"[3] as presently constituted, "periculosus et a catholicis evitandus." The term *viator* and its cognates appear no fewer than ten times,[4] a frequency suggesting a date in 1383 or 1384 – but it is not possible to be certain; nor can we firmly assert any connection other than the purely topical with **427**, below.[5]

VC: 3933 3935 4514 7980   Bale: 182   Sh: 61.5   Lo: 62.5

[1] "... disrumpamus" in ed., but MSS all agree on our reading.

[2] As demonstrated by Deanesly, *The Lollard Bible*, p. 246, n. 1; cf. also Severs, *Manual of Writings in Middle English* II: 525. Eng. version in Arnold, *Select English Works* III: 183-185.

[3] Cf. **50**, n. 6, above, etc.

[4] Cf. **47**, nn. 19, 20, above.

[5] Several of the *sermones* also focus on love: cf. **210**, **286**, **287**, above.

394. C11. *De gradibus cleri ecclesie.* Late 1382?

I. Inc.: Quidam secularis probus zelator veritatis fidei Christiane petit instanter quid requiratur ...

Expl.: × ... Et ista discrasia perturbat multipliciter istum mundum.

II. MSS:

i	Manchester, John Rylands Lib.	Eng. 86	f. 54v	xv/1	Unasc. Eng.[1]
ii	Praha, MK	D.123 (693)	ff. 84v-87v	xv/1	JW MS Boh.
iii	UK	V.F.9 (931)	ff. 39r-40v	1408	JW MS Boh.
iv			ff. 98v-100r		Asc.
v		X.E.9 (1910)	ff. 150v-151v	ca. 1420	JW MS Boh.[2]
vi	Wien, ÖNB	1337	ff. 36vb-37vb	ca. 1410	JW MS Boh.

vii	*1622*	ff. 180v-181v	1410	JW MS Boh.
viii	3927	ff. 8vb-9va	ca. 1410	JW MS Boh.
ix	3929	f. 215ra-vb	1409	JW MS Boh.
x	4527	ff. 83r-84v	1410	JW MS Boh.

III. Ed. J. Loserth, *Johannis Wyclif Opera Minora* (WS, 1913): 140-144†. From all MSS except ii and vii.

IV. Wyclyf is here concerned to answer an unnamed friend's queries touching the sacrament of ordination. As we might expect, he is highly critical of the proliferation of Scripturally unwarranted offices in the church, pleading that the only real distinctions recorded in the New Testament are between deacons on the one hand and priests and bishops (often interchangeably designated) on the other. Human laws and customary practices (by which he means canon law) are of no concern to him save insofar as they are clearly grounded in the law of Christ.

We may hazard a guess as to the identity of "quidam secularis": John Purvey, Wyclyf's faithful amanuensis and close companion in the Lutterworth years.[3] Evidently some "perversus magister" had approached him with a casuistic question intended to trap Wyclyf: perhaps certain of the Oxford masters, anxious to ingratiate themselves with Chancellor Rigg[4] and Archbishop Courtenay after the fifth congregation of the Blackfriars Synod (which met at Canterbury on 1 July 1382, and there condemned the work of Hereford and Repingdon), saw a way to generate an even more definitive disapprobation of their erstwhile colleague by using Purvey as a conduit. Perhaps late in 1382, if we rely on this *catena* of assumptions, would be the most defensible date for the *De gradibus cleri ecclesie*.

VC: 3933 3935 Bale: 97[5] Sh: 95 Lo: 96

[1] Same inc. as Bale; almost surely his source. No indication that the scribe was aware of his defective copy.

[2] Used in ed.; not in Lo.

[3] Cf. Deanesly, *The Lollard Bible*, 46 *passim*; *BRUO* III: 1527; above, Preface, n. 7.

[4] *BRUO* III: 1616; Dahmus, *The Prosecution of John Wyclyf*, 104 *passim* to 132.

[5] Tit. correct; inc.: "Videtur autem sanctis doctoribus..." (i.e., cap. iii).

395. C12. *Epistola missa archiepiscopo Cantuariensi*. Early 1383.

I. Inc.: Venerabilis in Christo pater et domino. Vester sacerdos pauper et humilis [4 wds.] pandit vestre reverencie hostiam cordis sui ...

Expl.: × ... et fieret in materia fidei extraneus legislator.

II. MSS:

i	Praha, MK	*O.29 (1613)*	ff. 227r-228r	ca. 1430	Unasc. Boh.[1]
ii	UK	X.E.9 (1910)	ff. 209r-210r	ca. 1420	JW MS Boh.
iii	*Vaticano*	*Borgh. lat. 29*	ff. 66v-67v	xv/1	JW MS Fr.[2]
iv	Wien, ÖNB	1337	ff. 51rb-52rb	ca. 1410	JW MS Boh.

v	1387	f. 105rb	ca. 1410	JW ms Boh.
vi	3927	ff. 10vb-11rb	ca. 1410	JW ms Boh.
vii	4527	f. 144r-v	1410	Asc. Boh.
viii	4937	ff. 82v-83v	ca. 1420	Asc. Boh.[3]

III. Ed. J. Loserth, *Johannis Wyclif Opera Minora* (WS, 1913): 3-6†. From all MSS except i and iii.

IV. Wyclyf speaks of himself throughout this letter to William Courtenay as "predictus [or: idem] sacerdos." We do not know whether the letter ever reached its intended recipient; of course Courtenay both as Bishop of London (1375-1381) and as the English primate after the murder of Sudbury during the Peasants' Revolt, was most unsympathetic to Wyclyf and took an aggressive part in bringing about his censure at Oxford, as well as in subsequent harrying of the Lollards on down to his death in 1396. The letter is, much like the non-epistolary *Epistola missa ad simplices sacerdotes* (**416**, below), a brief *Apologia pro doctrina sua*: Scripture, he avers, will be his sole bulwark. But it is not Scripture which impels him to judge the merits of the Flanders crusade ("ista crucis ereccio pro defensione cause pape," p. 4): he concludes syllogistically that "ista plebis occisio [et] terrarum depauperacio" probably does not flow from the charity of Christ; and in any case the present pope (i.e., Urban) is neither head nor member of the true Church. There follows his customary litany on the Eucharist (one passage, p. 4, ll. 25-32, much resembles a bold declaration in the *Trialogus* [**47**: p. 263]); and Wyclyf, all caution to the winds, urges Courtenay to write to the orders and such individuals under his jurisdiction, inquiring as to their doctrine in this vital area, "quia prelatus negligenter agens in ista materia est auctor criminis ex consensu."

VC: 3933 3935 4514   Bale: 181   Sh: 61.2   Lo: 62.2

[1] See Thomson, "Unnoticed MSS and Works of Wyclif," 36.
[2] Formerly ff. 6v-7v: see Stein, "The Vatican Manuscript....," 95.
[3] Cited as MS "F" in Loserth's introduction, p. IV, but apparently not collated. The MS is twice asc. in the *contenta*.

396. C13. *Epistola missa episcopo Lincolniensi.* 1382, or early 1384?

I. Inc.: Humilis servus Christi et devotus obedienciarius [9 wds.] petit in causa Christi istud suffragium ...
Expl.: × ... sub sigillo et testimonio confirmetur.

II. MSS:

i	*Praha, MK*	*O.29 (1613)*	f. 228r	ca. 1430	Asc. Boh.
ii	Wien, ÖNB	1337	f. 52rb-va	ca. 1410	JW ms Boh.
iii		1387	f. 105va	ca. 1410	JW ms Boh.
iv		3929	f. 208va-vb	1409	JW ms Boh.
v		4527	f. 147v	1410	Asc. Boh.

III. Ed. J. Loserth, *Johannis Wyclif Opera Minora* (WS, 1913): 6-7†. From all MSS except **i**.

IV. Wyclyf here requests of Bishop John of Buckingham (1363-1398)[1] that the friars, who had persecuted him for his Eucharistic beliefs, themselves declare under the seal of their orders ("sub sigillo suo generali") just what they professed touching that central dogma. If heretical, the good bishop should condemn it; or confirm it if orthodox. While Loserth confidently assigns this missive to 1383, in fact internal references are not so precise as to allow of that year exclusively: we might argue with equal force for 1382 or even early in 1384, before Buckingham moved vigorously against Wyclyf's obscure follower, John Corringham.[2]

VC: 3933 3935 4514 7980   Bale: deest   Sh: 61.3   Lo: 62.3

[1] His episcopal register is still in MS at Lincoln Cathedral. Of him, see M. M. C. Calthrop, "Ecclesiastical History (to A.D. 1600)," in William Page, ed., *The Victoria History of the Counties of England: Lincolnshire* II (London, 1906): 39-41; Workman, *JW* I: 154-156. (Not in DNB or *BRUO*.) Of course he had participated in the first session at Blackfriars, which condemned 24 of Wyclyf's teachings on 28 May 1382: *FZ*, 286.

[2] Cf. A. K. McHardy, "Bishop Buckingham and the Lollards of Lincoln Diocese," in *Schism, Heresy and Religious Protest*, 131-145. (See also **423**, n. 3, below.)

Section D

Homo publicus
General Petitions and Protestations

It is of course impossible to extricate the occasional pieces in this section altogether from the deeper contexts of Wyclyf's own intellectual evolution and the political events of the years between 1376 and 1384. A great deal has already been said by a multitude of scholars[1] on the activities and impact of Wyclyf *extra muros Oxoniensi* and *extra limites parochiae* during these years; yet much still remains controversial and far from settled. Rather than wading into these wide and treacherous waters, we shall confine our observations in the following commentaries to what can reasonably be inferred from the confirmed writings of Wyclyf himself.

[1] The first seriously to concern himself with this dimension of Wyclyf's career was the redoubtable martyrologist John Foxe; cf. below, **398**, n. 2. The biographical notices by Wirth, Lewis and Baber – not to mention Bale, Tanner and Leland – are often hopelessly confused, especially as to chronology. Robert Vaughan's two editions of *The Life and Opinions of John de Wycliffe, D.D.* (London, 1828 and 1853); Charles Le Bas' *The Life of Wiclif* (London, 1832); Oskar Jäger, *John Wycliffe und seine Bedeutung für die Reformation* (Halle, 1854), and other like ventures moved the issues only gradually into focus. Höfler (1870), Lechler (1873) and Buddensieg (1884, quincentenary small biography, London and Halle) accelerated our understanding appreciably. The many articles by Loserth (above, A12, n. 3, etc.) and of course Workman, *JW*, further refined the process. The most recent efforts of McFarlane, Dahmus, Daly, Wilks and Farr have brought us to our present level of awareness. – Concerning the sources of our image of Wyclyf, a superior essay is James Crompton, "John Wyclif. A Study in Mythology," *Transactions of the Leicestershire Archaeological and Historical Society* 42 (1966-1967): 6-34; and also Mudroch, *The Wyclyf Tradition*.

397. D1. [*De iuramento Arnaldi*]. Mid-1377.

I. Inc.: Hec est forma iuramenti Arnaldi de Granario ...[1]
Expl.: × ... post eius subtraccionem, postquam fuit gracius repetita.

II. MSS:

i	Praha, UK	III.G.11 (536)	ff. 230v-233v	xv/1	JW MS Boh.
ii		III.G.16 (541)	ff. 33r-35v	1414	Unasc. Boh.
iii	Wien, ÖNB	1337	ff. 115rb-117va	ca. 1410	JW MS Boh.
iv		3929	ff. 246ra-247va	1409	JW MS Boh.[2]

III. Ed. G. Lechler, *Johann von Wiclif und die Vorgeschichte der Reformation* II (Leipzig, 1873): 575-579. From **iv** only.

IV. Arnald Garnier was a particularly persistent papal collector who first showed his face in England in October of 1371, seeking clerical monies to help Gregory XI recover church lands in the territory of Milan.[3] On 13 February 1372 he was required to swear before nine of the king's officials at Westminster that he would act in no way prejudicially to the interests of the realm. Workman speculates that Wyclyf might have witnessed this impressive scene; in any case he took the trouble at some point to transcribe the document there drawn up.[4] But what is of greatest interest to us is his commentary on the oath. He finds Arnald's recent activities quite at variance with the letter of his solemn pledge;[5] the Frenchman has therefore perjured himself, and ought to be resisted throughout the land, "specialiter pensata natura legis caritatis et paciencie Christi vicarii et natura legis elemosine bonorum." (P. 579.) At this juncture Wyclyf obviously still trusts Gregory, even to granting the applicability of the hoary maxim from Roman law, "quod principi placuit, legis habet vigorem." [6] The publication of this political piece we may assign to the summer of 1377: whether officially solicited or not, it maintained his public visibility after the Bruges mission of 1374 and began to enhance his notoriety at the same time that he was conducting a series of heated debates *in scholis*.

It has not been hitherto noticed by Wyclyf scholars that the reformer actually knew Garnier. We have the evidence in the latter's record of his official acts in England. Late in 1373 or early in 1374 the collector noted in connection with his visit to the diocese of Lincoln: "Item Johanni Wiclif presbytero de canonicatu sub exspectatione prebende ecclesie Lincolniensis." [7] In the course of 1377, the two met again, and the question of the first fruits owing from Wyclyf's prebend at Aust in Westbury was adjudicated: he had paid £6/13/4, and was charged with a balance of £29/5/8 (another hand has written a laconic "vera" beside this last entry, indicating the formal character of the proceedings).[8] Finally, we discover that on 2 May 1377, at a subsequent hearing, the fruits of the Caistor prebend were sequestered, and Wyclyf was admonished. Two days later, Robert Wyclyf (his nephew?)[9] paid on his behalf £13/6/8; the balance then due was £32. Further resolution of the case was postponed until 13 January 1378, because the prebend soon came into the hands of Philip of Thornbury.[10] Wyclyf had therefore a very personal reason for exclaiming thus adversely on the doings of Arnald Garnier; beyond a doubt we witness here one of the most concrete of motives for Wyclyf's increasing disenchantment with the operations of the "clerus cesareus" of his later writings.

The king's council would soon request of him a further elaboration of his views: these he proffered in **398**, just below, wherein he begins to argue more strongly for disendowment.[11]

vc: 3933 3935 4714 7980   Bale: deest   Sh: 71   Lo: 72

---

[1] The name is garbled in all MSS.

[2] Buddensieg, *John Wiclif's Polemical Works in Latin* I: xxx says the folios are 259-260; this is, however, the older enumeration.

[3] Cf. Workman, *JW* I: 220, 270, 318; McKisack, *The Fourteenth Century*, 285, for narratives and sources. Essential primary material appears in the Vatican Archives, Collectoriae 12 and 13, ed. William E. Lunt (revised by Edgar B. Graves), *Accounts Rendered by Papal Collectors in England 1317-1378* (Philadelphia, 1968): 363-541. For detailed biography see ibid., pp. xxix-xlii. For papal

bulls, etc. relevant to Garnier's work both in England and on the Continent, see William H. Bliss and J. A. Twemlow, edd., *Calendar of Entries in the Papal Registers relating to Great Britain and Ireland. Papal Letters* IV: *A.D. 1362-1404* (London, 1902): 100-101, 105, 110, 113, 121, 142-143, 146, 148-153, 155-156, 159-160; L. Mirot, H. Jassemin, and J. Vielliard, edd., *Lettres secrètes et curiales du pape Grégoire XI (1370-1378) relatives à la France extraites de registres du Vatican* (Bibliothèque des Écoles Françaises d'Athènes et de Rome, 3ᵉ série: B.23: Paris, 1935-1957): nos. 442, 875, 1843, 1874, 2814; G. Mollat, ed., *Lettres secrètes et curiales du pape Grégoire XI (1370-1378) intéressant les pays autres que la France publiées ou analysées d'après des registres du Vatican* (as above, B.24: Paris, 1962-1965): nos. 378, 507, 508, 1292, 1455, 3285, 3327, 3328; for context also see W. E. Lunt, *Financial Relations of the Papacy with England, 1327-1534* (Cambridge, Mass., 1962): 6, 12, 51, 70-73, 103-114, 196-197, 203-204, 353n., 360-378, 534, 662-683.

⁴ French text in J. Caley, F. Holbrooke, edd., [Rymer and Sanderson], *Foedera, Conventiones, Litterae, et cujusque generis Acta Publica...*, 3rd ed., III/ii (London, 1830): 933-934. The question of Wyclyf's knowledge of French has seldom been explored; we can assume it was at least functional: cf. Helen Suggett, "The Use of French in England in the Later Middle Ages," in R. W. Southern, ed., *Essays in Medieval History selected from the Transactions of the Royal Historical Society on the Occasion of its Centenary* (London etc., 1968): 213-239. In this connection, it is not out of place to suggest that Wyclyf's concern to propagate Scripture among the laity in their own vernacular was not solely a reaction against the exclusivism of clerical Latin; it was also a direct challenge to the lingering penchant for Anglo-Norman among the upper strata.

⁵ Workman, *JW* I: 302-303.

⁶ Inst. 1.2.6. (Cf. J. A. C. Thomas, *The Institutes of Justinian. Text, Translation and Commentary* [Amsterdam and Oxford, 1975]: 5, 9.) For other references in Roman Law to this text of Ulpianus, see H. C. Black, ed., *Black's Law Dictionary*, 3rd ed. (St. Paul, 1953): 1488. The most significant recent study is Ewart Lewis, "King above Law ? 'Quod principi placuit' in Bracton," *Speculum* 39 (1964): 240-269.

⁷ Lunt/Graves, *Accounts Rendered...*, 430.

⁸ Ibid., p. 494.

⁹ Workman, *JW* I: 45-46, reviews known family connections.

¹⁰ The "ydiota" of the *De civili dominio* III (**28-30**, n. 33, above). Cf. also Workman, *JW* I: 204-206; Lunt/Graves, *Accounts Rendered...*, 504.

¹¹ Arnald's oath also comes under scrutiny in the *De officio regis* (**34**: p. 108, line 7), and he is evidently also the subject of the *De mandatis divinis* (**26**: p. 381).

This piece, as it appears in i, was evidently first noted by Constantin Höfler, "Anna von Luxemburg. Kaiser Karls IV. Tochter, König Richards II. Gemahlin, Königin von England 1382-1394," *Denkschriften der kaiserlichen Akademie der Wissenschaften, philosophisch-historischen Classe* (Wien) 20 (1871): 140. A good part of this pioneering article is devoted to Wyclyf's ecclesiology, doctrine of dominion and public disputations. And on pp. 235-238, Höfler transcribed the compendium of Wyclyf's "protestaciones" from 24 separate works, found on f. 58r of Praha, UK XI.E.3 (2050).

398. D2. [*Responsio*] *ad quesita regis et concilii* [*De questione utrum licet thesaurum retinere*]. November 1377.

1. Inc.: Dubium est utrum regnum Anglie possit legitime imminente necessitate sic defensionis thesaurum regni detinere ...

   Expl.: × ... vel lucrum privatum communem utilitatem regni impediat in futurum.

II. MSS:

i	Oxford, Bodleian	e Musaeo 86 (S.C. 3629)	ff. 66vb-69vb	1439	Asc. Eng.
ii	Praha, UK	III.B.5 (414)	ff. 3rb-5ra	xv/1	JW MS Boh.[1]
iii	Wien, ÖNB	1337	ff. 175ra-178va	ca. 1410	JW MS Boh.

III. Partial ed., John Foxe, *Rerum in Ecclesia gestarum, quae postremis et periculosis his temporibus evenerunt...* (Basel, 1559): 17;[2] complete ed., *FZ*, 258-271. From **i** only.

IV. Workman[3] has placed this piece in the context of the return to England and subsequent diligent inquests of the papal collector Arnald Garnier (see the preceding item); November of 1377 seems the likeliest time for its composition, since Richard's first parliament began to sit on 13 October, and in December Wyclyf first heard of Gregory's bulls censuring *liber* I of the *De civili dominio* (**28**; cf. **399-401**, below). He argues here on the bases of natural law, the law of the Gospel, and the law of conscience, that the papal rights to the goods of the *ecclesia anglicana* are severely restricted: "patet quod dominus papa non habet potestatem occupandi bona ecclesie ut dominus, sed tanquam gubernator, ministrator, et pauperum procurator."[4] *Dominium* was at this time preeminent in his thoughts; and we may furthermore assume that the king's council sought his opinion in the matter of papal exactions because of his acknowledged subtleties in the theoretical aspects thereof. Yet, despite Wyclyf's enthusiasm for the strength and autonomy of the English church, there were troubling elements in his *Responsio*: and so we read at the end of the Bodleian MS (the latest of the three known to us): "hic fuit impositum sibi silencium super premissis per dominum regem cum concilio regni." (P. 271.) If we may credit this addendum, it would appear that he had exceeded his mandate; but we have in actuality no firmer indication upon which to build a judgment.

VC: 3933 3935 4514 7980   Bale: 72   Sh: 65   Lo: 66

---

[1] Tit.: *De questione pro thesauris retinendis*.
[2] Other Latin eds. in 1563, 1570, 1576, 1583, 1596 and 1684. The first modern English version was ed. by S. R. Cattley, *The Acts and Monuments of John Foxe*, 8 vols. (London, 1837-1841; revised 1846-1849; cf. valuable note on subsequent eds. in the *Encyclopaedia Britannica*, 11th. ed., X: 771). The original MS of Foxe on Wyclyf is in London, BL Lansdowne 335; cf. description of this autograph in H. Ellis and F. Douce, *A Catalogue of the Lansdowne Manuscripts in the British Museum*, pt. II (London, 1819): 106; and of all edd., extracts, abridgements etc. of Foxe in the *British Museum General Catalogue of Printed Books to 1955* LXXVI (London, 1961): cols. 667-676. Substantial secondary coverage also in James Gairdner, *Lollardy and the Reformation in England. An Historical Survey* I (London, 1908): 333-365; William Haller, *The Elect Nation; the Meaning and Relevance of Foxe's Book of Martyrs* (New York, 1963): 160-167.
[3] *JW* I: 303-304.
[4] Pp. 260-261. He relies heavily here on the arguments of Bernard of Clairvaux' *De consideratione*; cf. above, **392**, n. 5.

399. D3.a. *Protestacio* [or: *Declaraciones*] *Johannis Wyclif*. Early 1378.

I. Inc.: In principio protestor publice sicut sepe feci alias ...
 Expl.: × ... quia tunc tota fides scripture foret damnabilis.

II. MSS:

i	London, BL	*Royal 13 E.IX*	ff. 250va-251vb	xiv/2	Asc. Eng.[1]
ii	College of Arms	*Arundel 7*	——[2]	xv/1	Asc. Eng.

III. Ed. [Matthew Parker], *Historia brevis Thomae Walsingham, ab Edwardo primo, ad Henricum quintum* (London, 1574): 206-209;[3] William Camden, *Anglica, Normannica, Hibernica, Cambrica, a veteribus scripta...* (Frankfurt, 1602; again in 1603): 206-208;[4] H. T. Riley, *Chronicon Monasterii S. Albani. Thomae Walsingham, quondam Monachi S. Albani, Historia Anglicana* I (RS, 1863): 357-363.[5] The last from **ii** only; MSS not ascertained from earlier eds.

IV. We are including the *Protestacio* and the *Libellus*[6] under a single rubric because of their closeness both in content and in time, although the MS history is sharply different. Considerable skepticism has developed of late concerning the validity of the ostensible circumstances (i.e., in Parliament) of the *Libellus*, but historians have seen no compelling reason to dispute the delivery of the *Protestacio* before the bishops at Lambeth late in March (?) of 1378, consequent upon his failure to appear at St Pauls in response to Bishop Sudbury's order of 18 December 1377, wherein he had been requested to clarify the meaning of the nineteen propositions that had been culled and paraphrased from the *De civili dominio* I.[7] The actual text of this *Protestacio*, because it is so obviously a transcription by some unknown third party, and because it appears in Walsingham's *Historia Anglicana* bracketed by scathing aspersions upon Wyclyf's motives and integrity, cannot be taken *prima facie* as an absolutely faithful rendition of his utterances on that occasion. But neither have we warrant to doubt that the text as we have it is *substantially* what Wyclyf did then declare and assert. Although the terminology and Scriptural and canonical citations correspond only roughly to those in his *Libellus*, there is no reason to see this variation as anything other than a further manifestation of Wyclyf's known penchant for restating his views, employing a different panoply of Scriptural armament to drive home the same conclusions. In this he had been thoroughly trained, and surely taught many others, *in scholis*.

VC: deest   Bale: 73[8]   Sh: 51   Lo: 52

---

[1] The basis for the Arundel MS; yet it is the latter which Riley used as his text.

[2] Not to be confused with the Arundel MSS in the BL; I was unable to examine this MS to ascertain proper folios for the *Protestacio*, and Riley did not note them in his marginalia. Cf. W. H. Black, *Catalogue of the Arundel Manuscripts in the Library of the College of Arms* (London, 1829).

[3] On Parker, see V. J. K. Brook, *A Life of Archbishop Parker* (Oxford, 1962); Elizabeth W. Perry, *Under Four Tudors, being the Story of Matthew Parker sometime Archbishop of Canterbury*, 2nd ed. (London, 1964); [R. I. Page and G. H. S. Bushnell,] *Matthew Parker's Legacy* (Cambridge, Eng., 1975).

[4] On Camden, see the article by E. M. Thompson in the DNB, VIII (1886-1887): 729-737; *Encyclopaedia Britannica*, 11th ed., V: 101.

[5] For Walsingham, see still V. H. Galbraith, ed., *The St Albans Chronicle, 1406-1420* (Oxford, 1936); the second vol. of Antonia Gransden's fine *Historical Writing in England* should soon refresh our perspective on the man.

[6] Both titles are rather arbitrary, but have become conventional since Workman's day (cf. *JW* I: 311): the preferred designation of *Protestacio* for the present piece derives from the three references in the *De veritate sacre scripture* I (**31**: 349); yet we must allow for the possibility that the *Libellus* is intended there. That one is not simply a copy or adaptation of the other is attested not only by the divergent content but also by the phrase in our inc., "... sicut sepe feci alias...."

[7] 30. Dahmus, *The Prosecution of John Wyclyf*, p. 51, n. 7, has tracked these down.

[8] Tit.: *Responsiones ad obiecta*; correct inc.

400. D3.b. [*Libellus*] *ad parliamentum regis*. Early 1378.

I. Inc.: Protestor publice ut sepe alias quod propono et volo esse Christianus ex integro ...

Expl.: × ... de amissione temporalium, stare pro evangelica paupertate.

II. MSS:

i	London, BL	Add. 5902[1]	ff. 36r-41v	xv/1	Unasc. Eng.
ii	Oxford, Bodleian	Arch. Selden B.26 (S.C. 3340)	ff. 83va-85va	xv/1	Asc. Eng.[2]
iii		e Musaeo 86 (S.C. 3629)	ff. 64va-66vb	1439	Asc. Eng.
iv	Paris, BN	f.l. 3184	ff. 53r-54v	1396	Asc. No. Fr.[3]
v	Praha, UK	V.F.9 *(931)*	ff. 101r-103v	1408[4]	JW MS Boh.
vi		XI.E.3 (2050)	ff. 59v-61r	1416	JW MS Boh.
vii	Vaticano	Borgh.lat. 29	ff. 45r-47v	xv/1	Asc. Fr.[5]
viii	Wien, ÖNB	1338	ff. 18ra-20va	ca. 1410	JW MS Boh.
ix		1387	ff. 134rb-135vb	ca. 1410	JW MS Boh.
x		3929	ff. 203vb-205va	1409	JW MS Boh.[6]

III. Ed. J. Lewis, *The History of the Life and Sufferings of the Reverend and Learned John Wicliffe, D.D.* ..., 1st ed. (London, 1720): 318-326; 2nd ed. (Oxford, 1820): 382-389; *FZ*, 245-257. From **ii** and **iii** only.

IV. The MS tradition of this *Libellus*[7] is appreciably more secure than for the closely related *Protestacio*, just above. It is fair to say that Wyclyf wrote it and either delivered it or prepared to deliver it in some public forum other than the episcopal convocation at Lambeth in the early spring of 1378. But it was not Parliament: Workman[8] has cast grave doubt on Netter's (scil.: Kenninghale's) date of 1377, and no Parliament met in April of 1378. The so-called "continual council"[9] (as opposed to the "Great Council"), in session during most of the regency of Richard II, may well have heard Wyclyf present this *pièce justificative* in March or April of 1378. That the council (or even the Great Council), despite

John of Gaunt and the queen mother (Joan of Kent, Princess of Wales, who intervened on Wyclyf's behalf more than once), might have seen fit to pursue the directive in Gregory XI's bull *Regum Anglie* of 22 May 1377,[10] is not altogether ruled out by the available evidence. That his arguments, either here or in the *Protestacio* – which for our purposes amounts to the same thing – were widely disseminated throughout the realm we may accept from the *De veritate sacre scripture* I (**31**: p. 349): "... non sum suspectus de formidine istarum conclusionum, cum transmisi illa per magnam partem Anglie et Christianismi et sic usque ad curiam romanam...."[11] But to brand the *Libellus*, as Workman did, a "shortened, popular form of the *Protestacio*,"[12] is too facile: the argumentation in the *Libellus*, while a bit briefer than in the corresponding portions of the *Protestacio*, is no less subtle or intricate in design.

VC: 3933 3935 4514[13]   Bale: deest   Sh: 50   Lo: 51

[1] Lo has 5092, f. 28. This MS was copied from **ii**. The foliation in an unpublished catalog was kindly reproduced for me by the Assistant Keeper of MSS, Dr. M. A. E. Vickson: there it is given as ff. 38r-45v.

[2] Besides the derivation in **i** (see the preceding note) this MS was also copied in Bodleian, James 3, pp. 304-314, ca. 1636.

[3] Tit.: *Protestacio*....

[4] A marginal note alludes to the year 1415.

[5] Tit.: *Ad parliamentum*; old foliation was 33r-35v: Stein, "The Vatican Manuscript...," 97.

[6] Tit.: *17* [sic] *conclusiones quas posuit Mgr. Johannis in parliamento regni Anglie.*

[7] On the title, see n. 6 to the preceding item.

[8] *JW* I: 311. Dahmus, *The Prosecution of John Wyclyf*, 57, basically agrees with Workman's judgment, though in my estimation for the wrong reasons.

[9] See N. B. Lewis, "The 'Continual Council' in the Early Years of Richard II, 1377-1380," *EHR* 41 (1926): 246-251.

[10] Translated in Dahmus, *The Prosecution of John Wyclyf*, 45-47; and see above, **28-30**, n. 21.

[11] Apparently a reference to the events described in one of the *Sermones* (**199**, above), though it appears there that the delation "ad curiam romanam" was of the *Libellus* itself. Cf. also **31**, I: 274, and Buddensieg's introduction, p. LI.

[12] *JW* I: 311.

[13] In all three tit.: *Decem et octo conclusiones.*

401. D3.c. *De condemnacione xix conclusionum.* Early to mid-1378.

I. Inc.: Cum secundum apostolum ad Hebreos 11 fides sit fundamentum Christiane religionis ...

Expl.: × ... et vivatur sobrie iuste et pie in evangelica paupertate.

II. MSS:

i	Oxford, Bodleian	Arch. Selden B.26 (S.C. 3340)	ff. 85va-87vb	xv/1	Asc. Eng.[1]
ii	Praha, MK	D.123 (693)	ff. 144bisr-149v	xv/1	JW MS Boh.[2]

iii	UK	III.B.5 (414)	ff. 5rb-7ra	xv/1	JW MS Boh.
iv		III.G.11 (536)	ff. 227r-230v	xv/1	JW MS Boh.[3]
v		IV.H.7 (771)	ff. 98v-102v	ca. 1410	JW MS Boh.
vi	Wien, ÖNB	1337	ff. 178va-181va	ca. 1410	JW MS Boh.
vii		1387	ff. 111va-113ra	ca. 1410	JW MS Boh.
viii		3929	ff. 215vb-217va	1409	JW MS Boh.
ix		3933	ff. 92ra-94ra	ca. 1415	JW MS Boh.
x	Wolfenbüttel, HzglB	Cod.Guelf. 306 (340)	ff. 210ra-213va	xv/1	Asc. Pol.[4]

III. Ed. *FZ*, 481-492. From **i** and **viii** only.

IV. This indignant *defensio* was in no sense an *epistola*, as averred in the later heading of the Oxford MS – but it was intended in all likelihood to circulate *in scholis* and beyond: cf. the exhortation on p. 408, "Eja, milites Christi, tam seculares quam clerici, et precipue professores paupertatis evangelice [!]...." It would therefore have served as a logical complement to the *Protestacio* and *Libellus*, just above. The *De condemnacione* is far from systematic: though he mentions the 19 propositions in Gregory's bulls, he addresses, in this sequence, only nos. 17, 19, 8, 11, 12 and 14. The tone is injured, the counterattack immoderate. What is of peculiar interest – and heretofore overlooked by Loserth[5] and Dahmus[6] – is *why* Wyclyf should himself have fastened onto *conclusiones* 17 and 19 as "duas precipue ... hereticas" (p. 484), and relegated the other four to a secondary rank. Nowhere in the five bulls of Gregory XI is any such hierarchy of perniciousness either stated or implied. (But such a determination might have been arrived at at some other stage of the proceedings.) We propose here one of two possibilities: either the proposition had fallen into the arena of general debate at Oxford, and one or more of Wyclyf's opponents (Aclyff? Crump?[7]) had contrived the sequence; or one or two of the masters-regent in theology, responding to Archbishop Sudbury's directive of 18 December 1377,[8] ventured some sort of confidential recommendation to the Chancellor, Adam de Tonworth, to identify propositions 17 and 19 as most *male sonantes* of all the *conclusiones*. There is, however, no real hint of either possibility in any source; yet the question surely deserves further consideration. Also, given the high proportion of MSS now extant which Shirley did not use in his edition, a new *textus criticus* might help to clarify a point or two, particularly the identity of the shadowy "quidam doctor mixtim theologus" on p. 483.

VC: 3933 3935 4514 7980   Bale: deest   Sh: 52   Lo: 53

---

[1] Copied from this codex in Bodleian, James 3, pp. 314-323, ca. 1636.

[2] Podlaha overlooks this piece but gives its expl. correctly; the reason may be that most of f. 144bis has been excised, leaving the "C" of "Cum ..." intact.

[3] Not III.G.1 (535) as in Lo.

[4] Cf. Kühn-Steinhausen, "Wyclif-Handschriften in Deutschland," 626.

[5] "Studien zur Kirchenpolitik Englands... I," 91-92. (Many errors.)

[6] *The Prosecution of John Wyclyf*, 37-38, 51-52. His thesis that Wyclyf found proposition 7 "embarrassing and difficult to defend" is thin, though we may accept his insistence that 19 is the correct number, as is so indicated in the present piece and in Gregory's bulls as well.

[7] See **28-30**, n. 23, above.

[8] Translated in Dahmus, *The Prosecution of John Wyclyf*, 64-66, from Sudbury's register; he corrects there some minor misreadings in Wilkins, *Concilia*... III: 123-124.

402. D4. *De paupertate Christi* [*conclusiones triginta tres*]. Early 1378.

I. Inc.: Christus deus noster caput universalis ecclesie fuit [4 wds.] homo pauperrimus ...

Expl.: × ... quod dominus undique compendiosius dabit pacem.

II. MSS:

i	Paris, BN	f.l. 3184	ff. 35v-46r	1396	Asc. No. Fr.
ii	*Praha, MK*	B.17.1 *(310)*	ff. 184v-209r	1414	Unasc. Boh.[1]
iii	UK	III.G.11 (536)	ff. 28r-49r	xv/1	JW MS Boh.[2]
iv		V.E.28 *(922)*	f. 159rb-va	ca. 1420	Asc. Boh.[3]
v		V.F.17 (939)	ff. 166r-194r	1412	JW MS Boh.
vi		X.D.10 (1889)	ff. 35vb-45va	ca. 1415	Asc. Boh.[4]
vii			ff. 179ra-180va		
viii	*Vaticano*	Borgh.lat. 29	ff. 24r-45r	xv/1	Asc. Fr.[5]
ix	Wien, ÖNB	1338	ff. 1ra-17vb	ca. 1410	JW MS Boh.
x		1387	ff. 126ra-134rb	ca. 1410	JW MS Boh.
xi		4343	ff. 236v-262r	1433	Asc. Boh.[6]

III. Ed. J. Loserth, *Johannis Wyclif Opera Minora* (WS, 1913): 19-73†. From all MSS except **ii, iv** and **viii**.

IV. As is not uncommon in the Wyclyf canon, the *De paupertate Christi* betrays no inner emblem of its contextual *raison d'être*. But in the *De veritate sacre scripture* we read: "Unde quia volui materiam communicatam clericis et laicis, collegi et communicavi triginta tres conclusiones illius materie in ligwa duplici." (**31**; I: 350.) So this work fits neatly into the *catena* of the *De civili dominio* (**28-30**) and the three items immediately above; it must therefore have been composed and circulated in the spring of 1378. (No English versions are extant.) The 33 conclusions themselves, dealing with the failings of the secular clergy, disendowment, and ideal poverty, are generically but not verbally related to the 19 propositions picked out of the *De civili dominio* and censured by Gregory XI on 22 May 1377. Via these intermediate links his argument culminated in the *De officio regis* (**33**) in 1379.

Two further points are noteworthy. The massive and deft array of supportive sources adduced – especially the *De consideratione*, St. Bernard's letter to Eugenius III, cited at least six times – canon law, and even Aquinas,[9] testify to the care with which he thus presented his brief. And then there is a mention of "cuiuslibet sacerdotis pauperis" on p. 55; surely this is one of the earliest uses of the term in the *corpus Wyclyfianum*.

vc: 3933 3935 4514 7980   Bale: deest   Sh: 64[10]   Lo: 65

[1] At the end is an anonymous *Conclusio de vita clericorum*: see Loserth ed., pp. VIII, 73n. It seems unlikely that this short piece was ever a part of Wyclyf's treatise; how it came to be added in this and several other MSS is not clear. Sedlák, *Studie a Texty*, XVII (interleaved), offers corrections to Loserth's ed. based on this MS.

[2] The *conclusio* follows, f. 49r-v.

[3] The *conclusio* only (acephalous).

[4] The *conclusio* on f. 45va-vb; also at the bottom of f. 180va (next entry). The text of **vii** is an extract from cap. xxvii in another hand, perhaps copied, as Loserth suggests in his introduction, p. IX, from the first part of the MS. But why?

[5] Previously designated ff. 25r-33r, 44r-48v (in reverse order, and commencing early in cap. iv: Stein, "The Vatican Manuscript...," 95-96. No *conclusio*.

[6] Ends with the *conclusio*.

[7] See **392**, n. 5, above.

[8] Pp. 23, 25, 27, 29, 30, 34, 36-43, 45, 47, 48-50, 58-60, 64; and cf. **28-30**, n. 25, above.

[9] P. 21: *Summa theologiae* IIa IIae 185.6.

[10] He remarks that it was "addressed apparently to the Duke of Lancaster. Written probably about 1380." Wrong on both counts.

403. D5. [*Peticio ad regem et parliamentum*]. Mid-1382.

I. Inc.: Placeat illustrissimo regi nostro tam Anglie quam Francie [44 wds.] condescendere pariter ...

Expl.: × ... quod istud venerabile sacramentum est panis verus et corpus Christi similiter.

II. MS:[1]

| i | Firenze, BLaur | Plut. XIX.33 | ff. 23v-26v | 1408 | Asc. Eng.[2] |

III. Ed. I. H. Stein, "The Latin Text of Wyclif's *Complaint*," *Speculum* 7 (1932): 87-94.

IV. Stein believed that this piece is reasonably complete as it stands in her Latin text, and disputed Workman's conclusion[3] that "there is no suitable ending" (i.e., in the English text known to him[4]). Wyclyf was capable of abruptness, and we need not challenge Stein's judgment on this point. Our scribe however was often careless: should another MS turn up, it would likely expose more anomalies in the Laurenziana text. At least in this case the two known MSS in Middle English do serve as useful controls.[5]

The occasion of the piece (whether originally in English or in Latin remains a nice question) was, it is generally agreed, the Parliament of May 7-22, 1382. Workman thought our piece was a sequel to an earlier petition, traceable now only in the *De blasfemia* (**37**: pp. 270-271) – a plausible hypothesis, but the reasons advanced above for a date of 1381 for this concluding treatise in the *Summa theologie* would seem to challenge this notion. In any case no official record even of the receipt of this *Peticio* exists. Some correlation with at least one of the *Sermones*[6] may likewise be urged – and remains equally unproven. Yet if we are to accept its composition in May of 1382, we cannot surely know even so whether it preceded or followed Parliament's denunciation of wandering preachers – the Lollards – which had itself been a political objective of Archbishop Courtenay at the Blackfriars Synod. (And that body, we remember, began to sit only on 17 May.) Throughout the language is careful, the substance predictable by this date: the rule of Christ; the usurpations of the mendicants; the royal rights *in temporalibus*; tithes; and the Eucharist.

VC: deest   Bale: 158   Sh: deest   Lo: deest

[1] According to Baber, *The New Testament...*, p. xl, there was in his day another Latin MS, "in the British Museum, Cott. MSS." He does not further specify this codex; perhaps a careful examination of the catalogs by Thomas Smith (1696) and J. Planta (1802) would uncover it. However it must be remembered that a great fire in 1731 "completely destroyed or seriously damaged nearly a quarter of the Cotton [MSS]" (Arundell Esdaile, *The British Museum Library; a short history and survey* [London, 1946]: 229), so that Baber's statement may perhaps be based on a *status quo ante*.

[2] First remarked in her "The Wyclif Manuscript in Florence," 97.

[3] *JW* II: 251.

[4] In Arnold, *Select English Works* III: 507-523. His preface is useful too.

[5] Severs, *Manual of Writings in Middle English* II: 365, 526.

[6] 171, above.

404. D6. *Epistola missa pape Urbano.* 1384.

I. Inc.: Gaudeo plane detegere cuicunque fidem quam teneo ...
   Expl.: × ... cum ista sit patens condicio Antichristi.

II. MSS:[1]

i	Brno, UK	*Mk II.24 (108)*	ff. 17v, 30r	ca. 1440	Asc. Boh.[2]
ii	München, BSB	*clm 15771*	f. 27r	ca. 1435	Asc. So. Ger.[3]
iii	Oxford, Bodleian	e Musaeo 86 (S.C. 3629)	f. 83ra-va	1439	Asc. Eng.
iv	Praha, MK	C.38 (462)	ff. 172vb-173ra	ca. 1410	JW MS Boh.[4]
v		*O.29 (1613)*	f. 226v ?[5]	ca. 1430	? Boh.
vi	Vaticano	Borgh.lat. 29	f. 67v	xv/1	Asc. Fr.[6]
vii	Wien, ÖNB	1337	f. 51ra-rb	ca. 1410	JW MS Boh.
viii		1387	f. 105ra	ca. 1410	JW MS Boh.
ix		3927	f. 11rb-va	ca. 1410	JW MS Boh.
x		4316	ff. 129v-130r	ca. 1430	JW MS Boh.
xi		4504	f. 114r	xv/1	Asc. Boh.
xii		4527	ff. 146v-147r	1410	JW MS Boh.
xiii		4937	f. 84r-v	ca. 1420	Asc. Boh.[7]
xiv	Wolfenbüttel, HzglB	*Cod.Guelf. 669 (719)*	ff. 219v-220r	1417	Asc. Boh.[8]

III. Ed. John Foxe, *Rerum in Ecclesia gestarum quae postremis et periculosis his temporibus evenerunt* ... 1st ed. (Basel, 1559): 16[9]; *FZ*, 341-342; G. Lechler, *Johann von Wiclif und die Vorgeschichte der Reformation* II (Leipzig, 1873): 633-634; J. Loserth, *Johannis Wyclif Opera Minora* (WS, 1913): 1-2†. The last from all MSS except **i, ii, iv, v, vi** and **xiv**. Translated by J. Dahmus, *The Prosecution of John Wyclyf* (New Haven, 1952): 141-142; Edward Peters, ed., *Heresy and Authority in Medieval Europe: Documents in Translation* (Philadelphia, 1980): 273-274.

IV. This piece, among the most widely disseminated of Wyclyf's shorter works both in Latin and in English,[10] was, as Loserth showed at some length both in his introduction (p. II) and in an earlier article,[11] not really a letter at all (despite the almost unanimous testimony of the MSS and the VC), but rather a kind of circular, designed to lay before interested parties in England Wyclyf's cardinal tenets of faith. Because Christ himself was "pro statu huius viacionis homo pauperrimus, omnem dominacionem mundanam abiciens," and His law is supreme, the pope, as "summus vicarius Christi in terris," is bound more tightly than any other man by both law and example. God, he declares, has prevented him from going to Rome in answer to a papal summons;[12] this is a veiled reference to the aftereffects of his first stroke, which he tells us elsewhere[13] left him "debilis et claudus." The tone is relatively restrained throughout – it is assuredly *not*, as one modern scholar has it, "nowhere [else] so pointed and unequivocal as in this letter"[14] – but this curious circumstance may readily be explained by the simple assumption that while the piece was structured in such a way as to encourage general distribution, it was nonetheless intended *at some time* to find its way to the Curia. Wyclyf had, after all, been summoned to appear; it would have been surprising indeed if we possessed no indication that he ever bothered to reply. Despite the preponderantly civil tone, there is yet a subtle threat of intransigence running through it: while he professes willingness to pay even unto death for any wrongful doctrine he might harbor, all the same it is God's will and not man's that he is most mindful of.

Loserth's strenuous advocacy of 1378, and Workman's less enthusiastic endorsement of that early date, are evidently predicated on the presumption that Urban never summoned Wyclyf; they urge that only Gregory XI did, at the time of the five bulls in May of 1377.[15] But the countervailing evidence of the *De citacionibus frivolis* (**413**) – both as to the summons and as to Wyclyf's physical incapacity – is too formidable. The assignment of 1384 (the year, besides, which appears quite legibly in the rubric of **iii**) to this "letter" puts us squarely in the camp of Shirley, Lechler, Buddensieg and Dahmus. Some Vatican scrap may someday vindicate us all.

VC: 3933 3935 4514 7980   Bale: 96[16]   Sh: 61.1   Lo: 62.2

[1] Bateson, *Catalogue of the Library of Syon Monastery*, no. N 28, ff. 114-115 ?, evidently contained "sentencie quarundam epistolarum Iohannis Wyclyff domino pape et aliis tam in anglico quam in latino;" this MS, as previously noted, is now lost.

According to the old *contenta* of Oxford, Bodleian Digby 98, "epistole multe Johannis Wytcliff" were at one time in that codex. Two folios are now missing, and it is those which evidently contained the "epistole"; we may presume them to have included the present piece, as well as **394** and **395**, above. A communication to the editor from the late Dr. Richard Hunt at Oxford revealed that Peter Partriche (cf. *BRUO* III: 1430-1431) wrote both the *contenta* and the text. There are also two pieces on ff. 200r-213v, *Declaracio magistri Johannis Whytheed de Hibernia in materia de mendicitate contra fratres*; and *De confessione et absolucione* by the same author. This Irish doctor continued Wyclyf's war against the mendicants in the first decade of the fifteenth century; his adversaries were the Franciscan Peter Russell and the Dominican William Edlesburgh. (For all three, see *BRUO* I: 625; III: 1611, 2037; and cf. also E. B. Fitzmaurice and A. G. Little, *Materials for the History of the Franciscan Province of Ireland A.D. 1230-1450* [British Society of Franciscan Studies 9: Manchester, 1920]: 172-176; Denifle and Chatelain, *Chartularium Universitatis Parisiensis* IV [1897]: no. 1868; Wilkins, *Concilia...* III: 324.)

[2] A fragment.

[3] Ibid.; see Kühn-Steinhausen, "Wyclif-Handschriften in Deutschland," 627.

[4] Inc.: "Audeo plane...."

[5] See above, **390**, n. 1. The f. is an estimate, based on known foliation of **394** and **395**, above.

[6] Formerly f. 7v; see Stein, "The Vatican Manuscript...," 95.

[7] Adds at end "servus ihesu xi et ecclesie sue Johannes" – the words also of **vii** and (without the name) **ix**. But this ending in **xiii** is not noted in Loserth's edition. If genuine, of course, we should have to rethink the question of the "letter's" actual identity.

[8] Noted in Otto von Heinemann, *Die Handschriften der Herzoglichen Bibliothek zu Wolfenbüttel. Die Helmstedter Handschriften* II/1 (Wolfenbüttel, 1888): 122. Cf. Kühn-Steinhausen, "Die Wyclif-Handschriften in Deutschland," 625.

[9] Eng. translations also in Eng. eds., 1563-1907; see above, **398**, n. 2. The Latin text in Foxe begins "Christus autem, qui evangelium illud ..." – i.e., p. 1, line 9 of Loserth ed.

[10] Arnold, *Select English Works* III: 504-506; cf. Severs, *Manual of Writings in Middle English* II: 365, 526. Both sources urge the priority of the Latin text.

[11] "Das vermeintliche Schreiben Wiclif's an Urban VI. und einige verlorene Flugschriften Wiclif's aus seinen letzten Lebenstagen," *Historische Zeitschrift* 75 (1895): 476-480.

[12] Not, as Loserth advocates, the summons of Gregory XI, but that of Urban VI; see text following, and also the *De citacionibus frivolis* (**413**), below. Urban's registers have not yet been published.

[13] *De citacionibus frivolis* (**413**: p. 556).

[14] Dahmus, *The Prosecution of John Wyclyf*, p. 147, n. 2. But his thorough canvassing of the questions surrounding this "letter" (pp. 141-150) is for the most part a helpful contribution.

[15] See **28-30**, n. 21; **399-402**, above.

[16] *Excusaciones ad Vrbanum*; correct inc.

Section E

Polemica contra Papatum I
On Disendowment, the Schism,
the Despenser Crusade

In the lesser pieces represented in these two concluding sections of *polemica*, Wyclyf seldom focused his reformer's zeal on any particular abuse within the *ecclesia militans*, but instead often seized upon an initial issue as emblematic of a general malady. He tended to see particular cases as connected elements in some larger pattern – indeed it is fair to say that his scholastic ambience nourished this habit. We should not expect any other *modus videndi* from a man who perceived "universals" and "ideas" as the ultimate matrices of the imperfect and transitory world of the senses.

As the contemporary Papacy cultivated endowment, tithes and indulgences as the surest material guarantees of its continued existence, so on the other side did it war against itself in the Schism, of which the Flanders campaign under the reckless direction of Bishop Henry Despenser of Norwich was only one among several grotesque outgrowths. And in like measure it was the Papacy which had legitimized and buttressed (some would say: sabotaged) with privilege both the mendicant orders and the older regular institutes, the objects of Wyclyf's slashing disparagement in our next section.

In the final resolution, then, we may vindicate our rubric in the analytic isolation of Wyclyf's *permanent* target: the *vicarius Christi* himself, who became in his eyes, with less and less equivocation, the bare-fanged *vicarius Antichristi hic in via*.

405. E1. *De servitute civili et dominio seculari.* Mid-1376? and early 1384.

I. Inc.: Cum secundum philosophos sit relativorum eadem disciplina [13 wds.] aliquid est dicendum ...

Expl.: × ... subiciat se martirio vel prosecucioni multiplici atque gravi.

II. MSS:

i	Firenze, BLaur	*Plut. XIX.33*	ff. 166r-173v	1408	JW MS Eng.[1]
ii	Manchester, John Rylands Lib.	Eng. 86	ff. 82v-89v	xv/1	JW MS Eng.

III. Ed. J. Loserth, *Johannis Wyclif Opera Minora* (WS, 1913): 145-164†; most of cap. v also in F. D. Matthew, *The English Works of Wyclif Hitherto Unprinted* (London, 1880): 483-485. From **ii** only.

IV. Loserth, following his strong antipathy against the year 1384 for both the *De citacionibus frivolis* (**413**) and the *Epistola missa pape Urbano* (**404**), finds instead much merit in 1378 as the probable date of composition of this piece. Capp. i-iv can unquestionably be linked both thematically and temperamentally with the analysis of slavery (i.e., serfdom) in the *De civili dominio* I (**28**), capp. xxxii and xxxiv. Although there are no *verbatim* correspondences, the parallelism is close enough even to substantiate a case for mid-1376 for these first four capp. But the very last sentence of cap. iv and the whole of capp. v and vi diverge so sharply both in content and in color as to compel the conclusion that they were added by Wyclyf years later, almost certainly early in 1384. The "four sects" are mentioned repeatedly,[2] as is "Antichrist" (i.e., the pope, or even the Papacy itself), and the term "refugam" (p. 161, line 26, *pace* Loserth,[3] clearly signifies Urban, at Naples).

vc: 3933 3935 4514 7980   Bale: 148   Sh: 68   Lo: 69

[1] First noted by Mabillon: see Stein, "The Wyclif Manuscript in Florence," 95-96.
[2] Cf. **46**, n. 2, and **50**, n. 6, above; Section F, below.
[3] P. xxviii. This designation is not uncommon in the latter part of his Lutterworth exile. It cannot in any single case be proven a conscious extrapolation from 2 Maccabees 5:8, as Loserth would have us believe. It seems most probable that it must always and exclusively apply to Urban vi in consequence of his departure from Rome for Naples in April of 1383, even though the ostensible purpose of his journey was to assert suzerainty over the cautious Charles iii of Durazzo (Carlo della Pace), whom he had installed as king of Naples prior to the assassination of Joanna i in 1382. From the point of view of an Englishman desirous of defending in any way the claims of "Urbanus noster" (as Wyclyf sometimes, and perhaps at times sardonically, called him) to be the one true pope, a stable residence in Rome was surely an important *sine qua non*. After it became apparent that Urban's Neapolitan stay was indefinite – and this impression could not have reached England before early 1384 – Wyclyf's opprobrious use of the term "iste refuga" reflected his final abandonment of hope that an end to the Schism might be near. When, in the summer of 1384, Urban was forced to leave Naples for Nocera, the die had already been cast; in any case word of this further migration would have reached Wyclyf too late to account for the several discrete pieces in which the epithet appears. — Clement vii, elected 20 September 1378, reinstituted the Avignonese Papacy on 20 June 1379; but his writ never ran at Oxford, where Wyclyf then was; he always served in the latter's polemical fulminations as a rather unreal paper foil for Urban. Indeed he almost invariably appears as "Robertus Gibbonensis," or, at best, one of "isti pape."

406. E2. *De officio regis conclusio*. 1379?

i. Inc.: Rex debet ex vi sui officii defendere legem dei ...
   Expl.: × ... quo fideliter servierit deo suo.[1]

ii. MSS:

i	Olomouc, Státní vě-decká Knihovna	I.V.34	f. 176r	1411	Unasc. Boh.[2]
ii	Praha, MK	D.123 (693)	f. 151r	xv/1	JW ms Boh.
iii	UK	X.C.23 (1876)	f. 195rb-va	1410	JW ms Boh.
iv		X.H.17 (1995)	f. 92v	ca. 1410	Unasc. Boh.
v		XI.E.3 (2050)	f. 59r	1416	JW ms Boh.
vi	Wien, ÖNB	1338	f. 30va	ca. 1410	JW ms Boh.
vii		1387	f. 107rb	ca. 1410	JW ms Boh.
viii		4515	f. 83v	ca. 1420	JW ms Boh.
ix		4527	f. 146r	1410	JW ms Boh.

iii. Ed. S. H. Thomson, "Three Unprinted Opuscula of John Wyclif," *Speculum* 3 (1928): 253. From **v** and **vi** only.

IV. Solomon was a good king, Wyclyf urges here and elsewhere,[3] because he did not hesitate to remove the priest Abiathar who opposed him (1 K 2:27). Disendowment was uppermost in Wyclyf's thought from 1377 to 1379; the latter year seems better to suit our text. At a later date Wyclyf did revert to "Christus rex pacificus" – an extension, it seems, from the example of Solomon.[4]

We should now seriously consider the possibility that Wyclyf's commentary in this very short piece – and on this subject in other works as well – may have derived in some fashion from an anonymous *Quaestio de potestate papae*, published in June of 1303 as a rejoinder to the overweening claims of Boniface VIII in *Unam sanctam*: its incipit, indeed, is "Rex pacificus Solomon, cui dedit dominus..."[5] and its tenor is quite in keeping with Wyclyf's own.

VC: deest   Bale: deest   Sh: 69   Lo: 70

[1] Expl. not uniform in all codices: **iii, v, vi** and **ix** all have "servieret ..."; Lo has "serviens."

[2] *Olim* I.V.34 of the Kaiserlich-königliche Studienbibliothek; now perhaps under a different shelfmark in the State Scientific Library there; editor possesses microfilm of whole codex.

[3] Cf. citations from the *De civili dominio* (**28-30**) and the *Dyalogus* (**408**) in the commentary on the ed., p. 252; add to these *De officio regis* (**33**: p. 258). Despite the close affinity in title and subject matter, it does not seem that our piece is either an extract from or an addendum to the larger treatise.

[4] *De vaticinacione sive de prophecia* (**45**: p. 167).

[5] See Walter Ullmann, "A Medieval Document on Papal Theories of Government," *EHR* 61 (1946): 180-201. One of the Paris MSS (BN, f.l. 3184, ff. 72r-79r) happens also to contain some Wyclyfiana. — The authorship of this important *quaestio* has very recently been assigned to John of Paris: Paul Saenger, "John of Paris, Principal Author of the *Quaestio de potestate papae* (*Rex pacificus*)," *Speculum* 56 (1981): 41-55; cf. on John above, **23-25**, n. 13.

407. E3. *De clavibus ecclesie* [*De potestate ligandi et solvendi*].[1] 1379.

I. Inc.: Quodcunque ligaverit vel solverit super terram conformiter ad Christi iudicium ...

Expl.: × ... quia tunc indubie foret papa impeccabilis.

II. MSS:

i	Wien, ÖNB	1337	f. 174va-vb	ca. 1410	JW MS Boh.
ii		1338	f. 30vb	ca. 1410	JW MS Boh.
iii		1387	f. 109ra[2]	ca. 1410	JW MS Boh.

III. Ed. S. H. Thomson, "Three Unprinted Opuscula of John Wyclif," *Speculum* 3 (1928): 251. From **i** and **ii**.

IV. The very construction of the opening sentence of this brief essay – not in fact a direct quote of Mt 16:19 – is conducive to the suspicion that it is, if not an extract (as Shirley believed), then at least wanting a proper introduction. Wyclyf did register a good many observations on the significance of the verse in question;[3] by examining these in roughly chronological sequence we may determine that the probable date of composition falls in 1379 (and not in 1383, as previously surmised). Cap. xxiii of the *De ecclesia* (**32**)[4] deals with indulgences at length, and as sharply as in the present piece, while the mention of "excommunicaciones huiusmodi vel censuras" is vague enough to have almost any conceivable application.

vc: deest   Bale: 178? 179?[5]   Sh: 70   Lo: 71

[1] Alternate title only in i; the designation *De clave celi*, ventured by both Sh and Lo, is in no known codex.
[2] Not 107, as in both Thomson ed. and Sh.
[3] Cf. **28**: pp. 281-285; **32**: pp. 9, 353, 557, 563, 579; **33**: p. 173; **34**: pp. 97-98; **37**: p. 37; **123**: pp. 62-63; **172**: p. 434; **246**: p. 102; **250**: p. 134; **254**: p. 175; **374**: pp. 39-40; **384**: p. 303; **388**: pp. 263-264, 270-271; **411**: pp. 624-625; **412**: p. 666; **414**: p. 131.
[4] See **32**, n. 13, above.
[5] 178 tit.: *De clauibus regni Dei*; 179 tit.: *De clauium potestate*; no incipits.

408. E4. *Dyalogus* [*Speculum ecclesie militantis*]. Late 1379?

I. Inc.: Cum ydempnitas sit mater fastidie ...
   Expl. cap. xxxvi: × ... ut veritati fructuose consenciant in hac parte.
   Inc. epil.: Restat finaliter perstringere totam istam sentenciam cum quodam epilogo ...
   Expl. epil.: × ... ut facilius a populo videantur et veritates eorum ut falsitates facilius cognoscantur.

II. MSS (those definitely known with the *epilogus* are marked with a ♦; those definitely lacking it, with a ◊; other MSS not examined in this particular):

i	Brno, UK	MK II, 44 (62)	ff. 1r-33v	xv/m[1]	Asc. Boh.
ii	Firenze, BLaur	Plut. XIX.33	ff. 38r-57r	1408	JW MS Eng.[2]
iii	BNC	Conv. Sopp. E.3.379	ff. 1r-15v ◊	?	Asc. ?[3]
iv	Manchester, John Rylands Lib.	Eng. 86	ff. 97r-116v, 118r-121r ◊	xv/1	JW MS Eng.[4]
v	München, BSB	clm 15771	ff. 35r-49r	ca. 1435	Asc. So. Ger.[5]
vi	Olomouc, KapK	C.O. 118	ff. 182r-198r ◊	xv/1	Asc. Boh.[6]
vii	Státní vědecka Knihovna	I.V.34	ff. 1r-23v ◊	1411	Asc. Boh.[7]
viii	Oxford, Bodleian	James 3 (S.C. 3840)	pp. 346-352	1636	Asc. Eng.[8]
ix	Praha, MK	B.17.1 (310)	ff. 134r-160v	1414	Asc. Boh.
x		C.38[9] (462)	ff. 159ra-172va	ca. 1410	JW MS Boh.
xi	UK	VIII.F.13 (1567)[10]	ff. 186r-211r ◊	ca. 1470	Asc. Boh.
xii		X.C.23 (1876)[11]	ff. 169ra-182vb ◊	1410	JW MS Boh.
xiii	Vaticano	Borgh.lat. 29	ff. 47v-66v	xv/1	Asc. Fr.[12]

xiv	Wien, ÖNB	1337	ff. 166ra-168va ◊	ca. 1410	JW MS Boh.[13]
xv		1338	ff. 55ra-81ra ♦	ca. 1410	JW MS Boh.
xvi		1387	ff. 109ra-110va ◊	ca. 1410	Asc. Boh.[14]
xvii			ff. 150ra-160vb ♦		
xviii		1622	ff. 133r-157v ◊	1410	Asc. Boh.
	[not in Wien, ÖNB 3929, ff. 107-109, *pace* Sh and Lo]				
xix		3930	ff. 3ra-22vb ◊	1412	JW MS Boh.
xx		*3932*	ff. 72rb-89vb ♦	1418	Asc. Boh.[15]
xxi		4302	ff. 25r-50r ◊	xv/m	Asc. Boh.
xxii		4505	ff. 1r-29v ♦	1439	Asc. Boh.
xxiii		4515[16]	ff. 1r-26v ◊	ca. 1420	Asc. Boh.
xxiv		4536	ff. 33r-67r ◊	xv/1	Asc. Boh.
xxv		*4701*	ff. 41r-57r ◊	ca. 1440	Unasc. Boh.[17]

III. Ed. Alfred W. Pollard, *Iohannis Wycliffe Dialogus sive Speculum Ecclesie Militantis* (WS, 1886).[18] From **iv, xv, xvii, xviii, xix** and **xxi-xxiv** only.

IV. It is a fair inference from the relatively simplistic – even caricatured – delineations of "Veritas" and "Mendacium" throughout this rambling exposition of Wyclyf's tenets on the Papacy, endowment, the friars, the Eucharist and the universities, that it must have preceded by a few seasons his considerably more finished effort in the *Trialogus* (**47**). Pollard's methodical canvas of the dating latitude in his preface (pp. xiii-xxi) led him to 1379; others have followed him in this.[19] No argument may now persuasively be entered against this choice, although I would allow that early 1380 remains arguable, as in several passages his language waxes pungent. There is only one canonical citation (p. 47, line 31), but it is sufficiently obscure to persuade us of his presence at Oxford at the time.[20]

Among the salient features of the *Dyalogus*[21] we may pick out its sustained concern with the real essence of poverty;[22] a startlingly cynical avowal that "canonisaciones istorum [i.e., of some saints] care pro pecunia erant empte" (p. 69); and a fascinating interpretation of the Magna Carta to harmonize with Wyclyf's own radical views on disendowment (p. 90). The epilogue (pp. 86-98) is neither summary nor retrospect, but a motley gathering of afterthoughts on several of the topics surveyed in the main body of the *Dyalogus* – a fact of little consequence in the MS tradition, but nevertheless of value in strengthening our sense that this piece was a kind of left-handed sketch, not on a level at all with the major works of the *Summa theologie*, for example, or with his architectonic Biblical commentaries of the same period.

It would appear that the unusually extensive and variegated MS tradition springs from both the relative brevity and the convenient omnibus compass of the *Dyalogus*.

VC: 3933 3935 4514 7980[23]   Bale: 17   Sh: 62, 63[24]   Lo: 63, 64[25]

---

[1] See **53**, n. 1, above, on the date.

[2] First noted by Mabillon in 1687; Stein, "The Wyclif Manuscript in Florence," 95-96.

[3] This MS was mentioned by Michael Bihl in his review of Richard Scholz, ed., *Marsilius von Padua, Defensor Pacis* (Hannover, 1932-1933) in *Archivum Franciscanum Historicum* 27 (1934): 284. The foliation is unique to that part of the codex; but further indications as to date and provenance are wanting. Editor unable to obtain further particulars.

[4] The basis for Pollard's ed.; it is, however, jumbled in the codex. On the intervening text on f. 117r, see **391**, above.

[5] Remarked in Kühn-Steinhausen, "Wyclif-Handschriften in Deutschland," 627-628. See also her comments on the abridgement of the piece in this MS.

[6] Kindly brought to my attention by the archivist at the Státní Archiv, Opava, where this collection is now (see above, **31**, n. 6, on another JW codex in the same series).

[7] See above, **53**, n. 2, and **406**, n. 2, for this MS. Asc. in Czech in marg., f. 10r; again in the colophon, and finally as part of a long biographical paean at the bottom of f. 24r – all in the hand of the rubricator.

[8] An extract from a BL Royal MS evidently no longer extant; cf. Sh.

[9] Misleadingly given as "CXXXVIII" in Lo.

[10] Listed as 1557 (= VII.F.3) in Lo.

[11] 1846 in Lo.

[12] *Olim* ff. 1r-6v, 13r-24r, 35v-36v; lacks capp. xxxi and xxxii. Cf. Stein, "The Vatican Manuscript...," 95-96.

[13] This is the treatise *De triplici ecclesia* (= Sh 63; Lo 64), published by S. H. Thomson, "Some Latin Works Erroneously Ascribed to Wyclif," 387-391. Although as it stands this piece was not written by Wyclyf, being a product of the Czech reform movement soon after 1408, yet it is for the greater part taken *verbatim* from the opening seven capp. of the *Dyalogus*.

[14] The first ff. are for the *De triplici ecclesia* (tit. here: *De tribus partibus ecclesie*): see the preceding note. Annotated by Peter Payne.

[15] Index, f. 90va-vb.

[16] Misnumbered 4514 (which is a JW MS) in Lo.

[17] Expl.: × "... quam graduati," corresponding to p. 53, line 28 in the ed. — The 1411 Oxford commission interested itself in this work: Wilkins, *Concilia*... III: 345-346 (nos. 141-155).

[18] There exists an almost complete translation of the *Dyalogus* by the Hussite Jakoubek of Stříbro: Milan Svoboda, ed., *Mistra Jakoubka ze Stříbra Překlad Viklefova Dialogu z Rukopisu Knihovny Musea Království Českého* (Praha, 1908): the text runs through p. 84, line 15 of the WS ed.

[19] E.g., Hodgkin, *Six Centuries of an Oxford College*, 27-37.

[20] Cf. **28-30**, n. 28, on his copy of the *Decretum*, from which this citation came.

[21] So spelled in several colophons. It is evident from his prol. to the *Trialogus* (**47**) that Wyclyf either honestly believed that the Greek root was "two" rather than "through"; or he did know the difference and was enjoying a modest *Wortspiel*. Of course his Greek was rudimentary: see **47**, n. 13, above.

[22] A substantial monograph on Wyclyf's attitude to poverty is today a prime *desideratum*. Already in his *Postilla super totam Bibliam* (esp. **345-371**) he displayed a keen interest in the matter; it is thematic throughout many of the *Sermones* and is especially prominent in his many attacks on the friars.

[23] All give 39 capp.; but even with the *epilogus*, Pollard finds only 37. Yet the expl. in the VC is as we have it. (Pollard does explore in his introduction the possibility that at some point around cap. xxx our text may have suffered. A close review of the MSS which he did not collate would perhaps clarify this.)

[24] No. 63 is listed under the title *De triplici ecclesia*. See nn. 13 and 14, above.

[25] See the preceding note.

409. E5. *Speculum secularium dominorum*. 1380 or 1381?

I. Inc.: Cum veritas fidei eo plus rutilat [23 wds.] necessitantur fideles sentenciam quam premittunt enucleare ...

Expl.: × ... et hoc movet fideles ad contra has sectas concorditer invehendum.

II. MSS:

i	Olomouc, KapK	O.C. 118	ff. 198v-202v	xv/1	Asc. Boh.[1]
ii	Praha, MK	D.123 (693)	ff. 183r-193v	xv/1	JW MS Boh.
iii	UK	III.G.11² (536)	ff. 62r-69v	xv/1	JW MS Boh.
iv		V.F.17 (939)[3]	ff. 157r-165v	1412	Asc. Boh.[4]
v	Wien, ÖNB	1338	ff. 20vb-26va	ca. 1410	JW MS Boh.
vi		1387	ff. 123rb-125vb	ca. 1410	JW MS Boh.
vii		4343	ff. 262v-270r[5]	1433	Asc. Boh.
viii		4522	ff. 133r-139v	1423	JW MS Boh.[6]

III. Ed. J. Loserth, *Johannis Wyclif Opera Minora* (WS, 1913): 74-91†. From all MSS except **i** and **ii**.

IV. The dating of this work is beset by more than the usual number of difficulties. Shirley called it "one of [his] latest writings;" Loserth, however (introduction, p. XI), denied this, and avowed (p. XII) that "its subject-matter not infrequently overlaps that" of the *De veritate sacre scripture* (**31**), which we have placed between late 1377 and the end of the following year. Loserth also argued that several passages in this *Speculum* bear directly on the five bulls promulgated in May of 1377 by Gregory XI against Wyclyf's teachings on dominion, and on the aftermath of that commotion. Unfortunately this line of reasoning is vulnerable on several points: there are in fact only two oblique references to papal bulls (pp. 86, 88), neither of which can support an exclusive signification. There are, on the other hand, at least half a dozen pejorative statements on the friars, which cannot possibly predate 1380 – yet none of these unmistakably engages their doctrine of the Eucharist.[7]

Wyclyf's attitude toward canon law is rather severe here: "Videtur autem primo ex papalis legis extollencia et mandati sui exequencia quod extollit se supra dominum Jesum Christum. Nam laborantes in lege sua plus premiat et clerus movetur per eum suos codices plus amplecti, plus studere, legere et auditorio allegare; quod videtur signum evidens quod homines plus amant istas tradiciones hominum quam diligunt legem Dei." (P. 88.) Such sentiments well accord with his remarks on the subject in the *De officio regis* (**33**) from the summer of 1379[8] – but with one important difference: there he still deployed Gratian, the *Decretales* and other canonical texts quite freely;[9] whereas in the *Speculum secularium dominorum* he has come to view the whole body of church law as deserving only of an incidental disparagement.[10] Exemplary poverty, however, is a recurrent theme – but that was likewise true as early as the *De paupertate Christi* (**402**), written in 1378.

There is one ostensibly solid clue in the extended discussion of an issue of papal politics on pp. 89-90: "Cum ergo vendicat ducatum tocius populi sequentis et tantum eclipsat vestigia Jesu Christi, patet quod huius ducis sequela sit in summitate periculi...." What was this unspecified duchy "sold" by an unnamed pope? Loserth asserts *en passant* that this relates to Gregory's running feud with the Florentines – but Florence was a republic. Milan was not yet a duchy (Václav IV bestowed the title in 1395). Flanders, of course – should we imagine the expression to apply somehow to Clement's maneuvers in 1383 – was a county. Naples, if we suspect the connection might be with Urban's designs in the interest of his scandalous nephew Butillo, was a kingdom. In fact there seems to exist no context which really fits this alleged transaction. But we do know of one instance which comes close: Clement's promise to Louis, Duke of Anjou and brother to King Charles v of France, that if by force of arms he could secure the Patrimony for the French claimant (i.e., Clement himself), a large part of it, to be designated the "Kingdom of Adria," would be granted him. This understanding had been reached at Sperlonga in April of 1379, but not until February of 1382 had a sizeable military body foregathered under the duke's banner at Avignon.[11] So this incident, which we would perhaps hope to furnish us with a precise *terminus a quo*, has perforce dissolved into an exasperating historical analogue to Heisenberg's indeterminacy principle: the closer we approach a clear focus on the movement of events, the farther we find ourselves from grasping the time and place of their occurrence! Even the term "hic refuga," so often a telltale fix on Urban in 1383 and 1384, seems intrusive in its isolated appearance on p. 81. Yet the plural "pseudovicarii perversi" and "isti pape" on p. 90 hint strongly at a plague-on-both-houses disenchantment; moreover, nowhere is "Urbanus noster" accorded that intermittent partiality we encounter even in some of the Lutterworth *polemica*. The Blackfriars Synod, the Flanders crusade, and his own failing health, customary harmonics in the writings after mid-1382, are nowhere to be found.

Weighing all of these arguments by extension or omission in the balance, I believe the most defensible date for the composition of the *Speculum secularium dominorum* was sometime in 1380 or early in 1381, before the Eucharistic commotion crowded *dominium* and endowment off the stage for a year or two, and while Wyclyf was yet optimistic that the secular powers in England could intervene disinterestedly in the alleviation of the church's grievous waywardness.[12]

VC: 3933 3935 4514   Bale: 147   Sh: 67[13]   Lo: 68

[1] First noticed in Sedlák, *Studie a Texty* I: p. XVII (interleaved). This collection is now at the Státní Archiv, Opava.
[2] Not 537, as in Lo.
[3] Not 932, as in Lo.
[4] Asc. to "J. Wenczlaw," a transparent camouflage.

⁵ Loserth read ff. 262v-269v.

⁶ Loserth called this (p. xiv) "a very bad transcription." Payne's notes crop up occasionally in the *marginalia*; it was written at Basel.

⁷ P. 77, lines 15, 30; p. 81, line 6; p. 90, line 35; p. 91, line 11; others less direct. The last, "has sectas," is very close to the "four sects" of his last years: cf. **46**, n. 2; **50**, n. 6, above; Section F, below.

⁸ At lines 35-37 of the *Speculum* there is a quotation from Pv 30:15, on the two leeches; this passage recurs in Wyclyf's works. Besides the two references in the *De officio regis* (pp. 270, 281), cf. also **48**: pp. 440, 447; **135**: p. 158; **153**: p. 326; **156**: p. 362; **166**: p. 384.

⁹ Cf. Pollard and Sayle ed., p. 237 (quoted above), and index references, pp. 287-288. Wyclyf still appealed to these sources extensively as late as the *De blasfemia* (**37**), in 1381: see Dziewicki ed., pp. 30, 55, 56, 81, 85, 89, 94, 104, 112, 117, 122, 124, 125, 128, 130-132, 135, 137, 158-160, 175, 180, 195, 225, 226, 232, 234, 237, 239, 249, 253, 255, 260, 261, 272, 279. (Listed here because inadequately indexed by Dziewicki.) There are fewer citations, but still an appreciable number, in the *De eucharistia* (**38**): also 1381.

¹⁰ As with **394**, above. (Cf. **28-30**, n. 28.)

¹¹ This basic chronology, with important bibliographical notes, appears in E. Delaruelle, E.-R. Labande, and P. Durliac, *L'Église au temps du Grand Schisme et de la crise conciliaire* I (Histoire de l'Église depuis ses origines jusqu'à nos jours 14: Tournai, 1962): 3-40. On the "Kingdom of Adria," see especially P. Durrieu, "Le royaume d'Adria. Épisode de la politique française en Italie sous le règne de Charles vi 1393-1394," *Revue des questions historiques* 28 (1880): 43-78. Our most vivid contemporary account of Urban's cruelty and caprice (perhaps it is he who is intended by Wyclyf's "hic papa superbissimus," immediately preceding our quotation on p. 89) is Dietrich of Niem's *De scismate*. For a fine study of this curialist turned conciliarist, see E. F. Jacob, *Essays in the Conciliar Epoch*, 3rd ed. (Notre Dame, 1963): 24-43. (I know of no comparable first-hand report from the pontificate of Clement vii).

On the whole labyrinthine tangle of papal finances in this period, besides the works cited in **397**, n. 3, above, see now J. Favier's massive *Les Finances pontificales à l'époque du Grand Schisme d'Occident, 1378-1409* (Bibliothèque des Écoles Françaises d'Athènes et de Rome, 211: Paris, 1967).

¹² Evidence of the later erosion of his reliance upon secular sturdiness in the face of ecclesiastical mischief is patent in several of the *Sermones*, as well as **421**, below. But at times his trust in the lords temporal burned more brightly.

¹³ Expl.: × "... contra fideles de ecclesia Jesu Christi. Amen." But none of the three mss cited by him (i.e., **v-vii**) matches this. — As to his remarking that it was "written 'tam in lingua latina quam eciam in vulgari'" (ed., p. 74), Wyclyf does not actually say that it was *written* in English, but only that "necessitantur fideles sentenciam quam premittunt *enucleare* tam ..." (emphasis added). In fact no English counterpart is known.

410. E6. *De scismate* [*De dissensione paparum*]. Late 1382.

I. Inc.: Quia ista monstruosa dissensio inter papas videtur significare tempora periculosa ...

Expl.: × ... sibi acquirere per simulata mendacia tamquam fidem.¹

II. MSS:²

i	London, BL	*Royal 7 E.x.*	ff. 74rb-75ra	xiv/2	Unasc. Eng.³
ii	Lambeth Pal.	*121*	ff. 238v-239v	xiv/2	Unasc. Eng.
iii	Oxford, Bodleian	52 (*S.C. 1969*)	ff. 100v-102v	ca. 1400	Asc. Eng.⁴
iv		James 3 (S.C. 3840)	pp. 228-229	ca. 1636	Asc. Eng.⁵

v	Praha, UK	X.E.9 (1910)	ff. 208r-209r	ca. 1420	JW ms Boh.
vi	Wien, ÖNB	1337[6]	ff. 67ra-68ra	ca. 1410	JW ms Boh.
vii		3929	ff. 217va-218ra	1409	JW ms Boh.
viii		4527	ff. 66r-67r	1410	Asc. Boh.

III. Ed. R. Buddensieg, *John Wiclif's Polemical Works in Latin* II (WS, 1883): 567-576. From **v-viii** only.

IV. Shirley believed this piece to be a letter sent to Bishop Despenser of Norwich regarding the impending crusade in Flanders;[7] but Buddensieg has demonstrated that, despite just such an indication in the explicits of **v** and **viii**, it is highly improbable that the *De scismate* was ever a letter at all. (We might add too that there is no evidence whatever that Wyclyf ever knew or communicated with Bishop Despenser.) Two more of Buddensieg's observations are worth reiterating: that the piece as we have it is virtually certain to be wanting a conclusion, a premise strengthened by the scribal note at the end of **vii**: "Non est hic finis quia deberent esse octo capitula";[8] and that it bears a close topical affinity to the *De cruciata*, our next item. As to its content, we may briefly note that Wyclyf asserts the Schism and all its doleful consequences to be directly traceable to the "cupiditatem mundani honoris et temporalium adiacencium papatui" – yet he still retains a faint partiality for "Urbanus noster" (p. 574), and the proximate blame for "hoc facinus" (i.e., the crusade) must be laid at the friars' feet, and at those of the "pseudocardinales et nostrates stantes in curia."[9] From its immediate association with the following piece and therefore with **248**, above, it must date from the early fall of 1382.

vc: 3933 3935 4514   Bale: 76[10]   Sh: 74   Lo: 75

[1] All three vc say 8 capp.; all mss have 7. The vc do supply another expl.: × "... est in clericis iam perversis." But see this expl. in Sec. G, Introduction, below.

[2] Our piece was at one time apparently in Syon Monastery O 36, ff. 11-22 (?): Bateson, *Catalogue of the Library of Syon Monastery*, 144. Now lost.

[3] See Thomson, "Unnoticed mss and Works of Wyclif," 31. Almost surely this is the ms cited as lost by Sh in his comments on **iv**.

[4] See Thomson, "Unnoticed mss and Works of Wyclif," 35-36. This ms was once owned by Merton College, the only Wyclyf text known today which is traceable to that library. (F. M. Powicke, *The Medieval Books of Merton College* [Oxford, 1931]: 35, 208).

[5] Three lines added *in finem*: "Et sic diabolus ... omnia regna mundi."

[6] Not 1437, as in Buddensieg's introduction, p. 569.

[7] See **48**, n. 4, above, *et frequenter alibi*.

[8] See n. 1, above; also Arnold's introduction to the considerably longer English version, *De pontificum romanorum schismate: Select English Works* III: 242; and cf. Severs, *Manual of Writings in Middle English* II: 366, 527.

[9] Most recently, the fine monograph by R. N. Swanson, *Universities, Academics and the Great Schism* (Cambridge, Eng., 1979): 52-53, has drawn attention to several implications in Wyclyf's attitude toward the Papacy during the Schism.

[10] Tit.: *De papa Romano*; inc.: "Pro eo quod haec insolita dissensio...."

411. E7. *De cruciata* [*Contra bella clericorum*]. Late 1382.

I. Inc.: Cum secundum fidem catholicam Rom. 8° [12 wds.] necesse est illos eventus ad bonum ecclesie provenire ...

Expl.: × ... ut dicit Apostolus Rom. 13, et gladium spiritualem sacerdotibus deputandum.

II. MSS:

i	*Praha, MK*	*D.50 (616)*	ff. 268r-279v	ca. 1430	Unasc. Boh.
ii	UK	V.F.9 (931)	ff. 54r-68r	1408	JW MS Boh.
iii	Wien, ÖNB	1337	ff. 57vb-67ra	ca. 1410	JW MS Boh.
iv		3929	ff. 233rb-239vb	1408	JW MS Boh.
v		3930	ff. 239vb-250va	1412	JW MS Boh.
vi		3933	ff. 63ra-70ra	ca. 1415	Asc. Boh.
vii		4527	ff. 134r-144r	1410	JW MS Boh.
viii		4536	ff. 237v-253r	xv/1	Asc. Boh.

III. Ed. R. Buddensieg, *John Wiclif's Polemical Works in Latin* II (WS, 1883): 588-632. From all MSS except **i** and **ii**.

IV. Buddensieg has in his usual style prepared a thorough summary of the contents of this diatribe, besides achieving his normal high level of editorial exactitude. We have elsewhere[1] already remarked Wyclyf's stridency against the ill-fated crusade of Bishop Despenser of Norwich in 1382-1383; the present piece is indeed the most sustained literary sortie in that campaign. We have to wonder how he could have expected his isolated vehemence on this subject – or on any other! – to have any measurable impact outside his own very restricted and suspect milieu. We are forced to allow room for the possibility that he reckoned, especially after his stroke late in 1382, on justification primarily *sub specie aeternitatis*. There exists in any case no tangible evidence that his plethora of *ad hoc* and *ad hominem* barrages at this late juncture circulated or was even known beyond his circle. It is to the uncritical fidelity and awesome industriousness of his Hussite admirers that we owe the preservation of almost every one of his *polemica*.

Cap. ix is an intriguing variation on his *De confessione* (**44**) of the year before. Here he maintains that the pope and many others trifle with this sacrament: "in locis subterraneis vel angulis absconditis seducunt homines, quos cum signis adulterinis frequenter sophistice assecurant." (P. 625.) Wyclyf employed this piece, finally, as a springboard into his *De Christo et suo adversario Antichristo*, our next item.

VC: 3933 3935 4514 7980   Bale: 190   Sh: 75   Lo: 76

---

[1] See above, **48**, n. 4, and **410**.

412. E8. *De Christo et suo adversario Antichristo.* Late 1382.

I. Inc.: Secundum catholicos ecclesia est predestinatorum universitas ...
Expl.: × ... posset licite a Christi vestigiis deviare.

II. MSS:

i	*Firenze, BLaur*	*Plut. XIX.33*	ff. 11r-18v	1408	JW MS Eng.[1]
ii	Praha, UK	III.G.16 (541)	ff. 36r-39r	1414	Asc. Boh.[2]
iii		V.F.9 (931)	ff. 41v-54r	1408	JW MS Boh.
iv		X.C.23 (1876)	ff. 203ra-206va	1410	JW MS Boh.[3]
v	Wien, ÖNB	1337	ff. 125ra-134vb	ca. 1410	JW MS Boh.
vi		3929	ff. 239vb-246ra	1409	JW MS Boh.[4]
vii		3930	ff. 230vb-239vb	1412	JW MS Boh.
viii		3933	ff. 70ra-76vb	ca. 1415	Asc. Boh.
ix		4527	ff. 124v-133v	1410	JW MS Boh.

III. Ed. R. Buddensieg, *Johann Wiclif's De Christo et adversario suo Antichristo* (Gotha, 1880);[5] idem, *John Wiclif's Polemical Works in Latin* II (WS, 1883): 653-692. From all MSS except **i**, **iii** and **iv**.

IV. This intense assault on the legitimacy of most papal claims might usefully be viewed as a kind of *De potestate pape* (**34**) revisited. In exile, ill, locked in mortal combat with the mendicants, galled by Despenser's bungling crusade, Wyclyf felt the need late in 1382 to restate in much sharper terms his deep reservations toward even the office of the Papacy itself. The piece also served as a generalized expansion of several arguments in the *De cruciata* of a few weeks previous.[6] It is a source of wonderment that even under these stern imperatives he was unable to see through the transparent anomalies of the Donation of Constantine in impugning Pope Sylvester's motives: "Supponi tamen potest, quod sanctus Silvester de isto crimine postmodum penitebat." (WS ed., p. 670.) That this Carolingian fantasy should finally have been demolished by a Roman rhetorician who was considerably less thoroughgoing in his antipapalism than Wyclyf, less than sixty years after the reformer's demise, only underscores a few of the oddities of intellectual history.[7]

VC: 3933 3935 7980   Bale: deest   Sh: 76   Lo: 77

[1] First noticed by Mabillon: Stein, "The Wyclif Manuscript in Florence," 95.

[2] Capp. xi-xv only.

[3] Expl.: × "... vel scriptura. Similiter ut fides...." Truhlař found this in cap. x; indeed it is at p. 378, line 10 of the WS ed.

[4] Buddensieg shows very clearly (pp. 642-643 in his WS introduction) how **vi** was at the elbow of the scribe of **v**.

[5] Commentaries on MSS are more general than in his later ed.; there he also acknowledges (p. 649) two useful reviews of the Gotha edition.

[6] **411**, just above. The immediate physical association of the two texts in **iii** and **v-ix** indicates that the scribes themselves perceived the continuity.

[7] Cf. now Wolfram Setz, *Lorenzo Vallas Schrift gegen die Konstantinische Schenkung* (Tübingen, 1975); idem, *Lorenzo Valla De Falso Credita et Ementita Constantini Donatione* (Weimar, 1976). Of

course this is not the only examination of the Donation in the Wyclyf corpus, but it is the closest. — An anonymous Italian, we now know, anticipated Valla by several decades in a *Liber dialogorum hierarchie subcelestis* (1388: 6 MSS extant today); ed. by Daniele Menozzi, "La critica alla autenticità della Donazione di Costantino in un manoscritto della fine del XIV secolo," *Cristianesimo nella Storia* 1 (1980): 123-154.

413. E9. *De citacionibus frivolis et aliis versuciis Antichristi.*[1] Late 1383?

I. Inc.: Si papa vel eius vicario citante virum legium regis, ut compareat [14 wds.] num predictus legius teneatur ...

Expl.: × ... et erroribus universis secura sibi serviat libertate.

II. MSS:

i	Firenze, BLaur	*Plut. XIX.33*	ff. 26v-29v	1408	JW MS Eng.[2]
ii	Manchester, John Rylands Lib.	Eng. 86	ff. 65r-68v	xv/1	JW MS Eng.[3]
iii	Oxford, Bodleian	James 3 (S.C. 3840)	p. 354	ca. 1636	Asc. Eng.[4]
iv	Praha, MK	D.123 (693)	ff. 136v-144v[5]	xv/1	JW MS Boh.
v	Národný Mus.	I.E.6 (*134*)	ff. 101r-104r	ca. 1420	Misasc. Boh.[6]
vi	UK	V.F.9 (931)	ff. 13r-18v	1408	JW MS Boh.
vii		X.E.9 (1910)	ff. 151v-156v	ca. 1420	JW MS Boh.
viii	Wien, ÖNB	1337	ff. 53vb-57vb	ca. 1410	JW MS Boh.
ix		3929	ff. 212ra-214vb	1409	JW MS Boh.
x		4527	ff. 79r-83v	1410	Asc. Boh.

III. Ed. R. Buddensieg, *John Wiclif's Polemical Works in Latin* II (WS, 1883): 546-564; partly in F. D. Matthew, *The English Works of Wyclif Hitherto Unprinted* (London, 1880): 485-487. WS edition from all MSS except **i** and **iii-vi**.

IV. The contents of this piece are adequately delineated in Buddensieg's customarily careful preface, pp. 539-541. (The two autobiographical indicia are also reviewed therein, pp. 541-542.) We read in cap. iv (p. 556): "Et sic dicit quidam debilis et claudus citatus ad hanc curiam [i.e., Romanam, per Urbanam papam]." From the reference to his paralysis and the papal citation we may with Buddensieg and Dahmus[7] agree on late 1383 or possibly early 1384 for the *De citacionibus*. It is interesting that at this twilight exilic hour Wyclyf still clings to the conviction that he is safe under the aegis of the king's law.[8]

VC: 3933 3935 4514   Bale: 219?[9]   Sh: 73   Lo: 73

[1] The concluding phrase is common in his later works; cf. **420**, below.
[2] First remarked by Mabillon: Stein, "The Wyclif Manuscript in Florence," 95.
[3] Begins on an inserted fragment between ff. 64v and 65r; titled simply "questio." The text begins again on f. 89v, and ends at p. 547, line 17 of our edition.
[4] Noted as "extracts from MS. now lost" in Sh; not in Lo.
[5] Podlaha erroneously ends this piece on f. 149v; see **401**, n. 1, above.
[6] Asc. "per Viklefistas heriticos editus." Correctly asc. in Bartoš, *Soupis Rukopisů Národního Musea v Praze* I.

[7] *The Prosecution of John Wyclyf*, 139-141.
[8] Cf. **409**, n. 11, above. The committee of 1411 censured four articles from the *De citacionibus*: Wilkins, *Concilia...* III: 349 (nos. 264-267).
[9] Tit.: *De bullis papalibus*; no inc.

414. E10. *De ordine Christiano*. Early 1384?

I. Inc.: Ad declarandum veritatem fidei et cum hoc errorem perfidie Christi ecclesiam perturbantem moventur quidam fideles videre ...
   Expl.: × ... quoad talem operam dimittenda et via melior est libere acceptanda.

II. MSS:

i	Karlsruhe, BLB	343	ff. 5r-8v	xv/1	JW MS Boh.[1]
ii	Manchester, John Rylands Lib.	Eng. 86	ff. 21v-24v	xv/1	JW MS Eng.
iii	Praha, MK	B.6.3 (293)	ff. 255r-261v	1421	Asc. Boh.
iv		D.123 (693)	ff. 63r-72v	xv/1	JW MS Boh.
v		O.29 (1613)	ff. 184r-187v	ca. 1430	Unasc. Boh.[2]
vi	UK	X.E.9 (1910)	ff. 146v-150r	xv/1	JW MS Boh.
vii	Vaticano	Borgh.lat. 29	ff. 4r-7r	xv/1	Asc. Fr.[3]
viii	Wien, ÖNB	1337	ff. 43va-47ra	ca. 1410	JW MS Boh.
ix		3927	ff. 3va-5vb	ca. 1410	JW MS Boh.
x		4527	ff. 120v-124r	1410	JW MS Boh.

III. Ed. J. Loserth, *Johannis Wyclif Opera Minora* (WS, 1913): 129-139†. From ii, vi, and viii-x only.

IV. This short piece weighs in the balance those well-worn arguments in favor of Petrine supremacy in the first flush of the Apostolic era (and by implication, therefore, of papal succession), and finds them of little worth. By now Wyclyf is indissolubly wedded to the notion of witholding obedience: "nemo obediret novis tradicionibus pape vel privati prelati que in lege Domini non fundantur ..." (p. 138). As to the date, Loserth ignored the two references to the "refuga" on p. 137; but we have already shown[4] that this phrase unerringly points to Urban's removal to Naples, and so our date must be very late in 1383 or early the following year. In tone and temper it is certainly compatible with the two works immediately preceding it in this Section.

VC: 3933 3935 4514 7980   Bale: 224   Sh: 77   Lo: 78

[1] First noticed in Kühn-Steinhausen, "Wyclif-Handschriften in Deutschland," 628. Tit. *De papa*; gives (incomplete) the *De eucharistia et penitencia* (**44**) as cap. vi. The hand is occasionally illegible.
[2] See Thomson, "Unnoticed MSS and Works of Wyclif," 36.
[3] Foliation given as 64r-67r in Stein, "The Vatican Manuscript...," 96.
[4] See **405**, n. 3, above.
[5] The Oxford commission of 1411 singled out some 13 objectionable expressions in this work (Wilkins, *Concilia...* III: 344; nos. 108-120); as usual the quotations are less than exact and always out of context.

Section F

Polemica contra Papatum II
On the "Four Sects" and the *Secta Christi*

When Wyclyf was not editing and arranging the *Sermones* (**54-299**), or grinding out the *Trialogus* (**47**), or with failing strength fashioning the *Opus evangelicum* (**374-377**), or attending as best he could to the daily needs of his modest parish at Lutterworth, he was ensnared in an interminable succession of rear-guard strikes against the Schism, the older orders and the mendicants. Some of these we have already assimilated; the rest lie ahead, the twenty-one pieces in this concluding arsenal of works surely from his pen.

But we slight the man in thus categorizing the majority of his final productions as a species of carping *feuilletonisme*. For there was a weighty counterbalance in the ongoing critique: the ideal of the *secta Christi*, embodied in the small bands of *sacerdotes simplices* (or: *pauperes*) who looked to him for at least the impression of guidance and justification. Of them we know concretely in truth even less than of Wyclyf himself. "Lollards," of course, was a scoffer's epithet; and to call them all "Lollards" is unquestionably an oversimplification. Time telescoped, from now to then, has compressed complexities and flattened individuation. It is most unlikely that John Wyclyf – never before celebrated for his organizing genius; a marginal diplomat; and a sick old don in semi-retirement – could have welded together under a single standard a whole regiment of dissident enthusiasts for any length of time at all. (But there were not so many of them, after all, and most fell away soon enough, after a season or two of sobering adversity.)

And so the *secta Christi* must have been, inescapably, another commanding abstraction, like his *status innocencie* or his *papa humilis et pauperrimus*. It was a socio-literary device, probably original with him, which in different hands or in a different setting might have culminated in the kindling of yet another fervent, shining institute – or in a mindless, rabid nihilism. As it was, this holy vision did at least dignify his indignation; and, at an unforeseeable but not too distant remove, it did stir the souls of brilliant Czech schoolmen. In the ashes of the greatest of them a nation was reborn even before Wyclyf's own remains were scattered upon the river Swift.

415. F1. *De nova prevaricancia mandatorum.* 1375? and late 1383.

I. Inc.: Cum secundum veritatis testimonium Matt. 19 ad ingressum in patriam sufficit et requiritur servancia mandatorum ...

Expl.: × ... dyabolus a bonis homines spoliantes.

II. MSS:

i	Firenze, BLaur	*Plut. XIX.33*	ff. 30r-38r	1408	JW MS Eng.[1]
ii	Karlsruhe, BLB	*343*	f. 1r	xv/1	Asc. Boh.[2]
iii	Manchester, John Rylands Lib.	Eng. 86[3]	ff. 90r-96v	xv/1	JW MS Eng.

iv	Praha, MK	B.6.3 (293)	ff. 242v-248v	1421	Asc. Boh.
v	Wien, ÖNB	1337	ff. 23va-24ra	ca. 1410	JW MS Boh.[4]
vi			ff. 117va-125ra		
vii		1387	ff. 108va-109ra	ca. 1410	JW MS Boh.[5]
viii		3929	ff. 187ra-192ra	1409	JW MS Boh.
ix		3930	ff. 264vb-271vb	1412	JW MS Boh.
x		3933	ff. 88vb-92ra	ca. 1415	JW MS Boh.
xi		4515	ff. 75r-83r	ca. 1420	JW MS Boh.
xii		4527	ff. 171r-178r	1410	JW MS Boh.
xiii		4536	ff. 122r-132v	xv/1	Asc. Boh.
xiv	Wolfenbüttel, HzglB	Cod.Guelf. 306 (340)	ff. 259ra-268rb	xv/1	Asc. Pol.[6]

III. Ed. R. Buddensieg, *John Wiclif's Polemical Works in Latin* I (WS, 1883): 116-150. From all MSS except **i, ii, iv, v** and **xiv**.

IV. Wyclyf examined the Decalogue in at least two other writings: the *De mandatis divinis* (**26**) and in the first volume of the *Sermones* (**67-75**). Capp. i-iii of the present treatise are reminiscent in tone (though not in phrasing) of the former (and of the immediately subsequent *De statu innocencie* [**27**] as well), and of minimal political content: they were perhaps part of the early drafting process for the *Summa theologie*, and date from 1375 or even 1374. But capp. iv-viii differ so dramatically in tenor and coloration that their composition and attachment to the first three capp. must date from late in 1383: "hic refuga" appears on p. 128, and that signifies Urban VI, as we have shown;[7] the crusade appears elliptically on the same page and again on p. 130. All four of the "sects" — secular clergy, canons, monks and mendicants — are systematically upbraided for their chronic violation of the commandments, in epithet and innuendo considerably surpassing the *sermones* mentioned above.

Cap. viii has experienced a separate MS tradition as the *De purgatorio*; see the germane notes below.

VC: 3933 3935 4514 7980[8]   Bale: 124?[9]   Sh: 31, 79[10]   Lo: 32, 80[11]

---

[1] See Stein, "The Wyclif Manuscript in Florence," 95.

[2] A fragment of cap. viii, inc.: "Hoc autem videtur ..." (= p. 148, line 16), *usque ad finem*. The asc. in a later hand: "Fragm. Johannis Wiclif," at the top of the page; and the colophon reads: "Explicit Tractatus de Prevaricacione decem mandatorum magistri Johannis Wykleff doctoris," in a contemporary hand.

[3] The old designation of Ashburnham xxvii is given in Lo as xxviii.

[4] This first is the *De purgatorio*.

[5] The *De purgatorio* only.

[6] Noticed in Kühn-Steinhausen, "Wyclif-Handschriften in Deutschland," 626.

[7] **405**, n. 3.

[8] All give 8 capp., with our expl.; none give the *De purgatorio* separately.

[9] Tit.: *De purgatorio piorum*; inc.: "Dona eis Domine requiem sempiter ...."

[10] The first is the *De purgatorio*; the second, the *De nova prevaricancia*.
[11] See the preceding note.

416. F2. *Epistola missa ad simplices sacerdotes*. Mid-1370s.

I. Inc.: Videtur meritorium bonos colligere sacerdotes ...
Expl.: × ... meritum caritative taliter operando.

II. MSS:[1]

i	Basel, Universitäts- und Öffent- liche Bibliothek	A.X.66	ff. 304r-305r	——[2]	
ii	Olomouc, Státní vědecká Knihovna	I.V.34	f. 176r	1411	Unasc. Boh.[3]
iii	Praha, MK	D.50 (616)	f. 23r	ca. 1430	Unasc. Boh.
iv		D.123 (693)[4]	f. 150v	xv/1	JW MS Boh.
v		N.48 (1572)	f. 175r	1422	Unasc. Boh.[5]
vi	UK	X.C.23 (1876)	f. 195va	1410	JW MS Boh.[6]
vii		X.H.17 (1995)[7]	f. 134v	ca. 1410	Asc. Boh.
viii	Wien, ÖNB	1337	f. 52va-vb	ca. 1410	JW MS Boh.
ix		1387	f. 105vb	ca. 1410	JW MS Boh.
x		3929	f. 207va-vb	1409	JW MS Boh.
xi		4515	f. 83r-v	ca. 1420	JW MS Boh.
xii		4527	ff. 145v-146r	1410	JW MS Boh.

III. Ed. *FZ*, p. xli n., from **viii** only; G. Lechler, *Johann von Wiclif und die Vorgeschichte der Reformation* II (Leipzig, 1873): 590-591, from **ix** and **x** only; J. Loserth, *Johannis Wyclif Opera Minora* (WS, 1913): 7-8†, from **vi-xii** only.

IV. Loserth's judgment as to the identity of this piece (introduction, p. v) is valid, as far as it goes: it is not, in fact, a letter to the poor priests at all, nor is it a fragment of a sermon. I would venture to say that it was most probably a memorandum to himself, an outline of something he intended later to amplify; or it may have been a transcription by some amanuensis – though there is no third-person indication that would point clearly to that characterization. In the form in which we have it, it is a convenient summary of what Wyclyf believed the ideal priest should be: removable – we would say "subject to recall"; sufficient to and solicitous of the needs of his flock; neither a frequenter of taverns nor avid in the chase, in games of chance, or even chess; and above all a preacher of the Gospel, as were the apostles: "qui autem non predicat publice, hortatur private ..." – a concluding observation calculated to inspire an active effort to bring about just this kind of priesthood, though it stops short of urging secular intervention, as he often did in other writings. Because of its brevity, it does not easily lend itself to dating; we are reduced to the kind of *argumentum ex silentio* which the scrupulous Buddensieg shunned. The friars are not mentioned, nor is the Eucharist or the Flanders crusade – and not even, save by implication, the Papacy. The tone is almost devotional. We are thus left with the strong likelihood that it belongs to a very early phase of his political (i.e., post-philosophical) involvement, perhaps at the very outset of his concern with the poor priests. This would take us back to 1374 or conceivably even 1373. Or, on the other hand, we may choose to treat it as a kind of sketch for the *De officio pastorali* (**53**), which we have placed around 1379. Even these two vague parameters do not, unfortunately, exclude a later composition *ad hoc*.

vc: 3933 3935 4514   Bale: 180   Sh: 61.4   Lo: 62.4

[1] There exists a late fourteenth-century English version of this piece, also titled *Epistola ad simplices sacerdotes*, and inc.: "Hit semes medeful to susteyne prestis togedre ..."; expl.: × "... what mon so euer he be," in London, BL Royal 17 B.XVII, unasc. Overlooked in Severs, *Manual of the Writings in Middle English* II; not the same as his no. 87 (pp. 375, 531).
[2] Other particulars not apparent from *Die Handschriften der Oeffentlichen Bibliothek der Universität Basel* I/1: *Die deutschen Handschriften* (Basel, 1907). (Not examined by the editor.)
[3] See Buddensieg, *John Wiclif's Polemical Works in Latin* I: LVII.
[4] Lo has D.693.
[5] Wrong expl. in Podlaha.
[6] After our expl., "Verba sunt anglica"; a reference to the English version?
[7] Lo has 1846; X.B.17 in his introduction, p. v.

417. F3. *Quattuor imprecaciones* [*De quattuor imprecacionibus*]. Late 1379?

I. Inc.: Quod clericus regni Anglie secundum ordinacionem quam Christus
   clero suo instituit reguletur ...
   Expl.: × ... Patet [huius] racionabilitas ex fide scripture.

II. MSS:

i	Olomouc, Státní vě-decká Knihovna	I.V.34	f. 176r	1411	Unasc. Boh.[1]
ii	Praha, MK	*O.29 (1613)*	f. 228r-v	ca. 1430	Unasc. Boh.
iii	UK	*V.F.9 (931)*	f. 97v	1408	Asc. Boh.
iv		X.C.23 (1876)	f. 195va	1410	JW MS Boh.[2]
v		X.H.17 (1995)	f. 92r	ca. 1410	Unasc. Boh.
vi	Wien, ÖNB	1337	f. 96vb	ca. 1410	JW MS Boh.
vii		1338	f. 30va-vb	ca. 1410	JW MS Boh.
viii		1387[3]	f. 107rb	ca. 1410	JW MS Boh.
ix		*1622*	f. 179v	1410	JW MS Boh.
x		3927	f. 24rb-va	ca. 1410	JW MS Boh.
xi		*3929*[4]	f. 207vb	1409	JW MS Boh.
xii		4515	f. 83v	ca. 1420	JW MS Boh.
xiii		4527[5]	f. 146r	1410	JW MS Boh.

III. Ed. R. Buddensieg, *John Wiclif's Polemical Works in Latin* II (WS, 1883): 713-714. From all MSS except **ii-v**, **ix** and **xi**.

IV. This terse, almost telegraphic series of four statements looks like nothing so much as heads of articles for disputation *in scholis*. Each of the four propositions begins "Quod ..." (or "item quod ..." in some MSS); three relate to the clergy in general, and the fourth to the friars in particular. Wyclyf's preeminent concern is with the manifest contradictions between clerical *dominium* and the *lex Christi*. These matters were much with him from 1376 through 1380; but from the inclusion of the mendicants under the lash of his disapprobation we may confidently assign these *imprecaciones* to late 1379 or early 1380.

vc: 3933 3935 4514[6]   Bale: deest   Sh: 93   Lo: 94

[1] First remarked in Buddensieg's edition, p. LVII. Not in Lo.
[2] Inc.: "Quia ...."
[3] Collated by Buddensieg; overlooked by Lo.
[4] Overlooked by both Buddensieg and Lo.
[5] Cf. n. 3, above.
[6] None give title.

418. F4. *De duobus generibus hereticorum*. Early 1380.

I. Inc.: Duo sunt genera hereticorum de quibus foret Anglia expurganda ...
Expl.: × ... quod finaliter oportet ut deo observiat paciendo.

II. MS:
i   Wien, ÖNB   1337   f. 181va-vb   ca. 1410 JW MS Boh.

III. Ed. R. Buddensieg, *John Wiclif's Polemical Works in Latin* II (WS, 1883): 431-432. From unique MS.

IV. On p. 430, Buddensieg remarks that this short piece is "probably an extract [Sh says the same] from one of W.'s sermons ...; it is, perhaps, a part of the *Opus Ewangel*. (De Sermone Domini in Monte) IV. part, *De Anticristo*, and seems to be taken from the 14th chapter ...." In fact there is no connection, and of course the *Opus evangelicum* (**374-377**) was not a collection of sermons.

The assignment of the *De duobus generibus hereticorum* we may modify somewhat. From its dual emphasis on simony and apostasy – as those terms were idiosyncratically conceived by Wyclyf – and with no discernible stress on the friars, we may place it sometime early in 1380. During that year, as we have seen, he completed also the tenth and eleventh libri of the *Summa theologie*: *De symonia* (**35**) and *De apostasia* (**36**).[1]

vc: 3933 3935 4514 7980[2]   Bale: deest   Sh: 96   Lo: 97

[1] English "translation" in Arnold, *Select English Works* III: 211-218 (actually a substantial expansion of our text); cf. Severs, *Manual of Writings in Middle English* II: 365, 526.
[2] Given in all vc without title.

419. F5. *De mendaciis fratrum*. Late 1381.

I. Inc.: Pseudofratres publicant [or: replicant] quod non licet sacerdotibus predicare ...
Expl.: × ... Ecce ergo Hieronymus et Gregorii omelia VI in fine.

II. MSS:

i	Praha, UK	X.C.23 (1876)	——[1]	1410	JW MS Boh.
ii	Wien, ÖNB	1338	f. 30rb	ca. 1410	JW MS Boh.[2]
iii		1387	f. 107ra	ca. 1410	JW MS Boh.
iv		3929	f. 208va	1409	JW MS Boh.
v		4527	f. 146v	1410	JW MS Boh.

III. Ed. R. Buddensieg, *John Wiclif's Polemical Works in Latin* II (WS, 1883): 405-406. From all MSS except i.

IV. The friars claim that priests may not preach among the people without special license from bishop or pope.[3] Wyclyf avers they lie in this matter, as in a multitude of others: none of the apostles, and particularly not Paul, required such license from Peter. The "father of lies," Satan, "qui est specialis patronus omnium talium pseudofratrum," lurks behind all their nefarious deceptions. Shirley and Buddensieg both thought this piece to be an extract. Perhaps so: but in this instance we confront no fewer than four Scriptural, three canonistic and one patristic reference *in textu*, and this particular configuration simply is not matched anywhere else in his known writings. His concentrated use of the *Decretum* urges a date just prior to his departure from Oxford late in 1381.

VC: 3933 3935 4514 7980[4]   Bale: deest   Sh: 88   Lo: 89

[1] Editor unable to locate; not in Truhlař.

[2] Collated in Buddensieg ed.; not in Lo.

[3] If we may presume the veracity of Wyclyf's charge, this represents a strange role reversal: from the outset (i.e., from the time of Innocent III) it had traditionally been the *friars'* right to preach that had been challenged. Canon x of III Lateran had stated: "... generali constitutione sancimus, ut episcopi viros idoneos ad sancte predicationis officium salubriter exequendum assumant ..."; a petition by several French prelates of Nicholas IV (himself a Franciscan) at the end of the century ventured to suggest "non quod fratres non predicent, quia multum placet eis [i.e., prelatis] quod predicent, sed petunt quod ipsi non predicent nisi de ipsorum licencia et assensu...." (A. G. Little, "Measures Taken by the Prelates of France against the Friars (c. A.D. 1289-1290)," in *Miscellanea Francesco Ehrle. Scritti di Storia e Paleografia* III: *Per la Storia ecclesiastica e civile dell'Età di Mezzo* [Studi e Testi 39: Vaticano, 1924]: 54.)

[4] All tit.: *De mendacio fratrum*; our tit. in ii and iii.

420. F6. *De versuciis Antichristi.* Late 1381 or early 1382.

I. Inc.: Quamvis dyabolus ex naturali ingenio multis cautelis superat viatores ...
   Expl.: × ... et sic desiderat solum beatitudinem cum mediis ad eandem.

II. MSS:

i	Vaticano	Borgh.lat. 29	ff. 68r-71r[1]	xv/1	Asc. Fr.

III. Ed. I. H. Stein, "The Vatican Manuscript Borghese 29 and the Tractate 'De Versuciis Anti-Christi,'" *EHR* 47 (1932): 98-103. From unique MS.

IV. The discovery of this ascribed text in a Vatican MS has confirmed the accuracy of the three early VC, all of which give the correct incipit and explicit. It is not, on the whole, a noteworthy addition to our *repertorium Wyclyfianum*: he is merely taking yet another polemical swipe at the "four sects," and dwelling one more time on the injustices of clerical dominion and the diabolical obfuscations of the friars *vis-à-vis* the Eucharist. Two authorities whom he cites, however, puzzle a bit: the first is Bernard de Gordon (fl. 1283-1308), the Montpellier doctor whose *Lilium medicinae sive de morborum prope omnium curatione* (1303) he evidently knew in some form (pp. 101-102);[2] the other is Galen himself (p. 102), who very rarely appears elsewhere in the Wyclyf canon.[3]

From the allusions to endowed colleges (p. 101), I would fix this short treatise sometime between the fall of 1381, when he left Oxford, and the middle of the following year, when he first heard of the proceedings against him at Blackfriars, of which we would have expected him to make some mention were this piece written subsequently.

VC: 3933 3935 4514   Bale: deest   Sh: deest   Lo: deest

[1] *Olim* ff. 8r-11r, as in Stein.

[2] On Bernard, see the commentary and thorough bibliography in Sarton, *Introduction to the History of Science* III/1 (1947): 873-876; Thorndike and Kibre, *Catalogue of Incipits*, cols. 772, 1811-1812; and, most definitively, Luke Demaitre, *Doctor Bernard de Gordon: Professor and Practitioner*, Studies and Texts 51 (Toronto, 1980).

[3] For Galen (whose only other citation by Wyclyf seems to have been in the early *De actibus anime* [4: p. 85]), see, as above, Sarton I (1927): 301-307; Thorndike and Kibre, cols. 1798-1802 (the index references); F. Kudlien and L. Wilson, "Galen," in DSB 5 (1972): 227-237.

There are at least two specific intermediary sources from which Wyclyf might have culled his knowledge of these two medical luminaries: the first – much the less likely – was the *Breviarium Bartholomei* of John of Mirfeld, which Sarton III/2 (1948): 1704-1706 believed to have been "written between 1380 and 1395" (cf. Thorndike and Kibre: col. 711); the second was John of Gaddesden (a Mertonian; d. 1361), whose *Rosa medicinae* (= *Rosa anglica*) was much read at Oxford; he was the first English court physician, and served Edward II. (Cf. Sarton III/1: 880-882; Thorndike and Kibre, cols. 552, 577; *BRUO* II: 739.) — Of course it is also possible that some other compendium may have been handy: see Loren C. MacKinney, "Medieval Medical Dictionaries and Glossaries," in J. L. Cate and E. N. Anderson, edd., *Medieval and Historiographical Essays in Honor of James Westfall Thompson* (Chicago, 1938): 244-268.

421. F7. *De deteccione perfidiarum Antichristi.* Late 1382.

I. Inc.: Paulus docet ad Ephesianos 4 quomodo Christi ecclesiam debet diligere ...

Expl.: × ... et de ipsa hostia questio est ventilata.

II. MSS:

i	Praha, MK	D.123 (693)	ff. 82v-84v	xv/1	JW MS Boh.
ii	UK	III.G.11 (536)	ff. 55v-56v	xv/1	JW MS Boh.

[not in IV.H.7 (771), *pace* Lo]

iii		V.F.9 (931)	f. 98r-v	1408	Asc. Boh.
	[unable to locate in X.H.23 (1991), *pace* Lo: contains few JW items]				
iv	Wien, ÖNB	1337	f. 36ra-vb	ca. 1410	JW MS Boh.
v		3927	f. 8rb-vb	ca. 1410	JW MS Boh.

III. Ed. R. Buddensieg, *John Wiclif's Polemical Works in Latin* I (WS, 1883): 380-384. From all MSS except **i** and **iii**.

IV. The unity of the church has been rent asunder by the "four sects"; so too has the realm been agitated by insidious heresies within. But Wyclyf's chief concern here is the false teaching on the Eucharist, "private in scolis suis" (p. 381: he does not single out the friars any more pointedly than this). The king's councillors ("legii homines regis nostri": p. 382) have the power to examine representatives of the "sects" to determine the particulars of their doctrine in this vital matter, and to regain for the kingdom (upon the presumed exposure of their heresies, and the consequent expulsion of the "sects") a great mass of ecclesial wealth. Failing that, he avows, "omnino debet fidelis populus prudenter examinare istos hereticos in hac parte ..." (p. 383).

This is, in sum, an odd exercise. It appears that Wyclyf had in mind at the outset some kind of *commentariolus* on 1 Co 13:13 (the three theological virtues), but brought that endeavor to an abrupt conclusion in order to exclaim upon the evident paralysis of the state in the face of massive churchly dissimulation; and at the end of that road he resolved to submit the whole question to the laity. But did he mean thereby the House of Commons, or some other quasi-judicial body ? This he does not bother to amplify – but this oversight is, we should add in all fairness, a common generic failing among reformers and revolutionaries both secular and spiritual. One phrase toward the end is perhaps revealing: "queratur ab ipsis hereticis si hoc credant, et ... quousque tota secta *sub sigillo suo generali* dederit fidem suam." In his letter to Bishop Buckingham of Lincoln (**396**, above), the same phrase recurs. May we presume that Wyclyf, disappointed in his hopes for episcopal remedy, is here extending his appeal to the incorruptible multitude of *fideles*? Or should we rather argue that the present work only mirrors his earliest, as yet unfocused, thinking on the appropriate strategies for curtailing the abuses of the "four sects"? Because the letter to Buckingham does deal with the friars specifically, we might be tempted to regard it as subsequent to the *De deteccione perfidiarum* – yet we cannot forget that while he was still at Oxford, the *De eucharistia* (**38**) already branded the mendicants as the chief root of sacramental mischief. And so surely the present broadside is not later than the end of 1382; it seems too schematic and tentative for 1383 or 1384, and there is no mention of the Despenser crusade. His evident trust in the virtues of the laity may even suggest the early months of his residence at Lutterworth.[1]

VC: 3933 3935 4514 7980[2]   Bale: deest   Sh: 86[3]   Lo: 87

[1] Buddensieg provides in his introduction (p. 378) and in the running notes a number of parallelisms with the *Trialogus* (**47**), and others of Wyclyf's polemical sallies. These are illuminating, but unfortunately prove nothing beyond a natural convergence of ideas. Yet we may note one additional correspondence: his initial concern with the unity of the church matches that of the *De religionibus vanis monachorum* (**434**, below) – which was, however, built around the Scriptural cornerstone of Mt 15:13, never mentioned in the *De deteccione*.

[2] All tit.: *Deteccio perfidie sectarum antichristi*. Our tit. only in **iv**; in **v** given as "Deteccio perfidie sectarum anticristi," as in the vc.

[3] "Probably an extract."

422. F8. *De novis ordinibus.* Mid-1382?

I. Inc.: Secundum apostolum ad Ephesianos 6 non est nobis colluctacio adversus carnem et sanguinem ...

Expl.: × ... quod viatores possunt in parte cognoscere ex scriptura.

II. MSS:

i	München, BSB	clm 15771	ff. 29v-31v	ca. 1435	Asc. So. Ger.[1]
ii	Praha, MK	D.123 (693)	ff. 100v-107v	xv/1	JW ms Boh.
iii	UK	III.G.11 (536)	ff. 56v-60r	xv/1	JW ms Boh.
iv		V.F.9 (931)	ff. 122v-126r	1408	Asc. Boh.[2]
v		XI.E.3 (2050)	ff. 12v-13v	1416	JW ms Boh.[3]
vi	Wien, ÖNB	1337	ff. 33ra-35vb	ca. 1410	JW ms Boh.

III. Ed. R. Buddensieg, *John Wiclif's Polemical Works in Latin* I (WS, 1883): 323-336. From **iii**, **iv** and **vi** only.

IV. There are here some peculiar turns of phrase and applications of argument not to be found in other of Wyclyf's writings against the "four sects." The train of thought is unusually difficult to follow, and it is far from evident what specific incident might have provoked the piece in the first place. The seemingly precise mention of a plot against John of Gaunt we have scrutinized in another place;[4] it remains inconclusive. The highly abbreviated reference to the Eucharistic imbroglio on p. 333 would appear to intimate that at the moment the matter has receded into Wyclyf's mental background. Yet the Despenser crusade and the *concilium terremotus* are nowhere in sight, and so probably mid-1382 is as safe a date of composition as any we might choose.

vc: 3933 3935   Bale: deest   Sh: 87[5]   Lo: 88

[1] See Kühn-Steinhausen, "Wyclif-Handschriften in Deutschland," 628.
[2] Tit.: *Tractatus de participacione tocius et partis in opere et in dignitate*.
[3] I suspect this text is somewhat condensed.
[4] **50**, n. 8, above.
[5] "This seems to be an extract."

423. F9. *De contrarietate duorum dominorum.* Mid-1382.

I. Inc.: Sicut est unus verus et summus dominus in celis residens ...

Expl.: × ... quia sic est in superiori triumphante ecclesia exemplante.

II. MSS:

i	Firenze, BLaur	Plut. XIX. 33	ff. 18v-22r	1408	Asc. Eng.[1]
ii	Manchester, John Rylands Lib.	Eng. 86	ff. 45r-48v	xv/1	JW MS Eng.

III. Ed. R. Buddensieg, *John Wiclif's Polemical Works in Latin* II (WS, 1883): 698-713. From **ii** only.

IV. Of the entire attested mass of Wyclyf's polemical outpourings, this is surely one of the most arresting. It was evidently provoked by his hearing of the statement by an anonymous friar that the customary division of society into clerics, knights and the common folk was inadequate, "cum femine sunt partes ecclesie et ipse non sunt aliqua istarum trium parcium." (P. 705; there is mention on p. 701 of "quidam ydiote" rationalizing endowment.) But in his retort to this, he does not really address the question of women at all; rather the entire piece descants upon the pervasiveness of *necromancy* among the orders. Nowhere else in his writings is this charge even brought up more than parenthetically.[2] That there abounded in the diocese of Lincoln a variety of religious aberrations, even beyond the norm, we may accept readily enough;[3] but that the clutch of unnamed mendicants fostered the perilous practice of necromancy affords a glimpse of something more extreme. We do know of one well-intentioned Spanish Dominican whose benign neutrality toward demon-worship brought the wrath of the Inquisition down upon his head sometime in the 1370s – and we must remember that the Inquisition was administered for the most part by other Dominicans.[4] The excavation of a real historical personage behind Wyclyf's startling "frater quidam nigromanticus" would justify considerably more than a footnote in any future appreciation of popular religion in fourteenth-century England.[5]

An isolated simile, comparing the current unrest in the church (by which we may infer the Schism generally) to the war "inter Gelvos et Gibilanos" (p. 771) would also appear to be unique to the *De contrarietate*. But because at this most apposite juncture the Flanders crusade is notably absent, we are probably on firm ground in assigning the publication of this strange essay to the early fall of 1382.

vc: 3933 3935[6] 4514 7980[7]   Bale: deest   Sh: 83   Lo: 84

---

[1] Noted by Mabillon in 1687; cf. Stein, "The Wyclif Manuscript in Florence," 95. It is most unlikely that the vc authors knew of either of these Eng. MSS; yet no Continental text is now known.

[2] Cf. *De dyabolo et membris eius* (**30**: p. 371). I am not at all sure that this dearth of subsequent reprises of the theme in any way implies a tacit repudiation of his polemical premise in the *De contrarietate duorum dominorum*. (The "two lords", incidentally, are Christ and Antichrist.)

[3] A slender reed, but probably sufficient to sustain this hypothesis, is Dorothy M. Owen, "Bacon and Eggs: Bishop Buckingham and Superstition in Lincolnshire," in G. J. Cuming and Derek Baker, edd., *Popular Belief and Practice* (SCH 8: Cambridge, Eng., 1972): 139-142.

[4] The case of Raymond of Tarrega is briefly reviewed in Jeffrey Burton Russell, *Witchcraft in the Middle Ages* (Ithaca, N. Y., 1972): 206. Two thoughtful generalized examinations of the psychological

impact of the Black Death – to which a rise in such excesses as necromancy may in part be attributed – are J. Huizinga, *The Waning of the Middle Ages: A Study of the Forms of Life, Thought and Art in France and the Netherlands in the XIVth and XVth Centuries* (original ed., 1924; several subsequent reprints): ch. XI, "The Vision of Death"; and Philip Ziegler, *The Black Death* (New York, 1969; reprinted 1971): ch. 17, "The Effects on the Church and Man's Mind." (See also above, **218**, n.) References to the subject of necromancy are scattered throughout Lynn Thorndike, *A History of Magic and Experimental Science* III (New York, 1934), though only on p. 36 is a specific case of English necromancy mentioned.

[5] Still illuminating is Bernard Manning, *The People's Faith in the Time of Wyclif* (Cambridge, Eng., 1919).

[6] Both tit. add: "... suarum partium ac eciam rerum."

[7] As an addendum, tit.: *Responsiones ad occultum*; no inc.

424. F10. *De oracione dominica.* Mid-1382.

I. Inc.: Cum heretici diebus istis novissimis [5 wds.] magis patenter inpugnant fidem [14 wds.] contra illos, iuvante Dei gracia, aliquid est dicendum ...

Expl.: × ... nec cognoscerent hominem facere opus aliquod laude dignum.

II. MSS:

i	Cambridge, Trinity Coll.	B.15.28	ff. 128r-130r[1]	xiv/ex	Unasc. Eng.
ii	Wien, ÖNB	1337	ff. 97ra-100va	ca. 1410	JW MS Boh.
iii		3929[2]	ff. 182ra-184rb	1409	JW MS Boh.

III. Ed. J. Loserth, *Johannes Wyclif Opera Minora* (WS, 1913): 383-392†. From all MSS.

IV. Loserth acknowledged in his introduction (p. XLVI) that this is a polemical piece; yet he retains it in his *Revision* in the section of "Sermons, Expositions and Practical Theology." He also recognized the similarity in temper and emphasis to Wyclyf's *De oracione et ecclesie purgacione* (**46**, above). We are impatient to discover just who the "heretics" were who in some way disparaged the centrality of the Lord's Prayer: he does mention the friars several times, scoffing at their assertion in the (first session?) of the Blackfriars Synod that their own "special prayers" were of equal effect (p. 387), and at their easy absolutions (p. 389). Almost as an afterthought he added that the last four *peticiones* (Mt 6:11-13) have a moralistic dimension in parallel with the four cardinal sins of sloth, avarice, gluttony and unchastity.

Midsummer of 1382, or slightly later, best fits this work, as well as the *De salutacione angelica*, our next item.[3]

VC: 3933 3935 4514 7980[4]   Bale: 106?[5]   Sh: 47   Lo: 48

[1] Does not appear to have been collated in ed., though mentioned in introduction.

[2] Mistakenly given as 3932 in Lo; yet he remarks Sh's mistaken listing of 4505.

[3] We have noted above (**46**, n. 4) that the *De oracione et purgacione ecclesie* is uniformly assigned seven capp. in the vc instead of the five we have today. The two capp. of the *De oracione dominica* seem at first glance to have a place between capp. iii and iv of the former work; but the continuity there is too pronounced.

[4] All specify 8 capp., but have our expl.

[5] Tit.: *Super oratione Dominica*; inc.: "Docet nos Dominus Iesus Christus ...."

425. F11. *De salutacione angelica*. Mid-1382.

I. Inc.: Quamvis autem salutacio angelica dicta ad beatam virginem sit communiter et laudabiliter usitata, non tamen videtur directe sonare in oracionem ...

Expl.: × ... Et sic est de aliis rosis et proprietatibus senciendum.

II. MSS:

i	Wien, ÖNB	1337	ff. 100va-102rb ca. 1410	JW MS Boh.
ii		3929[1]	ff. 184rb-185rb 1409	JW MS Boh.
iii		4505[2]	ff. 207r-209r 1439	JW MS Boh.

III. Ed. J. Loserth, *Johannis Wyclif Opera Minora* (WS, 1913): 393-397†. From **i** and **ii** only.

IV. Every indication as far back as the vc (and even a bit before, in the arrangement of both **i** and **ii**) points toward a close association of this and the preceding piece. It is ostensibly exegetical, but in fact polemical; the text of the "Hail Mary"[3] merely serves as an excuse for railing at the facile interpretations of the mendicants; and again Augustine is his sole support beyond the Scriptural texts themselves, Lk 1:28 and 2:33. The pope (unnamed, but probably Urban vi) comes under suspicion also for his emendation of the text. It was probably penned in the last half of 1382.

vc: 3933 3935[4] 4514   Bale: 174[5]   Sh: 48[6]   Lo: 49

[1] Omitted in Lo, though collated in his edition.

[2] Mentioned in Loserth's introduction and in Lo, though not collated.

[3] See commentary and bibliography in A. A. de Marco, "Hail Mary," *The New Catholic Encyclopedia* VI (New York etc., 1967): 898.

[4] Following tit.: "... que sequitur statim oracionem dominicam."

[5] Inc.: "Solent homines Christiparam sal. ..."

[6] "Evidently an extract."

426. F12. *De perfeccione statuum*. May 1383.

I. Inc.: Cum viantes et fratres specialiter contendant circa perfecciones [14 wds.] tractandum videtur parumper de ista materia ...

Expl.: × ... postponentes vel falsum ut fidem populo predicantes.

II. MSS:

i	Brno, UK	Mk II.44 (62)	ff. 233r-241r	xv/m	JW MS Boh.[1]
ii	Praha, UK	III.G.11 (536)	ff. 250r-260r	xv/1	JW MS Boh.
iii		IV.H.7 (771)	ff. 81r-92v	ca. 1410	JW MS Boh.
iv		V.F.9 (931)	ff. 104r-111v	1408	JW MS Boh.
v	Wien, ÖNB	1337	ff. 73ra-81va	1410	JW MS Boh.
vi		3927	ff. 37ra-43ra	ca. 1410	JW MS Boh.
vii		3930	ff. 178va-186vb	1412	JW MS Boh.
viii		4527	ff. 148v-156r	1410	JW MS Boh.

III. Ed. R. Buddensieg, *John Wiclif's Polemical Works in Latin* II (WS, 1883): 449-482. From all MSS except **i**, **iii**, and **iv**.

IV. Here Wyclyf clearly perceives that the struggle between Clement VII and Urban VI, as embodied in the organizing efforts of Bishop Despenser, was in actuality a civil war: he speaks several times of their authorizations to "slay one's brother." To a greater extent than in any other of his anti-crusade polemics, however, he links the friars with the execution of papal policies, and finds ample cause therein to sharpen his animosities against them. But at the outset, and again in capp. v and vi, he is more concerned to highlight the fallaciousness of the mendicant claim to a superior status among religious. Relying once again on those mighty pillars, Augustine and Chrysostom, he argues that "non sunt proprie Christiani, nisi imitantur Christum in moribus et in vita." (P. 456.) He never abandoned this premise, and it may safely be taken as emblematic of his reformist drive.

Buddensieg's note k, p. 455, is uncharacteristically careless: "omnes monachi ac canonici, albi vel nigri," cannot possibly signify Franciscans and Dominicans. He obviously meant the Cistercians and Benedictines, along with the Austin canons ("black") and the Norbertine (i.e., Premonstratensian, or "white") canons.[2]

There is a striking remark on p. 478: "Quando ergo forem excusabilis dogmatizando oppositum, ut si per valde contingens cognoscerem multos esse hereticos *in secta mea privata* ..." (emphasis added). It looks as if he is here assuming a greater personal responsibility for the Lollards (or at least the Poor Priests, if we are to distinguish the two)[3] than has of late been the fashion to ascribe to him.

Internal evidence points to May of 1383 as the date of composition of the *De perfeccione statuum*.

VC: 3933 3935 4514 7980   Bale: deest   Sh: 78   Lo: 79

---

[1] See **53**, n. 1, above, on the date. The foliation is incorrectly given in the otherwise excellent catalog by the current archivist, Dr. Vladislav Dokoupil, *Soupis Rukopisů Mikulovní Dietrichsteinské Knihovny* (and see **49**, n. 1, above, on Sedlák).

[2] Buddensieg does, however, identify most of the paraphrases of this work by the 1411 Oxford committee: Wilkins, *Concilia* ... III: 344 (nos. 99-107).

[3] See the introduction to this section, above.

427. F13. *De triplici vinculo amoris* [*sive caritatis*]. Mid- to late 1383.

I. Inc.: Tria sunt vincula amoris quibus fideles viantes ad invicem colligantur ...
Expl.: × ... esse distributa in seculo secundum regulam legis dei.

II. MSS:

i	München, BSB	clm 15771	ff. 19r-26r	ca. 1435	Asc. So. Ger.[1]
ii	Praha, UK	IV.H.7 (771)	ff. 31r-42r	ca. 1410	JW MS Boh.
iii		X.E.9 (1910)	ff. 137r-146r	ca. 1420	JW MS Boh.

[unable to locate in XI.E.3 (2050), mentioned only in Lo; it is MS γ in Buddensieg's general introduction, but is not cited in his specific introduction to the *De triplici vinculo amoris*, nor is it collated in his ed.]

iv	Wien, ÖNB	1337	ff. 25ra-33ra	ca. 1410	JW MS Boh.
v		3930	ff. 168vb-178va	1412	JW MS Boh.
vi		3933	ff. 80vb-86vb	ca. 1415	Asc. Boh.
vii		4527	ff. 162r-169r	1410	JW MS Boh.

III. Ed. R. Buddensieg, *John Wiclif's Polemical Works in Latin* I (WS, 1883): 161-198. From all MSS except **i** and **ii**.

IV. As was commonly the case in Wyclyf's *sermones*, the ostensible subject of this piece engages him only perfunctorily, through the first three (of ten) capp. The last seven focus on the "four sects," and especially on the friars: their pretensions and their invidious mendicancy come in for a predictable tide of abuse. Buddensieg's methodical touch is apparent throughout the introduction and notes, and so we shall comment here only on one allusion which could not have been comprehensible to him, and which has indeed escaped all commentators before now. On p. 188 we read: "Dicitur autem fratrem quendam publice in congregacione Oxoniensi taliter arguisse Christus cepit omnes infirmitates humanas, sed sic mendicare est quedam infirmitas ergo Christus taliter mendicavit." Although the wording does not match, the syllogistic thread closely parallels at least two *conclusiones* in Richard Maidstone's (O. Carm.) *Protectorium pauperis*, a series of *determinaciones* in rebuttal of John Ashwardby's anti-mendicant (and markedly Wyclyfite) positions late in 1380.[2] Our forcibly retired don was still settling scores.

There is no compelling reason to quarrel with Buddensieg's suggested date of late 1383, though a few months earlier is surely allowable. The parallels with the *Trialogus* (**47**) are numerous, though the line of development is seldom identical.[3] This we have learned to expect.

vc: 3933 3935 4514   Bale: deest   Sh: 49   Lo: 50

---

[1] This is the only Wyclyf piece in this codex correctly identified by C. Halm, G. Laubmann, etc., *Catalogus codicum latinorum Bibliothecae Regiae Monacensis* II/3 (München, 1876): 33, as indicated in Kühn-Steinhausen, "Wyclif-Handschriften in Deutschland," 627.

[2] We have already encountered Maidstone: cf. **47**, n. 19; **205**, n. 5; on Ashwardby, see *BRUO* I: 70.

[3] See, e.g., the phrase "Cum ergo non sunt est et non" (p. 190), as against the same passage in the *Trialogus*, p. 263: in the former mendicancy is at issue; in the latter, the metaphysics of the Eucharist.

428. F14 *Purgatorium secte Christi.* 1382 or 1383.

I. Inc.: Sepe assumptum est ut fides catholica quod Christus deus et homo sit potentissimus ...

   Expl.: × ... omissio minatur ruinam et destruccionem irremissibilem multis regnis.

II. MS:

i Manchester, John
   Rylands Lib.   Eng. 86   ff. 49r-54r   xv/1   JW MS Eng.

III. Ed. R. Buddensieg, *John Wiclif's Polemical Works in Latin* I (WS, 1883): 298-316. From unique MS.

IV. It seems peculiar that only one MS of this polemic is known to have survived. Neither in content nor in tone is it so extreme as most of his other writings (aside from the *Opus evangelicum* [**374-377**]) which we have assigned to the last two years of his life. It is however short enough to have perhaps escaped the catalogers' notice, and it may yet surface in Prague or Vienna.

Buddensieg's running notes adequately illustrate Wyclyf's habit of borrowing from himself. Obviously in dealing on several different occasions with the same restricted topic – in this case, the blatant defects of the "new orders"[1] – his thought would run in the same channels and even the same turns of phrase would recur. From this fact one might be tempted to construct a chronological sequence based on either: (1) an increasing elaboration and diversification of theses, culminating in an omnibus treatise such as the *Trialogus* (**47**); or (2) an increasing shorthand, codified simplification of theses, deriving from an *initial* omnibus of terminology and conclusions such as the *Trialogus*. Jacob's ladder confronts us – but instead of the Biblical angels ascending and descending, we see here a dynamic interaction of inductive and deductive ratiocination. Besides the obvious exclusionary rule that must apply in deciding between these two alternative models, having to consider such awkward matters as intended audience, state of draft from which any given text derives, subsequent emendation, interpolation and so on renders the whole enterprise very nearly nugatory. His frequent mentions of the *secta Christi* do not take us any closer in this instance to grasping the dimensions and precise identity of that amorphous group than we were at the outset of this section.

VC: 3933 3935 4514[2]   Bale: deest   Sh: deest   Lo: 98

[1] Cf., e.g., *De fundacione sectarum* (**431**); *De quattuor sectis novellis* (**429**), below; *De novis ordinibus* (**412**), above.
[2] Initial. tit. in all three: *Contra religiones privatas* ....

429. F15. *De quattuor sectis novellis*. Mid-1383.

I. Inc.: Secundum tres virtutes theologicas fideles quidam supponunt se moveri a domino ad fidem ...

Expl.: × ... potest movente dei gracia esse medium ad ecclesie prodessendum.

II. MSS:

i	Praha, MK	D.123 (693)	ff. 107v-136v	xv/1	JW MS Boh.
ii	UK	IV.H.7 (771)	ff. 13r-30r	ca. 1410	JW MS Boh.
iii		XI.E.3 (2050)	ff. 1r-5v	1416	JW MS Boh.
iv	Wien, ÖNB	1337	ff. 81va-95ra	ca. 1410	JW MS Boh.
v		3929	ff. 225ra-233rb	1409	JW MS Boh.
vi		4527	ff. 34v-46v	1410	JW MS Boh.
vii	Wolfenbüttel, HzglB	Cod.Guelf. 306 (340)	ff. 240vb-256vb	xv/1	Asc. Pol.[1]

III. Ed. R. Buddensieg, *John Wiclif's Polemical Works in Latin* I (WS, 1883): 241-290. From all MSS except **i**, **ii** and **vii**.

IV. Buddensieg has marshalled sufficient internal evidence to warrant a date of mid-1383 for this substantial diatribe. Here perhaps more than in any other single tractate Wyclyf strikes at the very bedrock of the institutional *ecclesia militans*. On p. 242 he states his thesis as straightforwardly as could be asked: "Quatuor autem sunt secte in Angliam et regna alia introducte, et ipse ex defectu fundacionis a Christo sunt ecclesie onerose et per consequens ad stabilicionem regni et ecclesie expurgande." His excoriation of each "sect" in turn is devastating, and none the less so for his dialectical skimming over contrary viewpoints in capp. v-x. At this late hour Wyclyf still upheld the conviction that the Crown should aggressively intervene to cut the church off from its fraudulently obtained temporalities; and his concern for the lot of the poor remains thematic. At one point, finally, he offered some of his clearest thought on the "priesthood of all believers," that cardinal Reformation tenet: "... quilibet *predestinatus* est sacerdos in patria nec debet propterea omnes ritus et opera sacerdotibus limitata exercere, nec debet fidelis *sine revelacione* consecracionem episcopi sui contempnare ..." (p. 259; emphasis added to underscore the crucially subjective elements in this definition).

VC: 3933 3935[2] 4514   Bale: deest   Sh: 85   Lo: 86

[1] See Kühn-Steinhausen, "Wyclif-Handschriften in Deutschland," 626.
[2] The first two VC add to the tit.: "... et eorum erroribus."

430. F16. *De dyabolo et membris eius.* 1383 or 1384.

I. Inc.: Fertur quendam fratrem inflatum superbia graviter [ferre] istam sentenciam orthodoxam ...

Expl.: × ... versucia dyaboli contra fideles de ecclesia Iesu Christi.

II. MSS:

i	London, BL	Cotton, Vesp. DXXIII	ff. 21r-29r	xv/1	Unasc. Eng.[1]
ii	Praha, UK	III.G.11 (536)	ff. 170v-174v	xv/1	JW MS Boh.
iii	Wien, ÖNB	1338	ff. 26va-29va	ca. 1410	JW MS Boh.
iv		4527	ff. 181r-184r	1410	Asc. Boh.[2]

III. Ed. R. Buddensieg, *John Wiclif's Polemical Works in Latin* I (WS, 1883): 361-374. From all MSS except i.

IV. This occasional piece was provoked by some unnamed friar's quite understandable denial that the mendicants were devils. Of course Wyclyf had been at war with them for several years by this time over the Eucharist, simony and poverty; it should come as no surprise that he was also roused to counterattack on this new front. It was most especially their chronic (where? at whose instigation?) harassment of the "simplices sacerdotes" – his own Poor Priests – which galled him: "fratres improperando eis dicunt, quod sunt heretici ydiote, cum ipsi non sciunt sensum scripture, sed thesaurus sensus domini est absconditus apus fratres." (Pp. 371-372.) Their professed poverty is a farce; they lie continually; they sow discord wherever they go; they extort alms even from the poor; in short, they burden the world grievously, and should be cut off utterly from it. Yet despite its uncompromising harshness, we cannot confidently bracket this tirade more precisely than sometime in the last two years of his life.

VC: 3933 3935 4514 7980   Bale: 4[3]   Sh: 29   Lo: 30

[1] First noticed in Thomson, "Unnoticed MSS and Works of Wyclif," 34.

[2] Wilkins, *Concilia* ... III: 348, lists five alleged extracts from this piece as among those singled out by the twelve doctors at Oxford in 1411. The first three correspond as follows to the pages of our ed.: 220:363; 221:365; 222:365. Nos. 223 and 224 are shabby bits of pantheism nowhere to be found in the *De dyabolo et membris eius*, and almost surely nowhere else in Wyclyf, save perhaps as straw men.

[3] Wrong inc.; correct inc. at no. 78, tit.: *Dialogu[s] de fratribus.*

431. F17 *De fundacione sectarum.* Late 1383.

I. Inc.: Motus sum per quosdam veritatis amicos originaliter detegere fundacionem fratrum ...

Expl.: × ... quantum ad firmitatem fidei de ecclesia sit ablata.

II. MSS:

i	Brno, UK	Mk II.44 (62)	ff. 217r-233r	xv/m	Asc. Boh.[1]
ii	Firenze, BLaur	Plut. XIX.33	ff. 1r-11v	1408	Asc. Eng.[2]

iii	Praha, UK	V.F.9³ (931)	ff. 83v-97v	1408	JW ᴍꜱ Boh.
iv		X.E.9 (1910)	ff. 174v-194r	ca. 1420	JW ᴍꜱ Boh.
v		XI.E.3⁴ (2050)	ff. 5v-11v	1416	JW ᴍꜱ Boh.
vi	Wien, ÖNB	1337	ff. 134vb-150va	ca. 1410	JW ᴍꜱ Boh.
vii		3927	ff. 25ra-36rb	ca. 1410	JW ᴍꜱ Boh.
viii		3930	ff. 250va-264vb	1412	JW ᴍꜱ Boh.
ix		4527	ff. 19r-34r	1410	JW ᴍꜱ Boh.
x		4536	ff. 98v-122r	xv/1	Asc. Boh.

III. Ed. R. Buddensieg, *John Wiclif's Polemical Works in Latin* I (WS, 1883): 13-80. From all ᴍꜱꜱ except **i-iii**.

IV. It is probable that almost every argument and innuendo against the friars which appears elsewhere in the Wyclyf canon has its moment in the sixteen capp. of this long invective. He is absorbed throughout in shoring up his contrary views by frequent reliance on Scripture. It is therefore enlightening to find him defending himself against the accusations of unspecified parties that he has read arbitrary meanings into certain passages: "In istis tamen protestor, quod nolo in hoc fide scripture quidquam temere diffinire, sed sive fratres, sive alii sensum alium *evidencius fundaverint*, humiliter eis consenciam, de quanto probabiliter fundaverint illud, quod dicunt." (P. 31; emphasis added.) Here are foreshadowings of Hus and Luther; and surely Wyclyf's sheer versatility with the *sacra pagina*, irrespective or his particular array of passages therefrom, far overmastered his anonymous adversaries.

Although he discarded much of the baggage of the schoolmen in his departure for Lutterworth late in 1381, certain irreducible axioms remained in his dialectical stock-in-trade; and one especially durable premise he voices here again: "Constat quidam ex principiis fidei, quod deus noster nec fecit nec facere potuit aliquid nisi probabile racione." (P. 25.) Repeatedly too he reverts to the burden which the friars wilfully impose on the poor; there can be no question that this issue was deeply real to him.

Buddensieg's suggested date between August and November of 1383 is eminently defensible.

vc: 3933 3935 4514 7980   Bale: 80⁵   Sh: 91   Lo: 92

[1] See **53**, n. 1, on the date; ᴍꜱ first identified in Sedlák, *Studie a Texty*, xvii (interleaved).
[2] Tit.: *De fundacione pseudofratrum*; cf. Stein, "The Wyclif Manuscript in Florence," 95.
[3] Erroneously given as V.E.9 in Lo.
[4] 2.E.9 in Sh.
[5] Tit.: *De origine sectarum*; no inc.

432. F18. *De concordacione fratrum* [*cum secta simplici Christi*] [*De sectis monachorum*] [*De ordinacione fratrum*]. Late 1383.

1. Inc.: Cum Christus sit primus et novissimus cuius perfecta sunt opera ...
   Expl.: × ... hoc sibi proprium quod super mendacio sit fundatum.

II. MSS:

i	Karlsruhe, BLB	*343*	ff. 1r-5r	xv/1	Asc. Boh.[1]
ii	München, BSB	*clm 15771*	ff. 32r-34v	ca. 1435	Asc. So. Ger.[2]
iii	Praha, MK	*B.6.3 (293)*	ff. 251v-255r	1421	Asc. Boh.
iv		D.123 (693)	ff. 52r-62v	xv/1	JW MS Boh.
v	UK	IV.H.7 (771)	ff. 43v-48r	ca. 1410	JW MS Boh.
vi	Wien, ÖNB	1337	ff. 39va-43va	ca. 1410	JW MS Boh.
vii		1622	ff. 183v-188r	1410	JW MS Boh.
viii		3927	ff. 1ra-3va	ca. 1410	JW MS Boh.
ix		3930	ff. 192va-196rb	1412	Asc. Boh.
x		4527	ff. 75v-79r	1410	Asc. Boh.

III. Ed. R. Buddensieg, *John Wiclif's Polemical Works in Latin* I (WS, 1883): 88-106. From **vi** and **viii-x** only.

IV. An oblique internal reference (rare in his *polemica*) to the *De fundacione sectarum* (**431**, just preceding) places this variously titled piece late in 1383. His attitude by this time is succinctly summarized in a single sentence on p. 101: "De papa autem et cardinalibus, monachis, canonicis atque fratribus non recolo, quod sit mencio in scriptura." Most noteworthy is however his invocation of Grosseteste,[3] William of St. Amour,[4] Bonaventure,[5] Ockham,[6] and FitzRalph[7] as witnesses against the excesses of the friars; it would indeed be of great value to us to ascertain whence he had gathered some of that evidence – especially William of St. Amour, who was little known in England.

The friars' alleged plot against John of Gaunt is trotted out one more time, with no more elaboration than before (p. 95).[8]

VC: 3933 3935 4514 7980   Bale: deest   Sh: 84   Lo: 85

---

[1] An extra sentence after our expl. Brambach's 1896 catalog used the tit.: *De ordinacione fratrum*, which does not appear in the MS; cf. Kühn-Steinhausen, "Wyclif-Handschriften in Deutschland," 628.

[2] Ibid., 627; this is a fragment.

[3] P. 92. (For this and the following four notes, older references appear in the edition.) This allusion must be to his deathbed exhortation to John of St. Giles OFM, as reported in Matthew Paris' *Chronica Majora* (ed. in RS by H. R. Luard, London, 1880) V: 400-402; episode reviewed in W. R. Thomson, "The Image of the Mendicants in the Chronicles of Matthew Paris," 22-23. For further bibliography on Grosseteste, see above, **4**, n. 2; **6**, n. 7; **9**, n. 1 and **26**, nn. 15, 16; etc.

[4] P. 92. – A secular master at Paris, William was in the forefront of the unsuccessful efforts to restrict the teaching rights of the mendicant scholars at the University. The major study of him is now M.-M. Dufeil, *Guillaume de Saint-Amour et la polémique universitaire Parisienne 1250-1259* (Paris, 1972); see too the discussion and further bibliography in Moorman, *A History of the Franciscan Order*, 124-131; and W. R. Thomson, "The Earliest Cardinal-Protectors of the Franciscan Order: A Study in Administrative History, 1210-1261," *Studies in Medieval and Renaissance History* 9 (1972): 63-71.

[5] (P. 94.) See above, **67**, n. But of course against this letter we must set the cardinal's many vigorous pleas for his order, most important of which was the *Apologia pauperum*, available now in translation: José de Vinck, *The Works of Bonaventure ... IV: Defense of the Mendicants* (Paterson, N. J., 1966).

[6] (Pp. 92, 94, 95: Ockham very seldom appears in Wyclyf's writings. See above, A7, n. 6.) Undoubtedly he implies here Ockham's *Epistola ad fratres minores* of early 1334: for successive editions of this letter, see Moorman, *A History of the Franciscan Order*, 324, n. 3.

[7] (P. 91.) See above, **23-25** and n. 12.
[8] See above, **50**, n. 8, and **422**.

433. F19. *Descripcio fratris*. 1382, 1383 or 1384.

I. [Entire piece:] Pseudofrater degens in [hoc] seculo est dyabolus incarnatus cum adinventis suis signis sensibilibus, desponsatus ad seminandum discordias in militante ecclesia, ex summa cautela sathane machinatus.

II. MSS:

i	Cambridge, Trinity Coll.	B.14.50	f. 20r	xv/1	Asc. Eng.[1]
ii	Praha, UK	X.C.23 (1876)	f. 196va	1410	JW MS Boh.
iii	Wien, ÖNB	1338	f. 30rb-va	ca. 1410	JW MS Boh.
iv		1387	f. 107rb	ca. 1410	JW MS Boh.
v	Wolfenbüttel, HzglB	Cod.Guelf. 306 (340)	f. 259ra	xv/1	Asc. Pol.[2]

III. Ed. R. Buddensieg, *John Wiclif's Polemical Works in Latin* II (WS, 1883): 407. From **iii** and **iv** only.

IV. This, the briefest of all the known writings of Wyclyf, has all the earmarks of an extract, but diligent perusal of his anti-mendicant invectives has not as yet isolated it. Doubtless it struck his followers as an apt summation of Wyclyf's manifold judgment upon the newer orders. It could have been penned at any time within the last three years of his life.[3]

VC: deest   Bale: deest   Sh: 89   Lo: 90

[1] Only recently noticed: Anne Hudson, "A Lollard Compilation and the Dissemination of Wycliffite Thought," p. 72 (and there transcribed with our variant).

[2] Noted in Kühn-Steinhausen, "Wyclif-Handschriften in Deutschland," 626.

[3] The phrase "cautela dyaboli" occurs in the *De concordacione fratrum* (**432**: p. 91, line 11), *et frequenter alibi*. Such turns of expression, idiosyncratic in his lexicon, can sometimes serve to identify, e.g., an acephalous piece as a bit of Wyclyfiana.

434. F20. *De religionibus vanis monachorum* [*De fundatore religionis*]. 1382, 1383 or 1384.

I. Inc.: Salvator noster diligens unitatem religionis [4 wds.] dicit in suo evangelio quod est sufficiens regula sue religionis ...

Expl.: × ... quoniam si cecus ceco ducatum prestet ambo in foveam cadunt.

II. MSS:

i	Basel, Universitäts- und Öffentliche B	A.X.66	f. 305v[1]		
ii	Olomouc, Státní vědecká Knihovna	I.V.34	f. 176r-v	1411	Asc. Boh.[2]

iii	Praha, UK	V.F.17 (939)	ff. 213v-214v	1412	JW MS Boh.
iv		X.C.23 (1876)	f. 195ra-rb	1410	JW MS Boh.
v		X.H.13 (1991)	ff. 184v-185v	ca. 1420	Unasc. Boh.
vi	Wien, ÖNB	1338[3]	ff. 29va-30ra	ca. 1410	JW MS Boh.
vii		3929	ff. 207vb-208rb	1409	JW MS Boh.
viii		3930	f. 166ra-va	1412	JW MS Boh.
ix		4515	ff. 83v-84v	ca. 1420	JW MS Boh.
x		4527[4]	f. 145r-v	1410	JW MS Boh.

III. Ed. R. Buddensieg, *John Wiclif's Polemical Works in Latin* II (WS, 1883): 435-440. From all MSS except i and iii-v.

IV. Both Shirley and Buddensieg (p. 436) believed that the *De religionibus* was "very probably a short fragment from some larger work." Of course it would be precipitous to rule out this possibility altogether, but the work is topically self-contained, and none of the five Scriptural citations *in textu* appear together in any of his later published polemics.[5] The message is elementary: no order, whether springing from the brow of Augustine, Benedict, Francis or Dominic, can muster an acceptable *raison d'être* when its practices wander from the *lex Christi*. His denunciations are merciless and sweeping; to judge from that alone, however, is insufficient to fix a date more exact than the last two and a half years of his life.

VC: deest   Bale: deest   Sh: 80   Lo: 81

[1] See **416**, n. 2, above.
[2] First noticed in Buddensieg's ed., p. I.VII: asc. "Johannes M[agister] Wyk." at bottom of f. 176v. Not in Sh or Lo.
[3] Only old (Denis) catalog no. given in Lo. Tit. in MS: *De fundacione religionis*.
[4] Collated by Buddensieg in ed.; overlooked by Sh and Lo.
[5] Mt 15:13 and 16:18; Ro 1:32; 1 Co 1:12-13; 3:6-8 and 10-11.

435. F21. *De solucione Sathane.* Late 1383, or 1384.

I. Inc.: Quantum ad obiectum fratrum, quod non sane intelligitur scriptura [32 wds.] hic oportet non millenario numero quantitatem temporis, sed universitatem, quo regnat ecclesiam, designari ...

Expl.: × ... excutite orthodoxe fidei lucem veram.

II. MSS:

i	Praha, MK	D.123 (693)	ff. 94v-100r	xv/1	JW MS Boh.
ii	UK	III.G.11 (536)	ff. 220v-223r	xv/1	JW MS Boh.
iii	Wien, ÖNB	1337	ff. 102rb-104vb	ca. 1410	JW MS Boh.
iv		1387	ff. 107rb-108va	ca. 1410	JW MS Boh.
v		3929	ff. 185va-187ra	1409	JW MS Boh.
vi		3930	ff. 166va-168vb	1412	JW MS Boh.
vii		4527	ff. 17r-19r	1410	JW MS Boh.

III. Ed. R. Buddensieg, *John Wiclif's Polemical Works in Latin* II (WS, 1883): 391-400. From all MSS except i.

iv. Rv 20:1-3, on the loosing of Satan, was a commonplace in medieval exegesis; here Wyclyf uses it as a platform for one of his last attacks on the "four sects," and particularly the mendicants. Rv 20:7, on Gog and Magog, buttressed his case: the church had entered that age of confusion and turmoil which they foreshadowed. The friars evade Christ's injunction (Mt 5:16) to let their light shine before men; instead they only disclose their true feelings on the Eucharist (for example) in their "private schools." His emphasis is conservative, to restore the church to its earlier purity.[1] Clearly the present piece fell within the last eighteen months of his life.

vc: deest   Bale: 135   Sh: 30   Lo: 31

[1] Some such image of the *ecclesia primitiva* was of course thematic among medieval reformers generally: see the exposition and extensive bibliographies in L. B. Pascoe, "Jean Gerson: The 'Ecclesia Primitiva' and Reform," *Traditio* 30 (1974): 379-409; S. H. Hendrix, "In Quest of the *Vera Ecclesia*: The Crises of Late Medieval Ecclesiology," *Viator* 7 (1976): 347-378. Of importance for its typology of historicism is Gordon Leff, "The Making of the Myth of a True Church in the Later Middle Ages," *Journal of Medieval and Renaissance Studies* 1 (1971): 1-15; see also his earlier "The Apostolic Ideal in Later Medieval Ecclesiology," *JTS*, new ser., 18 (1967): 58-82.

Section G

Dubia et spuria

Since the primary object of this enterprise has been to identify the MSS and substance of those works for which at least a strong argument can be made that they were indeed written by Wyclyf (or, in a few instances, transcribed in some form from one of his lectures or other public appearances), no pretense of completeness is offered for this section; neither do the items herein represented follow any discernible pattern. It is naturally the editor's expectation that non-Wyclyfian fourteenth-century specialists may refine at least some of the attributions – though it may well be that some of the *Dubia* are paraphrases of genuine Wyclyfiana.

Taking the VC as the most thorough and reliable of all the early listings of the reformer's works, we find that only three of the items ascribed to him in those lists do not correspond to anything in the established canon; of these the first two are found, with a reasonable congruency of titles, incipits and explicits, in all four of the VC, while the third appears only in 4514. The editor believes it quite probable that all three are true lost writings of John Wyclyf; they are consequently singled out here:

(1) *De duodecim legibus* – 8 capp.

Cum philosophi [or: pharisei] pseudo apostoli ... × ... in clericis iam perversis.

(2) *De dissensione facta in Romana ecclesia* [or: *curia*]

Iam incidit tractare de ista ... (no expl. given).

(3) *De quodam periculoso mendacio noviter practisato* – 7 capp.

Cum parvus error et missibilis ... × ... aliis modicum deleantur.

GDub.1. *De religione privata* [I]

Although this piece [In materia de religione privata ponit quedam posicio ... × ... cum responsione fideli ad argumenta reverendi monachi.] was edited by Buddensieg in his *John Wiclif's Polemical Works in Latin* II: 490-518, he himself declared that "[a]mongst all the polemical writings of W.'s, this is the least authenticated." (P. 486.) Workman, *JW* II: 124n., 309n., echoes him; Doyle, "William Woodford and Wyclif's *De religione*," 330, is stronger still: "In any case it is almost certain that the *De religione privata* was not written by Wyclif at all." It appears, however, in four almost exclusively Wyclyfite codices: Praha, UK III.G.11 (536), ff. 201r-208v; X.E.9 (1910), ff. 194r-202r; Wien, ÖNB 3929, ff. 261va-266rb; and 4527, ff. 184v-191r. (It is not in Wolfenbüttel, HzglB Cod. Guelf. 669 [719], *pace* Lo: 82.)

GDub.2. [*Tractatus*] *de probacionibus proposicionum*

On 29 July 1410 Master Simon of Tišnov defended "hic innocens et iustus tractatulus" at Prague. (His *protestacio* ed. Loserth, *Hus and Wiclif* [1st ed. only]:

271-276, from Wien, ÖNB 4002, ff. 38r-41r; also in Praha, UK X.E.24 [1925], ff. 133r-135v.) This was most likely the *De proposicionibus insolubilibus* (**5**); but cf. also Praha, UK VIII.F.16 (1570), ff. 1r-61v, and Truhlář's remarks.

G*Dub*.3, 4, 5. *Tractatus de deo*
Tractatus de potencia dei
Tractatus "de creancia"

These three successive pieces occupy ff. 210-226r of Praha, UK X.E.24 (1925) just mentioned. Truhlář observes parenthetically "Isti tres tractatus Johannis Wiclif esse videntur."

G*Dub*.6. *De ordine in peccato*

To be found in the JW MS Praha, UK X.C.23 (1876), ff. 196vb-197ra. [Sciendum quod per hunc modum fit ordo in peccato ... × ... absque dubio esset peccatum mortale.] Truhlář thought it might have been by Wyclyf.

G*Dub*.7. ———

Praha, UK IV.H.9 (773), ff. 258v-259r, contains this short and very elementary piece. [Tres sunt modi ... × ... deservierunt et tantum etc.] It deals with *obligaciones*, and cites Richard Swyneshed, though surely meant Roger: cf. J. A. Weisheipl, "Roger Swyneshed, O.S.B., Logician, Natural Philosopher, and Theologian," in *Oxford Studies Presented to Daniel Callus*, 231-252; Spade, *The Mediaeval Liar*, 102. ed. Dziewicki, *Johannis Wyclif Miscellanea Philosophica*, 152-156.

G*Dub*.8. *Epistola pulcra m. jo. anglici*

In Wien, ÖNB 3932, f. 89vb. Lechler asserted that one of Wyclyf's followers wrote this defense of the "pious" (Lollards?) against an unnamed persecutor: *Johannis Wiclif Trialogus cum Supplemento Trialogi*, 24.

G*Dub*.9. *Tractatus de restitucionibus*

In London, BL Arundel 458, ff. 68r-82r; unclear asc. in this Boh. MS.

G*Dub*.10. *Epistola ad ducem Lancastrensem*

Was f. 204 (?) in Syon Monastery, K 37, now lost: Bateson, *Catalogue of the Library of Syon Monastery*, 244. Perhaps a confusion with **402**, above.

G*Dub*.11. *De peregrinacione*

Was f. 179 (?) in Syon Monastery, D 49: see the preceding item.

GDub.12. *Decem necessaria ad perfeccionem hominis*

Asc. to Wyclyf in the *Tabulae codicum manuscriptorum praeter graecos et orientales in Bibliotheca Palatina Vindobonensi asservatorum* III (Wien, 1869): 246, from ÖNB 4343, ff. 235r-236r. [Notandum est ut homo possit amplius profitere et deo magis placere ... × ... omnis saporis suavitatem habentis.]

GDub.13. *Quomodo Christianus ad ministrandum disponi debet et digne recipiendum sacramentum corporis Christi*

In Wien, ÖNB 4316, ff. 125v-129r, in a different hand from the rest of this JW MS; also in ÖNB 4504, ff. 110v-113v, but in the same hand as in the preceding, and asc., *De verbi incarnacione* (**10**). [Docet apostolus prima cor. 11 sic dicens ... × ... iam audiendo sed bibendo didicisti.]

GDub.14. ——

The catalog affirms that the piece [Hic ostenditur que religio sit optima aliorum religionum ... × ... et subiectos subditum per [...] religiosis etc.], in ÖNB 4515, f. 193r, contains excerpts from Wyclyf (not further identified).

GDub.15. *Dubium de presciencia et predestinacione*

S. H. Thomson saw this piece in Oxford, Merton Coll. 113, ff. 107ra-116rb, in 1935, and observed at that time that it sounded very much like Wyclyf. It is unasc., and sandwiched between the *Super sentencias* of Robert Holcot OP and Alan de Lille, *De planctu naturae*. But Poole's commentary on this MS (*Iohannis Wycliffe De Dominio Divino*, pp. 263-264) glosses over the fact that these folios constitute a separate gathering, in a different hand from the Holcot work. [Utrum prescitus sicut et predestinatus faciens fructus bonos eterne vite meritorios ... × ... ac reprobacionis et paciencie quomodo non repugnarent hominis libertati virtualiter inquisivit etc.]

GDub.16. ——

In Wien, ÖNB 3928 (a Wyclyf MS), there is a short anonymous piece at ff. 189rb-190ra. [Discipulus quidam venerabilis doctoris ewangelici patet sex raciones ... × ... ad castigandum suos clericos mortaliter peccantes.] The same text appears again in 3932, ff. 155v-156r and in Praha, UK X.E.9 (1910), ff. 206r-207v. Whatever the precise character of this piece, its modern publication would surely throw some additional light on the tangled issue of Wyclyf and secular dominion.

GDub.17. ——

Praha, UK X.H.13 (1991), ff. 141v-158v and ff. 181r-184v contain "Excerpta theologica varia," unasc. There are also two unidentified short pieces on f. 92r of X.H.17 (1995). Both MSS do contain some JW material.

GDub.18. ——

In Wien, ÖNB 1622, ff. 127r-128r, and unasc. [Conclusio prima religio Christiana est quacumque privata ... × ... redderent sanem prepositum et subditum perfectos religiosos etc.] This is a predominantly JW MS.

***

G*Spur*.1. *De necessitate futurorum*

Sixteen years before the publication of his *Revision* of Sh, Loserth established that this piece could not possibly have been written by Wyclyf, but had to have been assembled by one of his disciples, incorporating the master's thought on the axiom "omnia que evenient de necessitate evenient." (Cf. above, **56**n.; we may add to those references the *De mandatis divinis* [**26**: pp. 393, 394] and the *Trialogus* [**47**: pp. 292-293].) Cf. Loserth, "Die ältesten Streitschriften Wiclifs," 68-70; also Lo: 99. MSS: Praha, UK V.F.9 (931), ff. 68v-75v; Wien, ÖNB 4937, ff. 28r-34v; credited to Wyclyf in all four VC. [Inpugnante quodam ingenioso magistro proposicionem venerabilis doctoris ewangelici quam in sua sancta senectute fideliter asseruit ... × ... tam in logica quam in veritate poterit defensari. Laus Christo.]

G*Spur*.2. *De ymaginibus*

Lo: 27 correctly states "[i]t is not a tract of Wyclif." The first few lines prove that it was, like the preceding item, by some disciple: [Ignorante quodam socio sentenciam Catholicam asserentem quod licet adorare sanctorum ymagines adoracione sanctis figuris debita, quam venerabilis doctor evangelicus usque ad suum felicem exitum docuit et defendit movetur quidam ruralis simplex discipulus dicti doctoris per declaracionem ... × ... ad dictam ignoranciam dei gracia poterit liberari adiuvante.] MSS: Brno, UK Mk II, 123 (102), ff. 99v-103r (incomplete and unasc.); Praha, UK X.E.9 (1910), ff. 210v-214v (a JW MS; Truhlař asc. to JW).

G*Spur*.3. *Super cantica canticorum*

Lo: 46 asserts that this "is not a work of Wyclif." The demonstration is in Loserth, "Die ältesten Streitschriften Wiclifs," 70-74, where it is edited in part. [Dilectis et prudentibus viris ... × ... regere in decore suo qui cum patre et spiritu sancto vivit et regnat in sancta sanctorum.] MSS: Wien, ÖNB 4514, ff. 1r-26v, asc.; 11635, ff. 1r-161r (xvi cent.), also asc. But the ascriptions are not as farfetched as might appear: we have noted above (**323**) that Wyclyf not only postillated sacred scripture, but also wrote two prologues to it, the second of which was his *principium* for the D.D.

G*Spur*.4. *Leccio* [or: *Commentarius*] *in Oseam et Danielem*

In Wien, ÖNB 3926, ff. 1r-187r; asc. to JW in binding by a much later hand. It is not at all the same piece as either **331** or **333**; it has furthermore a political cast to it which is absent from virtually all of Wyclyf's authenticated postills. It was in all likelihood a Hussite composition; Žižka is mentioned in a marginalium on f. 53r.

G*Spur*.5. *Commentarius in Apocalypsim*

On its face, this massive exegesis undoubtedly appealed to those scholars who sought to complete the known canon of Wyclyf's New Testament *Commentarius* (as it is listed in both Sh: 45 and Lo: 45, "praeter Apocalypsin"). But we now have two English MSS of Wyclyf on Rv (see **371**, above); and internal evidence in any case (particularly f. 86r of Wien, ÖNB 4526, where the death of Urban VI is mentioned) compels us to assign the work to Purvey sometime between 1385 and 1389. His source array, including Nicholas of Lyra, Grosseteste, and FitzRalph, is much as Wyclyf's own would have been in his later years. MSS: Brno, UK Mk II, 44 (62), ff. 85r-210r; Karlsruhe, BLB 346, ff. 1-120; Napoli, BN VII.A.34, ff. 69-90 (asc.); Praha, MK A.117 (219), ff. 15-146; A.163 (269), ff. 1-128; B.48.1 (351), ff. 1-161; B.48.2 (352), ff. 1-137; B.82.2 (395), ff. 1r-220v; UK III.G.17 (542), ff. 1-40 (incomplete); V.E.3 (895), ff. 13r-166r; Wien, ÖNB 4526, ff. 1r-131r; 4925, ff. 1r-134v (asc.). At least two of these texts mention imprisonment in the year 1390; this was Purvey. (Incomplete folio citations above derive from the list in Stegmüller, *Repertorium Biblicum Medii Aevi* III, no. 5118; he ventures no judgment as to the authenticity of the ascriptions.) [Opus arduum valde id est Apokalypsii videlicet ... × ... in nomine crucis sue finaliter triumphantis.]

G*Spur*.6. *Questiones xiii logice et philosophice*

Ed. Rudolf Beer, *Johannis Wiclif De Ente Praedicamentali ... Quaestiones XIII Logicae et Philosophicae* ... (WS, 1891): 223-293. S. H. Thomson established conclusively in his "Some Latin Works Erroneously Ascribed to Wyclif," 385-387, that several if not all of these miscellaneous *quaestiones* can not have been by Wyclyf. (To the MS Praha, UK V.E.14 [908], ff. 177r-202v, we may add for the third *quaestio*, UK X.E.24 [1925], ff. 295v-298r; cf. Truhlař.) It is virtually certain that these were all Hussite *quaestiones*.

G*Spur*.7, 8, 9. *De universalibus*
Replicacio de universalibus
De materia

These three items, corresponding to nos. 5, 6, and 8 in Lo, were all edited by M. H. Dziewicki, *Johannis Wyclif Miscellanea Philosophica* I (WS, 1901): 129-161; II (1905): 1-151; 170-188. They have been adequately disposed of in Thomson, "Some Latin Works Erroneously Ascribed to Wyclif," 383-385; cf. also Workman, *JW* II, 423-424.

G*Spur*.10. *De abominacione in loco sacro*

This piece was in actuality the fourth part of Matthew of Janov's *Regulae Veteris et Novi Testamenti* (written 1392; 1558 and 1715 edd. asc. this portion to Hus; latest ed. 4 vols., Innsbruck, 1908-1913); one of the three MSS, Praha MK O.11 (1595), originally had "Tractatus Johannis Wikleff heretici. Ideo caute legas, ne incidas in laqueum mortis;" but this asc. was later scratched out. Cf. Sarton, *Introduction to the History of Science*, III/2: 1352. Vlastimil Kybal was responsible for the Innsbruck ed.; see also his fine "Les origines du mouvement hussite en Bohème. Matthias de Ianov." *Revue historique* 103 (1910): 1-31.

G*Spur*.11. *Speculum peccatoris*

This piece, or parts of it, are extant in several MSS: London, BL Royal 6 E.III, ff. 105v-107r; 7 F.XI, ff. 259v-262v; and 17 B.XVII, ff. 69v-76r; Cambridge, Gonville & Gaius Coll., 353, 2, ff. 95r-102r, and others. Only the last named has been linked to Wyclyf, in M. R. James' catalogue; it is a crowded field. St. Bernard, Giles of Rome, and even Augustine (cf. Migne, *PL* 40: col. 983) have variously been taxed with its authorship; but the real author was most probably Richard Rolle of Hampole.

G*Spur*.12, 13, 14. ——

There are three short pieces asc. to JW in the VC, all in JW codd. The first two are from ÖNB, 3930, ff. 187ra-192va [Questio. Circa preparacionem ewangelii de qua dictum est ... × ... et per omnia argumenta que in opposicionem sunt adducta etc.] and f. 230ra-va [Dilecte fili dilige lacrimos ... × ... respicias vivendo condempnes etc.] – but the latter expl. is very plainly followed by "Explicit liber ambrosii de moribus ecclesie etc." The third is in ÖNB 4527, ff. 194v-209r [In materia de eukaristia est quedam posicio heretica ... × ... quam graciam sibi concedat dominus noster Ihesus Christus ... etc.]

Perhaps the ultimate Wyclyf *spurium* is "The Wife of Bath's Tale." Lucia B. Mirrielees claimed in her "John Wyclif's Freudian Complex," *University of California Chronicle* 32 (1930): 492-497, that an arcane 27-line code throughout the "Tale" betrays a ribald streak in our stern reformer!

Index of Manuscripts

Items enclosed in brackets are not *Wyclyfiana*. References are sequential within the given codices; lacunae are commonly non-Wyclyf items, or sometimes blank but numbered folios. The reader is directed both to the texts in question and to the various published manuscript catalogs of the respective collections for fuller particulars. NOTE: the VC listings appear *in textu* only; and for the few items in the Bateson book, see the General Index below. Finally, alternate shelfmarks (Oxford, Bodleian; Praha, UK and MK; etc.) are here omitted in the interests of compact citation.

ASSISI, Biblioteca Communale (BCommunale), 662: **2** (ff. 1ra-27rb), **3** (28va-109va)

BASEL, Universitäts- und öffentliche Bibliothek, A.X.66: **416** (ff. 304r-305r), **434** (305v)

BAUTZEN, Stadt- und Kreisbibliothek, M.St.8°.7: **44** (ff. 13r-19v)
Q° 24: **31** (ff. 228v-229v)

BERLIN-DAHLEM, Stiftung für Preussische Kulturbesitz, Theol. Fol. 580: [**48**n. (ff. 375r-401v)]

BRNO, Universitni Knihovna (UK), Mk II.24: **404** (ff. 17r, 30r)
Mk II.44: **408** (ff. 1r-33v), G*Spur*.5 (85r-210r), **53**n (210r), **431** (217r-233r), **426** (233r-241r), **49** (241v-252v), **53** (253r-276v)
Mk II.123: G*Spur*.2 (ff. 99v-103r)

BRUGES, Bibliothèque Publique, 497: [5n (ff. 46ra-59va)]

CAMBRIDGE, Corpus Christi College, 103: **4** (pp. 47a-87b), [**4**n (331a-415b)], **378** (419a-427b), **380** (428a-b)
180: **23-25**n
436: **53** (ff. 97r-135r)
——, Gonville and Caius College, 337: **11** (ff. 1r-47v), **11**n (47r-48v), **12** (48v), **23-25** (68r-127v), **22** (128r-178r), **26** (181r-277v), **27** (278r-287v)
353.2: G*Spur*.11 (ff. 95r-102r)
——, Jesus College, 59: **39** (ff. 140v-144v)

——, Peterhouse College, 223: **31** (ff. 179r-281v)
——, Queen's College, 15: **31** (ff. 1r-190r)
——, Trinity College, B.14.50: **433** (f. 20r), **40** (56r-58r)
B.15.28: **26** (ff. 1r-128r), **424** (128r-130r)
B.16.2: **7** (ff. 4ra-9va), **8** (9va-13rb), **9** (13va-16rb), **10** (16va-19va), **11** (23ra-44rb), **12** (46ra-57ra), **14** (59ra-66ra), **15** (66ra-82vb), **16** (83ra-104ra), **17** (108ra-127ra), **18** (131ra-137va), **19** (139vb-157ra), **55-111** (142ra-184rb [ink foliation]), **115-175** (184va-234va [i.f.]), **112-114** (234va-237rb [i.f.]), **176-229** (238ra-290va [i.f.]), **235-298** (290va-346rb [i.f.]), **230-234** (347ra-352bisr [i.f.]), **374-377** (353ra-437vb [i.f.])
O.4.43: **388** (pastedowns & front flyleaf)
——, University Library, Ff.i.21: **23-25**n
Ii.iii.29: **26** (ff. 2ra-45vb)
Ll.v.13: **26** (ff. 2ra-108va)

Città del Vaticano, see *Vaticano, Città del*

DUBLIN, Trinity College, A.5.3: **34** (pp. 176-179)
C.1.23: **374-377** (pp. 3a-332a), **27** (332b-350a), **12** (350a-386b), **12**n (387a), **180-182** (387a-396b), **185** (396b-398a), **32** (398b-403b), **235-236** (404a-413a), **374-377**n (414a-422b)
C.1.24: **31** (pp. 1-3), **31**n (4-7), **31** (8a-248b), **35** (249a-293a), **36** (293a-

310b), **35**n (310b-311b), **37** (312a-422b)
DURHAM, Cathedral Library, Dean and Chapter Muniments: **30** (ff. 110r-125v)
ERFURT, Wissenschaftliche Bibliothek der Stadt (SB Amplon.), Q° 253: **1** (ff. 1r-24v)
EL ESCORIAL, e.II.6: **2** (ff. 1ra-18vb), **3** (19ra-76vb), **20** (78ra-87rb), **21** (87va-97rb), **18** (97rb-103va), **11** (104ra-124rb)
ETON, College Library, 47: **39** (ff. 119r-121v)
FIRENZE, Biblioteca Medicea Laurenziana (BLaur), Plut.XIX.33: **431** (ff. 1r-11v), **412** (11r-18v), **423** (18v-22r), **383** (22r-23v), **403** (23v-26v), **413** (26v-29v), **32** (29v-30r), **415** (30r-38r), **408** (38r-57r), **47** (57v-165v), **405** (166r-173v), **30** (174r-182v)
——, Biblioteca Nazionale Centrale (BNC), Conv. Sopp. E.3.379: **408** (ff. 1r-15v)
HERRNHUT, Archiv der Brüder-Unität, ABII.R.1.16.a: **200-202** (ff. 35r-52r), **203** (55r-56v), **208** (145r-147v)
KARLSRUHE, Badische Landesbibliothek (BLB), 343: **415** (f. 1r), **432** (1r-5r), **414** (5r-8v), **44** (8v)
346: G*Spur*.6 (ff. 1-120)
KRAKÓW, Biblioteka Jagiellońska (BJag), 848: **11** (ff. 3ra-36ra), **18** (38ra-50rb), **21** (51ra-72ra), **12** (72va-96vb)
1855: **11** (ff. 86r-125v)
LINCOLN, Cathedral Chapter Library (Cath. Chap.), C.1.15: **11** (ff. 293ra-321va), **12** (325ra-339va), **12**n (339va-340ra)
LONDON, British Library (BL), Add. 5902: **400** (ff. 36r-41v)
Arundel 458: G*Dub*.9 (ff. 68r-82r)
Cotton, Vesp. DXXIII: **430** (ff. 21r-29r)
Harley 31: [**39**n]
Harley 206: [**39**n]
Harley 1731: [**47**n]
Lansdowne 409: [**23-25**n, **48**n (ff. 39r-69v)]
Royal 6 E.III: G*Spur*.11 (ff. 105v-107r)
Royal 7. B.III: **22** (ff. 66r-75r), **39** (75r-76v), **39**n (77r)
Royal 7 E.X: **410** (ff. 74rb-75ra), **31** (166ra-213vb)
Royal 7 F.XI: G*Spur*.11 (ff. 259v-262v)
Royal 10 E.II: [**28-30**n], [**38**n]
Royal 13 E.IX: **399** (ff. 250va-251vb)
Royal 17 B.XVII: G*Spur*.11 (ff. 69v-76r)
——, College of Arms, Arundel 7: **399**
——, Lambeth Palace, 23: **257-284** (ff. 258ra-280vb)
121: **410** (ff. 238v-239v)
537: **383** (pp. 1-24)
1058: **49** (pp. 1-23)
MANCHESTER, John Rylands Library, Eng. 86: **414** (ff. 21v-24v), **423** (45r-48v), **428** (49r-54r), **394** (54v), **373** (55r-64v), **413** (65r-68v), **372** (69r-82v), **405** (82v-89v), **413**n (89v), **415** (90r-96v), **408** (97r-116v), **391** (117r), **408** (118r-121r)
MELK, Stiftsbibliothek, E.20: [**47**n (ff. 173v-175v)]
MÜNCHEN, Bayerische Staatsbibliothek (BSB), clm 15771: **427** (ff. 19r-26r), **404** (27r), **300** (27r-28r), **422** (29v-31v), **432** (32r-34v), **408** (35r-49r)
NAPOLI, Biblioteca Nazionale (BN), VII.A.34: G*Spur*.5 (ff. 69-90)
OLOMOUC, Kapitolní Knihovna (KapK); now in OPAVA, Státní Archiv, C.O.115: **31** (ff. 2v-296v)
C.O.118: **408** (ff. 182r-198r), **409** (198v-202v), **202** (202v-204v)
——, Státní vědecká Knihovna, I.V.34: **408** (ff. 1r-23v), **53** (26r-48v), **416** (176r), **406** (176r), **417** (176r), **434** (176r-v)
OXFORD, Balliol College, 93: [**6**n (ff. 65ra, 67ra)]
——, Bodleian, 52: **410** (ff. 100v-102v)
333: **26** (ff. 109ra-186va)
703: **39** (ff. 57ra-58vb), [**39**n (59a-65vb)], **383** (66va-68vb), [**17**n (129r)]
716: **345-371** (ff. 1ra-171vb)
924: **31** (pp. 1-621)
Arch. Selden B.26: **400** (ff. 83va-85va), **401** (85va-87vb), **383** (88ra-90ra)
Ashmolean 424: [**4**n]
Canon misc. 219: [**5**n (ff. 102va-103rb)]

INDEX OF MANUSCRIPTS

Digby 49: [**6**n (f. 80r)]
e Musaeo 86: **41** (ff. 34va-35ra), **39** (36vb-39va), **400** (64va-66vb), **398** (66vb-69vb), **229** (71vb), **47** (71vb-72rb), **404** (83ra-va), **205** (?), **206** (?)
James 3: **26**n (pp. 89-106), **31**n (107-227), **410** (228-229), **39** (261-262), **400** (304-314), **401** (314-323), **408** (346-352), **413** (354)
James 12: [**39**n (pp. 103-107)]
Lat.th.C.32: [**5**n (f. 26vb)]
—, Corpus Christi College, 116: [**13**n (ff. 48r-56v, 132r-140r)]
—, Magdalen College, 38: **5** (ff. 23ra-28vb)
47: [**11**n (f. 53v)]
55: **328-332** (ff. 1ra-76vb), **345-371** (77ra-248va)
75: [**23-25**n]
97: [**11**n (ff. 102v-106r)]
98: **26** (ff. 117ra-206va)
117: **328-344** (ff. 1ra-273***ra), **320** (274ra-319ra)
—, Merton College, 113: G*Dub*.15 (ff. 107ra-116rb)
175: [**37**n]
308: [**4**n]
—, Oriel College, 15: **22** (ff. 225ra-243ra)
—, St John's College, 171: **320-344** (ff. 1r-374v)
PARIS, Bibliothèque Nationale (BN), f.l. 3183: [**381**n (ff. 160v-168v)]
f.l. 3184: **402** (ff. 35v-46r), **381** (46v-48r), **382-383** (49r-52v), **400** (53r-54v)
f.l. 3222: [**23-25**n (ff. 1-78)]
f.l. 14619: [**28-30**n], [**47**n (ff. 167v-168v)]
f.l. 15869: **28** (ff. 70r-103r), [**28-30**n (103r-108r)], **26** (109r-120v), **30** (120v-125r)
PAVIA, Biblioteca Universitaria (BU), 311: **11** (ff. 1ra-35va), **12** (38ra-42ra), **18** (42rb-47vb), **12** (48ra-61vb), **22** (62ra-71vb), **18** (72ra-76rb), **21** (76rb-91rb), **22** (91va-b), **21** (92), **22** (93ra-97vb, 108ra-130rb)
PRAHA, Knihovna Metropolitni Kapituli (MK), A.70: **26** (ff. 192r-275v), **51** (275v-276v), **26**n (277r-279v)

A.84: **31** (ff. 122ra-149rb)
A.117: G*Spur*.5 (ff. 15-146)
B.6.3: **300** (ff. 241r-242v), **415** (242v-248v), **432** (251v-255r), **414** (255r-261v)
B.17.1: **408** (ff. 134v-160v), **402** (184v-209r)
B.48.1: G*Spur*.5 (ff. 1-161)
B.48.2: G*Spur*.5 (ff. 1-137), **392** (137v-138v)
B.53: **31** (ff. 1r-274r), **31**n (274r-278r)
C.38: **26**n (ff. 1ra-17vb), **26** (18ra-107va), **31** (107va-158va), **408** (159ra-172va), **404** (172vb-173ra), **26**n (173ra-174va), **51** (182va-183rb)
C.73: **37** (ff. 11ra-86rb), **36** (86va-161ra), **41** (161ra), **34** (161rb-259va), **45** (259va-262vb), **34**n (263ra-264va)
C.116: **141-142**, **145-147** (ff. 333r-337r)
C.118: **38** (ff. 1r-?), **34** (96v), **36** (96v-110r), **23-25** (110r-130v)
D.35: **22** (ff. 1r-77v)
D.50: **416** (f. 23r), **411** (268r-279v)
D.123: **202** (ff. 23r-28v), **141-142**, **145-147** (29r-42r), **432** (52r-62v), **414** (63r-72v), **44** (72v-82v), **421** (82v-84v), **394** (84v-87v), **300** (87v-92v), **393** (92v-94v), **435** (94v-100r), **422** (100v-107v), **429** (107v-136v), **413** (136v-144v), **401** (144bisr-149v), **52** (150r), **416** (150v), **406** (151r), **387** (151r), **409** (183r-193v), **390** (?)
F.20: **53** (ff. 136r-155v)
L.36: **11** (ff. 139ra-169vb)
M.54: **11** (ff. 1r-106r), **18** (109r-144v), **20** (145r-169v), **12** (170r-210v)
M.136: [**5**n (ff. 59v-86v)]
N.19: **17** (ff. 13ra-57ra), **18** (59ra-71ra), **20** (71rb-88ra), **12** (88ra-110va), [**3**n (110vb-121ra)], **2** (129ra-166ra)
N.48: **141-142**, **145-147** (ff. 155r-160r), **416** (175r), **372** (175v-178r)
O.11: G*Spur*.10
O.29: **37** (ff. 118r-129v), **36** (142r-149r), **35** (149v-152v), **38** (153r-160v), **31** (161r-162r), **47** (162r-166r), **34** (166r-177v), **414** (184r-187v), **404** (226v?), **395** (227r-228r), **396** (228r),

52 (228r), **417** (228r-v), **28-30** (234v-236r)

—, Národný Museum (NM), I.E.6: **413** (ff. 101r-104r)

XXX.F.9: **348-370** (ff. 1r-191v)

—, Universitní Knihovna (UK), III.B.5: **31**n (ff. 1ra-3ra), **398** (3rb-5ra), **401** (5rb-7ra), **31** (7ra-155vb)

III.F.11: **37** (ff. 1ra-69va), **36** (69vb-134rb), **41** (134va), **34** (134vb-223ra), **45** (223va-226va), **34**n (226va-228rb)

III.F.20: **345-348** (ff. 3r-199r)

III.G.10: **20** (ff. 5r-30v), **12** (31r-69v), **11** (70r-104r), **18** (119r-139v)

III.G.11: **53** (ff. 1r-27v), **402** (28r-49v), **402**n (49r-v), **299** (52r-53v), **389** (53v-55v), **421** (55v-56v), **422** (56v-60r), **392** (60r-61v), **409** (62r-69v), **202** (69v-72r), **27** (72r-85v), **42** (86r), **237-239** (112r-122v), **241-244** (122v-137r), **247** (137r-141r), **50** (154r-160v), **386** (160v-170v), **430** (170v-174v), **372** (174v-178v), **372** (178v-190v), **373** (190v-201r), G*Dub*.1 (201r-208v), **36** (208v-220v), **435** (220v-223r), **45** (223r-227r), **401** (227r-230v), **397** (230v-233v), **44** (234r-238r), **49** (238v-250r), **426** (250r-260r), **255-256** (260v-268v), **246** (268v-271r)

III.G.16: **34** (f. 15v), **397** (33r-35v), **412** (36r-39r), **385** (86r-87v)

IV.A.18: **374-377** (ff. 1ra-202va)

IV.D.21: **26** (ff. 2ra-105vb)

IV.D.22: **26** (ff. 1ra-129va), **38** (130bis-ra-207rb)

IV.G.27: **26**n (ff. 1ra-35vb), **28-30** (36ra-124vb), **26** (125ra-146va)

IV.H.7: **429** (ff. 13r-30r), **427** (31r-42r), **432** (43v-48r), **49** (49r-55v), **372** (58r-80r), **426** (81r-92v), **44** (93r-98r), **401** (98v-102v), **373** (103r-116r)

IV.H.9: **11** (ff. 1ra-56vb), **20** (56vb-73va), **21** (73va-93rb), **12** (94ra-113vb), **18** (114r-130v), G*Dub*.7 (258v-259r), [**3**, **5**n (259r-262v)]

V.A.3: **26** (ff. 1r-121v)

V.E.3: G*Spur*.5 (ff. 13r-166r), **392** (166r-167v)

V.E.14: **2** (ff. 1r-32r), **3** (33r-176v), G*Spur*.6 (177r-202v)

V.E.17: **26** (ff. 2r-180r), **51** (180r-183v)

V.E.28: **402** (f. 159rb-va)

V.F.9: **413** (ff. 13r-18v), **388** (18v-39r), **394** (39r-40v), **412** (41v-54r), **411** (54r-68r), G*Spur*.1 (68v-75v), **431** (83v-97v), **417** (97v), **421** (98r-v), **394** (98v-100r), **393** (100r-101r), **400** (101r-103v), **426** (104r-111v), **49** (112r-122v), **422** (122v-126v), **44** (126r-130r), **50** (130v), **53** (131r-147r), **53**n (147v-148r)

V.F.17: **409** (ff. 157r-165v), **402** (166r-194r), **52** (213r-v), **434** (213v-214v)

V.G.10: **386** (ff. 138r-148v)

V.G.19: **385** (ff. 256v-258v)

V.H.16: **11** (ff. 1r-78r), **18** (79r-100r), **20** (100r-121v)

V.H.27: **29** (ff. 59r-65r), **241** (65v-68r), **273-275** (68v-77r)

V.H.33: **2** (ff. 1r-28r)

VIII.C.3: **31** (ff. 2ra-222rb)

VIII.E.11: **5** (ff. 55v-72v), [**5**n (140r)]

VIII.F.1: **11** (ff. 1ra-39rb), **20** (39rb-53rb), **21** (53va-73rb), **18** (73va-87rb), **12** (87rb-113ra)

VIII.F.9: **349-370** (ff. 1r-200r)

VIII.F.13: **408** (ff. 186r-211r)

VIII.F.16: G*Dub*.2 (ff. 1r-61v)

VIII.G.6: **11** (ff. 1r-57r), **20** (57r-79v), **21** (81r-109v)

VIII.G.23: **11** (ff. 1r-84r), **20** (211v-234v)

VIII.G.32: **38** (ff. 1r-82v), **17** (83r-143v)

IX.E.3: **3** (ff. 1r-176r)

IX.E.6: **14** (ff. 1r-15v), **15** (16r-51r), **19** (51r-55v), **16** (56r-96r)

X.C.23: **408** (ff. 169ra-182vb), **53** (183ra-194ra), **434** (195ra-b), **406** (195rb-va), **417** (195va), **416** (195va), **300** (195va-196va), **433** (196va), G*Dub*.6 (196vb-197ra), **412** (203ra-206va), **419** (?)

X.D.10: **402** (ff. 35vb-45va), **402**n (45va-b), **392** (106v-107r), **402** (179ra-180va)

X.D.11: **32** (ff. 1ra-130rb), **33** (130rb-210va), **33**n (210va-212ra), **32**n (212ra-214vb)

X.E.6: **30** (f. 61v)

X.E.9: **53** (ff. 37r-67r), **53**n (67r-68v), **35**n (69r-70r), **35** (70v-126r), **35**n (126r-131r), **50** (132r-136v), **427** (137r-146r), **414** (146v-150r), **394** (150v-151v), **413** (151v-156v), **388** (156v-174r), **431** (174v-194r), G*Dub*.1 (194r-202r), **204** (202r-206r), **410** (208r-209r), **395** (209r-210r), G*Spur*.2 (210v-214v)

X.E.11: **31** (ff. 1ra-30va), **32** (30vb-45rb), **33** (45va-55ra), **34** (55rb-72va), **35** (72va-76ra), **36** (76rb-92rb), **37** (92va-113vb), **47** (113rb-146ra), **38** (146rb-167va), **20** (167vb-173vb), **12** (174ra-175rb), **18** (175va-177ra), **20** (177rb-181va), **23-25** (183ra-205vb), **26** (206ra-230vb)

X.E.24: G*Dub*.2 (ff. 133r-135v), G*Dub*.3-5 (210r-226r), G*Spur*.6 (295v-298r)

X.G.1: **26**n (ff. 1ra-19rb), **26** (20r-158v)

X.G.11: **387** (f. 302r)

X.H.9: [**11**nn (ff. 1r-68r)]

X.H.13: G*Dub*.17 (ff. 141v-158v, 181r-184v), **434** (184v-185v)

X.H.17: **53** (ff. 37r-57r), **417** (92r), G*Dub*.17 (92r), **406** (92v), **416** (134v)

XI.E.3: **429** (ff. 1r-5v), **431** (5v-11v), **300** (11v-12r), **422** (12v-13v), **38** (15r-54r), **39** (54v-58r), **397**n (58r), **34** (58v), **406** (59r), **400** (59v-61r), **43** (61v), **39** (69r-76r)

XII.F.21: **53** (ff. 35r-61v)

XIV.C.26: **26** (ff. 141r-236v)

XXIII.F.58: **11** (ff. 3r-71r), **12** (75r-109r), **21** (109v-140v), **20** (141r-161v), **18** (162r-187r)

SALAMANCA, Biblioteca Universitaria (BU), 2358: **5** (ff. 33v-50r)

STOCKHOLM, Kunglig Bibliotheket (KunglB), Lat.A.164: **12** (ff. 1r-33v), **18** (34r-52v), **20** (53r-76r), **11** (87r-134r)

TŘEBOŇ, Státní Archiv, 17: [**12**n (ff. 160r-167v)]

VATICANO, CITTÀ DEL, Borgh.lat.29: **414** (ff. 4r-7r), **388** (7r-23v), **402** (24r-45r), **400** (45r-47v), **408** (47v-66v), **395** (66v-67v), **404** (67v), **420** (68r-71r), **300** (71r-72v)

Vat.lat.3065: [**5**n (ff. 21ra-31vb)]

Vat.lat.4313: **11** (ff. 1ra-31rb), **38** (31rb-70va)

VENEZIA, Biblioteca Nazionale Marciana (BMarc), Lat.VI.172: **12** (ff. 1ra-27va), **11** (27va-78va), **18**, **20**

Lat.VI.173: **6** (ff. 1ra-58vb)

Z.L.301: [**5**n (ff. 37rb-41rb)]

WIEN, Österreichische Nationalbibliothek (ÖNB) 1294: **31** (ff. 1ra-119vb), **31**n (120ra-127rb), **32** (128ra-207vb), **32**n (208ra-210va), **23-25** (212ra-251vb)

1337: **53** (ff. 1ra-20vb), **45** (20vb-23va), **415** (23va-24rb), **427** (25ra-33ra), **422** (33ra-35vb), **421** (36ra-vb), **394** (36vb-37vb), **432** (39va-43va), **414** (43va-47ra), **44** (47rb-50vb), **404** (51ra-b), **395** (51rb-52rb), **396** (52rb-va), **416** (52va-b), **393** (52vb-53va), **52** (53va-b), **413** (53vb-57vb), **411** (57vb-67va), **410** (67ra-68ra), **46** (68ra-71rb), **389** (71va-72vb), **426** (73ra-81va), **429** (81va-95ra), **299** (95ra-96vb), **417** (96vb), **424** (97ra-100va), **425** (100va-102rb), **435** 102rb-104va), **50** (104vb-110ra), **372** (110rb-114ra), **390** (114ra-115rb), **397** (115rb-117va), **415** (117va-125ra), **412** (125ra-134vb), **431** (134vb-150va), **49** (150va-161ra), **141-142**, **145-147** (161ra-165vb), **408** (166ra-168va), **202** (168va-170rb), **265** (170rb-174va), **407** (174va-b), **398** (175ra-178va), **401** (178va-181va), **418** (181va-b), **17** (182ra-243vb), **18** (244ra-258vb)

1338: **402** (ff. 1ra-17vb), **400** (18ra-20va), **409** (20vb-26va), **430** (26va-29va), **434** (29va-30ra), **387** (30rb), **419** (30rb), **433** (30rb-va), **406** (30va), **417** (30va-b), **407** (30vb), **372** (31ra-44va), **373** (44va-54ra), **408** (55ra-81ra), **48** (82ra-99rb), **388** (100ra-116ra), **386** (116ra-123vb), **384** (123va-141rb)

1339: **23-25** (ff. 1ra-89vb), **26** (91ra-234rb), **26**n (234rb-236rb), **27** (237ra-248vb)

INDEX OF MANUSCRIPTS

1340: **30** (ff. 1ra-260vb)
1341: **29** (ff. 1ra-144va), **28-30**n (144rb-152vb), **30** (153ra-251vb), **28-30**n (252vb-254vb)
1342: **345-370** (ff. 1ra-348vb)
1343: **35** (ff. 1ra-35rb), **35**n (35va-36vb), **36** (37ra-124vb), **37** (125ra-230va)
1387: **38** (ff. 1ra-43rb), **39** (43rb-46rb), **17** (47ra-74vb), **22** (75ra-104vb), **404** (105ra), **395** (105rb), **396** (105va), **416** (105vb), **393** (105vb-106rb), **390** (106rb-vb), **387** (107ra), **52** (107ra), **433** (107rb), **417** (107rb), **406** (107rb), **435** (107rb-108va), **415** (108va-109ra), **407** (109ra), **408** (109ra-110va), **202** (110va-111va), **401** (111va-113ra), **45** (113rb-114vb), **48** (115ra-123rb), **409** (123rb-125vb), **402** (126ra-134rb), **400** (134rb-135vb), **372** (138ra-144va), **373** (145ra-149rb), **408** (150ra-162vb), **47** (163ra-215ra)
1598: **26** (ff. 1r-78v)
1622: **35** (ff. 83r-127v), G*Dub*.18 (127v-128r), **408** (133r-157v), **384** (157v-179v), **417** (179v), **393** (179v-180r), **394** (180v-181v), **300** (181v-183v), **432** (183v-188r)
1647: **374-377** (ff. 1ra-298va)
1725: **23-25** (ff. 1r-31v), **26** (33r-67v), **28-30** (81r-236r)
1925: [**18**n (ff. 135v-139r)]
3926: G*Spur*.4 (ff. 1r-187r)
3927: **432** (ff. 1ra-3va), **414** (3va-5vb), **44** (5vb-8rb), **421** (8rb-vb), **394** (8vb-9va), **300** (9va-10vb), **395** (10vb-11rb), **404** (11rb-va), **384** (11va-24rb), **417** (24rb-va), **393** (24va-25ra), **431** (25ra-36rb), **426** (37ra-43ra), **49** (43ra-49vb), **35** (53ra-74rb), **35**n (74va-b), **38** (77ra-122ra), **38**n (122ra-123vb)
3928: **115-173** (ff. 1ra-123ra), **236** (123rb-126va), **245** (126va-128rb), **175** (128rb-131rb), **112-114** (131va-139ra), **252-256** (139ra-152va), **237-244** (152va-170rb), **246-251** (170vb-185ra), **299** (185ra-186rb), **141-142**, **145-147** (186va-189ra), G*Dub*.16 (189rb-190ra), **257-294** (193ra-253rb)
3929: **32** (ff. 1ra-114ra), **23-25** (114rb-170rb), **48** (170va-181vb), **424** (182ra-184rb), **425** (184rb-185rb), **435** (185va-187ra), **415** (187ra-192ra), **388** (192rb-203va), **400** (203vb-205va), **299** (205va-206va), **389** (206va-207va), **416** (207va-b), **417** (207vb), **434** (207vb-208rb), **52** (208rb-va), **419** (208va), **395** (208va-b), **387** (208vb), **50** (208vb-212ra), **413** (212ra-214vb), **394** (215ra-vb), **401** (215vb-217va), **410** (217va-218ra), **386** (218rb-223rb), **429** (225ra-233rb), **411** (233rb-239vb), **412** (239vb-246ra), **397** (246ra-247va), **372** (247va-250ra), G*Dub*.1 (261va-266rb), **390** (266rb-267ra), **27** (267rb-274va), **385** (274va-275ra)
3930: **47**n (ff. 1ra-2rb), **408** (3ra-22vb), **47** (23ra-124vb), **372** (125ra-141rb), **373** (141rb-150va), **434** (166ra-va), **435** (166va-168vb), **427** (168vb-178va), **426** (178va-186vb), G*Spur*.12 (187rb-192va), **432** (192va-196rb), **204** (197vb-202ra), **44** (217va-221ra), **49** (221ra-230va), G*Spur*.13 (230ra-va), **412** (230vb-239vb), **411** (239vb-250va), **431** (250va-264vb), **415** (264vb-271vb), **50** (300ra-303vb)
3931: **115-173** (ff. 1ra-137rb), **236** (137rb-140vb), **245** (140vb-142va), **175** (142va-145vb), **112-114** (145vb-153vb), **252-256** (153vb-167vb), **237-244** (167vb-186vb), **246-251** (186vb-201vb), **299** (201vb-203ra)
3932: **47** (ff. 1ra-72rb), **408** (72rb-89vb), G*Dub*.8 (89vb), **408**n (90va-b), **47**n (91ra-92ra), **257-295** (92va-152vb), **141-142**, **145-147** (153ra-155va), G*Dub*.16 (155v-156r), **38** (157ra-207va), **252** (207va-209rb)
3933: **33** (ff. 1ra-57rb), **33**n (58ra-62va), **411** (63ra-70ra), **412** (70ra-76vb), **50** (76vb-80vb), **427** (80vb-86vb), **389** (87ra-vb), **415** (88vb-92ra), **401** (92ra-94ra), **45** (99ra-101va), **53** (101va-117ra), **37** (117ra-183va), **37**n (185ra-195rb)
3934: **54-114** (ff. 1ra-132vb), **32** (148r-151r)

3935: **23-25**n (ff. 1ra-11va), **23-25** (13ra-48ra), **36** (49ra-128vb), **37** (129ra-223ra), **27** (225ra-231ra), **17** (237ra-271rb)
3937: **35** (ff. 115ra-137va)
4002: [**18**n (ff. 18r-23r)], G*Dub*.2 (38r-41r), **18** (42r-52r)
4302: **408** (ff. 25r-50r), **53** (53v-74r), **21** (75ra-96ra)
4307: **21** (ff. 38v-62r), **11** (62v-114r), **22** (115r-157v), **7** (158r-167v), **8** (167v-177r), **9** (177v-184r), **10** (185r-190v), **13** (190v-242v)
4308: **53** (ff. 133r-156v)
4316: **17** (ff. 1r-79v), **12** (85r-125r), G*Dub*.13 (125v-129r), **404** (129v-130r)
4343: **39** (ff. 225r-234r), **42** (234v-235r), G*Dub*.12 (235r-236r), **402** (236v-262r), **409** (262v-270r), **141-142**, **145-147** (270r-271v)
4483: **200** (ff. 67r-69r)
4488: **28-30** (ff. 11r, 36r)
4504: **35**n (ff. 1r-2r), **35** (2r-36r), **22** (37r-110v), G*Dub*.13 (110v-113v), **404** (114r), **21** (121r-153r)
4505: **408** (ff. 1r-29v), **47** (34r-187v), **48** (188r-207r), **425** (207r-209r), **47**n (209ra-227va)
4514: G*Spur*.3 (ff. 1r-26v), **37** (29r-86r), **37**n (86r-102v), **33** (105r-182v), **33**n (182r-184r)
4515: **408** (ff. 1r-26v), **35** (27r-67v), **415** (75r-83r), **416** (83r-v), **417** (83v), **406** (83v), **434** (83v-84r), G*Dub*.14 (193r), **50** (204v-207v, 210r-212ra)
4516: **47** (ff. 88r-203v)
4518: [**18**n (ff. 165v-169v)]
4522: **26**n (ff. 24r-108v), **53** (109r-131v), **409** (133r-139v), **42** (139v), **141-142**, **145-147** (139v-144v)
4523: **1** (ff. 1r-16r), **2** (16r-58r), **11** (58r-132v), **18** (133r-186r)
4526: G*Spur*.5 (ff. 1r-131r)
4527: **388** (ff. 1r-17r), **435** (17r-19r), **431** (19r-34r), **429** (34v-46v), **384** (46v-65v), **410** (66r-67r), **386** (67r-75v), **432** (75v-79r), **413** (79r-83r), **394** (83r-84v), **372** (85r-98v), **373** (98v-107r), **44** (107r-110v), **49** (110v-120v), **414** (120v-124r), **412** (124v-133v), **411** (134r-144r), **395** (144r-v), **434** (145r-v), **416** (145v-146r), **417** (146r), **406** (146r), **52** (146r-v), **419** (146v), **404** (146v-147r), **387** (147r), **396** (147v), **393** (147v-148r), **426** (148v-156r), **50** (157r-162r), **427** (162r-169r), **300** (169v-171r), **415** (171r-178r), **373** (178r-181r), **430** (181r-184r), G*Dub*.1 (184v-191r), **372** (191r-194v), G*Spur*.14 (194v-209r), **53** (209r-226ra), **53**n (226ra-vb), **204** (226v-229v)
4529: **54-114** (ff. 1r-165r)
4536: **408** (ff. 33r-67r), **53** (67v-96v), **53**n (96v-98v), **431** (98v-122r), **415** (122r-132v), **35** (132r-187va), **35**n (187va-191va), **388** (193r-216r), **411** (237r-253r)
4701: **408** (ff. 41r-57r)
4878: [**11**n (f. 4v)]
4925: G*Spur*.5 (ff. 1r-134v)
4937: **390** (ff. 26v-28r), G*Spur*.1 (28r-34v), **300** (80r-82v), **395** (82v-83v), **404** (84r-v)
5204: **11** (ff. 1r-65r), **5** (76r-96v)
5239: **5** (ff. 146r-147v)
11635: G*Spur*.3 (ff. 1r-161r)
WOLFENBÜTTEL, Herzog August Bibliothek (HzglB), Cod.Guelf.306: **176-234** (ff. 3ra-197vb), **235-236** (201rb-209va), **401** (210ra-213va), **372** (213va-229va), **373** (229va-240vb), **429** (240vb-256vb), **299** 256vb-259ra), **433** (259ra), **36** (268rb-369vb), **41** (369vb-370ra)
Cod.Guelf.565: **54-111** (ff. 1ra-109vb), **176-234** (110ra-292va), **235-236** (296r-303r)
Cod.Guelf.669: **204** (ff. 175v-179v), **404** (219v-220r)
Cod.Guelf.1126: **53** (ff. 1r-46r), **32** (46r-84v)
WORCESTER, Chapter Library (Cath. Chap.), F.118: [**5**n]
WROCŁAW, Biblioteka Uniwersytecka (BU), IV.F.7: **11** (ff. 304ra-351rb)

Index of Incipits

It is a fact well known to medievalists that many thousands of works appearing in codices of the fourteenth and fifteenth centuries are identifiable, if at all, only from the correspondence of their opening words (and hence the rest of the text, more or less) with verifiable titled copies. Shirley's "Index of first words to the extant works" (pp. 70-72) really only continued the practice of the compilers of the vc themselves. Here we have systematized and extended this practice, limiting the citation, however, to between three and five words as a rule. Fuller incipits, consonant with syntactical balance, will be found under the item headings themselves. Finally, italicized incipits correspond to those few extracts not spelled out in the text. Digests, indices, summaries and the like are here excluded.

Abdias prophetando contra ydumeos ...	336	Christus qui mentiri ...	298
Ad declarandum veritatem ...	414	Christus stabilit suam ecclesiam ...	131
Aggei prophecia dividitur ...	342	Claret historia quomodo ...	78
Aliqua in ista epistola ...	256	Communiter exponitur ista epistola ...	254
Alithia. Licet dixit insipiens ...	47	Completa tractatu primo ...	376
Amice carissime. Vobis in nomine ...	387	Conclusio prima religio ...	G*Dub*.18
Amice preclare ex scripturis ...	390	Conclusio quam intendit Johannes ...	371
Ante ascensionem valeficiens ...	174	Consequens ad dicta est tractare ...	19
Apostolus in ista epistola hortatur ...	226	Consequens est purgare errores ...	9
Apostolus in ista epistola instruit ...	186	Consequenter ad ordinem clericalem ...	33
Apostolus intendit pro finali ...	352	Constat ad literam quomodo ...	58
Apostolus noscens omnia ...	350	Constat ex dicta sanctorum ...	106
Apostolus scripsit hanc epistolam Hebreis ...	362	Constat ex dicto capitulo ...	292
Arguitur sic: ecclesia militans potuit ...	43	Constat ex doctrina Augustini ...	204
Asia Minor pars est ...	353	Constat ex evangelica historia quomodo ...	281
		Constat ex evangelio Matth. septimo ...	113
Beatus iste Johannes ...	201	Constat ex evangelio quod tribus ...	55
Beatus Johannes affectus ...	367	Constat ex evidencia huius scripture ...	252
Beatus Lucas intendit ...	363	Constat ex fide evangelii ...	236
Celestis medicus et incontaminibilis ...	89	Constat ex fide quod Christus ...	94
Christus consolando suos contra tribulaciones ...	126	Constat ex fide quod mundus ...	121
Christus Deus noster caput ...	402	Constat ex fide scripture Act. primo ...	124

Constat ex fide scripture cum pauca ...	255	Cum Deus undiquaque ...	54
Constat ex fide scripture quod ...	241	Cum duplex debet esse officium ...	53
Constat ex fundamento fidei ...	238	Cum exposicio huius libri ...	208
Constat ex historia quomodo dominus ...	261	Cum genealogia cuiuscunque persone ...	128
Constat ex multis capitulis ...	81	Cum heretici diebus istis ...	424
Constat ex parabola hac evangelica ...	87	Cum locucio ad personam ...	47
		Cum materia et forma ...	20
Constat ex processu epistole ...	205	Cum nemo salvabitur ...	214
Constat ex sensu literali ...	289	Cum parvus error et missibilis ...	GIntro.
Constat ex serie evangelii quod Christus ...	294	Cum philosophi [pharisei] pseudo apostoli ...	G.Intro.
Constat ex serie evangelii quod salvator ...	265	*Cum prelati contencionum non episcopi ...*	202n
		Cum quecunque scripta ...	215
Constat ex serie evangelii quomodo Christo ...	296	Cum quilibet Christianus et specialiter ...	23
Constat ex serie evangelii quomodo duo ...	284	Cum salvator ordinatus est ...	132
		Cum sapiencia Dei ...	372
Constat ex serie evangelii quomodo pharisei ...	287	Cum secundum apostolum ad Hebreos ...	401
Constat ex serie evangelii quomodo quidam ...	290	Cum secundum fidem catholicam ...	411
		Cum secundum philosophis sit relativorum ...	405
Constat ex serie evangelii quomodo salvator ...	285	Cum secundum sanctos spectat ...	45
Constat ex serie evangelii quomodo Veritas ...	263	Cum secundum veritatis testimonium ...	415
Constat ex serie huius epistole ...	197	Cum spiritus sit tercia ...	50
Constat ex testimonio scripture ...	288	Cum triplex dicatur martyrium ...	117
Constat ex textu evangelii quomodo ipsum ...	103	Cum veritas fidei eo plus ...	409
Constat iuxta historiam quod aliis ...	274	Cum viantes et fratres ...	426
Constat quod Christus intelligit ...	101	Cum ydempnitas sit mater ...	408
Constat quod ecclesia integratur ...	92		
Constat quod inter septem ...	172	Danielem prophetam iuxta Septuaginta ...	332
Constat quod in prima parte ...	104	De quinque festis beate virginis ...	137
Constat quod Lucas ex informacione ...	64	De sedecim partibus in quas ...	329
		Detectis utrumque parumper arris ...	26nn
Constat quod per pacienciam ...	260	Deus ut rex supereminens ...	332
Constat quod tota servitus ...	282	Dictum est dominica proxima ...	271
Constat quomodo Jacobus ...	133	Dictum est in proxima epistola ...	225
Consuetudo gentilis superstitum ...	235	Dictum est sermone duodecimo ...	190
Continuando sermones sanctorum ...	115	Dictum est superiori dominica ...	264
		Dictum est superius sermone ...	155
Convenimus ex mandato domini ...	32n	Dicturus de oracione suppono ...	46
Corinthi dicuntur esse ...	227	Dictus est in communi verbo ...	194
Cotidie legimus evangelium attestans ...	156	Dictus est superius quod tercius ...	377
		Die Parasceves dictum est ...	277
Cum Christi dileccio includit ...	85	Dilecte filii dilige ...	G*Spur*.13
Cum Christus sit primus ...	432	Dilectis et prudentibus ...	G*Spur*.3

Discipulus quidam venerabilis ...	G*Dub*.16
Dividitur autem liber iste in prohemium ...	331
Dividitur in prohemium ...	344
Docet apostolus prima ...	G*Dub*.13
Docet beatus Petrus ...	203
Doctor meus reverendus ...	381
Doctrina huius evangelii nedum ...	71
Dubium est utrum regnum ...	398
Duobus modis solet Christus ...	278
Duo sunt genera ...	418
Duo sunt quibus Christus ...	168
Duo sunt sacramenta precipua ...	44
Ecclesia facit hodie mencionem ...	257
Epistola ad Thymotheum ...	358
Epistola ista prophetica narrat ...	184
Eremias propheta cui hic ...	329
Est autem triplex calumpnia ...	328
Evangelium dicitur bonum ...	346
Evangelium Johannis ultimo ...	348
Ex dictis superius satis liquet ...	15
Exodi sexto et vicesimo describitur ...	269
Expedito superficialiter de sentencia ...	164
Exposicio huius evangelii dicta est ...	163
Exposicio huius evangelii patet in parte ...	165
Ex serie evangelii hodierni ...	293
Extenso ente secundum eius ...	8
Fertur quendam fratrem ...	430
Fidelibus recte evangelizantibus ...	136
Frons meretricis facta est ...	300
Gaudeo plane detegere ...	404
Genesis vicesimosecundo patet quod ...	320
Gracia dicendarum restat tractare ...	4
Habitacio patet ex predictis ...	353
Habito quod Deus est creativus ...	19
Hac prophecia dividitur in prohemium ...	335
Hanc secundam epistolam ...	368
Hanc terciam epistolam ...	369
Hec civitas primo dicta est ...	123
Hec est forma iuramenti ...	397
Hec est prima septem parabolarum ...	70
Hec septima epistola ...	370
Hic ostenditur que religio ...	G*Dub*.14
Hoc evangelium alludit fundacioni ...	175
Hoc evangelium continet legem ...	141
Hoc evangelium dat formam multiplicem ...	152
Hoc evangelium dat fulcimenta ...	244
Hoc evangelium dirigit amorem ...	160
Hoc evangelium docet apostolos ...	145
Hoc evangelium docet fideles formam ...	243
Hoc evangelium docet in exemplo ...	166
Hoc evangelium docet martyres ...	154
Hoc evangelium docet per que media ...	151
Hoc evangelium docet quale ministerium ...	146
Hoc evangelium docet quante ...	150
Hoc evangelium docet quomodo est ...	240
Hoc evangelium docet quomodo quicunque ...	169
Hoc evangelium docet statum ...	173
Hoc evangelium enucleat martyribus ...	159
Hoc evangelium et multa alia ...	79
Hoc evangelium excitat et informat ...	170
Hoc evangelium facit mencionem de crucifixione ...	138
Hoc evangelium facit mencionem de primo ...	57
Hoc evangelium facit mencionem de secunda ...	62
Hoc evangelium facit mencionem de tercio ...	56
Hoc evangelium narrat de triplici ...	118
Hoc evangelium narrat triplicem ...	72
Hoc evangelium notificat ecclesie ...	130
Hoc evangelium potest intelligi ...	134
Hoc evangelium sicut est clarissimum ...	80
Hoc evangelium ut priora docet formam ...	161
Hoc evangelium ut priora docet quomodo ...	162

Hoc evangelium ut priora hortatur ad paciendum ...	149
Hoc evangelium ut priora hortatur ad prudenter ...	158
Hoc regnum celorum est filius ...	69
Hoc regnum celorum est in predicacione ...	68
Homo iste est Christus indubie ...	120
Homo iste est indubie dominus ...	119
Homo iste singularis est Christus ...	88
Hostia consecrata quam videmus ...	41
Huius evangelii plana est historia ...	142
Humilis servus Christi ...	396
Iam incidit tractare ...	GIntro.
Iam secundo restat lacius disserere ...	24
Iam ultimo restat videre ...	34
Ignorante quodam socio ...	G*Spur*.2
Illa hostia alba et rotunda ...	40
Illa pauca que narrant ...	59
Illorum que insunt Deo communiter ...	14
Incipit ergo partem ...	354
In epistola hodierna tria genera ...	272
In fine patet ad literam ...	77
Informatis Corinthiis de quattuor ...	351
In hac epistola apostolus docet ...	196
In hac prima canonica ...	365
In hac secunda epistola ...	366
In hoc brevi evangelio notatur ...	60
In hoc capitulo primo describitur ...	337
In hoc evangelio cum sit in uno ...	84
In hoc evangelio exprimitur Matthei ...	139
In hoc evangelio narratur instructivum ...	66
In hoc evangelio ostenditur auctoritas ...	148
In hoc evangelio replicatur sentencia ...	63
In ista epistola apostolus hortatur ...	191
In ista epistola apostolus innuens ...	220
In ista epistola commendat ...	198
In ista epistola declarat apostolus libertatem ...	183
In ista epistola docemur ...	219
In ista epistola docet apostolus ipsos ...	224
In ista epistola docet apostolus nedum ...	209
In ista epistola docet apostolus quod ...	222
In ista epistola docet apostolus quomodo Christiani ...	229
In ista epistola docet apostolus quomodo vita ...	217
In ista epistola docet apostolus singulos ...	199
In ista epistola docet Paulus ...	182
In ista epistola hortatur apostolus fideles ...	232
In ista epistola hortatur apostolus quod ...	213
In ista epistola hortatur apostolus Thessalonicos ...	195
In ista epistola immediate sequente ...	188
In ista epistola intendit apostolus ...	223
In ista epistola ostendit apostolus ...	233
In ista epistola ostendit et exemplificat ...	231
In ista epistola pro finali ...	189
In ista epistola que immediate ...	187
In ista epistola videtur multis ...	192
In istis verbis patet primo ...	279
In istis verbis tria sunt ...	270
In isto evangelio docetur ecclesia ...	67
In isto evangelio exprimitur promissio ...	129
In isto evangelio monet Christus ...	147
In isto supponendo tempus esse ...	12
In materia de eukaristia est ...	G*Spur*.14
In materia de religione ...	G*Dub*.1
In prefacione huius libri ...	328
In primis supponatur ens esse ...	7
In primo capitulo ponitur ...	332
In primo ergo Dragmate ...	323
In principio protestor publice ...	399
In prohemio primo notatur tempus ...	343
In prohemio tanguntur ...	331n
In próphetando de exaltacione ...	328
Inpugnante quodam ingenioso ...	G*Spur*.1
In purgando errores circa universalia ...	11
In sermone proximo dicetur ...	258
Intencio apostoli in ista ...	361

Inter alia doctor meus ...	383	Licet regnum sumatur ...	295
Inter quinque festa beate Marie ...	122	Licet totum evangelium ...	374
In titulo enim describitur ...	321	Lira dividit hanc propheciam ...	341
In tractando de dominio oportet ...	23	Lira dividit hunc librum in duas ...	339
In tractando de tempore ...	12	Lira dividit hunc librum in prohemium ...	338
In tractatu vero informat ...	364	Lucas intendit principaliter ...	347
Ista contencio sicut filiorum ...	135		
Ista epistola dividitur in quattuor ...	355		
Ista epistola docet fideles quomodo ...	200	Magister reverende et amice ...	385
		Malachia ultimus duodecim ...	344
Ista epistola docet fideles viantes ...	230	Marcus fuit a domino ...	346
Ista epistola docet humilitatem ...	212	Matheus ex Judea ...	345
Ista epistola docet media ...	216	Matheus qui interpretatur ...	345
Ista epistola docet specialius ...	180	Miraculum huius evangelii creditur ...	65
Ista epistola magnificat caritatem ...	193		
Ista epistola multipliciter docet ...	221	Mos est Johannis inter ceteros ...	83
Ista epistola sicut multe alie ...	202	Motus sum per quosdam legis ...	1
Ista epistola sicut quelibet ...	177	Motus sum per quosdam veritatis ...	431
Ista epistola tamquam clavis ...	179	Multiplex ponitur causa ...	245
Ista epistola ut prior docet ...	181		
Istam questionem quam quesivit ...	286	Navicula ista potest intelligi ...	105
Ista sentencia reseratur sepe ...	157	Nemo cum prophetas ...	328n
Iste est secundus liber ...	323	Nemo peccat in spiritum sanctum ...	52
Iste fuit Herodes ...	251	Nota est historia Genesis decimoseptimo ...	268
Iste liber dicitur soliloquium ...	321		
Iste sanctus apostolus Andreas ...	248	Notandum est ut homo ...	GDub.12
Istud autem verbum fuit prophete ...	185	Notandum quo triplex est osculum ...	323
Istud creditur esse evangelium ...	153		
Istud est festum tercium ...	125	Nota quod prelati debent ...	363
Istud evangelium continet historice ...	262	Notata historia evangelii hodierni constat ...	280
Istum sermonem direxit dominus ...	76	Notata historia huius evangelii cum aliis ...	111
Iuvenum rogatibus quibus afficior ...	2		
		Notata historia huius evangelii patet ...	110
Johannis evangelista more suo ...	210	Notata historia patent tria ...	96
		Notata historia patet quomodo fidelis ...	97
Libellus de universalibus continet ...	11		
Liber Abacuch dividitur ...	340	Notata historia potest allegorice ...	98
Liber Amos propheta dividitur ...	335	Notata litera evangelium patet ad sensum ...	95
Liber Baruch dividitur ...	330		
Liber duodecim prophetarum dividitur ...	B4.VI.Prol.	Notatis verbis huius evangelii ...	90
		Notatur temporis adventus ...	347
Liber iste secundum Liram ...	340		
Liber Jeremie prophete dividitur ...	329	Obiciencium contra dicta de universalibus ...	10
Liber Osee dividitur ...	333		
Liber tercius hymnidicus ...	324	Octava et ultima pars ...	349
Licet capitulo septimo et tricesimo ...	29	Omnes isti quattuor apostoli ...	364
Licet hoc evangelium sit gravidatum ...	99	Omnes quatuordecim libri ...	176
		Omnia ista tria evangelia ...	114

INDEX OF INCIPITS

Opus arduum valde ...	GSpur.5
Ordo autem caritatis exigit ...	171
Osee fuit filius prophete ...	333
Paralipomenon sexto et tricesimo et Jeremie ...	342
Patenti litera potest hoc evangelium ...	112
Patet ex dictis quod regnum ...	108
Patet ex hoc evangelio quomodo pharisei ...	109
Patet ex processu evangelii ...	102
Patet prima notata historia ...	91
Patet quod in tribus commendatur ...	61
Paulus apostolus in salutando ...	357
Paulus docet ad Ephesianos ...	421
Paulus hortatur Philippenses ...	354
Paulus in ista epistola ...	218
Paulus in prohemio reddit ...	349
Paulus more solito ...	356
Paulus vero authonomatice ...	352
Phylosophia realis dividitur in tres ...	6
Placeat illustrissimo regi ...	403
Plana est historia quomodo ...	242
Post fructum benediccionis ...	389
Post generalem sentenciam ...	247
Post generalem sermonem de heresi ...	35
Post nativitatem sancti sanctorum ...	116
Prelibato tractatu de anima ...	22
Premissa sentencia de dominio ...	26
Premittit Christus specialiter ...	144
Prima pars Ezechielis divisi in septem ...	331
Prima pars Ezechielis introducit grande ...	331
Prima pars Johel est comminativa ...	334
Prima pars libri Danielis ...	332
Prima pars libri Jone ...	337
Prima pars prophecie Michee ...	338
Prima pars Sophonie ...	341
Primo genus hortatur ...	322
Pro exposicione illius epistole ...	228
Prophecia Naum dividitur ...	339
Prophecia Zacharie dividitur ...	343
Propheta Johannes in ista ...	297
Protestor publice ut sepe ...	400
Pro quo notandum ...	348
Proxima dominica dixi fraternitati ...	273
Proximo die dominico introducta ...	291
Pseudofrater degens in seculo ...	433
Pseudofratres publicant [replicant] quod ...	419
Quamvis autem salutacio ...	425
Quamvis autem sentencia ...	178
Quamvis dyabolus ex naturali ...	420
Quando fui iunior ...	167
Quantum ad obiectum ...	435
Quantum ad sensum literalem huius evangelii ...	73
Quarta vero pars scripture ...	322
Questio. Circa preparacionem ...	GSpur.12
Quia autem finis mandatorum ...	143
Quia autem spiritualiter viantibus ...	22
Quia conturbati sunt discipuli ...	140
Quia evangelium istud est multis ...	373
Quia fides trinitatis ...	86
Quia ista est ultima ...	234
Quia ista monstruosa dissensio ...	410
Quia nonnulli eciam illi ...	32
Quia omnes homines natura scire ...	5
Quia secundum philosophum ...	386
Quidam doctor utinam ...	384
Quidam fidelis in domino ...	393
Quidam secularis probus ...	394
Quidam socius quem suppono ...	388
Quid in natura sua est ...	42
Qui pasceret corporaliter ...	276
Quod clerus regni ...	417
Quodcunque ligaverit vel solverit ...	407
Quo supposito potest ...	362
Redeundo iam tercio ad materiam ...	25
Regulus iste potest notare ...	107
Restat finaliter perstringere ...	408
Restat nunc [promissa] discutere differenciam ...	51
Restat parumper discutere errores ...	31
Restat succincte de blasfemia ...	37
Restat ulterius ponere aliud ...	36
Rex debet ex vi ...	406
Salutacio patet ex predictis ...	353
Salvator noster diligens ...	434
Sciendum quod per hunc ...	GDub.6
Secunda epistola scribitur ...	359

Secundum apostolum ad Ephesianos ...	422	Tercium nidum supremum ...	380
Secundum catholicos ecclesia ...	412	Terminus large loquendo est diccio ...	1
Secundum doctores hebraicos ...	336	Titus fuit ordinatus ...	360
Secundum Jeronimum in epistola ...	334	Tractando de civili dominio ...	28
Secundum philosophos finis est ...	299	Tractando de eucharistia oportet premittere ...	38
Secundum philosophos patet ...	206	Tractando de volucione dei ...	16
Secundum tres virtutes ...	429	Tractando de ydeis primo oportet ...	18
Secundus doctor meus reverendus ...	382	Tractatus dividitur in tria ...	367
Sensus huius evangelii potest allegorice ...	100	Tres sunt modi ...	GDub.7
		Tres sunt nidi ...	378
Sensus istius evangelii est eiusdem ...	82	Tria movent me tractare ...	21
		Tria possunt dici caritati ...	283
Sensus literalis huius evangelii patet ...	75	Tria possunt notari super literalem ...	93
		Tria sunt que magis conferunt ...	323
Sentencia huius evangelii est inclusa ...	127	Tria sunt vincula ...	427
Sentenciam humani dominii sicut duorum ...	26	Triplex autem ponitur racio [causa] ...	345
Sentencia tractatus de eucharistia ...	38		
Sepe assumptum est ...	428	Unus amicus fidelis in domino ...	391
Sepe confessum sum et adhuc ...	39	Ut dicitur infra sermone nono et tricesimo ...	259
Sequitur de speciebus ypoteticarum ...	3	Utitur autem liber iste ...	324
Sequitur in textu ...	375	Utrum clerus debuit dotacionem ...	48
Sicut dictum est de sacramento ...	246	Utrum prescitus sicut et predestinatus ...	GDub.15
Sicut est unus verus ...	423		
Sicut iste textus potest ...	250	*Utrum religio privata ...*	204n
Si papa vel eius vicario ...	413	*Ut simplices sacerdotes zelo animarum ...*	141-142, 145-147
Sive autem a verisimili ...	249		
Subito aurugine prima ...	392	Ut supradicta de lege Christi ...	30
Superest investigare de distinccione ...	17	Ut supradicta magis appareant ...	27
Superiori dominica dictum est ...	267	Venerabilis in Christo pater ...	395
Superiori dominica docuit Christus ...	266	Verba huius epistole possunt ...	211
		Verbum istud prophete ...	237
Supponendum est ut fides ...	74	Videtur ex processu ...	253
Supponitur illud esse ultimum ...	275	Videtur meritorium bonos ...	416
Suppositis autem descripcionibus ...	2	Videtur sanctum prophetam ...	239
Suppositis dictis de fide ...	49		
Supposito ex superius declaratis ...	13	Ystoria actuum apostolorum ...	207
Tacto superficialiter de prima parte ...	53		
Tercia vero pars scripture ...	320		

Reverse Index of Explicits

The concept of this sort of reference tool has not, to the editor's knowledge, been hitherto applied in such a compendium as the present *Catalog*. Yet its utility should be obvious: because of wilful excision or simply accidents of time, as witness for example the fragment from **415** in Karlsruhe, BLB 343, f. 1r, the first part of a given piece may now be lost, but the last remain intact. With this kind of guide, working backward for four or five words from the last substantive word of a known work, identification of new copies may be facilitated. Stray "amens," "etc.s," and the like are here omitted.

431	. ablata sit ecclesia ...	101	. amissione in tribulacione finaliter ...
76	. abnegando elemosinam fictam faciliter ...	184	. animarum medico primo et confessione ...
414	. acceptanda libere est melior ...	77	. antecellunt malicia in veteris ...
41	. accidente perfeccior est natura ...	404	. Antichristi condicio patens ...
4	. accidentibus stantibus sensibilis ...	225	. Antichristi ecclesia tali ...
61	. activa quam melior sit ...	53	. Antichristi filii specialis ...
153	. adaptari temporis et loci ...	218	. Antichristi prepositos tales ...
74	. addiderit vulnus vulneri occisionem ...	115	. Antichristi spoliacionibus falsissimis ...
G*Spur*. 12	. adductu qua de evangelii ...	121	. Antichristo exhibent quam plurem ...
214	. adheretis indefectibiliter et formatam ...	368	. Apocalypsim scripsit quibus ...
227	. adiuvando ecclesiam sanctam ...	200	. apostoli sensu ex premissis ...
G*Spur*.2	. adiuvante per doctoris ...	23	. approbate ecclesiam aput doctorum ...
11	. agressuros aperit ista sentencia ...	82	. aptande sunt congruam capacitatem ...
247	. agunt quicquid demeritorium ...	164	. argumenta alia ad solucio ...
161	. alibi diffuse patet istorum ...	381	. argumenta subtilia et conclusiones ...
32	. alibi isto De . accidens per ...	132	. attendite septimo Matth. evangelium ...
26	. aliena discitur contemptu ista ...	154	. attingens non hominis statum ...
40	. aliis multis in et fidei ...		
352	. aliud sequitur et composita ...		
249	. alternasse femineo labore ...		
287n	. amabilem populi vocem ...		

377	. Augustinus Hec . disputator ...	133	. Christi legi conformiter virtuose ...
86	. beata sit finaliter quid deficere ...	163	. Christi legi observancie continuacionem ...
271	. beatitudinem adquiramus sic ...	183	. Christi legis simplicem ...
		91	. Christi vero in capiant ...
47	. beatorum sensum quemlibet satians ...	GSpur.1	. Christo Laus . defensari ...
		109	. Christum Jesum dominum cruciare ...
332n	. Belus est dictum ydolem ...	349	. Christum Jesum dominum per fit ...
344	. bene erit malo nulli ...		
97	. blasfemamus mendaciter temporalia ...	354	. Christum Jesum nostrum dominum ...
254	. blasfemiam istam contra viriliter ...	280	. Christus Jesus dominus conviva ...
92	. blasfemum et hereticum magis ...	GSpur.11	. Christus Jesus noster dominus concedat sibi ...
146	. bonum retribuere malum propter ...	261	. Christus Jesus perducat nos ...
		295	. Christus Jesus virginum sponsus ...
434	. cadunt foveam in ambo ...		
54	. capi possent evangelio ...	27	. clericorum dominio de pertractandum ...
343	. capitula ultima quattuor ...		
330	. captivis coram eam legit ...	408	. cognoscantur facilius falsitates ...
361	. carcere de veniendo onus ...		
174	. cardinali quadruplici vicio ...	22	. cognoscendum misterium incarnacionis ...
148	. caritatis regulas contra superbie ...	157	. cognoverunt domini revelacione ...
242	. causa sine reddiderimus ...	162	. comitetur prudencia particularis ...
386	. causativi ecclesie tocius ...		
105n	. cedunt cuncti argucie quibus ...	126	. communicant quibus cum decipiunt ...
211	. celorum regnum est que ...	328	. compendio in evangeliste ...
41	. Christiane fidei articulas quilibet ...	279	. commendat Deus quem sed ...
360	. Christiane fidei operum ...	391	. compleatur domini lex ...
58	. Christiani ceteri quam ipsa ...	352	. composita sua et sicut ...
		284	. concedat nobis quod consequente ...
98	. Christiani falsi ut culpabiles ...	259n	. concedat nobis quod faciemus ...
87	. Christiani ordinis limitibus ...	272	. concedat nobis quod te in requiescat ...
209	. Christi corpus est ipsis ...	255	. concessa sit indulgencia ...
29	. Christi crucis adversarios vincere ...	367	. conclusio doctrinalis est ideo ...
118	. Christi instar ad apostoli ...		
430	. Christi Jesu ecclesia de fideles ...	241	. conclusio patet et requiram ...
22	. Christi Jesu nostri domini eiusdem ...	GSpur.13	. condempnes vivendo respicias ...

145	. conducti ipso ab comminatorie ...	278n	. declaranda sentencia ista ...
352	. confirmacionem et prosecucionem ...	55	. declarandas alias relinquo materie ...
396	. confirmetur testimonio et sigillo ...	55	. declarandum aliis relinquo materie ...
256	. congregati indulgencie vocate ...	12	. declarat temporis quidditate ...
44	. confiteri constancius contrarium ...	330	. declinanda ydolatria pro captivitatis ...
15	. connotatum huiusmodi vel inevitabilitatem ...	177	. declinent ne perficere ...
117	. conquisitum dominium temporale ...	222	. defendunt vel facinora sua ...
238	. consenserit gratis nisi ...	173	. defensio diurnitate ex ...
385	. conservet et illuminet ...	427	. Dei legis regulam ...
27n	. consimilibus de sic et ...	104	. deitas quam minus est quod ...
89	. consolante reciproce se angeli ...	GIntro.	. deleantur modicum aliis ...
240	. conterendum crimine suo ...	250	. delinquunt sic domini ...
324	. contexerint metrico canticorum ...	18	. Deo in propriam ydeam habeat ...
23	. contingens sed simpliciter eternum ...	332	. deos omnes super magnus ...
323	. contra e et Deum ad ecclesia ...	411	. deputandum sacerdotibus spiritualem ...
1	. convertam me specialiter operis ...	226	. derivare alia vel fidei ...
285	. coronat dona propria ...	110	. detestantes repugnanciam tradicionis istam ...
171	. corporalem eciam quam spiritualem ...	68	. deturpare domini arma oportet ...
354	. corpus in redundanter ...	62	. deturpatur religio Christiana ...
19	. creandi genus aliud vel ...	266	. Deum laudat unanimiter ...
B4.VI.Prol.	. creaturas omnes suis pedibus ...	370	. Deum preter istorum ...
362	. Crisostomum secundum epistolam ...	288n	. Deus dominus primus concedat ...
359	. Crisostomus dicit ut Petrum ...	412	. deviare vestigiis Christi ...
107	. culpa a absolvendi potestatem ...	337	. deviliscentem iudicio viridis ...
95	. culpanda plus sollicitudo ...	85	. devitare sensibus hiis ...
237	. custoditur anima ubi ...	281	. dextris a collocabit iudicio ...
399	. damnabilis foret scripture ...	25	. dicitur donare humanam legem ...
229	. datas gratis elemosinas pure ...	GDub.13	. didicisti bibendo sed audiendo ...
26	. debet ecclesia quomodo iure ...	188	. differenda epistolas breviores ...
356	. decimo Marcum vide ...	252n	. dignitatis cesarie ablate ...
		424	. dignum laude aliquod opus ...
		278	. dilatanda sentencia ista ...

72	. dilatare auditorii pertinenciam ...	332	. evum in laus sit ...
130	. dimittentes residuum totum domini ...	423	. exemplante ecclesia triumphante ...
393	. dirrumpamus miserie statu ...	113	. exemplum et expetere auctoritatem ...
19	. dispensandum taliter ad ius ...	69	. exhortari continenciam continuam ...
181	. divina quam suspensio humana ...	46	. expellende ecclesia ab sunt ...
384	. dominetur nequicia mendacii ...	103	. expetere instanter Dei consilium ...
321	. dominum eternum in honor et laus ...	328	. extinguente aliquo sum templum ...
288n	. dominus primus concedat ...	191	. fabricare evangelio ex sua ...
364	. donative non sed instrumentaliter ...	222n	. facinora sua nutriant ...
334	. dulcedinem montes stillabunt ...	70	. falsa nimis contraria sibi ...
230	. dyaboli racionis participat ...	180	. feces suas destruit fundamentum ...
420	. eandem ad mediis ...	246	. fide in non superbia ...
213	. ecclesie activos decipiunt ...	351	. fideles uniendo in spiritus ...
219n	. ecclesie tardacionem ad graviter ...	410	. fidem tamquam mendacia ...
239	. eius locus perpetua ...	248	. fidem tamquam sentenciam istam ...
282	. elegerit ipsa cum partem ...	419	. fine in sexta omelia ...
106	. eligeret primum animatus fuerit ...	322	. finem in usque dominus dixit principio ...
187	. elevemur beatifice ultimum ...	372	. fine sine perfidiis ...
328	. eos in intret gaudat illud ...	6	. finis est sic et celestis ...
39	. eos vincet veritas finaliter ...	283	. flevit sic qui dominus ...
364	. epistolam hanc scripsit terrarum ...	186	. fovere et defendere ordinacionem ...
17	. essencie communicacione essenciam ...	159	. fraudat atque populum spoliat ...
376	. esse non se appetent ...	156	. fructuosius curati officio ...
378	. est consequens per et presens ...	179	. fundabuntur sanccius eo in ...
329	. est divisas quarta parte ...	432	. fundatum sit mendacio ...
39n	. est episcopis in quantum ...	262	. futuro in gloriam et presente ...
333	. eternam vitam ad eis in ambulantes ...	398	. futurum in impediat ...
323	. eternum in honor sit iudicanti ...	300	. germinare Anglia in caritatem ...
150	. evenire oppositum oportet ...	289	. gloria in autem surget ...
		288	. gloria in conregabimus ...
343	. evum in et nunc imperium ...	116	. gloriosum martyrum alios inter ...
		339	. graciarum accio sit ineternum ...

189	. gravata est veteris legis ...	3	. inponendo quiecius operis tocius ...
405	. gravi atque multiplici ...		
198	. gravissimum est inpenitencie ...	GDub.15	. inquisivit virtualiter libertati ...
267	. gula infert malum ...	165	. insordescat amplius ecclesia ...
GDub.12	. habentis suavitatem saporis ...	12	. instat modo consequens ...
		84	. insultantis dyaboli vel hominis ...
268	. heredes et filii ...		
25	. *hic habentur* ...	373	. intellecta melius sit evangelii ...
71	. homicide multipliciter sunt dominium ...	2	. intendo plurimum ut sentenciis ...
383	. honesta et racionabilis fuerit ...	290	. introducta gloriosius gaudiosos ...
199	. ignorant quam logicam et linguam ...	217	. introducte fallacie sectas ...
		83	. introducte noviter oracionis ...
172	. illudantur infidelibus ab ne ...	30	. introductis variacionibus suis ...
270	. illud custodiunt et Dei ...		
223	. illum sequi mistica ...	147	. introductos fallaciter Antichristi ...
38	. illusus est populus quibus ...		
291	. immortalis corporis vita ...	390	. introducunt insensibiliter ecclesie ...
407	. impeccabilis papa foret ...		
114	. impercepta inanicio sua est ethica ...	323	. intuentes indefectibiliter iste ...
371	. imponit finem gracia ...	409	. invehendum concorditer sectas ...
169	. improbare sufficere procuratorem ...	206	. invehendum efficaciter vel ...
342	. incarnandus sciencie eius ...		
208	. incastrata negligenciam fratrum ...	14	. involuti multipliciter sumus rixosas ...
345	. inchoati cardinalibus virtutibus ...	279n	. ipso cum sit eternam ...
		193	. ista ambo superat patria ...
134	. inductiva plurima peccata ...	333	. ista intelligit et sapiens ...
336	. ineternum regnum omne domino ...	294	. iudicii diem post sabbatum ...
234	. inferius isto De ...	125	. iuvat satis virginis Marie ...
34	. infernum ad dyaboli membrum ...	321	. Jeronimum sanctum vanitatum ...
108	. infinitam palam contradiccionem ...	341	. Jerusalem dicetur illa ...
320	. infra declaratur ut penalia ...	284	. Jesus Christus concedat nobis quod ...
363	. ingrediebantur qui omnes ...		
99	. iniquus est receptabilis spoliorum ...	347	. Johannem ad usque ...
		231	. laborare acutissime contrarii ...
277	. iniuriam manifestam proximo ...		
		395	. legislator extraneus fidei ...
346	. innovando veteri ut conformando ...	197	. libertate facili et pulcra ...

413	. libertate serviat sibi ...	335	. nono capitulo Christum ...
143	. libet sicut sentenciam istam ...	366	. noscibiles nobis sunt ...
		265	. noster Deus dominus concedat nobis ...
37	. limitare ministerium hoc ad placuerit ...	274	. nostra redempcione est passus ...
196	. lucet que in omnium ...		
387	. Lutterworth de curatus ...	141-142.	
10	. Lyncolniensis textus est iste ...	145-147	. novitates huiusmodi contra ...
		96	. novitatem ordinis vel religionis ...
433	. machinatus sathane cautela ...		
149	. manifesta heresis sit contrarians ...	38	. observare finaliter Jesu Christo ...
277n	. manifestam iniuriam proximo ...	260	. observasse impositum eis regimen ...
215	. mendicare licite et clamorosa ...	252	. observavit apostolis suis ...
		349	. octavo interpretacionem et undecimo ...
207	. mensura in facere hoc ...		
90	. merendum amplius ad medium ...	332	. odiunt quod vituperant ...
		212	. omisse sunt attencio ista ...
355	. me visitastis et carcere ...	362	. omnes salutati apostoli ...
219	. militantis ecclesie retardaciones ...	416	. operando taliter caritative ...
		9	. oportet signa talia propter ...
368	. Minoris Asie tocius ...	347	. oracione in pentacostes ...
365	. mixtis in aqua ...	83	. oracionis vendicione in sophisticatur ...
160	. moderanda prudencia cum alios ...	30	. orare sic procuratorie necesse ...
GDub.1	. monachi reverendi argumenta ...	144	. ordinandi utile bonum ...
16	. morere et Deo benedic ...	348	. orditur sic esse Dei filium ...
245	. mori male poterit ...	382	. originale Vide . septimo ...
GDub.6	. mortale peccatum esset ...	202n	*. otiose plurimum forent ...*
124	. mortalis et dampnabilis sit ...	402	. pacem dabit compendiosius ...
127	. mortiferi informative virtute ...	233	. paciendo humiliter poterunt ...
119	. mortis hora habuit quam fervide ...	418	. paciendo observiat Deo ...
131	. mortis horam singuli ignoramus ...	100	. palliatur hodie sicut confessione ...
56	. motor primus mobilium omnium ...	408	. parte hac in consenciant ...
		346	. partes undeviginti in dividitur ...
394	. mundum istum multipliciter ...	152	. partis prime tricesimo sermone ...
24	. nature et homine noto ...	258	. patria in corporalis ...
178	. negant ipsam infideliter ...	292	. patria in materiale gaudium ...
51	. nesciuntur discrimine sine quando ...	293	. patria in plene ditabitur ...

67	. patria in statum ad reservatum ...	73	. prelatorum latrocinii generibus ...
142	. paulative inducere suis filiis ...	388	. presenti pro sufficiant dicta ...
400	. paupertate evangelica et stare ...	374	. presenti pro sufficiunt tres ...
401	. paupertate evangelica in pie ...	323	. prima exposicione in supra ...
8	. peccandi occasio indirecte sumitur ...	141	. prima parte superius patet ...
GDub.16	. peccantes mortaliter clericos ...	351	. primo Hebreos vide ...
		294n	. principio in videatur licet ...
323n	. peccati originalis sorde ...	204	. privati sunt ordines quare ...
261	. perducat nos quam ad novissimam ...	102	. procurantes dominium contra sua ...
271	. perducat quam ad beatitudinem ...	429	. prodessendum ecclesie ad medium ...
168	. perpetue dampnacionis pena ...	64	. prodessentem temporis processu ...
128	. personarum accepcio est exhinc ...	59	. prodesse plus eis fuerit ...
		90	. promerendum amplius ad medium ...
151	. pertractanda aliis relinquo pauca ...	176	. promerendum graciam ad quantum ...
31	. pertractare diffusius propono voluerit ...	81	. promoverent discenciam eius ad quanto ...
273	. perveniet necessarie est ingressus ...	345	. prophetarum more verbum ...
410n, GIntro.	. perversis iam clericis ...	50	. prophetavit multipliciter errorem ...
363	. Petro cum fuisse martirisatum ...	65	. proscripta est silencio ...
		158	. prosecuta aviduis pharisaicis ...
1	. Petrus quam perfeccior erit ...	275	. proximo sermone superius ...
31n	. *plurima ut sonat istud et* ...		
201	. politicas probaciones omnes ...	202	. puniendi acucius suos legios ...
2	. pono finem tractatui meo ...		
269	. populi tocius et suo peccati ...	367	. quattuordecimo Marco simulacris ...
329n	. post diu sed Abrahe ...	350	. quindecimo Romanos ad octavo ...
7	. post patet ut genere in ...		
48	. postulando adiutorio Dei ...	346	. quinto Job universa ...
194	. potuit non peccare ...	348	. quinto Luce vide ...
251	. prediandus taliter est ...		
93	. predicandum aspere foret ...	66	. racionem disparem vel noticie ...
426	. predicantes populo fidem ...		
221	. predicetur dominis secularibus ...	121	. rapinam promovent et ...
		232	. raptores et heretici ...
52	. prelati sunt cuiusmodi ecclesiam ...	139	. recompensam retribuit spiritualem ...

263	. redigere spiritui servitorem ...	336	. salvacio erit Syon ...
140	. regis tanti heredibus iniurietur ...	42	. salvatoris corpore melior est que ...
328n	. regnat et vivat fine sine perducat eos ...	138	. sanctis istis conformiter vivunt ...
344	. regnat et vivit fine sine qui concedat nobis ...	GSpur.3	. sanctorum sancta in regnat ...
322	. regnat et vivit fine sine qui perducat nos ...	195	. sanatus sit finaliter medici ...
35	. regnat semper ecclesiam totam ...	259	. sanctus spiritus et filius et pater ...
287	. regnaturi eternaliter domino ...	422	. scriptura ex cognoscere ...
428	. regnis multis irremissibilem ...	185	. scriptura in fuerint fundate ...
140	. regni tanti heredibus iniurietur ...	166	. scriptura in includitur philosophica ...
297	. regnum stabit potissime ...	32n	. *scripturarum catholicum sensum* ...
298	. regulantem domini legem ...	417	. scripture fide ex racionabilitas ...
53	. regum regis domini nostri ...	342	. secula in benedictum sit nomen ...
257	. re in ius plenum habebimus ...	341	. secula in benedictus est que veritas ...
210	. religio eorum est vana ...	264	. seculorum secula in benedictus Deus ...
GDub.18	. religiosos perfectos subditum ...	20	. seculorum secula in benedictus sit ...
GDub.14	. religiosos [...] per subditum ...	296	. seculorum secula in diligendum ...
122	. removendo necessitancia hoc ad alia ...	324	. seculorum secula infinita per gloria ...
253	. renuebat dyabolo ipso ...	335	. seculorum secula in gloria et honor ei sit ...
397	. repetita gracius fuit ...	337	. seculorum secula in gloria et honor sit cantantibus ...
5	. requirit intellectus clarificacione ...	334	. seculorum secula in gloria et honor sit cui beatifica ...
224	. reserare modestia cum Christi ...	338	. seculorum secula in gloria et honor sit cui Christo ...
60	. respondentes varie varii sunt ...	340	. seculorum secula in gloria et honor sit cui gaudebo ...
299	. resumendum corpore cum vivencium ...	331	. seculorum secula in gloria et honor sit qui omnia ...
375	. resurgere Dei gracia ...	330	. seculorum secula in latera ...
146	. retribuere malum propter ...	320	. seculorum secula omnia per durat ...
190	. revocaret cicius nostri Christi ...	112	. secundo Petri prima et ...
78	. sacramenta huiusmodi accipere ...	106n	. secundum non eligeret primum ...
36	. sacramento venerabili hoc in varietas ...	216	. secura est docuit Christus ...

45	. sedata sit ecclesia perturbacio ...	203	. suum Deum timeant principaliter ...
136	. seducta est ecclesia adulteram ...	380	. tamen Hoc . ecclesiam ...
105	. seducuntur cuncte argucie quibus ...	G*Dub*.7	. tantum et deservierunt ...
		339	. te a resiliet te videret ...
243	. seminare mendacia periculosa ...	129	. tempus quoad instantibus ...
		167	. tenebrarum principis perpetuus ...
111	. sempiternum regnum ad perveniatur ...		
		340	. tercio capitulo componentem ...
425	. senciendum proprietatibus et rosis ...		
		331	. terra in et celo in potestas ...
353	. sensibilitate eius et scripture ...	57	. terris in hic perpetuum ...
		236	. testamenti veteris similibus ...
135	. sentencia ista in illustret ...		
21	. sepe satis alibi et octavi ...	367	. testificandi verbum omne ...
338	. septimi capituli fine in tua ...	155	. tollerando fideliter membrorum ...
363	. septimo Luce vide soli ...		
345	. sepulti filii tunc personam ...	358	. toxicos fructus ad quo ...
369	. sequente proximo prologo ...	11	. tractatui isti finem imponit ...
164	. sequuntur que argumenta alia ...	235	. trinitati specialiter fuit ...
		120	. triumphantes ecclesie partes scandalizant ...
170	. sequuntur que inconveniencia ...		
		G*Spur*.5	. triumphantis finaliter sue ...
88	. seta sicut generant ...		
403	. similiter Christi corpus ...	228	. ultimo Thessalonicos ad secunda ...
75	. simulatur dyabolo quod per hominis ...		
		353	. unctus est qui Christum ...
63	. singillatim observancias religionum ...	182	. unionis gracie et hominum ...
415	. spoliantes homines bonis ...	392	. valeatis videar scripsisse ...
49	. stabilire diaboli et Christi ...	421	. ventilata est questio ...
79	. stabilitus amplius fide et laudibus ...	435	. veram lucem fidei ...
		47	. veritatem decideret Phronesis ...
286	. sua bona omnia constituit ...		
33	. suam partem defendere Christianos ...	123	. Veritati contrarii ypocrite sunt ...
329	. sua peccata quidam magnalia ...	389	. Veritatis dominus concedat nobis ...
175	. subiectante aliquo sine accidens ...	329	. Veritatis dominus sit benedictus ...
43	. successorum commiserunt determinacioni ...	192	. viante in copiosius habitet ...
		205	. viatores obligat generaliter ...
12	. suffragia oracionis eo ab ...		
94	. suis bonis omnibus fidelium ...	137	. virtutes ad dirigi debet ...
		276	. vita et veritas via ...
13	. sunt vere tunc Deum aput ...	220	. vita in quam concilio ...
406	. suo Deo servierit [servieret; serviens] ...	28	. vite liber conferat nobis ...
		244	. vocalis quam placencior ...

Alphabetical Index of Wyclyf's Latin Writings

Ad argumenta Wilelmi Vyrinham determinacio[nes]: **382, 383**
De actibus anime: **4**
De amore [Ad quinque questiones]: **393**
De apostasia: **36**
De blasfemia: **37**
De Christo et suo adversario Antichristo: **412**
De citacionibus frivolis et aliis versuciis Antichristi: **413**
De civili dominio [De dominio civili] [De dominio humano]: **28, 29, 30**
De clavibus ecclesie [De potestate ligandi et solvendi]: **407**
De composicione hominis: **21**
De concordacione fratrum [cum secta simplici Christi] [De sectis monachorum] [De ordinacione fratrum]: **432**
De condemnacione xix conclusiones: **401**
De contrarietate duorum dominorum: **423**
De cruciata [Contra bella clericorum]: **411**
De demonio meridiano: **300**
De deteccione perfidiarum Antichristi: **421**
De dominio divino: **23, 24, 25**
De dotacione ecclesie [Supplementum trialogi]: **48**
De duobus generibus hereticorum: **418**
De dyabolo et membris eius: **430**
De ecclesia: **32**
De ente in communi: **7**
De ente predicamentali: **13**
De ente primo in communi: **8**
De eucharistia [tractatus maior]: **38**
De eucharistia conclusiones duodecim [or: quindecim]: **41**
De eucharistia et penitencia [Confessio]: **44**
De eucharistia minor confessio [De corpore Christi]: **39**
De fide catholica [De ecclesia (tractatus minor)]: **49**
De fide sacramenti [De eucharistia confessio]: **40**
De fratribus ad scholares: **392**
De fundacione sectarum: **431**
De gradibus cleri ecclesie: **394**
De intelleccione dei: **14**
[De iuramento Arnaldi]: **397**
De logica: **1**
De logica tractatus tercius: **3**
De mandatis divinis [Decalogus]: **26**
De materia et forma: **20**
De mendaciis fratrum: **419**
De nova prevaricancia mandatorum: **415**
De novis ordinibus: **422**
De octo questionibus pulchris: **390**
De officio pastorali: **53**
De officio regis: **33**
De officio regis conclusio: **406**
De oracione dominica: **424**
De oracione et ecclesie purgacione: **46**
De ordine Christiano: **414**
De paupertate Christi [conclusiones triginta tres]: **402**
De peccato in spiritum sanctum: **52**
De perfeccione statuum: **426**
De potencia productiva dei ad extra: **19**
De potestate pape: **34**
De proposicionibus insolubilibus: **5**
De quattuor sectis novellis: **429**
De religionibus vanis monachorum [De fundatore religionis: **434**
De salutacione angelica: **425**
De sciencia dei: **15**
De scismate [De dissensione paparum]: **410**
De septem donis spiritus sancti: **50**
De servitute civili et dominio seculari: **405**
De solucione Sathane: **435**
De statu innocencie: **27**
De symonia: **35**
De tempore [De individuacione temporis]: **12**
De trinitate [De personarum distinccione]: **17**
De triplici vinculo amoris [sive caritatis]: **427**
De universalibus: **11**

De vaticinacione sive de prophecia: **45**
De verbi incarnacione [De benedicta incarnacione]: **22**
De veritate sacre scripture: **31**
De versuciis Antichristi: **420**
De volucione dei: **16**
De ydeis: **18**
Descripcio fratris: **433**
Determinacio ad argumenta magistri Outredi: **381**
Determinaciones contra Kylyngham Carmelitam: **378, 379, 380**
[Differencia inter peccatum mortale et veniale]: **51**
Dubia: GDub.1-18
Dyalogus [Speculum ecclesie militantis]: **408**
[Epistola ad quendam socium de sensu mistico Matt. 21º]: **391**
Epistola missa ad simplices sacerdotes: **416**
Epistola missa archiepiscopo Cantuariensi: **395**
Epistola missa episcopo Lincolniensi: **396**
Epistola missa pape Urbano: **404**
Errare in materia fidei quod possit ecclesia militans: **43**
Exhortacio cuiusdam doctoris: **389**
Exposicio textus Matthei xxiii [De ve octuplici]: **372**
Exposicio textus Matthei xxiv [Longum evangelium] [De Antichristo]: **373**
[Libellus] ad parliamentum regis: **400**
Litera parva ad quendam socium [Strode]: **387**
Logice continuacio: **2**
Opus evangelicum I, II [De sermone domini in monte]: **374, 375**
Opus evangelicum III, IV [De Antichristo I, II]: **376, 377**
[Peticio ad regem et parliamentum]: **403**
[Postilla super totam Bibliam]:
  [Chronica sive historica?]: **306-319**
  [Dialectica sive disputativa?], Jb, Ec: **320-321**
  [Epistolaria], Ro, 1 Co, 2 Co, Gl, Ep, Php, Cl, 1 Th, 2 Th, 1 Tm, Phm, He, Ac, Ja, 1 P, 2 P, 1 Jn, 2 Jn, 3 Jn, Jde, Rv: **349-371**

[Evangelica?], Mt, Mk, Lk, Jn: **345-348**
[Hymnidica et quasi poetica et decantativa], Ps, SS, Lm: **322-324**
[Monastica sive ethica?]: *325-327*
[Politica et legislativa?]: *301-305*
[Prophetica], Is, Jr, Baruch, Ezk, Dn, Ho, Jl, Am, Ob, Jnh, Mi, Na, Hk, Zp, Hg, Ze, Ml: **328-344**
Protestacio [or: Declaraciones] Johannis Wyclif: **399**
Purgans errores circa veritates in communi: **9**
Purgans errores circa universalia in communi: **10**
Purgatorium secte Christi: **428**
Quattuor imprecaciones [De quattuor imprecacionibus]: **417**
Questio ad fratres de sacramento altaris: **42**
[Questiones et dubia super viii libros physicorum]: **6**
Responsio ad decem questiones [magistri Strode]: **385**
[Responsio] ad quesita regis et concilii [De questione utrum licet thesaurum retinere]: **398**
Responsiones ad argumenta cuiusdam emuli veritatis [id est magistri Strode]: **388**
Responsiones ad [xviii] argumenta Radulphi Strode: **386**
Responsiones ad xliv conclusiones [Responsio ad argucias monachales]: **384**
Sermones miscellanei: **235-299**
Sermones super epistolas: **176-234**
Sermones super evangelia dominicalia: **54-114**
Sermones super evangelia de sanctis: **115-175**
Speculum secularium dominorum: **409**
Spuria: GSpur.1-14
Summa de ente [Summa intellectualium]: **7-19**
Summa theologie: **26-37**
Trialogus [Summa summe]: **47**

Index of Wyclyf's Writings

This index lists citations of works in this catalog in other entries in the catalog. For other information about Wyclyf, see the General Index.

1: 2, 11n, 12, 15
2: 3
3: 5, 6, A7n, 19n, 22n, 23-25n, 27, 47n
4: 2, 7, 12, 15, 16, 22n, 51n, 79, 166n, 167, 205n, 374-377n, 420n, 432n
5: 3, 4, 23-25n, G*Dub*.2
6: 10, 28-30n, 51n, 374-377n, 432n
7: Pref., 11n, 12, 15, 18n
8: Pref., 11n, 12.
9: 15, 432
10: 6n, A7, 11n, 15, 16, 18n, G*Dub*.13
11: Pref., 4, 7, 9, 10, 13-16, 20n, 21n, 22n, 55n, 209
12: 4, 11, 13, 15, 18n, 19nn, 20n, 22n, 23-25n, 26n, 39n, 55, 373n
13: 6, 10, 12, 14, 19n
14: 7-9, 13, 15, 16n, 21n
15: 7, 12, 14, 16, 19n, 373n
16: 9, 13, 14n, 15, 205n, 373n
17: A7, 7-10, 11n, 19, 20n, 21n, 44n, 47n, 49n, 207, 374-377n, 382-383n
18: Pref., A7, 8, 9, 12-14, 19, 20n, 23-25n, 36n
19: 12, 22, 27, 38, 53n
20: 12
22: A7, 11n, 12, 14, 17n, 19, 20n, 21n, A12, 47n, 209
23-25: 6n, 22, 26n, 28-30, 31nn, 34nn, 47n, 280, CIntro., 381nn, 406n, 432n
26: 44n, 47nn, 67, 72, 374-377n, 392n, 415, 432n, G*Spur*.1
27: 26n, 202n, 415
28-30: 4n, 6n, 12, 21n, 22, 26, 31n, 32, 33, 36n, 37n, 38n, 47n, 51, 52, 171, 280, CIntro., 381-383
31: 6n, 26n, 32, 34, 44nn, 51, 149n, 261, 372n, 389, 399n, 400, 402, 408n, 409
32: 12, 17n, 26n, 28-30, 33, 34, 38, 42n, 46n, 49, 386, 388, 392n, 407
33: 26n, 34, 38, 53, 171, 373, 392n, 402, 406n, 407n, 409
34: 26n, 28-30, 38, 52n, 382-383n, 388, 392n, 397n, 407n
35: 34, 38, 157, 235, 392n, 418
36: 26n, 28-30n, 37-40, 47n, 233, 235, 418
37: 26n, 47n, 235, 403, 407n, 409n
38: 6n, 17, 19, 26, 39-42, BIntro.n, 175n, 204, 276, 388, 409n, 421
39: 28-30n, 31n, 38nn, 42, 53, 175n
40: 38nn, 175n
41: 38nn, 53, 175n
42: 32nn, 38nn, 175n
43: 38n, 175n
44: 38nn, 47n, 78, 132, 175n, 388n, 411, 414
45: 57n, 406n
46: 50n, 73, 372n, 384n, 405n, 409n, 424, 425n
47: 1n, 26n, 27, 38n, 48, 49, 51, 53, 81, 85, 127, 175n, 179, 205n, 217n, 239, 345n, 373-377, 390n, 392n, 393n, 395, 408, FIntro., 421n, 427, 428, G*Spur*.1
48: 37n, 47nn, 409n, 410n
49: 26n, 47n, 193n
50: 38n, 372n, 384n, 388n, 393n, 405n, 409n, 422n, 432n

51:	52, 198	180:	49n
53:	36n, BIntro., 80, 408n, 416, 431n	182:	362n
54:	66, 112	187:	49n, 190
55:	374-377n	188:	238
56:	373n, G*Spur*.1	189:	238
57:	159	190:	238
60:	6n	191:	238
61:	47n	193:	49n
62:	58, 175n	198:	51
63:	175n	202:	27n, B2.III
64:	175n	204:	B2.III
67:	159, 415, 432n	205:	216n, 392nn, 427n
68:	415	206:	216n
69:	415	208:	47n
70:	415	209:	175n
71:	50n, 415	210:	393n
72:	415	214:	211
73:	415	216:	41n, 210
74:	415	218:	41n, 210
75:	72, 415	219:	41n, 50n, 210, 237
79:	47n	224:	191n, 217n
87:	161	225:	41n
91:	93	228:	288
93:	101	229:	210, 390n
96:	283	236:	245
97:	287	238:	49n, 217n
109:	400n	239:	299
112:	54, 175n	246:	49n, 240, 407n
113:	54, 175n	247:	390n
114:	54, 175n, 179	248:	410
123:	407n	250:	407n
135:	409n	254:	407n
141:	49n, 142n, 145n, 146n, 147n, 153	255:	49n
142:	141n	257:	218
145:	141n	258:	256
146:	141n	264:	272
147:	141n	265:	49n, 204, 299
148:	49n	266:	272
153:	173, 409n	271:	265
156:	409n	284:	283
160:	373n	286:	383n
161:	189	287:	204, 393n
162:	373n	291:	290
165:	373n	299:	265n
166:	168, 409n	301-305:	55n
167:	166, 168	323:	G*Spur*.3
171:	403n	331:	G*Spur*.4
173:	407n	333:	G*Spur*.4
175:	209	345:	372n, 373
179:	47n	359:	389

363: 349n
371: G*Spur*.5
372: 373
373: 6n, 45, 56n, 161, 372, 374-377n
374-377: 6n, 45, 49n, 52n, 56n, 166n, 234n, 372, 373, 384n, 388, 407n, FIntro., **418**, **428**
378-380: 21n, 28-30n, 385
381: 23-25, 382-383nn
382-383: 23-25, 34n, 385
384: 28-30nn, 44n, 388n, 390n, 392n, 407n
385: 386
388: 44n, 56n, 384, 390n, 407n
390: 404n
391: 408n
392: 41n, 402n
394: 46n, 372n, 404n, 409n
395: 26n, 47n, 404n
396: 47n, 421
397: 26n, 28-30n, 72, 227, 332n, 409n
398: 28-30n, 392n, DIntro.n, 397, 404n
399: 28-30, CIntro., 385n, 398, 400-402, 404n
400: 28-30, 199, CIntro., 385n, 390n, 398, 399, 401, 402, 404n
401: 28-30, 385n, 398, 402, 404n, 413n
402: 26n, 33, 42, 392n, 404n, 409, G*Dub*.10
403: 171
404: 405
406: 408n
408: 47, 49n, CIntro., **382-383**, 390n, 406n
409: BIntro.n, CIntro., **413n**
410: 411n
411: 248, 407n, 410, 412
412: 208, 234n, 248, 313n, 392n, 407n, 411, 414, 428n
413: 388n, 404, 405, 414
414: 290, 407n
416: 372n, 395, 434n
418: 35n
420: 47n, 374-377n, 384n
421: 409n
422: 373, 432n
423: 136n, 396n
424: 44n, 83
425: 424
427: 26n, 47n, 393
429: 50n, 428n
430: 423n
431: 49n, 50n, 52n, 373, 428n
432: 433n
433: 40n, 432
434: 421n
435: 47n
G*Dub*.1: **204**
G*Spur*.5: 370n
English writings: Pref., B2n, **382-383**, 403, 404, 409n, 410n, 416n, 418n

General Index

Besides the customary alphabetical references to persons, places and concepts, short-title bibliographical citations are integrated by author (asterisked throughout). A note of caution is in order regarding the headings under the entry "Wyclyf, John: Doctrines of." Wyclyf certainly discussed, for example, the Eucharist, or dominion, or the "four sects" in other than just the writings indicated – but the works cited are *only* those explicitly identified in that connection in the commentary (IV) section of the text. Further, St. Paul and Jesus are of course engaged much more frequently than this Index would lead us to believe; and specific Bible citations throughout the entire *corpus Wyclyfianum* eminently merit an omnibus treatment elsewhere.

Aclyff, John de, **28-30**, **401**
Adam de Tonworth, **401**
*Affeldt, Werner: "Verzeichnis der Römerbriefkommentare...," **349**n
*Agaësse, P., and A. Solignac: *Œuvres de Saint Augustin* XLVIII, XLIX, 55n
Alain de Lille, G*Dub*.15
Alhazen, **4**n
Alpetragius, **4**n
*Anstey, H.: *Munimenta Academica...* I, **3**n
Aquinas, Thomas, St., **9**, **61**n, **66**n, **107**, **300**n, **402**
*Arbesmann, Rudolf, "The 'Daemonium Meridianum' ...," **300**n
*Ariew, Roger: "Did Ockham Use...," **378-380**n
Aristotle, **4**, **5**, **18**n, **23-25**, **33**n, **107**
*Arnold, Thomas: *Select English Works...* I-III, Pref.n, **50**n, **51**n, B2Intro., **55-234**, **236**, **240**, **242-244**, **298**, **393**n, **403**n, **404**n, **410**n, **418**n
Arundel, Thomas, **47**n
Ashwardby, John **427**
*Aston, T. H.: *History of the University...,* **3**n
Augustine of Hippo, St., **4**n, **12**n, **17**n, **18**n, **22**, **23-25**, **32**, **45**, **51**, **52**, BIntro.n, **54**, **55**, **66**n, **75**, **78**, **154**, **266**, **374-377**, **425**, **426**, **434**
*Auksi, Peter: "Wyclif's Sermons...," BIntro.n

*Baber, Henry Hervey: *The New Testament...,* Pref.n, DIntro.n, **403**n
Baconthorpe, John **23-25**n
*Bale, John: *Index Britanniae Scriptorum...,* Pref.n; *Scriptorum illustrium...,* Pref.n, and text, *passim*
Barton, William, **31**n, **39**, **41**
*Bartoš, František M.: *Literární Činnost...,* **17**nn, **32**n, **374-377**n; *M. Petr Payne...,* **17**n; *Soupis Rukopisů Národního...* I, II, B4n, **413**n; *Viklef a Čechy...,* **32**n
Basel, **47**n
Basil of Caesarea, St., **211**
*Bateson, M.: *Catalogue of the Library...,* **6**n, **17**n, **22**n, **42**n, **382-383**n, **404**n, G*Dub*.10, G*Dub*.11
*Baudry, L.: "À propos de Guillaume...," A7n
*Bäumker, C.: *Witelo, ein Philosoph...,* **4**n
Bede, the Venerable, **266**

*Bednarski, A.: "Die astronomischen Augenbilder...," **4n**
*Beer, Rudolf: *Johannis Wyclif De Compositione...*, **21**; *Johannis Wyclif De Ente...*, **13**, G*Spur*.6
Beguines and Beghards, **191**
Benedict of Nursia, St., **434**
*Benrath, Gustav A.: *Wyclifs Bibelkommentar*, B2.IVn, **257-259, 285, 289-291, 293-296, B4, 320-325, 328-371**; "Wyclif und Hus," **32n**
*Benzing, Josef: *Buchdruckerlexikon...*, **47n**
*Berkhout, Carl, and J. B. Russell: *Medieval Heresies...*, **32n**
Bernard of Clairvaux, St., **392, 398n, 402**
Bernard de Gordon, **420**
*Betts, Reginald R.: "English and Čech Influences...," **42n**; *Essays in Czech History...*, A7n, **11n, 12n, 23-25n, 42n**; "Peter Payne...," **12n**; "Richard fitz-Ralph...," **23-25n**; "The Great Debate...," A7n, **11n**; "The Influence...," A7n, **11n**
*Bigne, Margarin de la: *Maxima Bibliotheca...* XXV, BIntro.n
Binham, William, **23-25, 28-30, 378, 380, 382-383**
*Black, H. C.: *Black's Law Dictionary*, **397n**
*Black, W. H.: *Catalogue of the Arundel...*, **399n**
Black Death, **28-30n, 218**
Blackfriars (Earthquake) Synod, **39n, 40, 41, 45, 47, 120, 203, 210, 216, 218, 219, 225, 372, 392, 394, 403, 409, 420, 422, 424**
*Blanciotti, B.: *Doctrinale Fidei...*I, **17n**
*Bleienstein, Fritz: *Johannes Quidort...*, **23-25n**
*Bliss, William H., and J. A. Twemlow: *Calendar of Entries...* IV, **397n**
*Block, Edward: *John Wyclif...*, **28-30n**
*Bloomfield, Morton W.: "A Preliminary List ....," A12n
*Bocheński, I. M.: *A History...*, **5n**
Boethius, Anicius Manlius Severinus, **266**
Bonaventura da Bagnorea, St., **67n, 432**
Boniface VIII, **406**

*Boor, Friedrich de: *Wyclifs Simoniebegriff...*, **35n**
*Bowman, John Wick: *Hebrews James...*, **182n**
Bradwardine, Thomas, Pref., **15, 16, 373n**
*Brambach, Wilhelm: *Die Handschriften...* IV, **44n, 432n**
Brandeis, Lucas, **51n**
*Brandt, William J.: "Remarks on Bishop Thomas...," B2n
*Breck, Allen DuPont: ed. of JW *De Tempore*, **12n**; *Johannis Wyclyf Tractatus...*, **17**; "John Wyclyf and Time," **12n**; "The Manuscripts...," **12n**
Brinton, Thomas, B2n
British Museum General Catalogue... LXXVI, **398n**
*Brock, R. O., Jr.: *An Edition of Richard...*, **23-25n**
*Bronowski, Jacob: *The Ascent of Man...*, **4n**
*Brook, V. J. K.: *A Life of Archbishop...*, **399n**
*Brown, Edward: *Fasciculus Rerum...* I, II, **23-25n, 28-30n, 47n**
*Bruce, F. F.: *History of the Bible...*, Pref.n
Brunfels, Otto, **47**
*Buddensieg, Rudolf: *Johann Wiclif's De Christo...*, **412**; *John Wiclif's Polemical...* I, II, Pref.n, **46, 50, 53n, 204n, 392n, 397n, 410-413, 415, 416n, 417, 418, 421-423, 427-435,** G*Dub*.1; *John Wyclif's De Veritate...*I-III, **28-30n, 31**
*Bühler, Curt F.: "Greek Philosophers...," **51n**
Burley, Walter, Pref., **4, 6n, 33n, 51n**
*Burr, D.: "Scotus and Transubstantiation," **16n**

*Caillois, Roger: "Les démons de midi," **300n**
Cajetan of Thiene, **385n**
*Camden, William: *Anglica, Normannica, Hibernica...*, **399**
*Cannon, H. L.: "The Poor Priests...," **38n**
*Cannon, W. R.: "John Wyclif...," **32n**
*Caplan, Harry: *Mediaeval Artes Prae-*

dicandi..., BIntro.n; *Mediaeval Artes Praedicandi... Supplementary...*, BIntro.n
*Carmody, J. J.: *Al-Bitruji...*, **4**n
*Charland, T.-M.: *Artes Praedicandi...*, BIntro.n
Charles III of Durazzo, **405**n
Chaucer, Geoffrey, **385**, G*Spur*.concl.
*Chenu, Marie-Dominique: "Le Traité 'De Tempore'...," **12**n
Chronicon Anglie, **48**n
Chrysostom, St. John, **55**, **74**, **374-377**, **426**
Clement VII, **31**, **37**n, **48**, **405**n, **409**
*Coleman, Janet: *Medieval Readers...*, BIntro.n
Constance, Council of, **32**
Constantine, Donation of, **120**, **234**, **352**, **412**
conversion, spiritual, **19**n
*Cook, William R.: "John Wyclif...," **32**n, **42**n; "The Eucharist...," **42**n
*Copleston, Frederick J.: *A History of Philosophy* I-VIII, A**7**n
Corringham, John, **396**
*Coulton, George G.: *Chaucer and His England*, **385**n
Courtenay, William, **28-30**n, **41**, **394**, **395**, **403**
*Courtenay, William J.: "The Effect...," **218**n
*Cox, J. Charles: *The Sanctuaries...*, **32**n
*Coxe, H. O.: *Catalogus codicum manuscriptorum...* II, B**4**n, **374-377**n
*Crombie, A. C.: *Medieval and Early Modern...*, **4**n; *Robert Grosseteste...*, **4**n
*Crompton, James: "Fasciculi Zizaniorum I, II," **12**n; "John Wyclif...," DIntro.n; "Wyclif, John," **17**n
*Cronin, H. S.: "John Wycliffe...," **28-30**n; "Wycliffe's Canonry...," **28-30**n
*Cross, Claire: " 'Great reasoners...'," **136**n
Crump, Henry, **28-30**n, **401**
crusade (Flanders, 1383), **37**n, **47-49**, **188**, **235**, **238**, **247**, **249-252**, **254**, **256**, **372**, **373**, **384**, **388**, **390**, **395**, **409**, EIntro., **410-412**, **416**, **421-423**, **426**

*Dahmus, Joseph H.: "Further Evidence...," Pref.n; *The Prosecution of John...*, **28-30**n, **32**n, **39**n, **41**n, DIntro.n, **399**n, **400**nn, **401**nn, **404**, **413**n; *William Courtenay...*, **28-30**n, **41**n; "Wyclyf was a Negligent...," **28-30**n
*Dakin, A.: *Die Beziehungen...*, **28-30**n
*Dales, Richard C.: *Commentarius in viii libros...*, **6**n
*Daly, Lowrie J.: *The Political Theory...*, **28-30**nn, **33**n, DIntro.n; "Walter Burley...," **28-30**n, **33**n
*D'Avray, D. L.: "Sermons to the upper...," BIntro.n
*Deanesly, Margaret: *The Lollard Bible...*, Pref.n, **393**n, **394**n
Decretales (of Gregory IX), **28-30**, **33**
Decretum (of Gratian), **28-30**, **38**n, **40**
*Delaruelle, E., E.-R. Labande and P. Durliac: *L'Église au temps...*I, **409**n
*Delorme, F. M.: *Collationes in Hexaemeron...*, **55**n
*Demaitre, Luke E.: *Doctor Bernard de Gordon...*, **420**n
*Denifle, Henri, and Émile Chatelain: *Chartularium Universitatis...* I, **9**n
Despenser, Henry, **37**n, **47**, **48**, EIntro., **410-412**, **426**
*Devlin, Mary A.: "Bishop Thomas Brunton...," B**2**n
*Díaz y Díaz, M. C.: *Index Scriptorum...* II, **4**n
*Dickinson, F. H.: *Missale ad Usum...*, B**2**n
Die Handschriften der Oeffentlichen... I/1, **416**n
*Diels, Hermann: *Die Fragmente...*I, **51**n
Dietrich of Niem, **409**n
*Dijksterhuis, E. J.: *The Mechanization...*, **4**n
*Dokoupil, Vladislav: *Soupis Rukopisů Mikulovní...*, **49**n, **426**n
Dominic Guzman, St., **212**, **434**
*Doyle, Eric: "A Manuscript...," **23-25**n; "William Woodford, O.F.M.....," **28-30**n, G*Dub*.1; "William Woodford's *De dominio*..." **23-25**n, **48**n
*Dudik, B.: *Forschungen in Schweden...*, **11**n

*Dufeil, M.-M.: *Guillaume de Saint-Amour*..., **432**n
*Duhem, Pierre M.: *Le système*... III, V, VI, **4**n, **9**n
*Dunbabin, Jean: "Aristotle in the Schools," **33**n
*Durrieu, P.: "Le royaume d'Adria...," **409**n
*Dziewicki, Michael Henry: *Johannis Wyclif De Ente*..., **9, 10, 14, 16, 19**; *Johannis Wyclif Miscellanea Philosophica* I, II, **4**, A**7**n, **11, 20**, G*Dub*.7, G*Spur*.9; *Iohannis Wyclif Tractatus de Apostasia*..., **36**; *Iohannis Wyclif Tractatus de Blasphemia*..., **37**; *Johannis Wyclif Tractatus de Logica* I-III, **1-3**

*Eckermann, W.: "Augustus Favaroni...," **32**n
Edlesburgh, William, **404**n
Edward, the Black Prince, **300**
Edward II, **420**n
*Edwards, R. A.: "Henry Despenser...," **48**n
Egidio de' Colonna (Giles of Rome), **11**n, **23-25**
*Ehrle, Franz: "Der Kampf...," **9**n
*Ellis, H., and F. Douce: *A Catalogue*..., **398**n
*Emden, Alfred Brotherston: *A Biographical Register*... I-III, AbbrL, Pref.n, **4**n, **5**nn, A**7**nn, **11**nn, **12**n, **15**n, **17**nn, **23-25**nn, **28-30**nn, **39**n, **41**n, **42**n, **48**n, **199**n, **205**nn, **384**n, **385**n, **394**n, **396**n, **404**n, **420**n, **427**n; "Additions and Corrections...," **5**n
Empedocles, **51**n
Encyclopedia of World Art IV, **4**n
*Erb, Peter C.: "Vernacular Material...," BIntro.n
*Erben, Wilhelm, and Anton Kern, "Johann Loserth...," Pref.n
*Erickson, Carolly: "The Fourteenth-Century Franciscans...," **381**n
*Etzweiler, James: "Baconthorpe...," **23-25**n; "John Baconthorpe...," **23-25**n
Eusebius of Caesarea, **374-377**n

al-Fârâbî, **107**
*Farr, William: *John Wyclif as Legal*..., A**12**n, DIntro.n
Faulfiš, Mikuláš, **23-25**n, **32**n
*Favier, J.: *Les finances pontificales*..., **409**n
*Fischer, B., et al.: *Biblia Sacra* I-II, B**4**n
Fitzmaurice, E. B., and A. G. Little: *Materials for the History*..., **404**n
FitzRalph, Richard, **16, 23-25**, **32**n, **34**n, **47, 381**n, **432**, G*Spur*.5
*Forte, S. L.: "A Cambridge Dominican Collectio...," BIntro.n
*Foxe, John: *Rerum in Ecclesia*..., DIntro.n, **398, 404**
Francis of Assisi, St., **212, 251, 434**
*Frere, Walter Howard: *The Use of Sarum* I-II, B**2**n
*Friedberg, A. [Emil]: *Corpus Iuris Canonici* II, **44**n
*Fristedt, Sven L.: *The Wycliffe Bible*..., Pref.n
Froben, Johann, **47**
*Fürstenau, Heinrich: *Johann von Wiclifs*..., **32**n

*Gairdner, James: *Lollardy and the Reformation*... I, **398**n
*Galbraith, V. H.: *The St Albans Chronicle*, **399**n
Galen(us), Claudius, **420**
Garnier, Arnold, **26, 72, 397, 398**
*Geanakoplos, Deno J.: *Interaction*..., **47**n
*Geraedts, Ignatius: "Gedachten rond 'De Consideratione'," **392**n
*Gewirth, A.: "John of Jandun...," **28-30**n
*Geyer, Bernhard: *Friedrich Ueberwegs Grundriss*... I-V, A**7**n
*Gilchrist, John: "The Social Doctrine...," **23-25**n, **28-30**n
*Gilson, Etienne: *History of Christian Philosophy*..., A**7**nn, **9**n, **16**n, **28-30**n, **385**n; *Introduction à l'étude*..., **55**n; *Jean Duns Scot*..., **16**n
Good Parliament (1376), **28-30**
*Grant, Michael: *Jesus*..., **301**
Gratian(us), Franciscus, **28-30**, **33**
Gregory I, **279**

Gregory XI, **28-30**, **32**, **385**, **397**, **400-402**, **404**, **409**
Grosseteste, Robert, **4**n, **9**, **26**, **47**, **55**n, **70**, **72**, **149**, **191**, **265**, **432**, G*Spur*.5
*Gwynn, Aubrey: several articles in *Studies...*, **23-25**n; *The English Austin Friars...*, **22**n, **39**n, **199**n; "The Sermon-Diary...," **23-25**nn; "Two Sermons...," **23-25**n

*Haller, William: *The Elect Nation...*, **398**n
*Halm, C., and G. Laubmann: *Catalogus codicum latinorum...* II/3, **427**n
*Hammerich, L. L.: *The Beginning...*, **23-25**n
*Hanrahan, T. J.: "John Wyclif's Political Activity...," **28-30**n
*Hargreaves, Henry: "The Wycliffite Versions," Pref.n
*Harris, E.: *Johannis Wyclif Tractatus de Benedicta...*, **22**, A12
Haulay, John, **32**
*Heitz, P., and C. C. Bernouilli: *Basler Büchermarken...*, **47**n
*Heinemann, Otto von: *Die Handschriften...* II/1, **404**n
*Heitzman, M.: "Jana Wyclefa traktat....," **11**n
*Hendrix, Scott H.: "In Quest....," **435**n
Henry VIII, **48**
Henry of Ghent, **34**n
Hereford, Nicholas, Pref., **38**, CIntro., **394**
*Hérold, V.: prospective ed. of *De ydeis*, **18**n
*Herzberg-Fränkel, S., and M. H. Dziewicki: *Iohannis Wyclif Tractatus de Simonia*, **35**
Higden, Ranulf, **6**n, **78**
Hildegard of Bingen, **45**
*Hodgkin, R. H.: *Six Centuries...*, **22**n, **408**n
*Höfler, Constantin: "Anna von Luxemburg....," **397**n
Holcot, Robert, G*Dub*.15
*Holtzmann, Walther, and Rafaello Morghen: *Repertorium Fontium...* II, **4**n, **23-25**n
Hostiensis (Sinibaldo Fieschi), **28-30**

*Hudson, Anne: "A Lollard Compilation...," **374-377**n, **433**n; "A Lollard Sermon-Cycle...," B2n; "John Purvey...," Pref.n; *Selections from English...*, Pref.n, **40**nn
Hugh of St. Victor, **66**n
*Huizinga, Jan: *The Waning...*, **423**n
Humbert de Romans, BIntro.n
Hundred Years' War, A12, **33**
*Hurley, Michael: "'Scriptura Sola'...," **28-30**n, **31**nn
Hus, Jan, **11**, **17**n, **32**, **42**n, **47**n, **374-377**n, FIntro., **431**
Hussites, **12**, **42**, **47**n, BIntro., **279**n, **408**nn, **411**, FIntro., G*Spur*.6
*Hüttebräuker, Otto: *Der Minoritenorden...*, **381**n

Ibn Sînâ, **107**
Illyrius, Matthias Flacius, **18**n, **36**n, **53**n
Innocent III, **44**, **78**, **419**
Inquisition, Papal, **423**
insolubilia, **3**, **5**

*Jacob, Ernest F.: *Essays in the Conciliar...*, **409**n
*Jäger, Oskar: *John Wycliffe...*, DIntro.n
Jakoubek of Stříbro, **26**n, **408**n
*James, Montague Rhodes: *A Descriptive Catalogus... Corpus Christi...* I, **4**n; *A Descriptive Catalogue... Gonville & Caius...* I, **11**n, G*Spur*.11; *Catalogue of the Manuscripts...*, A7n; *The Western Manuscripts...* I, III, **4**n, **40**n, **388**n
James, Richard, **26**n, **31**n, **39**n, **382-383**n
James, Thomas, **382-383**n
James of Venice, **51**n
*Janssen, V. F.: "Die Four Sects....," **50**n
*Jellouschek, Carl J.: "Ein mittelalterliches Gutachten....," Pref.n
Jerome, St., **55**, **74**, **332**n, **333**n, **374-377**
Jiří of Kněhnic, **23-25**n, **32**n
Joan of Kent, **400**
John XXII, **382-383**n
John of Buckingham, **396**, **421**
John of Gaddesden, **420**n
John of Gaunt, **39**, **47**, **50**n, **382-383**, **402**n, **421**n, **432**

John of Jičin, **20**n
John of Jandun, **28-30**
John of Mirfeld, **420**n
John of St. Giles, **432**n
John Quidort of Paris, **23-25**n, **109**, **406**n
*Johnson, A. F., and Victor Scholderer: *Short-Title Catalogue*..., **47**n
*Jones, E. D.: "The Authenticity....," Pref.n

*Kalivoda, Robert: "Johannes Wyclifs Metaphysik....," A7n
*Kaminsky, Howard: *A History*..., **32**n, **42**n; "Wyclifism as Ideology....," **28-30**nn
*Kaňak, M.: *John Viklef*..., **32**n
*Kantorowicz, Ernest H.: *The King's Two Bodies*..., **28-30**n
Keninghale, John, **20**, **41**, **400**
*Kennan, Elizabeth T.: "Antithesis and Argument....," **392**n; "The *De Consideratione*....," **392**n
Kenningham, John, **12**, **42**, CIntro., **378**, **380**
*Ker, Neil: *Medieval Manuscripts*... II, **39**n; "Wyclif Manuscripts....," **26**n, **28-30**n
Kilingham, Richard, **12**n
Kilwardby, Robert, **12**n
*Kirk, G. S., and J. E. Raven: *The Presocratic Philosophers*, **51**n
*Kitchel, M. J.: "The 'De potentiis...'," **4**n
*Knapp, Peggy Ann: "John Wyclif...," Pref.n; *The Style*..., Pref.n, **70**n
Knighton, Henry, **48**n
*Knowles, Michael David: *Saints and Scholars*..., **23-25**n, **28-30**n; "The Censured Opinions....," **23-25**n; *The Religious Orders*... II, **23-25**n
*Kraus, H. P.: *The Cradle of Printing*..., **47**n
*Kropatschek, F.: *Das Schriftprinzip*..., **31**n
*Kudlien, F., and L. Wilson: "Galen," **420**n
*Kühn-Steinhausen, H. [= I. H. Stein]: "Wyclif-Handschriften....," **1**n, **32**n, **41**n, **44**n, **53**n, B2.In, B2.IIIn, **300**nn, **372**n, **401**n, **403**n, **404**n, **408**n, **414**n, **415**n, **422**n, **427**n, **429**n, **432**n, **433**n
*Kvačala, J.: "Wiclef a Hus....," **1**n, A7n

*Kybal, Vlastimil: "Etude sur les origines....," **42**n; "Les origines du mouvement....," G*Spur*.10

*Labriolle, Pierre de: "Le démon de midi," **300**n
*Ladner, Gerhardt: "*Homo Viator*....," **47**n
*Lambert, Malcolm D.: *Franciscan Poverty*..., **34**n, **382-383**n
*Lampe, G. W. H.: *The Cambridge History*... II, Pref.n, **31**n
*Landeman, Charles: *The Problem of Universals*, A7n
*Lang, Albert, J. Lechner, and M. Schmaus: *Aus der Geisteswelt*..., Pref.n, **12**n, **15**n
Langham, Simon, **381**
Latemar, John, **50**n
Lateran IV (1215), **44**, **419**
*Laun, Justus F.: "Die Prädestination....," **15**n; "Thomas von Bradwardin....," **15**n
Lavenham, Richard, **11**n
*Le Bas, Charles Webb: *The Life of Wiclif*, Pref.n, DIntro.n
*Lechler, Gotthard: *Johannis de Wiclif Tractatus*..., **53**; *Joannis Wiclif Trialogus*..., **47**, **48**, G*Dub*.8; *Johann von Wiclif*... I-II, A7n, **31**n, **32**n, **47**n, **141**n, **205**, **265**n, DIntro.n, **397**, **404**, **416**
*Leclercq, Jean: *Jean de Paris*..., **23-25**n; "Les controverses....," **112**n; and H. M. Rochais: *S. Bernardi Opera* III..., **392**n
*Leff, Gordon: *Bradwardine and the Pelagians*..., **15**n; "John Wyclif....," **23-25**n; *Paris and Oxford*..., **9**n; "The Apostolic Ideal....," **435**n; *The Dissolution*..., A7n, **9**n, **16**n; "The Making....," **435**n; *William of Ockham*..., A7n, **31**n; "Wyclif and Hus....," **32**n; "Wyclif and the Augustinian....," **17**n
*Legg, J. Wickham: *The Sarum Missal*..., B2n
*Lewis, Ewart: "King above Law....," **397**n
*Lewis, John: *The History*..., 1st, 2nd eds., **39**, **41**, **47**n, **382-383**, DIntro.n, **400**
*Lewis, N. B.: "The 'Continual Council'....," **400**n

light metaphysics, 4n, **166-169**
*Lindberg, David C.: *A Catalogue*..., 4n; "Lines of Influence...," 4n; "Witelo," 4n
*Little, Andrew G.: *Liber Exemplorum*..., BIntro.n; "Measures Taken...," **419**n
*Little, Lester K.: *Religious Poverty*..., 34n, **191**n
*Lloyd, M. E. H.: "John Wyclif...," **28-30**n
*Lodge, E. C., and R. Somerville: *John of Gaunt's Register*..., **50**n
*Loewe, J. H.: "Der Kampf...," A7n
*Lohr, Charles H.: "Commentaries...," AbbrL, 4n, **6**n, **9**n, **11**n, **12**n, **15**n, **16**n, **28-30**n, **51**n
Lollards, 48, BIntro., 395, 403, FIntro., 426, G*Dub*.8
Lombard, Peter, A7, **22**, 47
*Loofs, F.: *Leitfaden zum Studien*..., 17n
*Loserth, Johann: "Das vermeintliche Schreiben Wiclif's...," **404**n; "Die ältesten Streitschriften...," **23-25**nn, 381, G*Spur*.1, G*Spur*.3; "Die Wiclif'sche Abendmahlslehre...," **42**n; *Hus und Wiclif* 1st, 2nd eds., **11**n, **12**n, **18**n, **20**n, **26**n, **32**n; *Iohannis Wyclif De Civili*... II-IV, **29-30**; *Iohannis Wyclif De Eucharistia*..., 38, **42**, 44; *Iohannis Wyclif Opus Evangelicum* I, II, **374-377**; *Iohannis Wyclif Tractatus de Ecclesia*..., **28-30**n, **32**, **33**n; *Johannis Wyclif Opera Minora*, **23-25**nn, **33**n, 45, 49, 52, BIntro.n, 372, 373, 381-390, 392-396, 402, 404, 405, 409, 414, 416, 424; *Johannis Wyclif Sermones*... I-IV, **47**n, **54-299**, **389**n; *Johannis Wyclif Tractatus de Potestate*..., 34; "Johann von Wiclif and Guilelmus...," A12n; "Johann von Wiclif und Robert...," **9**n; *Shirley's Catalogue*..., AbbrL, Pref.n, and text, *passim*; "Studien zur Kirchenpolitik*... I, II," A7n, A12n, **401**n; "The Beginnings...," **382-383**; "Wiclifs Sendschreiben...," AbbrL, **45**, **49**, **52**, 202, 372, 373, 384-388, 390, 392-396, 402, 404, 405, 409, 414, 416; "Zur Kritik...," Pref.n; and F. D. Matthew: *Johannis Wyclif Tractatus de Mandatis*..., **26**, **27**, **51**

Louis d'Anjou, **401**
*Lunt, William E.: *Accounts Rendered*..., **397**nn; *Financial Relations*..., **397**n; *Studies in Anglo-Papal*... II, **37**n
Luther, Martin, 44n, 47n, **431**
Lutterworth, **28-30**n, **38**, **39**, **44**, **55**, **282**, 373, 384, 387, 390, 394, **405**n, 409, FIntro., 421, 431
*Lutz, Cora E.: "Walter Burley's...," **51**n

*Mabillon, Jean: *Museum Italicum*... I, 47n, **405**n, **408**n, **412**n, **413**n, **423**n
*MacClintock, Stuart: "John of Jandun," **28-30**n
*MacKinney, Loren C.: "Medieval Medical Dictionaries...," **420**n
*Madan, F., and H. H. E. Craster: *A Summary Catalogue*... II/1, B4n
Maidstone, Richard, 205, 427
*Maier, Anneliese: *Codices Burghesiani*..., **388**n; " 'Ergebnisse' der spätscholastischen...," **11**n
*Mallard, William: "Charity and Dilemma...," B2.IVn; "Dating the *Sermones*...," B2.IVn, **257-296**; "John Wyclif...," **31**n
Mankswell, Andrew, **28-30**n
*Manning, Bernard C.: *The People's Faith*..., **70**n, **423**n; "Wyclif and the House...," **378-380**n
*Mansi, J. D.: *Sacrorum conciliorum*... XXVI, **28-30**n
*Mantello, Frank: "The Endleaves...," **388**n
*Marcett, Mildred E.: *Uthred of Boldon*..., **23-25**n, **47**n
*Marco, A. A. de: "Hail Mary," **425**n
*Markowski, M.: "Problematyka uniwersialów...," A7n, **11**n
*Marrone, John: "The Absolute...," **34**n
Marsiglio of Padua, **28-30**
*Martin, A. R.: *Franciscan Architecture*..., **67**n
*Martin, C.: "Walter Burley...," 4n
Mary, St., 122, 125, 137, 282, 425
*Mathis, Burkhard: *Die Privilegien*..., **382-383**n
*Matthew, F. D.: "The Date...," **38**n; *The English Works*..., Pref.n, 47n, **382-383**, **405**, **413**

Matthew of Janov, G*Spur*.10
*Maurer, Arnold A.: "Some Aspects...," A7n
*Mazzeo, Joseph A.: "Light metaphysics...," 4n
*McCready, William D.: "Papalists and Antipapalists...," 34n
*McCristal, J. F.: *A Study*..., 26n
*McDonnell, Ernest W.: *The Beguines and Beghards*..., 191n
*McFarlane, K. B.: *John Wycliffe*..., 28-30n
*McGinn, Bernard: "Angel Pope...," 45n
*McGrade, Arthur S.: *The Political Thought*..., A7n
*McHardy, A. K.: "Bishop Buckingham...," 396n
*McKisack, May: *The Fourteenth Century*..., 28-30n, 397n
*McShane, Eduardo D.: *A Critical Appraisal*..., 28-30n, 45n
Melanchthon, Philip, 4n
*Meneghin, V.: *Scritti inediti*..., 4n
*Menozzi, Daniele: "La critica alla autenticità...," 412n
*Metlitzki, Dorothee: *The Matter of Araby*..., 4n
*Michałski, Konstanty: several articles, 11n
*Migne, Jacques P.: *Patrologiae...scriptores latini*... CLXXVI, 47n
Milverley, William, 5n, 11n
*Minio-Paluello, L.: "Michael Scot," 4n; "Two Erasures...," 22n
*Mirbt, Carl: *Quellen zur Geschichte*..., 44n
*Mirot, L., H. Jassemin and J. Vielliard: *Lettres secrètes*..., 397n
*Mirrielees, Lucia B.: "John Wyclif's Freudian Complex," G*Spur*.concl.
*Mitterer, Albert: *Die Entwicklungslehre Augustins*..., 55n
*Mollat, Guy: *Lettres secrètes*..., 397n
*Mollat, Michel: *Études sur l'histoire*... I-II, 34n, 112n
*Molnár, Amedeo: "Recent Literature...," A12n
*Molnar, E. S.: "Marsiglio of Padua...," 28-30n

*de Montfaucon, Bernard: Τοῦ ἐν Πατρὸς...VII, 374-377n
*Moody, Ernest A.: *Truth and Consequence*..., 385n
*Moorman, John: *A History*..., 217n, 432nn
More, John, 28-30n
*Mourelatos, Alexander P. D.: *The Pre-Socratics*..., 51n
*Muckle, J. T.: "Robert Grosseteste's Use...," 55n; "The Hexameron...," 55n
*Mudroch, Vaclav: *The Wyclyf Tradition*..., Pref.n, DIntro.n
*Mueller, Ivan: ed. of *De universalibus*, 11n
*Myers, Alexander R.: *English Historical Documents IV*..., 28-30n
*Mynors, R. H. B.: *Catalogue of Manuscripts*..., 5n

*Nasr, Seyyed Hossein: *Islamic Science*..., 4n
necromancy, 423
Nicholas II, 233
Nicholas IV, 419n
Nicholas of Lyra, 55, B4, G*Spur*.4, G*Spur*.5
*Nichols, John: *The History and Antiquities*... IV, 38n
Nicolas de Clamanges, 28-30n
*Nimmo, Duncan: "Poverty and Politics...," 251n
*Novotný, J.: "Peter Payne...," 17n
*Nygren, Gotthard: *Das Prädestinationsproblem*..., 17n

*Oberman, Heiko O.: *Archbishop Thomas Bradwardine*..., 15n; " 'Et tibi dabo...," 34n; Fourteenth-Century Religious Thought...," A7n; *The Harvest*..., 31n
*Odložilík, Otakar: "Wycliffe's Influence...," 32n
*Oliger, Livario: "Liber Exemplorum...," BIntro.n
*Owen, Dorothy M.: "Bacon and Eggs...," 423n

*Owen, J. and L. H. Starkey: "Realism," A7n
*Owst, G. R.: *Literature and Pulpit...*, BIntro.n; *Preaching in Medieval England*, BIntro.n
Oxford University, A12, **32**n, **38**, **41**, **43**, **53**n, **55**, **373**, **381**, **384**-**386**, **392**, **395**, DIntro., **401**, **405**n, **408**, **419**-**421**, **427**; Balliol College, **5**n; "Commission of twelve" (1380), **3**n, **39**; "Commission of twelve" (1411), **3**n, **28**-**30**n, **35**n, **39**n, **47**n, **206**n, **384**, **386**, **408**n, **413**n, **414**n, **426**n, **430**n; Oriel College, **28**-**30**n; Merton College, **31**n, **385**n, **387**, **410**n, **420**n; Queen's College, **37**n

*Page, R. I., and G. H. S. Bushnell: *Matthew Parker's Legacy*, **399**n
*Page, William: *The Victoria History...* II, **396**n
*Palacký, František: *Documenta Mag. Joannis...*, **11**n
Páleč, Stephen, **11**n, **12**n
*Pantin, William A.: "A Benedictine Opponent...," **28**-**30**n; *Oxford Life...*, **47**n; *The English Church...*, **23**-**25**n; "Two Treatises...," **23**-**25**n, **381**n
Paris, **32**n, **34**n, **432**n
Paris, Matthew, **432**n
*Parker, Matthew: *Historia brevis Thomae Walsingham...*, **399**
Partriche, Peter, **404**n
*Pascoe, Louis B.: "Jean Gerson...," **435**n
Patrington, Stephen, **205**, **216**, **392**
Paul, St., **121**, **220**, **419**
Paul of Venice, **385**n
Payne, Peter, **12**n, **17**n, **18**n, **20**n, **22**n, **23**-**25**nn, **26**nn, **28**-**30**nn, **31**n, **33**, **34**nn, **35**nn, **36**nn, **37**nn, **38**nn, **47**nn, **48**nn, **50**n, B2.IIn, B2.IVn, **388**n, **409**n
Peasants' Revolt (1381), A12, **37**
*Pegis, Anton C.: "Concerning William...," A7n
*Peirce, C. S.: "Insolubilia," **5**n
Pelayo (Pais), Álvaro, **4**n
*Pelikan, Jaroslav, *The Preaching of Chrysostom*, **374**-**377**n
Peraldus, Guilelmus, A12n

*Perroy, Édouard: "Gras profits et rançons...," **32**n; *L'Angleterre...*, **48**n; *The Anglo-French Negotiations...*, **23**-**25**n
*Perry, Elizabeth W.: *Under Four Tudors...*, **399**n
*Peschke, E.: "Die Bedeutung Wiclefs...," **42**n
Peter of Časlav, **9**, **13**
Peter of Mantua, **5**n
*Peters, Edward: *Heresy and Authority...*, **404**
*Pfander, Hans G.: *The Popular Sermon...*, BIntro.n
Philip de Thornbury, **28**-**30**n, **397**
*Phillips, Heather: *John Wyclif's Eucharistic Doctrines*, **38**n
*Pincin, Carlo: *Marsiglio*, **28**-**30**n
*Podlaha, A.: *Soupis Rukopisů knihovny...* I-II, AbbrL, **372**n, **390**n, **401**n, **413**n, **416**n
*Pollard, A. F.: "Uhtred...," **23**-**25**n
*Pollard, Alfred W.: *Iohannis Wycliffe Dialogus...*, **408**; and Charles Sayle: *Iohannis Wyclif Tractatus de Officio...*, **33**
*Poole, Reginald L.: "Binham or Bynham...," **23**-**25**n; *Iohannis Wycliffe Tractatus de Civili...* I, **28**; *Johannis Wyclif De Dominio...*, **22**n, **23**-**25**, GDub.15; "Wyclif's Doctrine of Dominion," **28**-**30**n; and Mary Bateson: *Index Britanniae...*, **5**n
Poor Priests, **38**, BIntro., **97**, **120**, **185**, **384**, **402**, FIntro., **416**, **426**, **430**
*Poschmann, B.: *Penance and the Anointing...*, **44**n
*Post, Gaines: *Studies in Medieval...*, **28**-**30**n; "Vincentius Hispanus...," **28**-**30**n
*Powicke, Frederick M.: "Master Simon...," **11**n; *The Medieval Books...* **410**n
Prague, **11**, **23**-**25**n, **26**n
*Prantl, C.: *Geschichte der Logik...* IV, **5**n, **385**n
*Pressfield, Harry: "Wyclif and the Common...," **28**-**30**n
*Previté-Orton, C.W.: "Marsilius of Padua," **28**-**30**n

Prokop of Plzeň, **18**n
Purvey, John, Pref., **38**, CIntro., **394**, G*Spur*.5

*Quain, Edwin A.: "The Medieval Accessus...," Pref.n

Radcliff, Nicholas, **39**n
*Ransom, Margaret W.: "The Chronology...," B**2**n
*Rashdall, L. H.: *The Universities of Europe*... III, A**7**n
*Rauh, H. D.: *Das Bild des Antichrist*..., **45**n
Raymond of Tarrega, **423**n
*Reeves, W. P.: "A Second MS...," **28-30**n
*Renan, Ernest: *Vie de Jésus*, **137**n
Repingdon, Philip, **394**
*Reusch, Heinrich: *Die Indices Librorum*..., **47**nn
Richard II, **41**n, **50**n, **120**, **235**, **400**
*Riedl, C. C.: *Robert Grosseteste*..., **4**n
Rigg, Robert, **394**n
*Riley, H. T.: *Chronicon Monasterii*..., **399**
*Robson, John A.: *Wyclif and the Oxford*..., **1**n, **6**n, A**7**, **13**nn, **15**n, **17**n, **22**n, **31**n
*Roensch, Frederick J.: *Early Thomistic School*..., **9**n
*Rubinstein, Nicolai: "Marsilius of Padua...," **28-30**n
*Russell, Frederick H.: *The Just War*..., **188**n
*Russell, Jeffrey Burton: *Witchcraft*..., **423**n
Russell, Peter, **404**n
*Ryan, J. K., and B. M. Bonansea: *John Duns Scotus*..., I-V, **16**n
*Rymer, Thomas, and Robert Sanderson: *Foedera, Conventiones*..., 3rd ed., III/ii, **397**n

*Saenger, Paul: "John of Paris...," **406**n
*Salter, H. E.: "John Wyclif...," **28-30**n; *Medieval Archives*..., **28-30**n, **41**n; *Medieval Oxford*, **3**n; and W. A. Pantin and H. G. Richardson: *Formularies*... I, **28-30**n
*Samsó, Julio: "Al-Bitruji...," **4**n
*Sarton, George: *Introduction to the History*... I-III, **4**n, **6**n, **23-25**n, **28-30**n, **47**n, **385**n, **420**nn, G*Spur*.10
Sarum Missal, B**2**
Scharpe, John, **6**n, **37**n
*Scheible, H.: *Die Anfänge*..., **36**n
Schism, A**12**, **31-33**, **238**, **241**, **253**, **256**, **372**, EIntro., **405**n, FIntro., **423**
*Schlauch, Margaret: "A Polish Vernacular...," **11**n
*Schmidt, M.: "John Wyclifs Kirchenbegriff...," **17**n
*Schneyer, Johann B.: *Die Unterweisung*..., BIntro.n; *Repertorium der lateinischen Sermones*... I-VIII, BIntro.n
Schöffer, Peter, **47**n
*Scholz, Richard: *Aegidius Romanus*..., **23-25**n
*Schrader, M., and A. Führkötter: *Die Echtheit des Schrifttums*..., **45**n
*Schüssler, Hermann: *Der Primat*..., **31**n
Scot, Michael, **4**n, **51**n
Scotus, Duns, **16**, **205**
*Sedlák, Jan: *Studie a Texty*..., I, II **11**n, **49**n, B**2**.IIIn, **402**n, **409**n, **426**n, **431**n
*Seńko, Władysław: "Un traité inconnu...," **11**nn
*Setz, Wolfram: *Lorenzo Valla De Falso*..., **412**n; *Lorenzo Vallas Schrift*..., **412**n
*Severs, Burke: *A Manual*... II, Pref.n, **382-383**n, **385**n, **393**, **403**n, **404**n, **410**n, **418**n
Shakyl, Richard, **32**
*Shapiro, Herman: "Walter Burley...," **4**n
*Sharp, D. E.: *Franciscan Philosophy*..., **16**n
*Shirley, Walter Waddington: *A Catalogue*..., Pref.n, and text *passim*; *Fasciculi Zizaniorum*..., **12**, **17**n, **20**n, **39**, **41**, **42**, B**2**.IIIn, **205**nn, **206**n, **378**, **380**, **396**n, **398**, **400**, **401**, **404**, **416**
Simon of Tišnov, G*Dub*.2
*Skalweit, Gerhard: *Der Kreuzzug*..., **48**n
*Šmahel, F.: " 'Doctor evangelicus...'," **32**n
*Smalley, Beryl: "Church and State...," **28-30**n; "John Wyclif's *Postilla*...," B**4**; "Oxford University Sermons...," BIntro.n; "The Bible and Eternity...," B**4**n; "The Biblical Scholar...," **26**n, **149**n; *The Study*..., **31**n; "Wyclif's *Postilla*...," B**4**, **323**, **324**, **329**, **335**

*Smith, Lucy T.: "English Popular Preaching...," BIntro.n
*Solignac, Aimé: "Analyse et sources...," 18n
Solomon, **406**
*Southey, Robert: *The Book...,* I **38n**
*Spade, Paul V.: *The Mediaeval Liar...,* **5nn**, **385n**, G*Dub*.7
*Spinka, Matthew: *Advocates of Reform,* **38**, **53**; *John Hus...,* **32n**; *John Hus' Concept...,* **11n**, **32n**
*Stacey, John: *Wyclif and Reform,* A12n
*Stalder, R.: "Le concept de l'église...," **32n**
Stanislav of Znojmo, **11**
*Stannard, Jerry: "Brunfels, Otto," **47n**
*Stegmüller, Friedrich: *Repertorium Biblicum...* I-VII, **31n**, B4, **320-324**, **328-371**, G*Spur*.5
*Stein, I. H.: "Another 'Lost' Chapter...," **14n**; "The Latin Text...," **403**; "The Vatican Manuscript...," **300n**, **388n**, **395n**, **400n**, **402n**, **404n**, **414n**, **420**; "The Wyclif Manuscript...," **28-30n**, **47n**, **382-383n**, **405n**, **408n**, **412n**, **413n**, **415n**, **423n**, **431n**; "Two Notes on Wyclif," **11n**, **21n**, **34n**, **38n**
*Stephens, G.: *Förteckening öfver de förnämsta...,* **11n**
*Stigall, John O.: "The Manuscript Tradition...," **51n**
Stokes, Peter, **205**, **209**, **216**, **392**
*Strayer, Joseph R.: *On the Medieval Origins...,* **28-30n**
Strode, Ralph, **44n**, CIntro, **385-390**
Sudbury, Simon, **37**, **395**, **399**, **401**
*Suggett, Helen: "The Use of French...," **397n**
*Svoboda, Milan: *Mistra Jakoubka...,* **408n**
*Swanson, R. N.: *Universities, Academics...,* **410n**
Swynshed, Roger, G*Dub*.7

Tabulae codicum manuscriptorum... III, G*Dub*.12, G*Dub*.14
*Talbert, Ernest W.: "The Date...," B2n
*Tanner, Thomas: *Bibliotheca Brittanico-Hibernica...,* Pref.n, DIntro.n
Tartys, John, **5**

*Tatnall, Edith C.: article on *De officio regis,* **33n**; *Church and State...,* **33n**; "John Wyclif...," **28-30n**; "The Condemnation...," **32n**
Tempier, William, **9**
*Theiner, Paul: *Walter Burley...,* **51n**
*Theisen, Wilfrid: "*Liber de Visu*...," **4n**; "Witelo's Recension...," **4n**
Theutonicus, Michael, **11n**
Thomas Netter of Walden, **3n**, **12n**, **17n**, **400**
Thomas of Walsingham, **399**
*Thompson, A. Hamilton: *The English Clergy...,* **28-30n**
*Thompson, C. H.: *Uthred of Boldon...,* **23-25n**, **381**
*Thomson, Samuel Harrison: miscellaneous mentions, Pref., **4**, **7n**, **11**, **18**, **388n**, G*Dub*.15; "A Gonville and Gaius...," **11n**, **21n**, **22n**, **26n**; "A Lost Chapter...," **10n**; "A Note on Peter...," **17n**, **28-30n**; "Cultural Relations...," **11n**; *Europe in Renaissance...,* Pref.n; *Johannis Wyclif Summa...,* Pref.n; **7**, **8**; "John Wyclif's 'Lost'...," **40**; "John Wyclyf," Pref.n; *Latin Bookhands...,* Pref.n, **11n**, **374-377n**; "Learning at the Court...," **11n**; *Magistri Johannis Hus...,* **32n**; "Pre-Hussite Heresy...," **42n**; "Scot, Michael," **4n**; "Some Latin Works...," **11n**, **408n**, G*Spur*.6; "The Influence of Augustine...," **17n**; "The Order of Writing...," A7n, **11n**, **13n**, **15n**, **18n**; "The Philosophical Basis...," Pref.n, A7n; "The *Summa in VIII*...," **6n**; *The Theological Doctrines...,* Pref.n; *The Writings of Robert...,* Pref.n, **4n**, **6n**, **9n**, **26n**, **55n**, **149n**; "Three Unpublished Opuscula...," **43**, **406**, **407**; "Unnoticed Manuscripts...," **31nn**; "Unnoticed MSS and Works...," **1n**, **2n**, **3n**, **5n**, **6n**, **11nn**, **18nn**, **20nn**, **21nn**, **26n**, **28-30n**, **31nn**, **34n**, **39n**, **300n**, B4nn, **390n**, **392n**, **395n**, **410n**, **414n**, **430n**; "Unnoticed *Quaestiones*...," **6n**; "Wyclyf, John," Pref.n; "Wyclyf or Wyclif?" Pref.n; and E. W. Talbert: "Wyclif and his Followers...," Pref.n

*Thomson, Williell R.: "An Unknown Letter...," **261**, **391**; "The Earliest Cardinal-Protectors...," **432**n; "The Image...," **67**n, **432**n

*Thonnard, F.-J.: "La notion...," **4**n, **79**

*Thorndike, Lynn: *A History of Magic*... III, **4**n, **423**n; *Michael Scot*, **4**n; and Pearl Kibre: *A Catalogue of Incipits*..., **4**nn, **6**n, **420**nn

*Tierney, Brian: *Foundations of the Conciliar*..., **23-25**n; "Ockham, the Conciliar Theory...," A7n; *Origins of Papal Infallibility*..., **34**n

Tissington, John, **39**, **42**, **382-383**n

*Totok, Wilhelm: *Handbuch der Geschichte*... II, A7n

*Trapp, Damasus: "Clm 27034...," **11**n

*Truhlař, J.: *Catalogus codicum*..., AbbrL, **14**n, **202**n, B4n, **348**n, **386**n, G*Dub*.2-6, G*Spur*.2, G*Spur*.6

*Twemlow, S. A.: "Wycliffe's Preferments...," **28-30**n

Ullerston, Richard, **48**

*Ullmann, W.: *A History of Political*..., **28-30**n; "A Medieval Document...," **406**n; "John Baconthorpe...," **23-25**n

Urban VI, **31**, **32**, **37**n, **45**, **48**, **49**, **124**, **202**, **208**, **373**, **395**, **404**, **405**, **409**, **410**, **413-416**

Uthred of Boldon, **23-25**, **28-30**n, **47**n, **378**, **380-383**

*van Hove, A.: *De Privilegiis*..., **382-383**n

*Vattier, Victor: *John Wyclyff D.D.*..., A7n

*Vaughan, Robert: *John de Wycliffe*..., **39**, **41**, DIntro.n; *The Life and Opinions*... II, **39**, **41**, DIntro.n

*Vermaseren, B.A.: "Nieuwe Studies...," **32**n

*Vinck, José de: *The Works of Bonaventure*... IV, **432**n

Vojtěch Raňků of Ježov, **32**n

*Vooght, Paul de: "Hus et Wiclif...," **32**n; *Hussiana*, **31**n, **32**nn, **35**n, **42**n; "La notion wiclifienne...," **32**n; "La 'simoniaca haeresis'...," **35**n; "Le caractère sacerdotal...," **32**n; *Les sources*..., **31**n; *L'Hérésie de Jean Hus*, **32**n, **42**n

*Walsh, Katherine: "Archbishop Fitz-Ralph...," **23-25**n; "The *De Vita evangelica*...," **23-25**n

Walsingham, Thomas, **48**n

*Walzer, Richard: *Greek into Arabic*..., **6**n

Waldby, Robert, **199**

*Wanley, G. H.: *A Catalogue*... I, **47**n

*Weber, J.: "Soupis Rukopisů...," **12**n

*Weisheipl, James A.: "*Repertorium Mertonense*...," **4**nn, **5**n; "Roger Swyneshed...," G*Dub*.7

Wells, John, **205**, **206**, **216**

*Welter, J. T.: "Un nouveau recueil...," BIntro.n; "Un recueil...," BIntro.n

*Weltsch, Ruben E.: *Archbishop John*..., **11**n

*Werner, Karl: *Die Scholastik*..., III, IV/1 **15**n

*Westin, Gunnar: *John Wyclif*..., A12n, **28-30**n

*Whitney, James P.: "A Note...," **199**n

Whytheed, John, **404**n

*Wiegand, Friedrich: *De Ecclesiae Notione*..., **32**n

*Wilkins, David: *Concilia Magnae Britanniae*... III, **3**n, **28-30**n, **35**n, **39**n, **47**n, **48**, **374-377**n, **384**n, **386**n, **401**n, **404**n, **408**n, **413**n, **426**n, **430**n

*Wilkins, J. J.: *Was John Wycliffe*..., **28-30**n

*Wilks, Michael J.: "Misleading Manuscripts...," Pref.n; "Predestination...," **23-25**n, **28-30**n; "*Reformatio regni*...," **32**n, DIntro.n; "The *Apostolicus*...," **34**n; "The Early Oxford Wyclif...," A7n; *The Problem of Sovereignty*..., **28-30**n

William of Auvergne, **109**

William of Ockham, A7n, **378**, **380**, **432**

William de Rymyngton, **384**

William of St. Amour, **432**

*Williams, Arnold: "Protectorium pauperis...," **47**n, **205**n; "Relations between the Mendicant...," **382-383**n

*Winster, H. J. J.: "The Optical Researches...," **4**n

Winnerton, Thomas, **39**, **42**

*Wirth, L. P.: *Iohannis Wiclefi viri*..., **47**, DIntro.n

*Wisłocki, Władysław: *Katalog Rękopisów...* I, **11n**
Witelo (Erazm Ciołek, Witek?), 4, 167, 205
*Wolfenschiessen, Burkhard von: "Das franziskanische Privilegienrecht," **382-383n**
*Wolter, Allan B.: "Duns Scotus, John," **16n**
Woodford, William, 17, 23-25, 28-30, **39n**, 42, **47n**, 382-383
*Woolley, Reginald M.: *Catalogue of the Manuscripts...*, **11n**
*Woozley, A. D.: "Universals," **A7n**
*Wordsworth, C.: *The Ancient Kalendar...*, **38n**
*Workman, Herbert B.: *John Wyclif...* I-II, AbbrL, **4n, 6n, A7n, 22n, 23-25nn, A12n, 26n, 28-30nn, 32n, 34n, 38, 39n, 41n, 45n, 47nn, 205nn, 300n, 374-377nn, 378-380n, 381n, 382-383, 384n, 385n, 386n, 387n, 396n, DIntro.n, 397, 398, 400, 403, 404, G*Dub*.1, G*Spur*.9**
*Wright, Thomas: *Political Poems...* I, **41n**
*Wrong, George M.: *The Crusade of MCCCLXXXIII...*, **48n**
*Wroth, Lawrence C.: *A History...*, **47n**
*Wulf, Maurice de: *Histoire de la philosophie...* I-III, **A7n**
Wyche, Richard, 42
Wyche, Thomas, **28-30n**
Wyclyf, John: and Aquinas: **9n**; and Aristotle, 6, **51n**; and Augustine, **12n**, 17, 19, **44n**, 47, 51, 52, BIntro.n, 54, 55, 79; and Baconthorpe, **23-25n**; and Bradwardine, 15, 16, 19; and Burley, 4, **6n**; and Egidio de' Colonna, **23-25n**; And FitzRalph, 16, 19; and French, **397n**; and Grosseteste, 9, 19, **26n, 55n**, 70, 72; and Greek, **47n, 408n**; and Hus, **17n**, 32, **374-377n**; and Jewish/Muslim thought, **4n**, 76, 84, 155; and Joachim of Fiore, **6n**; and Ockham, **A7n**; and Peraldus, **A12n**; and Scripture, 19, 26, **28-31, 33, 40, 47, 49, 50, 52**, BIntro, **54-299, B4, 300-377, 394, 395, 397n, 399, 405n, 406-408, 419, 421, 424, 425, 431, 432, 434, 435**; and Woodford, 23-25, **28-30n**
Wyclyf, doctrines of: *caritas*, 49, 83, 104, 143, 155, 167, 177, 193, 210, 211, 224, 286, 287, 300, 386, 393, 395, 397; dominion, disendowment, 12, 21, 23-25, 28-31, 45, 48, 49, 53, 77, 95, 101, 109, 113, 119, 120, 133, 150, 164, 165, 180, 201, 208, 215, 223, 231, 254, 261, 280, 381, 385, 386, **390n**, 397, 398, 402, 403, 406, 408, 409, 417, 420, 421, 429, G*Dub*.16; Eucharist, 3, 12, 17, 20, 22, 27, 34, 36-44, 49, 53, 64, 67, 78, 82, 114, 126, 138, 140, 175, 193, 200, 204, 209, 217, 220, 223, 225, 226, 229, 233, 236, 276, 297, 300, **350n**, 372, 395, 396, 403, 408, 409, 416, 420-422, 427, 430, 435; "four sects," etc., 46, 50, 53, 109, 128, 158, 194, 197, 208, 214, 222, 227, 230, 265, 298, 372, 384, 388, 391, 393, 405, FIntro., 415, 420-422, 427, 430, 435; "lex Christi" — canon and secular law, 28-30, **31n**, 33, 38, 44, BIntro., 64, 65, 99, 111, 123, 129, 131, 135, 165, 168, 178, 183, 197, 207, 216, 221, 222, 240, 254, 261, 384, 385, 387, 394, 397-399, 402-404, 408, 409, 414, 419, 434; "omnia quod fuit...," etc., 56, 373, 375, 388, G*Spur*.1; poverty and the mendicants, 15, 28-30, 34-38, 42, 44, 45, 47-49, BIntro., 53, 57, 58, 60-63, 65, 67, 69, 73, 76, 78, 87, 92-94, 97, 99, 101, 105, 112, 114, 115, 121, 122, 126, 129-131, 133, 139, 145, 146, 156, 159-161, 170, 172, 180, 189, 192, 196, 204, 210-215, 217, 231, 232, 236, 238, 240, 241, 247, 249, 255, 256, 289, 297, 300, 372, 374-377, 381-383, 388, 392, 396, 402-404, EIntro., 408-410, 412, FIntro., 415-421, 424-428, 430-433, 435; papacy, 15, 31, 34, 48, 105, 115, 123, 138, 159, 162, 163, 170, 172, 183, 195, 234, 250, 254, 297, 385, 388, 398, 404, EIntro., 405, 408, 412, 414; prayer, 46, 73, 214, 219, 237, 243, 296, 424, 425; prea-

ching, pastoral duties, **44**, BIntro., **53**, **70**, **80**, **90**, **122**, **127**, **130**, **146**, **152**, **174**, **185**, **265**, **286**, **416**, **419**; predestination, foreordination, **15**n, **16**, **17**n, **32**, **47**, **49**, **56**n, **83**, **88**, **96**, **106**, **148**, **151**, **180**, **193**, **239**, **270**, **373**, **386**, **429**; realism, universals, ideas, A7, **9-11**, **15**, **17-19**, **38**, **47**, EIntro; simony, **35**, **94**, **298**; "viator," **47**, **50**, BIntro., **53**n, **81**, **127**, **164**, **166**, **239**, **374-377**, **393**

Wyclyf, life events of: appearance at St Pauls, **28-30**, **399**; at Parliament, Gloucester, **32**; at Westminster, **397**; debates with John Kenningham, **12**, **378**, **380**, **397**; first stroke (1382), **76**, **390**, **404**, **411**, **413**; five bulls of Gregory xi, **28-31**, **398**, **409**; holding of various prebends, **28-30**, **397**; *magister artium*, **1**; regent-doctor, **22**; retirement to Lutterworth, **28-30**n, **38**, **43**, **44**, **387**, **405**n, **418**, **431**; second stroke in 1384, **374-377**; trip to Bruges, **23-25**, **397**

Wyclif, writings: *see* Index of Wyclyf's Writings

Wyclyf, Robert, **397**

*Wynar, Lubomyr R.: *S. Harrison Thomson...*, Pref.n

*Xiberta, Bartolomeu Maria: *De Scriptoribus Scholasticis...*, **11**n, **23-25**n; "Fragments d'una qüestió...," **15**n

*Young, Robert F.: "Bohemian Scholars...," **42**n

Zdislav of Zvířetice, **11**n
*Ziegler, Philip: *The Black Death...*, **423**n
Žižka, Jan, G*Spur*.4

RAYMOND H. FOGLER LIBRARY
DATE DUE

BOOKS ARE SUBJECT TO